Encyclopedia of the
AMERICAN
JUDICIAL
SYSTEM

Encyclopedia of the
AMERICAN JUDICIAL SYSTEM

*Studies of the Principal
Institutions and Processes of Law*

Robert J. Janosik, *EDITOR*

Occidental College

Volume III

CHARLES SCRIBNER'S SONS · NEW YORK

Copyright © 1987 Charles Scribner's Sons

Encyclopedia of the American judicial system.

Includes bibliographies and index.
1. Law—United States—Dictionaries. 2. Justice,
Administration of—United States—Dictionaries.
3. United States—Constitutional law—Dictionaries.
I. Janosik, Robert J. (Robert Joseph)
KF154.E53   1987   349.73′0321   87–4742
ISBN 0–684–17807–9 Set   347.300321
ISBN 0–684–18858–9 Volume I
ISBN 0–684–18859–7 Volume II
ISBN 0–684–18860–0 Volume III

Published simultaneously in Canada
by Collier Macmillan Canada, Inc.

1 3 5 7 9 11 13 15 17 19 V/C 20 18 16 14 12 10 8 6 4 2

Printed in the United States of America.

"Amendments to the Constitution" has been adapted from Clement E. Vose,
Constitutional Change: Amendment Politics and Supreme Court Litigation Since 1900,
A Twentieth Century Fund Study, © 1972, The Twentieth Century Fund, New York.

The paper in this book meets the guidelines for permanence and
durability of the Committee on Production Guidelines for Book Longevity
of the Council on Library Resources.

CONTENTS

v

CONTENTS

CONTENTS

CONTENTS

Encyclopedia of the
AMERICAN
JUDICIAL
SYSTEM

Part V
CONSTITUTIONAL LAW AND ISSUES

AMENDMENTS TO THE CONSTITUTION

Clement E. Vose

ARTICLE V of the United States Constitution provides a formal mechanism for amendment of that document. The process is legislative; the executive is given no formal role in the process. One route to amendment begins in Congress. The Constitution allows a two-thirds majority in both the Senate and the House of Representatives to propose an amendment. Once such a proposal receives the requisite two-thirds quorum in both houses, it is sent to the state legislatures for ratification. Three-fourths of all the legislatures of the states, or of the conventions called in the states especially for the purpose of considering the proposal, must then ratify the proposed amendment within a "reasonable time," as determined by Congress, before the amendment is incorporated into the Constitution.

A second mechanism for amendment is also noted in the Constitution. The legislatures of two-thirds of the states may petition the Congress to call a convention to consider a proposed amendment. Though this mechanism has never in fact been used, calls for a convention have been heard and widely considered regarding proposed balanced-budget and abortion issues.

Despite congressional suggestions for thousands of amendments, only a handful have actually been formally proposed. The rarity of formal amendment under the American Constitution has been directly connected to the blossoming of judicial review in 1803, even though amendment was expressly provided for while judicial review was not. It has been argued that the triumph of judicial review was in keeping with the goal of the framers to make the Constitution open to change. Provision for any change was an eighteenth-century novelty, but the experience of only a decade led Americans to accept judicial

action as a better mode of change than amendment.

The small number of amendments adopted in the twentieth century—only eleven—attests to national satisfaction with governance by regular legislation, administration, and judicial review. In contrast to these governing routines the amendment process is treacherous because it is so little used. Because amendments are needed only when other modes fail, they tend to deal with extreme situations and are thus either very concrete or quite abstract. So much can be accomplished in American government by regularly used means that special circumstances account for amendments.

Advocacy of constitutional change by amendment is often emblematic of frustrated causes. An amendment may be a last resort, a means of dramatizing a need, and a claim on the future for the legitimacy of certain goals and values. Controversy over an amendment is ordinarily simply one part of wider political conflict but a part that is often highly symbolic. The amendments advocated by Progressives symbolized a distrust of the judiciary and of ordinary legislation in much the same way as the initiative, referendum, recall, taxpayer suits, and other popular government programs of the day did. In the same spirit, since World War II conservatives have claimed that the president and the Supreme Court were out of touch with the people and that constitutional amendments afforded a means of redress. If an amendment then fails even to be proposed, its supporters—like true believers in a small sect—will remain undaunted and be likely to persist and become ever more zealous in carrying a conviction about the constitutional legitimacy of their position. They believe—and there are occasional historical proofs to give substance to their view—that they will someday overcome. Meanwhile, their amendment stands in their minds as a symbolic alternative to prevailing but, as they see it, illegitimate constitutional policy.

Discussions of the amendment process have been perennially couched in terms of whether it is too easy or difficult. When the Supreme Court treated ambiguities in the amendment procedure as political questions, academic regrets were offered. Interest in amendments has often been in arid legality rather than in political realities. There has been insufficient recognition that controversy over the amendment process is a function of something else, a commitment for' or against a government policy on social, economic, or political matters. If a given amending procedure is deemed more or less likely to result in a certain amendment's proposal and ratification, then the attitudes about process have an anchor in policy preferences.

Amendment controversialists usually differ over social policy, government organization, power, and procedure. Opponents of the Fifteenth, Eighteenth, and Nineteenth Amendments and child-labor regulation insisted that conventions in the states were an essential ingredient of the constitutionality of the process. They pointed to legislatures as easy marks for lobbyists and argued that state legislatures were often not representative of the people. They urged in unsuccessful litigation that the process of ratification was a justiciable question, properly resolved by the Supreme Court rather than by the political branches. But the great affection of these same interests and individuals for the "popular will," conventions, and judicial review of amendments crumbled when American politics was transformed in the 1930s. Then they attacked the Court, sought amendments themselves, and found the state legislatures more dependable allies than the people who elected Roosevelt, Truman, Eisenhower, Kennedy, and Johnson.

In the period 1910–1940, the Progressive spirit expressed itself by supporting a string of constitutional amendments that were anathema to the social-conservative, states'-rights mind. The circumstances of power distribution among major governmental institutions in the United States during this era, though complex and changing, made possible the formal proposal by Congress of several constitutional amendments. State legislatures, elected on a district basis,

rightly were deemed sufficient carriers of the middle-class virtues to act as ratifying bodies for the prohibition and woman-suffrage amendments. Surprisingly, because of their origins as Progressive reform mechanisms, taxpayer suits and statewide referenda became favorite weapons of opponents of these amendments. When a federal child-labor amendment was proposed to the legislatures in 1924, popular opposition was dramatized by a statewide advisory referendum in Massachusetts. In 1933, when repeal of Prohibition could muster the requisite vote in Congress, "wets" regarded the legislatures as heavily weighted against them. Because legislatures were seen as obstacles to ratification of repeal, Congress specified the state-convention method. This was in response to the urgings of the Association Against the Prohibition Amendment and the Voluntary Committee of Lawyers, who recommended at-large election of delegates to ratify the Twenty-first Amendment. This method worked.

That men opposing national constitutional regulation of suffrage, alcoholic beverages, or child labor made the wisest strategic and tactical moves possible for them occasions no surprise. But they were shortsighted in defining democracy essentially in terms of their temporary strategic posture. They attacked state-legislative ratification in the federal judiciary. They praised state ratifying conventions and referenda until times changed and President Roosevelt's popularity at the polls dictated a strategy of legislative ratification of the Twenty-second Amendment, which limited a president to two terms. In this instance, the content of the amendment and the procedure for ratification showed the sponsors' distrust of popular, at-large elections.

Constitutional amendments are a form of legislation to be studied empirically by students of elections, pressure groups, and lawmaking institutions. A knowledge of Congress, propaganda, and the climate of state legislation are all essential.

From the portrayal of amendment politics between 1910 and the 1940s, six characteristics can be distilled. First, a constitutional amendment is legislative in character, with specific alternative procedures so that proponents will choose strategies for proposal in Congress and ratification in the states that maximize support.

Second, advocates of states' rights and state sovereignty during the period from 1865 to 1937 counted on the Supreme Court and judicial review as the best means to curb claims made for national power over social, economic, and political subjects. Their basic position and theory was antagonistic to the growth of national authority, whether by acts of Congress or by constitutional amendments.

Third, Populists and Progressives, who favored the extension of government power to regulate and correct social ills, tended in these years to have the greatest leverage in Congress and the state legislatures, relative to other governmental institutions. As these institutions represented one path to constitutional amendment, this form of legislation became a viable means for seeking reform. Many ideas for progressive amendments failed in Congress. The child-labor amendment succeeded there but failed ratification in the state legislatures. The amendments for Prohibition, the income tax, the popular election of senators, and woman suffrage must be counted as essentially Progressive amendments.

Fourth, in defense of state sovereignty, a group of conservative lawyers spelled out a legal theory that placed intrinsic limits on constitutional amendments. By their theory, for example, enlargement of a state's constituency through suffrage amendments was not permissible. The total body of writing on the permissible scope of amendments shows this theory to be a transparent attack on the participation of blacks or women in elections and on government prohibition of liquor or child labor.

Fifth, convention ratification was championed by critics of amendments proposed between 1918 and 1924 and by proponents of repeal in 1933 because of its strategic value. At-large election of convention delegates was preferred over district voting. In the 1940s, conservatives shifted from this preference to favor legislative ratification. They also objected to at-large voting in presidential elections and favored an electoral college constituted by district elections. There is sufficient continuity among men and organizations with a states'-rights outlook to indicate that the preference for convention ratifications was strategic, not principled, as time and circumstance saw the preference evaporate.

Last, the comparative merits of legislatures and conventions as state ratifying bodies depend on the electoral system, the campaign, and internal practices. Many considerations, such as the enormous experience Americans have had with legislatures, as opposed to special ratifying conventions, should enter into the assessment. The single experience with convention ratification in 1933, where pledged delegations elected at large were the rule, was much like a straight referendum. By so classifying the convention, the basic issue becomes one of comparing the referendum to the legislature as an instrument of the popular will. The literature on this subject is large and complex, but it strongly questions a conclusion that the referendum or the convention represents the millennium for democracy.

The written Constitution of the United States needs constantly to be revised, and its revisions, whether by amendment, statute, ruling, or order, also need clarification. The number of changes advocated is exceedingly high, compared to the number acceded to. This has been a general condition of American constitutional law throughout its history. While the ten amendments embodying the Bill of Rights were adopted early in the 1790s, only five amendments were added in the nineteenth century and eleven more in the twentieth century (as of 1986). Since the 1950s the best-known measures, mostly nonamendments, have been provoked by the decisions of the Supreme Court and by presidential action. This is because of American reverence for the Constitution and the amendment procedure itself.

Reverence for the American Constitution is akin to the reliance of religious fundamentalism on biblical texts, for it assumes that a written instrument has easily discernible meanings. It rests also on the inescapable fact that certain textual language is so specific that close to 100 percent of the public is in agreement. For those parts especially concerning dates, very specific changes and rules of eligibility may be advocated. Otherwise, amendments are urged on occasions when the Court or the president has been thought to have misinterpreted the original, true meaning of the text. A clarifying amendment may be needed.

An attachment to formal amendments as having a pedigree, a virtue, and a legitimacy superior to the decisions of judges or presidents is normal. When a group gains satisfaction from the judges and president in power, it ordinarily sheds its preoccupation with formal amendment. The heirs of the Progressives were not much interested in amendments after about 1941, by which time the Supreme Court had upheld the constitutionality of federal power to regulate child labor and other New Deal measures.

After one studies amendment politics for the period 1910 to 1970, it comes as a surprise to conclude that a historical treatment of constitutional amendments—advocated, proposed, or ratified—explains less about amendments themselves than about governmental structure and procedure. The subject matter, the motivations, and the alliance of interests vary over the years, but the procedures, the arguments, the strategies, and the tactics have a certain consistency attached to the constitutional order itself. A large time frame is critical to understanding this conclusion because it shows how the same substantive sides reverse their procedural positions. Observations limited to one era will confuse this picture by making particular criticisms of institutions appear timeless when they are not.

Advocacy of an amendment to the Constitution usually stems from one or a combination of these five considerations: (1) As a higher law, the existing constitutional text cannot be changed by ordinary legislation, and so, both in a symbolic sense and in a technical sense, an amendment appears to be required. (2) As a federal constitutional system in which some state practices cannot be reached by ordinary acts of the national government, an amendment may be required to apply practices of some states to recalcitrant states. (3) The reverse may come into play when frustrated provincial interests seek amendments to regulate or limit national power. (4) Amendments are aimed at specific national institutions, occasionally Congress but more commonly the Supreme Court and the presidency; one purpose of such amendments is to alter the method of selection of, the authority of, or procedures followed by the president and the Supreme Court. (5) Amendments may also be limited to overcoming particular acts or rulings of a governmental body, especially those of the Supreme Court and the president.

PRESIDENTIAL TENURE AND THE BRICKER AMENDMENT

Franklin D. Roosevelt's bid in 1940 for a third term first evoked a rather comic effort to return to the "true principles of the Constitution" even though the text set no limit of presidential tenure. Opponents in Congress hastily called hearings to record their offense at Roosevelt's audacity. Those testifying had remarkable genealogical credentials but little else. Among them was a small collection of descendants of American presidents. After Roosevelt was elected to both a third term and a fourth, this opposition turned out to be something more than lampoon. The Republican-dominated Eightieth Congress in 1947 voted to propose an amendment limiting a president to two terms, and the requisite number of states completed ratification in 1951. This Twenty-second Amendment did not apply to Harry Truman, who was then president, but it was otherwise strict by providing that "no person shall be elected to the office of the President more than twice, and no person who has held the office of President, or acted as President, for more than two years of a term to which some other person was elected President shall be elected to the office of President more than once."

Although Dwight D. Eisenhower, the first president to be elected after the ratification of the Twenty-second Amendment, later repudiated this measure, there appears little chance for its repeal.

Champions of presidential power as asserted by Roosevelt, Truman, and, in the domestic field, Kennedy and Johnson have been largely disenchanted with this resource. Where they once saw eternal verities, they have come to see human failings and have turned against the presidency as an institution in much the same way that conservative critics did in the 1930s and 1940s.

A second amendment effort should also be noted in this context. As a constitutional barrier to the president and the national government, no proposal generated as much political heat in the 1950s as an amendment formulated by Senator John Bricker of Ohio. The Bricker amendment became a rallying point for the modern states'-rights forces because it seemed calculated to give to the rural areas in the sparsely populated states some veto over the national government's treaty-making power, by declaring that no treaty shall affect the internal law of an individual state without the approval of the state.

The movement for the Bricker amendment was driven by a constitutional myth that formal limitations are more important than capabilities of power. One section of the proposal provided that any treaty contrary to constitutional restrictions would be void. Critics argued that this was already the case, but defenders pointed to the incontrovertible fact that no treaty had ever been declared unconstitutional. Despite the fact that no treaty can become the law of the land without presidential endorsement and a two-thirds vote of the United States Senate, proponents of the Bricker scheme insisted that an amendment was needed to require review by the Supreme Court in case the Constitution were violated.

Although constitutional limitations would have been reinforced, the most significant goal was to cut into the power and independence of the president in foreign policy. The amendment was aimed at any president aggressive enough to favor agreements of consequence with other nations.

Bricker's departure from the Senate in 1958 ended the active campaign for this amendment. Eisenhower's style and his luck in international diplomacy helped quell the movement. But a decade later the Vietnam War ended Johnson's chance for a second elected term as president and was feeding Senate Democrats with a fear of power in the White House. This did not take the form of advocacy of a constitutional amendment. Instead, efforts were made to cut asunder the Tonkin Gulf Resolution of 1964—which was the basis of President Johnson's military buildup and engagement in Vietnam—through the War Powers Act of 1973.

AMENDMENTS AND DECISIONS OF THE SUPREME COURT

There is such wide opportunity for those unhappy with the Supreme Court to express their dissatisfaction that constitutional amendments must be understood to be only one opportunity to do so. Article III of the Constitution merely says that there shall be "one supreme Court," leaving Congress with broad powers over the number of justices, their compensation, and the Court's budget. Congress also has considerable control over the Court's jurisdiction and over the establishment of other federal courts. Since first exercising this authority by enacting the Judiciary Act of 1789, Congress has developed a complete statutory code, Title XVI of the *United States Code,* regulating numerous aspects of the business of the Supreme Court. Even in times of great constitutional crisis, as in 1937, the proposals of President Roosevelt to curb the Court took the form of a legislative bill rather than a constitutional amendment. Indeed, particular judicial decisions objected to by Congress may often be altered or countermanded by statutes.

Statutes are only one means Congress has to correct, to modulate, or to harass the Court. Another means was shown by the Senate's refusal in 1968 to act favorably on President Johnson's elevation of Abe Fortas to be chief justice of the United States, followed by its outright rejection in 1969 and 1970 of President Richard Nixon's nominations of Clement Haynesworth and G. Harrold Carswell to be associate justices of the Supreme Court. A possibly more explosive and damaging move lay in Congressman Gerald Ford's efforts to have the House of Representatives vote to impeach Associate Justice William O. Douglas. There are also the routine matters of authorizing new federal judgeships, action on nominees to fill those and other vacant seats, annual consideration of appropriations for the judiciary, and committee investigations of subjects bearing on the courts.

Constitutional amendments may nevertheless be needed to deal with limited situations. It is remarkable how many amendments have followed an unyielding Supreme Court ruling. Oftentimes the Court ruling has been only a minor obstacle faced by a cause. This seems true of the *Dred Scott* v. *Sandford* decision in 1857, which is sometimes pictured as a cause of the Civil War, which in turn was corrected by the Northern victory in the field and then the Thirteenth, Fourteenth, and Fifteenth Amendments. A decision with an incidental effect was *Minor* v. *Happersett* (1875), wherein the Court ruled that the Fourteenth and Fifteenth Amendments did not afford women the right to vote. This made certain the need of a woman-suffrage amendment, ratified as the Nineteenth Amendment in 1920.

The equal rights amendment (ERA) went to the states for ratification on 22 March 1972 when the required two-thirds vote was achieved in the Senate, having been passed by the House of Representatives in October 1971. As finally approved for action by the states the key section of the ERA read, "Equality of rights under the law shall not be denied or abridged by the United States or by any State on account of sex." Congress would have the power to legislate under the amendment but not until two years after ratification.

Senator Sam Ervin of North Carolina insisted to the end of debate that women were adequately protected against sex discrimination by the due process clause of the Fifth Amendment and the equal protection clause of the Fourteenth Amendment. But women despaired of this and insisted that a primary reason why the ERA was needed was the Court's record. The issue was often cast as an amendment to overcome Supreme Court unwillingness to apply the Constitution to women's rights. By the end of 1973, twenty-two states had ratified the ERA, but this initial rush of support engendered strong opposition outside Congress. In the South particularly, state ratification movements bogged down in heated debate on the wisdom and utility of the amendment.

By 1979 the state ratification movement was languishing. In all, thirty-five states had voted to ratify, but four of those states then rescinded their approval. Since Congress had originally allowed the usual seven years for the state ratification process, it became necessary to extend that period to 30 June 1982, to allow the requisite thirty-eight states to ratify. But by the expiration of the extended period, the amendment still lacked the necessary state support, and so the ERA failed to achieve constitutional status.

The Sixteenth Amendment, which was ratified in 1913 and permitted the United States government to levy an income tax, is the only clear instance in the twentieth century of ratification of an amendment that was virtually required by a Supreme Court ruling. In one of its most famous cases, *Pollock* v. *Farmers' Loan and Trust Co.* (1895), the Court, voting 5–4, held that an income tax enacted in 1894 was beyond the power of Congress. In 1913 the income tax was adopted in the Sixteenth Amendment and upheld as valid by the Supreme Court in *Dodge* v. *Brady* (1916).

Much is made of the unratified child-labor amendment, as it should be, for its proposal in 1924 by Congress followed the Supreme Court's invalidation of two successive child-labor statutes. But when Congress finally enacted a third

law regulating child labor, the Court, in *United States* v. *Darby* (1941), changed its position and overruled the *Hammer* v. *Dagenhart* decision of 1918. This quite correctly suggests that given time, the Court might have cooperated with Congress in permitting an income tax and even in watering down the prohibition amendment. These are all instances in which congressional leadership and willpower may do things eventually accepted by the Court, even if reluctantly.

The number of would-be amendments aimed at the Supreme Court is too large to attempt a review, but a few failures achieved sufficient prominence to require mention. Although each is a complicated story in itself, they may be condensed to indicate their essence as protests against judicial rulings. Those to be reviewed here are the Becker amendment to overcome decisions forbidding prayers in public school and the Dirksen amendments in response to reapportionment and religious cases. Each has so far failed but has gained considerable attention. It should be added that the failure of these amendments gives a certain negative endorsement by Congress and the states of the judicial decisions that provoked them. This is true also for the civil rights rulings of the Supreme Court so commonly attacked by southerners in Congress, for here again the majority not only acquiesced but, in voting overwhelmingly for the Civil Rights Act of 1964 and the Voting Rights Act of 1965, really supported rulings of the Warren Court on race relations.

Becker School-Prayer Amendment. The impression that American politicians prefer God as a running mate was mightily reinforced during 1963–1964, when some two hundred separate House joint resolutions were proposed to provide for the constitutionality of prayers and Bible reading in the public schools. This avalanche of amendments was triggered by three Supreme Court decisions. A denominationally neutral prayer adopted by the New York State Board of Regents for a program of daily classroom prayers in public schools was ruled invalid by the Supreme Court in the case of *Engle* v. *Vitale* (1962). The Court ruled 6–1 that this was inconsistent with the First Amendment, which prohibits laws respecting an establishment of religion. The following year, the Court upset Bible reading and the unison recitation of the Lord's Prayer by students prescribed by a Pennsylvania statute and by a rule of the school board in Baltimore.

These cases, *Abington School District* v. *Schempp* and *Murray* v. *Curlett,* were decided together in a flurry of opinions in which the Supreme Court held, 8–1, that the establishment clause of the First Amendment, as applied to the states through the Fourteenth Amendment, had been unconstitutionally breached. There was an immediate outcry against the New York decision, intensified a year later by the Pennsylvania and Maryland cases. The criticism of the Court reached such an intensity that the phlegmatic chairman of the House Judiciary Committee, Emanuel R. Celler, finally called hearings to consider the hundreds of amendments put forward by members of Congress.

Representative Frank J. Becker, a Republican from Nassau County, New York, formulated the amendments that became the focus of the hearings. A Roman Catholic and a veteran of World War I, Becker was prominent in the Knights of Columbus and the American Legion, and it was thought that his motions were representative of the wishes and perhaps even directions of leading critics of the prayer decisions, such as Cardinal Spellman of New York. Becker was the first member of the House to submit an amendment in the Eighty-eighth Congress, which opened in January 1963. This was just a sentence that read, "Prayers may be offered in the course of any program in any public school or other public place in the United States."

This was sufficient in response to *Engle,* but when the Supreme Court reinforced that ruling in its decision in the *Schempp* and *Curlett* cases, Becker submitted a more elaborate resolution. This revised Becker amendment was drafted by an ad hoc committee of congressmen to satisfy all critics of the Court's rulings with a single resolution they could all support. The wording thus became more elaborate in a resolution submitted on 10 September 1963 which included this provision: "Nothing in this Constitution shall be deemed to prohibit making reference to belief in, reliance upon, or invoking the aid of God or a Supreme Being in any governmental or public document, proceeding, activity, ceremony, school institution, or place, or upon any coinage, currency, or obligation of the United States."

The perfected Becker amendment of September 1963 had the stated support of 58 other House members, but Chairman Celler opposed it and would not call hearings. In a familiar routine, efforts were made to bypass Celler by a petition to discharge the Judiciary Committee from considering it. But 218 signatures were needed. Had the measure come to the House floor, it probably would have won many votes. Yet Celler gauged there was solid, if not vocal, support for his position, and he held his ground. By April 1964 the discharge petition had gained 157 signatures, and Celler felt it wise to hold hearings in the hope of stopping the amendment. The hearings in April, May, and June 1964 are printed in three volumes, containing nearly 2,774 pages of testimony, exhibits, and documents. But after the hearings ended on 3 June 1964, the House Judiciary Committee took no further action and Congressman Becker's discharge petition drive also failed.

Ardor for the Becker school-prayer amendment had peaked early, and gradually it became evident through the 1964 hearings that it was insufficient. Mail to the Judiciary Committee changed from pro to anti, and Catholic interests especially retreated from support of Becker. The ideal of church-state separation was clearly strongly supported, and while the Supreme Court's application of this ideal to exclude prayers from school was widely criticized, the decisions also were persuasive. Eventually opponents to these decisions were made to look like opponents of the First Amendment. Attacking the justices for their godlessness was one thing, but amending the Constitution's First Amendment came to seem like medicine too strong for the malady.

Dirksen Apportionment Convention Amendment. Senator Everett McKinley Dirksen's death on 7 September 1969 ended an intriguing crusade over several years to overturn the Supreme Court's "one man, one vote" ruling on apportionment of state legislatures. He had sought to accomplish this amendment to be proposed by a special constitutional convention, an untried method of proposal provided by Article V of the Constitution. Dirksen was reacting to the reapportionment rulings of *Baker* v. *Carr* (1962) and *Reynolds* v. *Sims* (1964). The Court had alarmed Dirksen by taking jurisdiction of cases where malapportionment was claimed and then, in *Reynolds,* declaring that the equal protection clause requires that the seats of both houses of a bicameral state legislature be apportioned on a population basis. As the strongest objections to these rulings were from state legislators, especially those with rural constituencies, Dirksen and others determined that their initiative could register most effectively through voting to call a special constitutional convention to deal with this outrage. A majority of legislative bodies in thirty-four states (two-thirds of the fifty states in the Union after 1959) would be needed to support the petition.

In seeking to employ the untried procedure of having the state legislators apply to Congress to call a federal convention to consider an apportionment amendment, Senator Dirksen chose the most favorable procedural path to his goal. He had already failed to persuade congressional colleagues to order a delay in court-ordered reapportionment. Dirksen quietly took an unused route, one that was most suited to capturing the political strength of hostility to the Supreme Court apportionment rulings. State chapters of the American Farm Bureau Federation worked closely with Dirksen through the entire campaign. In 1964 the general assembly of the Council of State Governments passed a resolution favoring an application to Congress for a constitutional amendment on apportionment. Almost before it was announced, sixteen state legislatures had voted for the Dirksen petition to Congress. This swift start led to an awareness of danger, which provoked supporters of reapportionment to worry about the procedures for a convention as well as the substance of any amendment that might be proposed.

The Constitution provides that upon application of two-thirds of the states, Congress "shall call a convention." Dirksen's opponents began to talk darkly about the possible nightmare of a "runaway" convention, one that might propose any number of amendments or even an entirely new constitution. As the number of state legislatures to pass a "Dirksen resolution" increased to twenty and then twenty-five, the most constructive response to the threat of an unbridled constitutional convention was the introduction by Senator Sam Ervin of a bill to provide procedures for such an eventuality.

Ervin's "federal constitutional act" would have required, particularly in the amendment or amendments to be proposed, uniformity in each application to Congress, placed a six-year life on such applications, and permitted a state to rescind its application. When two-thirds of the states had made proper application, certified by the clerk of the House and the secretary of the Senate, each house would be duty bound to agree to a concurrent resolution calling for the convening of a federal constitutional convention on the designated subject. Such a resolution would designate the place and time of meeting of the convention, set forth the nature of the amendment or amendments for consideration, specify the means of ratification, and provide that the convention be convened within one year. Any such convention would "be composed of as many delegates from each State as it is entitled to Representatives in Congress." The states themselves would govern the method for selecting delegates, and the vice-president of the United States would convene the constitutional convention. The state delegations would each have but a single vote, but in case "the delegates from any State present are evenly divided on any question before the convention, the vote of that State shall not be cast on the question." Ervin's bill also ruled out proposing an amendment "of a general nature different from that stated in the concurrent resolution calling the convention." This measure was not acted upon, even though the number of Dirksen resolutions rose to thirty.

By June 1969 thirty-three states had passed resolutions to apply to Congress for a special constitutional convention to propose the Dirksen apportionment amendment. There was fear that the Senate might be obliged to drop other business to engage in "a chaotic fight over basic Constitutional law."

Meanwhile, an increasing number of states—more than forty—were complying with *Reynolds*, and second thoughts about an amendment were spreading to the state legislatures. The North Carolina legislature rescinded its earlier resolution, and the number of states was suddenly down to thirty-two. The campaign continued in the summer of 1969, but legislatures were going out of session without acting, and then, Senator Dirksen died in September. Finally, on 4 November 1969, the Wisconsin assembly refused by a vote of 62–36 to support the Dirksen resolution, and the idea of such an amendment was virtually abandoned.

AMENDMENTS TO THE CONSTITUTION

AMENDMENTS AND THE STATES

When several states do not follow strong trends in the rest of the nation a federal constitutional amendment may be advanced to bring them to heel. This was achieved in a number of instances, beginning with the constitutional policy of racial equality set forth at the end of the Civil War in the Thirteenth, Fourteenth, and Fifteenth Amendments. The provision that the states stop electing United States senators by vote of their legislatures and do so by popular ballot stemmed partially from a similar animus. As has been seen, prior to World War I most states had adopted prohibition laws and permitted women to vote, but the Eighteenth and Nineteenth Amendments were essential to enforce this policy in a few remaining states. The Twenty-fourth Amendment, which provides that the right to vote shall not be abridged by reason of failure to pay a poll tax, has a kinship with the Civil War Amendments, as it was directed primarily at a few southern states.

This is not to say that amendments are often inspired by a single objective. They ordinarily have a complex purpose, usually a mixture of aims. Thus, the amendment for equal rights for women, adopted by the House in August 1970 but defeated in the Senate, was aimed at broadening congressional power, overcoming some state practices, and augmenting the authority of the Supreme Court.

There are also amendments geared to changing constitutional provisions, whether vague or specific, which cannot be altered by an ordinary statute. The Twentieth Amendment in 1933 exemplified this by resetting exact dates for assembling Congress (from 4 March to 3 January) and for inaugurating the president and vice-president (from 4 March to 20 January). The two-term limit for president could not have been set by statute—hence, the Twenty-second Amendment. While the admission of new states into the Union is a subject of ordinary legislation, provisions for District of Columbia representation in Congress and participation in presidential elections are subjects requiring constitutional amendments. The District was, for example, granted electors for president by the Twenty-third Amendment, ratified in 1961. Another illustration of a technical amendment, one needed because no other form of legislation could legitimately achieve the objective in mind, is the Twenty-fifth Amendment, put forward by Senator Birch Bayh of Indiana to clear up ambiguity over presidential disability, removal, and succession. This was ratified in 1967.

The question of whether a problem can be dealt with by a statute instead of a constitutional amendment recurs often. The child-labor issue early in the twentieth century shows how changing times and outlooks gave this question different answers. In 1916, Congress and President Woodrow Wilson believed the commerce clause justified a child-labor law, but the Supreme Court said no in 1918 in *Hammer*. After another law (this one based on the tax power) and another judicial invalidation, the country was treated to fifteen years of controversy over the wisdom of a child-labor amendment proposed by Congress in 1924. Then Congress again passed a child-labor statute based on the commerce clause, and this time the Supreme Court upheld it and overruled *Hammer*. In years when the Supreme Court is indulgent toward congressional power—when the justices have a spirit of restraint regarding the national legislature, in other words—much can be done by statute that might in another era call for an amendment. If the Supreme Court had not taken a generous view of the authority of Congress, there are many basic statutes that would have had to await adoption of new amendments. Since the 1930s these include the National Labor Relations Act and the Social Security Act of 1935, the Fair Labor Standards Act of 1938, and the Civil Rights Act of 1964.

THE EIGHTEEN-YEAR-OLD VOTE

It is clear that these and many other statutes are directed in part at bringing a few recalcitrant states into line, at setting national standards in a particular field, and at ensuring that the sanctions are sufficient to bring the desired result. The legal mind is stretched and the lay mind bewildered by a statute-or-amendment cacophony. There seems little doubt that a national act to legalize abortions throughout the United States or Supreme Court rulings holding anti-abortion statutes invalid would make the slow, state-by-state process of reform unnecessary. But very serious doubt about the constitutionality of reducing the voting age to eighteen in federal, state, and local elections by means of a simple statute led to the passage of the Twenty-sixth Amendment.

The eighteen-year-old vote was granted by Title III of the Voting Rights Act Amendments of 1970, approved by President Nixon 22 June 1970. The key part of the text is as follows:

> Sec. 302. Except as required by the Constitution, no citizen of the United States who is otherwise qualified to vote in any State or political subdivision in any primary or in any election shall be denied the right to vote in any such primary or election on account of age if such citizen is eighteen years of age or older.

Senator Edward Kennedy of Massachusetts had championed this statutory solution by contending that the approval of the Voting Rights Act of 1965 in the case of *Katzenbach* v. *Morgan* (1966) explicitly recognized that Congress had broad power to legislate to enforce the equal protection clause. The Court by a 7–2 margin upheld the provision that no person who has completed the sixth grade in Puerto Rico shall be denied the right to vote in any election because of his inability to read or write English. Yet there was sufficient doubt within Congress about the limits of its powers that the measure had to be tacked on to the extension of the Voting Rights Act and also had to include a proviso for enforcement that anticipated a Supreme Court test. Congress could not, directly and explicitly, seek from the Supreme Court an advisory opinion on the eighteen-year-old-vote statute. It could, and did, authorize and direct the attorney general "to institute in the name of the United States such actions against states or political subdivisions, including actions for injunctive relief, as he may determine to be necessary to implement" the law.

While Senator Kennedy argued that a statute was adequate and constitutional, the Department of Justice and President Nixon insisted that an amendment was required. President Nixon canvassed "many of the nation's leading constitutional scholars" and found that the "great majority" regarded providing for the eighteen-year-old vote by statute "as unconstitutional."

The tactic of placing the eighteen-year-old-vote provision in the Voting Rights Act amendments of 1970 helped ensure its adoption by both houses of Congress. It is interesting to observe how this tactic affected the president, the attorney general, state compliance, the development of litigation, and the response of the courts. President Nixon favored voting at age eighteen but believed this should be done state by state or by federal constitutional amendment, and yet he signed the measure because he lacked an item veto and could not have killed Title III without vetoing the first two titles of the Voting Rights Act amendments. Attorney General John Mitchell promptly sought letters of compliance from all governors and had received positive assurances from twenty by the end of July 1970.

The Supreme Court held in *Oregon* v. *Mitchell* (1970) that Congress could validly lower the voting age to eighteen for federal, but not state and local, elections. This decision presented state and local election officials with the expensive prospect of providing separate balloting arrangements for voters of different ages whenever national and state elections coincided. This would next occur across the nation in 1972. Many persons who had been reluctant to afford the vote to eighteen-year-olds now agreed to move swiftly toward a constitutional amendment to make voting eligibility by age equivalent in all elections. In March 1971, Congress approved and thus officially proposed this amendment to the states: "The right of Citizens of the United States, who are 18 years of age or older, to vote shall not be denied or abridged by the United States or by any state on account of age." The two-thirds majority was easily achieved: the Senate vote on 10 March was unanimous at 94–0, and the House vote on 23 March was 401–19. Ratification began immediately and was completed in the record time of three months on 30 June 1971, when Ohio became the thirty-eighth and final state to approve the amendment.

CASES

Abington School District v. Schempp, 374 U.S. 203 (1963)
Baker v. Carr, 369 U.S. 186 (1962)
Dodge v. Brady, 240 U.S. 122 (1916)
Dred Scott v. Sandford, 19 Howard 393 (1857)

Engle v. Vitale, 370 U.S. 421 (1962)
Hammer v. Dagenhart, 247 U.S. 251 (1918)
Katzenbach v. Morgan, 384 U.S. 641 (1966)
Minor v. Happersett, 88 U.S. 162 (1875)
Murray v. Curlett, 374 U.S. 203 (1963)
Oregon v. Mitchell, 400 U.S. 112 (1970)
Pollock v. Farmers' Loan and Trust Company, 157 U.S. 429;
    158 U.S. 601 (1895)
Reynolds v. Sims, 377 U.S. 533 (1964)
United States v. Darby, 312 U.S. 100 (1941)

BIBLIOGRAPHY

Tip H. Allen and Coleman B. Ransone, *Constitutional Revision in Theory and Practice* (1962), provides a useful starting point for analysis. Comment, "Congressional Reversal of Supreme Court Decisions, 1945–1957," in *Harvard Law Review*, 81 (1955), offers an excellent, though hardly exhaustive, summary of twenty-five instances of objectionable judicial decisions altered or countermanded by congressional statute. Wilbur Edel, *A Constitutional Convention: Threat or Challenge?* (1981), surveys the arguments for a rethinking of the entire Constitution.

Gerald Gunther, "The Convention Method of Amending the United States Constitution," in *Georgia Law Review*, 14 (1979), surveys some of the problems involved in the fears of a "runaway" constitutional convention. Paul Kauper, ed., *The Article V Convention Process: A Symposium* (1971), a reprint from *Michigan Law Review*, 66 (1968), is a useful collection of essays on various aspects of the process. Lester B. Orfield, *The Amending of the Federal Constitution* (1942; repr., 1971), serves as a basic reference source on the subject.

Richard Polenberg, "The National Committee to Uphold Constitutional Government, 1937–1941," in *Journal of American History*, 52 (1965), provides information on the link between the American Liberty League and support for an anti-third-term amendment. Herman Pritchett, "Congress and Article V Conventions," in *Western Political Quarterly*, 35 (1982), highlights some of the national political issues involved. Donald Robinson, ed., *Reforming American Government: The Bicentennial Papers of the Committee on the Constitutional System* (1985), collects essays on amendment issues. Paul G. Willis and George L. Willis, "The Politics of the Twenty-second Amendment," in *Western Political Quarterly*, 5 (1952), illuminates the amendment process.

[See also CONGRESS; CRIMINAL PROCEDURE; EXECUTIVE AND DOMESTIC AFFAIRS; EXECUTIVE AND FOREIGN AFFAIRS; JUDICIAL REVIEW; RELIGIOUS LIBERTY; and SUPREME COURT OF THE UNITED STATES.]

THE COMMERCE CLAUSE

Paul R. Benson, Jr.

T HE story of the commerce clause of the United States Constitution is both interesting and important. It is interesting because the genius of the Constitution—its flexibility and adaptability as a practical instrument of public policy—is clearly revealed in the evolution of the interpretation of the clause by the Supreme Court. It is important because the history of the commerce clause is to a large extent the history of the great growth of national power over domestic affairs, particularly since the Civil War. Article I, Section 8 of the Constitution makes the seemingly innocuous assertion that "the Congress shall have Power . . . To regulate Commerce with foreign Nations, and among the several States, and with the Indian Tribes." As will be seen, Congress has used this authority to give the national government vast power to regulate every aspect of American business and the economy and even to achieve goals of social welfare and individual rights where these have had an economic impact or connection.

THE BEGINNINGS

The history of the commerce clause properly begins with the great steamboat case, *Gibbons* v. *Ogden* (1824), and with the powerful pen of Chief Justice John Marshall. The New York legislature had given a business partnership the exclusive right to operate steamboats on the state's waterways, and this monopoly granted a license to Aaron Ogden to run steamboats on New York Bay. Then, Thomas Gibbons, an adventurer, began to operate a steamboat ferry service between New Jersey and New York on the basis of a federal coasting license issued under the Federal Coasting Act of 1793. Ogden sued Gibbons

in the state courts and obtained an injunction against the interloper; Gibbons appealed.

In a unanimous decision the Supreme Court found for Gibbons and struck down the New York monopoly laws. Chief Justice Marshall wrote the majority opinion. For the first time, he carefully defined the three main parts of the commerce clause. He began by giving the term *commerce* a broad and expansive meaning: "Commerce, undoubtedly, is traffic, but it is something more; it is intercourse. It describes the commercial intercourse between nations, and parts of nations, in all its branches, and is regulated by prescribing rules for carrying on that intercourse." And, Marshall continued, commerce had always been understood to include navigation. Now, to what commerce did this regulatory power extend? Commerce, as used in the Constitution, was a unit and carried the same meaning throughout the clause. Commerce with foreign nations included every species of commercial intercourse; the same was true with the states: "The word 'among' means intermingled with. . . . Commerce among the States, cannot stop at the external boundary line of each State, but may be introduced into the interior." However, noted Marshall, there were limits to the reach of federal power: "Comprehensive as the word 'among' is, it may very properly be restricted to that commerce which concerns more States than one. . . . The completely internal commerce of a State, then, may be considered as reserved for the State itself."

Finally, Marshall asked just what that power is and then answered in sweeping terms:

> It is the power to regulate; that is, to prescribe the rule by which commerce is to be governed. This power, like all others vested in Congress,

938

is complete in itself, may be exercised to its utmost extent, and acknowledges no limitations, other than are prescribed in the constitution. . . . If . . . the sovereignty of Congress, though limited to specified objects, is plenary as to those objects, the power over commerce with foreign nations, and among the several States, is vested in Congress as absolutely as it would be in a single government.

Realizing the scope of this definition and the tremendous grant of power to Congress, he went on to acknowledge that the real restraints on the commerce power were political, not textual.

Having defined the commerce clause in broad and comprehensive terms, the chief justice faced the question of whether the power to regulate commerce is exclusive to the national government or shared with the state governments. But Marshall, the great nation-builder who usually delighted in expounding national power under the Constitution, became uncharacteristically guarded and held that the matter could be dismissed because Congress had already legislated. The only question that remained was whether a state could regulate commerce at the same time that Congress was doing so. Here again, however, Marshall was reluctant to give a straightforward answer. Instead, he stated that if a state passed a law of the same nature as an act of Congress, the state did not derive its authority from the delegated congressional power but from some other power that was reserved to the state. This was an oblique reference to what would come to be called the "police power" of the states—the inherent power to legislate for the health, safety, morals, and general welfare of the people.

Marshall was now in a position to consider the question of whether the New York monopoly laws conflicted with the Federal Coasting Act of 1793. He had no trouble in finding that the latter granted to licensed vessels the privilege of carrying on the coasting trade and hence the right to navigate the coastal waters of the United States. Thus, the state acts came into direct collision with the act of Congress and would therefore have to fall. The monopoly was declared at an end, and commerce by steamboat was free.

The importance of *Gibbons* for the subsequent development of the commerce clause in constitutional adjudication cannot be overstated. In one of his great nationalistic opinions, Chief Justice Marshall interpreted broadly all parts of the enumerated power. He thereby handed Congress a tremendous grant of power to control the American economy in all its parts and facets, to regulate all types of businesses, and to apply these rules to the ever-changing conditions created by new technologies or new social and political circumstances.

But Marshall did not decide the question of whether power over commerce was exclusive to Congress or shared by Congress and the state legislatures. Instead, he left this question unanswered and introduced into constitutional law the concept of the inherent "police power" of the states. This concept appears again in the chief justice's decision in *Willson* v. *Black Bird Creek Marsh Co.* (1829), in which he upheld a Delaware law that authorized a dam across a navigable tidal creek flowing into the Delaware River, even though the dam obstructed navigation of the creek by a vessel holding a federal coasting license identical to the one employed by Thomas Gibbons. Marshall reasoned that the state statute was designed to improve health conditions and to enhance property values in the area and that it was therefore a valid regulatory measure; furthermore, it was not in conflict with any act of Congress. Marshall obviously regarded the legislation as a legitimate exercise of the state's police power.

In 1835, Roger Brooke Taney became chief justice, and the Supreme Court fell into confusion regarding the nature of the commerce power and its relation to the police power of the states. But, finally, in the landmark case of *Cooley* v. *Board of Wardens of the Port of Philadelphia* (1852), the Court cleared up much of this confusion. At stake was the constitutionality of a Pennsylvania act of 1803 that required ships entering or leaving the port of Philadelphia to take on local pilots. Justice Benjamin R. Curtis met the issue squarely: he held that Pennsylvania had enacted a regulation of commerce and that thus the question was whether the grant of the commercial power to Congress deprived the states of all power to regulate pilots. He answered this as follows:

The grant of commercial power to Congress does not contain any terms which expressly exclude the states from exercising an authority over its subject matter. If they are excluded, it must be because the nature of the power, thus granted to Congress, requires that a similar authority should not exist in the States. . . . But when the nature of a power like this is spoken of, when it is said that the nature of the power requires that it should be exercised exclusively by Congress, it must be intended to refer to the subjects of that power, and to say they are of such a nature as to require exclusive legislation by Congress.

Having turned attention from the nature of the power (a philosophical question) to the subjects of the power (a pragmatic inquiry), Curtis found that commercial regulation covered a vast field that contained many different subjects. Some of these were national in character and demanded the uniform regulation that only Congress could provide; here federal power was properly exclusive. Others were essentially local in nature (although still connected with interstate commerce) and required diverse regulation; and as to such local matters, the states had concurrent power over commerce in the absence of any conflicting congressional action.

Curtis looked to an act of Congress of 7 August 1789 that left the regulation of pilotage to the states until such time as Congress might legislate further; he had no difficulty in finding that the Pennsylvania statute accorded with the sense of Congress that pilotage was a local subject that could best be regulated by the individual states according to the "local peculiarities" of their own ports. The state law was constitutional, but Curtis was careful to confine his decision to pilotage and to emphasize the point that the Court's opinion did not extend

> to the question what other subjects, under the commercial power, are within the exclusive control of Congress, or may be regulated by the States in the absence of all congressional legislation; nor to the general question how far any regulation of a subject by Congress, may be deemed to operate as an exclusion of all legislation by the States upon the same subject.

The decision in *Cooley* is important for two reasons. First, the Court answered the question that Marshall had left open in *Gibbons*. It adopted in effect a "selectively exclusive" theory, holding that some aspects of commerce were of national importance and required uniform, or "exclusive," congressional regulation, whereas other aspects were primarily of local concern and permitted diverse, or "concurrent," state regulation. This compromise theory of the commerce power proved to be very practical and enduring. It gave to the national government all the power necessary to regulate an expanding, increasingly industrialized, and interdependent economy, and at the same time, it allowed the states to remain viable partners in the American federal system of shared governmental power.

Second, in focusing attention on the subjects of the commerce power, the Court set itself in the position of ultimate arbiter of the boundaries of national and state power by reserving to itself final determination of the classification of those subjects. The real significance of the *Cooley* case is that it gave to the Court great and far-reaching power to make decisions that would affect the very heart of American federalism. Justice Curtis had enunciated a formula—the *Cooley* rule—that established the Supreme Court as the umpire of the nation and the states.

FEDERAL POWER TO 1937

For more than sixty years after the *Gibbons* case, Congress did not make much use of its power to regulate commerce. After the Civil War, however, Americans turned their energies toward economic expansion and the creation of material wealth. Business boomed, and with it came the rise of large corporations and trusts that monopolized industries, fixed prices, discriminated against customers, and effectively excluded any real competitors. Some of the worst of these abuses were in the railroad industry with its many discriminatory practices involving rate rebates, pooling agreements, and the like.

Interstate Commerce Act. In response to a growing public demand for an end to these exploitative actions, Congress, in 1887, passed the Interstate Commerce Act, which provided for "reasonable and just" rail rates, prohibited the worst of the other abuses, and established a five-man Interstate Commerce Commission (ICC) to police the industry. The act was upheld in *Interstate Commerce Commission* v. *Brimson* (1894) as a necessary and proper regulation by Congress of commercial transportation. However, the Court generally interpreted the statute's regulatory provisions so narrowly that it required several later enactments to make the commission an effective governing body.

As the ICC began to be strengthened, some of its most notable successes came in cases in which the Court upheld its authority to control intrastate rail rates where these could be shown to have an adverse effect upon interstate commerce. The leading decision is *Houston, East & West Texas Railway* v. *United States* (1914), better known as the *Shreveport Case*. Texas railroads were charging more for short hauls between Shreveport, Louisiana, and points in eastern Texas than for longer hauls west from those places to Dallas and Houston. Thus, Texas merchants enjoyed an unfair advantage over their out-of-state competitors; to correct this discrimination, the ICC issued an order requiring the equalization of the intrastate rates and the interstate rates. This was appealed on the grounds that the federal agency had no jurisdiction over intrastate rates.

Justice Charles Evans Hughes wrote the strongly worded opinion, which upheld the ICC. Emphasizing the paramount power of Congress "to provide the law for the government of interstate commerce," he argued that Congress's right to regulate was broad and penetrating:

> Its authority, extending to these interstate carriers as instruments of interstate commerce, necessarily embraces the right to control their operations in all matters having such a close and substantial relation to interstate traffic that the control is essential or appropriate to the security of that traffic, to the efficiency of the interstate service, and to the maintenance of conditions under which interstate commerce may be conducted upon fair terms and without molestation or hindrance. . . . Wherever the interstate and intrastate transactions of carriers are so related that the government of the one involves the control of the other, it is Congress, and not the State, that is entitled to prescribe the final and dominant rule.

The *Shreveport* decision is an early high-water mark in the Supreme Court's adjudication of national power under the commerce clause; it enunciates the proposition that federal authority can reach to essentially intrastate matters if the regulation of these is necessary to the effective protection or control of interstate commerce. Furthermore, in case of conflict, it is Congress (and not the states) that is empowered under the commerce clause to make the final determination both as to the effect of, and the remedy for, local discriminations or obstructions. In short, the *Shreveport* "affectation" doctrine demonstrates the Court's awareness that the United States economy was becoming increasingly nationalized and interdependent and thus, in constitutional terms, would provide the basis for the future expansion of national control over that economy.

Sherman Antitrust Act. At the same time that Congress moved to regulate the railroad industry, it also formulated legislation to curb the formation of the large trusts and monopolies that were threatening to control many of the nation's major industries and thereby stifle the free-enterprise system. To maintain a competitive economy, Congress, in 1890, passed the Sherman Antitrust Act, which made illegal "every contract, combination in the form of trust or otherwise, or conspiracy, in restraint of trade or commerce among the several States," and which prohibited any person from monopolizing or attempting to monopolize "any part of the trade or commerce among the several States." The law provided suitable punishments for violations of its provisions, and it contained the stipulation that the government could bring suits in equity to dissolve illegal combinations.

The first antitrust case to come before the Supreme Court was *United States* v. *E. C. Knight Co.* (1895), also known as the *Sugar Trust Case*. The American Sugar Refining Company had purchased the E. C. Knight Company and three other companies and thereby gained control of more than 90 percent of all sugar refining in the country. The government petitioned under the Sherman Act for a court order to cancel the sale agreements. In an 8–1 decision Chief Justice Melville W. Fuller denied the government's claim. Drawing a sharp distinction between commerce and manufacturing, he argued that the congressional power to regulate commerce was independent of the police power of the states to suppress monopolies in manufacturing or other productive enterprises and that the two powers should therefore be kept separate in order to preserve "the automony of the States as required by our dual form of government." To the government's contention that a business combination to control domestic production might lead to a restraint of trade among the states, Fuller answered that any such result or effect on commerce would be only "indirect" and beyond the reach of federal power. Thus, the Sherman Act could not be extended to monopolies in manufacturing, and the national government was without authority to regulate the Sugar Trust.

The *Knight* decision is important because it is the first case in which the Supreme Court used the doctrine of dual federalism and its corollary, the distinction between "direct" and "indirect" effects on commerce, to limit the delegated powers of the national government. This judicially contrived doctrine and its obviously pernicious results will be examined in more detail shortly.

Despite its early loss in *E. C. Knight Co.,* the federal government was able to use the Sherman Act to win an expanded interpretation of its power to regulate commerce. In *Northern Securities Co.* v. *United States* (1904) the Court applied the antitrust prohibitions of the act to a railroad holding company that controlled both the Northern Pacific and Great Northern roads. Justice John Marshall Harlan rejected the argument that Northern Securities was merely a stock investment company, not itself in commerce, and held that the Sherman Act made illegal "every contract, combination, or conspiracy, in whatever form, of whatever nature, and whoever may be parties to it, which directly or necessarily operates *in restraint* of trade or commerce *among the several states or with foreign nations"* (emphasis in original). Thus, it was necessary only for the government to make the factual showing that the railroad combination operated in restraint of commerce, and that had been done.

The next year in *Swift & Co.* v. *United States* (1905) the Court formulated the "stream of commerce" doctrine to expand further Congress's power under the commerce clause. The government brought suit to enjoin Swift and other meatpackers from conspiring to control the price of livestock in the stockyards. The companies argued that any combinations affecting sales had taken place in local yards and that the transfers of title were therefore local transactions, which were exempt from federal control. In a unanimous opinion Justice Oliver Wendell Holmes, Jr., looked to the extensive interstate movement of live animals and dressed meat and held that

such activities constituted "a current of commerce among the States." The application of the Sherman Act was therefore a valid exercise of federal power, and the packers could be enjoined from price-fixing. More important, the creation of the stream-of-commerce doctrine signaled a new extension of congressional authority under the commerce clause.

Federal Police Power. At the same time that Congress was beginning to regulate the worst abuses by American industry, it also began to develop, using its delegated powers to tax and to regulate commerce, the equivalent of a federal police power. If this appears to be a somewhat indirect approach, it must be remembered that constitutional theory holds that the national government (a government of enumerated powers), unlike the state governments, possesses no inherent police power with which to legislate for the health, safety, good morals, and general welfare of the people. But there was an increasing demand on the part of the public that something be done about a number of national problems of an essentially social and/or moral nature, and thus, Congress was moved to use its commerce power in particular to solve these problems.

Congress first struck at national gambling with the passage of the Federal Lottery Act of 1895, which prohibited the importation, mailing, or transporting of lottery tickets from one state to another. The act was sustained in *Champion* v. *Ames* (1903), often called the *Lottery Case.* Justice Harlan spoke for the five-man majority and, in a strongly worded opinion, held that the power to regulate commerce includes the power to prohibit it and that the Tenth Amendment does not derogate an expressly delegated power of the national government. Furthermore, prevention of harm to the public morals is a proper objective of the commerce power; if the states are free to forbid the sale of lottery tickets within their own borders, Harlan reasoned, then "Congress, for the purpose of guarding the people of the United States against the 'widespread pestilence of lotteries' and to protect the commerce which concerns all the States, may prohibit the carrying of lottery tickets from one State to another."

Harlan's opinion, which opted for a broad and unfettered view of the commerce power, represents a landmark in commerce clause adjudication. It demonstrates the Supreme Court's awareness that if Congress cannot prohibit the interstate transportation of lottery tickets, no one can do so; therefore, both federal and state regulation will be frustrated, and there will be a no-man's-land free from control by any government.

Congress was quick to use the ruling in the *Lottery Case* to reach other evils. In 1906 it passed the Pure Food and Drugs Act, which prohibited shipping adulterated and misbranded foods and drugs in interstate commerce. In 1910, Congress attacked the problem of prostitution via the White-Slave Traffic Act. Often known as the Mann Act, it proscribed the transportation of women in interstate or foreign commerce for immoral purposes. Finally, in 1919, Congress enacted the National Motor Vehicle Theft Act, which barred the movement of stolen automobiles across state lines, a measure designed actually to prevent or discourage vehicle thievery before any interstate movement occurred. The Court made clear its approval of the moral purpose behind these enactments and upheld their constitutionality in a series of decisions.

Dual Federalism. Simultaneously with the Supreme Court's development of expanded interpretations of national power under the commerce clause, including the *Shreveport* affectation doctrine and the *Swift* stream-of-commerce doctrine, the justices also erected a bar to federal authority in the doctrine of dual federalism. This judicial formulation rested on the premise—faulty as a matter of long-accepted historical understanding—that the reserved powers of the states under the Tenth Amendment limit or restrict the delegated powers of the national government. There is not space here to review in detail the validity of this proposition; suffice it to say that for at least the first one hundred years of the existence of the United States as a constitutional republic, such an interpretation of the Tenth Amendment had not been given serious consideration by the Court. In fact, two eminent chief justices, Marshall and Taney, and a renowned associate justice and legal scholar, Joseph Story, had all taken the view that the Tenth Amendment was but declaratory of the original distribution of powers in the Constitution and thus did not abridge any of the powers granted to the national government.

In spite of the lack of supporting precedent, however, the Supreme Court (under the influence of many essentially conservative justices in the period 1895–1936) used the doctrine of dual federalism to create a second line of cases in which the power of Congress under the commerce clause was limited and in which federal authority over certain economic conditions was therefore frustrated for a time. The first of these cases is *E. C. Knight Co.*, already detailed, in which the Court held that the suppression of monopolies in productive enterprise is a local matter left to state control under the Tenth Amendment and thus not subject to congressional regulation.

The next instance of the use of the doctrine of dual federalism came in *Hammer v. Dagenhart* (1918), which involved the constitutionality of the Child Labor Act of 1916. The act prohibited for thirty days the shipment in interstate commerce of products made with child labor. By a vote of 5–4 the Court struck down the statute. Speaking for the majority, Justice William R. Day first invoked the old discredited distinction between the power to regulate and the power to prohibit. He distinguished contrary precedents such as *Champion* on the ground that in those cases the restricted products were "harmful" and thus prohibition of them was the only way to protect commerce from becoming contaminated; here, however, the cotton goods were "of themselves harmless." Then Day took up the question of congressional purpose, which, in his view, was "to standardize the ages at which children may be employed in mining and manufacturing." But employment in such production was not part of commerce, and Day was adamant in his denunciation of the act: "The grant of power to Congress over the subject of interstate commerce was to enable it to regulate such commerce, and not to give it authority to control the States in their exercise of the police power over local trade and manufacture." Therefore, the statute unconstitutionally invaded the reserved powers of the states under the Tenth Amendment and was invalid.

Probably the best example of the Supreme Court's invocation of the doctrine of dual federalism, however, occurs in *Carter v. Carter Coal Co.* (1936), a case involving the validity of the Bituminous Coal Conservation Act of 1935 (often called the Guffey-Snyder Coal Act), which provided for a coal code to regulate the industry. Justice George Sutherland, writing for the majority, began with a general defense of dual federalism, moved on to reiterate the *E. C. Knight Co.* holding that mining is not commerce, and finally came to the government's contention that the production of coal did "bear upon and directly affect" interstate traffic in coal. Sutherland's answer was to resurrect the distinction between direct and indirect effects on commerce and then to drive that dichotomy to its logical conclusion. Because the alleged harmful consequences of labor-management disputes in the coal industry (even though they might result in work stoppages and a reduced volume of coal mined and shipped) were "all local evils," their effect upon commerce, regardless of the extent, could only be "secondary and indirect" and thus beyond the reach of federal legislative control. The national government was powerless to regulate an important sector of the nation's economy —the entire soft-coal industry.

The decision in the *Carter* case threw into stark relief the absurdity of the Court's distinctions between manufacturing and commerce and between direct and indirect effects. Neither was based on economic reality; both were artificial formulas designed to allow the justices to write their own predilections concerning governmental regulation into constitutional law. But beyond these considerations the doctrine of dual federalism created a no-man's-land between the jurisdictions of the national government and the states in which neither could regulate. In other words, dual federalism frustrated both governments in their efforts to confront and solve modern economic problems.

FEDERAL POWER AFTER 1937

Reality intruded into the judicial chambers after the outcome of the 1936 presidential elections. Franklin D. Roosevelt won overwhelmingly, vindicating public support for his New Deal program, and promptly turned his fire on the Supreme Court in the form of his famous Court-packing plan of 1937. It is difficult to assess the influence that the plan had on some of the more centrist justices, but suffice it to say that between 1937 and 1942 the Supreme Court repudiated the doctrine of dual federalism, opted for the broadest kind of national power over commerce, and withdrew almost entirely from its previous role as a censor of governmen-

tal economic policy. The story of how Congress has come to have virtually unlimited regulatory power over every aspect of the American economy follows.

National Labor Relations Act. In 1935, Congress passed the National Labor Relations Act, popularly known as the Wagner Act, which imposed extensive regulations on labor-management relations in industry and which created the National Labor Relations Board (NLRB) to police such relations and specifically to prevent certain "unfair labor practices," including interference with employees forming their own unions and bargaining collectively with employers. The key jurisdictional provision in the act empowered the NLRB to issue cease-and-desist orders against any person or company engaging in any unfair labor practice "affecting commerce."

The constitutionality of the Wagner Act was first tested in *National Labor Relations Board* v. *Jones and Laughlin Steel Corp.* (1937). Jones and Laughlin, the nation's fourth-largest steel producer and one with extensive interstate operations, was charged with committing certain unfair labor practices at its big Aliquippa plant in Pennsylvania. The question became whether Congress could control labor-management relations in "local" industrial production that affected commerce. Chief Justice Charles Evans Hughes answered in the affirmative and gave broad scope to the power of Congress over commerce: If production activities had "such a close and substantial relation" to interstate commerce that it was essential to regulate the former in order to protect the latter, Congress could not be denied "the power to exercise that control." Clearly, Jones and Laughlin's multifaceted nationwide operations exhibited just such a relationship.

Hughes faced one final hurdle—the steel company's claim that any effects on commerce would be only indirect and therefore not subject to congressional authority. The chief justice responded succinctly, "In view of respondent's far-flung activities, it is idle to say that the effect would be indirect or remote. It is obvious that it would be immediate and might be catastrophic." This decided the case; the National Labor Relations Act was a constitutional exercise of the power of Congress to regulate commerce among the several states. In another case decided the same day, *National Labor Relations Board* v. *Friedman-Harry*

944

Marks Clothing Co., the Court upheld the application of the Wagner Act to a small clothing manufacturer. Size was obviously unimportant if the business had a "close and substantial" relationship to interstate commerce.

The great significance of the *Jones and Laughlin* decision is that in it the Supreme Court dealt a body blow to the doctrine of dual federalism. Congress now had power under the commerce clause to regulate labor-management relations in certain manufacturing activities that had previously been considered "local" and therefore beyond the reach of federal power. Furthermore, in a number of cases over the next few years, the Court uniformly sanctioned the jurisdiction of the NLRB in a variety of industries; and in *National Labor Relations Board* v. *Fainblatt* (1939), Justice Harlan Fiske Stone accepted the board's contention that its authority extended to a small New Jersey processor of women's sports garments, even though the company had no title or interest in the cloth or finished goods that moved interstate. Fainblatt's unfair labor practices might lead to a cessation of manufacture and, consequently, to a suspension in interstate commerce. This circumstance, Stone reasoned, brought Fainblatt's enterprise under federal regulation.

The Supreme Court's decision in the *Fainblatt* case effectively closed the question of the NLRB's jurisdiction; after 1939, no serious argument was advanced that the NLRB lacks authority to investigate charges of unfair labor practices and to issue cease-and-desist orders. In fact, the NLRB has voluntarily placed limits on its own jurisdiction by creating categories of cases that it could accept but would not. The only valid conclusion to be drawn is that under the commerce clause, Congress has plenary power over the conduct of labor-management relations in American industry.

Fair Labor Standards Act. In 1938, Congress passed the Fair Labor Standards Act, which prescribed minimum wages and maximum hours (subject to time-and-a-half for overtime) for all employees engaged in interstate commerce or in the production of goods for that commerce. The act made it unlawful for an employer to ship or sell in interstate commerce any goods produced under substandard labor conditions and to violate the wage and hour provisions for employees engaged in production for such commerce. This comprehensive labor legislation was quickly subjected to a test of its constitutionality by the owner of a Georgia sawmill engaged in shipping lumber out of state.

Justice Stone wrote the unanimous opinion in *United States* v. *Darby* (1941), undoubtedly one of the half-dozen most important cases in Supreme Court history. He first took up the question of whether Congress could prohibit the shipment in interstate commerce of lumber produced under substandard labor conditions, and he answered it in the affirmative. Quoting John Marshall's powerful language from *Gibbons*, Stone reasoned, "The power to regulate commerce is the power 'to prescribe the rule by which commerce is governed.' . . . It extends not only to those regulations which aid, foster and protect the commerce, but embraces those which prohibit it." Responding to the objection that the act was in reality designed to regulate wages and hours, control of which was reserved to the individual states, Stone was blunt and unequivocal:

> The power of Congress over interstate commerce . . . can neither be enlarged nor diminished by the exercise or non-exercise of state power. . . . Congress . . . is free to exclude from the commerce articles whose use in the states for which they are destined it may conceive to be injurious to the public health, morals or welfare, even though the state has not sought to regulate their use. . . . It is no objection to the assertion of the power to regulate interstate commerce that its exercise is attended by the same incidents which attend the exercise of the police power of the states.

Then he expressly overruled *Hammer*, arguing that it rested on a distinction (between harmful and harmless goods) that had long since been abandoned.

Stone then took up the question whether Congress could prohibit the employment under substandard labor conditions of workmen in the production of goods for interstate commerce. He cited with approval the *Shreveport* affectation doctrine and held that Congress had the power, through the commerce clause, to prevent the evils of substandard labor conditions and unfair competition.

Finally, Stone faced his last obstacle—the claim that the Tenth Amendment limited the delegated powers of the federal government. In a now-famous statement he met this issue squarely and disposed of it:

> Our conclusion is unaffected by the Tenth Amendment. . . . The amendment states but a truism that all is retained which has not been surrendered. . . . From the beginning and for many years the amendment has been construed as not depriving the national government of authority to resort to all means for the exercise of a granted power which are appropriate and plainly adapted to the permitted end.

Stone's conclusion, solidly based on history and case precedent, laid to rest the doctrine of dual federalism for another thirty-five years. A somewhat abortive attempt was made by conservative justices on the Court to reestablish its respectability in 1976 (an incident recounted below), but the doctrine has lost its former vitality and properly so. As in the beginning, the delegated powers of the national government are complete in themselves and may be exercised to their utmost extent.

As clear and as powerful as were the holdings in the *Darby* case, however, they did not close the question of the jurisdictional reach of the Fair Labor Standards Act. There were two reasons for this. First, the act created no administrative agency that could make initial expert judgments on questions of fact. Second, Congress had not attempted to exercise its power over commerce to its fullest extent; the provisions of the act were applicable only to employees "engaged in commerce or in the production of goods for commerce." Thus, there was a continuing stream of cases after 1941 involving interpretation of this language.

The first test came in *A. B. Kirschbaum Co.* v. *Walling* (1942). Kirschbaum owned a building that was rented to garment manufacturers who produced clothing for interstate commerce. He employed twelve maintenance men at substandard wages to produce heat and hot water, to keep elevators and the power system in working order, and to make necessary repairs. The question was whether their activities brought them within the protection of the act, and the Court ruled in the affirmative. Justice Felix Frankfurter argued that the tenants could not engage in manufacturing without a habitable building and that the work of the employees therefore had

"such a close and immediate tie with the process of production for commerce" that the employees must be regarded as engaged in an occupation "necessary to the production of goods for commerce." This broad interpretation of the act furnished the Department of Labor with a far-reaching grant of constitutional power to enforce the congressionally prescribed labor standards against employers in all areas of the economy.

Over time, Congress has broadened the reach of the statute. In 1961 it amended the act and extended its coverage to all employees of any "enterprise" engaged in commerce or production for commerce. In 1966, Congress added to its list any enterprise engaged in the operation of a hospital, a school for special children, an elementary or secondary school, or an institution of higher learning, regardless of whether the enterprise is public or private, profit or nonprofit. Simultaneously, Congress terminated its exemption of the states and their political subdivisions as "employers" within the meaning of the earlier statute.

Critical reaction was immediate, and these amendments were challenged as to their constitutionality by twenty-eight states. In *Maryland* v. *Wirtz* (1968) the Supreme Court upheld the statutory changes. Speaking for a 6–2 majority, Justice John Marshall Harlan first looked to the fact that schools and hospitals are large users of goods that move in interstate commerce. Because strikes and work stoppages could obviously interrupt and burden this flow of goods, Congress had a "rational basis" for extending the act's coverage to workers in these enterprises. Then he took up Maryland's contention that the federal commerce power had to yield to state sovereignty. Harlan refused to "carve up the commerce power to protect enterprises indistinguishable in their effect on commerce from private businesses, simply because those enterprises happen to be run by the States for the benefit of their citizens."

Harlan's strong and well-reasoned opinion merely reaffirmed the plenary nature of the power of Congress to regulate commerce. This understanding was reiterated again in *Fry* v. *United States* (1975), in which the Court upheld the Economic Stabilization Act of 1970, which temporarily froze the wages of state and local government workers, against the claim that it intruded upon a protected area of state sovereignty.

Then, one year later, the case of *National League of Cities* v. *Usery* (1976) was decided, and for the first time in forty years, the Supreme Court resurrected the doctrine of dual federalism to strike down congressional legislation based on the commerce clause. In 1974, Congress amended the Fair Labor Standards Act to extend federal wage and hour requirements to almost all employees of the states and their political subdivisions. These provisions were attacked as repugnant to the reserved powers of the states under the Tenth Amendment.

Writing for a five-man majority, Justice William H. Rehnquist agreed with critics of the provisions. Because one "undoubted attribute" of state sovereignty was the power to determine the wages and hours of state employees and because this was a function essential to the "separate and independent existence" of the states, Congress could not (even under the commerce power) abrogate state authority in the matter. Having declared unconstitutional the act's amendments, Rehnquist proceeded to distinguish the *Fry* decision (the Economic Stabilization Act of 1970 was an emergency measure that displaced state power only for a limited time) and to overrule the Court's decision in *Maryland* v. *Wirtz* (the operation of schools and hospitals is an integral governmental function of the states). Justice William J. Brennan, Jr., wrote a scathing dissent in which he accused the majority of disregarding all of the Court's most notable commerce clause decisions since *Gibbons,* and reading its own conception of what constitutes a "desirable governmental structure" into the Constitution.

The decision in the case evoked a large volume of constitutional commentary, most of it critical. Indeed, it is difficult to know where to begin in criticizing Justice Rehnquist's opinion; but a few comments will highlight the fallacies and misconceptions that underlie his reasoning. First, he disregarded the plain meaning of John Marshall's seminal interpretation in *Gibbons* of the broad congressional power to regulate commerce. Second, he overrode in the most casual fashion the accepted notion that the power of Congress over interstate commerce cannot be diminished by the exercise of state power. Finally, Rehnquist simply ignored the nation's entire constitutional history in holding that the Tenth Amendment may be invoked as a limitation on the exercise of a delegated power of Congress.

The principle enunciated in *National League of Cities* has not been followed in subsequent cases. In *Hodel* v. *Virginia Surface Mining and Reclamation Assn.* (1981) the Court upheld a federal law regulating surface mining on steep slopes as a valid exercise of national legislative power under the commerce clause. Justice Thurgood Marshall emphasized the congressional findings of fact about the substantial adverse effects of surface mining on interstate commerce, and he rebuffed the Virginia coal producers' claim that the act sought to regulate private land use, a traditional state function, and thus was unconstitutional under the Tenth Amendment. The statute did not attempt to regulate the "States as States"; rather, Congress had simply used its commerce power "to pre-empt or displace state regulation of private activities affecting interstate commerce," clearly a legitimate federal objective.

A second case, *Equal Employment Opportunity Commission* v. *Wyoming* (1983), also failed to follow the doctrine enunciated in *National League of Cities.* At stake was the constitutionality of a 1967 federal law that makes it unlawful for employers to discriminate against persons between the ages of forty and seventy on the basis of age and that in 1974 was extended to include state and local governments. Speaking for a five-man majority, Justice William J. Brennan, Jr., held that the act did not "directly impair" the ability of the states to "structure integral operations in areas of traditional governmental functions" and thus was "a valid exercise of Congress's powers under the Commerce Clause." Justice John Paul Stevens, in a concurring opinion, spoke even more to the point. He argued that because of the interdependence of the segments of the economy and the magnitude of government employment, Congress, in exercising its power to control the labor market, may regulate both the private and public sectors of that market; he specifically rejected what he viewed as *National League of Cities'* modern embodiment of the doctrine of dual federalism.

But more was to come. Almost two years later, the Court decided *Garcia* v. *San Antonio Metropolitan Transit Authority* (1985). At stake was the constitutionality of the Fair Labor Standards Act as applied to a municipally owned and operated mass-transit system. In a 5–4 decision, Justice Harry A. Blackmun held that the transit authority was not immune from the requirements of the federal act, because the concept of "traditional governmental function" is not only unworkable in determining state immunity from federal regulation but is also inconsistent with "established principles of federalism" and because there is "nothing in the overtime and minimum-wage requirements of the FLSA, as applied to SAMTA, that is destructive of state sovereignty or violative of any constitutional provision." Then he specifically overruled *National League of Cities* and thereby rejected once again the long-discredited doctrine of dual federalism.

Regulation of Agriculture. The first response of President Franklin D. Roosevelt's New Deal to the depressed condition of American agriculture was the Agricultural Adjustment Act of 1933. This measure, based on a tax levied on processors of farm products, was declared unconstitutional by the Supreme Court in *United States* v. *Butler* (1936). Congress responded by passing the Agricultural Adjustment Act of 1938, which was based on a system of marketing quotas for several major crops. The first test of the law came in *Mulford* v. *Smith* (1939). Justice Owen J. Roberts wrote the 7–2 majority opinion, which upheld the application of the act to the marketing of tobacco. He stressed the fact that it was not production that was regulated but only the sale of tobacco in interstate commerce "to prevent the flow of commerce from working harm to the people of the nation" in the form of ruinous prices and the disorderly marketing of agricultural commodities. Agriculture, like business and labor, had come under federal regulation.

There was, however, another and more comprehensive test of the 1938 act. In 1941 an Ohio farmer exceeded his wheat production quota and was fined by the Department of Agriculture. He challenged the constitutionality of the act on the ground that his crop was grown for use on his own farm and therefore did not affect interstate commerce in wheat. Justice Robert H. Jackson wrote the unanimous opinion in the important case of *Wickard* v. *Filburn* (1942). He threw out all the distinctions between manufacturing and commerce and between direct and indirect effects. Congress thus possessed plenary power to regulate agricultural production; henceforth, no farmer could possibly regard himself as immune from the dictates of the Department of Agriculture.

Civil Rights. One of the most interesting chapters in the long history of the commerce clause concerns its use, first by the Supreme Court and then by Congress in the years since World War II, to advance and expand the civil rights of American minorities, particularly blacks. In the early case of *Morgan* v. *Virginia* (1946) the Court struck down a state statute that required all interstate motor buses to seat passengers in such a way that contiguous seats would not be occupied by persons of different races at the same time. For a 6–1 majority, Justice Stanley F. Reed found that the law put an undue burden on commerce in a matter that required national uniformity—namely, regulations for interstate travel.

In 1963 the Court decided in *Colorado Anti-Discrimination Commission* v. *Continental Air Lines* that the interstate airline was subject to a state act that prohibited employers from discriminating against job applicants on the basis of race, color, or ancestry. Justice Hugo L. Black reasoned in his unanimous opinion that the mandated hiring practices did not unconstitutionally burden the operation of commercial air travel and did not conflict with any relevant federal laws. Thus, in the years following World War II, the Supreme Court took the lead at the national level in attacking racial discrimination, and its initial weapon of choice was the commerce clause.

As the 1960s wore on and the demands of blacks and other minorities for equality of treatment and opportunity became more insistent, the scene of civil rights action shifted to the legislative branch. In 1964, Congress passed the omnibus Civil Rights Act, which was designed to advance a number of basic legal, economic, and educational human rights. The "symbolic heart" of the statute was Title II, which guaranteed the positive right of free and equal access to privately owned public accommodations such as hotels, motels, restaurants, gasoline stations, and places of amusement that lodged transient guests, served food or other products that had "moved in commerce," or presented films or sport teams that move interstate. The act was based squarely on the commerce power.

The constitutionality of Title II was immediately tested in the companion cases of *Heart of*

Atlanta Motel v. *United States* (1964) and *Katzenbach* v. *McClung* (1964). In his affirmative opinions for the Court, Justice Tom C. Clark first looked to "the meaning of the Commerce Clause" and, in doing so, quoted extensively from earlier opinions. Then he cited some of the evidence of the disruptive effect that racial discrimination has had on commercial intercourse. Clark concluded that Congress had a "rational basis" for finding its regulatory scheme "necessary to the protection of commerce." Because the means selected to eliminate the evil were reasonable and appropriate, the only remaining question was whether the act applied to the two businesses. It clearly did; approximately 75 percent of the motel's guests came from out of state, and about 46 percent of the meat served by Ollie McClung's barbecue restaurant moved in interstate commerce. This closed the issue; Title II was a valid exercise of the congressional power to regulate commerce.

In sum, Congress, under the Supreme Court's interpretation of the commerce clause, has the power to regulate all aspects of American economic life. This tremendous power extends also to matters of a social and/or moral nature if they embody some economic effect on commerce that "concerns more states than one." Thus, it is easy to understand how the commerce clause has become one of the major vehicles for the expansion of national power in the twentieth century.

STATE POWER

The second part of the story of the commerce clause is the way in which the Supreme Court has played its role as arbiter of the American federal system—that is, the way in which it has interpreted state power under this provision. Out of the landmark case of *Cooley* v. *Board of Wardens* (1852) came the *Cooley* rule, which holds that a state can regulate aspects of interstate commerce if the subject is more "local" than national in nature, there is an absence of conflicting federal legislation, and the matter comes within the scope of traditional state regulation. This three-pronged doctrine gives to the states a partially concurrent power over commerce but leaves to the Court the all-important task of working out a system of adequate declarations with respect to the precise limitations on state action. The result

has been the formulation over time of a number of judicial doctrines and positions in the area, the most important of which are the direct-indirect effects test, the no-discrimination doctrine, and the intent-of-Congress or silence-of-Congress standard. A brief explication of each follows.

Direct-Indirect Effects Test. One of the first formulas to evolve was that of the direct and indirect effects upon interstate commerce. If the Court considered the economic activity to be of essentially national interest, state regulation of it was held to exert a "direct" effect on the commerce and had to fall; however, if the Court viewed the matter as basically local in nature, state control was regarded as having only an "indirect" or "incidental" effect and could stand. A corollary to this dichotomy was the concept of a burden on commerce. The Court often took the position that a state regulation that had a direct effect on commerce ipso facto placed an "undue burden" upon it and thus was unconstitutional.

A good example of this is *Reading Railroad* v. *Pennsylvania* (1873), often referred to as the *State Freight Tax Case,* which involved a state act requiring transportation companies to pay a tax on every ton of freight, whether carried wholly within the state or in interstate trade. The tax was held invalid as applied to the latter; Justice William Strong reasoned that the state legislature had made payment of the tax a condition for transporting goods into or out of Pennsylvania and that this constituted a burden on the conduct of such commerce, which was in conflict with the need for national uniform regulation.

No-Discrimination Doctrine. A second formula involved the matter of discrimination against commerce. If the Court found that a state regulation "discriminated against" out-of-state commerce in favor of in-state business, the legislation was likely to be struck down; if the act was evenhanded in its application, then it could be sustained (all other things being equal). Closely associated with this doctrine was the concept of freedom of commerce—the proposition that the commerce clause in and of itself demands "free" or unfettered commercial intercourse within the United States and automatically prohibits state attempts to interfere with or restrict the flow of goods and services interstate. An early application of the no-discrimination doctrine occurred in *Welton* v.

Missouri (1876). The state passed a law that required any person selling merchandise not grown, produced, or manufactured in Missouri to obtain a peddler's license; no such license was required of those dealing in goods produced within the state. The Court found the act to be unconstitutional and void; Justice Stephen J. Field held that the license tax amounted to an impost on goods coming into the state, that it could serve as an "absolute exclusion" on such goods, and that it could give rise to "all the evils of discriminating State legislation . . . which existed previous to the adoption of the Constitution." Missouri could not so burden "foreign" commodities.

A later case also well illustrates the use of the no-discrimination doctrine. In *West* v. *Kansas Natural Gas Co.* (1911) the Court denied Oklahoma the right to keep for its own local consumers natural gas produced within the state. Justice Joseph McKenna found that the state regulation was discriminatory and thus unconstitutional.

Intent-of-Congress Standard. The third formula adopted for determining the permissibility of state power was that of the intent of Congress and its corollary, the silence of Congress. After the *Cooley* case, the Supreme Court turned its attention from the nature of the commerce power to the subjects upon which it operated. Concomitantly, it assumed the role of arbiter over whether the subjects were "national" or "local" in character and therefore over what belonged to the nation and what to the states. One way in which it could make this determination was to refer to congressional intent, if any. If Congress had spoken on a subject, this usually settled the matter. If, however, Congress had remained silent (which was normally the case before 1900), then the Court could assume that its judicial wisdom would coincide with the unexpressed will of the legislative branch. Furthermore, because many of the justices in the last third of the nineteenth century were economic conservatives who generally disapproved of any governmental interference with business, the Court usually took the view that the silence of Congress meant that the subject was to remain free and unregulated.

The best example of the use of the silence-of-Congress standard is *Leisy* v. *Hardin* (1890). An Iowa statute prohibited the manufacture, sale, or dispensing of intoxicating liquors except under very stringent conditions. Leisy, an Illinois brewer of beer, violated the law and then challenged its validity. Chief Justice Melville W. Fuller wrote the majority opinion, which voided the state enactment. He began by looking to the intent of Congress:

> Whenever . . . Congress remains silent . . . the only legitimate conclusion is that the general government intended that power should not be affirmatively exercised, and the action of the States cannot be permitted to effect that which would be incompatible with such intention. Hence, inasmuch as interstate commerce . . . is national in its character, . . . so long as Congress does not pass any law to regulate it, or allowing the States so to do, it thereby indicates its will that such commerce shall be free and untrammelled.

Fuller then had no trouble in finding that beer is an article of commerce whose importation and sale Iowa could not interdict; to allow this would be to concede to a majority in that one state the power over commercial intercourse, which the Constitution granted to all of "the people of the United States." Therefore, the Iowa "dry" law could not stand.

THREE THEORIES OF THE 1940S

Although the various doctrines just discussed were generally utilized in a conscientious and informed manner, occasionally they were applied in a rather mechanical and perfunctory fashion, most often to strike down state legislation. As a reaction to this, beginning in the late 1920s and extending through the 1940s, three distinct theories developed on the Supreme Court to answer the perennial question, What does the commerce clause by its own force prohibit the states from doing? The theories are associated with three prominent justices—Harlan Fiske Stone, Hugo L. Black, and Robert H. Jackson. Each approach will now be examined briefly.

The Stone View. Harlan Fiske Stone was a hard-headed realist who took a commonsense approach to the problem of the negative effect of the commerce clause on state power. He believed that the purpose of the commerce clause was to prevent state discrimination and the erection of local barriers to the flow of commerce. Furthermore, he would substitute extensive factual analysis and pragmatic reasoning for the mere incantation of mechanistic legal formulas. Thus, the justices would be required to weigh competing demands and to determine economic effects before striking a final "balance" between the state and national interests involved.

Two cases in particular well illustrate Stone's use of this balancing-of-interests doctrine. The first is *Parker* v. *Brown* (1943), in which he upheld a California law that regulated the production and price of raisins, over 90 percent of which move in interstate and foreign commerce. Stone, now chief justice, found that the California Agricultural Prorate Act was consistent with national agricultural policy and did not conflict with any federal legislation. Then, he carefully analyzed the California raisin industry to show its need for the economic protection that the state regulations provided. In short, California's interest in maintaining its raisin production outweighed any interest consumers might have in greater immediate volume and temporarily lower prices.

The second case is *Southern Pacific Co.* v. *Arizona* (1945), often called the *Arizona Train Case*. The state passed a law limiting the lengths of trains to seventy freight cars or fourteen passenger cars; it defended this regulation on the basis of the need to protect railroad employees from injuries resulting from "slack-action" accidents, which increase in severity with train length. Southern Pacific attacked the limitations as undue interferences with an economical and efficient national rail transportation service. In a 7–2 majority opinion, Chief Justice Stone struck down the state act. He recognized the power of the state "to make laws governing matters of local concern," but he asserted that the Court was the ultimate authority in balancing national and state interests in commerce.

Stone then weighed the "serious burden" put on railroad service against the claimed safety factor. Shorter trains meant less slack action but also more trains and thus more grade-crossing accidents and other severe injuries. Therefore, the effect of the law as a safety measure was "so slight or problematical" that it could not outweigh the national interest in "an adequate, economical and efficient railway transportation service."

The Black View. Hugo L. Black was an old Populist from Alabama who believed very much in rule by the people (or their elected legislative representatives) in economic matters and who also had a generally unfavorable opinion of businessmen and their practices. Therefore, he took the view that in the absence of relevant congressional legislation, the commerce clause by its own force only prohibits the states from patently discriminating against interstate commerce in favor of local business, and he would limit judicial review (by appointed justices) of state economic regulation and taxation to this single inquiry.

Perhaps as good an example as any of the Black philosophy is found in his dissenting opinion in the *Arizona Train Case*. After accusing the Court of acting as a "super-legislature" and arguing that elected officials were best qualified to make public policy regarding governmental regulation of train lengths, he went on to assert that the alleged "serious burden" on commerce reduced itself to one of "mere cost"; he thought that it was reprehensible for the majority to favor "an economical national railroad system" at the expense of "the personal safety of railway employees." He would have upheld the Arizona train-limit law. It must be said that not only would Black allow very wide scope for state power, but he was also never very concerned about the financial costs to business of state regulation.

The Jackson View. Robert H. Jackson had been solicitor general and attorney general under Franklin Roosevelt before going to the Supreme Court, and he possessed some well-defined and strongly held notions about the extent of state power. Specifically, Jackson believed that the commerce clause had been designed to create in the United States one great free-trade area and that it therefore prohibited state restraints upon the free movement of goods and services nationally. He took what could be designated a "hard line" toward exercises of state power; therefore, he always scrutinized state acts with a very suspicious eye, ready to strike down almost any obstruction to the freedom of interstate commerce. Furthermore, as he saw it, it was preeminently the duty of the Court to protect this commerce from state interference.

Probably the best exposition of Jackson's philosophy is to be seen in *H. P. Hood & Sons* v. *Du*

Mond (1949). A New York law forbade any dealer to buy milk from in-state producers unless licensed to do so. Hood, a Boston-area milk distributor, applied for a license to establish a fourth milk-receiving plant in New York and was turned down on the ground that another plant would create "destructive competition" in the marketplace. Hood appealed, and writing for a 5–4 majority, Justice Jackson overturned the state requirement. He began with an extensive history of the Constitutional Convention to show that the framers had intended the commerce clause to prevent any one state from erecting "an economic barrier against competition with the products of another state"; then he argued that the Court's steadfast adherence to that interpretation had resulted in a "federal free trade unit" that had brought to the American people the most impressive economic prosperity "in the history of commerce." Finally, Jackson summed up this line of reasoning in a now-famous declaration:

> Our system, fostered by the Commerce Clause, is that every farmer and every craftsman shall be encouraged to produce by the certainty that he will have free access to every market in the Nation, that no home embargoes will withhold his exports, and no foreign state will by customs duties or regulations exclude them. Likewise, every consumer may look to the free competition from every producing area in the Nation to protect him from exploitation by any. Such was the vision of the Founders; such has been the doctrine of this Court which has given it reality.

Against the backdrop of this sweeping statement, he had no trouble in finding that the New York statute as applied was repugnant to the national commerce power and therefore invalid.

A word of summary is now in order regarding these three theories. The ongoing controversy among the justices has been over the extent to which state economic action can be sanctioned constitutionally in order to create and maintain a fair and workable balance between state and national interests. It can be argued that among the modern judges, Chief Justice Stone stands out with his pragmatic, fairly executed, and intellectually tenable balancing-of-interests doctrine. Justice Jackson's views, although they carry a strong patriotic appeal, are probably too restrictive of state power and would not give the states enough flexibility to control effectively commercial activities of an essentially local and diverse nature. In contrast, although the position of Justice Black appears to be one of judicial self-restraint and "liberal" in the sense of granting wide latitude to the states in the management of their economic affairs, it actually calls for the exercise of the same judicial discretion as the other two (merely biased toward the states) and ignores the fact that Congress is unlikely to act to overturn state actions that adversely affect interstate commerce.

Given the fact that in a federal system someone has to have final authority to settle the inevitable disputes between the two levels of government and the fact that the Supreme Court has long since been invested with that authority, the real question then becomes, What guidelines should the Court use in the execution of its constitutional responsibility? The argument of this essay is that the Stone approach (which embodies a deference to legislative judgments, a clearheaded appreciation of the complexities endemic in federalism, and a sympathy for the legitimate needs of the states) results in the most acceptable resolution of the whole vexatious problem.

STATE REGULATION OF INTERSTATE COMMERCE

The Supreme Court has been called upon to decide hundreds of commerce clause cases involving questions of state power, and it has developed a number of formulations and positions with which to carry out its role as arbiter of the American federal system. Broadly speaking, the cases have been of two kinds: those in which state regulation that affects interstate commerce is challenged and there is no conflicting federal legislation and those in which state economic action is objected to as being in conflict with an act of Congress. It is obvious that both categories present complicated and complex issues for the Court to resolve, and thus, its decisions often rest on the combination of concepts or principles that can command a majority of nine independent and strong-minded individuals.

Superficially, it might appear that the main controversy has been between the kind of broad nationalism exhibited by Marshall and the states'-rights position of Taney; but this by itself is too simplistic an explanation. Nearly all the justices have been nationalists in the sense that they have appreciated the need to prevent the fractionalization of the United States economy. A second factor in the conflict has been the ideological regard for government regulation of business. "Liberal" justices favor government control at both the national and state levels and therefore try to minimize the negative effect of the commerce clause on exercises of state power. "Conservative" justices opt for a minimum of governmental authority at both levels and thus emphasize the commerce clause as a limitation per se on state regulation or taxation. Finally, the fact must be faced that judicial decisions do not always reflect only logic and/or ideology; they are often the result of conscious policy choices that have resulted from the grinding necessities of maintaining a working and evolving federal system. A brief survey of the various categories of cases will demonstrate the accuracy of this analysis.

State Power in the Absence of Federal Legislation. In spite of the decision in *Hood,* some states have continued to try to regulate the flow of milk across state lines but, appropriately enough, with a notable lack of success. In *Dean Milk Co.* v. *City of Madison* (1951) the Court examined an ordinance of Madison, Wisconsin, which prohibited the sale of milk unless it had been pasteurized and bottled within five miles of the center of the city. Justice Clark had no trouble in finding that the regulation, as applied to the Illinois company, imposed "an undue burden on interstate commerce" and was invalid. Similarly, a Florida Milk Commission order that required distributors in the Pensacola area to buy all their class-I milk from local producers first was struck down by Justice Byron R. White in *Polar Ice Cream & Creamery Co.* v. *Andrews* (1964) as an "unreasonable clog upon the mobility of commerce." Finally, the Court held in *Great Atlantic and Pacific Tea Co.* v. *Cottrell* (1976) that Mississippi could not prohibit the sale of Louisiana milk that met Mississippi health standards solely because Louisiana had not signed a reciprocity agreement with Mississippi; Justice Brennan was succinct in his conclusion that the state's mandatory requirement "unduly burdens the free flow of commerce."

A second area that has occasioned dispute is the regulation of motor vehicles, particularly trucks. An early, seminal case is *South Carolina State Highway Department* v. *Barnwell Bros.* (1938), in which Justice Stone upheld a state act that limited trucks to a width of ninety inches and a loaded weight of twenty thousand pounds. Making careful use of his balancing-of-interests doctrine, Stone reasoned that the restrictions were nondiscriminatory and did not result in a constitutionally forbidden burden on interstate commerce. But in *Bibb* v. *Navajo Freight Lines, Inc.* (1959) the Court invalidated an Illinois law that required the use of specially contoured mudguards on all trucks and trailers. Justice William O. Douglas looked to the evidence of a "heavy burden" on efficient trucking operations and an inconclusive safety factor to find a deleterious—and thus unconstitutional—effect on commerce. And in a third case, *Raymond Motor Transportation, Inc.* v. *Rice* (1978), Justice Lewis F. Powell struck down a Wisconsin statute that prohibited sixty-five-foot double-trailer truck units on the state's interstate highways. Raymond presented evidence, uncontroverted by Wisconsin, to show both the economy and safety of the sixty-five-foot rigs, and Powell easily concluded that "the challenged regulations violate the Commerce Clause because they place a substantial burden on interstate commerce and they cannot be said to make more than the most speculative contribution to highway safety."

A third category of cases has involved attempts by the states either to keep out or to disadvantage products from rival states. For example, in *Pike* v. *Bruce Church, Inc.* (1970), Arizona, pursuant to a statute forbidding cantaloupes from leaving the state unless packed in regular arrangement in closed containers, ordered Bruce Church, which had been shipping from its packing plant in California in identical containers, to pack its melons in Arizona. Because it would have cost about $200,000 to build an in-state packing shed, the company contested the order. For a unanimous Court, Justice Potter Stewart annulled the state order; the real purpose of the state action was to enhance the reputation of Arizona growers through the national recognition enjoyed by Bruce Church's superior produce, but such a state interest was too "tenuous" to justify an unneeded packing facility. In short, the Arizona order imposed "an unlawful burden upon interstate commerce" and could not stand.

In a slightly different vein, the Supreme Court has had to deal with the attempts of states to insulate themselves from interstate involvements. Thus, *Hughes* v. *Alexandria Scrap Corp.* (1976) upheld a Maryland law that provided monetary bounties for the destruction of hulks (old, inoperable automobiles) and that favored in-state scrap-metal processors over out-of-state ones. Justice Powell advanced the novel idea that Maryland was a "market participant" rather than the usual market regulator in order to sanction the state's program.

Four years later, in *Reeves, Inc.* v. *Stake* (1980), Justice Blackmun used the same concept to sustain the policy of the South Dakota Cement Commission, as applied in time of shortage, of limiting the sale of cement from a state-owned plant to state residents only. But in *City of Philadelphia* v. *New Jersey* (1978) the Court rebuffed an attempt by New Jersey to prohibit the importation of solid or liquid waste collected outside the state. To Justice Stewart, such a legislative embargo was "clearly impermissible under the Commerce Clause." Thus, generally speaking, the justices may be seen as having acted to keep open the channels of national commerce and have rather regularly frustrated parochial, self-seeking state action designed to interdict or close them.

State Power in the Presence of Federal Legislation. The second broad grouping of cases—somewhat smaller in size—is that in which state legislation is challenged as being in collision with an act of Congress. In these cases the Supreme Court has generally framed its decisions in terms of the theory of preemption, according to which when Congress has legislated comprehensively on a subject, it is presumed to have "occupied the field" to the exclusion of all contrary state legislation. Thus, the Court must answer the question, Does either the nature of the subject matter or a declaration of congressional purpose operate to supersede state regulation? Because Congress almost never makes its intent explicit, it follows that the Court is forced to do much the same thing as in other commerce clause cases: it must balance the national and state interests involved. Two cases in particular illustrate the process.

Huron Portland Cement Co. v. *City of Detroit* (1960) concerned the constitutionality of a municipal smoke abatement code that provided for stricter standards than those imposed on Huron's vessels by the United States Coast Guard. Justice Stewart upheld the Detroit ordinance as a legitimate exercise of traditional police power "to protect the health and enhance the cleanliness of the local community" and reasoned that it did not unduly burden the company's federal license to operate on the Great Lakes.

A case that is even more supportive of state power is *Florida Lime & Avocado Growers, Inc.* v. *Paul* (1963). At issue was the validity of California maturity standards for avocados sold in the state, which were different from those promulgated by the secretary of agriculture (under amendments to the Agricultural Adjustment Act passed in 1935) and which excluded more than 6 percent of Florida's avocados from the California market. Speaking for a 5–4 majority, Justice Brennan let the state maturity tests stand. The subject did not demand "exclusive federal regulation in order to achieve uniformity vital to national interests"; the supervision of readying foodstuffs for market had always been "a matter of peculiarly local concern"; and there was nothing in the 1935 act that indicated a congressional design to displace traditional state power.

These two cases are representative of a trend on the Court. The justices have become more and more reluctant to strike down state regulations on the ground that they conflict with federal statutory provisions in the same subject-matter areas. As a result, the states have enjoyed increased control over essentially national commercial concerns.

STATE TAXATION OF INTERSTATE COMMERCE

Over time, the Supreme Court has decided an exceedingly large number of cases involving the impact of state taxes on interstate commerce. It would not be very useful in a general survey to try to cover even the more important aspects of this subject, for they are too numerous. But several of the leading cases will be examined and a few main principles will be delineated.

To begin with, the Court has operated from two basic but obviously somewhat contradictory assumptions: the states may not use their taxing power to discriminate against interstate commerce, but interstate commerce may be made "to pay its own way," in the sense that interstate businesses must pay their fair share of the local tax burden. The practical application of these conflicting principles to concrete cases has been very difficult, partly because it is often almost impossible to determine where the actual incidence (or effect) of a state tax lies.

As was shown in *Reading Railroad* in 1873, the Court has adhered to the rule that property cannot be taxed while it is being transported in interstate commerce. Once it reaches its final destination and becomes mixed up with the general mass of property in the state, however, it loses its immunity. In *Robbins* v. *Shelby County Taxing District* (1887) the Court struck down a Tennessee tax on traveling salesmen levied for the privilege of taking orders for goods to be delivered from another state. But the states have blocked this escape from a sales tax by the imposition of "use" taxes; in *Henneford* v. *Silas Mason Co.* (1937), Justice Benjamin N. Cardozo upheld a 2 percent Washington state tax on "the privilege of using within this state any article of tangible personal property." An exemption was provided for goods that had already been subjected to an equal or greater tax; the tax was nondiscriminatory and was applied only after goods had come to rest in the state; and the tax was not a "protective tariff."

The trend of decision since World War II has been clearly in the direction of granting to the states greater freedom to tax various aspects of interstate and foreign commerce. Two examples illustrate this leniency on the part of the Court. *Complete Auto Transit, Inc.* v. *Brady* (1977) sustained a Mississippi sales tax levied on the transportation services (delivery of vehicles from a railroad terminal to General Motors dealers) performed by a Michigan corporation. Justice Blackmun drew on a long line of decisions to frame a four-part test for a state tax, and in the present instance, he found that the activity in question is sufficiently connected to the state to justify the tax; the tax is fairly apportioned to the amount of business conducted; the tax does not discriminate against interstate commerce; and the tax is fairly related to the benefits provided by the state. The company had made no claims to the contrary, and the rule to be enforced was

that "interstate commerce may be made to pay its way."

Four years later, in *Commonwealth Edison Co.* v. *Montana* (1981), the Court validated a 30 percent severance tax on all coal mined in the state. Justice Thurgood Marshall relied on the *Complete Auto Transit* tests, but when he reached the fourth one—a fair relation to state benefits—he ducked the issue by ruling that this was "essentially a matter for legislative, not judicial, resolution." Justice Blackmun, joined by Justices Powell and Stevens, dissented on the ground that the tax was supplying one-fifth of Montana's total revenue and bore no reasonable relation to the services provided by the state. The *Commonwealth Edison* holding is quite representative of the Court's desire since the 1930s to avoid striking down state tax laws as repugnant to the commerce clause.

CONCLUSION

A few summary statements need now be made. First and foremost, it is an accepted fact that Congress, under the authority of the commerce clause as interpreted by the Supreme Court, has plenary power to regulate every aspect of commercial enterprise in the United States. Congress has unquestioned control over any business activity that in any manner "affects" commerce, regardless of how "local" that activity may be or how "remote" the effect. And Congress is not limited to the regulation of purely economic matters; by virtue of its commerce power, it can strike at the primarily moral evils of gambling, prostitution, and racial discrimination if it can be shown that there is a connection between the prohibited activity and any commerce that "concerns more states than one."

Second, in the same way that the Supreme Court has expanded national power over commerce, it has become increasingly tolerant toward exercises of state power, both regulation and taxation, and has allowed the states wide authority in the commercial realm. This latter trend undoubtedly results not only from the fact that the Court has ceased to act generally as a censor on economic legislation but also because the justices have remained sensitive to the need to preserve the states as viable elements in the American scheme of government. At the same time, however, the Court has not abdicated its historic role as umpire of the federal system, and it continues to function as the final arbiter of national and state interests.

Finally, the record of the Supreme Court in its interpretation of the commerce clause has been commendable. One of the main animating reasons for the framing of the Constitution was to promote the general welfare and ensure domestic tranquility in economic and social relationships, and in furtherance of these objectives, the Court has construed the commerce clause to be both a vast reservoir of positive national power and a limitation on divisive and parochial state power. Thus, it may be argued that over the long stretch of American history the Court has been remarkably faithful in utilizing the commerce clause to advance the best interests of all the people of the United States.

CASES

A. B. Kirschbaum Co. v. Walling, 316 U.S. 517 (1942)
Bibb v. Navajo Freight Lines, Inc., 359 U.S. 520 (1959)
Carter v. Carter Coal Co., 298 U.S. 238 (1936)
Champion v. Ames, 188 U.S. 321 (1903)
City of Philadelphia v. New Jersey, 437 U.S. 617 (1978)
Colorado Anti-Discrimination Commission v. Continental Air Lines, 372 U.S. 714 (1963)
Commonwealth Edison Co. v. Montana, 453 U.S. 609 (1981)
Complete Auto Transit, Inc. v. Brady, 430 U.S. 274 (1977)
Cooley v. Board of Wardens of the Port of Philadelphia, 12 Howard 299 (1852)
Dean Milk Co. v. City of Madison, 340 U.S. 349 (1951)
Equal Employment Opportunity Commission v. Wyoming, 460 U.S. 226 (1983)
Florida Lime & Avocado Growers, Inc. v. Paul, 373 U.S. 132 (1963)
Fry v. United States, 421 U.S. 542 (1975)
Garcia v. San Antonio Metropolitan Transit Authority, 105 S.Ct. 1005 (1985)
Gibbons v. Ogden, 9 Wheaton 1 (1824)
Great Atlantic and Pacific Tea Co. v. Cottrell, 424 U.S. 366 (1976)
Hammer v. Dagenhart, 247 U.S. 251 (1918)
Heart of Atlanta Motel v. United States, 379 U.S. 241 (1964)
Henneford v. Silas Mason Co., 300 U.S. 577 (1937)
Hodel v. Virginia Surface Mining and Reclamation Assn., 452 U.S. 264 (1981)
H. P. Hood & Sons v. Du Mond, 336 U.S. 525 (1949)
Hughes v. Alexandria Scrap Corp., 426 U.S. 794 (1976)
Huron Portland Cement Co. v. City of Detroit, 362 U.S. 440 (1960)
Interstate Commerce Commission v. Brimson, 154 U.S. 447 (1894)

Katzenbach v. McClung, 379 U.S. 294 (1964)
Leisy v. Hardin, 135 U.S. 100 (1890)
Maryland v. Wirtz, 392 U.S. 183 (1968)
Morgan v. Virginia, 328 U.S. 373 (1946)
Mulford v. Smith, 307 U.S. 38 (1939)
National Labor Relations Board v. Fainblatt, 306 U.S. 601 (1939)
National Labor Relations Board v. Friedman-Harry Marks Clothing Co., 301 U.S. 58 (1937)
National Labor Relations Board v. Jones and Laughlin Steel Corp., 301 U.S. 1 (1937)
National League of Cities v. Usery, 426 U.S. 833 (1976)
Northern Securities Co. v. United States, 193 U.S. 197 (1904)
Parker v. Brown, 317 U.S. 341 (1943)
Pike v. Bruce Church, Inc., 397 U.S. 137 (1970)
Polar Ice Cream & Creamery Co. v. Andrews, 375 U.S. 361 (1964)
Raymond Motor Transportation, Inc. v. Rice, 434 U.S. 429 (1978)
Reading Railroad v. Pennsylvania, 15 Wallace 232 (1873)
Reeves, Inc. v. Stake, 447 U.S. 429 (1980)
Robbins v. Shelby County Taxing District, 120 U.S. 489 (1887)
Shreveport Case, 234 U.S. 342 (1914)
South Carolina State Highway Department v. Barnwell Bros., 303 U.S. 177 (1938)
Southern Pacific Co. v. Arizona, 325 U.S. 761 (1945)
Swift & Co. v. United States, 196 U.S. 375 (1905)
United States v. Butler, 297 U.S. 1 (1936)
United States v. Darby, 312 U.S. 100 (1941)
United States v. E. C. Knight Co., 156 U.S. 1 (1895)
Welton v. Missouri, 91 U.S. 275 (1876)
West v. Kansas Natural Gas Co., 221 U.S. 229 (1911)
Wickard v. Filburn, 317 U.S. 111 (1942)
Willson v. Black Bird Creek Marsh Co., 2 Peters 245 (1829)

BIBLIOGRAPHY

Albert S. Abel, "The Commerce Clause in the Constitutional Convention and in Contemporary Comment," in *Minnesota Law Review*, 25 (1941), argues that the framers viewed the commerce power as a "mild, modest little power" but also as one "exclusive" to Congress. Dean Alfange, Jr., "Congressional Regulation of the 'States *qua* States': From *National League of Cities* to *EEOC* v. *Wyoming*," in *The Supreme Court Review: 1983*, edited by Philip B. Kirkland et al. (1984), criticizes the decision in *National League of Cities* but avers that through 1983 the Supreme Court had not cleared up the problems presented by its reasoning in the case. Leonard Baker, *John Marshall: A Life in Law* (1974), an excellent one-volume biography of the chief justice, includes his judicial philosophy.

Paul R. Benson, Jr., *The Supreme Court and the Commerce Clause, 1937–1970* (1970), analyzes in depth the major trends in commerce clause adjudication in the period indicated. Walter Berns, "The Meaning of the Tenth Amendment," in Robert A. Goldwin, ed., *A Nation of States: Essays on the American Federal System* (1963), argues convincingly that the Tenth

THE COMMERCE CLAUSE

Amendment is merely declaratory of the division of powers made between the nation and the states in the original, unamended Constitution.

Edward S. Corwin, *The Commerce Power Versus States Rights* (1936), elucidates the conflicting interpretations of the commerce clause that preceded the Supreme Court's constitutional crisis with the New Deal; and "The Passing of Dual Federalism," in Robert G. McCloskey, ed., *Essays in Constitutional Law* (1957), traces the history of the Court's use of the doctrine of dual federalism and posits that by 1950 it had long since lost its force. William W. Crosskey, *Politics and the Constitution in the History of the United States,* 2 vols. (1953), argues the insupportable thesis that the United States Constitution was intended to establish a unitary state, but he includes an informative analysis of the *Gibbons* case.

George Dangerfield, "The Steamboat Case," in John A. Garraty, ed., *Quarrels That Have Shaped the Constitution* (1964), highlights in delightful form the factual background of *Gibbons* v. *Ogden,* with an emphasis on the personalities involved. Felix Frankfurter, *The Commerce Clause Under Marshall, Taney and Waite* (1937), details the historical interpretation of the commerce power in the nineteenth century by three prominent chief justices. George L. Haskins, "John Marshall and the Commerce Clause of the Constitution," in *University of Pennsylvania Law Review,* 104 (1955), affirms the importance of Marshall's decision in the *Gibbons* case and its great impact both as a source of federal power and as a restriction upon state powers. Robert H. Jackson, *The Struggle for Judicial Supremacy: A Study of a Crisis in American Power Politics* (1941), relates the story of the political and constitutional conflict between the Roosevelt administration and the Supreme Court from the perspective of a participant.

Alfred H. Kelly, Winfred A. Harbison, and Herman Belz, *The American Constitution: Its Origins and Development* (6th ed., 1983), provides perhaps the best one-volume history of the Supreme Court, including its interpretations of the commerce clause over time. W. Howard Mann, "The Marshall Court: Nationalization of Private Rights and Personal Liberty from the Authority of the Commerce Clause," in *Indiana Law Journal,* 38 (1963), holds that in *Gibbons* v. *Ogden* the Court used the commerce clause to secure the jurisdictional authority to nationalize and enforce private rights and to curb state power over such rights. Robert F. Nagel, "Federalism as a Fundamental Value: *National League of Cities* in Perspective," in *The Supreme Court Review: 1981,* edited by Philip B. Kurland et al. (1982), defends this decision and asserts that it is misunderstood because today's scholars are preoccupied with individual rights to the exclusion of constitutional structure (that is, federalism).

Mary Cornelia Porter, "That Commerce Shall Be Free: A New Look at the Old *Laissez-Faire* Court," in *The Supreme Court Review: 1976,* edited by Philip B. Kurland (1977), argues that the Supreme Court of 1890–1936 was not as economically conservative as it has been painted and that it rather effectively balanced the interests of investors and the consuming public. Frederick D. G. Ribble, *State and National Power over Commerce* (1937), is a most authoritative history of the commerce clause up to 1937. Robert L. Stern, "The Problems of Yesteryear—Commerce and Due Process," in Robert G. McCloskey, ed., *Essays in Constitutional Law* (1957), discusses the Court's holdings in the economic area with respect to both congressional and state legislation and concludes that the problems of the 1930s are no more.

[*See also* CIVIL LIBERTIES AFTER 1937; FEDERALISM; HUGHES COURT AND ERA; MARSHALL COURT AND ERA; *and* TANEY COURT AND ERA.]

CONGRESS

Louis Fisher

T HE U.S. Congress continues to be the most powerful legislature in the world. Congressional influence is based not merely on explicit and implicit constitutional powers but also on an imposing array of institutional and staff resources. Offsetting this congressional influence are the powers of the presidency, the courts, and the combined forces of the media and public opinion, as well as divisions and disagreements within Congress.

This essay explores congressional power within the context of the American system of separated powers. The principal focus is on three functions. First is the legislative power, including discussion on the nondelegation doctrine, nonstatutory controls, the legislative veto, and various forms of administrative legislation (executive orders, proclamations, and rule-making). The second section covers the investigative power, executive privilege, and the immunity of members of Congress under the speech-or-debate clause. The final section analyzes the power of the purse, concentrating on executive-legislative conflicts over the impoundment of funds and the congressional budget process.

SEPARATION OF POWERS

Congressional powers function within the framework of the theory of separated powers. Although the Constitution does not explicitly provide for a division of powers among separate branches, Article I confers legislative powers on Congress, Article II vests executive powers in the president, and Article III places judicial powers "in one supreme Court, and in such inferior Courts as the Congress may from time to time ordain and establish."

The actual operation of this system of separated powers is far more complex than it initially appears to be. First, the doctrine of the separation of powers works in tandem with the principle of checks and balances. An institution cannot check unless it has some measure of independence; it cannot retain that independence without the power to check. To accommodate these two principles, the Constitution created what appears to be a contradiction: a system of separated powers and a system of overlapping powers. To protect its independence and coequal status, each branch necessarily shares in the powers of the other branches. The president can veto legislation submitted to him by Congress, Congress can override the veto, the Senate must give its advice and consent to treaties and appointments recommended by the president, the judiciary may decide that legislative and executive acts are unconstitutional, and a number of other restraints serve to rein in the activities of each branch.

In the *Federalist Papers* (no. 48), James Madison explained the theory behind the system of checks and balances. Unless the departments of government were connected and blended to give each a constitutional control over the others, "the degree of separation, . . . essential to a free government, can never in practice be duly maintained." Power was of an encroaching nature, he said, and had to be restrained. Mere parchment barriers, as set forth in the Constitution, would be insufficient protection against "the encroaching spirit of power."

Although these checks are essential for the maintenance of separated powers, it is a mistake to emphasize the restraining nature of the Constitution and conclude that it is designed to thwart effective government. This is the impression one would have from a famous dictum by Justice Louis D. Brandeis in his dissenting opinion in *Myers* v. *United States* (1926): "The doctrine of the separation of powers was adopted by the Convention of 1787, not to promote efficiency but to preclude the exercise of arbitrary power."

Brandeis spoke a half-truth. The framers wanted to prevent the exercise of arbitrary power but not at the cost of efficient government. They did not deliberately construct a system of government that would lead to stalemate and deadlock. If they had wanted inefficient government, they could have retained the Articles of Confederation. The record is clear that the framers regarded the Confederation's form of government unacceptably weak and searched for a more vigorous, effective alternative.

On the basis of their experience with the Continental Congress from 1774 to 1787, the framers concluded that a one-branch government was too inefficient to meet the needs of an emerging nation. Members of the Continental Congress had to legislate, administer, and adjudicate. To relieve themselves of some of those burdens, they experimented with administrative boards staffed by men recruited from outside Congress. When that proved ineffective, they turned to single executives in an effort to impart efficiency and accountability to government. Gradually they turned over their adjudicatory duties to courts of admiralty. This separation of powers, based on the search for a more efficient system, occurred long before the delegates met at the Philadelphia convention to draft a new constitution. It was well said by the historian Francis Wharton that the Constitution "did not make this distribution of power. It would be more proper to say that this distribution of power made the Constitution of the United States."

It is also a misconception to believe that the framers borrowed the theory of separated powers from the French political theorist Montesquieu. The framers relied more on firsthand experience than on borrowed theory. Theory played a role, but it was always tested and circumscribed by experience. Madison pointed out in the *Federalist Papers* (no. 47) that while the accumulation of all powers in the same hands "may justly be pronounced the very definition of tyranny," he did not agree that the three powers of government should be kept totally distinct and separate. Nor did he believe that the British Constitution, on which Montesquieu had relied for his model, preserved a separation between the three powers. Moreover, Madison reviewed the state constitutions to show the degree to which the powers overlapped in those documents.

Finally, it is a fallacy to believe that the theory of separated powers guarantees the protection of individual liberties. Too much separation can just as easily undermine liberties by making government unworkable. The deep swings in France between executive and legislature, characterized by an oscillation between administrative and representative forms of government, offer a classic example of the danger of extreme separation. The constitutions of 1791 and 1848 represented the most ambitious attempts in France to establish a pure separation of powers. The result in the first case was the Committee on Public Safety, the Directory, and the reign of Napoleon Bonaparte, while the second experiment led to Louis Napoleon, reaction, and the Second Empire. "It is hardly surprising," M. J. C. Vile has observed, "that this last flirtation with the pure doctrine ended in the same way as others had ended in France—in absolutism."

The framers wanted to avoid this kind of political fragmentation and paralysis of power. Justice Joseph Story said that the framers adopted a separation of powers but "endeavored to prove that a rigid adherence to it in all cases would be subversive of the efficiency of the government, and result in the destruction of the public liberties." In an oft-quoted statement, Justice Robert Jackson said in *Youngstown Sheet and Tube Co.* v. *Sawyer* (1952) that "while the Constitution diffuses power the better to secure liberty, it also contemplates that practice will integrate the dispersed powers into a workable government. It enjoins upon its branches separateness but interdependence, autonomy but reciprocity."

Although the framers marked out the general boundaries of the three departments of government, the powers are not enumerated in detail. Much is left to the growth of implied powers, requiring compromise and accommodation among the three branches of government. In the *Federalist Papers* (no. 37), Madison drew an analogy to naturalists who found it difficult to distinguish between vegetable life and the animal world. So was it an even greater task, he said, to draw the boundary between the departments of government or "even the privileges and powers of the different legislative branches. Questions daily occur in the course of practice which prove the obscurity which reigns in these subjects, and which puzzle the greatest adepts in political science." Justice Oliver Wendell Holmes remarked in *Springer* v. *Philippine Islands* (1928), "However we may disguise it by veiling words we do not and cannot carry out the distinction between legislative and executive action with mathematical precision and divide the branches into watertight compartments, were it ever so desirable to do so, which I am far from believing that it is, or that the Constitution requires."

There is little that one branch can do without the active cooperation and support of the others. Only Congress can declare war, but the president acts as commander in chief. Only Congress can appropriate money, and yet it is the executive that expends the funds. The president can claim exclusive power to negotiate treaties and to nominate officers. Still, he depends on the Senate for advice and consent and on the House for implementing funds and the definition of official duties. The "exclusive" powers amount to a rather brief list: the president's power to pardon, the power of the House of Representatives to impeach and of the Senate to try all impeachments, the power of the judiciary to decide what constitutes a "case or controversy," and a few other prerogatives. But even in these areas the branches overlap to a considerable extent.

Part of the complexity results from the growth of "implied powers." Some constitutional scholars have argued that an act of the federal government is invalid unless based on a power specifically enumerated in the Constitution, but such a doctrine would bring government to a standstill. Even these scholars must admit to the existence of some implied powers: the power of Congress to investigate, the power of the president to remove executive officials, and the power of the Supreme Court to review executive and legislative actions. The picture grows more complex once we add powers that are considered "inherent," "incidental," "inferred," "emergency," and "aggregate," complicated still further by the "glosses," "penumbras," and "interstices" that have been discovered in the Constitution.

The U.S. Constitution cannot survive purely on the basis of express powers, or "strict constructionism." Implied powers are required for any government. Madison noted in the *Federalist Papers* (no. 44), "No axiom is more clearly established in law, or in reason, than that whenever the end is required, the means are authorized; whenever a general power to do a thing is given, every particular power necessary for doing it is included." Chief Justice John Marshall said in *McCulloch* v. *Maryland* (1819) that a constitution represents a general structure, not a detailed manual of instruction:

> A constitution, to contain an accurate detail of all the subdivisions of which its great powers will admit, and of all the means by which they may be carried into execution, would partake of the prolixity of a legal code, and could scarcely be embraced by the human mind. It would, probably, never be understood by the public. Its nature, therefore, requires, that only its great outlines should be marked, its important objects designated, and the minor ingredients which compose those objects, be deduced from the nature of the objects themselves.

LEGISLATIVE POWERS

Article I of the Constitution provides that "all legislative Powers herein granted shall be vested in a Congress of the United States." The powers expressly granted are fundamental in nature. Congress has the power to tax, to borrow money, and to regulate commerce with foreign nations and among the various states. It has the power to declare war, to raise and support the military, and to call forth the militia to suppress insurrections and repel invasions. To carry these and other powers into execution, Congress is authorized to make all laws "which shall be necessary and proper."

Strict interpretation would prohibit Congress from delegating its power to another branch. This notion finds expression in the ancient maxim "Delegated power cannot be delegated." Adherence to this doctrine would mean that power delegated by the people to Congress cannot be transferred elsewhere.

Delegation. Notwithstanding the doctrine that Congress may not surrender its legislative power to other agencies, vast congressional powers have been delegated to the president, to executive agencies, and to independent regulatory commissions. Delegations are supposed to be accompanied by legislative standards that define congressional policy and protect the essential law-making function of Congress. However, standardless delegations are increasingly common. Delegations are upheld even when the statutory language is vague and ill defined, such as general guidelines of "excessive profits," "reasonable rates," "unjust discrimination," and "in the public interest."

Although the Supreme Court frequently pays homage to the nondelegation doctrine, announcing on various occasions that it would be a breach of fundamental law were Congress to transfer its legislative power to the president, the Court typically upholds the delegation in question. Only on two occasions, both occurring in 1935, did the Supreme Court strike down a delegation of legislative authority to the president— in *Panama Refining Co.* v. *Ryan* and in *Schechter Poultry Corp.* v. *United States.* On all other challenges the Court recognizes that the nature of government requires Congress to pass general legislation and rely on other branches to fill in the details.

The tension between the nondelegation doctrine and the practical needs of government is relieved by some creative rationalizations. Robert Cushman offered this amusing but accurate syllogism: (1) *Major premise*: Legislative power cannot be constitutionally delegated by Congress; (2) *Minor premise*: It is essential that certain powers be delegated to administrative officers and regulatory commissions; (3) *Conclusion*: Therefore, the powers thus delegated are not legislative powers. Standardless delegations survive court scrutiny in part because of procedural safeguards written into the statute (such as the right of judicial review), various guidelines that can be discovered in the legislative history of a statute (including committee reports and floor debates), and certain customs and traditions that help confine executive discretion (Fisher, 100– 123).

The Administrative Procedure Act of 1946 established rules and standards for agency rulemaking, in order to promote fairness and equitable treatment. Agencies are required to give notice and a hearing prior to issuing a rule or regulation. Through such procedural standards, Congress tries to eliminate or minimize the opportunity for executive caprice and arbitrariness.

The problem of delegation is compounded when the agent of Congress transfers the responsibility to a subordinate. The Supreme Court has been as lenient toward subdelegation as delegation. A number of decisions have recognized that the president and department heads cannot personally discharge all of the statutory tasks assigned to them. A congressional survey after World War II revealed that President Harry Truman had to act, either expressly or by inference, under at least 1,100 statutes. In 1950, on the basis of that study, Congress authorized the president to subdelegate functions to his department heads or to agency officials on the condition that the officer discharging those tasks be someone who had been confirmed by the Senate. In this way Congress hoped to maintain some system of accountability to elected representatives.

The Supreme Court has never discarded the nondelegation doctrine. However, justices who raise that banner do so usually in dissenting opinions. The majority uses the doctrine indirectly to restrict the reach of a statute until Congress deliberately, consciously, and explicitly expands its coverage. For example, in 1958 the Court decided that Congress had not intended in the Immigration and Nationality Act to give the Secretary of State the discretion he claimed: the power to deny passports to persons with alleged Communist beliefs and associations. Referring to *Panama Refining*, the Court said it would "construe narrowly all delegated powers that curtail or dilute" such basic freedoms as the right to travel (*Kent* v. *Dulles*).

A similar approach was used by the Court in 1980 to invalidate a safety standard promulgated by the Secretary of Labor. Justice John Paul Stevens, joined by Chief Justice Warren Burger and Justice Potter Stewart, agreed that the construction placed upon the statute by the government would have represented an unconstitutional delegation of legislative power. Justice William Rehnquist, in a separate opinion, wrote an even stronger critique of the delegation in *Industrial Union Dept., AFL-CIO* v. *American Petroleum Institute* (1980).

Nonstatutory Controls. Vagueness in legislation is remedied in part by details that appear in the legislative history, such as committee reports, committee hearings, floor debates, and correspondence from review committees. This material substantially narrows the range of agency discretion. For example, the energy appropriations act for fiscal 1984 contained what appears to be an extraordinary grant of power: a lump sum of $884 million for construction by the Corps of Engineers. However, the two houses of Congress had definite projects in mind when they arrived at that sum. The projects are itemized in the conference report and listed state by state so that each member of Congress was aware of the projects to be carried out.

Nonstatutory controls satisfy the needs of both the legislative and executive branches. Neither Congress nor the agencies are always certain of the specifics to be included in a statute. When judgments and predictions are wrong, rigid statutory language must be rewritten. Putting guidelines and details in nonstatutory sources adds valuable flexibility to the legislative and administrative process. If an adjustment is necessary after a law is passed, committees and agencies can depart from the nonstatutory scheme without having to pass new legislation.

The system of nonstatutory controls is fragile. Much depends on a "keep the faith" attitude among agency officials. They must want to maintain the integrity of their budget presentations and preserve a relationship of trust and confidence with their review committees. Violation of that trust may result in budget cutbacks, restrictive language in statutes, and line-item appropriations.

The evolution of nonstatutory controls is illustrated by the history of funds that are "reprogrammed" by the Defense Department. Reprogramming consists of the shift of funds within an appropriation account (for example, within "Aircraft Procurement, Army"). Shifts from one account to another (as from "Aircraft Procurement, Navy" to "Weapons Procurement, Navy") are called "transfers" and require statutory authority. Reprogramming is essentially a nonstatutory development. Control is exercised for the most part through committee reports, agency directives, and a complicated set of understandings between the two branches.

Several decades ago the extent of legislative control over defense reprogramming consisted basically of review by two members from each of the Appropriations Committees: the chairman of the defense appropriations subcommittee and the ranking minority member. Often the review was farmed out to staff. Gradually the subcommittees began to place restrictions in the committee reports, and the Defense Department incorporated these restrictions into its directives and instructions to agency officials. In time, congressional review included a greater number of committee members (extending to the full subcommittee and sometimes the full committee) and eventually the authorization committees (Armed Services). On occasion the committees agreed that the decision was of such fundamental importance that it should be made on the floor of Congress by the entire membership rather than be worked out as an agency-subcommittee agreement.

The tenuous nature of nonstatutory controls is underscored by an incident that occurred in 1975. The conference report on the defense appropriations bill had directed the Navy Department to produce as its air combat fighter a derivative of the plane to be selected by the air force. The purpose was to increase commonality between the two services and save money. Instead, the navy picked an aircraft that was not a derivative. A contractor, who had bid on the expectation that the navy would follow the understanding in the conference report, lodged a formal protest with the General Accounting Office (GAO), claiming that the contract was null and void. The contractor insisted that the directives placed in the conference report were binding on the navy.

The GAO disagreed, ruling that such directives have legal force only when some ambiguity in the language of a public law requires recourse to the legislative history. Otherwise, agencies follow nonstatutory controls for practical, not legal, reasons. Agencies may ignore nonstatutory controls but only "at the peril of strained relations with the Congress." To be legally binding, the directive on the navy aircraft had to appear in the public law.

Administrative Legislation. Presidents are obligated under the Constitution to take care that the laws be "faithfully executed." The often conflicting and ambiguous passages within a law must be interpreted by executive officials to construct the purpose and intent of Congress. When based on statutory authority, agency rules and regulations are binding on the public.

In theory, agency regulations carry into effect the will of Congress as expressed in a statute: "A regulation which does not do this, but operates to create a rule out of harmony with the statute, is a mere nullity" *Manhattan General Equipment Co.*

v. *Commissioner of Internal Revenue* (1936). In practice, ambiguities and vagueness in statutes create opportunities, if not the necessity, for creative rule-making by agencies.

Added to the list of administrative regulations are the proclamations and executive orders issued by the president. Some proclamations are merely declaratory in effect, such as the designation of Law Day and other issues of general interest. Other proclamations have substantive impact on agencies and the public.

A good example of the range of presidential proclamations is the "New Economic Policy," unveiled by President Richard Nixon in 1971. He placed a 10 percent surcharge on articles imported into the United States, ostensibly for the purpose of ensuring that American products would not be at a disadvantage because of "unfair exchange rates." The more immediate concern was a deterioration of the American balance of payments. Importers immediately filed appeals with the Customs Bureau and later with the Customs Court, claiming that the scope of the proclamation exceeded any power delegated by Congress to the president.

In 1974 the Customs Court agreed with the importers and declared the surcharge invalid. Had this decision prevailed, the federal government could have had to repay about $500 million that it had collected. However, a year later the Court of Customs and Patent Appeals reversed the decision. Although the appellate court subscribed to the theory that the president did not possess any undelegated power to regulate commerce or to set tariffs and that no such inherent power existed for the president, it concluded that he had acted within the Trading with the Enemy Act.

Neither Nixon's proclamation nor the administration's legal defense had ever referred to the act. Moreover, nothing in the act specifically authorized or prohibited the imposition of a surcharge. The opinion of the appellate court appeared to be influenced by the questions of foreign relations and foreign policy that were at stake. Foreign exchange rates, international monetary reserves, balance of payments, and trade barriers had become increasingly intertwined. The court held that Congress could delegate more broadly in foreign affairs than in domestic affairs, in *United States* v. *Yoshida International, Inc.* (1975).

Less successful was Proclamation 4744, issued by President Jimmy Carter in 1980 to impose a fee on imported oil. This action, which would have increased the price of gasoline by 10 cents a gallon, was meant to lower domestic gasoline consumption. A district court ruled that the proclamation "does not fall within the inherent powers of the president, is not sanctioned by the statutes cited by Defendants [the Department of Energy], and is contrary to manifest Congressional intent" in *Independent Gasoline Marketers Council* v. *Duncan* (1980). At the time the court handed down its decision, Congress was about to strip Carter of his authority to impose fees or quotas on imported oil.

Another far-reaching instrument for administrative legislation is the executive order. In June 1941, before the Japanese attack on Pearl Harbor and America's entry into World War II, President Franklin Roosevelt resorted to an executive order to seize a defense industry plant in California (Executive Order 8773). He acted not on statutory authority but on the general powers vested in him "by the Constitution and laws of the United States, as President of the United States of America and Commander in Chief of the Army and Navy of the United States." He invoked those powers again when he seized shipbuilding companies, a cable company, a shell plant, and almost 4,000 coal companies. Not until 1943 did Congress pass the War Labor Disputes Act to provide statutory authority for presidential seizure of plants, mines, and other facilities.

Also beginning with Franklin Roosevelt, presidents have used executive orders to articulate and implement an antidiscrimination policy for the federal government. Roosevelt threatened to withhold contracts from employers who failed to satisfy equal-employment provisions in federal contracts. Presidents Harry Truman and Dwight Eisenhower continued that policy, and President John F. Kennedy threatened to cancel contracts as a means of forcing compliance with federal equal-employment standards. Executive Order 11246, issued by President Lyndon Johnson, established the administrative structure for carrying out the nondiscrimination policy and provided the basis for a preferential hiring system ("affirmative action"). To the extent that Congress provides appropriations for the agencies that administer the executive order, it sanctions, or at least acquiesces in, the affirmative-action policy.

In 1969 the comptroller general challenged the nondiscrimination policy of the Nixon Administration. Under the "Philadelphia Plan," which was issued pursuant to Executive Order 11246, contractors had to set specific goals for hiring members of minority groups as a condition for working on federally assisted projects. The comptroller general decided that the plan conflicted with Title VII of the Civil Rights Act of 1964, which prohibited discrimination on the basis of race, color, or national origin. The administration claimed that interpretation of the Civil Rights Act had been vested by Congress in the Department of Justice, which had approved the plan as consistent with the act. Federal courts upheld the legality of the plan as well as the executive order that placed it in operation, in *Contractors Ass'n. of Eastern Pennsylvania* v. *Secretary of Labor* (1971).

Executive orders are a source of law only when they draw upon the constitutional powers of the president or powers expressly delegated by Congress. Actions that exceed those bounds have been struck down by the courts. Executive orders may not supersede a statute or override contradictory congressional expressions (*Marks* v. *CIA,* 1978). The major example is the *Youngstown* case of 1952, which held that President Truman's attempt to seize the steel mills of the nation had no basis in statute or in the Constitution.

For a number of decades, study commissions have recommended that the rule-making functions of all agencies (including the independent regulatory commissions) be placed directly under the president. Congress has consistently refused to delegate to the president a general supervisory function over all federal regulations. Nevertheless, President Ronald Reagan issued Executive Order 12291 in 1981 to authorize the Office of Management and Budget (OMB) to review major regulations and subject them to cost-benefit analysis. By making the OMB the central clearinghouse and arming it with a vague cost-benefit weapon, the order opened the door to *ex parte* (off-the-record) contacts between industry spokesmen and federal officials and allowed the OMB to use the cost-benefit concept as a way to delay or kill regulations that the administration did not want. The unrecorded communications between White House and agency officials and between executive officials and industry representatives raised serious questions of due process and deprived the rule-making docket of information needed for judicial review.

Executive Order 12291 applied only to executive departments and agencies, not to the independent regulatory commissions. However, the latter are subject to the OMB's supervision under the Paperwork Reduction Plan Act of 1980. The OMB puts a control number on federal requests for information from the private sector. Without a control number, agency requests for information can be ignored. By using cost-benefit and paperwork-review procedures, the OMB was able to pursue Reagan's policy of substituting free market controls for federal regulation.

Legislative Veto. Until the Supreme Court's decision in *INS* v. *Chadha* (1983), Congress had access to the "legislative veto" to control agency actions. This device came into use in 1932 as an accommodation between the executive and legislative branches: the executive gained authority that Congress would otherwise not have delegated, while Congress retained for itself the ability to disapprove the use of that authority by a two-house veto (concurrent resolution), a one-house veto (simple resolution), and even a committee veto. The Court struck down these legislative vetoes because they violated the Constitution in two respects. All of them violated the presentment clause, which requires bills to be presented to the president for his signature or veto. And some of them violated the principle of bicameralism.

The Supreme Court asserted that the legislative veto's efficiency or convenience would not save it "if it is contrary to the Constitution. Convenience and efficiency are not the primary objectives—or the hallmarks—of democratic government." The Court said that although the legislative veto might be a "convenient shortcut" and an "appealing compromise," it was "crystal clear from the records of the Convention, contemporaneous writings and debates, that the Framers ranked other values higher than efficiency." Here the Court played loose with history. The record amply demonstrates that governmental efficiency was a key consideration for the framers.

The Court also claimed that the framers had

unmistakably expressed their "determination that legislation by the national Congress be a step-by-step, deliberate and deliberative process." However, both houses of Congress regularly use "shortcut" methods that pose no problems under *Chadha*: suspending the rules, asking for unanimous consent, placing legislative riders on appropriations bills, and even passing bills that have never been sent to committee. Congress even affects the rights and duties of individuals outside the legislative branch without abiding by the principles of bicameralism and presentment, such as when a committee issues a subpoena during its investigative effort or when one house of Congress passes a resolution holding an executive officer in contempt. Furthermore, legal rights and duties are affected through unilateral executive orders, proclamations, agency rule-making, and court decisions concerning constitutional rights and statutory interpretations.

The Court's theory of government contradicted practices that had developed over a period of decades by the political branches. Neither administrators nor members of Congress want the static, formalistic model adopted by the Court. The conditions that spawned the legislative veto have not disappeared: executive officials still want substantial latitude in administering delegated authority, and legislators still want to maintain control over that authority without having to pass new legislation subject to the president's veto.

The executive and legislative branches will develop substitutes to satisfy the need for congressional control and administrative discretion. On many fronts, Congress will do indirectly what it did directly through the legislative veto. Most of the legislative controls will continue to be exercised at the committee and subcommittee levels, usually through a mix of informal and nonstatutory techniques. To the extent that these controls are omitted from statutes and rely on good-faith relationships between executive agencies and congressional committees, *Chadha* will not stand in their way. Nonstatutory legislative vetoes existed in the past and will persist in the future, perhaps in even greater numbers because of the Court's decision. They are not legal in effect. They are, however, in effect, legal.

Congress can also place language in an appropriations bill to prohibit an objectionable agency rule or regulation. Presidents are unlikely to veto an entire appropriations bill because of an offensive limitation or rider. The practical effect is therefore at least a two-house legislative veto, and because of House-Senate accommodations the result in many cases will be a one-house veto. Another fallout from *Chadha* may be a decision on the part of members to maintain their present reliance on short-term authorizations and appropriations. This will put the burden on agencies to secure legislative support in advance rather than requiring Congress to stop agency actions through a legislative veto. In some cases, Congress may be able to write more specific language into statutes to guide administrative behavior.

Statutes can also rely more heavily on requirements that agencies first "notify" committees before they act. Notification does not raise a constitutional issue, since it falls within the report-and-wait category already sanctioned by prior court rulings. Nevertheless, notification can easily become a code word for committee prior approval. Only in highly unusual circumstances would an agency defy its oversight committees.

After the Court had handed down the *Chadha* decision, Congress began to delete legislative vetoes from statutes and replace them with joint resolutions. Since a joint resolution must pass both houses of Congress and be presented to the president for his signature or veto, it conforms to the Court's insistence on bicameralism and presentment. If Congress decides on a joint resolution of approval, this will shift the power advantage to Congress. Presidents or executive officials would have to secure congressional approval within a specific number of days. If one house withheld its support, the joint resolution could not pass and the administration would be faced with what would be essentially a one-house veto.

To the surprise of some observers, Congress continued to place legislative vetoes in bills after *Chadha* and they have been signed into law. Most of these legislative vetoes are of the committee-veto variety. President Reagan and the Justice Department have objected to this development. The White House and the Justice Department will probably continue to adopt a theoretical position on the doctrine of separated powers, insisting that Congress should not interfere with administrative duties and functions. Such a position mirrors the formalistic model of the Constitution announced in *Chadha*. At the agency level, however, the position is more likely to be one of pragmatism and accommodation, accepting congressional committee involvement in certain agency decisions as the necessary price to pay for greater administrative authority and discretion.

The Supreme Court treated a complex issue in simple terms. The unfortunate effect was to convey to the country an impression of government that does not, and cannot, exist in practice. We should not be too surprised or disconcerted if, after the Court closed the door to the legislative veto, we hear a number of windows being raised and perhaps new doors constructed, making the executive-legislative structure as accommodating as before for shared power. It may not be a house of aesthetic quality and certainly will not resemble the neat model envisioned by the Court, but it will accommodate a reconciliation of administrative discretion and congressional control, allowing government to operate in an effective manner.

INVESTIGATIVE POWER

The Constitution does not explicitly grant Congress the power to investigate, but since its beginning, Congress has used the investigative power for four main purposes: to enact legislation, to oversee the administration of programs, to inform the public, and to protect its integrity, dignity, reputation, and privileges. To enforce these essential duties, Congress possesses an inherent power to punish for contempt. In 1927 the Supreme Court recognized that the investigative power is implied in the Constitution; it said that a legislative body "cannot legislate wisely or effectively in the absence of information respecting the conditions which the legislation is intended to affect or change," *McGrain* v. *Daugherty* (1927).

Although Congress has an inherent power to punish for contempt, the decision in *Anderson* v. *Dunn* (1821) required each house of Congress to exercise the least possible power adequate to the end proposed (usually the power of imprisonment) and to limit the period of punishment for the life of the legislative body (that is, imprisonment would have to end at the time of congressional adjournment). Because of *Anderson*, it was possible for someone to violate the dignity of one of the houses of Congress in the closing days of a Congress and be punished only during that period. For that reason, as well as a desire to delegate such matters to the courts, Congress passed legislation in 1857 to enforce the attendance of witnesses on the summons of either house. Failure to appear or refusal to answer pertinent questions could lead to indictment as a misdemeanor in the courts.

The investigative power is interpreted broadly by the courts to permit Congress to carry out its legislative functions. Zealous or careless investigations, however, can violate individual freedoms protected by the Constitution. Witnesses cannot be compelled to give evidence against themselves. They cannot be subjected to unreasonable search and seizure. Their freedoms of speech, press, religion, and political belief and association cannot be abridged. Congressional investigations must be properly authorized by Congress. Questions put to witnesses by congressional committees must be pertinent and relevant to the committee's work and the purpose of the hearings.

In conducting congressional investigations, members of Congress have an immunity under Article I, Section 6, of the Constitution, which provides that "for any Speech or Debate in either House," senators and representatives "shall not be questioned in any other Place." The courts have consistently held that the immunities of the speech-or-debate clause exist not simply for the personal or private benefit of members "but to protect the integrity of the legislative process by insuring the independence of individual legislators," *United States* v. *Brewster* (1972).

The speech-or-debate clause is read broadly by the courts to include not only words spoken in debate but also anything "done in a session of the House by one of its members in relation to the business before it" (*Kilbourn* v. *Thompson*, 1881). The clause protects members for remarks made in the course of committee hearings or in committee reports (*Doe* v. *McMillan*, 1973). Speeches printed in the *Congressional Record* are covered, whether delivered or not (*Hutchinson* v. *Proxmire*, 1979). The acquisition of information by congressional staff, obtained formally or informally, is a necessary stage of legislative conduct that is generally protected by the speech-or-debate clause (*Tavouraleas* v. *Piro*, 1981).

A number of other activities, designated by the courts as "political" rather than "legislative," are not protected: contacts with executive agencies, assistance to individuals who seek federal contracts, preparing news releases and newsletters for constituents, and speeches delivered outside the Congress (*Brewster; Hutchinson*). Nor is there any legislative immunity when disseminating documents and information outside Congress (*Doe; Gravel* v. *United States,* 1972).

In some early cases the courts afforded legislators more protection under the speech-or-debate clause than their aides (*Dombrowski* v. *Eastland,* 1967). In *Gravel,* however, members of Congress and their aides were treated "as one" when an aide carries out a task that would have been a legislative act if performed personally by the member. When performing these tasks, aides become members' "alter egos" (*Gravel; Doe*). But even in the case of legislative acts, the speech-or-debate clause does not extend a privilege to members or aides who "violate an otherwise valid criminal law in preparing for or implementing legislative acts" (*Gravel*).

Executive Privilege. The claim of executive privilege sets the stage for a confrontation between two "absolutes": the power of Congress to investigate and the power of a president to withhold information. Although these prerogatives are often cast in unqualified and unconditional terms, generally there are opportunities to negotiate a settlement that is satisfactory to both branches. If the two branches cannot agree, the matter may find its way into the courts, but even at that point the role of a federal judge may be one of mediating the dispute and encouraging adversaries to compromise.

The House of Representatives has the "sole Power of Impeachment." It cannot fulfill that responsibility unless it has full access to materials needed for an investigation. Even short of impeachment, executive privilege is inappropriate when there are charges of administrative malfeasance. Attorney General William French Smith, while upholding a very broad theory of executive privilege in 1982, admitted that he would not try "to shield documents [from Congress] which contain evidence of criminal or unethical conduct by agency officials from proper review." During a news conference in 1983, President Reagan said "we will never invoke executive privilege to cover up wrongdoing."

Several barriers stand in the way of full disclosure to Congress. The Supreme Court noted in 1959 that Congress "cannot inquire into matters which are within the exclusive province of one of the other branches of the Government" (*Barenblatt* v. *United States,* 1959). Were Congress to seek information concerning a pardon, the president could decline on the ground that the matter is solely executive in nature and of no concern to Congress (unless the pardon required appropriations for an amnesty program). The president need not disclose to anyone in Congress the details of a treaty being negotiated. He may do so to enlist the support of legislators, but the invitation is voluntary on his part. Nor is the president under any obligation to share with members of Congress the plans of tactical military operations.

Similarly, until the president submits to the Senate the name of a nominee, Congress has no grounds for gaining access to the person's file. Requests for personnel and medical files might also be regarded by the president as an unwarranted intrusion into personal privacy. The removal power over executive officials is strongly attached to the president's office. Grover Cleveland withheld from the Senate various papers and documents that pertained to a suspended official. The power to remove, he said, was solely an executive prerogative and could not be shared or compromised with the Senate.

Formulation of a policy requires trust and confidentiality among presidential aides. In 1974 the Supreme Court decided that the president's interest in withholding information for the purpose of confidentiality is implied in the Constitution, "to the extent this interest relates to the effective discharge of a President's powers, it is constitutionally based" (*United States* v. *Nixon,* 1974).

Kilbourn and other early decisions suggested that a congressional investigation could not interfere with matters pending before a court. Under that doctrine, however, legislative inquiries could be frustrated for years while awaiting the outcome of a lawsuit. Congress is free to investigate a matter even if it results in publicity that is prejudicial to a defendant. In such situations a court may find it necessary to postpone a trial until the prejudice has been removed (*Delaney* v. *United States,* 1952). When Congress seeks a document that it could have had in the absence of a lawsuit, the mere existence of a suit or grand jury action is inadequate reason to withhold information from Congress.

In 1982 the Reagan Administration provoked a confrontation with Congress by announcing that Congress could not see documents in active litigation files. The announcement followed the investigation by a number of committees looking into the $1.6 billion "Superfund" program established to clean up hazardous-waste sites and to prosecute companies responsible for illegal dumping. Anne Gorsuch, administrator of the Environmental Protection Agency (EPA), followed President Reagan's instructions that "sensitive documents found in open law enforcement files" should not be turned over to congressional committees. The result of this policy would be to forestall congressional oversight for years until the government had completed its enforcement actions.

After the House Public Works Committee held Gorsuch in contempt, the House of Representatives voted 259 to 105 to support the contempt citation. Although partisan overtones were present, 55 Republicans joined 204 Democrats to build the majority. Following the statutory procedure for contempt citations, the Speaker of the House certified the facts and referred them to the U.S. Attorney for presentation to a grand jury. Instead, the Administration asked a district court to declare the House action an unconstitutional intrusion into the president's authority to withhold information from Congress. In 1983 the court dismissed the government's suit on the ground that judicial intervention in executive-legislative disputes "should be delayed until all possibilities for settlement have been exhausted" (*United States* v. *House of Representatives*, 1983).

The Reagan Administration subsequently agreed to release "enforcement-sensitive" documents to Congress but only in a series of steps, beginning with briefings and edited versions and ending with the unedited documents. Congress then moved to clarify the duty of the U.S. Attorney to bring contempt actions before the grand jury. Legislation under consideration would make that duty nondiscretionary, to be carried out not later than sixty days after a contempt citation had been certified.

Efforts by the executive branch to withhold information may have to give ground in case of criminal prosecution. Attorneys for President Nixon claimed that the president, not the courts, should determine whether information fell within the scope of the executive privilege. In its unanimous decision in *United States* v. *Nixon*, the Supreme Court rejected this theory and required Nixon to produce certain Watergate tape recordings and documents relating to his conversations with aides. Shortly after this decision, and under pressure of certain impeachment by the House of Representatives, Nixon resigned from the presidency.

POWER OF THE PURSE

In the *Federalist Papers* (no. 58), James Madison remarked that the power of the purse represents the "most complete and effectual weapon with which any constitution can arm the immediate representatives of the people, for obtaining a redress of every grievance, and for carrying into effect every just and salutary measure." Article I, Section 9 of the Constitution places this weapon squarely in the hands of Congress: "No Money shall be drawn from the Treasury, but in Consequence of Appropriations made by Law."

The appropriations power, while broad, is restricted by other provisions in the Constitution. Congress cannot lawfully use its funding power to establish a religion, diminish the compensation of members of the federal judiciary, or take other actions specifically proscribed by the Constitution. Congress may not impose unconstitutional conditions on recipients of federal funds. The flow of federal money is not "the final arbiter of constitutionally protected rights" (*Clark* v. *Board of Education of Little Rock Sch. Dist.*, 1967). A rider to an appropriations bill, seeking to prohibit the payment of federal salaries to three named "subversives," was struck down in 1946 as a bill of attainder in *United States* v. *Lovett*. Congress could not use its power of the purse to inflict punishment on individuals.

The distribution of the power of the purse has been shaped by two landmark statutes: the Budget and Accounting Act of 1921 and the Congressional Budget and Impoundment Control Act of 1974. Both statutes attempted to contribute accountability to the budgetary process.

The 1921 statute made the president responsible for submitting a national budget each year. It replaced a process that had become fragmented and decentralized among the various federal agencies. Congress created the Bureau of the Budget (now the Office of Management and Budget) to assist the president in the formulation of budget estimates. The purpose was to fix upon the president the responsibility for subjecting agency estimates to scrutiny, revision, and correlation.

This structure of presidential accountability has gradually eroded over the years. A number of statutes now prohibit the president from altering the budget estimates of certain agencies. Today the president does not submit a budget of his own making, representing in aggregate and in detail what he believes to be best for the nation. He does not, and cannot, defend the contents. For the most part he presents estimates for programs over which he has no direct control, particularly the entitlement programs (such as social security, federal disability, and unemployment compensation), interest on the public debt, and other "uncontrollables," which constitute about three-fourths of the budget. *Uncontrollable* is one of the more unfortunate terms used in budgeting, because the budget is controllable. Congress and the president simply choose to make it largely uncontrollable. Nothing in the idea of entitlement prevents the president from recommending less than projected outlays and submitting remedial legislation to Congress to change the law on benefit levels.

Under Carter and Reagan, the President's budget seemed at times little more than a meaningless ritual. Carter's budget in 1980 was moribund the moment it reached Capitol Hill. Several months later he sent up a new budget. Reagan used the budget to great advantage in 1981, cutting deeply into entitlements, reducing taxes, and raising defense spending, but in 1982, 1983, 1984, and 1985, his budgets were virtually ignored by Congress, including the Republican-controlled Senate. The link between the president's budget and presidential responsibility seemed all but severed.

The Congressional Budget. The Budget and Accounting Act of 1921 provided for an "executive budget" only in the sense that the president initiated the budget and took responsibility for it. The act allowed members of Congress full freedom, either in committee or on the floor, to decrease or increase the president's estimates. As part of budget reform during this period, in 1920 the House of Representatives centralized all appropriations power

in a single committee; the Senate adopted the same reform in 1922.

The jurisdiction of the appropriations committees was undercut within a matter of decades as Congress instituted various "backdoor" devices, allowing the authorizing committees to give spending authority to the agencies. Moreover, the appropriations committees decided to act not through a single bill but through thirteen separate appropriations bills, and at no time was this action on appropriations linked in any formal sense to revenue actions. As a consequence, members of Congress did not vote explicitly on the aggregate federal budget or the budget deficit and surplus.

During the "battle of the budget" in 1972, President Nixon publicly ridiculed the "hoary and traditional procedure of the Congress, which now permits action on the various spending programs as if they were unrelated and independent actions." Partly because of these deficiencies in the congressional budget process, Nixon justified his withholding of billions of dollars from domestic programs.

In response to these massive impoundments by the Nixon Administration, Congress passed the Congressional Budget and Impoundment Control Act of 1974. The act required the president to submit special messages whenever he proposed to rescind (cancel) or defer (delay) appropriations. To rescind funds, both houses of Congress had to complete action on a bill or joint resolution within forty-five days of continuous session. In the case of a deferral, it would remain in effect unless one house passed a resolution of disapproval. The Supreme Court's decision in *Chadha* in 1983, striking down the legislative veto, invalidated the one-house disapproval over deferrals.

The 1974 act contained a number of other provisions designed to strengthen legislative control. It created budget committees in the House and the Senate, established the Congressional Budget Office (CBO) to supply technical support, and required the adoption of budget resolutions to set overall limits on budget aggregates (such as total outlays and revenues) and to permit debate on spending priorities. Following the model of an executive budget in the 1921 act, Congress assumed that congressional control and responsibility would be improved by centralizing the budget process in the legislative branch. In essence, the act of 1974 anticipated a contest between two budgets: presidential and congressional.

The analogy was weak because the president heads an executive branch fortified by a central budget office. This hierarchical system restricts the size of budget requests as they move upward from bureaus and departments to the OMB and the president. But there is no head in Congress and no possibility of a central budget office. Congress is decentralized, and no amount of procedural innovation can disguise that reality. Bicameralism, weak leadership, and committee and subcommittee autonomy are facts of life.

Technical and procedural complexities of the 1974 act have helped obscure its effectiveness. Members of Congress complimented the new process but condemned the budget resolutions it produced. Senator Robert Packwood announced in 1976, "Although I can commend the process wholeheartedly, it is with reluctance that I cannot support the result."

Many of the compliments depended on illusion, for behind all the talk of "comprehensiveness" and "accountability" was the fact that the budget committees provided a new access point for members who had been rebuffed by authorization and appropriations committees. To gain sufficient votes to pass the budget resolutions, the budget committees had to accommodate these spending interests (especially in the House of Representatives). The totals in budget resolutions were set at generous levels, adding a new rationale for higher spending. The appropriations committees found it difficult to argue against amendments to increase spending when their bills provided less than the amounts allowed in a budget resolution. The new process therefore tolerated higher spending than would have been acceptable in the past.

The "current services budget," adopted by the 1974 statute, became a handy concept to legitimate annual, automatic adjustments for inflation. The concept helped shelter federal programs from budget-cutting drives. Other innovations, such as the reports submitted every March by authorizing committees, stimulated program advocacy. Forced to issue recommendations early in the year, authorizing and appropriations committees inflated their estimates beyond likely needs. Their behavior allowed the budget committees to put together resolutions substantially lower than the sum of the March requests. Members could then claim "savings" through these make-believe reductions. Instead of keeping within the president's aggregates, members voted on generous ceilings in budget resolutions and then announced to their constituents that they had "stayed within the budget." Which budget—the president's or Congress'—was never made clear.

Although the framers of the 1974 statute knew that entitlements and uncontrollables constituted the most disturbing pressure for higher spending, entitlements received a preferred status in the budget act and were subjected to little discipline. Serious efforts to constrain entitlements were not made until 1980 and 1981.

Action on budget resolutions consumed increasing amounts of time, leading to delay in the passage of appropriations bills and increasing reliance on continuing resolutions as temporary funding instruments once the fiscal year began. The problem with a compressed schedule grew worse when Congress decided to use "reconciliation" to control entitlements and federal spending. Under reconciliation, Congress seeks budget savings by changing benefit levels and benefit criteria for social welfare programs. Senator Lowell Weicker voted against reconciliation instructions in 1981 "because of the precipitate, injudicious way the president's spending reduction package has been considered in the body. We are supposed to be a deliberative body but, instead, we have been a mirror to the administration's program." Members of Congress voted on a massive reconciliation bill with practically no opportunity for amendment and little understanding of its impact on agencies and programs.

The 1974 budget act assumed that members of Congress would behave more responsibly by having to vote explicitly on budget aggregates, facing up to totals rather than deciding in piecemeal fashion the spending actions in separate appropriations and authorizations. However, the record since 1974 demonstrates that members do not want to vote on aggregates when the aggregates represent high levels of outlays or huge deficits. Instead, members will avoid a vote or will vote for unrealistic estimates. The result is escapist budgeting, and members become less, not more, responsible.

With budget deficits growing to alarming magnitudes, in 1985 Congress passed the

Gramm-Rudman-Hollings Act to establish a statutory schedule to bring the deficit to zero by fiscal 1991. The act provided that if the president and Congress fail to adhere to the schedule, an automatic "sequestration" report is to be prepared by the comptroller general, to eliminate the excess spending. In 1986 the Supreme Court, in *Bowsher* v. *Synar,* declared the sequestration process unconstitutional because it placed executive duties on the comptroller general, who could not be removed by the president. The decision forced Congress to meet the deficit targets through the regular legislative process or discover an automatic mechanism for cutting spending that would conform to the Court's ruling.

CONCLUSIONS

The subtleties and complexities of the American system of separated powers cannot be captured by a simple formula. Neither in theory nor in practice have the branches of government ever been distinct or compartmentalized. Overlapping powers have been necessary for settling boundary disputes and breaking deadlocks. So long as each branch maintains the capacity to resist encroachments and preserve its status as a coequal branch, the American system tolerates a substantial amount of shared power and joint effort. Different kinds of accommodations and intermediate positions have allowed government to operate effectively without sacrificing or compromising basic constitutional values.

CASES

Anderson v. Dunn, 6 Wheaton 204 (1821)
Barenblatt v. United States, 360 U.S. 109 (1959)
Bowsher v. Synar, 54 U.S.L.W. 5064 (1986)
Clark v. Board of Education of Little Rock Sch. Dist., 374 F.2d 569 (8th Cir. 1967)
Contractors Ass'n. of Eastern Pennsylvania v. Secretary of Labor, 442 F.2d 159 (3rd Cir. 1971)
Delaney v. United States, 199 F.2d 107 (1st Cir. 1952)
Doe v. McMillan, 412 U.S. 306 (1973)
Dombrowski v. Eastland, 387 U.S. 82 (1967)
Gravel v. United States, 408 U.S. 606 (1972)
Hutchinson v. Proxmire, 443 U.S. 111 (1979)
Independent Gasoline Marketers Council v. Duncan, 492 F.Supp. 614 (D.D.C. 1980)
Industrial Union Dept., AFL-CIO v. American Petroleum Institute, 448 U.S. 607 (1980)
INS v. Chadha, 462 U.S. 919 (1983)
Kent v. Dulles, 357 U.S. 116 (1958)
Kilbourn v. Thompson, 103 U.S. 168 (1881)
McCulloch v. Maryland, 4 Wheaton 316 (1819)
McGrain v. Daugherty, 273 U.S. 135 (1927)
Manhattan General Equipment Co. v. Commissioner of Internal Revenue, 297 U.S. 129 (1936)
Marks v. CIA, 590 F.2d 997 (D.C. Cir. 1978)
Myers v. United States, 272 U.S. 52 (1926)
Panama Refining Co. v. Ryan, 293 U.S. 388 (1935)
Schechter Poultry Corp. v. United States, 295 U.S. 495 (1935)
Springer v. Philippine Islands, 277 U.S. 189 (1928)
Tavouraleas v. Piro, 527 F.Supp. 676 (D.D.C. 1981)
United States v. Brewster, 408 U.S. 501 (1972)
United States v. House of Representatives, 556 F.Supp. 150 (D.D.C. 1983)
United States v. Lovett, 328 U.S. 303 (1946)
United States v. Nixon, 418 U.S. 683 (1974)
United States v. Yoshida International, Inc., 526 F.2d 560 (Ct. Cust. & Pat. App. 1975)
Youngstown Sheet and Tube Co. v. Sawyer, 343 U.S. 579 (1952)

BIBLIOGRAPHY

John L. Blackman, *Presidential Seizure in Labor Disputes* (1967). Grover Cleveland, *The Independence of the Executive* (1913). Robert E. Cushman, *The Independent Regulatory Commissions* (1941). Louis Fisher, *Constitutional Conflicts Between Congress and the President* (1985). Morton Rosenberg, "Beyond the Limits of Executive Power: Presidential Control of Agency Rulemaking Under Executive Order 12,291" in *Michigan Law Review,* 80 (1981).

Allen Schick, *Congress and Money* (1980). Joseph Story, *Commentaries on the Constitution of the United States,* 2 vols., 5th ed. (1905). M.J.C. Vile, *Constitutionalism and the Separation of Powers* (1967). Francis Wharton, *The Revolutionary Diplomatic Correspondence of the United States*, 6 vols. (1889).

[*See also* ADMINISTRATIVE AGENCIES; ARTICLES OF CONFEDERATION; EXECUTIVE AND DOMESTIC AFFAIRS; *and* EXECUTIVE AND FOREIGN AFFAIRS.]

CONSTITUTIONAL INTERPRETATION

Craig R. Ducat

CONSTITUTIONAL interpretation is concerned with the justification, standards, and methods by which a court exercises the power of judicial review. Judicial review, simply, is the practice used by courts to pass upon the constitutionality of actions taken by any of the coordinate branches of government. The exercise of this power, whose broad scope and substantial impact on the determination of public policy appear to be unique to the American political system, poses a genuine problem for a democracy. In a nation that presumably emphasizes the responsiveness of officeholders to the wishes of the people as expressed through the ballot box, by what authority do appointed, life-tenured judges sit in judgment on the validity of policies enacted by those democratically elected officeholders?

The acuteness of the inconsistency of judicial review with democratic institutions deepens further once we recognize that nowhere does the Constitution explicitly authorize the Supreme Court, or any other institution for that matter, to engage in any sort of constitutional review. When the Supreme Court laid claim to the practice of judicial review and first confronted the legitimacy of that power in *Marbury* v. *Madison* (1803), the justification that it offered necessarily lay in arguments beyond the text of the Constitution. Although British, colonial, and state courts had occasionally asserted the power of judicial review and the Supreme Court itself apparently had assumed such a power to lie within its grasp even before 1803, the Court's disposition of *Marbury* is regarded as both its first and most authoritative statement in justification of this apparently extra-constitutional practice. Because the traditional argument in support of judicial review, as presented in *Marbury* and as supplemented by the writings of later proponents, has

long been thought to be fatally defective in certain important respects, the controversy surrounding judicial review continues unabated.

The study of constitutional interpretation, then, concerns itself with several alternative theories by which the practice of judicial review might ostensibly be harmonized with democratic institutions; but that is not all there is to it. How the power of judicial review is justified has an important and inevitable effect on the standard that the courts will apply to assess whether a given legislative, executive, administrative, or judicial action contravenes the Constitution. In sum, constitutional interpretation focuses on alternative frameworks of judicial review that describe the logical interconnections among the justification for the review power, the standard of constitutionality to be applied by the court, and the method according to which the judges reach their conclusion that a certain governmental action does or does not violate the Constitution.

THE TRADITIONAL THEORY OF JUDICIAL REVIEW: CONSTITUTIONAL ABSOLUTISM

It makes sense to begin consideration of constitutional interpretation with the theory articulated by Chief Justice John Marshall, speaking for the Court in *Marbury* v. *Madison*, not only because it is the oldest of the alternative formulations but also because it is the view that still dominates teaching about the Supreme Court in American elementary and secondary education. In the discussion that follows, strands of arguments advanced by Justice Hugo Black, the only member of the Court in modern times to completely embrace this point of view, are woven together with those of Marshall to lend clarity, coherence, and contemporary relevance.

The traditional theory of constitutional interpretation ultimately rests on the contention that there is no inconsistency between the practice of judicial review and the basic tenets of the American system. This is so, the advocates of the traditional view argue, because of an important distinction that must be made between parliamentary systems on the one hand and constitutional systems on the other. Although both are varieties of democratic systems, a parliamentary system, such as Great Britain's or those of continental Europe, is characterized by the fact that acts passed by the legislature stand on an equal footing with the other written and unwritten components of the Constitution. It is this parity that makes for parliamentary supremacy, since the legislative branch can enact changes in such component parts of the Constitution at will. In a constitutional system such as ours, however, it is the written Constitution that is supreme, not actions taken by a coordinate branch of government. The supremacy clause of the Constitution (Article VI, paragraph 2) tells us so.

The connection between constitutional supremacy and judicial review requires two important arguments and several key assumptions. The first critical assumption is that the Constitution is a collection of rules. The contention that ours is a constitutional (as distinguished from a parliamentary) system merely makes the point that the rules contained in the Constitution are to be regarded as supreme. When Congress passes a bill and that bill is duly approved by the president or his veto of it is overridden, the resulting legislation also contains rules. In a constitutional system, it is imperative that we distinguish between these two sets of rules. The rules contained in the Constitution are superior; the rules embodied in legislation are inferior. The first in the resulting sequence of arguments made by the traditionalists then runs as follows: legislation passed by Congress may conflict with the Constitution. When this happens, the conflict must be resolved. If these two kinds of rules do conflict, then, as the supremacy clause of the Constitution dictates, the inferior rules must give way to the superior ones. The provisions of the Constitution must prevail over legislation enacted by Congress because "[t]his Constitu-

tion, and the laws of the United States which shall be made in pursuance thereof; . . . shall be the supreme law of the land . . . ." Unless elaborated, this argument simply warrants the conclusion that a constitutional system implies some kind of constitutional review, but it does not itself furnish a justification for judicial review.

The second argument of the series seeks to address why such a constitutional determination is the function of courts, particularly the Supreme Court. This argument is based on the assumption that judicial power, which is given to the federal courts under Article III of the Constitution, is that of deciding real cases and controversies. The decision of cases entails the judge's application of rules to facts in order to reach a decision. Where the facts of a case call into play two contradictory rules, the judge must decide which is the valid rule before he or she can apply it. Thus, to use Marshall's words in *Marbury*, "It is emphatically, the province of the judicial department, to say what the law is." As the supremacy clause also makes undeniably clear, when a collision occurs between a constitutional rule and a statutory one, judges are duty-bound to respect the Constitution. Thus it is that judges have the power of judicial review. This line of argument, it should be pointed out, sidesteps the serious problem posed at its outset by adopting the position that the democratic quality of the American system is limited by its constitutional character.

In order for the Constitution itself to be supreme, the traditional theory of constitutional interpretation requires additional stipulations. The most important of these stipulations bears upon the relationship of judges to the constitutional rule that they are applying. It is the relevant text of the Constitution that provides the standards for evaluating rules laid down by Congress or the president. The standard for assessing constitutionality, in other words, must bè the words of the Constitution, not what the judges would prefer the Constitution to mean. Constitutional supremacy necessarily assumes that a superior rule is what the Constitution says it is, not what the judges prefer it to be.

How then, it might be asked, can such an objective meaning of constitutional provisions be ascertained? The answer lies in two tools of constitutional interpretation, the "plain meaning" rule and the "intentions of the Framers." The former signifies the notion that the words of the Constitution are to be taken at face value and are to be given their "ordinary," "accepted" meaning; the latter requires fidelity to what those who wrote the Constitution intended its provisions to mean. By relying upon these two tools, advocates of the traditional theory of constitutional interpretation seek to constrain the judges to act only as faithful conduits of the document and thus effect the reality of constitutional rather than judicial supremacy.

Although Marshall's decisions largely stressed the broad interpretation of constitutional provisions, use of this traditional approach to constitutional interpretation quite often has amounted to what we know more familiarly as "strict construction," a concept that has been criticized as misleading, a cover for much that is inconsistent and devoid of real meaning (Dworkin). The link between constitutional absolutism and strict construction is a common suspicion of governmental power. Several examples demonstrate this link. Perhaps the most famous is Justice Black's reading of the First Amendment in 1959, in which he held the constitutional guaranties of free speech and press to be absolute prohibitions against governmental regulation (*Barenblatt* v. *United States* [dissenting opinion]). Another is Black's position that the word "liberty" in the due process clause of the Fourteenth Amendment was meant to include all the protections contained in the Bill of Rights and thus safeguard them against state as well as federal infringement (*Adamson* v. *California,* 1947 [dissenting opinion]). Other illustrations can easily be found among those decisions rendered by the Supreme Court, interpreting both the commerce clause and the taxing and spending powers, which confined Congress to regulating only those features of the economy bearing upon the interstate distribution of goods and services, while assigning to the states the constitutional power of regulating the various means of production, such as manufacturing, mining, and farming (*United States* v. *E. C. Knight Co.,* 1895; *Hammer* v. *Dagenhart,* 1918; *Schechter Poultry Corp.* v. *United States,* 1935; *Carter* v. *Carter Coal Co.,* 1936). The feature common to all these examples is the interpretation of the right or prerogative discussed in black-or-white terms. Such positions appear to manifest a mechanical quality of decision-making in which the judge seems de-

tached from the process of adjudication so that only the constitutional rules seem to control the decision. The approach is perhaps best reflected in a now-famous passage from Justice Owen Roberts' opinion for the Court in *United States* v. *Butler* (1936):

> There should be no misunderstanding as to the function of this court in such a case. It is sometimes said that the court assumes a power to overrule or control the action of the people's representatives. This is a misconception. The Constitution is the supreme law of the land ordained and established by the people. All legislation must conform to the principles it lays down. When an act of Congress is appropriately challenged in the courts as not conforming to the constitutional mandate, the judicial branch of the government has only one duty; to lay the article of the Constitution which is invoked beside the statute which is challenged and to decide whether the latter squares with the former. All the court does, or can do, is to announce its considered judgment upon the question. The only power it has, if such it may be called, is the power of judgment. This court neither approves nor condemns any legislative policy. Its delicate and difficult office is to ascertain and declare whether the legislation is in accordance with, or in contravention of, the provisions of the Constitution; and, having done that, its duty ends.
> (pp. 62–63)

As noted before, however, this theory of constitutional interpretation is not without serious flaws. In the first place, the contention that provisions of the Constitution are capable of objective definition is dubious at best. Research by many political scientists (the works of Schubert and Spaeth are illustrative) has amassed overwhelming evidence that demonstrates that the different political attitudes and values of judges are closely related to their voting behavior in cases that are decided nonunanimously. The fact that such evidence clearly supports the conclusion that judges do not decide controversial cases "objectively" effectively refutes the pretensions of constitutional absolutists that adjudication is detached and mechanical. Nor is the prospect particularly good for reversing this reality of judicial behavior, at least by any use of interpretive tools such as the plain meaning rule or the intentions of the Framers, for these purported instruments to the attainment of constitutional objectivity have been withered by a devastating barrage of criticism (Anderson; Carter).

Equally vulnerable, as Dworkin has shown, is the absolutists' portrayal of the Constitution as a mere collection of rules that bear more weight than ordinary legislation. Recall that this assumption was crucial because such a characterization of constitutional provisions was essential to the subsequent assertion that judges just apply these rules to decide cases. Dworkin has demonstrated that the defect in this assumption is simply that not all the provisions in the Constitution can be accurately described as rules. While some provisions, such as those specifying that a senator's term shall be six years or that the president shall be at least thirty-five years old, are rules, others are not. The guaranties, for example, that no person shall be deprived of life, liberty, or property without due process of law, or that no person shall be subjected to cruel or unusual punishment, or that private property shall not be taken for public use without just compensation, embody constitutional principles, not rules.

The difference between principles and rules, as Dworkin has pointed out, is significant and has important consequences for the arguments of the constitutional absolutists. Assuming that any definitional problems in terms have been resolved, rules identify specific consequences that must be accepted if a given rule is to be regarded as relevant to deciding the case at hand. This is what leads us to say that rules have an absolute or either-or quality: if a given rule is relevant to the facts of a case, the consequences it specifies must be accepted. Principles have no such quality because they do not identify specific consequences. Since principles are capable of statement only in general terms, their meaning and consequences are ambiguous. It is this combination of generality and ambiguity in principles that makes them more or less applicable. Thus due process or equal protection of the laws, for example, may be more or less present in a variety of situations and the burden of deciding how and whether they apply rests with the judges. Consequently, principles afford judges far greater latitude in interpretation. Recognizing that the Constitution contains principles as well as rules means that the reality of greater interpretive freedom must be accepted and addressed.

The cumulative impact of these criticisms is lethal for constitutional absolutism, at least in anything like its traditional posture, since the cornerstone of the theory is the tacit but crucial assumption that judges do not exercise discretion. It was the implicit denial that judges have important matters of choice in interpretation which permitted the assertion that the Constitution itself was supreme and that the judge was merely a conduit through which it spoke. But the Constitution is an inanimate object and cannot speak, and the instruments for divining its "objective" meaning have now been completely discredited. Additionally, since the most important provisions of the Constitution declare principles, not rules, the toll taken on constitutional absolutism is heavy indeed. Principles necessarily require interpretive discretion if their meaning is to be made clear in particular and varying circumstances. Although Dworkin would disagree with this conclusion, most political scientists and apparently most justices appointed since the Great Depression have recognized that the exercise of significant amounts of discretion is inevitable, and in the exercise of that discretion the judges' behavior will be substantially affected by their political values and attitudes—something not lost on most presidents, who pick their nominees to the Court with precisely that aim in mind.

It is therefore quite inaccurate to say, as Marshall did in *Marbury,* that the power of judicial review is justified because the judge confronts an immutable collision between an inferior rule and a superior one, and that, in order to apply it to the case at hand, he or she must first decide which is the valid rule. In light of these criticisms of constitutional absolutism, the fact is surely otherwise. The collision that Marshall portrays is by no means inevitable, as Marshall's performance in that very case reveals (Ducat). Throughout American history, the reason why legislation has periodically been declared unconstitutional is not because of its collision with certain fixed rules of the Constitution, but because the justices have read into the principles of the Constitution interpretive doctrines of their own creation with which the policies endorsed by other branches of the government are then seen as inconsistent. It is the principles, not the rules of the Constitution, which have been the perennial sources of litigation and the occasions of judicial review, and those principles mean what the justices say they mean. In short, the collision of which Marshall speaks is not a collision between a statute (or executive order or administrative regulation) and the Constitution, but between the statute and some doctrine created by the justices to interpret the Constitution. All constitutional collisions are man-made, involving, as they do, substantial judicial discretion.

Ultimately, it is the failure of constitutional absolutism to recognize and address the reality of judicial discretion which dooms the traditional theory of constitutional interpretation. Subsequent modes of constitutional interpretation have profited from the realization and thus begin by accepting this premise. In doing so, however, they cannot escape—as the constitutional absolutists sought to—the riddle of the undemocratic character of judicial review.

THE BALANCING OF INTERESTS, OR JUDICIAL SELF-RESTRAINT

Although the two remaining frameworks of constitutional interpretation (discussed in this section and the next) differ significantly in the enthusiasm with which they embrace judicial review, they share the candid acknowledgment that courts are political institutions; that is, that judges, like other government officials, have a wide range of choice in the decisions they make, and in making such choices, their values and attitudes have a substantial and often preponderant influence. This concession activates the dilemma posed by judicial review in a democratic society for the simple reason that, if the justices can be said to have the last word on the constitutionality of policy and if that judgment is informed principally by personal political values, some overarching authority must be identified that sanctions the substitution of judicial policy preferences for those of governmental officials responsible to the electorate. Failing this, judicial review is open to the simple rebuttal, "Who elected you?" —to use the words we are fond of using against any self-serving claim of prerogative. To those judges and scholars whom we call the interest balancers or advocates of judicial self-restraint, that simple rebuttal is virtually unanswerable because, although they have accepted the premise that courts are political institutions, they feel bound by the fundamental assumption that public policy ought to be expressed through the actions of elected representatives.

That courts are political institutions is, for the interest balancers, an undeniable fact of life. Although the quaint trappings and peculiar format of the judicial process make it appear unique, in fact the act of judging is really very much like the act of legislating. Every case, the interest balancers contend, presents a conflict of competing social interests among which a choice must be made. Even an apparently uncomplicated personal injury case, in which a pedestrian sues an automobile driver, can be said to involve contending social interests, for in such a case, although the litigants represent themselves, they personify the classes of pedestrians and drivers. To decide, as the judge might, that the defendant must compensate the injured plaintiff is to hold that pedestrians and drivers have certain respective rights and obligations. Such statements, to be applied as precedent in future like cases, distributing as they do benefits and burdens, are statements of public policy. Every case, then, calls upon a judge to weigh conflicting social claims and to apportion gains and losses. This process of balancing competing social interests, influenced as it is by the values of the decision maker, demonstrates the essential similarity between judges and other political functionaries. In accordance with the fundamental tenets of democracy, the judge should strive to satisfy as many of these conflicting claims as is possible, since the happiness of the many is to be preferred over the satisfaction of the few.

This interest-balancing perspective readily translates into judicial self-restraint. Where the constitutionality of a law is called into question, judges in a democratic system are duty-bound to respect the balance among interests embodied in the statute for the logical reason that, having been passed by a majority in the legislative branch, it presumably satisfies more rather than fewer interests. For this reason, statutes are presumptively constitutional.

Does this consequently call for the renunciation or the minimization of judicial review, and, if only its minimization, on what basis consistent with democratic theory could judicial review legitimately be invoked? According to Justice Felix Frankfurter, who was at least as great an apostle of judicial self-restraint as Black was of absolutism, the uneasy answer was minimization: minimization, rather than complete renunciation, because of the impact of the due process clauses of the Fifth and Fourteenth Amendments; uneasy, because although "one's own opinion about the wisdom or evil of a law should be excluded altogether when one is doing one's duty on the bench" (*West Virginia State Board of Education* v. *Barnette,* 1943) such a division of personal and professional minds is not always or entirely possible.

According to the restraintists, the due process clauses furnish both the only possible justification for judicial review and the only relevant standard for undertaking it. The guaranty of due process supplies a justification for the exercise of judicial review because due process by definition refers to the assurance of procedural regularity. The restraintists' test of constitutionality follows directly from this. As noted earlier, a statute is presumed to be constitutional, which means that the burden of proof rests on the attacking party. That burden can be successfully discharged only by showing that the law in question is unreasonable: that is, that the enactment is arbitrary, capricious, or patently discriminatory. This constitutional standard is known as the test of reasonableness.

A judgment of reasonableness is not to be confused with an opinion about the wisdom or desirability of a law. In no sense is the question one of whether the legislative branch enacted the best policy. If one visualizes the enactment of a law as the legislature's response to a given problem pressing for its attention, it is usually the case that the policy selected was one option among many. In applying the test of reasonableness, the restraintists assert, a judge must focus on the policy alternative enacted by the legislature and answer the single question, whether a body of reasonable men and women could have selected that policy as a reasonable response to the problem. Under no circumstances is a judge entitled to engage in comparing the policy selected by the legislature with other policies it might have chosen, for this would not be a test of whether the policy enacted was reasonable but whether it was the best policy. In a democracy, the choice as to which is the best policy is reserved for officeholders who are popularly elected. When the justices engage in comparative assessments to see whether the legislative branch enacted the best policy, the Court in effect substitutes its judgment about the wisdom of policy for that of the people's elected representatives and assumes the role of a "super-legislature."

Discussion of the method by which the restraintists engage in interest balancing in constitutional cases would not be complete without two additional observations. First, all interests are to be treated equally. Since the Fifth and Fourteenth Amendments place life, liberty, and property on the same footing—that is, none is to be denied without due process of law—the test of reasonableness is to be applied to all statutes regardless of the different interests they touch, with no exceptions. Second, the statistical effect of applying the test will be such as to produce an exceedingly high proportion of decisions in which the constitutionality of statutes is upheld. This result is hardly surprising since, as should be clear from the foregoing discussion, lessening the mortality rate of statutes was one of the principal aims of this mode of constitutional interpretation.

Although a perpetual refrain of deference to majority rule dominates the case to be made for judicial self-restraint and that theme ought not to be minimized, there are additional arguments of substantial weight that are generally thought to contribute to the attractiveness of this theory of constitutional interpretation. For the sake of clarity, these arguments can perhaps best be apportioned and summarized according to three general issues: the functioning of the democratic system, the institutional capacity of the judiciary, and political prudence. The lines of advocacy that follow are drawn principally but by no means exclusively from the writings of two celebrated proponents of self-restraint: Frankfurter, mentioned earlier, and Alexander Bickel, late Yale law professor and former Frankfurter law clerk. Frankfurter penned two famous opinions that are particularly acclaimed as insightful and eloquent statements in behalf of judicial self-restraint: *West Virginia State Board of Education* v. *Barnette* (dissenting opinion) and *Baker* v. *Carr* (1962) (dissenting opinion). Bickel's contributions to the cause consist principally of two books, *The Least Dangerous Branch* and *The Supreme*

Court and the Idea of Progress. The strands of argument summarized below, which mesh to make the case for judicial self-restraint, reflect a fabric woven of different threads, each of which has been spun by these and other proponents.

While the insistence on respect for majority rule, and the converse contention that anything less is tantamount to sanctioning minority rule, constitute the flagship argument for judicial self-restraint, it is bolstered by a related assertion about the detrimental impact that the active use of judicial review has on the effectiveness of the democratic system. Large-scale reliance upon the courts for the resolution of public problems, the restraintists argue, will lead in the long run to the atrophy of institutions of popular government. Even if political parties and legislative institutions do not fall into disuse and slowly fade away because of the emerging reliance on the courts to do their job, there is a distinct possibility that minorities, long estranged from popular political participation because of extensive discrimination, may, by taking their demands to the courts rather than to parties and legislatures, consign the mechanisms of popular governance to perpetual control by narrow, special interests, thus collapsing the broad-based policy perspective and popular accountability that are the lifeblood of the democratic system.

The judicial restraint school develops a two-pronged argument: it asserts both that courts do not have the power to decide many issues and that courts do not have the capacity to do so. Restraintists like to point out that courts, after all, are institutions with peculiar structural features such as presentation of information through the adversary format and solution of problems by reliance upon rules and principles that minimize divergence from what has been done previously. These institutional attributes limit the kinds of things courts can do well or even do at all. As Bickel (1970, 175) put it:

> The judicial process is too principle-prone and principle-bound—it has to be, there is no other justification or explanation for the role it plays. It is also too remote from conditions, and deals, case by case, with too narrow a slice of reality. It is not accessible to all the varied interests that are in play in any decision of great consequence. It is, very properly, independent. It is passive. It has difficulty controlling the stages by which it approaches a problem. It rushes forward too fast, or it lags; its pace hardly ever seems just right. For all these reasons, it is, in a vast, complex, changeable society, a most unsuitable instrument for the formation of policy.

Sometimes matters have a structure so foreign to adjudication that courts cannot begin to tackle them, as Lon Fuller has shown with respect to what is called a polycentric problem, which Lieberman argues is increasingly the form taken by our social and economic difficulties. Moreover, when courts render judgments and then are limited in their capacity to follow through, judicial decisions may convey the impression that the problem has been solved when in fact it persists, sometimes in a more virulent form. And the notoriously conservative character of the judicial process (Ducat) may make bedfellows of judicial self-restraintists and political radicals who may wisely suspect that, when minorities take their demands for change to the courts, any victory may well ring hollow. The fruits of litigation are substantially less likely to produce significant change than otherwise could be achieved through the sort of popular political action necessary to gain control of a party organization or a legislature. Frankfurter put it both succinctly and eloquently when, dissenting from the Court's initial legislative reapportionment decision in *Baker* v. *Carr* (p. 270), he wrote:

> In this situation, as in others of like nature, appeal for relief does not belong here. Appeal must be to an informed, civically militant electorate. In a democratic society like ours, relief must come through an aroused popular conscience that sears the conscience of the people's representatives. In any event there is nothing judicially more unseemly nor more self-defeating than for this Court to make *in terrorem* pronouncements, to indulge in merely empty rhetoric, sounding a word of promise to the ear, sure to be disappointing to the hope.

Even if these arguments can somehow be surmounted, there remain substantial considerations of political prudence. If the judiciary is, to use Alexander Hamilton's phrase in the *Federalist* (no. 78), "the least dangerous" branch, that is because it is the weakest. In perhaps an unintended sense, Justice Roberts was right when, in the passage from the *Butler* case quoted earlier, he characterized the judicial power as "only . . . the power of judgment." Courts may decide things, but the power to enforce them always lies in the hands of the executive branch. It may be part of our political mythology that Andrew Jackson once said of our greatest chief justice in the wake of a decision that particularly irked the feisty president, "John Marshall has made his decision, now let him enforce it." The point of that comment is nonetheless valid. It was precisely such an understanding that enforcement is just as important to the success of a judicial decision as the Court's rendering of judgment that moved Justice Frankfurter, during oral argument in the school desegregation cases in 1952, to wonder aloud from the bench, "Nothing could be worse from my point of view than for this Court to make an abstract declaration that segregation is bad and then have it evaded by tricks." The point here is a simple but effective one. The Court should select occasions for the exercise of its power with care, in the full realization that the effectiveness of its decisions bears an important relation to what the market will bear, not only in the prospect of essential cooperation from officers of the executive branch but also with respect to the likelihood that the people will more or less willingly submit to its judgments. Above all, the Court should avoid putting itself in the humiliating posture of announcing an important ruling and then having its command ignored.

Keenly aware of the weapons that stock the legislative arsenal, the restraintists also counsel prudence because of the damage to both the Court's power and reputation that can result when congressional dismay with its decisions triggers congressional retaliation. Although impeachment has never really been very credible as a political weapon, several more realistic Court-curbing options are available and have been employed by Congress either to threaten the judiciary or to effect change, or both. These include such options as proposing constitutional amendments, increasing the number of justices, and withdrawing some of the Court's appellate jurisdiction. If it is true that in any war with Congress the Court will surely come out the loser, then due regard for the vulnerability of its political position should lead those on the Court to choose their battles wisely and conduct them carefully. Frankfurter again probably summed it

up best in *Baker* when he warned (p. 267): "The Court's authority—possessed of neither the purse nor the sword—ultimately rests on sustained public confidence in its moral sanction. Such feeling must be nourished by the Court's complete detachment, in fact and in appearance, from political entanglements and by abstention from injecting itself into the clash of political forces in political settlements."

Despite the strength of these arguments, interest balancing has itself been weighed and found wanting. A source of difficulty, common to several of the more serious misgivings prompted by this theory of constitutional interpretation, lies in the restraintists' reading of both democratic theory and practice.

Regardless of the lengths to which it has been embellished, the democratic theory argument offered by the restraintists is reduced to the seemingly intractable dilemma of the Court as an undemocratic institution in a democratic society. Thus, they argue, because Congress is a democratic institution and the Court is an undemocratic institution, the latter should defer to the former. Assuming that responsiveness to the people is the litmus by which democratic institutions are exclusively to be tested, it would require either an astonishing or willful ignorance of the workings of Congress to contend that its legislative process so superbly measures up to the majority-rule criterion as to warrant all the deference the restraintists claim in the name of majority rule. As Shapiro has forcefully argued, several features of Congress, such as the committee system, seniority, the filibuster, plurality election and low voter turnout, and the dominance of the trustee model of representation, work to frustrate what might uncritically be called "the popular will." By what strain of logic, then, should the Court feel compelled to defer to an institution whose various features, redeemable perhaps by other standards, fail the restraintists' own test of representativeness and "prevent the full play of the democratic process"—to use Frankfurter's words in the *Barnette* dissent (p.650). Nonmajoritarian traits also characterize practices or institutions in all three branches of government: the judiciary, the legislative branch (as we have just seen), and the executive branch (with its Electoral College and tenured federal civil service), for different and very defensible reasons.

But the real fallacy of the restraintists' conclusion about the Court emanates from their badly flawed definition of democracy. The characterization of the Court as undemocratic because its members are not elected and therefore are not responsive to the popular will assumes that democracy can be defined simply as majority rule. Few of us would care to defend such a grossly inadequate definition. It is by now fairly elementary political science that the concept of democracy must include a provision of those rights which make it possible for minorities to become majorities. The problem, in short, is that the restraintists have forgotten the minority rights component in the democratic equation. Is the Court an undemocratic institution? Whether it is depends upon what it does. If the Court uses the power of judicial review to guarantee the free exercise of rights such as speech, press, and association so that political coalitions of citizens can be formed to influence the making of public policy, isn't the Court just as democratic as Congress? This possibility never seems to occur to the restraintists, however, because their too-limited conception of democracy has left out the rights that make the decision-making procedure possible.

Democracy is a term that describes a process by which citizens compete for the power to turn their preferences into law. It is a game of numbers. Several important assumptions underlie these political intramurals: that all votes are equal; that citizens have an equal right to participate; that the resources necessary to political competition are relatively evenly spread; and that the wins and losses will be more or less evenly distributed over the populace. Political majorities, it was expected, would rise and fall with the issues. Above all, the Founders supposed this to be a system that would avoid the spectre of perpetual winners who made policy at the expense of perpetual losers, for this constitutes exploitation or, as the Founders were wont to say, "tyranny." Since the principles of judicial self-restraint convert the Court into a virtual rubber stamp of Congress, this constitutional theory necessarily must either accept these assumptions as accurate statements about the realities of the political process or else, to the extent they are not, accept the judgment that routine judicial deference to congressional decisions countenances judicial participation in a process of polit-

ical exploitation. It is a political truth too obvious to require demonstration here that blacks, women, Hispanics, and other social groups have traditionally been victimized by such pervasive discrimination and they have not enjoyed "equal" opportunity. The political process has instead perpetuated a number of permanent minorities who have been repeatedly exploited by a majoritarian political process in which the restraintists would have the Court acquiesce. And the fine impartiality—with which the restraintists maintain that abridgements of free speech, press, association, and other basic constitutional rights should be given the same deference as is accorded legislation affecting property rights—is likely to do little else than ensure the effective suppression of political grievances. It is unclear whether any of these considerations crossed Frankfurter's mind when he admonished his brethren in *Baker* to make judicious use of their "moral sanction" lest "sustained public confidence" in the Court be eroded.

The institutional and prudential arguments with which judicial self-restraint fortifies itself are not beyond criticism either. Portraying the Court rather like a patient in delicate condition, the restraintists, like so many constitutional physicians, prescribe plenty of bed rest. But is the Court so weak? Shapiro argues that the malady is largely psychosomatic. The restraintists, he argues, are less accomplished at expert diagnosis than at self-fulfilling prophecy. Because they never tire of saying that the Court is a fragile institution, endless repetition of that shibboleth makes it so. Their admonition to husband Court resources for a rare exertion leads Shapiro to ask whether the building of political muscle isn't instead the result of vigorous daily exercise.

Indicting the Court for failure to deliver on public policy all by itself seems equally suspect. That the Court should not involve itself with the bigger problems of the day because it cannot solve them all alone seems weak and fatalistic. Of course the Court cannot solve problems all by itself; no institution of American government can. A system founded on doctrines such as the separation of powers and checks and balances necessarily calls for cooperation among governing institutions, not unilateral policy making. In such a system the Court has a useful—indeed indispensable—role as the legitimator of political claims and as a catalyst for the aggrieved to coalesce and assert themselves in the democratic process (Ducat).

STRICT SCRUTINY, OR THE PREFERRED FREEDOMS APPROACH

It was especially the problem of permanent minorities that gave rise to the brand of judicial activism with which we are familiar today. In its modern garb, the active use of judicial review, which constitutes the third school of constitutional interpretation, casts the Court as the institutional defender of the politically disadvantaged. It was not always so with judicial activism. Until the triumph of New Deal liberalism over the staunch conservatism of the old Court in the late 1930s, the Supreme Court maintained a virtually unblemished record throughout most of American history of defending the rich and powerful, something Roosevelt's political lieutenants never tired of pointing out. There was complete agreement among the Roosevelt appointees, who soon inundated the Court, that a restraintist posture in the evaluation of administration economic policies should replace the activist constitutional doctrines through which the old Court had effected its finger-in-the-dike defense of laissez-faire capitalism. These same appointees, however, broke into warring factions over whether similar deference was due legislation directly bearing on constitutional guaranties of the First Amendment variety.

Because the wording of the Fifth and Fourteenth Amendments seemed to accord the interests of life, liberty, and property equal weight, Frankfurter and others, as noted earlier, asserted that all legislation must be judged by the same due process standard. Justices such as William O. Douglas, Frank Murphy, and Wiley Rutledge, however, argued that all constitutional rights were not equal. Embracing the premise that minority rights were absolutely essential to the democratic enterprise, these modern-day activists enthusiastically carried the implications of the argument to their natural constitutional conclusion. Since First Amendment rights and other like freedoms were fundamental to the democratic process, legislation affecting their exercise was entitled to substantially less deference than that accorded statutes regulating property rights and economic liberties. A democracy could still function without vigilant protection of economic rights associated with a capitalistic system, but not without those communicative and associational freedoms which make it possible for political coalitions to form. The rights of speech, press, association, assembly, and other liberties necessary to the democratic process constitute "preferred" freedoms.

The essential link between protection of these fundamental rights and ending the problem of permanent minorities was first alluded to by Justice Harlan Stone in his now-famous footnote to an otherwise undistinguished opinion disposing of a perfectly anonymous business regulation case, *United States* v. *Carolene Products Co.* (1938). Stone mused (p. 152):

> There may be narrower scope for operation of the presumption of constitutionality when legislation appears on its face to be within a specific prohibition of the Constitution, such as those of the first ten Amendments, which are deemed equally specific when held to be embraced within the Fourteenth. . . .
>
> It is unnecessary to consider now whether legislation which restricts those political processes which can ordinarily be expected to bring about repeal of undesirable legislation, is to be subjected to more exacting judicial scrutiny under the general prohibitions of the Fourteenth Amendment than are most other types of legislation. . . .
>
> Nor need we enquire whether similar considerations enter into the review of statutes directed at particular religious, . . . or national, . . . or racial minorities . . . whether prejudice against discrete and insular minorities may be a special condition, which tends seriously to curtail the operation of those political processes ordinarily to be relied upon to protect minorities, and which may call for a correspondingly more searching judicial inquiry.

However tentatively expressed, the connection is nonetheless apparent. Precisely because the Court is not a majoritarian institution, it has a constitutional responsibility to carefully scrutinize majority-passed legislation that directly impinges upon the exercise of those rights by minorities through which their political demands can be expressed. Given the social isolation and prejudice encountered by easily identifiable minorities, without the guarantee of these fundamental rights their participation in the political process will be effectively muted and conditions of exploitation will be perpetuated.

Although judicial practitioners of strict scrutiny agree with the restraintists that, in the area of economic policy and other legislation bearing on nonfundamental rights, the standard of mere reasonableness is justified, constitutional evaluation of legislation directly abridging those liberties fundamental to a democratic system must clear a higher hurdle. In the interest of clarity, it may prove helpful to see the standard as a tripartite test, although its employment by the justices does not necessarily proceed in this neat and orderly fashion and from time to time is undertaken using slightly different words. Nevertheless, the component parts of this test of constitutionality can be set out as follows:

1. Where legislation or other statement of policy abridges a preferred freedom on its face, the usual presumption of constitutionality is reversed; that is, the statute or other enactment is assumed to be unconstitutional, and that presumption can be dislodged only when the government has successfully discharged its burden of proof.

2. The government must show that the exercise of the fundamental right in the case in question constitutes "a clear and present danger" or that the legislation implicating that liberty advances "a compelling interest."

3. The legislation or other regulation must be drawn in such a way as to present a precisely tailored response to the problem and not burden basic liberties by its overbreadth; that means, the policy adopted by the government must constitute the least restrictive alternative.

As compared with the test of reasonableness employed by the restraintists, this constitutional standard imposing strict scrutiny surely does demand, in one sense at least, that governmental policy be the best, not merely a plausible alternative. Where the best policy is defined as that which effectively meets the problem and maximizes the freedom remaining, it is clear that only the "best" policy can be constitutional.

Strict scrutiny can be contrasted with judicial self-restraint in another important sense. It is readily apparent that problems of conflict between governmental power and civil liberties cannot be resolved by somehow merely maximizing satisfaction of the competing interests. At least if strict scrutiny maximizes, it does so in a much more sophisticated way than that suggested by interest balancing. If some rights occupy a preferred position, it stands to reason that everyone is entitled to those rights before claims to nonfundamental liberties can be granted. In any conflict, then, between persons attempting to have their claims to basic rights satisfied and other citizens seeking to have less important rights extended, such as an owner's right to do with his property as he wishes, the claims of the former must prevail over the claims of the latter, even if the number of individuals in the first group is significantly fewer than that of the second.

The logic of Stone's *Carolene Products* footnote, however, carries the activists beyond the concept of preferred freedoms. The problem of permanent minorities requires more than just applying strict scrutiny to legislation directly impinging on the mechanisms by which inputs in a democratic system are conveyed to policy makers; it also frequently mandates exacting constitutional evaluation of the outputs of the process. All legislation creates categories according to which rights and obligations, benefits and burdens are distributed. All legislation therefore necessarily discriminates. The equal protection clause of the Fourteenth Amendment and the due process clause of the Fifth Amendment guarantee that neither the states nor the national government may invidiously discriminate. This does not mean that government may make no distinctions in the way it treats people. Categories in law cannot, however, be created for reasons that bear no convincing relationship to the problem for which the legislation furnishes an ostensible response when the statutory benefits and burdens are assigned along lines traditionally constituting avenues of social prejudice and are to the detriment of "discrete and insular minorities," to use Stone's phrase. Legal categories drawn on the basis of race or alienage, for example, are said to constitute "suspect classifications."

The justification for strict scrutiny of legislation that apportions benefits and burdens according to suspect classifications can be traced directly to the problem of permanent minorities. If the "discrete and insular minorities" have been denied fundamental rights and are therefore precluded from access to the democratic process, the chances for their being victimized by "unfriendly" legislation are multiplied, if not ensured. Until the impediments to equal access have been removed, the Court owes an equal obligation to the permanent minorities to carefully scrutinize legislation that imposes suspect class-based burdens upon them.

In applying strict scrutiny to legislation that employs a suspect classification, the judicial activists basically apply the same three-part constitutional standard used to evaluate legislation infringing a preferred freedom. A statute that explicitly discriminates on the basis of race, for example, is presumed to be unconstitutional. Government bears the burden of demonstrating that it has a compelling interest for distinguishing among citizens on that basis. Finally, it must also show that no other basis for categorization in the law could serve that compelling interest.

In the period 1943–1949, when judicial activists often exercised effective control of the Court, strict scrutiny was employed mainly in defense of preferred freedoms. Perhaps its clearest statement during this time came from Justice Rutledge in his opinion for the Court in *Thomas v. Collins* (1945). Struggle for control of the Court intensified between the activist and restraintist factions in the ensuing years, and the activists did not return to a clearly dominant position until the time of the later Warren Court, 1962–1969. During this era the activist majority resumed its employment of strict scrutiny to preferred freedoms and significantly extended its application to suspect classifications. Although it can accurately be said that the Burger Court of the 1980s did not share the enthusiasm of the Warren Court's activist majority for expanding the number of both fundamental rights and suspect classes, the beachhead of strict scrutiny established during the Warren years did hold. Contemporary arguments between activists and self-restraintists are more often on the order of holding the line than of repealing the past.

Impressive as these arguments drawn from democratic theory and practice may be, strict scrutiny exhibits a number of serious shortcomings, several of which are closely associated with the process-based justification offered for judicial review. In the first place, contemporary judicial activists such as Justices William Brennan and Thurgood Marshall, and modern activist advocates of a bygone day such as Justice Douglas,

placed the imprimatur of fundamentality on rights that, whatever their importance when judged by another yardstick, have little if anything to do with the democratic process. When freedoms such as the right to interstate travel and the right to privacy are also acknowledged to be fundamental, it shows that the class of liberties so identified has outstripped the democratic process criterion. It is therefore incumbent upon the activists to reformulate their justifications for determining that certain rights are fundamental while others are not. In the absence of any adequate reformulation, labeling diverse freedoms as "preferred" smacks of subjectivity and arbitrariness, and the determination of which rights are in or out becomes rudderless.

The process-based justification of strict scrutiny rooted in democratic theory is not only insufficient, it is objectionable. To argue that the right to free speech, for example, depends upon the importance of free speech to the democratic process puts the cart before the horse. Human happiness is the end and democracy is a method for attaining that end, not vice versa. This misconception of democracy as end rather than method has important consequences for the exercise of free speech and other fundamental liberties as individual rights. Justifying the status of a liberty in terms of its contribution to democracy necessarily leads to the conclusion that its permissible exercise hangs upon its utility to others. Thus the Court has said on occasion that impermissible speech, such as obscenity or libel, is distinguishable from permissible speech on the grounds that the former is "without redeeming social importance" (*Roth* v. *United States*, 1957). The notion that the right to speak hangs upon whether what you say is useful to your neighbor is repressive, much along the same majoritarian lines we consider interest balancing vulnerable. It is also offensive to anyone who subscribes to the basic belief that a free society is ultimately to be distinguished from a totalitarian one on the grounds that the former assumes individuals are ends in themselves and not merely means to an end, while the latter proceeds on reverse expectations. It is individual rights, after all, which the Constitution guarantees, not social rights.

In addition to these problems, strict scrutiny leaves unanswered two difficulties that, as practical matters, the Court has yet to address. One of these asks what we are to do when two fundamental liberties collide, as when freedom of the press conflicts with guaranteeing a fair trial or when facilitating the free exercise of religious beliefs becomes tantamount to establishing a state religion. Strict scrutiny can guide our judgment when it is a matter of governmental regulatory power versus the exercise of civil liberties, but what are we to do when the case is pitched in terms of one preferred freedom against another?

Finally, there remains the genuine political vulnerability of the Court. Repeatedly invoking strict scrutiny will turn the court into an institution almost exclusively representative of the underdogs. Even if it is conceded that there are a number of permanent minorities, it does not follow that gathering all of them together will produce a viable political base from which the Court can hope to withstand the inevitable conflict with a largely unblack, unhispanic, unpoor, and unweak electorate. The permanent minorities are "discrete and insular," in the most important political sense, only in relation to the white, middle-class bulk of society. In relation to each other, the permanent minorities consist of many members who share characteristics of more than one group, so that when one sums the minorities, the increment gained by adding another group is offset by the fact that many of those individuals have already been counted. Then, too, there is the obvious point that, even if adding the minorities together did create a majority as a matter of numbers, they are politically disadvantaged and powerless, which is why the activists involved the Court in their behalf in the first place. At any rate, suffice it to say that demonstrating perpetual favoritism with regard to permanent minorities may well jeopardize broad-based respect for the Court as an even-handed and principled institution: such a reputation was not insignificant in weathering the Court-curbing storm of the 1930s. Injudicious and unrestrained applications of strict scrutiny could well provoke popular political campaigns against the Court from politicians anxious to curry favor with the middle of American society. A case in point consists of the attacks made on the judiciary during the 1968 presidential campaign and the consequent decline in public respect for the Court.

IS CONSTITUTIONAL THEORY POSSIBLE?

The preceding discussion yields a conclusion that is both distressing and challenging. What is disconcerting is not merely the scope and gravity of the imperfection in each theory, but the intertwined character of the strengths and weaknesses that plague these approaches to constitutional interpretation. The assets of any one interpretive framework appear to address the liabilities of the others with a disturbing degree of interconnection. Yet given the contradictions among the premises of these modes of interpretation, it seems unimaginable that any patchwork, resulting from an attempt to borrow a little from this approach and take a little from that, could produce a defensible and coherent theory of constitutional interpretation. On the other hand, choosing one from among the existing three modes of interpretation means accepting a seriously defective framework. It appears constitutional theory has reached an impasse.

On the assumption that the most desirable response lies in renovating the third framework, Ely in *Democracy and Distrust* attempts to remodel strict scrutiny. However, retaining the process-based justification, as he does, appears to warrant the conclusion that, although he has replaced an occasional stud and modified the floor plan, little has been done to save the crumbling foundation. Tushnet has argued that the problems that haunt this old house are less attributable to deficiencies in Ely's carpentry than fundamental defects of structural design. Judicial review cannot be justified, he contends, if we insist on satisfying three incompatible assumptions: (1) "that there are occasions when judicial displacement of legislative decisions—judicial review—is justified"; (2) "that judges cannot justifiably do whatever they want, but must respect some constraints on their behavior as judges"; and (3) "that in a pluralist society, objective values are not available as the basis for ordering social institutions" (Tushnet, 1037–1038). For reasons he elaborates, particularly with regard to Ely's effort, constitutional theory that fulfills all three demands is not possible. This, he argues, is not because of anything peculiar to judicial review but because of certain basic contradictions in liberalism.

CONSTITUTIONAL INTERPRETATION

Acclaimed as perhaps the most promising effort in resolving these problems of constitutional architecture is the approach set out by Dworkin in *Taking Rights Seriously*. Although agreeing with the critics of absolutism that the Constitution is composed more significantly of principles than rules, Dworkin denies that this entitles judges to "exercise discretion," if the term means that they may rely on their own value preferences in reading vague constitutional provisions. Constitutional provisions, Dworkin argues, are not vague; they are ambiguous. Vagueness suggests the absence of meaning, so the judge is called upon to furnish his own meaning; ambiguity suggests remoteness but completeness in a general statement that is capable of lending guidance, so the judge must operationalize constitutional guaranties. It is the function of judges to give effect to the logical theory contained in the Constitution that animates and binds together its provisions. Because the Constitution is a document of liberal principles, predicated on the primacy of a person's worth, it is the function of judges, as instruments of the Constitution's logic, to give effect to preexisting individual rights in the decision of cases. Given the limitations of this essay, this presentation of what Dworkin has named "the rights thesis" is no more than the barest of summaries; but it does suggest the sort of innovative and insightful thinking necessary to overcome the problems of constitutional theory.

It remains to be seen whether Dworkin or any other creative thinker can furnish a coherent, defensible, and workable blueprint of constitutional interpretation. Meanwhile, the application of constitutional guaranties will continue according to the three interpretive modes that have been the focus of this essay.

CASES

Adamson v. California, 332 U.S. 46 (1947)
Baker v. Carr, 369 U.S. 186 (1962)
Barenblatt v. United States, 360 U.S. 109 (1959)
Carter v. Carter Coal Co., 298 U.S. 238 (1936)
Hammer v. Dagenhart, 247 U.S. 251 (1918)
Marbury v. Madison, 5 U.S. (1 Cranch) 137 (1803)
Roth v. United States, 354 U.S. 476 (1957)
Schechter Poultry Corp. v. United States, 295 U.S. 495 (1935)

Thomas v. Collins, 323 U.S. 516 (1945)
United States v. Butler, 297 U.S. 1 (1936)
United States v. Carolene Products Co., 304 U.S. 144 (1938)
United States v. E. C. Knight Co., 156 U.S. 1 (1895)
West Virginia State Board of Education v. Barnette, 319 U.S. 624 (1943), 21 U.S.L.W. 3164 (1952)

BIBLIOGRAPHY

William Anderson, "The Intention of the Framers: A Note on Constitutional Interpretation," *American Political Science Review*, 49 (1955), makes one of the most comprehensive yet concise statements on the fallacies of relying on the intentions of the Framers as an interpretive guide to construing the Constitution. Alexander M. Bickel, *The Least Dangerous Branch* (1962), argues in this early statement of judicial self-restraint that the Court can and should sidestep many problems using discretionary devices that do not require principled justification. Alexander M. Bickel, *The Supreme Court and the Idea of Progress* (1970), trains the big guns of judicial self-restraint on the activism of the Warren Court. Hugo L. Black, *A Constitutional Faith* (1968), provides, in the series of lectures that this book comprises, one of the most integrated statements available of his version of constitutional absolutism. Lief H. Carter, *Reason in Law* (1984), gives a clearly written, well illustrated, and easily understood exposition of how lawyers reason. Jesse H. Choper, *Judicial Review and the National Political Process: A Functional Reconsideration of the Role of the Supreme Court* (1980), discusses extensively the role of the Supreme Court in the political system, which accepts the characterization of the Court as an undemocratic institution, yet argues for the necessity of judicial review to protect individual rights.

Craig R. Ducat, *Modes of Constitutional Interpretation* (1978), provides a detailed discussion of the three interpretive frameworks with many illustrations of their use. Ronald Dworkin, *Taking Rights Seriously* (1977), offers a sophisticated, well written, and closely reasoned philosophical treatment and reformulation of traditional problems that have long dominated jurisprudence. His formulation of "the rights thesis" has clear and immediate consequences for the practice of judicial review, as several chapters explain. John Hart Ely, *Democracy and Distrust: A Theory of Judicial Review* (1980), makes perhaps the most convincing statement yet of judicial activism based on a defense of those rights as necessary to the democratic process. Lon L. Fuller, "The Forms and Limits of Adjudication," *Harvard Law Review*, 92 (1978), gives us, in this posthumous publication, his definitive statement of just what we mean by adjudication, what cultural and structural assumptions underlie it, and what kinds of problems it cannot solve. Charles G. Haines, *The American Doctrine of Judicial Supremacy* (1959), presents one of the best histories of judicial review. Jethro K. Lieberman, *The Litigious Society* (1981), argues that although increasingly courts govern America, the nature of the problems we are asking them to resolve reaches beyond their institutional capacity. Arthur S. Miller and Ronald Howell, "The Myth of Neutrality in Constitutional Adjudication," *University of Chicago Law Review*, 27

(1960), responds to constitutional absolutism's insistence on neutrality and objectivity and defends a result-oriented jurisprudence.

Glendon A. Schubert, *The Judicial Mind* (1965), demonstrates, in a very sophisticated and impressive quantitative manner, the relationship between judicial voting patterns and the personal values and attitudes of the justices. Martin Shapiro, *Freedom of Speech: The Supreme Court and Judicial Review* (1966), defends judicial activism as undertaken through the Supreme Court's treatment of freedom of speech, conducting an all-out attack on judicial self-restraint and taking no prisoners. Harold J. Spaeth, *Supreme Court Policy Making* (1979), introduces the reader to the judicial process of the Supreme Court from a political science perspective, emphasizing the importance of the justices' attitudes and values in decision making and viewing their formal opinions as rationalizations of political choices. Mark Tushnet, "Darkness on the Edge of Town: The Contributions of John Hart Ely to Constitutional Theory," *Yale Law Journal*, 89 (1980), critically evaluates Ely's process-based judicial activism, arguing that constitutional theory in service of liberal values is not possible. Herbert Wechsler, "Toward Neutral Principles of Constitutional Law," *Harvard Law Review*, 73 (1959), makes the classic statement, in what Judge Wright calls "the scholarly tradition," defining and developing the expectation that the Supreme Court be entirely principled in the justifications it offers for the constitutional decisions it makes. J. Skelly Wright, "Professor Bickel, the Scholarly Tradition, and the Supreme Court," *Harvard Law Review*, 84 (1971), delivers an activist federal judge's devastating response to Bickel's position.

[*See also* AMERICAN JURISPRUDENCE; AMERICAN LEGAL CULTURE; BURGER COURT AND ERA; COURTS AND CONSTITUTIONALISM; JUDICIAL REVIEW; LEGAL REASONING; MARSHALL COURT AND ERA; *and* SUPREME COURT OF THE UNITED STATES.]

THE COURTS AND CONSTITUTIONALISM

James Magee

Though much of what we tend to identify as the American Constitution consists of the customs and practices of the American polity, constitutional law in the United States, at least in its most visible form, is principally the work of the Supreme Court. Through its power of judicial review of the actions of other participants in the political system, the Court wields great political power. In 1954, for example, the Court held that segregated public schools were impermissible. In 1974 the Court directed President Richard M. Nixon to relinquish tape-recorded conversations concealing his involvement in the Watergate cover-up, a directive that ultimately forced the first resignation of an American president. In 1973 the Court invalidated the antiabortion laws of nearly every state in the Union. Judicial review has placed in the hands of justices of the Supreme Court a formidable political power.

Yet, there is nothing in the Constitution that clearly authorizes this power. The language of the text explicitly recognizes the veto power of the president but is silent as to the veto power of the Court. Such an assumed power poses serious problems in a democratic political system in which policy is to be made not by a Court consisting of unelected and essentially life-tenured justices but by the people through their elected representatives, who can be held accountable for their decisions. Nevertheless, the Court has proclaimed that it is the "ultimate interpreter" of the Constitution.

There is a certain logic that supports judicial review narrowly conceived as the duty of the Court to refuse enforcement of an unconstitutional act of Congress—for instance, in deciding a case properly brought to the Court for resolution. By this logic, if A rests his or her claim on a provision of the Constitution and B relies on an act of Congress, the Court is obligated to refuse to enforce the act of Congress if it collides with the paramount law, the Constitution. This was the argument of Chief Justice John Marshall in *Marbury* v. *Madison* (1803). But the logic that supports this duty does not justify the supremacy of judicial interpretations of the meaning of constitutional provisions. Yet this supremacy has evolved as an inevitable dogma; that is, the Court's version of the Constitution is presumed to be preeminent and binding on all participants in the political system. If this is so, President Abraham Lincoln's Emancipation Proclamation, which freed the slaves, was unconstitutional because it collided with the Court's holding in *Dred Scott* v. *Sandford* (1857), which denied the federal government any power to prohibit or curb slavery.

Several factors have invited the Court to play this role in American history. Unless the Constitution is to speak with multiple meanings (one for the president, another for Congress, and a third for the judiciary), some institution must be final and supreme in its interpretation of the document. The Court has assumed this role. Its detachment from politics was intended by the framers of the Constitution when they stipulated that the justices of the Court be appointed (rather than elected) and that their commissions be practically for life. But the role of judicial supremacy in the field of constitutional interpretation embroils the Court in American politics, and the insularity of the justices makes the Court's position all the more problematic in a democracy, for the justices are not held accountable on election day.

THE COURTS AND CONSTITUTIONALISM

APPROACHES TO CONSTITUTIONALISM

The traditional model of constitutional decision-making has been the most publicized explanation of the Court's work in constitutional law. The Court consults the constitutional text and /or the intentions of those who designed the constitutional plan, which are recorded in James Madison's notes on the Constitutional Convention and in the *Annals of Congress,* especially for the First Congress. When the Court invalidates a law (for instance, a state law prohibiting abortions), it links its conclusion to a norm in the Constitution; otherwise, the law should prevail, however unwise or imprudent it may be. This is the interpretivist model of judicial decision-making. Interpretivism is a concept that tries to accommodate judicial review with democratic government; judicial intervention is seen as nothing more than an obligation to uphold the Constitution.

The difficulty with interpretivism is clear: in a constitutional law case, the meaning of a provision of the Constitution is itself the issue. What is meant by the Fourth Amendment's prohibition against "unreasonable" searches and seizures? What is the "free exercise" of religion that the First Amendment expressly forbids the government to prohibit? Only where the constitutional text or the intent of those who drafted it is clear does interpretivism assist the justices who must resolve constitutional law disputes. Those circumstances, however, are not the soil that produces disagreements as to the meaning of a constitutional term. No one has been heard to contend in court, for instance, that a person could, even if elected, serve as the nation's president if his or her age is less than thirty-five years or could become a United States senator at age twenty-five. The Constitution clearly settles these matters. The cases that the Supreme Court selects for review tend to be atypical; only infrequently do they involve legal disputes resolvable merely by citing precedent. Instead, these cases reveal questions in which at least two plausible and conflicting resolutions exist. Such cases have already filtered through the lower judiciary, either state or federal and sometimes both. The justices are confronted with situations in which lower courts have disagreed, where contending litigants press on and invest heavily in legal fees in the hope of convincing the "ultimate interpreter" of the merits of their side in the dispute. Interpretivism, then, entails judicial choices, and this results in judicial policymaking. The problem is how much policymaking is compatible with the principles of democratic government.

One alternative to judicial policymaking in the area of constitutional review can be found in the jurisprudence of Justice Felix Frankfurter, one of the twentieth century's most distinguished jurists. He acted on the assumption that only legislators are legitimate policymakers in a democracy and that these legislators must be presumed to act in accordance with the Constitution. Legislation is thus presumed to be constitutional (short of an obvious collision with the Constitution), and the Court would be justified in nullifying such legislation only if there is no reasonable basis for it. In other words, as long as the goal of the legislation in question is permissible, any means chosen by the legislature that rationally or conceivably furthers that goal is thereby constitutional. Adhering to this measure of constitutionality, Frankfurter was able to join in upholding the Smith Act of 1940, which made it a crime, among other things, to advocate the violent overthrow of the government. Since Congress has as a legitimate goal the prevention of the overthrow of the government, it could punish persons who advocated overthrow because there is a rational relationship between advocacy and overthrow. Someone who reads the First Amendment might think that a law punishing advocacy (short of any actions designed to overthrow) without more is surely unconstitutional.

Frankfurter's "reasonableness" test would uphold virtually every law passed, for lawmakers do not often make laws that are irrationally related to permissible governmental objectives. Strict adherence to this test of constitutionality would in fact preclude judicial policymaking, by destroying the power of judicial review itself. In *West Virginia State Board of Education* v. *Barnette* (1943) the Court denied government the power to compel schoolchildren to salute the American flag. Frankfurter dissented, basing his vote to uphold the state law on the ground that national uniformity is a legitimate goal of government, and compulsory flag saluting is rationally related to the furtherance of that goal. There is no opportunity for judicial policymaking here.

Interpretivism and unbending allegiance to

988

the reasonableness test present problematic consequences for judicial review. Interpretivism inescapably involves the Court in the creation of public policy. Yet, pure interpretivism would seem to preclude most of the major constitutional holdings of the twentieth century protecting individual rights and liberties. Michael J. Perry argues that almost no decision in favor of civil rights and liberties in the twentieth century can be justified according to the tenets of interpretive review, not even the momentous holding outlawing segregated public schools. Rigorous application of the reasonableness test would have obliterated the gains in human rights fashioned by the Court, for this test all but amputates the power of the Court to curtail the will of the majority in society.

Both approaches are efforts to achieve the same goal; both are in search of a judicial role compatible with the demands of democratic government. And both seek judicial objectivity but exact heavy prices for it. Pure interpretivism is unrealistic; flexible interpretivism clearly requires the Court to make public policy. The reasonableness test, if faithfully followed, abolishes any effective judicial review of legislation.

Thus, some middle ground must exist, for the search for objectivity in constitutional adjudication is illusory, and the value of judicial protection against majoritarianism, though anomalous in a democracy, is nonetheless important and often very desirable. After all, the provisions of the Constitution must mean something, and surely their meanings cannot be left to the very majoritarian impulses that a constitution, almost by definition, is designed to circumscribe. This middle ground, sometimes called "line-drawing" or the "balancing of interests" doctrine, involves the Court in making public-policy choices in the name of constitutional construction. Some of these choices have been of little consequence to the American people generally; others have been highly beneficial; still others have been disastrous. One important scholarly position is worth briefly noting here, for it is central and simple, and its weakness reveals important features of the Court's abilities in the realm of constitutional lawmaking.

Alexander M. Bickel, whose untimely death at age forty-nine did not diminish his stature as one of the preeminent constitutional authorities in America, defended judicial review within American democracy because of "the Court's peculiar capacity to enunciate basic principles." Because the Court is alleged to have this capacity, democratic government can accommodate judicial review. Bickel knew that at times principle had to be moderated to keep society viable, but "when it strikes down legislative policy, the Court must act rigorously on principle, else it undermines the justification for its power." Bickel recognized that a pure interpretive model was a chimera, that the constitutional text was not a repository of answers to constitutional questions. He saw the Court's creativity in the constitution of "open texture" and held that the authority underlying the Court's creativity resides in its "certain capacities for dealing with matters of principle that legislatures and executives do not possess" (1962, 69–70).

Advocates of Bickel's principled adjudication offer examples to prove that the process of judgment is within the reach of the justices acting together as a court. Herbert Wechsler, for instance, suggested that First Amendment freedom of speech claims could be settled through the use of the "clear and present danger" test, developed by Justices Oliver Wendell Holmes and Louis D. Brandeis (almost exclusively in dissenting opinions). That test stipulates that speech is protected until it can be shown that the speech is likely to provoke a danger to society that is clear, imminent, and sufficient to warrant government interference with expression. The problem with this test is that it suffers from the same illusory nature as interpretivism. One can argue that citing the First Amendment itself is as useful. As Paul Freund said of the clear-and-present-danger test, no matter how fast or frequently we repeat its words, it is no substitute for judicial balancing of interests. The Court must determine if a clear danger exists, whether it is imminent, and whether it is sufficient.

Constitutional law in the United States has thus evolved through history as a set of public-policy choices made by the Supreme Court in its self-proclaimed role as "ultimate interpreter" of the Constitution. Some of its choices can be linked with the Constitution—either the text itself or the radiations from the text (Bickel's constitution of "open texture"). Others have been choices imposed by a prevailing majority of justices and traceable to nothing save their own values. Some others have, in fact, been distortions of the Constitution. In the nineteenth century, constitutional issues were rarely raised in American courts. In the twentieth century, however, especially since World War II, there has been an exponential increase in the number of constitutional issues brought into the courts and ultimately to the Supreme Court. In deciding these matters, the justices, to be sure, have insisted that their holdings were constitutionally rooted. Dissenting justices have accused the majority of ignoring constitutional values and substituting instead their own views on what is best for society. Legal critics have pierced through the Court's proffered analyses to expose some of the policy choices for what they really are.

THE COURT AND CONSTITUTIONALISM

With the model of "principled adjudication" as a backdrop against which to measure the performance of the Court, major doctrinal developments can be explored. Obviously, no exhaustive treatment can be undertaken here; instead, the most pronounced, if not the most important, policies of the Court in American history will be reviewed.

Constitutional history can be divided into three great eras: the period from the founding until the Civil War; from 1865 until 1937; and from 1937 until the present. The major issue confronting the Court during the first era was the federal-state relationship. The power of government to regulate the economy preoccupied the judiciary during the second period, and the principal concern of the Court in constitutional law since 1937 has been individual rights and liberties. Though each era has been dominated by one major constitutional question, sprinklings of other issues can be found in all three periods.

The First Era: Constitutionalism and National Supremacy. During the early period the Court sought to ensure national supremacy against the possibility of fragmentations that might occur under the pressures of the doctrine of states' rights. Probably the most important decision during this formative era was *McCulloch* v. *Maryland* (1819). There the Court held that Congress had the power to create the Bank of the United States and that no state could tax that bank or

any other instrumentality of the United States. The most significant aspect of the Court's holding was that in carrying out its enumerated powers, Congress must have the power to choose whatever means it deems appropriate unless plainly forbidden by the Constitution. The Court expressly rejected Maryland's literal argument (which was also Thomas Jefferson's) that Congress may do only that which is absolutely necessary to implement one of its delegated powers. Article I, Section 8, ends with a clause that states that Congress shall have the power to make all laws "which shall be necessary and proper for carrying into Execution" its enumerated powers. Maryland insisted that the word *necessary* severely restricted legislative choice to that which is absolutely necessary. But Chief Justice Marshall and his Court saw this construction as essentially defeating the purpose of a constitution designed to endure for ages to come and held that the legislature must have a range of choice to effectuate its powers.

It is difficult to imagine what the United States would be like today if the Court had ruled in favor of Maryland. The tone of the opinion was clearly one of national supremacy. In fact, Chief Justice Marshall's unanimous opinion for the Court stated that for purposes of the Union, the states were not sovereign, thus dealing a serious blow to the states'-rights movement.

In another major decision the Court broadly defined perhaps Congress' most important regulatory power: to regulate commerce. Article I, Section 8, gives Congress the power to regulate commerce among the states, with foreign nations, and with the Indian tribes. The power to regulate interstate commerce has perhaps been the most widely used national power. In *Gibbons* v. *Ogden* (1824) the Court invalidated a state steamboat monopoly as colliding with a congressional law granting licenses to individuals to travel on navigable waterways of the United States. Congress was clearly within its power to regulate commerce here, but the Court, speaking again through Marshall, defined the national commerce power in extremely generous terms. The power, he said, can be exercised to its utmost and subject to no limitations except those prescribed in the Constitution itself. The Court seemed to suggest that the reach of this power was to be determined by Congress itself.

The Court also entertained the idea that only

Congress could regulate matters affecting interstate commerce—that the power, in other words, was exclusive to Congress and the states could not regulate even if Congress were silent. This was the position of concurring Justice William Johnson, but Marshall avoided committing the Court to this interpretation of the commerce power.

President Andrew Jackson, who was not as enthused about national supremacy as were Marshall and his brethren on the Court, was in the position to nominate Marshall's successor when the great chief justice died in 1835. Jackson named Roger B. Taney, his attorney general and the first Catholic to serve on the Court, as the new chief justice. Fervent federalists feared that Jackson's appointment power would work in such a way as to undo the nationalist gains of the Marshall Court. With the exception of the *Dred Scott* decision, which to that date represented only the second time that an act of Congress had been held unconstitutional, the values nurtured by the Taney Court did not undermine the legacy of Marshall's strong nationalism. In all other significant cases involving concepts of national power, the Taney Court's disposition, from the perspective of those who worshiped the jurisprudence of John Marshall, can be seen as at worst reconciling prior doctrine with resurgent state power concerns. For example, on the matter of whether Congress' commerce power was exclusive (a matter that had not been settled by the Marshall Court), the Taney Court decided that congressional power was "selectively" exclusive. In *Cooley* v. *Board of Wardens of the Port of Philadelphia* (1852) the Court held that when Congress is silent regarding a particular matter affecting commerce, the states may regulate that matter if it does not require a uniform national rule. If it is a subject that can tolerate various standards from state to state, then it does not lie exclusively in the domain of Congress. In *Cooley*, not only did the Court not weaken national power (for the Court left free Congress' power to act), but it also expanded national judicial power, for the Court would decide which subjects required local and which national legislation. This increase in judicial power would serve the Court well when, in the second great period of constitutional history, the Court embarked on a course of overseeing the national economy.

The Court's prestige was high during the Taney era, in which the justices maneuvered creatively within the boundaries of inherited doctrine. The Court even felt able to provide a constitutional solution to the most wrenching social and political problem that was dividing the nation: slavery. In *Dred Scott* the Court could have, consistent with precedent, avoided the issue altogether for want of jurisdiction. Instead, it chose to step in and resolve a matter that seemed to defy the political process. In that case the Court ruled that black slaves were not, never had been, and could never become citizens of the United States; that they were property owned by others; that Congress could not take away that property; and that Congress was powerless to prevent the spread of slavery among the states and federal territories. Ultimately, the nation, in search of a solution to this immoral and divisive disgrace to humanity, would risk drowning itself in its own blood on the battlefields of the Civil War. Under the leadership of Abraham Lincoln, the nation did not emerge unscathed, but the secessionist states were restored to the empire and slavery was abolished.

As the Civil War came to an end the Court's prestige plummeted to its lowest depths since Justice John Rutledge resigned from the Court (without ever having sat) in order to accept a state judicial appointment. The first great era of constitutional and judicial history ended with the Court, the erstwhile outspoken proponent of national authority, seemingly reduced to ruin in post–Civil War America.

The Second Era: Capitalism and the Economy. The Court rebounded to play a significant role in the second era of constitutional law development. The driving issue became the extent to which government could control what some earnestly believed should remain unfettered: capitalism and the entrepreneur. Initially, the Court refused to interfere with the use of legislation to regulate the growing economy; from soon after the Civil War until 1890, the Court's self-assigned function was to restrain itself. But beginning in 1890, judicial review became an instrument enlisted by private enterprise to shield itself from a political process, in which legislative majorities had increasingly succeeded in passing laws designed to protect society from the harmful aspects of a burgeoning capitalist economy.

At the bidding of corporate lawyers, the Supreme Court adjusted the Constitution to find a

991

comfortable and secure place in that document for the theory of laissez-faire liberalism, the doctrine maintaining that government should leave the economy alone. Private property interests had been very important to the Marshall and Taney Courts, but judicial concern for property during that earlier period did not become the crusade that unfolded after 1890. (Marshall's decision in *Gibbons,* after all, had collided with the vested interests of the Livingston and Fulton steamboat monopoly.) As both state and federal government expanded to cope with the rise of big business, through the use of powers (such as the commerce power) previously dormant, the Court was equal to the task of developing constitutional weapons created to beat back regulation of the economy. Constitutional doctrines could be conceived and made ready for use by justices conditioned to believe that Communism and unprecedented constraints on capitalism were one and the same. Needless to say, in the midst of battle the justices denied that they were usurping legislative prerogatives in the guise of constitutional interpretation. They claimed that it was merely the sworn duty of the justices to uphold the Constitution, which seemed to limit the regulatory powers of government. Justice David J. Brewer, an apostle of unrestrained free enterprise (except where governmental controls might further business interests), insisted in a 1983 address to the New York State Bar association, that "courts . . . make no laws, they establish no policy, they never enter the domain of public action. They do not govern." Despite a rising tide of criticism, it was clear to the judicial eye that the policies of the Court from 1890 until 1937, though apparently inconsistent, were compelled by an objective reading of the Constitution of the United States.

Immediately after the Civil War, Congress engineered three amendments to the Constitution. The Thirteenth Amendment (1865) abolished slavery and prohibited involuntary servitude (except military conscription) everywhere in the country. The Fifteenth Amendment (1870) prohibited voter discrimination on account of race, color, or previous condition of servitude. The most ambiguous, and thus inevitably the most litigated, was the Fourteenth Amendment (1868), which among other things abolished *Dred Scott* by stating that "all persons born or naturalized in the United States, and subject to the jurisdiction thereof, are citizens of the United States and of the State wherein they reside." Another important component of the Fourteenth Amendment is the package of general and undefined but potentially limitless individual-rights claims against state power. Prior to this the only civil rights and liberties guaranties against the states were the handful of restrictions found in the original Constitution, such as the ban against ex post facto laws and bills of attainder. Provisions of the Bill of Rights, such as the right of free speech and religion, were binding only on the national government. But the Fourteenth Amendment prohibited each state from abridging "the privileges or immunities of citizens of the United States"; from depriving "any person of life, liberty, or property, without due process of law"; or from denying "to any person within its jurisdiction the equal protection of the laws."

There is some evidence that in writing these provisions of the Fourteenth Amendment, Congress intended to impose on the states the rights and liberties contained in the Bill of Rights. But this evidence is fragmentary and unconvincing. Still, the amendment speaks in very spacious language and was ratified in the aftermath of a bloody and dislocating civil war; and the Congress that formulated the amendments was led by the Radical Republicans, who seemed determined to punish the confederate states.

In the *Slaughterhouse Cases* (1873) the Court first confronted the meaning of the Fourteenth Amendment. A post–Civil War Louisiana law gave, in effect, a monopoly to one corporation engaged in the butchering business in metropolitan New Orleans. More than one thousand other butchers were prevented from practicing their trade as butchers in Louisiana; they eventually found themselves challenging the law as a violation of the Thirteenth and Fourteenth Amendments before the Supreme Court. Their claim was that they had a right "to exercise their trade." In a 5–4 decision upholding the law, Justice Samuel F. Miller dismissed all the constitutional arguments. The Thirteenth Amendment addressed slavery and involuntary servitude, which was not involved here. Reliance on the equal protection clause was given short shrift, for the Court stated that it applied only to racial discrimination; and the due process clause was read as a procedural, not substantive, guaranty: liberty could be deprived as long as the state acted according to a process worthy of "due process of law," which had been shown here. When he came upon the argument that the right to exercise a trade is a "privilege" or an "immunity" of citizens of the United States, Miller elaborated a position for the Court that stripped the privileges and immunities clause of any significant substance. That clause, he said, guarantees against state abridgment of those privileges and immunities that attach to national, as distinct from state, citizenship. That reading reduced the reach of that clause almost to naught, an interpretation that remains intact today.

Four years later the Court was presented with another claim arising in a case involving an Illinois law that regulated the rates that railroad companies could charge for the use of grain elevators. In *Munn* v. *Illinois* (1877) Chief Justice Morrison Waite, for a majority of his colleagues, sustained the law against a charge that it contravened the due process clause of the Fourteenth Amendment. Waite stated that the law regulated a matter "affected with a public interest." A law may be imprudent or unwise, he said, but not thereby unconstitutional; and removal of such legislation should be undertaken by way of the political, not judicial, process. Waite left open the possibility that an outrageous regulatory law might collide with the due process clause.

In 1877, when the Granger movement was at its height, it seemed that legislatures could interfere in the economy and that states could set "reasonable" rates to be charged by an industry such as the railroads. In a year or two, however, corporate lawyers, in conjunction with the newly organized American Bar Association, soon challenged governmental restrictions and ultimately induced the Court to change its rendition of the Fourteenth Amendment. As a political minority, entrepreneurs could not prevail in the majoritarian democratic process; their logical recourse was to the antimajoritarian power of the federal judiciary. Persistently pressing the Court with horrible possibilities of reckless interference with free enterprise if a majority of justices continued to uphold regulatory legislation, corporate lawyers convinced the Court to intervene —on behalf of the Constitution, of course.

In the watershed *Minnesota Rate Cases* (1890) the Court for the first time struck down a state law establishing maximum railway rates as violative of the due process clause. The rates were held unreasonable and thus invalid. This action was the realization of a doctrine that transferred to the Court unbridled supervisory power to uphold or veto both state and federal legislation: the doctrine of substantive due process. This doctrine maintains that legislation can be declared unconstitutional because of its substance rather than for want of fair procedure. The Court isolated the word *liberty* from the procedural context of the amendment and acted as if the clause said that government shall not interfere with individual freedom (as defined by the Court). The procedural guaranty of the clause was transformed into a reservoir of substantive rights existing at the discretion of the Court. Such a distortion of the Constitution was successfully pushed upon the Court, despite earlier and resolute judicial refusals. In 1878, in *Davidson* v. *New Orleans,* the Court refused to accede to that "strange misconception" of the due process guaranty. And in the *Slaughterhouse Cases* (1873), as noted, Justice Miller rejected the butchers' claim the right to work was harbored within the due process clause when he responded "that under no construction of that provision that we have ever seen, or any that we deem admissible," can the clause be construed as a substantive check on state power.

State and federal laws could now be held void if either government infringed on something viewed as a fundamental right by a majority of justices. Moreover, with no formal argument about its merits, the proposition that a corporation is a "person" within the meaning of that term in the due process clause was casually accepted by the Court, thus widening the sweep of judicial supervision of regulatory measures. "Liberty of contract," a right judge-made and later judge-destroyed, became the preeminent freedom sanctified by the bench and bar as deserving of the constitutional shield that emerged from the Court's disfiguration of the due process clauses in the Fourteenth and Fifth Amendments. Any law that could be seen as infringing on the right of anyone to contract independently with another—for example, a law regulating the terms of a work schedule, salaries, wages, prices, or rates—was now subject to the threat of judicial veto.

It is ironic that the Court aborted the substantive possibilities of the privileges and immunities clause only later to manipulate the due process clause into a substantive tool. Such are the ways of an institution whose role as overseer of the constitutional system, according to Alexander Bickel (1932), is justified by its peculiar capacity to generate principled conclusions.

Between 1890 and 1937 the Court invoked substantive due process to fend off what it saw as undesirable socialist legislation. In *Lochner* v. *New York* (1905), in a 5–4 decision, the Court held unconstitutional a New York law fixing the maximum hours of bakers. Dismissing New York's legislative findings that these maximum hours were reasonably related to the health of bakers, the Court majority treated the measure as an undue interference with the liberty of contract of both employees and employers. The newly created judicial weapon of substantive due process was not wielded exclusively against government and in favor of liberty of contract, however. As if *Lochner* had never been decided, the Court upheld laws imposing maximum working hours on women and their employers. The point is that substantive due process gave the Court nearly complete discretion either to accept or to reject legislation displeasing to a majority of justices in a given case. Substantive due process allowed the Court to uphold whatever values it thought deserved protection from what it perceived as socialist tendencies in the political process.

Another tool at the disposal of the justices to circumscribe state involvement in economic regulation stemmed from the *Cooley* rule. In the absence of congressional legislation, states could regulate a matter affecting interstate commerce if the matter was local in character; that is, state-by-state standards could be tolerated. If the matter was not local, it was exclusively a matter for Congress and required a uniform national rule. Whether a national rule was necessary was for the Court to decide. The most famous example is *Wabash, St. Louis & Pacific Railway* v. *Illinois* (1886), in which the Court denied states the power to set railway rates; this, it was held, was a subject requiring national regulation. There were other cases in which the Court sat in the pivotal position.

Having had little prior interest in using its regulatory powers, Congress became involved in the national economy just a few months after the *Wabash* decision when it passed the momentous Interstate Commerce Act of 1887. This was the beginning of what would become deep and rou-

tine involvement in the national economy and the rise of the welfare state. Digging in its heels to resist this movement, the Court tempered the tide of federal power with innovative and imaginative readings of congressional power under the Constitution.

Confronting concentrated corporate capital, an unregulated economy (in part because the Court denied the states such authority in many cases), and the undesirable social costs of the rapid expansion of unregulated American business and industry, Congress increasingly resorted to the commerce power and the sweeping definition assigned to it by the Marshall Court in the *Gibbons* case in 1824. In the nineteenth century, Congress seldom exploited the vast reserve of power contained in the prevailing judicial interpretation of the commerce clause. Beginning with the Interstate Commerce Act, however, Congress, encouraged by Populists and Progressives, asserted itself to curb corporate giants and to ameliorate the hardships suffered by the lower classes. But rather than abide by the promise of *Gibbons*, between 1895 and 1937 the Court reneged and developed two sets of precedents to define the national commerce power—one endorsing broad authority, the other severely curtailing it. Like the flexibility of substantive due process, this arrangement facilitated judicial ability either to uphold or to strike down acts of Congress under the commerce power.

What arose in the case law of the commerce power was a series of "concepts" constructed by the Court as supposed measures of the reach of congressional authority. Of these concepts, only one served as any realistic and understandable indicator of the purposes and limits of the commerce power; the others were judicial creations designed either to authorize or to retard the exercise of federal power. The broad grant of authority in *Gibbons* was lost beneath the Court's strained attempts to define the parameters of national economic regulation.

In 1890, Congress passed the Sherman Antitrust Act, which in part prohibited monopolies or combinations of business "in restraint of trade or commerce among the several states." E. C. Knight Company was a conglomerate that, through the acquisition of the stock of other companies, succeeded in controlling 98 percent of the sugar-refining industry in the United States. Under the Sherman Act, the government tried to prevent this monopoly by preventing the acquisition of the stock. In *United States* v. *E. C. Knight Co.* (1895) the Court concluded that commerce was not involved. Speaking through Chief Justice Melville W. Fuller, the Court argued that manufacturing and refining precedes commerce and is not part of it. Congress could regulate only "direct" effects on interstate commerce and could not regulate "indirect" effects. Manufacturing, refining, and production were merely indirect effects on interstate commerce. The fact that E. C. Knight Company could have a drastic effect on the price of sugar sold in the United States was immaterial to the chief justice. As Thomas Reed Powell, law professor at the Harvard Law School, quipped, only a "legal mind" could comprehend the distinction, and a legal' mind is one that can extricate something from that from which it is inextricable.

Ten years later the Court invented a new measure, this time to support national action. In *Swift* v. *United States* (1905) a unanimous Court held that activities of the meat-packing houses, located primarily in Chicago, constituted interstate commerce. Congress had sought to check collusion and corruption in the meat-packing industry. Justice Holmes, who wrote for the Court, reasoned that this ostensibly local industry was a "throat" through which interstate commerce passes, that the butchering and packaging of meat products in Chicago was a "stream" through which the great flow of interstate commerce (presumably from the grazing lands of the Southwest to retailers elsewhere) must inevitably pass. Thus Congress could reach through its power to regulate interstate commerce. This reasoning fails to explain why Philadelphia, the location of E. C. Knight's sugar-refining business, was not a similar "current of commerce" (presumably beginning in the cane fields of Louisiana and ending on the tables of homemakers). If the stream-of-commerce test could justify federal intervention in butchering and meat-packing concerns in Chicago, it stands to reason that the refining of sugar in Philadelphia was equally within the reach of the interstate commerce power. In spite of the apparent inconsistency, the holding and reasoning in *E. C. Knight* were left undisturbed and available for later use as negative precedent.

Armed with two different and contradictory techniques for defining the scope of the commerce power, the Court nonetheless produced a third measure—the substantial effects test. In the *Shreveport Case* (1914) Justice Charles Evans Hughes announced that federal power could be exercised over any seemingly local matter that has a "substantial effect" (meaning substantial impact) on interstate commerce. The Court upheld an order by the Interstate Commerce Commission (ICC) that would not permit intrastate railway rates between eastern Texas and Dallas, which were lower than the maximum interstate rates between eastern Texas and Shreveport, Louisiana. The existing arrangement shut off Shreveport from effective access to goods shipped from eastern Texas. The ICC found that these Texas intrastate rates constituted a substantial burden on the free flow of interstate commerce, and the Supreme Court agreed, even though the Texas rate schedule operated directly only upon intrastate rail movement. The Court correctly recognized that a matter appearing to be local in character may nonetheless have a real impact on interstate commerce.

By now the Court could swing in either direction in reviewing assertions of federal power based on the commerce clause. This is exactly what the Court did between 1895 and 1937. The substantial-effects test permitted the Court great discretion, but at least it allowed the government to present evidence of impacts on interstate commerce; to that extent, it served as a legitimate standard. But the stream-of-commerce test was artificial and a measure of almost nothing, for nearly every matter could somehow be in some "stream" through which commerce passes. And the "direct-indirect effects" criterion was apparently comprehensible only to those who supported it, for it made little sense to conclude that a monopoly controlling 98 percent of the sugar-refining industry did not directly affect interstate commerce. The only clarity that surfaced from that doctrine was the Court's absolute, though certainly unpersuasive, conclusion that manufacturing, mining, refining, production, and so forth were not matters of interstate commerce; they were activities or events that took place before commerce commenced or after it had come to an end. However, the reasoning in *Swift* supports the argument that some manufacturing and production were events within certain streams through which interstate commerce must pass.

The Court developed another doctrine that greatly enabled the judiciary to preclude federal regulation altogether in certain subject matters.

This derived from the Court's befuddling reading of the Tenth Amendment, which says, "The powers not delegated to the United States by the Constitution, nor prohibited by it to the States, are reserved to the States respectively, or to the people." This declaration does not, by itself, demarcate the scope of all or any of Congress' powers; it merely asserts that federal powers are limited to the powers enumerated in the document. If Congress exceeds its powers, the Tenth Amendment has been violated; but the amendment has nothing to do with discerning the outer boundaries of each or any of the enumerated powers delegated to the national government.

During this period of economically conservative judicial activism, however, the Court distorted the Tenth Amendment in much the same way as it treated the due process clause. The Court infused substantive content into the Tenth Amendment, against which it would assess the constitutionality of challenged legislation. The Court identified certain subjects as local, thereby reserved to the states, and making such subjects immune from federal oversight; the Court did this without addressing the outer boundaries of individual enumerated powers, as if the Tenth Amendment were like the First Amendment—laced with specific substantive exclusions, such as speech, press, religion, and assembly. Edward S. Corwin dubbed this practice the doctrine of "dual federalism," whereby the Court abstracted certain powers and called them local in nature and exercisable only by the states.

Between 1935 and 1936, in response to New Deal economic measures, the Court pursued a course of unbending resistance, mobilizing its arsenal of restrictive precedents to disarm both state and federal governments in their attempts to cope with economic catastrophe. Typical of the Court's posture was its holding in *United States* v. *Butler* (1936), which invalidated the first Agricultural Adjustment Act, passed in 1933. This law taxed processors of agricultural products to generate a pool of federal funds to be used to purchase from farmers crops produced in excess of established federal quotas. The purchasing was based on the congressional spending power, and the goal was to ensure a stable price for agricultural crops, thus maintaining an incentive for farmers to remain in business so as to generate food supplies for the nation as a whole. For the first time, the Court ruled that the

spending power is independent of any other power, that Congress could constitutionally spend money not only in conjunction with another enumerated power but independently—as long as it were "for the general welfare," as stipulated in the Constitution. The Court adopted the version of that power advocated by Alexander Hamilton and Justice Joseph Story in his famed treatise on the Constitution. Thus, the only question before the Court was whether this expenditure was for the general welfare; the only answer was yes, inasmuch as the law was designed to preserve the flow of food to feed the nation. However, Justice Owen J. Roberts, disclaiming anything but judicial duty, insisted that the Court need not answer this question because Congress had invaded the reserve powers of the states sheltered by the Tenth Amendment. Once more, this was preposterous, for if the spending here were, in fact, for the general welfare, the Tenth Amendment would not have been assaulted. Invasion of the amendment materializes only if the expenditure is not for the general welfare.

The Court's impoverished reasoning in a series of cases prompted critics to protest that the Court was usurping the governmental powers of Congress. This in turn led President Franklin D. Roosevelt, in one of his famed "fireside chats," to accuse the Court of stifling the national will and any prospects for economic recovery and then to submit his "Court-packing" plan.

The Court survived this invasion of its independence, even though the Court had nearly destroyed the New Deal recovery program with its bankrupt judicial reasoning. However, without a single change in membership, in the spring of 1937 the Court began systematically to validate what was left of the New Deal and any measures that would come later. In fact, between 1937 and 1941, fifty years of discordant case law were abandoned. This was the judicial revolution that caused the second great era of constitutional law to pass into history.

"Liberty of contract" was destroyed in the same manner in which it had been born—by judicial stroke of the pen. In *West Coast Hotel Co.* v. *Parrish* (1937) the Court overruled *Adkins* v. *Children's Hospital* (1923) and allowed government to regulate minimum wages. In rejecting pleas on behalf of freedom of contract, Chief Justice Hughes denied that such a freedom could even be found in the Constitution. In a series of commerce-power cases between 1937 and 1942, the Court dismantled all the old "concepts" except the only legitimate measure of authority: the substantial-effects test.

The combination of a desperate economic situation and the hard-line, uncompromising posture of the Court in 1935 and 1936 resulted in nearly complete judicial withdrawal from an area of public law that it had dominated for almost fifty years. The question of the extent of governmental authority to manage the economy had been settled. Since 1937 the Court has evolved a position in which it applies the reasonableness test to locate the outer limits of the commerce, spending, and taxing powers—the three most important regulatory powers available to Congress in the realm of political economy. As noted earlier, this test assures that legislation will be upheld and that judicial policymaking will be reduced to almost nothing. In fact, since 1937 only one economic regulation of Congress has been held unconstitutional by the Court, but this isolated aberration was overruled in 1985. While no longer supervising the power-conferring provisions of the Constitution, the post-1937 Court has become preoccupied with the power-limiting aspects of the document, such as the Bill of Rights, which restricts governmental powers no matter how extensive the scope of such powers might be.

Post-1937 Constitutionalism: Civil Rights and Liberties. The third great epoch of constitutional development is now in place and still unfolding. Its principal concerns are the rights and liberties of individuals, particularly minorities, against the powers of both state and federal governments. These concerns have appeared before, but with few exceptions the Court's disposition (except for economic freedoms) was unfavorable toward the individual. What characterizes the present era is the predominance of civil liberties issues before the Court and its generally favorable response. Although it is obviously impossible to survey thoroughly this vast enterprise of the modern Court, we can examine two of the most important developments to illustrate the role now played by the Court.

One of the basic problems of constitutional interpretation that first confronts the justification of this new role arises from the fact that the states, rather than the federal government, are more likely to confine individual freedom. Yet the Bill of Rights (the only place in the Constitution where a specific body of rights can be found) was never intended to bind the states. The Fourteenth Amendment does, but it speaks in general terms. As stated earlier, some evidence supports the proposition that the amendment was intended to apply the Bill of Rights against the states, but this evidence is overshadowed by the fact that the drafters did not explicitly make this major change and by the fact that post-1868 developments in the states reveal almost no attempt to comply with the demands of the Bill of Rights.

To solve this problem, after 1937 the Court could have repeated the process that created "liberty of contract," but that avenue had apparently been closed by the Court's burial of freedom of contract in *West Coast Hotel.* The Court's initial solution was ambiguous and came early in the 1937 Court term, just months after the judicial revolution, in *Palko* v. *Connecticut* (1937).

Frank Palko had been convicted of second-degree murder only because the trial judge had excluded evidence that might have brought a conviction of first-degree murder. On appeal the state succeeded in reversing the trial judge's evidentiary ruling and had Palko retried; Palko was then convicted of first-degree murder and sentenced to death. On appeal to the Supreme Court he argued not only that these events constituted double jeopardy, which the Fifth Amendment forbids, but also that the entire Bill of Rights is applicable against the states.

Palko's claims were not supported by precedent. In *Hurtado* v. *California* (1884) the Court had rejected a claim that provision for grand jury indictment in the Fifth Amendment was required of the states. The Court in *Hurtado,* moreover, seemed to insist that none of the provisions in the Bill of Rights could apply against the states through the Fourteenth Amendment. Nonetheless, in *Palko,* which has basically been the guiding precedent in defining the due process clause since 1937, Justice Benjamin N. Cardozo agreed that the due process clause does protect freedom of speech and the right to counsel, among other rights. However, he held that certain matters, such as trial by jury, grand jury indictment, and double jeopardy (as in this case), were excluded. Only rights that are "of the very essence of a system of ordered liberty" are protected. The question arises whether these precious rights are found only in the Bill of Rights. Cardozo's illustrations of what is and is not included in this scheme of freedom come from the Bill of Rights. Are basic rights protected because they are found in the Bill of Rights, or is that a mere coincidence? Perhaps freedom of speech would have been deemed fundamental, regardless of its location. Yet Cardozo spoke of "the privileges and immunities that have been taken over from the earlier articles of the federal bill of rights and brought within the Fourteenth Amendment by a process of absorption." Furthermore, in a footnote to an otherwise unimportant case, *United States* v. *Carolene Products Co.* (1938) (a footnote that Chief Justice Hughes may actually have written), Justice Harlan Fiske Stone referred to "specific prohibitions," such as those in the Bill of Rights, which are equally specific when "embraced within the Fourteenth."

Palko has been read by later Courts in two different ways. One, known as "selective incorporation," stipulates that certain provisions of the Bill of Rights are fundamental or essential and thus literally transferred over to the Fourteenth Amendment and applied against the states exactly as they would be against the federal government. Moreover, the meaning of the due process clause of the Fourteenth Amendment is confined to those fundamental provisions of the Bill of Rights. The second version treats the Bill of Rights and the Fourteenth Amendment as independent of each other, although the two may overlap coincidentally. In this reading, the due process clause becomes an evolving concept whose content is neither confined to the Bill of Rights nor fixed in any way.

The Court subscribed to the latter reading during the 1940s and 1950s. This was the view of Justice Felix Frankfurter, who commanded a majority of justices during this period. After his retirement, the Court adhered to the selective-incorporation version of *Palko* during the 1960s. Justice Hugo L. Black, who had joined the Court in *Palko*, by the late 1940s argued that the intentions of the framers of the Fourteenth Amendment were to incorporate no more and no less than the first eight amendments and that these provisions were to be applied equally to the states and the federal government. Rather than select fundamental parts of the Bill of Rights,

Black insisted on them all—but no more. Thus, his later position is similar to selective incorporation, and no doubt he was instrumental in pushing the Court in the 1960s into officially accepting that doctrine. Black's principal goal was to confine judicial discretion, and confinement to the Bill of Rights in defining the due process clause, however inaccurate it might have been, at least did accomplish that goal.

By the end of the 1960s the Court under Chief Justice Earl Warren had nationalized, through the due process clause, most of the provisions of the Bill of Rights. This was one of the great feats of the post-1937 Court. Not only were these rights applied against the states, but they were reinterpreted in the 1960s in a far more libertarian way than ever before. This was true not only in the area of criminal procedure, where the Court revolutionized the constitutional law of criminal justice, but also in the substantive areas of freedom of speech, press, and religion; the separation of church and state; and freedom of assembly. The 1940s saw the Court actively protecting freedom of speech; in the 1950s the Court was very reluctant to assert itself outside the realm of racial equality; in the 1960s the Court actively pursued libertarian values on every front of civil rights and liberties.

A problem arose for the Court in its claim to adhere to the tenets of selective incorporation. In *Griswold* v. *Connecticut* (1965) the Court faced a law punishing individuals who use, or counsel in the use of, contraceptives. Knowing that nothing in the Bill of Rights addresses the use of birth control devices, litigant Griswold requested the Court to nullify the law in the same way in which the "old Court" had struck down laws colliding with freedom of contract. But Justice William O. Douglas, who spoke for the Court, disowned any such power and rejected the discredited device of substantive due process as practiced in *Lochner*. Instead, he claimed allegiance to selective incorporation and its confinement to the Bill of Rights. The problem was that nothing in the Bill of Rights could be enlisted to help the Court in its holding that the law was unconstitutional. The Court argued that the important right of privacy was not specifically written in the Bill of Rights but was lodged among the penumbras of several guaranties therein. Douglas even argued that the right to use contraceptives could be found in the Fifth Amendment right not to be compelled to be a witness against oneself in a criminal case. It was obvious that the Court was using the doctrine it professed to avoid: substantive due process.

When the Warren era ended in 1969, its admirers feared the worst when President Richard M. Nixon succeeded in appointing what he called four "strict constructionists" to the Court during his first three years in office. He replaced the retiring chief justice with Warren E. Burger. The Burger Court did indeed curtail many of the Warren Court's reforms in the realm of criminal procedure. In other matters, the Court was not as unwilling to protect individual rights as some of its unfriendly critics had predicted. For example, it was the Burger Court that fashioned a libertarian abortion policy in its decision in *Roe* v. *Wade* (1973) and subsequent cases.

Roe was an undisguised use of substantive due process, and the opinion was written by one of Nixon's strict constructionists, Justice Harry A. Blackmun. Because of its importance and the fact that the right to abortion cannot be linked to anything specific in the Constitution, *Roe* has generated a round of debate over what Justice Byron White, in dissent, described as "an exercise of raw judicial power."

The attempt at principle proved problematic for the Court. Blackmun found the right to abort a fetus in the right of privacy, which he asserted was basic to the word *liberty* of the due process clause (an undisguised departure from selective incorporation). Thus, privacy obviously included more than abortion, but when homosexuals challenged a Virginia law that punished as criminal conduct certain sexual practices between consenting adults, even in the privacy of their own homes, the Court upheld the law and offered not a word explaining why (*Doe* v. *Commonwealth's Attorney*, 1976). Even if the Court could reject the assertions of privacy of homosexual relations between adults, the Court—equipped with the capacity for principled decisions—owed at least an explanation distinguishing the privacy implications of the destruction of a fetus from those involved in the private sexual relations of consenting adults.

Thus, the corpse of substantive due process has been deliberately exhumed and revitalized. The Court has been entrusted with tremendous policy discretion, as is evident in the inconsistent application of the judge-made right of privacy.

How far the Court will travel with the power of substantive due process will depend on the future composition of its membership.

The second major constitutional instrument of reform used by the Court to promote civil rights and liberties has been the equal protection clause of the Fourteenth Amendment. Its original purpose, as the Court in the *Slaughterhouse Cases* stated, was to protect against racial discrimination, but its language speaks very broadly, and since the 1960s the body of constitutional law attached to that clause has grown enormously and includes many more matters than racial discrimination.

Though perjorative in connotation, the word *discrimination* means classification. In making laws governments must classify, for they cannot govern people one at a time. The task of a reviewing court is to determine whether classifications are so invidious as to collide with the equal protection clause. The court must also find that the discriminatory action is "state action" because the clause is addressed to states.

Prior to the 1960s, the Supreme Court confined the reach of the clause primarily to racial matters. And before World War II, the Court found racial violations only under egregious circumstances. In fact, while the Court manipulated the Constitution in favor of property and business interests, it ignored the Constitution when it approved in *Plessy* v. *Ferguson* (1896) the "separate but equal" doctrine, which legitimized racial segregation imposed by the states, allowed such practices to become socially entrenched, and thereby made the eventual process of desegregation that much more difficult.

World War II helped to spark the American conscience (including that of its judges) into the realization that racism at home could no longer be sanctioned. At least until the 1960s, the political process seemed unable to make the needed changes. It was the Court that began to lead the way. It found state action more easily and more frequently; it ate away at the separate-but-equal doctrine, finding more and more that separate facilities were not equal. Then, triumphantly, in *Brown* v. *Board of Education of Topeka* (1954) the Court abolished the doctrine altogether, at least in the field of public education. Since then, the federal courts have been actively involved in the task of integrating public school systems throughout the United States.

Problems of principle and practicality abound in the constitutional law of race relations. Why the Court ordered integration (facilitated through busing) rather than simply command that enforced segregation cease is unclear. Also, the constitutional limit to government action in the way of providing advantages to blacks and other previously excluded minorities is an issue. (In other words, when does "affirmative action" become invidious "reverse discrimination"?) These problems continue to face the country and the Court when dealing with the original, limited purpose of the equal protection clause. Problems also arise when that clause is read to reach matters beyond race.

In the mid-1960s the Warren Court developed an extended equal protection analysis by appearing to expand the concept of "suspect" classifications (previously only race) and by creating a "fundamental rights" component of equal protection. Ordinary classifications would be subjected to the easily satisfied reasonableness test. Other classifications would undergo the nearly impossible "compelling state interest" test, which requires that government put forth an overwhelming goal achievable in virtually no other way than through the challenged classification. Governmental classifications that the Court defines as "suspect" categories, or classifications that impinge on what the Court holds to be "fundamental rights or interests," would be constitutional only if such classifications could shoulder the burden of the compelling-state-interest test.

The list of suspect categories has not included much more than race and national origin (although for some purposes "alienage" was added by the Burger Court). The Court has never made it clear whether "illegitimacy" was a suspect classification even though it has invalidated numerous laws discriminating against illegitimate children. Both the Warren and Burger Courts were guarded in extending the list of suspect classifications. But during the 1970s the Burger Court made gender a "semisuspect" category and developed a third, more refined test in the equal protection field. This third test falls in between the all-or-nothing alternatives resulting from applying either the reasonableness test (which government could hardly fail) or the test of compelling state interest (which government could hardly pass). This middle-level test requires that

government demonstrate that its classification substantially further a specifically articulated state objective. This test provides flexibility, which increases judicial power. So far, the Court has been careful to confine the new measure to sex discrimination (and perhaps illegitimacy, though inconsistently). The Burger Court eliminated many sexually discriminatory laws that reflected sexual stereotypes in American culture.

Under the fundamental-rights element of this new equal protection analysis, the Court claims that such rights are constitutionally derived. But, if so, the Court need not venture through the equal protection clause to bar governmental classifications that infringe these rights. It could simply nullify the law as colliding with the right itself. If, for example, a state law allowed only Catholics to practice their religion, a court could veto the law as a direct violation of the First Amendment clause protecting the free exercise of religion, which is applicable against the states. Thus, the fundamental-rights element of equal protection seems entirely redundant.

The Warren Court used this analysis to engineer social and political changes. It was obvious that it developed the fundamental-rights analysis to protect interests that the Court felt to be important but not explicitly or even implicitly traceable to the Constitution. Justice John M. Harlan criticized his colleagues for using this approach to become a superlegislature, for every law affects important individual interests and the Court should not be free to pick and choose which interests deserve strict judicial scrutiny. But the Warren Court energetically employed this dimension of its newly created analysis to effect social and political reforms. For example, in *Shapiro* v. *Thompson* (1969), under the auspices of a Court-created "right to travel," state laws requiring minimum residency requirements before otherwise eligible persons could receive welfare benefits were held unconstitutional. However, the Burger Court did very little to further the fundamental-rights element of equal protection law.

Clearly the most sweeping changes occurring as a result of this analysis of the equal protection clause came in the field of voting and legislative apportionment. After years of refusing to review the validity of malapportioned legislative electoral districts, the Court entered this area and concluded that the equal protection clause demands that electoral districts in both houses of each state be equal in size. This was the momentous holding in *Reynolds* v. *Sims* (1964). The Court would tolerate deviations only for compelling and unavoidable reasons. It insisted that the Constitution required the standard of "one person, one vote" and that these votes were to be as mathematically equal as possible.

A complete reading of the Fourteenth Amendment would indicate that the equal protection clause was never intended to reach malapportioned electoral districts. In fact, Section 2 of the amendment seems clearly to permit the states the right to deprive people of the right to vote altogether, provided that the states are willing to accept a reduction in representation in Congress. Moreover, it would hardly seem necessary to have added the Fifteenth Amendment, which prohibits discrimination in voting on account of race or color, if the Fourteenth Amendment, whose primary beneficiaries were to be blacks, had already reached voting rights. The Court's intrusion in the name of constitutional interpretation was clearly illegitimate from the standpoint of traditional intepretive review. Nevertheless, despite initial negative reaction, judicially mandated reapportionment has been one of the great successes of the Court. Compliance has been widespread and has resulted in a more egalitarian reallocation of political power throughout the United States.

THE DILEMMAS OF CONSTITUTIONALISM

Frustrated by the failure of the Warren Court to deliver principled reasoning and generally to act like a court of law, Philip Kurland wrote in 1970 that the nation will have to learn live with a political Court, and he foresaw great dilemmas. The fact is that the Court has always been a political court, and the American people have endured it as such.

We have traced constitutional history through the values that the Supreme Court has tried to foster and protect through its assumed role as "ultimate interpreter" of the Constitution—an interpreter whose determinations are binding on all other participants in the body politic. It is clear that the Court has adjusted its readings of the Constitution from a political perspective far more than from a traditional legal perspective. Many of the Court's great decisions cannot withstand even rudimentary analysis under traditional, interpretivist standards of legal criticism, and many are barren of anything resembling principle. Some of the holdings, in fact, would be thoroughly incomprehensible to those unexposed to the political nature of the Court's work.

The myth of dispassionate judicial decision-making may still persist, not in the academic community but perhaps among the American people in general—at least among those not driven to cynicism by unpleasant and often unexplainable judicial policy. A different confusion has afflicted professional critics of the Court, a confusion that attends overly high expectations concerning the institutional abilities of that tribunal. Alexander Bickel, Philip Kurland, Archibald Cox, and other like-minded critics have exposed the failures of the Court to reach the standards that they have set; what they have asked of the Court is that its decisions be based on principled analysis.

That the Court does not always measure up to this standard is obvious; the question is whether it can do so. The atypical nature of the cases decided by the Court makes principled decision-making very difficult. The difficulty is multiplied by the presence of nine independent justices appointed by various presidents ordinarily for very different reasons. Some are meek and ineffectual; others are iron-willed, domineering, and diplomatic. They all have strongly held values regarding public-policy matters. In other words, group dynamics can easily shape the published reasoning offered by the Court to defend its holdings in any given case. Anthony Amsterdam has aptly explained, in a humorous analogy, the inherent distortion of principle resulting from the diverse composition of the Court. The justices are commissioned to paint a portrait of a horse; this is the task before them. With the individual justices each involved in the enterprise, each helping to brush on the paint, the emerging creature on the canvas resembles a camel, not a horse. When the finished product is released for public display, eager critics demonstrate that the camel is not a horse. The reasoning offered by the Court is analytically deficient; the "principle" offered by the Court cannot withstand scrutiny. When Justice Potter Stewart retired from the Court in 1981 after more than twenty years

1001

of service, he was asked if the Court would benefit if additional justices came to the Court to help with the mounting case loads. Stewart responded that he would have found his job easier if he had had no judicial colleagues at all.

The limitations of the judicial process itself often make the task even more susceptible to failure from the perspective of the advocates of principled adjudication. For example, the Court must decide a case on the basis of the record in which the case is presented. The Court may generate a principle by way of a proposition that is not applicable to other situations. The Court is not an administrative agency or a congressional committee that is permitted to hold extensive investigations before making a ruling that has widespread applicability.

Four years before his death and one year after the Warren Court had come to an end, Alexander Bickel conceded the difficulty of the demand of his standard and publicly questioned the Court's ability to do what he insisted was the only legitimate justification for its role in a democratic society. "I have come to doubt in many instances the Court's capacity to develop 'durable principles,' and to doubt, therefore, that judicial supremacy can work and is tolerable in broad areas of social policy" (1970). Bickel also made it clear that in the long run the results—the policies pursued by the Court—will matter far more than the process of judgment utilized by the Court. Of the Warren Court's clear tendency toward libertarian and egalitarian public policy, Bickel acknowledged that if that policy prevails, "little else will matter" (1970).

Prior to the Warren Court's revolutionary interpretation of the Constitution, the more optimistic Bickel rightly criticized those who look for nothing but results in the Court's work and care not at all about the integrity of the process of judgment. He held that the justices of the Supreme Court should strive to produce principled decisions derivable from the Constitution. But as Bickel himself came to conclude, that is not always possible.

Constitutional law as created by the Supreme Court unfolds in the intersection of two legitimacies—the process of judgment and the judgment itself. The Court is at once both a court and a political branch of the government. History judges the Court's contribution by the results it achieves, not the methodology that brought about the contribution. But, from the perspective of democratic government, a greater justification is needed for the Court's role. Constitutional theorists abound; some are more persuasive than others, but none is immune from serious criticism. Whether or not a coherent theory exists to defend the role played by the Court in the evolution of constitutional law, it is clear that the Court is an aberration in a democratic polity. Bickel's demand for principled adjudication has been unmet, as he himself recognized. The Court either refuses to submit to its constraints or is inherently unable to measure up.

But the political legitimacy that the Court can galvanize is weightier than the legitimacy of process. The fact that the Court continues to function undisturbed as a powerful policymaker is proof enough of that, especially in the wake of policies that do not easily fit the Constitution. The "ultimate interpreter" has been an important and permanent policymaker in a political system that theoretically cannot tolerate such power. The Court functions amidst a contradiction: it must act as a court to maintain its legal legitimacy, but by acting as a court it may not be able to arrive at results that reinforce its political legitimacy. The tension has not been and most likely cannot be reconciled, yet the Court continues to function. Myth and respect, in part, perpetuate the power of the Court. But that power survives also because the Court has played its role well.

CASES

Adkins v. Children's Hospital, 261 U.S. 525 (1923)

Brown v. Board of Education of Topeka, 347 U.S. 483 (1954)

Cooley v. Board of Wardens of the Port of Philadelphia, 12 Howard 299 (1852)

Davidson v. New Orleans, 96 U.S. 97 (1878)

Doe v. Commonwealth's Attorney, 425 U.S. 901 (1976)

Dred Scott v. Sandford, 19 Howard 393 (1857)

Gibbons v. Ogden, 9 Wheaton 1 (1824)

Griswold v. Connecticut, 381 U.S. 479 (1965)

Hurtado v. California, 110 U.S. 516 (1884)

Lochner v. New York, 198 U.S. 45 (1905)

McCulloch v. Maryland, 4 Wheaton 316 (1819)

Marbury v. Madison, 1 Cranch 137 (1803)

Minnesota Rate Cases [Chicago, Milwaukee & St. Paul Railway Co. v. Minnesota], 134 U.S. 418 (1890)

Munn v. Illinois, 94 U.S. 113 (1877)

Palko v. Connecticut, 302 U.S. 319 (1937)

Plessy v. Ferguson, 163 U.S. 537 (1896)

Pollock v. Farmers' Loan & Trust Co., 158 U.S. 601 (1895)

Reynolds v. Sims, 377 U.S. 533 (1964)

Roe v. Wade, 410 U.S. 113 (1973)

Shapiro v. Thompson, 394 U.S. 618 (1969)

Shreveport Case, 234 U.S. 342 (1914)

Slaughterhouse Cases, 16 Wallace 36 (1873)

Swift v. United States, 196 U.S. 375 (1905)

United States v. Butler, 297 U.S. 1 (1936)

United States v. Carolene Products Co., 304 U.S. 144 (1938)

United States v. E. C. Knight Co., 156 U.S. 1 (1895)

United States v. Nixon, 418 U.S. 683 (1974)

Wabash, St. Louis & Pacific Railway v. Illinois, 118 U.S. 557 (1886)

West Coast Hotel Co. v. Parrish, 300 U.S. 379 (1937)

West Virginia State Board of Education v. Barnette, 319 U.S. 624 (1943)

BIBLIOGRAPHY

Henry J. Abraham, *Freedom and the Court,* 4th ed. (1982), analyzes the constitutional law of civil rights and liberties in the United States; and *The Judicial Process,* 4th ed. (1980), contains a massive bibliography of public law and judicial process literature. John Agresto, *The Supreme Court and Constitutional Democracy* (1984), presents a brilliant argument that contradicts the notion of judicial supremacy. Dean Alfange, *The Supreme Court and the National Will* (1937), is an award-winning study of the Court's role, as it culminated in the Judicial Revolution of 1937. Anthony Amsterdam, "Perspectives on the Fourth Amendment," in *Minnesota Law Review,* 58 (1974), is an acute study.

Raoul Berger, *Government by Judiciary* (1977), written from the perspective of pure interpretivism, attacks the modern Court's interpretation of the Fourteenth Amendment. Alexander M. Bickel, *The Least Dangerous Branch* (1962), contains the author's most comprehensive discussion and defense of judicial review; *The Supreme Court and the Idea of Progress* (1970), is a critical analysis of the Warren Court from the perspective of both process and the impact of decisions; and *The Morality of Consent* (1975), published posthumously, is a statement of Bickel's mature views on democracy and the Constitution. Philip Bobbitt, *Constitutional Fate* (1982), offers a theoretical analysis of the meaning of the Constitution and explores various models of constitutional argument.

Archibald Cox, *The Role of the Supreme Court in American Government* (1976), analyzes the dilemmas of the Court's role in American government, with illustrations from the Burger Court. John Hart Ely, *Democracy and Distrust* (1980), attempts in a highly provocative manner to develop a theory of judicial review. Michael Kammen, *A Machine That Would Go of Itself: The Constitution in American Culture* (1986), is a detailed survey of the Constitution as a cultural phenomenon in the United States. Alfred H. Kelly, Winfred Harbison, and Herman Belz, *The American Constitution,* 6th ed. (1983), is the definitive single-volume history of constitutional development. Philip Kurland, *Politics, the Constitution, and the Warren Court* (1970), offers an analytical commentary on the Warren Court and a general discussion of the problems of a political Court. Robert G. McCloskey, *The American Supreme Court* (1960), is a brief but excellent account of the Court's political role in American history.

Michael J. Perry, *The Constitution, the Courts, and Human Rights* (1982), attacks the interpretivist defense of contemporary civil liberties doctrine and imaginatively defends judicial review as the work of the Court as "moral leader" of the nation. C. Herman Pritchett, *Constitutional Law of the Federal System* (1984), gives a topical analysis of the constitutional law of the separation of powers and federalism; and *Constitutional Civil Liberties* (1984), focuses on the examination of the constitutional law of individual rights and liberties. Herbert Wechsler, "Toward Neutral Principles of Constitutional Law," in *Harvard Law Review,* 73 (1959), is a discussion of some core issues of constitutionalism.

[*See also* CIVIL LIBERTIES AFTER 1937; COMMERCE CLAUSE; CONSTITUTIONAL INTERPRETATION; FEDERALISM; FREE SPEECH AND EXPRESSION; HUGHES COURT AND ERA; JUDICIAL REVIEW; RACIAL DISCRIMINATION AND EQUAL OPPORTUNITY; *and* SUPREME COURT OF THE UNITED STATES.]

CRIMINAL PROCEDURE

Nicholas N. Kittrie

CRIMINAL procedure is the enforcement process utilized by agencies and agents of government to implement the prohibitions contained in the criminal law. The process is usually thought to include investigatory functions, the initiation of prosecutions, trial management, sentencing procedures, and appellate review. These stages are followed by the corrections process, which some commentators include in criminal procedure.

CHARACTERISTICS OF THE AMERICAN CRIMINAL PROCESS

One may describe criminal procedure primarily as a people-processing system. Under it, various agencies of government—the police, prosecutor, courts, and corrections—take into custody or otherwise subject to their authority individuals suspected of, charged with, or convicted of crime. Each of these agencies utilizes distinct standards and rules at its particular stage in the processing of suspects or convicts.

The Funnel Effect. Commentators have portrayed the American criminal procedure as a sampling process rather than a comprehensive system. One notes at the outset that there is a wide disparity in the numbers of persons coming into contact with crime and with each stage or agency of criminal justice. The criminal justice process has consequently been described as a funnel. At each stage of the process, significant numbers of those previously brought in touch with government authority are discharged or otherwise terminated. As a result, the number of persons exposed to the initial stages of criminal procedure far exceeds the number involved in the final stages. President Lyndon Johnson's Commission on Law Enforcement and Administration of Justice reported as early as 1965 that of a sample of 467,000 offenders apprehended on suspicion of committing serious crimes, approximately 177,000 were formally charged, only 38,000 went to trial, and of those some 30,000 were finally convicted.

More-recent statistics, derived from the 1976 and 1983 Uniform Crime Reports, paint a similar picture of fragmentary justice. The two decades following the Johnson Commission saw a well-financed national campaign for better reporting of crime and more-vigorous policing, prosecution, and trial; the campaign resulted in significantly increased activity but produced little change in the funnel function of the criminal justice process. Although police received reports of some 12 million serious crimes annually, the estimated figures for 1976 and 1983 indicate that the police made arrests only in about 19.4 percent of all reported crimes. Prosecutions occurred in 9.2 percent of all reported crimes, and convictions as charged were reached in less than 700,000 cases, or a mere 5.96 percent of all crimes reported to the police. It is noteworthy also that 92 percent of all convictions resulted not from court trials but were secured through plea bargaining and negotiated guilty pleas. Criminal procedure's implementation of criminal law has therefore been viewed as occasional and selective rather than constant and total. This fragmentary or "symbolic" implementation, contrasted with what is described as comprehensive enforcement under most foreign systems, has become the hallmark of American criminal justice.

To appreciate fully the selectivity of the criminal process, one must point out that even in the initial instances the agencies of American criminal justice respond to only a segment of all crimes committed in society. Many, if not most, crimes go unreported because victims or citizens fail to alert the police out of embarrassment, fear, ignorance, or a sense of futility. One can merely speculate, therefore, on the "dark" numbers of crimes that occur but are not made part of the official criminal justice record. Only in recent years have victimization studies, utilizing random community interviews, given greater insight into the amount of unreported criminality in America. Current estimates put the annual number of serious criminal victimizations near 40 million, with only approximately 12 million of these being reported to the authorities. Taking into account the estimated number of victimizations in America, the country's clearance rate for criminality appears even more appalling than before. Only 6.3 percent of all victimizations are followed by arrests, only 2.8 percent result in a prosecution, and less than 2.1 percent end in a conviction.

Due Process Versus Efficiency. In seeking the causes for the funnel effect, identified by the constantly declining number of persons processed by the successive stages of criminal procedure, one gains a greater understanding of the basic makeup of the American criminal justice system. The decline in numbers not only testifies to personnel shortages and to other shortcomings (financial, scientific, and the like) that prevent criminal justice agencies from "clearing" and processing every reported crime but also speaks to the stringent burdens of proof placed upon the government in the criminal arena. To take even preliminary action against suspects and to proceed from one stage of criminal justice to another, government agents must deal with such burdensome questions as those relating to "probable cause," "unreasonable search and seizure," "due process," and certainty "beyond a reasonable doubt." Moreover, the numerical attrition is also due in great part to the American insistence upon law officers' compliance with procedural proprieties (such as magistrate-issued warrants and the implementation of the right to counsel), rather than being satisfied with mere evidentiary reliability and procedural efficiency. Some underpinnings of these procedural proprieties are derived from the early Anglo-American traditions embodied in common law, but most are founded on state or federal consti-

tutional safeguards and their judicial interpretations. These will be more elaborately discussed later at the applicable stages of the criminal process.

Students of the American criminal process have not agreed on the significance of the funnel effect in the measuring of the system's success or failure. Some argue that the constant decrease in the number of persons processed through the successive stages of criminal procedure is testimony to the system's inadequacy. They point to the high number of cases terminated without reaching the final stages as supporting the argument that suspects "get off easy" and that crime frequently does "pay."

Yet a different perspective on the realities of criminal justice enforcement gives rise to a counterconclusion. The processing of a suspect through even the initial stages of criminal procedure may at times be impossible, as when implicating evidence is lacking or weak. In some cases, advanced processing is undesirable or not cost-effective, as when the merits or attainment of enforcement are overcome by more pressing prosecutorial interests. In many other instances, full processing may also be unnecessary to accomplish the ultimate goals of criminal justice.

It may be erroneous to assume that the success of the criminal process can best be measured by the percentage of suspects whose cases are continued through all stages to the final serving of the sentence. If the preventive rather than retributive goals of criminal justice are considered, the prompt institution and early termination of criminal procedures might constitute a cost-effective policy. Consider the following preliminary events in the criminal process: the police patrol a crime-ridden area; a police officer admonishes a petty offender; the police raid a gambling establishment; a suspect is frisked; a disorderly person is confined overnight; a grand jury is convened and investigates suspected wrongdoing. Each of these events is likely to have a preventive and deterring impact, even if the process does not reach the concluding stages of trial, sentencing, and corrections. Recognizing the potential impact of such efforts, police and prosecutorial agencies have from time to time relied on preliminary procedural stages, not followed up by further processing, as a means for telegraphing new or more stringent enforcement policies.

The ability of criminal justice agencies to engage deliberately in these preventive or deterrent practices is due in great part to the nation's adherence to the principle of "opportunity," as contrasted with the principle of "legality," in the enforcement of the criminal law. The countries of continental Europe embrace what they describe as the "principle of legality" in their criminal procedure. This designation stands for the proposition of total and unflinching implementation of the criminal law. Once the process of enforcement has commenced, it cannot be readily terminated before it reaches the final judicial stage. Only a judicial officer may examine the accumulated evidence and determine to dispense with the trial and subsequent stages. The American doctrine of "opportunity," on the other hand, vests a great amount of discretion (based on whether successive action is deemed "opportune") in the hands of the police and prosecuting agencies. These agencies consequently possess the power to search or not to search, to arrest or to release, to prosecute or to terminate the charges. The high degree of decentralized discretion that results accounts for the view of American criminal justice not as a single, continuous, and integrated system but as a combination or conglomeration of relatively independent criminal stages and procedures.

Finally, criminal procedure in the United States must be understood in light of the American political commitment, reinforced by the Constitution, to a government by "checks and balances." The concept stands not only for a division of powers between the legislative, executive, and judicial branches; it also suggests ongoing interaction and a continuing interplay of power between these branches. In actual implementation, the concept of checks and balances means that the legislature, the police, the prosecution, and the courts are not free of scrutiny by each other. The police powers in investigating crime are thus subject to prescription by the legislature and review by the courts. The prosecutor's authority may likewise be legislatively and judicially controlled. Even the power of the courts is impacted by legislative enactments. This American proclivity for checks and balances is manifested not only in interagency review (described as intermural checks) but also in a multiplicity of provisions for review and appeal within each agency of justice (what might be called intramural checks).

The ever-present emphasis on checks and balances distinguishes American criminal procedure and makes it a system committed more to due process than to efficiency. The emphasis on intermural checks is manifested in the requirement of approval by an independent magistrate (an agent of the judicial branch) for police search and arrest warrants, for a suspect's continuing detention, and for the setting of bail for those arrested. Similarly, the prosecutor's authority to prosecute often must be preceded by an intermural grand jury return of an indictment, and discontinuance of the prosecution requires judicial approval. Even the courts, exempt from intermural checks and scrutiny, find their judgments reviewed not only by higher courts in the state hierarchy but also by federal tribunals. Often, the outcome of this elaborate and sometimes perplexing system of decentralized and discretionary authority is inefficiency and delay. On the other hand, the existing process is generally seen by most Americans as a necessary protection for the rights of the citizen and as an indispensable safeguard against the excesses of governmental power.

The Adversary Process. To appreciate fully the nature of the safeguards and checks imposed upon the various stages of the American criminal process, one should seek out their doctrinal background in the long contest between the adversary and inquisitorial systems of justice. American criminal procedure is, in the main, an adversary system. Recently, this system has been coming under growing criticism for its perceived inability to channel effectively the growing numbers of defendants through the criminal justice process. In the face of the burgeoning criminal case loads and the proliferation of plea-bargaining agreements as a means of avoiding trial, many legal scholars and administrators have been looking to continental Europe for a more effective system of justice. Some see in the inquisitorial process of these civil law countries possibilities for improving the adversary system of justice as developed under the Anglo-American common law.

An initial definition of terms is necessary to delineate properly the adversary process from the inquisitorial process. The adversarial method of resolving disputes takes its guidance from the parties in the contest: police and prosecution versus the accused. The approach is premised on the notion of a power equilibrium between those policing and those policed that should not be disturbed by the state's role as a final arbiter. At the heart of this approach is the presumption that the accused is innocent until proven guilty, with the burden of establishing guilt resting exclusively on the state. In this adversary process, the lawyers for the prosecution and the accused aggressively challenge each other and thereby define the parameters of the contest. Theoretically, the judge is a neutral figure, despite state service. The court's major function is the mediation of the trial and its outcome of guilt or innocence.

The inquisitorial system, on the other hand, adheres to the concept of the state, not the parties, as having the overriding responsibility for eliciting the facts and implementing the criminal law. The goals of the inquisitorial system can thus be distinguished dramatically from those of the adversary system. The continental process aims primarily at determining the truth through the inquisition of all relevant parties, while the adversary system's primary goal is to mediate and settle the dispute between contestants. This is not to suggest that the inquisitorial system is not interested in settling disputes or that the adversary system does not seek truth. Rather, in each instance the ranking of dispute settlement versus the pursuit of truth is a question of priorities, of primary and secondary goals. These diverse perspectives of the process help explain why pretrial negotiations and settlement (in the form of a plea bargain) are more favorably viewed in the American legal system, while the inquisitorial system insists on the ongoing pursuit of truth through the final stages of the trial process.

In terms of criminal administration, the adversary approach puts each of the parties completely in charge of preparing and pursuing its own case. On the other hand, the dominant mode in the inquisitorial system is state control of the entire process, with such control being exercised though the judiciary. Continental judges, both at the pretrial investigation and the adjudicatory stage, are more than neutral umpires and are expected to take the initiative in extracting evidence as well as determining guilt and punishment.

Not only American scholars but also American jurists have long and vigorously insisted on a commitment to the adversary system and the preservation of its integrity. Speaking in *Miranda*

v. *Arizona* (1966), the Supreme Court of the United States strongly emphasized that "our adversary system of criminal proceedings" is distinguished "from the inquisitorial system recognized in some countries."

Critics of American criminal procedure point to the preponderance of plea bargaining and nontrial dispositions in criminal cases. The adversary approach is said to have made trials a very cumbersome process, overburdened with complex rules and procedural safeguards. Jury trials, in particular, are extremely costly in terms of time, labor, and money. The pressure on the accused to forgo a trial is enormous, and one commentator, pointing to the resulting predominance of plea bargaining in America, concluded, "The admirable American preoccupation with safeguarding the individual's procedural rights has backfired. By affording the whole collection of procedural rights to a small minority of defendants, the system deprives the great majority of rights available to the accused in most civilized countries" (Weigand, 421). The criticism cannot be ignored. Only a few observers have questioned the fairness of the adversary trial, under which the sharp two-party contest of evidence and arguments serves to sensitize the judge and jury and to heighten their cognizance of the alternative conclusions and dispositions available to them. But where the vast majority of criminal suspects never enjoy the benefit of the full-dress adversary trial, its efficacy and value border on the moot.

While inquisitorial procedures have gained increased attention, it is doubtful that the inquisitorial style of trial, with its drastically different allocation of functions to the participants, is transplantable to the United States. Reforms of the adversary process in America, however, must be distilled from the current framework of the adversary system. This inward-directed reform is mandated particularly by the American criminal procedure's constitutional underpinnings, which cannot be readily undone. These underlying constitutional requirements, again, will be more elaborately discussed in the pages that follow.

MAJOR STAGES IN THE CRIMINAL PROCESS

The procedures utilized by the various agencies of justice at the diverse stages of the American criminal process do not have a uniform parentage. Some of these procedures have been formulated by the involved agencies themselves: police, prosecutorial, or judicial. Others have been determined by the jurisdiction's legislative branch: the federal Congress, the state legislature, or the municipal council. Still others have been mandated by the safeguards contained in the federal or state constitutions, as they are judicially interpreted. Finally, some of the procedures are a product of the "supervisory power" exercised by high courts upon lesser tribunals. These complex origins of criminal procedure thus reflect the American pattern of both intra- and intermural checks and balances imposed upon the administration of criminal justice.

Throughout most of American history the procedural safeguards included in the federal Bill of Rights were interpreted as applicable only to federal agencies and their criminal procedures. State criminal procedures were subject only to standards required under state constitutions, state legislation, or state executive practices. By and large, state criminal procedures were therefore immune from federal scrutiny. Various federal criminal procedures, moreover, were generally assumed to come under intra-agency review and were not subjected to judicial and intermural checks.

The adoption of the Fourteenth Amendment to the federal Constitution after the Civil War drastically changed this situation by recognizing the rights of a national citizenship from which flowed an entitlement of all American citizens to "due process." It was thereafter only a question of time before the various protections long before included in the federal Bill of Rights (in particular the Fourth Amendment requirements of reasonableness and probable cause to justify arrests and searches, the Fifth Amendment protection against self-incrimination, and the Sixth Amendment recognition of the right to counsel) began to be extended to the conduct of state criminal justice agencies.

Since the 1930s, there has been a growing merger between the standards of state criminal procedure and the federal standards. This joining of standards, or "federalization," has been the outcome of judicial activism. Beginning particularly in the middle of the twentieth century but drawing on earlier manifestations of this role, the United States Supreme Court con-

stantly expanded, by interpretation, the applicability and binding power of federal constitutional criminal standards to state procedures. As a consequence, criminal procedures nationwide were increasingly made to fit within a new federal mode.

The Supreme Court's interpretive process also impacted upon the substance of both federal and state criminal procedures, a process that can be described as "constitutionalization." As the content of the federal constitutional language was constantly broadened, state and federal procedures had to be modified in order to comply with what the courts considered fundamental requirements under the Constitution. The outcome of this federalization and constitutionalization of criminal procedure standards will be detailed in the accounts of the various stages of the criminal process that follow.

Electronic Surveillance. Before police agencies secure sufficient evidence to confront a suspect by means of an arrest or a search, they frequently resort to other, preliminary investigatory methods. These might include contacts with informants, the examination of evidence voluntarily submitted, and the utilization of various surveillance techniques. As long as the suspect's physical property or personal freedom is not infringed upon, these investigatory procedures are left solely to the discretion of the police.

Wiretapping and electronic eavesdropping are modern methods employed by law enforcement officials to gather evidence of illegal activities, particularly with regard to victimless crimes, organized crime, and national security. Under the common law, an informant overhearing a criminal conversation could communicate information to the police. Similarly, the police could engage in eavesdropping as long as no physical invasion (or trespass) of the suspect's property occurred. The conclusion that electronic surveillance, as long as it was carried out without a trespass, did not constitute a search and was therefore exempt from the Fourth Amendment safeguards was approved in 1928 by a majority of the Supreme Court in *Olmstead* v. *United States.*

The potential for widespread abuse of privacy by new technological surveillance tools caused the Supreme Court in 1967 to reverse its previous stance. In *Katz* v. *United States* the Court held that in addition to safeguarding against physical trespass, such as manifested by search and seizure, the Fourth Amendment protects an individual's reasonable expectations of privacy. Electronic information-gathering techniques that invade such privacy must therefore comply with the Fourth Amendment standard of reasonableness, as well as the requirement for warrants supported by probable cause.

Pursuant to the Supreme Court's conclusion in *Katz,* Congress, in 1968, passed Title III of the Omnibus Crime Control and Safe Streets Act, which specifies the circumstances and procedures for obtaining a warrant for the initiation of electronic surveillance. The act limits this type of investigation to crimes of treason, espionage, narcotics, gambling, violence, and other specified felonies typically related to organized crime. Before a federal official may commence wiretapping or other electronic surveillance, he must submit an application to a high-ranking prosecutor, who in turn must receive approval from the United States attorney general (or a specially designated assistant). The latter must then petition a federal district or circuit-court judge for a surveillance warrant. Similar and not less stringent procedures are required for state investigations utilizing electronic surveillance.

The petition must set forth the crime under investigation, the location of the phone to be tapped, and the identity, if known, of the suspected offenders. Finally, the petition must inform the judge of all previous wiretap authorizations that involved the same person, their location, and the facilities involved. The petitioned judge must be satisfied there is probable cause that one of the specified offenses was committed and that evidence of the crime will be obtained from the requested surveillance. The judge may issue a warrant only if he is also satisfied that there is no other legal way to gather the information sought.

The warrant issued expires as soon as the police obtain the evidence specified or thirty days after issuance, whichever is sooner. The warrant may be renewed for one additional thirty-day period, provided the state makes a new showing of probable cause. Upon the issuance of a warrant, the law enforcement officials need not obtain an additional search warrant to enter the premises under investigation in order to install the requisite eavesdropping equipment. The Supreme Court held in *Dalia* v. *United States* (1979) that such authority to enter is implied.

Despite its authorization of electronic surveillance, Congress has directed law enforcement agencies to "minimize the interception of communications." The Supreme Court has similarly directed participating officers to practice "intrinsic" minimization by ceasing to listen and record conversations that have no relevance to the ongoing investigation (*Berger* v. *New York,* 1967). Officers are nevertheless permitted to listen periodically to nonpertinent conversations to assess whether the conversants have shifted to a relevant topic. For the further protection of the public, the issuing judge must seal the recordings of communications and preserve them for a minimum period of ten years. Access to the recordings may be gained only through a court order.

Failure to comply with any of the rigid safeguards imposed by the electronic-surveillance law will result in suppression of all evidence gathered. A motion to suppress such evidence may be filed in court by any party able to establish an invasion of his constitutional right to privacy. Any participant in a recorded conversation, the owner of a tapped telephone, or a resident of the premises on which the tapped telephone is located may request suppression.

Not all electronically secured communications, however, are subject to these safeguards of privacy. Since the Fourth Amendment has been interpreted to protect only reasonable expectations of privacy, when one party to a conversation consents in advance to the recording or transmission of the exchange, a surveillance warrant is no longer required. This exception is founded on the premise that since a speaker cannot prevent a person in whom he or she is confiding from repeating the conversation orally at a later date, neither can the listener be prevented from surreptitiously recording the exchange by electronic means and playing it back to others. Most states uphold this one-party waiver to the warrant requirement, but a few insist that the permission of a party to the conversation cannot be substituted for a judicially issued warrant.

Other exceptions to the requirement of the 1968 law are contained in the Foreign Intelligence Surveillance Act of 1978, which applies to investigations undertaken in the interest of national security and carried out against foreign agents. Federal investigators in these cases may obtain a surveillance warrant from a member of a specially designated panel of federal judges and need not comply with the rigid standards set forth in Title III. Such lesser standards for the protection of national security against foreign agents were recognized by the Supreme Court in *United States* v. *United States District Court* (1972).

Arrest and Lesser Detentions. Criminal justice experts have never reached consensus on a single purpose or justification for arrest. This process, whereby a government agent deprives an individual of personal liberty, has been supported on diverse grounds: the interruption of an ongoing crime; the prevention of a future offense; the restraining of a suspect in preparation for an upcoming search; detention to enable a detainee's further interrogation; and confinement to prevent a suspect's escape and guarantee his or her appearance at a trial. Arrests have in fact been carried out to serve any and all of these objectives. Yet both the common law and the subsequent constitutional standards have failed to differentiate between permissible and unpermissible objectives, dwelling instead on the amount of evidence required to justify the restraint.

The common law permitted all persons, whether police officials or private citizens, to make an arrest without a warrant for any crime (felony or misdemeanor) committed in their presence. Police officers, as distinct from private individuals, were permitted also to make warrantless arrests for felonies, but not misdemeanors, undertaken outside their presence. For all offenses not committed in their presence, private individuals were required first to secure a warrant. The common law, however, left unresolved the questions of whether arrests could be carried out to prevent potential rather than completed crimes and whether arrests with warrants were generally preferable, in doctrine and in practice, to warrantless arrests.

Currently, when and how a suspect may be arrested, whether by state or federal agents, is increasingly governed by the federal Constitution's Fourth Amendment, which prohibits unreasonable searches and seizures and prescribes the standards for the issuance of warrants. This federal dominance is due to the fact that the Fourth Amendment protections were extended from federal to state practices by the Supreme Court in *Wolf* v. *Colorado* (1949).

Generally, although the Fourth Amendment specifies that all warrants must be based on probable cause, it does not prohibit arrests or searches without such warrants. In practice, most arrests have been, and continue to be, made without a warrant. Although warrants are considered the rule for carrying out a search, arrests are conceded not to require a warrant except in specified situations. The police thus do not need a warrant to arrest a suspect in a public place or even in a private place to which the person retreated after his arrest was attempted in public (*United States* v. *Watson,* 1976). Nor is a warrant required for an emergency arrest in the suspect's own home (*Payton* v. *New York,* 1980). Police, moreover, may proceed to make a warrantless arrest on private premises other than the suspect's home when exigent circumstances militate against the issuance of a warrant. Such circumstances are considered to exist if the offense is grave; the police reasonably believe the suspect is armed; there is a high degree of probable cause to believe the suspect did in fact commit a crime; the police strongly believe the suspect will be found on the premises; the police fear the suspect will probably flee; and the police believe they can enter the premises to make the arrest peaceably (*Dorman* v. *United States,* 1970).

When the police seek to arrest a suspect in his own home, absent exigent circumstances, they must first obtain a valid arrest warrant. Since warrants are subject to intermural checks, they must be issued by a "neutral and detached" magistrate (*Shadwick* v. *City of Tampa,* 1972). Prior to issuing the warrant, the magistrate is charged with determining whether, based on the evidence submitted, there is probable cause that a crime has been committed and that the sought suspect committed the crime. To support probable cause, the evidence must go beyond mere or vague suspicion and must contain specific data with regard to both the crime and the suspect to persuade the magistrate. For probable cause, the magistrate may consider a wide variety of evidence, including hearsay, the suspect's arrest record, and other evidence that would not be admissible at trial. The determination is made in a nonadversary hearing, where only the police, not the suspect, are represented.

The finding of probable cause may be based on personal knowledge of an individual testifying before a magistrate, such as the victim, a police officer, or any other person who witnessed the crime. But the finding may rely also on assertions by an absent informant relayed to the magistrate by the police. When the request for a warrant is based on assertions of an absent informant, who may be neither identified to the magistrate nor able to reveal the sources of his or her information, the magistrate must evaluate the "totality of the circumstances" to determine whether probable cause has been satisfactorily established (*Illinois* v. *Gates,* 1983). The magistrate in such instances is to make a commonsense determination of probable cause based on all the information presented, including the "veracity" and "basis of knowledge" of the informant, as well as the reliability of past tips supplied to the police by the informant.

Probable cause is a prerequisite for all arrests, whether with or without a warrant. But the United States Supreme Court has upheld a lesser interference with personal liberty, defined as a "stop," which may be carried out on lesser grounds than probable cause. Beginning with *Terry* v. *Ohio* (1968), the Court has sanctioned the practice of stops, or brief detentions of suspects for the sole purpose of identification or a weapons search, even in the absence of the evidentiary criteria required for a full arrest. A police officer who has mere "reasonable suspicion" to believe a person has committed, or is about to commit, a crime and is armed may detain such subject briefly for the purposes previously specified.

Similar exceptions to the probable-cause requirement have also been recognized with regard to the temporary stopping of motor vehicle drivers for purposes such as the checking of license registrations or driver sobriety. These stops, however, may not be ordered or carried out in an arbitrary manner. To be upheld, the police must conduct systematic stops of passing automobiles, investigating every car or every few cars that pass the checkpoint (*Delaware* v. *Prouse,* 1979).

An additional exception to the requirement of probable cause applies to suspects and others ordered to appear before a grand jury. The courts have favored the investigatory duties and powers of grand juries and have refrained from restricting them through the imposition of the probable-cause requirement. By holding that compelled grand jury appearances do not constitute arrests, the courts have permitted grand juries to order appearances on lesser standards of evidence (*United States* v. *Calandra,* 1974).

Arrest warrants must specifically name or otherwise identify the person to be apprehended. Police in possession of an arrest warrant must comply strictly with arrest procedures established by federal and state law. Officers must usually identify themselves and state their purpose, even if they confront an unlocked door, before requesting entry into the premises. If entry is refused, the police may force a door or window. However, some jurisdictions authorize unannounced, or "no-knock," entry whenever the police suspect that evidence might be otherwise destroyed (*Ker* v. *California,* 1963).

Police, in specified situations, may use deadly force for the apprehension of a suspect. Most jurisdictions follow guidelines set forth by statute or by police department regulations that describe the circumstances under which resort to deadly force is permissible. The American Law Institute guidelines, for example, permit the use of deadly force only when the proposed arrest is for the commission of a felony; there is reasonable police belief that the suspect's crime involved the use, or threat of use, of force or that a substantial risk of imminent serious bodily harm exists to the arresting police or others; and the police force poses no substantial risk to bystanders.

The execution of an arrest might also require, at times, the securing of a search warrant. If the arrest is to be carried out in the residence of a third party, the officers must, in the absence of exigent circumstances, obtain a search warrant for entry into such premises to arrest a suspect (*Steagald* v. *United States,* 1981). Conversely, no arrest warrant is required for apprehending those found on searched premises pursuant to a valid search warrant. This waiver of an arrest warrant is attributed to the desire to prevent the flight of occupants, minimize potential risk to the searching police, and otherwise expedite the carrying out of an orderly search (*Michigan* v. *Summers,* 1981).

If the police have made an arrest without prior determination of probable cause by either a magistrate or a grand jury, a probable-cause hearing is required to validate the suspect's continuing detention (*Gerstein* v. *Pugh,* 1975). At such a hearing, either the police or the prosecutor must establish probable cause before a judge, who must both decide if the evidence justifies restraint and determine the availability of bail.

A suspect arrested in violation of the Fourth Amendment requirements may not insist that the arrest is unconstitutional. A suspect whose arrest was unlawful—because a warrant was lacking, probable cause was absent, or even the very detention was secured by kidnapping—can be compelled to stand trial (*Ker* v. *Illinois,* 1886; *Frisbie* v. *Collins,* 1952). The only relief available to one arrested in violation of his constitutional rights is a civil suit for false arrest against the offending officers and their superiors.

Search and Lesser Seizures. Although no single or even predominant objective has been articulated for the arrest process, the purpose underlying the search is more clear. The goal of the search is the discovery and seizure of the tools or fruits of a crime and any other evidence relevant to the proof of a criminal event. Though the search process, in the main, invades only rights of property while arrest affects personal liberty, more-stringent standards have been imposed in the United States on the search process than on the arrest. In particular, resort to a judicial warrant is indispensable for all searches except in a few specified circumstances, while no such insistence on warrants exists with regard to arrests *(Watson).* Police possessing probable cause are therefore required to go before a magistrate to secure a warrant prior to conducting a search, but they may make an arrest without such authorization.

The process of federalization and constitutionalization that has affected the law of arrest has also been repeated with regard to the law of search. Since the very same provisions of the Fourth Amendment protect individuals against both unreasonable arrests and searches, judicial activism regarding arrests has affected in like manner the standards for searches.

The protection against unreasonable searches accorded by the Fourth Amendment to "persons, houses, papers, and effects" applies to the human body as well as to the property owned or possessed by an individual. To be protected, the searched place must be one in which a person has a reasonable expectation of privacy. Excluded are such properties as an open field, paint on the exterior of an automobile, or one's handwriting *(Katz).*

To secure a valid search warrant, the police must present a magistrate with evidence to es-

tablish probable cause that evidence of a crime is located in a particular place. They must also specify the items to be sought. The procedure for securing a search warrant is identical to that previously discussed for obtaining an arrest warrant. But while only an actual suspect of the crime is subject to arrest and not others able to testify to the offense, a search is more far-reaching. The premises and properties sought to be searched by the police need not belong to one suspected of a crime. It is sufficient that the police establish that evidence of a crime is to be found at such location.

The execution of a search warrant, unlike the making of an arrest, may be undertaken only by a police officer. A search must be conducted as soon as possible after the issuance of the warrant (*United States* v. *Nepstead,* 1970). The timeliness requirement is to ensure that probable cause still exists and that evidence is not removed. As in the case of the arrest warrant, the police must identify themselves before entering the premises to be searched. Once inside, they may seize all tools, fruits, and other evidence of crime that they discover within the searched area, regardless of whether such items were specified in the warrant (*Coolidge* v. *New Hampshire,* 1971). Police do not need a separate arrest warrant to detain, for the duration of the search, individuals found on the searched premises. The authority to do so is implied in the search warrant itself. The police may search any persons who are found on the premises and are named in the search warrant. The police may also arrest others present if there exists probable cause to do so, and in such a case they may search the arrestees as incident to the arrest.

In only few specified instances may the police conduct a warrantless search. These exceptions to the warrant requirement are limited and require strict conformity with applicable guidelines. The first exception, being a search incident to an arrest, is permissible following all lawful arrests. Viewed as a necessary precaution, such searches are permitted as a matter of course and do not depend on police knowledge that the suspect was armed or in possession of criminal evidence (*United States* v. *Robinson,* 1973). Searches incident to an arrest extend to those areas within reach, the "wingspan," of the suspect at the time of the arrest (*Chimel* v. *California,* 1969). Should the arrestee move during the period of arrest, his wingspan moves with him. For a suspect arrested in his automobile, the search area extends to the complete interior of the vehicle. For one arrested in a particular room in his house, the search may not go beyond that room. An incidental search, however, is valid only if it is conducted at the time of the arrest and cannot be undertaken after the arrestee's removal.

A second exception to the warrant requirement is known as the plain-view doctrine. Under it, police who are lawfully on certain premises and inadvertently encounter fruits or instrumentalities of a crime that are "in plain view" may seize such evidence without resort to a warrant. This exception would apply whenever the police unexpectedly discover contraband while executing an arrest or search warrant.

An automobile search is the third exception to the search-warrant requirement. Pursuant to it, police officers possessing probable cause that evidence of a crime is contained in an automobile or any other type of vehicle are permitted to search the vehicle without first securing a warrant (*Carroll* v. *United States,* 1925). This waiver of the warrant is justified by the mobile character of the premises to be searched and the consequent exigency of the situation. An automobile search is not confined to the interior of the vehicle. The search may extend to the trunk or any container in which suspected evidence might be held, as long as probable cause exists. A warrantless automobile search may be conducted at the time the vehicle is stopped, or the automobile may be towed promptly to a police station for a later search (*Chambers* v. *Maroney,* 1970).

Warrantless searches are also permitted in other situations classified as "emergencies." Several circumstances have been recognized by the courts as justifying warrantless searches because of their exigent nature. The police, when in "hot pursuit" of a suspected felon who flees into nearby premises, may enter the premises to search for the suspect without first obtaining a warrant. Another exception is the case of evidence that is likely to disappear if time is allowed to elapse; the police may thus administer a blood alcohol test without a warrant, because the blood alcohol content is likely to diminish with the passage of time.

Finally, the so-called stop-and-frisk rule is yet another exception not only to the warrant requirement for searches but also to the probable cause standard. This rule permits a police officer to stop briefly and frisk superficially a person without first possessing either a warrant or probable cause if the officer has a "reasonable suspicion" that the individual engaged in, or is about to engage in, criminal activity (*Terry*). The detention permitted under this exception must be brief, and the search likewise is limited to a protective frisk, a patting-down of the suspect's outer clothing if the officer believes the suspect to be armed and dangerous. Evidence seized as a result of a stop-and-frisk is admissible only if the officer searched exclusively those areas capable of concealing a weapon. If the search was so limited, all evidence secured, whether weapons or other contraband, will be admissible in court.

Evidence that is seized in the absence of a warrant or in the pursuit of a defective warrant is subject to suppression or exclusion from the subsequent trial (*Mapp* v. *Ohio,* 1961). But the suppression of illegally obtained evidence, mandated by the "exclusionary rule" of the United States Supreme Court, has been undergoing drastic changes in recent years. Detailed discussion of the exclusionary rule's current content appears below.

Eyewitness Identification. Once a crime has been reported and a suspect has been seized, victims and other witnesses may be called upon to identify the suspect as part of the police and prosecution's investigatory process. Eyewitness identification may take various forms, including lineups, showups, and photographic displays. Although a suspect may not refuse to take part in identification procedures prior to trial, he or she must be accorded certain constitutional protections while undergoing any such process. These protections are to assure that the identification methods comply with the Fourteenth Amendment requirement of due process as well as with the Sixth Amendment right to counsel.

The most common method for identifying crime suspects is the lineup, a practice of placing the suspect, along with several others, on exhibition before the witness. Lineups may not be unnecessarily suggestive, or else they become violative of the suspect's constitutional right to due process (*United States* v. *Wade,* 1967). Although no clear-cut definition of suggestibility has been articulated, the placing of a black suspect in an otherwise all-white lineup is an example.

A second method of eyewitness identification, the one-person showup, has been greatly discouraged by the courts. Embodying a high degree of suggestibility and posing a considerable risk of misidentification, this practice relies on a one-to-one confrontation in which the witness is asked to identify one suspect only. Not only are the opportunities for misidentification by the witness enhanced under these circumstances, but the very fact that a suspect is held in police custody is considered unduly suggestive of the detainee's guilt. The Supreme Court has nevertheless upheld police showups if the practice is limited to exigent circumstances, such as when the impending death of a witness permits no time for a lineup (*Stovall* v. *Denno*, 1967).

A third common pretrial identification method is the photographic display. In lieu of personal identification, the witness in this instance is shown photographs of either the suspect only or of the suspect and others, for the purpose of identifying the perpetrator of the crime. Despite the suggestibility of this procedure, the Supreme Court has upheld it (*Simmons* v. *United States,* 1968). Unlike the lineup and showup, the witness in the photographic display does not actually confront the suspect. Accordingly, the courts have considered this procedure part of the intra-agency police investigatory work and exempt from the safeguards (including due process and the right to counsel) that are applicable during the adversary stages of the criminal process.

The dominant technique employed at lineup or showup to safeguard the rights of the suspect against unnecessary suggestiveness is the presence of counsel. The suspect's right to counsel as an observer and advocate is limited, however, to identification procedures conducted after the criminal case has entered a "critical stage" (*Wade*). The critical stage commences at the institution of the adversary criminal proceedings, such as when formal charges are entered against the accused with the return of an indictment or the filing of the "information," a criminal complaint issued at the exclusive discretion of the prosecutor. Arraignments and other preliminary judicial hearings have also been considered as commencing the adversary stage. Police identification procedures prior to that time are viewed as part of the intra-agency investigatory stage and are exempt from the safeguards applicable during the later stages.

Whether or not represented by counsel at lineup or showup, the suspect may have due process rights at the identification stage judicially reviewed at a pretrial hearing. A finding of abuse may result in the suppression of the identification. At the hearing, the likelihood of misidentification will be weighed against other factors, such as the previous opportunity by the witness to observe the suspect at the scene of the crime; the clarity of such observation; the accuracy of the witness's preidentification description of the defendant; the certainty of the witness's identification of the suspect; and the length of time elapsed between the commission of the crime and the witness identification (*Manson* v. *Brathwaite,* 1977).

Although entitled to presence of counsel, a suspect at a postindictment lineup may waive this right. To constitute an intelligent waiver, the defendant must be advised first of the right to counsel. In the absence of a waiver, the government may not offer at trial identification evidence obtained at a lawyerless lineup. Moreover, even an in-court identification by witnesses who took part in such illegal prior identification is likely to be disallowed. Only if the prosecution can satisfy the court that the witness's later in-court identification was based on independent knowledge and was not tainted by the pretrial procedure will such subsequent identification be allowed into evidence (*Wade*).

Police Interrogations. The interrogation of the suspect is one phase of the criminal procedure that most clearly distinguishes between the adversary and inquisitorial systems of justice. While the inquisitorial system harbors no fundamental misgivings regarding the accused's conviction through the words of his own mouth, such an outcome is contrary to the fundamental premises of the adversary process. Moreover, self-incrimination by the suspect challenges also the constitutional doctrine against compelling an individual "to be a witness against himself" contained in the Fifth Amendment.

However, since voluntary self-incrimination is prohibited neither by adversary doctrines nor by constitutional doctrines, American criminal procedure has sought to overcome its initial misgivings against compulsory testimony, by increasingly refining the definitions of voluntariness. The most comprehensive development took place in a 1966 decision by the Supreme Court. But in *Miranda* v. *Arizona* (1966) the opposition to inquisitorial techniques gained an even more dramatic victory. The Supreme Court articulated in *Miranda* comprehensive standards regarding all interrogations of suspects held in custody. As a safeguard against coerced "confessions," these standards established the suspect's right to the presence of counsel during all custodial police questioning. In requiring counsel, the Court acted contrary to strong law enforcement concerns that such presence would not only guard against coerced statements but would also militate against all confessions. The decline in confessions, it was feared, would force the criminal justice system to rely on extrinsically obtained evidence alone and thus increase the difficulty in securing convictions.

Relying on the Fifth Amendment protection against self-incrimination, which had been extended to the states by *Malloy* v. *Hogan* (1964), the *Miranda* Court mandated that suspects interrogated while in police custody are entitled to be advised, orally or in writing, that they have the right to remain silent, that anything said by them may be used against them in court, that they have the right to presence of counsel during police questioning, and that counsel will be appointed by the court in cases of indigency.

Nevertheless, *Miranda* did not foreclose all police communications with either the community at large or a suspect. The right to counsel applies only when a suspect is in police "custody" and is about to undergo police "interrogation." A person is considered in custody whenever, due to police presence, he or she cannot voluntarily leave an existing location, whether that be a jail, a police station, a hotel, or a home (*Orozco* v. *Texas,* 1969). A suspect is not considered in custody, however, if he voluntarily goes to the police station to make a statement. The police, accordingly, need not warn a confessant of *Miranda* rights.

Before the *Miranda* warnings are required, the suspect must not only be in custody but also subject to police interrogation. A person in custody who freely chooses to confess to a crime need not be advised of the right to remain silent. But any questions regarding the crime posed to a suspect by a police officer are considered an interrogation. Questions asked by police officers after a suspect renders a voluntary confession and that seek to expand on the information already offered by the suspect also constitute an interrogation and must be preceded by the *Miranda* warning. Even a nonverbal action on the part of police officers seeking to elicit incriminating statements from a suspect (such as a suspect's confrontation with incriminating evidence) will be considered an interrogation if the officers knew, or should have known, that such action was "reasonably likely to elicit an incriminating response" (*Rhode Island* v. *Innis,* 1980).

Further definitions of the point at which a suspect's right to presence of counsel commences have come forth from the Supreme Court in subsequent decisions. Once the adversary criminal stages have begun, whether through the return of an indictment, the filing of an information, or any preliminary appearance before a magistrate, the police may not elicit information from a suspect, overtly or covertly, without the presence of counsel. This is true whether the suspect is in custody or at large, subject to interrogation or not (*Brewer* v. *Williams,* 1977).

Police questioning of detained suspects might take place, off and on, over the course of several hours or days. Under such circumstances, once a suspect requests legal representation pursuant to *Miranda,* police may not continue questioning him on subsequent occasions without ensuring the presence of counsel. This is not the case, however, if the suspect himself freely initiates further communications to the police. The Supreme Court held also that an initial confession, made without the required warnings, would not "taint" or adversely affect the admissibility of a second confession given after an appropriate administration of the *Miranda* warnings (*Oregon* v. *Elstad,* 1985).

After being constitutionally advised, the suspect may waive the right to counsel. To be valid, the waiver must be made voluntarily and be founded on the defendant's actual knowledge of constitutional rights, including the right to appointed counsel if the suspect is indigent. The waiver need not be made in writing, but the government must meet the burden of establishing that the decision to waive was both voluntary and knowing (*North Carolina* v. *Butler,* 1979). Moreover, the defendant's subsequent request for an attorney negates any previous evidence of a waiver and invalidates confessions obtained without the presence of counsel (*Edwards* v. *Arizona,* 1981).

Preliminary Hearings and Bail. Federal and most state statutes require that persons held in police custody, whether arrested pursuant to a warrant or without a warrant, whether apprehended on the basis of a grand jury's indictment or a prosecutor's information, be brought before a magistrate. This appearance is usually referred to as a "preliminary hearing" if it is conducted after a police arrest or as an "arraignment" if it takes place after the initiation of the prosecution.

The taking of the suspect before a magistrate must usually be done without unnecessary delay. Failure of the police to do so does not necessarily taint the confession or evidence secured from the accused in the interim, since the hearing is not constitutionally mandated. But the Supreme Court, in its "supervisory authority," has insisted on prompt hearings in federal cases and has invalidated confessions obtained at interrogations during a violation of this requirement (*McNabb* v. *United States,* 1943; *Mallory* v. *United States,* 1957).

It is the magistrate's function at such preliminary appearances to advise the prisoner of his or her rights, ensure representation by counsel, and set bail. If the appearance takes place after the initiation of the prosecution, through an indictment or an information, the magistrate may also ask the prisoner for a plea—guilty or not guilty.

If the police took custody of the suspect without a warrant or if arrest was secured on the basis of a prosecutor's information, the hearing before the magistrate must first address itself to the existence of probable cause to support the prisoner's continuing confinement (*Gerstein*). If any confrontation between the defendant and the accuser is likely to take place at these hearings, presence of counsel for the accused is mandatory.

The release of a detainee on bail is not specifically authorized or required by the Constitution, although the Eighth Amendment prohibits the setting of "excessive bail." Bail, however, has a long history in the common law and has traditionally consisted of requiring the defendant to furnish a valuable collateral or guarantee to the court, in the belief that its value will induce the accused to appear in court to face the pending charges. Courts generally consider bail excessive if it is set above the amount considered reasonable to ensure the defendant's appearance at trial.

Despite the constitutional silence regarding the right to bail and the further failure of the courts expressly to extend the Eighth Amendment bail reference to the states (*Schilb* v. *Kuebel,* 1971), the federal government and most states have established bail systems. Some jurisdictions, however, do not permit bail releases of suspects in capital cases because of the concern that no security would ensure the return of an accused facing a possible death penalty.

Two major bail systems operate in the United States. The traditional, or money-based, system has its roots in the notion that the risk of forfeiting a substantial sum of money will prevent a suspect from flight and will assure appearance at trial. Under this system a magistrate sets the sum of the bail according to the severity of the crime charged, with the funds being payable or guaranteed prior to release from jail. In practice, an indigent suspect, who is unable to raise the funds, remains in prison awaiting trial, while an individual of means is released through arrangements with a bail bondsman, who for a designated fee guarantees the amount of the bond. Under this system, the bondsman is frequently not only the guarantor but also the implementer of the bailed suspect's appearance in court. To avoid financial loss, bondsmen make it their business from time to time to apprehend and deliver to the authorities tardy or escaped suspects.

Complaints against the economic inequality inherent in the money-bail system resulted in bail reform in most jurisdictions. The federal Bail Reform Act of 1966, for example, permits the release of a suspect in the case of a noncapital offense either on the word of the suspect or on an unsecured appearance bond. When the court determines that the suspect is likely to flee the jurisdiction, the judge may resort to alternative methods for guaranteeing appearance at trial, including placing the defendant in the custody of another person, imposing travel restrictions, or requiring the posting of a secured appearance bond with the court. Practices similar to the federal model have been adopted in many states in an effort to permit indigent defendants' release from confinement prior to trial and the determination of their guilt. Finally, in considering a suspect's availability for bail, the magistrate usually may only take into account the likelihood of escape. In most jurisdictions, no consideration may be given to whether the released suspect is likely to pose a public danger through resort to new crime.

The Initiation of Prosecutions: Indictment and Information. Just as the arrest and search powers of the police are limited by the requirement of a warrant issued by an independent magistrate, so, too, the prosecutor's power is often controlled by the requirement of a grand jury indictment to lodge formally the complaint against the suspect. An indictment by a grand jury, which ranges from sixteen to twenty-three members and is subject to judicial supervision, contrasts with the less formal initiation of prosecutions by an information.

The right of one accused of a felony not to be prosecuted except by a grand jury indictment is specified in the Fifth Amendment to the Constitution and is enforceable in federal cases. The Supreme Court, however, has not applied this right to state criminal procedures. Resort to a grand jury indictment is therefore not necessary in ensuring an accused in state procedures his due process protection (*Hurtado* v. *California,* 1884). Nevertheless, many states, particularly those east of the Mississippi, require by either state constitution or statute a grand jury indictment in felony cases.

The grand jury function of determining probable cause to indict a suspect is one of its three major responsibilities. The other two functions relate more directly to the investigation of crimes: initiating such investigations or carrying them out upon judicial or prosecutorial request. Vested with broad investigatory powers, the grand jury is free to consider any crimes committed within its jurisdiction. It may call witnesses and gather evidence freely, and at the conclusion of its investigation, if a determination of probable cause has been made, it will hand down its indictments to the prosecutor. In its investigative role, the grand jury may also serve as a check on the conduct of government agencies and agents, in matters such as legislative and executive corruption or overcrowding in jails. But the investigatory function, vesting in the grand jury supervisory authority over other branches of government, is usually narrowly defined by law.

Grand jury work is conducted with greater procedural latitude than are police arrests and interrogations, prosecutorial investigations, and court trials. A grand jury, unlike the police and prosecutor, may order witnesses to testify before it. In summoning a witness to testify, the grand jury need not, in most cases, inform the witness of the subject matter of the inquiry. A witness ignoring a grand jury subpoena or refusing to respond to its questioning may be held in contempt and be confined in jail until he or she cooperates or until the term of the grand jury expires. If a subsequent grand jury again subpoenas the same witness and he or she refuses to testify, the witness can again be held in contempt.

Grand juries are also empowered to issue subpoenae duces tecum, which compel witnesses to produce documents required for the investigation. To allow them the broadest investigatory latitude, grand juries are permitted to examine and consider all available evidence, whether hearsay or not, whether legally or illegally obtained, whether admissible or inadmissible in a court of law (*Calandra; Costello* v. *United States,* 1956).

Since the filing of an information by the prosecutor frequently serves as an alternative to a grand jury indictment, requisite safeguards have been introduced to check on this prosecutorial power. Anyone arrested after being accused by an information is entitled to be brought for a preliminary hearing before a magistrate (*Gerstein*). At this hearing the prosecutor's evidence against the accused and the determination of probable cause must be subjected to judicial review.

Suppression of Illegally Obtained Evidence. Prior to appearance for trial, a suspect who has been subjected to earlier police or prosecutorial actions has available procedural remedies for any previous official misconduct. To ensure that the constitutional rights of the accused are respected by law enforcement officials, the Supreme Court fashioned in 1914 the exclusionary rule, also known as the suppression doctrine (*Weeks* v. *United States*). The rule stands for the proposition that the federal courts will not permit into evidence at a criminal trial any evidence obtained in violation of the defendant's constitutional rights. Most commonly invoked for violations of the Fourth and Fifth Amendments (regarding arrest and search procedures, as well as the safeguards against self-incrimination), this rule has severe consequences for the police and prosecution. Relying on the rule, the courts may eliminate all incriminating evidence, including a confession or the very murder weapon, from the legal consideration of guilt or innocence.

Extended to state criminal procedures in 1961 through *Mapp,* the exclusionary rule may be invoked only where the violation of the defendant's rights have been carried out by law enforcement officials or their agents. The rule's limitation to instances of "state action" is based on the premise that this remedy is intended to protect individuals from overzealous and unlawful police activities, but not against the world at large. Some states have nevertheless extended the exclusionary rule to any evidence illegally seized, whether by a government agent or a private citizen. In either event, when illegal evidence is obtained by law enforcement officers who collaborate with nongovernment agents, the collusive product is equally tainted.

Various rationales have been advanced by the Supreme Court for its exclusionary rule. Initially, the rule was sometimes characterized as a rule of evidence, falling within the court's supervisory power over lower federal tribunals *(Weeks).* Subsequently, the rule was supported as a constitutionally mandated tool for deterring police misconduct *(Wolf),* as well as a redress-granting remedy for the aggrieved citizen *(Alderman* v. *United States,* 1969). Finally, the rule has been advocated as necessary for the maintenance of judicial integrity and the preservation of the state as a model of lawfulness *(Elkins* v. *United States,* 1960).

The suppression doctrine, as previously noted, has not been applied to proceedings before the grand jury. A witness before the grand jury, therefore, may be confronted by evidence secured through illegal means. In reaching this outcome, the Supreme Court concluded that the enhancement of the grand jury's investigatory role, by permitting such tainted evidence, "outweighs" the deterrent benefits to be derived from the application of the rule *(Calandra).*

Further limiting the suppression doctrine is the requirement that the accused must have standing to challenge the legality of the police conduct. Standing is satisfied when the unconstitutional police activity took place on a person's property or involved personal belongings or the accused. An individual thus may not challenge and seek to exclude evidence obtained in violation of another person's property rights *(Alderman).* Some states, however, have abolished the standing requirement, in order to broaden the protection offered by this constitutional safeguard. This reform allows any person who is adversely affected by illegally obtained evidence, whether involving his or a third party's rights, to invoke the exclusionary rule.

When illegally obtained confessions or unlawfully seized goods lead the police to further evidence of a crime, the defendant may seek to have such "derivative" evidence suppressed as well. A murder weapon discovered through an unlawful confession exemplifies such derivative discovery. Often called the "fruits of the poisonous tree," such secondary evidence will be suppressed or not depending on whether it was obtained "by exploitation of . . . [the] illegality or instead by means sufficiently distinguishable to be purged of the primary taint." *(Wong Sun* v. *United States,* 1963).

Because of the drastic effects of the exclusionary rule, under which reliable evidence is excluded in deference to due process considerations, its scope has been subjected to growing judicial restrictions. Under an increasing number of circumstances, the courts have modified the exclusionary rule to permit collateral utilization of illegally seized evidence. Thus, although a suspect's statement to the police made in violation of *Miranda* cannot be introduced by the prosecution as part of its case-in-chief, it may nevertheless be utilized to impeach the defendant's conflicting courtroom testimony *(Walder* v. *United States,* 1954). Similar exceptions have been extended to physical evidence secured in violation of the Fourth Amendment. Despite the illegality in obtaining such evidence, the courts have permitted its utilization when such evidence ultimately and inevitably would have been discovered in the regular and lawful course of police investigations *(Nix* v. *Williams,* 1984).

In 1984 the Supreme Court set forth the so-called good-faith exception to the exclusionary rule in *United States* v. *Leon.* Under this exception, when a police officer acting in good faith executes a search warrant that he believed to be valid but later proves to be deficient as a result of error on the part of the issuing magistrate, the seized evidence will be admissible in court. The deterrence rationale of the exclusionary rule, the Supreme Court reasoned, was meant to apply to the police and not to magistrates, who play a neutral role in the adversary process. Errors in the issuance of the warrant, accordingly, should not affect the admissibility of evidence secured by an otherwise lawful search on the part of a police officer.

To many observers of the American criminal process, the increasing exceptions to the exclusionary rule do not appear as merely marginal curtailments. There is a growing fear that these are indeed the first indications of a deliberate campaign to reinforce the powers of the police and to reduce the safeguards of the accused.

Speedy Trial. Once formally charged with a crime, the accused is guaranteed a speedy trial by the Sixth Amendment. The Supreme Court has extended this right to state trials as well (*Klopfer* v. *North Carolina,* 1967). Several considerations underlie this insistence on a speedy trial: the desire to protect the unbailed accused from lingering in jail; the protection of society against new crimes by a dangerous offender free on bail; and the concern that witnesses may forget occurrences, move away, or die prior to testifying at trial.

To determine whether a defendant has been denied a speedy trial, the Supreme Court established a four-part test in which each element is to be weighed on a case-by-case basis. To be considered are the following: the length of the delay; the reasons for the delay; whether the defendant has asserted this right to a speedy trial; and the actual prejudice to the defendant caused by the delay (*Barker* v. *Wingo,* 1972).

An accused's allegations of denial of a speedy trial may be rebutted by the prosecution. The court will usually tolerate delays of less than one year between indictment and trial. It also will consider, as a mitigating factor, that requests for postponement originated with defense counsel and that the defendant demonstrated little or no insistence for a speedy fashion. Conversely, a defendant's claim is likely to be upheld if the delay was in excess of one year, postponements were requested by the prosecution, and the defendant emphatically insisted on a speedy trial. To be weighed also is whether defendant's case was prejudiced by, for example, the death or unavailability of one or more witnesses. If a violation of the Sixth Amendment right to a speedy trial is ascertained, the defendant is entitled to the dismissal of the pending charges. Since little guidance has been furnished prosecutors to put them on notice regarding criteria for determining unreasonable delays, the dismissal remedy has been generally viewed as unduly harsh.

The federal Speedy Trial Act of 1974 addressed this inadequacy. Applying to federal criminal courts only, the act establishes a time frame of one hundred days within which a confined accused must be indicted and brought to trial. But allowances are made for permissible delays such as those caused in the convening of the grand jury, defendant's need for a competency hearing or trial on other charges, the unavailability of witnesses, and postponements requested by the prosecution and agreed to by defense counsel and the court.

Pleas and Plea Bargains. Prior to the commencement of a criminal trial, but after the return of an indictment or the filing of an information, the accused is brought before a magistrate for arraignment. At that time, the accused is asked to enter a plea. The arraignment represents a critical stage in the criminal process and the defendant is therefore entitled to the assistance of counsel in deciding how to plead and in making the plea.

The defendant may plead not guilty, nolo contendere, or guilty. If he or she chooses to plead not guilty, a full criminal trial will ensue. For the purpose of imposing punishment, a plea of nolo contendere resembles a guilty plea, although it differs in some respects. The nolo contendere plea may not be construed as an admission of guilt at subsequent legal proceedings, whether criminal or civil. Not all jurisdictions recognize this plea, and the federal as well as state courts that permit it require prior judicial approval. By entering a plea of guilty or pleading nolo contendere, the defendant not only waives the Sixth Amendment right to a jury trial but dispenses with a court trial altogether.

Although the great majority of those charged with crimes plead guilty and are relieved of trial, the due process protections of the Fourteenth Amendment impose certain procedural safeguards on the plea-bargaining process. Before accepting a plea, the judge must address the accused in open court to determine whether the plea is made "voluntarily" and "intelligently." The judge must assess the defendant's awareness and understanding of the following issues: the nature of the crime charged, particularly the requirement of criminal intent; the maximum and mandatory minimum penalties faced by the defendant; the defendant's right to plead not guilty; and the plea's effect on defendant's right to a trial. A defendant who pleads guilty without compliance with these procedural requirements may have the plea withdrawn.

Trial by Jury. The Sixth Amendment guarantees the right of the accused to a jury trial "in all criminal prosecutions." But the common-law tradition exempts "petty offenses" from trials by jury, and an accused in a federal criminal case is similarly accorded a jury only if a punishment of at least a six-month imprisonment is possible in the case. The Sixth Amendment right to a jury has been applied to the states in *Duncan* v. *Louisiana* (1968), and most states have followed the federal practice of restricting juries to the more serious crimes only. A few states, however, permit the defendant a jury trial on lesser offenses, including misdemeanors.

The contemporary jury is viewed as supplying a popular input into the administration of criminal justice, continuing the accused's traditional right to be tried by an impartial tribunal of his peers. However, since the jury is designed to afford protection for the accused, there is an absolute right to assert or to waive this right. The prosecutor, on the other hand, has no authority to insist on a jury trial.

Once a jury is selected and hears the evidence in the case, it is required to conduct its deliberations in private. The United States Constitution does not require a jury verdict to be unanimous, although federal and most state practices impose such a requirement. When jury unanimity (in favor of either conviction or acquittal) is lacking, the jury will be considered a "hung jury" and will be dismissed. To avoid a hung jury and the expenses of a retrial, some states have done away with the requirement of unanimous verdicts in noncapital cases. While majority verdicts by a twelve-member tribunal have been upheld by the Supreme Court, unanimity continues to be required in trials by a six-member jury (*Burch* v. *Louisiana,* 1979).

The Prohibition of Double Jeopardy. Once a suspect has been brought to trial to face charges, any subsequent attempt to try that individual again for the same offense must overcome the Fifth Amendment prohibition against double jeopardy. The prohibition, extended by the Supreme Court to the states in *Benton* v. *Maryland* (1969), specifies that no person shall "be subject for the same offense to be twice put in jeopardy of life or limb." The concern underlying this language is that the inequality in resources between the state-financed prosecution and the private defendant is likely to result in injustice, should the government be permitted to try and retry an accused. Accordingly, the Supreme Court has held that a defendant is protected from reprosecution for the same offense after either an earlier acquittal or conviction. Neither may a defendant receive multiple penalties for the same offense (*North Carolina* v. *Pearce,* 1969). Double jeopardy does not apply, however, unless an individual has been previously placed in jeopardy. Police arrests, searches, interrogations, identifications, and prosecutorial informations and indictments are not viewed as placing one in jeopardy. Only when a trial jury is sworn or when the first witness takes the oath in a non-jury trial does jeopardy "attach," meaning that the accused is placed in jeopardy.

The prohibition against double jeopardy is not absolute. Under some specified circumstances, an accused may be placed on trial again, despite an earlier acquittal, conviction, or mistrial. Whether a second trial is permissible depends on which party, the prosecution or the defense, requests the new trial or accounts for the need to have the case retried. To understand when and why a reprosecution of an offense will be allowed, it is necessary to consider the specific disposition of the first trial, whether through mistrial, acquittal, or conviction.

A mistrial is the judicial termination of a criminal case without an ultimate jury or court decision regarding guilt or innocence. When at the conclusion of the evidence a jury cannot reach a verdict of either guilt or innocence, the judge is obliged to dismiss it as hung and declare a mistrial. A judge may also declare a mistrial at an earlier stage if in the interest of public justice there is a "manifest necessity" for the discontinuation of the ongoing proceeding (*United States* v. *Perez,* 1824). A mistrial may also be required where some members of the jury die or become seriously ill either during the trial or the jury deliberations. Once a mistrial is declared through no fault of the prosecution, the state may seek a retrial, despite the earlier attachment of jeopardy (*Abney* v. *United States,* 1977).

Once a defendant is acquitted, any retrial is barred. Acquittal can be manifested by a jury's or judge's not-guilty verdict at the conclusion of the trial or the defendant's discharge by the judge prior to or during trial. A discharge based on a judicial determination negating guilt, such as a finding of insanity or entrapment, will bar reprosecution.

When a trial ends in a conviction, retrial on the same charges is generally barred. The prosecution, furthermore, is prevented from charging the previously convicted offender with a more serious connected offense. Once an accused, for example, is indicted for second-degree murder and is convicted of the lesser crime of manslaughter, he or she may never be tried again for first- or second-degree murder of the same victim. The failure of the original indictment or information to charge a higher offense and the jury's finding of yet a lesser charge prevent the state from going back to a potentially more severe prosecution (*Brown* v. *Ohio,* 1977).

If the convicted person, however, chooses to appeal and prevails, a new trial may be ordered at the discretion of the appellate judge. Such a retrial is not viewed as constituting jeopardy, because it is attributed to the voluntary action of the accused. If the defendant's appeal results in a reversal of the conviction, the prosecution is not barred from further appealing that decision if the reversal is based on an error in the proceedings. Such prosecutorial action is viewed not as the pursuit of a new finding of guilt but as a request for the reinstatement of the original verdict (*United States* v. *Ball,* 1896). If, however, the reversal is based on a judicial determination that there is not sufficient evidence to merit conviction, reprosecution will be disallowed (*Burks* v. *United States,* 1978).

Prosecution for two or more separate crimes one of which is viewed as a lesser included offense of the other is also barred by the double-jeopardy clause. To determine whether two separate crimes exist or whether one crime is the lesser of a larger offense, the court must decide "whether each . . . [crime] requires proof of an additional fact which the other does not" (*Blockburger* v. *United States,* 1932). An accused thus cannot be tried, based on the same incident, for the crime of possession of narcotics as well as the crime of possession of narcotics with intent to sell. Since all elements of the former crime are included in the latter, the crime of possession is viewed as a lesser included offense.

A major exception to the prohibition against double jeopardy comes into play when the same acts of the defendant violate both state and federal law. Since the states and the federal government are considered separate sovereignties, each may undertake prosecution for the violation of its laws without confronting the double-jeopardy safeguards. For the assassination of specified federal officials, for example, an accused may be tried separately under federal and under state laws (*Abbate* v. *United States,* 1959). In practice, however, neither the state nor the federal government usually choose to duplicate the expense, time, and effort in pursuing separate prosecutions based on the same offending act. Approximately half the states, moreover, have passed legislation barring such repetitive, although constitutionally permissible, double prosecutions.

One remaining double-jeopardy problem concerns the permissibility of multiple prosecutions and trials for a series of factually related yet legally distinct crimes. An offender charged with the robbery of several victims at the same place and time may be prosecuted separately for each without violating the double-jeopardy clause. However, the offender's multiple prosecutions may be barred under the related doctrine of "collateral estoppel." Borrowed from civil, as distinct from criminal, procedure, this doctrine is designed to protect the accused against unduly burdensome prosecutions. If one accused of such multiple robberies is acquitted in the first trial because of the failure of proof of the suspect's presence at the scene of the crime, the prosecution cannot again prosecute for the robbery of a second or other victims at a subsequent trial (*Ashe* v. *Swenson,* 1970).

Sentencing. After the return of a guilty verdict by the jury or a conviction by a judge, the criminal process reaches its ultimate stage: sentencing, or the imposition of sanctions on the convicted offender. Sentencing may take place immediately after the jury's or judge's verdict or at a later, separate sentencing hearing. The defendant does not have a constitutional right to a separate adversarial sentencing proceeding. Moreover, although the defendant's Sixth Amendment right to counsel at sentencing has been recognized (*Mempa* v. *Rhay,* 1967), many other procedural safeguards afforded at trial, including the right to confront and cross-examine witnesses, do not extend beyond the trial into the sentencing stage (*Williams* v. *New York*, 1949).

Judges exercise wide procedural discretion at sentencing hearings. Often they rely on reports prepared by probation officers and containing uncontested and unverified information gathered from prosecution and defense witnesses, victims, the offender's neighbors, and even unidentified informants. These probation reports need not be made available to the accused and his counsel, who are therefore in no position to contest or explain them.

Although a separate sentencing hearing is not constitutionally mandated, the sentencing judge may hold a sentencing hearing and permit the opposing parties to review all or some of the reports before the court. Some jurisdictions allow the defendant at such hearings to present witnesses and other evidence in an effort to mitigate the sentence. In most states the convicted offender is merely asked if he or she wishes to address the court with regard to the imposition of the sentence, without any further effort on the part of the court to widen the sentencing inquiry.

Where the accused is subject to particularly harsh sanctions under special laws, such as those applicable to habitual offenders, the sentencing procedure may take the form of a trial and be accompanied by many of the procedural protections afforded at trial. Several jurisdictions impose harsher penalties not only on habitual offenders but also on dangerous offenders, sex offenders, and drug-dependent offenders. At the sentencing of such offenders, the prosecution must establish additional facts, such as habitual criminality, which are viewed as prejudicial and excludable at the original trial. When such new evidentiary materials are presented at sentencing, the defendant is afforded most of the procedural safeguards available at trial, including the right to confront and cross-examine witnesses, to introduce evidence, and to be heard in self-defense (*Specht* v. *Patterson*, 1967).

Sentencing in death-penalty cases carries even greater procedural safeguards for the defendant because of the severity of the penalty and the fear of error. A defendant sentenced to death may challenge the sentencing procedures, under both the constitutional requirement of due process and prohibition of cruel and unusual punishment, if the convicted individual believes the sentence was imposed arbitrarily. A jury, which is asked to make recommendations with regard to the imposition of the death penalty, must articulate the aggravating and mitigating circumstances considered by it. In addition, a defendant sentenced to death is entitled to examine presentence reports, including any confidential sections, and must be afforded an opportunity to appeal the sentence on the basis of a sentencing record setting forth the court's reasons for imposing the death penalty (*Gardner* v. *Florida*, 1977).

Appeal and Habeas Corpus. The United States Constitution does not specify an offender's right to an appeal. Sentences in most courts are not subject to appeal, and the judge need not state orally or in writing the reasons for imposing a particular sentence. In jurisdictions that allow appeals, the judge is usually required to include a statement in the record to explain the court's choice of the particular sentence, and this pronouncement can later serve as a basis for appeal.

An indirect and increasingly utilized method of appeal open to those convicted of a crime is the writ of habeas corpus, recognized in Article I, Section 9 of the United States Constitution. Originally designed as a remedy against arbitrary detention practices prevailing in the common law, the writ orders any person responsible for the custody of a prisoner to bring the latter before a judge to determine the lawfulness of the confinement. The writ of habeas corpus may be served on any individual charged with the administration of detention facilities, be he a prison warden, jailer, parole officer, or probation officer. The petitioner for the writ may allege unlawful detention by either federal or state authorities. A petitioner confined for a federal crime must address the petition to a federal court, but if convicted of a state crime, the petitioner may seek relief in either a federal or state court.

To assert unlawful detention, the petitioner must first establish that he or she is "in custody." Custody, for this purpose, may be imprisonment, parole, or probation (*Jones* v. *Cunningham*, 1963). The petitioner has the further burden of proving the detention to be unlawful.

Prior to challenging a state detention in a federal court, the petitioner must have exhausted all available state remedies. If the appeal has not been taken as far as possible within the state judicial system, the federal court will refrain from considering the petition, in order to afford every opportunity to the state courts to remedy the asserted violation (*Ex parte Hawk*, 1944).

The federal court holding a habeas corpus hearing must abide by any findings of fact made by the state trial court, unless the federal judge determines the petitioner was not granted a full and fair state trial. In granting a writ of habeas corpus to one confined on a state sentence, the federal court must find, furthermore, that the state violated the prisoner's federal constitutional rights (*Stone* v. *Powell*, 1976). If the federal court finds, for example, that the state denied the petitioner's Fourteenth Amendment right to due process by allowing a racially discriminatory jury to hear his case, the writ may be issued.

A state prisoner who petitions a federal court but has failed previously to comply with the state procedures for asserting federal constitutional claims will have an additional burden to meet at the federal habeas corpus hearing. Under the "cause and prejudice" standard, the petitioner will be required to show not only a violation of federal constitutional rights but also satisfactory reasons for the previous noncompliance with state procedural requirements. Should a petitioner in federal court, for example, assert a state violation of Fifth Amendment rights, it would be necessary to explain to the federal tribunal why the violation was not raised at the initial trial and to establish prejudice by virtue of the state violation.

The increasing burdens that resort to the writ of habeas corpus have placed on the federal judiciary in recent decades have produced efforts to curtail this remedy. Not only have many scholars and policymakers expressed their distaste for this indirect method of appeal, but the Supreme Court also has endeavored to restrict the availability of this ancient relief, as in *Engle* v. *Isaac* (1982).

ADEQUACIES AND INADEQUACIES OF AMERICAN PROCEDURE

The American criminal process is committed to the adversary persuasion and subjected to a complex system of checks and balances. It has been divided, furthermore, into three stages for the purpose of determining the character and intensity of the safeguards required at the vari-

ous points of the process. Courts and scholars have differentiated between the investigatory, the adjudicatory, and the postadjudicatory stages, endowing the defendant in each with a different degree of constitutional safeguards.

The investigatory stage, the earliest of the three, is thought to include police surveillance, search and seizure, and grand jury investigations. The burden of proof placed on the police and prosecution during this stage is to show probable cause and reasonableness, as specified in the Fourth Amendment. Resort to uncontested and hearsay evidence is tolerated at this point. In the conduct of the investigatory stage, moreover, notice to the suspect need not necessarily be given, hearings may be conducted ex parte (without the presence of the suspect), and the suspect's protection against self-incrimination and the right to counsel are usually considered inapplicable.

Once the adjudicatory stage commences or is being approached (through the initiation of custodial interrogation or through the return of an indictment or information), the process is considered "critical" and requires the full panoply of constitutional rights for the accused. This means that no interrogation or identification procedures involving the accused may be carried out without the presence of counsel. Moreover, the accused's protection against self-incrimination must be scrupulously observed, and complete adherence to the adversary process is required. At this stage, hearsay may not be relied on and the finding of guilt requires proof "beyond a reasonable doubt" (a standard developed in the common law).

Once adjudication is terminated with a verdict of guilty, the process once more changes into a less procedure-laden style. Throughout sentencing and the correctional stages that follow (in such matters as offender classification, discipline, probation, and parole), the adversary methods give way to less-stringent and less-protective procedures. Presence of counsel is not always necessary, cross-examination may not be permitted, and the other formal evidentiary requirements of the adjudicatory stage will not be observed.

Although this classification of the criminal process into three categories or stages has been accepted without much criticism and although the Supreme Court has not only refined it repeatedly but also relied on it to justify diverse procedural standards, its very theoretical foundations are in question. There is no adequate policy or constitutional support for the proposition that only the middle segment of the criminal process requires strict adherence to adversary standards. To justify the existing differentiation by insisting that the issue of guilt or innocence in the adjudicatory stage is more critical than the question of specific sanctions in the sentencing stage is to emphasize form and tradition over substance and contemporary realities. Moreover, the extension of some constitutional safeguards, such as the right to counsel, to certain investigatory stages that are tagged "critical" but not to others is difficult to justify. Why counsel is mandated to protect the rights of the accused at a postindictment identification but not at a preindictment parade has not been satisfactorily explained.

To this day, the question of whether the whole range of criminal procedure should be treated more uniformly and consistently remains unaddressed. The existing pattern of distinct checks and balances designed for the various stages of the criminal process is not only doctrinally unsupported but also confusing to both citizens and criminal justice officials. The current patchwork quilt is based on some historical foundations. But in the face of the contemporary quest for greater effectiveness in law enforcement and criminal justice, the diversity of the criminal process and its ever-changing flux present an unmatched and confusing obstacle course.

Observing the fragmentary character of American procedure, where only a minute segment of all committed and reported crimes come to a final and satisfactory closing, one should not be surprised by the popular cynical assertion that in America crime does indeed pay. The complex and sometimes inconsistent standards required of the police; the contemporary laxity of bail, which often releases habitual offenders to the community pending trial; and the judiciary's permission for appeals and particularly habeas corpus to become the new tool for the denial of guilt have all contributed to the inadequacies of criminal justice in America. Public confidence in the state's ability to maintain law and order has been gravely shaken. Vigilantism is on the rise. But for every citizen activist willing to take the law into his or her hands, there are scores of unfortunate victims who merely groan in the face of the greatest contemporary invasion of privacy and the quality of life in America—rampant crime, which threatens a citizen's life, person, home, and business.

Reform must concentrate on crafting a new procedural balance between the state as the accuser and the individual as the suspect and accused. In particular, there is a need for legislative and self-regulatory action to formulate streamlined prescriptive standards for the operation of criminal justice agencies, as well as for the training of their personnel. The record of the past, in which the courts have been relied upon to supply post facto remedies for defective or unlawful police and prosecutorial practices, has created too much havoc with both the citizenry and the agencies of law. The future of American criminal justice requires not only a new balancing of citizen and community rights and duties but also a clear and reliable codification of this balance by the legislative and executive branches. Criminal justice's current erratic practice of awaiting the judiciary's delphic decisions must give way to a more permanent and predictable code of standards that both citizens and criminal justice officials could be made to learn and master—for the common welfare of the Republic.

CASES

Abbate v. United States, 359 U.S. 187 (1959)
Abney v. United States, 431 U.S. 651 (1977)
Alderman v. United States, 394 U.S. 165 (1969)
Ashe v. Swenson, 397 U.S. 436 (1970)
Barker v. Wingo, 407 U.S. 514 (1972)
Benton v. Maryland, 395 U.S. 784 (1969)
Berger v. New York, 388 U.S. 41 (1967)
Blockburger v. United States, 284 U.S. 299 (1932)
Brewer v. Williams, 430 U.S. 387 (1977)
Brown v. Ohio, 432 U.S. 161 (1977)
Burch v. Louisiana, 441 U.S. 130 (1979)
Burks v. United States, 437 U.S. 1 (1978)
Carroll v. United States, 267 U.S. 132 (1925)
Chambers v. Maroney, 399 U.S. 42 (1970)
Chimel v. California, 395 U.S. 752 (1969)
Coolidge v. New Hampshire, 403 U.S. 443 (1971)
Costello v. United States, 350 U.S. 359 (1956)
Dalia v. United States, 441 U.S. 238 (1979)
Delaware v. Prouse, 440 U.S. 648 (1979)
Dorman v. United States, 435 F.2d 385 (D.C. Cir. 1970)
Duncan v. Louisiana, 391 U.S. 145 (1968)
Edwards v. Arizona, 451 U.S. 477 (1981)
Elkins v. United States, 364 U.S. 206 (1960)
Engle v. Isaac, 456 U.S. 107 (1982)

Frisbie v. Collins, 342 U.S. 519 (1952)
Gardner v. Florida, 430 U.S. 349 (1977)
Gerstein v. Pugh, 420 U.S. 103 (1975)
Ex parte Hawk, 321 U.S. 114 (1944)
Hurtado v. California, 110 U.S. 516 (1884)
Illinois v. Gates, 462 U.S. 213 (1983)
Jones v. Cunningham, 371 U.S. 236 (1963)
Katz v. United States, 389 U.S. 347 (1967)
Ker v. California, 374 U.S. 23 (1963)
Ker v. Illinois, 119 U.S. 436 (1886)
Klopfer v. North Carolina, 386 U.S. 213 (1967)
McNabb v. United States, 318 U.S. 332 (1943)
Mallory v. United States, 354 U.S. 449 (1957)
Malloy v. Hogan, 378 U.S. 1 (1964)
Manson v. Brathwaite, 432 U.S. 98 (1977)
Mapp v. Ohio, 367 U.S. 643 (1961)
Mempa v. Rhay, 389 U.S. 128 (1967)
Michigan v. Summers, 452 U.S. 692 (1981)
Miranda v. Arizona, 384 U.S. 436 (1966)
Nix v. Williams, 467 U.S. 431 (1984)
North Carolina v. Butler, 441 U.S. 369 (1979)
North Carolina v. Pearce, 395 U.S. 711 (1969)
Olmstead v. United States, 277 U.S. 438 (1928)
Oregon v. Elstad, 470 U.S. 289 (1985)
Orozco v. Texas, 394 U.S. 324 (1969)
Payton v. New York, 445 U.S. 573 (1980)
Rhode Island v. Innis, 446 U.S. 291 (1980)
Schilb v. Kuebel, 404 U.S. 357 (1971)
Shadwick v. City of Tampa, 407 U.S. 345 (1972)
Simmons v. United States, 390 U.S. 377 (1968)
Specht v. Patterson, 386 U.S. 605 (1967)
Steagald v. United States, 451 U.S. 204 (1981)
Stone v. Powell, 428 U.S. 465 (1976)
Stovall v. Denno, 388 U.S. 293 (1967)
Terry v. Ohio, 392 U.S. 1 (1968)
United States v. Ball, 163 U.S. 662 (1896)
United States v. Calandra, 414 U.S. 338 (1974)
United States v. Leon, 468 U.S. 897 (1984)
United States v. Nepstead, 424 F.2d 269 (9th Cir. 1970)
United States v. Perez, 9 Wheaton 579 (1824)
United States v. Robinson, 414 U.S. 218 (1973)
United States v. United States District Court, 407 U.S. 297 (1972)
United States v. Wade, 388 U.S. 218 (1967)
United States v. Watson, 423 U.S. 411 (1976)
Walder v. United States, 347 U.S. 62 (1954)
Weeks v. United States, 232 U.S. 383 (1914)
Williams v. New York, 337 U.S. 241 (1949)
Wolf v. Colorado, 338 U.S. 25 (1949)
Wong Sun v. United States, 371 U.S. 471 (1963)

BIBLIOGRAPHY

Albert W. Alshuler, "Plea Bargaining and Its History," in *Columbia Law Review*, 79 (1979), presents an excellent overview of the plea-bargaining phenomenon. A. G. Amsterdam, "Speedy Criminal Trials: Rights and Remedies," in *Stanford Law Review*, 27 (1975), explores the transformation of this Sixth Amendment right. Edwin D. Driver, "Confessions and the Social Psychology of Coercion," in *Harvard Law Review*, 82 (1968), surveys police tactics and the inherently coercive nature of questioning.

William Geller, "Enforcing the Fourth Amendment: The Exclusionary Rule and Its Alternatives," in *Washington University Law Quarterly* (1975), is an important discussion of legal doctrines surrounding the suppression of evidence. B. J. George, Jr., "From Warren to Burger to Chance: Future Trends in the Administration of Criminal Justice," in *Criminal Law Bulletin*, 12 (1976), is a broad analysis of criminal procedure cases of the period. Erwin N. Griswold, *Search and Seizures: A Dilemma for the Supreme Court* (1975), is a scholarly treatment of Fourth Amendment law in this important area.

Wayne R. La Fave, "The Prosecutor's Discretion in the United States," in *American Journal of Comparative Law*, 18 (1970), is a comprehensive overview of prosecutorial discretion. Wayne R. La Fave and Jerolde H. Israel, *Criminal Procedure* (1985), is an indispensable and comprehensive study. Edmund F. McGarrell and Timothy J. Flanagan, eds., *Sourcebook of Criminal Justice Statistics*, published annually, is an essential compilation. Paul J. Mishkin, "Forward, the High Court, the Great Writ, and Due Process of Time and Law," in *Harvard Law Review*, 79 (1965), focuses on the applicability of due process standards to habeas corpus petitions.

Walker V. Shaefer, "Unresolved Issues in the Law of Double Jeopardy," in *California Law Review*, 58 (1970), discusses forcing states to raise all claims against a defendant in a single trial. Jerome H. Skolnick, *Justice Without Trial: Law Enforcement in Democratic Society* (1966), is a scholarly treatment of the tension between law enforcement and individual rights. Thomas Weigand, "Continental Cures for American Ailments: European Criminal Procedure as a Model for Law Reform," in *Crimes and Justice*, 2 (1980), provides an important critical analysis of the American criminal justice system. Charles H. Whitebread and Christofer Slobogin, *Criminal Procedure* (1986), provides an excellent understanding of the system.

[*See also* ADVERSARY SYSTEM; CRIMINAL JUSTICE SYSTEM; CRIMINAL LAW; DUE PROCESS OF LAW; PLEA BARGAINING; POLICE; PROSECUTORS; SENTENCING ALTERNATIVES; *and* STATE CONSTITUTIONAL LAW.]

DUE PROCESS OF LAW

David Fellman

THE concept of due process of law is firmly lodged in the text of the Constitution of the United States. The Fifth Amendment of the Constitution provides that "no person shall . . . be deprived of life, liberty, or property, without due process of law." This provision applies only to the national government (*Barron* v. *Baltimore,* 1833). The states, however, are limited by the express language of the Fourteenth Amendment, which stipulates "nor shall any State deprive any person of life, liberty, or property, without due process of law." Thus, the due process guaranty, which is part of the supreme law of the land, is binding upon all public officials, national and state.

The due process clauses must be understood in the light of several basic doctrines of American constitutional theory. The first is that the Constitution is a law and not a mere collection of theoretical or abstract political principles. The second is that the Constitution, as declared in Article VI, is the supreme law of the land, binding upon all public officials at every level of authority. The third is that the United States Supreme Court is the final judge of the meaning of that supreme law. That the courts have the authority to hold unenforceable any statutes or executive acts that they find in contravention of the Constitution (the power of judicial review) is the key to the American system of public law.

In addition, every state of the American union has a bill of rights, most of which include due process clauses stated in much the same language as that employed in the federal Constitution. Indeed, even where a state constitution does not explicitly contain a due process clause (as in the case of Wisconsin), the concept is embraced within the state's constitutional law.

The definition of due process is one of the chief problems in American constitutional law, for its character is such that it qualifies most other constitutional guaranties. Due process applies to a wide range of issues, including the administration of justice, criminal law, police power, taxation, administrative procedures, corporate enterprises, and eminent domain. It has been observed that the study of due process is *de rebus omnibus* (Hough, 222). American constitutions do not spell out the meaning of due process of law. The problem of definition has been left to the courts as they decide specific cases.

ENGLISH ORIGINS AND USAGES

The origin of the phrase "due process of law" is generally assigned to the Magna Charta, which the rebellious English nobility compelled King John to accept at Runnymede in 1215. In the Great Charter, the king was compelled to agree to respect certain ancient and important rights and privileges of the feudal nobility. The Great Charter contained an important guaranty that was destined to develop into a mighty doctrine: the king agreed that "no freeman shall be taken or imprisoned or disseised or exiled or in any way destroyed, nor will we go upon him nor send upon him, except by the lawful judgment of his peers and by the law of the land." Since the expression "by the law of the land" *(per legem terrae)* was merely part of a treaty between king and nobles guaranteeing certain procedural rights of a technical character—that is, judicial proceedings according to the nature of the case—there was no suggestion of trial by jury or any other popular liberty. But with time, Magna Charta acquired greater significance as successive kings reissued or reconfirmed its principles.

DUE PROCESS OF LAW

The phrase "due process of law" was first used in 1354, in the Statute of Westminster. There Edward III affirmed "that no man of what estate or condition that he be, shall be put out of land or tenement, nor taken, nor imprisoned, nor disinherited, nor put to death, without being brought to answer by due process of law." Thus, "due process of law" and "law of the land" came to mean the same thing.

The British constitution was transformed by the revolutions of 1640 and 1688. It was this new constitution that was so masterfully expounded by Sir William Blackstone, who published his influential *Commentaries on the Laws of England* in 1765–1769. In that great treatise, the due process clause acquired a firm position in the English legal system. Blackstone said, "It were endless to enumerate all the affirmative acts of parliament wherein justice is directed to be done according to the law of the land: and what that law is, every subject knows, or may know if he pleases; for it depends not upon the arbitrary will of any judge, but is permanent, fixed, and unchangeable, unless by authority of parliament."

The limitations of Magna Charta applied to the king and not to Parliament. Since Parliament is legally omnipotent, its decisions are not amenable to the judgment of the courts, and even today the courts do not have the power to refuse to enforce acts of Parliament on any constitutional ground, including due process grounds.

Even so, English judges can and do resort to the concept of natural justice, which is an aspect of natural law, especially where the absence of specific statutory directives affords them scope for the affirmation of general principles of justice. Of course, English judges are bound by what Parliament declares, but as A. L. Goodhart has observed, "By a convenient fiction it [the House of Lords] assumes that Parliament always intends that its statutes will accord with natural justice; no statute will therefore be construed to be retrospective or to deprive a person of a fair hearing or to prevent freedom of speech unless Parliament has so provided in the most specific terms."

The concept of natural justice serves various due process purposes in English courts. It is well established, for example, that the principle of natural justice requires administrative boards to give hearings to affected parties. The concept of natural justice has also been applied by English judges in criminal cases.

In many ways, the concept of natural justice is comparable to the American doctrine of due process of law. The English barrister E. B. Simmons wrote that the concept comes to three points essentially: "(1) No man may seem to act as judge in his own cause. (2) Every accused person has a right to hear the whole case against him. (3) No man may be condemned unheard." Of course, this is not the whole of due process as construed by American courts, but it is a good part of it. What gives the doctrine of due process of law greater force in the United States than in England is that American courts may employ it to declare federal and state statutes and administrative acts to be unenforceable because of their unconstitutionality. To be sure, these courts do not repeal or expunge an unconstitutional statute; they merely refuse to enforce it.

THE RISE OF DUE PROCESS IN AMERICAN COURTS

It is settled beyond question that the principle of due process came from England to America as part of the common law and has been a fundamental rule in the judicial system of every state. It is clear that in their legislation, the American colonists gave evidence of the importance they attached to the due process notion, for particularly in the later days of the colonial empire, the words of Magna Charta were closely paraphrased. Later on, in the more controversial stage of the prerevolutionary debate, the due process concept was frequently restated and emphasized. Thus, in 1774, the First Continental Congress declared "that the respective colonies are entitled to the common law of England, and more especially to the great and inestimable privilege of being tried by their peers of the vicinage, according to the course of that law."

While no specific mention was made of the right to due process of law in the Declaration of Independence, which was drawn up by the Second Continental Congress in 1776, the "due process of law" clause received specific treatment in the first state constitutions. Thus, the Virginia Bill of Rights, which was drafted by George Mason in 1776 and afterward made a part of the first Virginia Constitution, provided "that no man be deprived of his liberty, except by the law of the land or the judgment of his peers." Seven other states followed suit. By the time the federal Bill of Rights was added to the Constitution with the adoption of the first ten amendments in 1791, eight of the thirteen states had constitutions that contained due process clauses. Today almost all state constitutions include such clauses.

Section 1 of the Fourteenth Amendment added a new weapon to those available to American courts involved in cases dealing with the limits on governmental power, by providing that no state shall "deprive any person of life, liberty, or property, without due process of law." However, despite its enormous importance today, Section 1 was little debated in Congress.

Not only did the members of the Thirty-Ninth Congress who participated in the debate on Section 1 of the Fourteenth Amendment fail to spell out the specific meaning of due process of law, but it is equally true that the United States Supreme Court has never committed itself to a precise, all-embracing definition. In the leading case of *Davidson* v. *New Orleans* (1878), Justice Miller expressed the conviction that it was neither possible nor wise to attempt a definition of due process "at once perspicuous, comprehensive and satisfactory." He went on to say, "There is wisdom, we think, in the ascertaining of the intent and application of such an important phrase in the Federal Constitution, by the gradual process of judicial inclusion and exclusion, as the cases presented for decision shall require, with the reasoning on which such decisions may be founded."

As Justice John Marshall Harlan wrote in a distinguished dissenting opinion in *Poe* v. *Ullman* (1961), the Fourteenth Amendment was intended "to embrace those rights 'which are . . . *fundamental;* which belong . . . to the citizens of all free governments.'" He went on to say,

> Due Process has not been reduced to any formula; its content cannot be determined by reference to any code. The best that can be said is that through the course of this Court's decisions it has represented the balance which our Nation, built upon postulates of respect for the liberty of the individual, has struck between that liberty and the demands of organized society.

Similarly, Justice Felix Frankfurter, who thought deeply on this subject, once declared that "due process of law is a summarized constitutional guarantee of respect for those personal immunities which, as Mr. Justice Cardozo twice wrote for the Court, are 'so rooted in the traditions and conscience of our people as to be ranked as fundamental,' . . . or are 'implicit in the concept of ordered liberty.'" As Justice Harlan argued, so Justice Frankfurter pointed out that "the vague contours of the Due Process Clause do not leave judges at large. We may not draw on our merely personal and private notions and disregard the limits that bind judges in their judicial function. Even though the concept of due process of law is not final and fixed, these limits are derived from considerations that are fused in the whole nature of our judicial process" (*Rochin* v. *California,* 1952).

Clearly, American courts, in deciding concrete cases, have construed due process of law by the judicial process of gradual inclusion and exclusion on the basis of traditional values, philosophy, logic, ethical principles, and a large measure of social expediency. The courts have always maintained that this approach conforms with the elastic nature of the common law. In a case involving the problem of self-incrimination, *Twining* v. *New Jersey* (1908), the Court held that due process is to be construed in the light of the circumstances of each case, without reference to a particular status of the law in the past. Justice William H. Moody wrote,

> It does not follow that a procedure settled in English law at the time of the emigration, and brought to this country and practiced by our ancestors, is an essential element of due process of law. If that were so, the procedure of the first half of the seventeenth century would be fastened upon the American jurisprudence like a straight-jacket, only to be unloosed by constitutional amendment.

Manifestly, the sheer weight of long-established historical practice makes a difference, but history is an aid to construction and does not supply an imperative guide. Due process of law is basically a flexible process because conditions change. Thus, as a general rule, American judges do not attempt to define the concept of due process of law with any precision. It is considered an impracticable thing to try to do. Indeed, the New Jersey Supreme Court once observed that "it certainly would be presumptuous, to attempt to frame a definition of 'due process of law,' which shall embrace all and only all the cases which a just mind will perceive to be included in it" (*Moore* v. *State,* 1881).

Even so, there have been a number of attempts to define due process of law, at least in a general way, although their very generality seems to substitute vagueness for vagueness. Thus, in a famous statement expressed as counsel in presenting *Dartmouth College* v. *Woodward* (1819), Daniel Webster asserted, "By the law of the land is most clearly intended the general law; a law which hears before it condemns; which proceeds upon inquiry, and renders judgment only after trial. The meaning is, that every citizen shall hold his life, liberty, property, and immunities, under the protection of the general rules which govern society." To be sure, this is by no means a definition utterly devoid of meaning, but its lack of specificity reduces its value in a considerable measure.

The position that has found the largest measure of acceptance by the justices of the nation's highest court was that which Justice Frankfurter spelled out so eloquently in his concurring opinion in *Joint Anti-Fascist Refugee Committee* v. *McGrath* (1951):

> Representing a profound attitude of fairness between man and man, and more particularly between the individual and government, "due process" is compounded of history, reason, the past course of decisions, and stout confidence in the strength of the democratic faith which we profess. Due process is not a mechanical instrument. It is not a yardstick. It is a process. It is a delicate process of adjustment inescapably involving the exercise of judgment by those whom the Constitution entrusted with the unfolding of the process. . . . The precise nature of the interest that has been adversely affected, the manner in which this was done, the reasons for doing it, the available alternatives to the procedure that was followed, the protection implicit in the office of the functionary whose conduct is challenged, the balance of hurt complained of and good accomplished—these are some of the considerations that must enter into the judicial judgment.

DUE PROCESS AS FAIR PROCEDURE

Unquestionably, the due process clause of the Fifth Amendment got off to a slow start. The early legal history of the United States bears out the fact that little importance was attached to the due process clause during the formative period of its institutions. All that Justice Joseph Story had to say about the clause when he published the first edition of his treatise on the Constitution in 1833 was the following: "This clause in effect affirms the right of trial according to the process and proceedings of the common law" (vol. 3, 661). Had the clause attained more significance, undoubtedly it would not have escaped the attention of such a learned legal scholar. Thus, in the early years under the Constitution, the due process concept was applied only to secure procedural regularity or fairness and had nothing to do with the adjudication of substantive rights. The early cases dealt with questions of notice, personal service, the right to a hearing, and taxation procedures. Accordingly, the Supreme Court found it easy to define due process in 1855 as merely implying "regular allegations, opportunity to answer and a trial according to some settled course of judicial proceedings" (*Murray* v. *Hoboken Land and Improvement Co.*). Furthermore, since the national government, in the years prior to the Civil War, rarely enacted legislation affecting the basic liberties of the citizen, there was little occasion to invoke broader protection of the Fifth Amendment.

From the point of view of the process considered as a guaranty of procedural regularity or fairness, the principal requirements are adequate notice and a fair hearing. For example, in 1969, in the case of *Sniadach* v. *Family Finance Corp.,* the United States Supreme Court ruled that for a state to permit the freezing of wages in a garnishment proceeding without first giving the debtor notice and a hearing is a violation of fundamental principles of due process. It was asserted that a prejudgment garnishment of this type constituted a taking of property that may impose tremendous hardship on wage earners and their families. In other words, a debtor has a right to notice and a hearing before he can be deprived of the unrestricted use of his property. There are situations, however, where summary action by government may be justified, as in the case of the summary destruction by public officials of spoiled food on the ground that in the case of such a dangerous nuisance, the protection of public health is a more compelling interest than the property owner's right to prior notice and a hearing. Of course, he can get a judicial hearing afterward, but in such cases the public officials involved have very strong good-faith defenses in damage suits (*North American Cold Storage Co.* v. *Chicago,* 1908).

Procedural due process was thoroughly reviewed by the Supreme Court in 1967, in the case of *In re Gault.* This case involved a challenge to the juvenile-court proceedings of the state of Arizona. A fifteen-year-old boy was taken into custody by the police on the charge of having made obscene telephone calls. The Supreme Court ruled that in this case due process had clearly been denied. There had been no notice of charges to the boy or his parents; no counsel was offered or provided; the accused was not warned of his privilege against self-incrimination, and the privilege of silence was not knowingly waived. Moreover, because no witnesses were sworn, the accused had been denied the right of cross-examining his accusers (that is, the right of confrontation), so vitally required to validate a judicial hearing. Said Justice Abe Fortas, "Due process of law is the primary and indispensable foundation of individual freedom. It is the basis and essential term in the social compact which defines the rights of the individual and delimits the powers which the state may exercise." He insisted that the constitutional domestication of juvenile-court proceedings will not damage the procedure for handling juveniles, since it is still possible to deal with juveniles separately from adults under the supervision of the "kindly judge."

The meaning of due process as a guaranty of fundamental fairness in criminal cases involving adults has been explored by the Supreme Court in numerous important decisions. Thus, it is a violation of due process to permit a conviction for a crime where the courtroom was under mob domination (*Moore* v. *Dempsey,* 1923). Similarly, due process means that an accused has a right to be present at every stage of the proceedings, although he may forfeit that right by disorderly, disrespectful, and disruptive behavior in the courtroom (*Illinois* v. *Allen,* 1970) or by voluntary

absence from the courtroom (*Taylor* v. *United States,* 1973). Furthermore, a defendant has been denied due process if he was tried by a judge who had a direct financial stake in the outcome of the case (*Tumey* v. *Ohio,* 1927).

The right to an impartial judge is an essential ingredient of the due process guaranty of fundamental fairness. Similarly, it is a violation of due process to convict a defendant on the basis of no corroborative evidence at all (*Thompson* v. *Louisville,* 1960). Due process also protects the defendant's right to an impartial jury (*Irvin* v. *Dowd,* 1961).

In the celebrated case of *Mooney* v. *Holohan* (1935), the Supreme Court ruled that due process has been denied if the prosecution presented testimony that it knew was perjured. Due process is also violated if the prosecution suppresses evidence in its possession that is favorable to the accused (*Brady* v. *Maryland,* 1963). In short, the prosecution may strike hard blows, but not foul blows.

Whatever else due process assures to the accused, it stands for the proposition that a defendant is entitled to a fair hearing, and the concept of a fair hearing has many dimensions. For example, before being punished for disrupting a legislative sitting, the accused is entitled to a notice of charges and a hearing on the charges (*Groppi* v. *Leslie,* 1972). While there is no mechanical formula for due process, the Court agreed that all the rights accorded to a defendant in a criminal trial are not necessary in legislative contempt proceedings. Even so, notice of charges and an opportunity to reply to them are absolutely fundamental. It was pointed out in *Groppi* that if given a hearing, the putative contemnor might prove mistaken identity or mental incompetence or might offer mitigating circumstances.

Similarly, it is established that an accused is constitutionally entitled to a hearing on the issue of his mental competence to stand trial (*Pate* v. *Robinson,* 1966). Since it is a violation of due process for a state to convict an accused person while he is legally incompetent, the Court held that it follows that state procedures must be adequate to protect this right. The Court has also ruled that it is a denial of due process to revoke a parole without a hearing (*Morrissey* v. *Brewer,* 1972). In addition, a fair hearing means that the presiding judge in a criminal trial has denied due process if, through threatening remarks from the bench, he in effect drove a witness from the stand (*Webb* v. *Texas*, 1972).

The due process requirement of a fair trial is denied if there has been such a clear buildup of prejudice in the community through massive adverse publicity as to raise serious doubts regarding the impartiality of the jury *(Irvin)*. Thus, in a notorious case where a socially prominent doctor was convicted of murdering his wife, the Supreme Court reversed the conviction because, prior to the trial, there had been massive newspaper, radio, and television publicity, which included many matters unfavorable to the defendant that were never presented in court (*Sheppard* v. *Maxwell*, 1966). The Supreme Court ruled that the trial judge had failed to fulfill his duty to protect the defendant from the inherently prejudicial publicity that had saturated the community and to control disruptive influences in the courtroom, which had created an atmosphere of bedlam. Finally, it is to be noted that the right to a fair trial implies the right to a public trial, since due process frowns on the dangers inherent in holding secret trials, which in the past have been instruments for the suppression of political and religious heresies (*In re Oliver*, 1948).

It is well understood, however, that an accused may waive his right to a full trial by entering a plea of guilty, and many defendants do in fact waive their trial rights by making such a plea. But due process has been violated if the plea was not voluntary, and a plea may be regarded as involuntary if the accused did not understand the nature of the constitutional rights he was waiving or the nature of the charge against him (*Henderson* v. *Morgan*, 1976).

A basic requirement of procedural due process is that a court that has given judgment in a case must have had jurisdiction of the case. Lack of jurisdiction clearly negates any decision the court may have made. Thus, in *Kinsella* v. *United States ex rel. Singleton* (1960), the Supreme Court set aside the conviction of a woman who was married to an American soldier and who had been convicted of murder under the Uniform Code of Military Justice by a court-martial sitting in Germany. The Court held that since the accused was not a member of the armed forces, she was not triable by a court-martial, whose jurisdiction has always been based on the status of the accused rather than the nature of the offense.

In addition to the requirement that a court must have proper jurisdiction over cases it tries, procedural due process also assures to a defendant specific notice of charges so that he may know in advance precisely what he has to respond to. Thus, on several occasions the Supreme Court has set aside convictions for violating statutes that were so vaguely worded as not to give adequate notice of just what was forbidden. In the famous case of *Lanzetta* v. *New Jersey* (1939), the Court ruled unconstitutional, on the grounds of vagueness, a state statute that made it a crime to be a "member of a gang." The Court has ruled a number of times that where a statute is so vague that persons of ordinary intelligence can only guess as to its meaning, the statute is invalid for lack of adequate notice. For example, in *Coates* v. *Cincinnati* (1971) the Court ruled unconstitutionally vague a city ordinance that made it a criminal offense for "three or more persons to assemble . . . on any of the sidewalks . . . and there conduct themselves in a manner annoying to persons passing by." It was held that the statute was invalid because it was based upon "an unascertainable standard": because conduct that annoys some people does not annoy others, the ordinance does not specify any standard of conduct at all.

Although most statutes survive the challenge of vagueness, the doctrine that statutes must not be so vague as to provide no ascertainable standard of conduct for individuals, the police, and trial judges still has some vitality. For example, the Supreme Court of Massachusetts ruled invalid a statute making it an offense for one "known to be a thief or a burglar" to act "in a suspicious manner around a store" (*Alegata* v. *Massachusetts*, 1967). However, statutes forbidding "disorderly conduct" are usually upheld by the courts on the grounds that the phrase has acquired a well-established meaning through "common usage and our legal tradition" (*State* v. *Reynaldo*, 1954).

Just as courts and legislative bodies are obliged to observe the fundamental notice and fair-hearing requirements of due process, so are administrative agencies required to observe the amenities of due process of law. For example, before welfare payments can be discontinued by an administrative official, he is obliged to conduct an evidentiary hearing (*Goldberg* v. *Kelly*, 1970). Similarly, students may not be suspended from a public school without some sort of hearing appropriate to the circumstances (*Goss* v. *Lopez,* 1975), and a tenured professor may not be dismissed from the faculty of a state college without a hearing (*Perry* v. *Sindermann,* 1972). It has also been established in many cases that an occupational or professional license may not be revoked by administrative act without due notice and a fair hearing. Speaking generally, administrative agencies must observe various procedural rights, including rights to specific notice of charges, to present evidence and argument, to challenge adverse evidence through cross-examination, to appear with counsel, to have the decision based upon the evidence in the record, and to have a complete record of the proceedings.

In conclusion, it would be appropriate to take note of an observation that Justice Harlan F. Stone made in *Missouri ex rel. Hurwitz* v. *North* (1926):

> The Fourteenth Amendment is concerned with the substance and not with the forms of procedure. . . . The due process clause does not guarantee to a citizen of a state any particular form or method of state procedure. Its requirements are satisfied if he has reasonable notice, and reasonable opportunity to be heard and to present his claim or defense, due regard being had to the nature of the proceedings and the character of the rights which may be affected by it.

SUBSTANTIVE DUE PROCESS

As long as the courts construed due process as a guaranty only of procedural rights, particularly those rights which had achieved a well-defined place in the common law, the judicial interpretation of due process did not stir up much public controversy. In fact, it has always been felt that judges are especially competent experts insofar as procedural law is concerned. As Justice Robert H. Jackson explained in his dissenting opinion in *Shaughnessy* v. *United States ex rel. Mezei* (1953),

> Procedural fairness, if not all that originally was meant by due process of law, is at least what it most uncompromisingly requires. Procedural due process is more elemental and less flexible than substantive due process. It yields less to the times, varies less with conditions, and defers much less to legislative judgment. Insofar as it is technical law, it must be a specialized responsibility within the competence of the judiciary on which they do not bend before political branches of the Government, as they should on matters of policy which comprise substantive law.

Due process of law serves to protect two important sets of rights, the right to procedural fairness and the right to be free from arbitrary or unreasonable regulations by government. The latter right is called a substantive right, since no procedural question may be involved. For example, even where there had been no procedural flaw, a holding that the rates imposed on a public utility by a regulatory commission or legislative body are so low as to amount to taking of private property involves a substantive right.

A new point of view that extended the concept of due process to include judicial scrutiny of the substantive content of law as well as procedural rights appeared gradually in the state courts. The New York Court of Appeals, one of the nation's most prestigious state appellate courts, began to break new ground in the mid-nineteenth century in several important decisions. In 1856, in *Wynehamer* v. *New York,* the New York Court of Appeals ruled that a statute that established prohibition constituted an unconstitutional taking of the property of those already in the liquor business, contrary to due process of law. In other words, the court ruled that the substantive right to own and sell property lawfully acquired was protected by the due process clause of the state constitution. The court held that the legislature does not have an absolute discretion to subvert property rights, that all property rights are inviolable, and that while the legislature may regulate the liquor business, it cannot confiscate and destroy property lawfully acquired. "All property," the court declared, "is equally sacred in the view of the constitution." The legislature is not omnipotent, the court observed, and the due process clause forbids it to exercise arbitrary power.

When the United States Supreme Court was first called upon to construe the due process clause of the Fourteenth Amendment, in the celebrated *Slaughterhouse Cases* (1873), the Court backed away from construing due process broadly, by ruling constitutional an act of the

New Orleans City Council that gave a virtual monopoly to one slaughterhouse, thus putting many independent butchers and slaughterers out of business. In denying their appeal, the Court ruled that Section 1 of the Fourteenth Amendment was designed to uphold only the newborn rights of blacks, not those of anyone else.

This position had a short life. The rapid increase of the population and the growth of the economy, particularly after the panic of 1873 had run its course, created the need for more social control by means of governmental regulation through the expansion of the state's police power. Judicial intervention was soon to follow, and in 1884, in *Hurtado* v. *California,* wherein the Court sustained the validity of a state statute that abolished indictment by grand jury in the state courts over due process objections, the Court warned, "But it is not to be supposed that these legislative powers are absolute and despotic, and that the amendment prescribing due process of law is too vague and indefinite to operate as a practical restraint. It is not every act, legislative in form, that is law. Law is something more than mere will exerted as an act of power."

The floodgates opened a few years later, when cases arose that challenged as arbitrary the decisions of the burgeoning state railroad or public utility commissions. In the *Railroad Commission Cases* (1886) the Supreme Court served notice that it is not to be inferred that the power of regulation is without limit:

> This power to regulate is not a power to destroy, and limitation is not the equivalent of confiscation. Under pretence of regulating fares and freights, the State cannot require a railroad corporation to carry persons or property without reward; neither can it do that which in law amounts to a taking of private property for public use without just compensation, or without due process of law.

In the earliest railroad rate cases, while the Court asserted the power of judicial review of rates, it exercised that power only as to those rates which were so low as to be regarded as confiscatory in their effect upon the railroads. The next logical step was taken in *Chicago, Milwaukee & St. Paul Railway* v. *Minnesota* (1890), wherein the Court declared invalid a certain rate

that, although it allowed a net profit to the railroad, did not permit a profit large enough to constitute what the justices thought was a fair return on the investment. Above all, the Court made it clear that "the question of the reasonableness of a rate of charge for transportation by a railroad company, involving, as it does, the element of reasonableness both as regards the company and as regards the public, is eminently a question for judicial investigation, requiring due process of law for its determination." The Court therefore held that because the statute, as construed by Minnesota's highest court, made rates determined by the state railroad commission final, conclusive, and unreviewable by the courts, it denied due process of law. To put it somewhat differently, the right of a judicial investigation of rates determined by an administrative agency is assured to the railroad by due process of law. A flood of appeals began to pour into the calendars of the United States Supreme Court. From then on, the courts were willing to look into the underlying reasons for statutes and to make judgments regarding the substantive quality of legislation. In the years 1890–1900, the United States Supreme Court heard 197 appeals that invoked the due process clauses.

Thus, due process of law became something more than a guaranty of procedural regularity. The Supreme Court opened the door to independent judicial review of the reasonableness of legislation in the light of conditions and values as understood by the judges. In short, the courts became the judges of legislative wisdom. In a sense, the Supreme Court became, in fact if not in theory, a third branch of the legislature—indeed, a sort of perpetual constitutional convention. In the due process cases, the judicial veto became judicial supremacy. A striking example of the construction of due process to defeat important social legislation was the decision of the New York Court of Appeals in 1911, in *Ives* v. *South Buffalo Railway,* which held the state's workman's compensation law unconstitutional. Because the statute imposed upon employers liability without fault for injuries occurring to workers in the course of employment, the Court ruled that this constituted an unreasonable taking of private property without due process of law.

It was in the area of labor legislation that the United States Supreme Court exercised its widest discretion in ruling on statutes on the basis of substantive due process. A majority of the Court soon began to rule corrective labor legislation invalid on such grounds. Thus, in 1908, the Court held that a statute that outlawed a "yellow dog" contract for railroad employees (a contract of employment in which the worker had to pledge not to join a union) was unconstitutional on the ground that such a restriction was an "arbitrary interference with the liberty of contract" of both employers and employees (*Adair* v. *United States*). There soon followed a series of cases in which the Court ruled unconstitutional state statutes that sought to regulate a wide variety of commercial transactions.

The decisions that stirred up the greatest controversy were *Lochner* v. *New York* (1905), which, by a 5–4 vote, invalidated a state statute that provided for a ten-hour work day and a sixty-hour work week for bakers, on the ground that these regulations were "mere meddlesome interferences with the rights of the individual," and two later cases that, by 5–4 votes, held unconstitutional on substantive due process grounds a minimum-wage law for women, *Adkins* v. *Children's Hospital* (1923) and *Morehead* v. *Tipaldo* (1936).

However, responding to the pressures generated by the Great Depression, legislative bodies, state and federal, began to enact various price-fixing statutes, and the Supreme Court slowly modified its views on the due process issue. Thus, in 1934, by a 5–4 vote, the Court upheld the regulation of milk prices as being "a reasonable exertion of governmental authority" (*Nebbia* v. *New York*). Soon thereafter, the Court sustained the validity of statutes that regulated maximum warehouse charges (*Townsend* v. *Yeomans*, 1937), minimum prices for milk sold in interstate commerce (*United States* v. *Rock Royal Co-Operative, Inc.*, 1939), and price-fixing for coal moving in interstate commerce (*Sunshine Anthracite Coal Co.* v. *Adkins*, 1940). Reversing two recent precedents, the Supreme Court ruled in 1937 that a minimum-wage law for women was consistent with due process (*West Coast Hotel Co.* v. *Parrish*) and in 1941 the Court sustained the constitutionality of the Fair Labor Standards Act of 1938 (the so-called Wages and Hours Bill) enacted under the commerce power of Congress (*United States* v. *Darby Lumber Co.*). In 1963, in upholding a state statute that provided that only lawyers

may engage in the business of "debt adjustment," Justice Black declared, "It is up to the legislatures, not courts, to decide on the wisdom and utility of legislation" (*Ferguson* v. *Skrupa*). The notion that due process authorizes courts to hold statutes unconstitutional when they believe that legislatures have acted unwisely, said Justice Black, has long since been discarded: "We have returned to the original constitutional proposition that courts do not substitute their social and economic beliefs for the judgment of legislative bodies, who are elected to pass laws."

THE SURVIVAL OF SUBSTANTIVE DUE PROCESS

The United States Supreme Court is no longer willing to substitute its judgment regarding the reasonableness of economic legislation for that of the legislative bodies. To this extent, the concept of substantive due process, as a basis for the exercise of judicial review, has lost its vitality. But substantive due process is still invoked by the courts, for in a considerable variety of cases involving what are regarded as "fundamental rights" the Supreme Court has established on a wide front the judicial power to strike down restrictive legislation.

One of the earliest decisions to take this line of thought was *Meyer* v. *Nebraska* (1923), wherein the Court ruled unconstitutional a state statute that required that all instruction through the eighth grade, in all schools, whether private or public, be in the English language. Although it was conceded that the state may regulate various aspects of schooling, such as the certification of teachers, "fundamental rights," such as that involved in this instance, are protected by due process. Justice James McReynolds, who spoke for the Court, declared that the liberty protected by the Fourteenth Amendment includes

> not merely freedom from bodily restraint, but also the right of the individual to contract, to engage in any of the common occupations of life, to acquire useful knowledge, to marry, establish a home and bring up children, to worship God according to the dictates of his own conscience, and generally to enjoy those privileges long recognized at common law as essential to the orderly pursuit of happiness by free men.

In fact, Justice Stone set the intellectual tone for the "fundamental rights" approach to due process in a famous footnote he wrote into the opinion in *United States* v. *Carolene Products Co.* (1938). In that case, the Court upheld the constitutionality of a federal statute that forbade the shipment of filled milk in interstate commerce on the ground that the wisdom of this sort of legislation is a matter for the judgment of the legislature and not that of the courts. But Justice Stone went on to explain that there "may be narrower scope for operation of the presumption of constitutionality" in several situations: (1) when the legislation on its face appears to be within a specific prohibition of the Constitution; (2) when legislation restricts those political processes which can ordinarily be expected to bring about repeal of undesirable legislation, such as the right to vote or to disseminate information, interference with political organizations, or prohibition of peaceable assembly; and (3) when legislation is directed against particular religious or racial minorities, or embodies prejudice against "discrete and insular minorities . . . which tends seriously to curtail the operation of those political processes ordinarily to be relied upon to protect minorities." In these situations, a more searching judicial inquiry than is usually appropriate is called for.

The concept of fundamental rights as a basis for activist judicial review of substantive legislation was greatly strengthened in 1942, in *Skinner* v. *Oklahoma*, wherein a statute that provided for the sexual sterilization of certain classes of habitual criminals was ruled unconstitutional. The Court based its decision on the equal protection clause rather than the due process clause but said that the statute in question denied a "basic liberty," because "marriage and procreation are fundamental to the very existence and survival of the race." Since a fundamental right was involved, the statute could not survive the "strict scrutiny" to which such statutes are subjected by reviewing courts.

In a series of cases the Supreme Court developed the concept of a right to privacy as one that falls within the scope of substantive due process. In *Griswold* v. *Connecticut* (1965) the Court ruled invalid a state statute that prohibited the use of contraceptives or the giving of advice as to their use, as an interference with the right of privacy, a right that Justice Douglas asserted was "older

than the Bill of Rights." Although he was reluctant to revive substantive due process language and preferred to link the idea of privacy to other sections of the Bill of Rights, such as the Third, Fourth, and Ninth Amendments, two other justices of the Court, Harlan and White, thought that the statute clearly violated due process of law.

The newly developed concept of the right of privacy was expanded in 1973 in *Roe* v. *Wade*, which ruled unconstitutional a state statute forbidding abortions at any stage of pregnancy except to save the life of the mother. Speaking for the Court, Justice Harry A. Blackmun argued that the right at stake was founded in the personal liberty concept of the due process clause of the Fourteenth Amendment.

The Court has also judged the substantive merit of legislation regarding voting. In *Baker* v. *Carr* (1962) the Supreme Court ruled unconstitutional state legislative apportionments that result in unequal voting power for various citizens. The concept of "one man, one vote" became the watchword of a long series of decisions that sought to protect equality of voting power. The Court chose to rest its decision on the equal protection clause, but the result was the same as that which invocation of substantive due process would have produced. Indeed, many constitutional law writers now speak of substantive equal protection, according to which discriminations based on sex, race, financial status, or youth are ruled invalid. A good example is a series of decisions that ruled invalid legislation hostile to the interests of illegitimate children. For example, in 1983 the Court ruled unconstitutional a Tennessee statute that barred paternity suits or child-support actions brought on behalf of illegitimate children more than two years after birth *(Pickett* v. *Brown)*. The Court thought that the state's asserted interest in preventing the litigation of stale or fraudulent claims was outweighed by the importance of providing children an adequate opportunity to secure support.

The continuing vitality of the principle of due process of law is strikingly reflected in the Supreme Court's gradual expansion of the thrust of the due process clause of the Fourteenth Amendment with regard to various forms of state action. It must be recalled that this amendment provides that no *state* shall "deprive any person of life, liberty, or property without due process of law." It should also be recalled that the first eight amendments to the Constitution are not addressed to the states but only to the national government.

However, the adoption of Section 1 of the Fourteenth Amendment in 1868 drastically changed the legal picture with regard to civil liberties. Initially, the provision was read restrictively when, in the *Slaughterhouse Cases,* the Court refused to hold that a citizen who had lost his employment because of a state-created monopoly was protected by a federal right or privilege. The Court's determination during Reconstruction to limit the thrust of the Fourteenth Amendment was underscored ten years later when, in the *Civil Rights Cases* (1883), it ruled that the legislative power of Congress to enforce Section 1 of the Fourteenth Amendment was limited to action by a state and did not extend to ordinary relations between private individuals, such as racial discrimination by innkeepers, theater owners, and public conveyances.

The "liberty" phrase in the due process clause did nonetheless generate the possibility of reading various provisions of the Bill of Rights into Section 1 of the Fourteenth Amendment. The Supreme Court took a first hesitant step in the direction of incorporating provisions of the Bill of Rights into the demands of the Fourteenth Amendment in 1897, when it decided that the Fifth Amendment requirement of just compensation for private property taken by a state for a public use applied to the state through the due process clause *(Chicago, Burlington & Quincy Railroad* v. *Chicago).* Above all, in 1925, in the celebrated case of *Gitlow* v. *New York,* the Court ruled squarely, without even arguing the point, that the freedom of speech protected by the First Amendment from abridgment by Congress was one of the fundamental personal liberties protected by the due process clause of the Fourteenth Amendment from impairment by the states. Gitlow lost his appeal from a conviction in the New York courts for violating a state criminal anarchy statute, but the long-term significance of the case lies in the fact that the Supreme Court was willing to take jurisdiction of the appeal. Since then, decisions have underscored the proposition that a state denial of liberty of speech and press presented questions of federal constitutional law, over which the Supreme Court may take jurisdiction. In 1940 the Court

held that the liberty secured by Fourteenth Amendment due process included the First Amendment guaranty of religious freedom *(Cantwell* v. *Connecticut).* Today all parts of the First Amendment, relating to freedom of speech, the press, religion, assembly and petition, and the prohibition of an establishment of religion, now apply as federally enforceable limitations on the states.

Most of the provisions of the federal Bill of Rights deal with the rights of persons accused of crime, and until 1923 the Supreme Court was unwilling to review state appellate court decisions in criminal matters. In the leading case of *Moore* v. *Dempsey* (1923), however, the Supreme Court ruled that where a person convicted in a state court petitions for a writ of habeas corpus in a federal district court on the ground that the trial court had been dominated by overwhelming mob pressures, the district judge must make an independent evaluation of the facts, even though the state appellate court had previously reviewed the facts and upheld the verdict. This decision opened the door to a significant expansion of federal control over state criminal procedures, through review by the Supreme Court on the basis of the due process clause. Most, though not all, of the provisions of the Bill of Rights have now been incorporated into the due process clause, but a few have not been regarded as essential to justice and remain unincorporated, such as the Fifth Amendment guaranty of indictment by grand jury.

While the Court has not read into the due process concept all of the guaranties of the federal Bill of Rights, it has also not limited the meaning of due process to principles specifically enumerated in the Constitution, for due process is construed as a guaranty of a fair trial, in accordance with the principles of fundamental justice, and thus the due process clause is read as including rights not stated in the Constitution. An important example is the famous 1935 case of *Mooney* v. *Holohan,* wherein the Court ruled that where the prosecution has deliberately deceived the court and jury by presenting testimony known to be perjured, the state has denied due process. Later, the Court extended the *Mooney* rule to include the suppression by the prosecution of evidence favorable to the accused.

The net result of the decisions rendered in the twentieth century has been to constitute the

DUE PROCESS OF LAW

United States Supreme Court as a veritable court of criminal appeals. While the states still handle most criminal litigation and are deeply involved in the area of basic human rights, there is now available a considerable array of corrective federal judicial remedies, largely under the rubric of due process of law, as well as a growing body of federal civil rights legislation.

CASES

Adair v. United States, 208 U.S. 161 (1908)
Adkins v. Children's Hospital, 261 U.S. 525 (1923)
Alegata v. Massachusetts, 335 Mass. 287, 23, N.E.2d 201 (1967)
Baker v. Carr, 369 U.S. 186 (1962)
Barron v. Baltimore, 7 Peters 243 (1833)
Brady v. Maryland, 373 U.S. 83 (1963)
Cantwell v. Connecticut, 310 U.S. 296 (1940)
Chicago, Burlington & Quincy Railroad v. Chicago, 166 U.S. 226 (1897)
Chicago, Milwaukee & St. Paul Railway v. Minnesota, 134 U.S. 418 (1890)
Civil Rights Cases, 109 U.S. 3 (1883)
Coates v. Cincinnati, 402 U.S. 611 (1971)
Dartmouth College v. Woodward, 4 Wheaton 518 (1819)
Davidson v. New Orleans, 96 U.S. 97 (1878)
Ferguson v. Skrupa, 372 U.S. 726 (1963)
In re Gault, 387 U.S. 1 (1967)
Gitlow v. New York, 268 U.S. 652 (1925)
Goldberg v. Kelly, 397 U.S. 254 (1970)
Goss v. Lopez, 419 U.S. 565 (1975)
Griswold v. Connecticut, 381 U.S. 479 (1965)
Groppi v. Leslie, 404 U.S. 496 (1972)
Henderson v. Morgan, 426 U.S. 637 (1976)
Hurtado v. California, 110 U.S. 516 (1884)
Illinois v. Allen, 397 U.S. 337 (1970)
Irvin v. Dowd, 366 U.S. 717 (1961)
Ives v. South Buffalo Railway, 201 N.Y. 271, 94 N.E. 439 (1911)
Joint Anti-Fascist Refugee Committee v. McGrath, 341 U.S. 123 (1951)
Kinsella v. United States ex rel. Singleton, 361 U.S. 234 (1960)
Lanzetta v. New Jersey, 306 U.S. 451 (1939)
Lochner v. New York, 198 U.S. 45 (1905)
Meyer v. Nebraska, 262 U.S. 390 (1923)
Missouri ex rel. Hurwitz v. North, 271 U.S. 40 (1926)
Mooney v. Holohan, 294 U.S. 103 (1935)
Moore v. Dempsey, 261 U.S. 96 (1923)
Moore v. State, 43 N.J.L. 203 (1881)
Morehead v. Tipaldo, 298 U.S. 587 (1936)
Morrissey v. Brewer, 408 U.S. 471 (1972)
Murray v. Hoboken Land and Improvement Co., 18 Howard 272 (1855)
Nebbia v. New York, 291 U.S. 502 (1934)
North American Cold Storage Co. v. Chicago, 211 U.S. 306 (1908)

In re Oliver, 333 U.S. 257 (1948)
Pate v. Robinson, 383 U.S. 375 (1966)
Perry v. Sindermann, 408 U.S. 593 (1972)
Pickett v. Brown, 462 U.S. 1 (1983)
Poe v. Ullman, 367 U.S. 497 (1961)
Railroad Commission Cases, 116 U.S. 307 (1886)
Rochin v. California, 342 U.S. 165 (1952)
Roe v. Wade, 410 U.S. 113 (1973)
Shaughnessy v. United States ex rel. Mezei, 345 U.S. 206 (1953)
Sheppard v. Maxwell, 384 U.S. 333 (1966)
Skinner v. Oklahoma, 316 U.S. 535 (1942)
Slaughterhouse Cases, 16 Wallace 36 (1873)
Sniadach v. Family Finance Corp., 395 U.S. 337 (1969)
State v. Reynaldo, 243 Minn. 196, 66 N.W.2d 868 (1954)
Sunshine Anthracite Coal Co. v. Adkins, 310 U.S. 381 (1940)
Taylor v. United States, 414 U.S. 17 (1973)
Thompson v. Louisville, 362 U.S. 199 (1960)
Townsend v. Yeomans, 301 U.S. 441 (1937)
Tumey v. Ohio, 273 U.S. 510 (1927)
Twining v. New Jersey, 211 U.S. 78 (1908)
United States v. Carolene Products Co., 304 U.S. 144 (1938)
United States v. Darby Lumber Co., 312 U.S. 100 (1941)
United States v. Rock Royal Co-Operative, Inc., 307 U.S. 533 (1939)
Webb v. Texas, 409 U.S. 95 (1972)
West Coast Hotel Co. v. Parrish, 300 U.S. 379 (1937)
Wynehamer v. New York, 13 N.Y. 378 (1856)

BIBLIOGRAPHY

Daniel A. Farber and John E. Muench, "The Ideological Origins of the Fourteenth Amendment," in *Constitutional Commentary,* 1 (1984), is a scholarly analysis of the theoretical background of the Fourteenth Amendment in its formative historical period. A. L. Goodhart, "Legal Procedure and Democracy," in *Cambridge Law Journal* (1964), is an analysis of the concept of natural justice as employed by English judges. Charles M. Hough, "Due Process of Law—Today," in *Harvard Law Review,* 32 (1919), examines the concept of due process. Sanford H. Kadish, "Methodology and Criteria in Due Process Adjudication—A Survey and Criticism," in *Yale Law Journal,* 66 (1957), is a scholarly analysis of due process adjudication. James Kent, *Commentaries on American Law,* 14th ed. (1896), is one of the leading treatises on American constitutional law.

Rodney L. Mott, *Due Process of Law* (1926), the first large-scale treatise on the concept of due process, although dated, is still valuable for background material. E. B. Simmons, "Natural Justice," in *Justice of the Peace and Local Government Review,* 127 (1963), summarizes the concept of natural justice as employed by English judges. Virginia Wood, *Due Process of Law, 1932–1949* (1972), is a learned text covering the history of due process in an important formative period.
[*See also* ADMINISTRATIVE LAW; COURTS AND CONSTITUTIONALISM; CRIMINAL PROCEDURE; EQUAL PROTECTION CLAUSE; FRANCHISE; HUGHES COURT AND ERA; JUDICIAL REVIEW; JUVENILE LAW; *and* PRIVACY.]

THE EQUAL PROTECTION CLAUSE

Jeffrey M. Shaman

THE equal protection clause is contained in the Fourteenth Amendment to the Constitution, which was proposed by Congress in 1866 and ratified by the necessary three-fourths of the states in 1868. The equal protection clause provides that no state shall deny to any person within its jurisdiction the equal protection of the laws. By its terms, the equal protection clause is directed only to the action of state governments and not to the action of the federal government. However, the Supreme Court has ruled that the due process clause of the Fifth Amendment, which is directed to the federal government, serves purposes similar to the equal protection clause and therefore can be said to include an equal-protection component. As a result, both the state governments and the federal government are prohibited by the Constitution from denying to persons the equal protection of the laws.

The equal protection clause was one of the Civil War Amendments. As such, its primary purpose, as envisioned by its framers, was to protect the rights of the newly freed slaves by prohibiting racial discrimination against them. However, unlike the other Civil War Amendments (the Thirteenth and Fifteenth), the Fourteenth Amendment makes no mention of race or slavery. Regardless of the intent to ban racial discrimination, which inspired the enactment of the Fourteenth Amendment, its wording would seem to prohibit all forms of unjust discrimination by guaranteeing equal protection of the laws to "all persons." Despite this all-inclusive language, the Supreme Court, when first called upon to interpret the Fourteenth Amendment in the years shortly after its enactment, stressed the historical background of the amendment and ruled that it applied only to racial discrimination.

Other forms of discrimination, the Court ruled, were not prohibited by the equal protection clause. In fact, for some years the Supreme Court was so unimpressed with attempts by litigants to use the equal protection clause to deal with other forms of discrimination that by 1927 the Court described the clause as "the usual last resort of constitutional arguments."

In more recent years, however, the Supreme Court has reversed itself on this issue. While continuing to recognize that the primary purpose of the Fourteenth Amendment is to ban racial discrimination, the Court has held that, given the encompassing language of the amendment, it serves other purposes as well. Thus, the Court has used the equal protection clause to strike down not only racial discrimination but also gender-based discrimination, discrimination against illegitimate children, discrimination against aliens, and discrimination that deprives individuals of their fundamental rights.

Although the Supreme Court has given a wider application to the equal protection clause, the Court has never held that the clause prohibits the government from using classifications in its laws. This is so because classification is a necessary ingredient of laws. Virtually all laws create distinctions between persons or groups. For example, many laws create distinctions by classifying which persons are eligible for certain benefits or subject to certain penalties. If the equal protection clause were interpreted as proscribing all classifications, it would be impossible for the government to enact any legislation whatsoever. Therefore, the Supreme Court has consistently taken the position that the equal protection clause prohibits only unjust classifications in legislation.

In determining whether a legislative classifica-

1038

tion is unjust and therefore violative of the equal protection clause, the Supreme Court has developed three different standards of judicial review, which are referred to as strict scrutiny, intermediate scrutiny, and minimal scrutiny. Strict scrutiny is used to evaluate the constitutionality of legislative classifications that are suspect because they are directed against minorities who have experienced a history of purposeful unequal treatment or have been subjected to unique disabilities on the basis of stereotyped characteristics not truly indicative of their abilities. Classifications based upon race, national origin, and alienage all have been found to be suspect and therefore subject to strict scrutiny. Strict scrutiny is also used to evaluate the constitutionality of legislative classifications that impinge upon fundamental rights, such as the right to privacy, the right to vote, and the right to interstate travel. Under strict scrutiny, legislation will be struck down as violative of the equal protection clause unless the government can show that the legislation is necessarily related to a compelling governmental purpose.

Intermediate scrutiny is used to evaluate the constitutionality of legislative classifications based upon gender or illegitimacy of birth, which are similar to suspect classifications. Under intermediate scrutiny, legislation will be held to violate the equal protection clause unless the government can show that it is substantially related to an important governmental purpose.

Minimal scrutiny is used to evaluate the constitutionality of all other legislative classifications. Under minimal scrutiny, there is a presumption that the legislation in question does not violate the equal protection clause, and hence, it will be upheld as constitutional unless the party challenging it can show that it is completely unrelated to any valid governmental purpose.

Because the Fourteenth Amendment provides that "no state" shall deny equal protection of the laws to any person, the Supreme Court has ruled that the amendment "erects no shield against merely private conduct however discriminatory or wrongful" (*Shelley* v. *Kraemer*, 1948). Ordinarily, private individuals and organizations are not subject to the equal protection clause and may engage in discriminatory behavior unless it is prohibited by statute. However, there are occasions when private conduct is either connected to or supported by the government to such an extent that it is tantamount to state action and therefore comes within the ambit of the equal protection clause. When, for instance, a private party engages in conduct that historically has been a virtually exclusive prerogative of sovereign government, that conduct will be considered state action that is subject to the equal protection clause. Thus, it has been ruled that when private parties conduct a primary election, govern a company town, or operate a public park, their activity is the functional equivalent of state action that must meet the dictates of the equal protection clause.

State action may also be present in a nexus of private and governmental action. For instance, the operation of a privately owned restaurant that leased space in a government parking facility was found to amount to state action because a "symbiotic relationship" or joint venture had been formed between the restaurant and the government (*Burton* v. *Wilmington Parking Authority*, 1961). Where there are sufficient contacts between a private actor and the government, the former takes on the appearance and perhaps the actual authority of the state and will be treated as an agent of the government.

The existence of state action may also be established through government support of private activities. For example, restrictive covenants in deeds or contracts that bar the sale of property to minorities are private arrangements between individuals that do not involve the government. But if an attempt is made to enforce such covenants by court order, the once private arrangement becomes invested with state action by virtue of the court's participation in it. However, it has been held by the Supreme Court that the fact that a private party is licensed, regulated, or financed by the government does not imbue all of that party's activities with state action: only an action of the private party that is specifically required or enforced by the government will be considered state action.

CLASSIFICATIONS BASED UPON RACE

The Supreme Court has always recognized that the primary purpose of the equal protection clause is to prohibit racial discrimination. This principle was followed by the Court in 1880 in the case of *Strauder* v. *West Virginia,* in which the Court ruled that a state statute excluding blacks from juries was a violation of the equal protection clause. In its opinion the Court stated that the clause secures to black persons "all the civil rights" enjoyed by white persons. The Court further explained that the equal protection clause requires that laws be the same for all, regardless of their race.

In 1896, however, the Court decided the case of *Plessy* v. *Ferguson,* in which it severely limited the effectiveness of the equal protection clause as a means of combatting racial discrimination. In *Plessy* the Court was faced with a state statute that required all railway companies to provide separate but equal cars for white and black passengers. The statute further imposed criminal penalties upon railway officials who failed to obey its dictates. The Court upheld the constitutionality of the statute by adopting the doctrine that separate but equal facilities for the races did not violate the equal protection clause.

In embracing the separate-but-equal doctrine in *Plessy,* the Court relied upon several questionable propositions. First, the Court asserted that laws mandating racial separation "do not imply the inferiority of either race." This assertion, which was belied by common knowledge, would be emphatically disavowed by the Court fifty-eight years later in the case of *Brown* v. *Board of Education* (1954). Second, the Court in *Plessy* incorrectly assumed that racial segregation was a natural state of affairs. Third, the Court granted undue deference to the legislature by maintaining that "there must necessarily be a large discretion on the part of the legislature" to enact regulations. Finally, the justices added that in determining whether a regulation is reasonable, the legislature "is at liberty to act with reference to the established usages, customs and traditions of the people." By thus equating the reasonableness of legislation—and hence its constitutionality—with usage, custom, and tradition, the Court permitted the use of discriminatory classifications, no matter how pernicious, so long as they were customary or traditional in society. Obviously, this had the effect of eroding the capacity of the equal protection clause to challenge the status quo.

Before the separate-but-equal doctrine was abandoned, it was used to uphold racial segrega-tion in public schools and other state institu-tions. During this period the Court decided several cases in which it ruled that state statutes mandating racial segregation in schools did not violate the equal protection clause. At the same time, the Court did not accept all forms of racial discrimination. In *Buchanan* v. *Warley* (1917) the equal protection clause was held to be violated by an ordinance that barred blacks from moving into predominantly white neighborhoods and whites from moving into predominantly black neighborhoods.

Beginning in 1938, the Court, while still ad-hering to the separate-but-equal doctrine, began to place more emphasis upon the equality com-ponent of the doctrine. In several cases involving racially segregated schooling, the Court found violations of the equal protection clause, because the education available to blacks in separate schools was not truly equal to that available to whites in their schools.

A turning point in the treatment of racial clas-sifications was reached in the case of *Korematsu* v. *United States* (1944). In *Korematsu* the Court upheld the constitutionality of a federal order requiring the detention of persons of Japanese ancestry in "relocation centers" during World War II. However, in upholding the order, the Court stated that only a grave national emer-gency, such as the war, could justify such an ex-treme measure. Moreover, the Court held for the first time that classifications based upon race are suspect and therefore subject to strict scrutiny under the equal protection clause.

Nevertheless, close examination of the major-ity opinion in *Korematsu* reveals that the Court was less than rigorous in its application of strict scrutiny—a failure that would eventually be cor-rected. But in *Korematsu* the Court deviated from true strict scrutiny by readily acquiescing to the judgment of military authorities that wholesale internment of Japanese-Americans was neces-sary because significant numbers of them might engage in sabotage or espionage against the United States. Justice Frank Murphy, who was one of three dissenters in the case, pointed out that this judgment was based upon "an accumu-lation of misinformation, half-truths and insinua-tions that for years have been directed against Japanese-Americans by people with racial and economic prejudices."

Finally, in 1954, in the famous case of *Brown*

v. *Board of Education,* the Supreme Court over-turned the separate-but-equal doctrine. In *Brown* the Court faced the question of whether segregation of children in public schools solely on the basis of race violates the equal protection clause even though the tangible characteristics of the schools, such as books, equipment, buildings, and teachers, are equal in quality. It ruled unanimously that such segregation did violate the equal protection clause: "In the field of education, the doctrine of 'separate but equal' has no place." The Court explained that separate schooling is "inherently unequal" for two reasons. First, it is unequal because even though the tangible characteristics of separate schools may be similar, their intangible characteristics can never be equalized. Second, to separate black children "from others of similar age and qualifications solely because of their race generates a feeling of inferiority as to their status in the community that may affect their hearts and minds in a way unlikely ever to be undone."

The decision in *Brown* dealt with de jure racial segregation—that is, racial segregation caused by law. De facto racial segregation, which is caused by housing and migration patterns rather than by law, has never been held to violate the equal protection clause. Because de facto segregation does not violate the Constitution, school districts are under no legal obligation to change it. But de jure segregation does violate the Constitution, and steps must be taken to replace it with a racially integrated school system.

In a series of cases after *Brown,* the Court ruled that the equal protection clause also prohibits racial segregation at public beaches, municipal golf courses, parks, airport restaurants, athletic contests, municipal auditoriums, and courthouses. In addition, the Court has ruled that the equal protection clause does not allow a state to ban interracial marriage or award custody of a child to a divorced parent because the other parent has subsequently entered an interracial marriage.

Where a law is racially neutral on its face but has a racially disparate impact, it is not subject to strict scrutiny unless it can be shown that the law was adopted with an intent to cause racial discrimination. For example, in *Washington* v. *Davis* (1976) the Supreme Court used minimal scrutiny and upheld the use of a personnel test that was failed by a higher percentage of blacks than whites. The Court refused to use strict scrutiny in that case because there was no showing that the test had been adopted for the purpose of causing racial discrimination. At times, a law that is racially neutral on its face may have a racially disproportionate effect that is so clear that it reveals an unmistakable intent to racially discriminate. But where this is not so, the Supreme Court has ruled in several cases that a racially disparate impact alone does not call into play strict scrutiny. The Court's position in these cases has been criticized on the ground that it ignores subtle forms of invidious racial discrimination.

Although the Supreme Court has held that racial classifications are suspect, it has never held that they are unconstitutional per se. Nor has the Court ruled that all government action must be racially neutral or "color-blind." In fact, the government at times needs to take race into account in order to counteract the invidious racial discrimination that exists in American society. Therefore, color-blindness on the part of the government must remain a goal for the future when racial discrimination is less pervasive in society.

In that context, the Court has upheld the constitutionality of benign racial classifications or so-called affirmative-action programs, which use racial classifications to extend benefits previously denied to racial or ethnic minority groups. Some persons object to affirmative-action programs on the ground that they appear similar to quota systems used in the past to discriminate invidiously against racial or ethnic minorities. However, affirmative action programs are essentially different from past quota systems because they are designed to benefit individuals rather than hinder them and are directed toward integrating the races rather than segregating them. For these reasons, affirmative-action programs are not violative of the equal protection clause so long as they are properly designed as a means of remedying the effects of invidious racial discrimination.

The Supreme Court's first pronouncement on an affirmative-action program employing a benign racial classification occurred in 1978 in the case of *Regents of the University of California* v. *Bakke.* The *Bakke* case involved an affirmative-action program adopted by a state medical school whereby a certain number of places in the entering class were reserved for minority or disadvantaged students. Although the Court struck down this particular affirmative-action program because it was not properly tailored, a majority of the justices agreed that affirmative-action programs, if properly devised, are a constitutional means of counteracting invidious racial discrimination. Hence, in a case decided two years later, *Fullilove* v. *Klutznick,* the Court upheld the constitutionality of an affirmative-action program designed to ensure minority participation in federal public works projects by requiring that 10 percent of the federal grants for such projects be awarded to minority-owned businesses. The Court also has upheld the use of benign racial classifications to realign voting districts to achieve fair representation of minority groups.

CLASSIFICATIONS BASED UPON ALIENAGE

In the early 1970s the Supreme Court held that classifications based upon alienage, like those based upon race, are suspect and therefore subject to strict scrutiny. Under strict scrutiny, the Court has struck down state laws that preclude aliens from eligibility for welfare benefits, civil service employment, admission to the bar, scholarships, and the practice of civil engineering. More recently, though, the Court has stated that it is inappropriate to subject all state exclusions of aliens to strict scrutiny because "to do so would obliterate all the distinctions between citizens and aliens." Therefore, the Court has exempted alienage classifications from strict scrutiny when they concern "matters firmly within a State's constitutional prerogatives" (*Foley* v. *Connelie,* 1978). Using only minimal scrutiny for such matters, the Court has upheld state laws that bar aliens from employment as state troopers, public school teachers, and deputy probation officers. By the Court's own admission, its decisions concerning alienage classifications "have not formed an unwavering line." And some justices who have dissented from the majority approach maintain that the decisions concerning alienage are impossible to reconcile, in that a state has no greater interest in excluding aliens from employment as state troopers, teachers, or probation officers than it does in excluding them from employment as civil servants, attorneys, or engineers. Nonetheless, a slim majority of the Court continues to follow this approach.

The Court has also used minimal scrutiny in evaluating alienage classifications that are contained in federal statutes. This stance has been taken because Article I of the Constitution grants to Congress the authority to regulate immigration and naturalization. Given this "paramount federal power over immigration and naturalization," the Court has been more tolerant of federal than state regulations of aliens. A regulation of the Civil Service Commission barring aliens from federal employment was declared unconstitutional on the ground that the commission lacked the power to issue such a regulation. The Court at the same time suggested that Congress could exclude aliens from the civil service. In addition, the Court has upheld a federal provision denying medicare benefits to aliens unless they had been admitted for permanent residence in the United States and been residents for at least five years.

CLASSIFICATIONS THAT ABRIDGE FUNDAMENTAL RIGHTS

Legislative classifications that abridge fundamental rights also are subject to strict scrutiny under the equal protection clause and will be held unconstitutional unless shown to be necessary to achieve a compelling state interest.

Personal Autonomy. In *Skinner* v. *Oklahoma* (1942) the Supreme Court ruled that the right to procreate was fundamental and accordingly struck down a statute that provided for the sterilization of persons convicted two or more times of certain felonies involving moral turpitude. Characterizing procreation as "a basic civil right" and "fundamental to the very existence and survival of the race," the Court ruled that the statute unjustly discriminated against the right to procreate by imposing the penalty of sterilization upon some criminal offenders but not others.

Just as the right to procreate is fundamental, so is the right not to procreate. In *Eisenstadt* v. *Baird* (1972) the Court held that the equal protection clause was violated by a statute that prohibited the distribution of contraceptives to unmarried persons. In its opinion in *Eisenstadt* the Court described the right of privacy as a right to be "free from unwarranted governmental intrusion into matters so fundamentally affecting a person as the decision whether to bear or beget a child." This right belongs to unmarried persons as well as married ones. Therefore, the statute could not be justified as a means of preventing extramarital sex, because that purpose was in direct conflict with an individual's right to privacy. Nor could the statute be justified as a health measure, because there was no reason to single out unmarried persons, as distinct from married ones, for health purposes.

The right to marry was considered by the Court in *Zablocki* v. *Redhail* (1978). In *Zablocki* a state law provided that any person under an obligation to support a child not in his or her custody could not marry without first obtaining approval from a court. Furthermore, to obtain such approval, the applicant had to show that his or her obligation of support for the child was being met and that the child was not and was unlikely to become a public charge. In striking down the law, the Court applied strict scrutiny because the right to marry is of fundamental importance, and the classification significantly interfered with the exercise of that right. Although the Court recognized that the state law in question was aimed at protecting the financial welfare of children, which is a strong state interest, it held that the law was an unduly harsh method of accomplishing that interest, given that there were other means to achieve it that did not penalize the right to marry.

Political Participation. A second cluster of rights that have been recognized as fundamental under the equal protection clause involves participation in the political process. Although the right to vote is not explicitly guaranteed by the Constitution, several provisions in it do imply the existence of a right to vote. In addition, as the Supreme Court has said, the right to vote "is preservative of other basic civil and political rights." Therefore, it is of fundamental importance and is protected by the use of strict scrutiny under the equal protection clause.

The importance of the right to vote was recognized in *Reynolds* v. *Sims* (1964), which established the principle of "one person, one vote." The *Reynolds* case dealt with a constitutional challenge to the gross malapportionment that then existed in the Alabama legislature. This ap-

portionment scheme was considered to be a violation of the equal protection clause.

Under the ruling in *Reynolds,* the seats in all state legislative chambers must be apportioned on the basis of one person, one vote. This principle also applies to the apportionment of congressional seats, although not to the United States Senate, because its composition is expressly governed by Article I of the Constitution. The one-person, one-vote rule also applies to elections for county, municipal, and other local legislators and to elections for governor, mayor, and other executive officers. Whenever a state or local government decides to choose legislative or executive officials by popular election, the equal protection clause requires that all votes be treated with equal weight. One exception that the Supreme Court has allowed to the one-person, one-vote principle is the election of state judges, who may be chosen from electoral districts without regard for population patterns.

The equal protection clause provides additional protection for the fundamental right to vote. In *Kramer* v. *Union Free School District* (1969) it was held that the equal protection clause was violated by a state law that prohibited persons from voting in school district elections unless they owned or leased property in the district or had children enrolled in the district schools. In support of the law, the state argued that it had proper reason to restrict the franchise to persons interested in school affairs who would therefore have a better understanding of the matters upon which they were voting. Nevertheless, the Supreme Court ruled that the state law in question was unconstitutional because it was not adequately related to the state purpose of restricting the franchise to interested voters. The law was found to be both underinclusive and overinclusive in regard to that purpose because it allowed some persons with no interest to vote in school elections while precluding others with bona fide interests. Thus, the law was found to discriminate unjustly against the right to vote.

In the case of *Harper* v. *Virginia Board of Elections* (1966) the Supreme Court held that the equal protection clause was violated by poll taxes that condition the right to vote. As the Court reasoned in *Harper,* the ability to pay taxes has no relationship to vote, and therefore the requirement of paying a fee to vote is unconstitutional. The Court has also used the equal protection clause to strike down state laws that barred members of the armed services from voting and that conditioned the right to vote on a residency requirement. Both a one-year residency requirement and a three-month one have been held by the Court to violate the equal protection clause. On the other hand, a fifty-day residency requirement as a condition to vote has been upheld by the Court as necessary to serve the important state interest in having accurate voter lists.

Other limitations upon the right to vote have occasionally been upheld as constitutional by the Supreme Court. The Court has ruled that literacy tests, so long as they are not administered in a discriminatory manner, are not prohibited by the equal protection clause. Despite this ruling, when Congress later enacted a statute outlawing the use of literacy tests as a voting prerequisite, the Court upheld the statute as properly within the authority of Congress. This means that although literacy tests are not necessarily unconstitutional, they may be prohibited by federal statute if Congress sees fit to do so.

Related to the right to vote is the right to be a candidate. Although the states have authority to set qualifications for candidates for public office, those qualifications must comply with the equal protection clause. In several instances the Supreme Court has ruled that the Constitution is violated by state laws that require the payment of a filing fee as a prerequisite for a candidate to be listed on the ballot. Recognizing that filing fees may serve the need of a state to keep the size of a ballot manageable, the Court held that such fees are unconstitutional where they have the effect of excluding qualified candidates from an election. Thus, election filing fees that are unduly high or make no exceptions for indigent candidates are unconstitutional.

The equal protection clause also prohibits laws that place unduly burdensome obstacles upon the ability of political parties to place their candidates on the ballot. In *Williams* v. *Rhodes* (1968) the clause was violated by a state law that strongly favored established political parties to the detriment of other political groups. Under the law, established political parties retained their position on the ballot merely by garnering 10 percent of the votes cast in the preceding gubernatorial election. For other parties to gain a position on the ballot, though, they had to submit petitions signed by a total of 15 percent of the voters in the last election. Moreover, the petition had to be filed early in February of the election year. These and other burdens, such as elaborate primary and party-organization requirements, "made it virtually impossible for a new political party, even though it has hundreds of thousands of members, or an old party, which has a very small number of members, to be placed on the state ballots." The state failed to show any compelling reasons for imposing such heavy burdens upon minority political parties.

In subsequent cases, however, the Supreme Court has sustained the constitutionality of state laws that place less-restrictive limits upon access to the ballot. In one case, the Court upheld a law that denied ballot access to independent candidates unless they obtained a petition signed by 5 percent of the persons registered to vote in the previous election. In another case, the Court upheld a statute that denied ballot position to any political party that had neither secured 2 percent of the vote in the previous general election nor obtained a petition signed by registered voters equal in number to at least 1 percent of the votes cast in the prior general election. Taken together, the Court's decisions in this area seem to mean that in order to keep ballots manageable and to protect the integrity of elections, the states may condition access to the ballot upon the demonstration of a "significant, measurable quantum of community support" but may not require a demonstration of support so great that independent candidates and minority political parties have no realistic chance to obtain ballot positions.

The Right to Travel. The Supreme Court has also held that the right to travel from state to state is a fundamental right entitled to the protection of strict scrutiny under the equal protection clause. Although this right is not expressly guaranteed by the Constitution, it is clearly implied by the fact that the Constitution creates a federated nation and grants citizenship to individuals on a national basis. An individual is a citizen of the United States, not merely of the particular state in which he or she resides. As a result, there is a fundamental interest in being able to travel freely throughout the country.

An important decision involving the right to interstate travel was rendered by the Supreme Court in 1969 in *Shapiro* v. *Thompson.* This case concerned statutes in several jurisdictions that denied welfare benefits to persons who had not resided in a jurisdiction for at least one year. The Court struck down the statutes as violative of the equal protection clause, reasoning that the one-year residency requirements abridged the fundamental right to travel from state to state. The argument that the statutes were a justifiable means of deterring indigent persons from entering a state was rejected by the Court on the ground that no state had the right to exclude persons from entering it. The Court also took the position that it was constitutionally impermissible for the state to distinguish between old and new residents in a manner that impinges upon a fundamental right, such as the right to interstate travel. Although a state may enforce some conditions upon the granting of welfare benefits in order to ensure that applicants are bona fide residents of the state, a state may not create subclasses of state citizenship based upon the length of time a person has lived in the state.

Following the decision in *Shapiro,* the Supreme Court has used the equal protection clause to strike down statutes that placed one-year residency requirements upon the right to vote and the right of indigent persons to obtain free medical care. On the other hand, the Court has upheld some residency requirements that were challenged under the equal protection clause. In a summary decision, the Court sustained the decision of a lower court upholding the practice of a state university charging higher tuition rates to nonresidents than to persons who had resided in the state for one year or more. In a later case the Court commented that strict scrutiny is applicable only to residency requirements that penalize the right to interstate travel by denying another fundamental right, such as the right to vote, or a necessity of life, such as welfare or medical care.

The Court departed from this standard in the case of *Sosna* v. *Iowa* (1975). In that case the Court sustained a requirement that a person reside in the state for one year before being allowed to file a divorce action against a nonresident. Although the state residency requirement at question in *Sosna* affected two fundamental interests—the right to interstate travel and the right to marital association—the Court saw fit to use only minimal scrutiny to review the residency requirement, on the ground that the area of domestic relations "has long been re-

garded as a virtually exclusive province of the States." Although in many other modern cases the court has not deferred to the authority of the states over domestic relations, in *Sosna* the Court did so in order to allow the states control over when a divorce may be granted.

Six years later, the approach taken in *Sosna* was eschewed in *Jones* v. *Helms,* which involved a state statute that made it a crime for a parent to willfully abandon a dependent child. According to the statute, the crime was a misdemeanor unless the parent left the state after abandoning the child, in which case it was raised to a felony with a more strict penalty. Although the statute obviously concerned domestic relations, the Court made no reference to the *Sosna* rationale, choosing instead to take a different approach to uphold the statute. Although the right to travel is fundamental, the Court explained, it is not "unqualified" and may be lost, as it was here, through the commission of a crime. Therefore, it was concluded that strict scrutiny would not be applied to the state statute because it "did not penalize the exercise of the constitutional right to travel." In other words, the right to interstate travel is fundamental except when it has been forfeited through the commission of a crime. Although the Court's decision in this case may well be correct, its reasoning in reaching the decision is open to question. The premise of the Court's reasoning seems to be tautological: the right to travel is fundamental when it is fundamental. The court could have avoided this tautology and still reached the same result in *Jones* by reasoning that under strict scrutiny the fundamental right to interstate travel is outweighed by the compelling state interest in protecting dependent children.

The cases dealing with the right to interstate travel illustrate that it is difficult to square the Court's decisions in this area. However, it is possible to extract some general principles from the cases. Laws that place barriers upon the ability to migrate into a state or that allocate essential government benefits on the basis of length of residency are in all probability violative of the equal protection clause. But laws that restrict the capacity to migrate without seriously impairing it are probably not in violation of the equal protection clause. Finally, even laws that seriously impair the right to interstate travel will be found not to violate the equal protection clause if they can be shown to be necessary to accomplish a compelling state interest.

Treatment of Those Accused of Crime. In another series of cases the Supreme Court has suggested that there is a fundamental right to equality of treatment in the criminal justice system. When a state engages in action that causes inequitable treatment of individuals in the criminal justice system, the state action will be subject to strict scrutiny under the equal protection clause. This principle was established in *Griffin* v. *Illinois* (1956), wherein the Court struck down a state statute that restricted the right of indigent defendants to obtain free transcripts of their criminal trials, which were necessary to appeal their convictions. The Court held that the equal protection clause is violated when a state places conditions upon the right to appellate review in a way that discriminates against convicted defendants on account of their inability to pay for trial transcripts. As the Court pointed out, there can be no equal justice where the kind of appeal that a person is entitled to depends upon the amount of money he or she has.

The *Griffin* ruling was extended seven years later in *Douglas* v. *California,* a case concerning a state statute that permitted the denial of free counsel to indigent defendants on appeal if a state court had gone through the record of a case and decided that in its view no good would be served by the appointment of counsel. The statute was held by the Supreme Court to violate the equal protection clause. The Court noted that although a state may have no constitutional obligation to provide appellate review in criminal cases, once it does allow such review, it cannot condition the right to appeal on a person's financial ability to pay for court costs or counsel.

However, in *Ross* v. *Moffitt* (1974) the Supreme Court held that its ruling in *Douglas* did not apply to a second appeal. Thus, even where persons who can afford to hire their own attorneys enjoy the opportunity of appealing their criminal convictions a second time, the equal protection clause does not require that indigent defendants be afforded free counsel for a second appeal. In the Court's view, then, although the equal protection clause requires some degree of equality of treatment in the criminal justice system, it does not require perfect equality.

The right to equal treatment in the criminal justice system also applies to equality in sentenc-ing. The equal protection clause prohibits the practice of imposing harsher penalties upon criminal defendants because they are indigent. Therefore, it is unconstitutional to imprison criminal defendants merely because they are unable to pay a fine, which otherwise would be their only penalty. Further, it is unconstitutional to increase a defendant's jail term beyond the maximum statutory period because the defendant cannot afford to pay a fine. It is not a violation of the equal protection clause, however, for a state to require an indigent defendant to later repay the state for the services of appointed counsel.

Limitations. Beginning in the early 1970s the Supreme Court moved in the direction of restricting the recognition of further fundamental rights by stating that only those rights explicitly or implicitly guaranteed by the Constitution would henceforth be protected as fundamental under the equal protection clause. It would not be used as the source of constitutional protection for any right unless the right could be shown to have a definite connection to some other provision in the Constitution. The Supreme Court has held that education, housing, subsistence, and employment, although undeniably of extreme importance, are not fundamental rights entitled to the protection of strict scrutiny under the equal protection clause.

One of the most significant cases decided by the Supreme Court in this regard is *San Antonio Independent School District* v. *Rodriguez* (1973). The *Rodriguez* case concerned a challenge under the equal protection clause to a state system of financing public schools through local property taxes. According to the system, the state allocated approximately $225 per pupil per year to each local school district and empowered each district to raise additional funds through local property taxes, which were by law the only other means the school districts could use to raise funds and which by law could not exceed a designated percentage of the value of the property in the district. Because the value of property varied from district to district, so did the amount of money available for school financing. The school district where the plaintiffs resided was able to raise only $356 per pupil, whereas one of the other districts, with more valuable property, was able to raise $594 per pupil. Plaintiffs asserted that this gross disparity in education spending, which was the result of tying educational financing to the value of property in the district where a student lived, was violative of the equal protection clause.

The Supreme Court, in a 5–4 decision, ruled that this school financing system was not unconstitutional. The majority reached this outcome by first holding that only minimal scrutiny would be applied to the financing system because the right to an education was not a fundamental right. Although the Court quoted with approval the statement in *Brown* v. *Board of Education* that "education is perhaps the most important function of state and local governments," the Court went on to say that "the importance of a service performed by the State does not determine whether it must be regarded as fundamental for purposes of examination under the Equal Protection Clause." Only those rights, the Court continued, which are explicitly or implicitly guaranteed by the Constitution are fundamental, and the right to an education is not among them. Therefore, the fact that some children in the state received a better than adequate education while others did not was not sufficient reason for strict scrutiny.

Applying minimal scrutiny in *Rodriguez,* the Court found that the state financing system was a constitutional means of advancing the goal of local control of schools. As is the practice under minimal scrutiny, the Court accepted this goal without critically examining it and did not evaluate whether the disparities in the state school financing system were truly justified. Thus, when it comes to the allocation of scarce resources for school financing, the Court will ordinarily grant considerable deference to the other branches of government.

Following its ruling that education is not a fundamental right, the Supreme Court has also upheld the authority of a state to deny tuition-free public education to children who are not bona fide residents of the state. On the other hand, the Court has held that although education is not a fundamental right, a state may not deny public education to a student because he or she is the child of an illegal alien. The latter ruling was based upon the principle that there is insufficient justification to deny something as important as education to children because of their status as illegal aliens, for which they cannot be held responsible.

Another right that the Supreme Court has refused to recognize as fundamental because it is not guaranteed by the Constitution is the right to housing. Using only minimal scrutiny, the Court has upheld summary eviction statutes that give landlords the power to repossess premises without providing prior notice and a hearing to tenants and that preclude tenants from defending their failure to pay rent on the ground that the landlord had failed to comply with the requirements of the building code. The Court additionally has upheld the constitutionality of a statute that prohibited unrelated persons from living together in the same household. Taken together, these decisions are a clear indication that unless a statute is completely irrational, the Court will defer to the other branches of government insofar as the regulation of housing is concerned.

The same sort of deference will be shown to regulations that affect the right to subsistence, as can be seen in several cases in which the Supreme Court applied mere minimal scrutiny to review the constitutionality of statutes controlling the allocation of welfare benefits. Using minimal scrutiny, the Court has ruled that it does not violate the equal protection clause to provide different amounts of welfare benefits according to family size or according to the kind of welfare program in which a person participates. In this area and in the area of school financing, the Court seems to have been taking the approach that the allocation of scarce resources is primarily a matter to be determined by the other branches of government as long as they do not act in a manner that is entirely irrational.

The Supreme Court has also held that the right to employment is not fundamental, because it is neither explicitly nor implicitly guaranteed by the Constitution. This ruling occurred in several cases in which the Court held that mandatory retirement provisions do not violate the equal protection clause. In the first of these cases, *Massachusetts Board of Retirement* v. *Murgia* (1976), the Court sustained the constitutionality of a state statute requiring the retirement at age fifty of state police officers on the ground that it was a valid means of ensuring that police officers are of sufficient physical fitness to perform the duties of their work. Although the Court admitted that individual physical examinations would have been a more precise means of determining physical fitness, it nevertheless held that under minimal scrutiny the mandatory retirement provision was rationally related to the purpose of achieving a physically fit state police force.

When the *Murgia* case was first decided, many persons believed that the decision applied only to mandatory retirement provisions for jobs that especially required physical fitness because of their strenuous nature. However, the Supreme Court dispelled this notion three years later in *Vance* v. *Bradley* by holding that the equal protection clause was not violated by a federal statute that mandated retirement at age sixty for officers in the Foreign Service. The Court upheld this mandatory retirement provision on the ground that it helped to maintain the quality of the Foreign Service, which otherwise would suffer, the Court asserted, because at age sixty there is a decline in the physical and mental abilities needed for job performance. The Court made this assertion despite the fact that it is contrary to established medical knowledge, in addition to being inconsistent with a federal statute that prohibits age discrimination in employment.

It is apparent from the cases dealing with education, housing, subsistence, and employment that the Supreme Court currently is most reluctant to expand the recognition of fundamental rights under the equal protection clause. However, those rights that already have been recognized as fundamental—the right to privacy, the right to vote, the right to interstate travel, and the right to equal treatment in the criminal justice system—will continue to be accorded the protection of strict scrutiny under the Fourteenth Amendment's provisions.

CLASSIFICATIONS BASED UPON GENDER

At one time the Supreme Court saw nothing unconstitutional about classifications based upon gender. In fact, until 1971 the Court consistently upheld the constitutionality of statutes that contained such classifications. Most of these statutes discriminated against women by, for example, denying them the right to enter a profession, to serve on juries, or to obtain employment. These statutes and others like them were upheld against challenges under the equal protection clause on the ground that gender was a permissible classification properly within the discretion of the legislature.

The Court's early view is illustrated by an infamous concurring opinion authored by Justice Joseph P. Bradley in the case of *Bradwell* v. *State,* an 1873 decision sustaining the constitutionality of a state statute that prohibited women from the practice of law. Justice Bradley stated that "the natural and proper timidity and delicacy which belongs to the female sex evidently unfits it for many of the occupations of civil life." It was this sort of rigid thinking about women that led to the approval of many forms of invidious sexual discrimination.

In *Muller* v. *Oregon* (1908) the Supreme Court established a constitutional doctrine that would be relied upon to uphold sexual discrimination until the 1970s. The *Muller* case, unlike most other early cases involving gender-based classification, concerned legislation that was beneficial to women—to wit, legislation that mandated maximum working hours for women but not for men. The legislation was challenged by an employer of women who argued that it amounted to gender discrimination, which was a violation of the equal protection clause. The Supreme Court sustained the constitutionality of the legislation on the ground that it was a permissible means of improving health and working conditions. In the course of its opinion upholding the legislation, the Court stated that "sex is a valid basis for classification" and thereby established the new doctrine.

Although the Supreme Court's decision in *Muller* was directed only to a protective labor statute, thereafter the statement that "sex is a valid basis of classification" was mechanically followed in later cases by the Supreme Court and other courts to approve laws that severely disadvantaged women by, for instance, denying them admission to colleges and universities, denying them the right to make a will without the consent of their husbands, and in some instances subjecting them to harsher criminal penalties than those for men.

The Supreme Court continued to adhere to the doctrine that sex is a valid basis of classification through the 1960s. In *Goesaert* v. *Cleary* (1948) the Court upheld a state statute that prohibited the licensing of a woman as a bartender unless she was the wife or daughter of the male owner of the bar in which she would work. Assuming without question that the state could prohibit all women from working as bartenders, the Court concluded that the statute was a reasonable means of preventing the "moral and social problems" that could arise through the employment of female bartenders. Similarly, in *Hoyt* v. *Florida* (1961) the Court sustained a state statute that included all men on jury lists unless they requested an exemption but excluded all women from the lists unless they volunteered for jury duty. Despite what the Court referred to as the "enlightened emancipation of women from the restrictions and protections of bygone years," the justices nonetheless felt that women were "still regarded as the center of the home and family life," and it was therefore justifiable for a state to relieve them of the civic obligation of jury duty.

A breakthrough in the Supreme Court's treatment of classifications based upon gender occurred in *Reed* v. *Reed* (1971), which involved a challenge under the equal protection clause to a statutory scheme for the selection of administrators of intestate estates. According to the scheme, eligible persons were grouped into eleven categories, depending upon their relationship to the decedent. Those persons in categories most closely related to the decedent were given priority to be selected as administrators. However, where it was necessary to select between two or more persons in the same category, the statute provided that males were to be chosen first. For example, where a son and a daughter both applied to administer an estate, the statute directed that the male was to be chosen. The supposed purpose of the preference for males was to reduce the work load of state probate courts by eliminating the need to decide between persons who were equally entitled to appointment.

In a unanimous decision, the Supreme Court held that this form of sexual discrimination was an infringement of the equal protection clause. The Court stated that the objective of reducing the work load of probate courts was not without legitimacy but to accomplish that objective by giving a mandatory preference solely on the basis of sex was "to make the very kind of arbitrary legislative choice forbidden by the Equal Protection Clause."

Despite the court's ruling in *Reed,* its written opinion in the case was puzzling. In the first place, the opinion made no mention of prevailing precedents holding that sex is a valid basis of classification, and the opinion's silence on this matter raised the question of whether the doctrine was still viable. Second, the opinion adopted the terminology of minimal scrutiny but did not show the degree of deference to legislation that is usually associated with that level of scrutiny. In cases following *Reed* it became apparent that the doctrine that sex is a valid basis of classification was being overruled sub silentio and that gender-based classifications were being reviewed at a level of justification more demanding than the minimal scrutiny test.

In 1973 the Supreme Court decided its next case involving a gender classification, *Frontiero* v. *Richardson.* In this case the Court struck down a federal statute that provided that the wives of male members of the armed services would automatically be considered dependent upon their husbands for the purpose of obtaining military benefits, whereas the husbands of female members of the armed services would not be considered dependent upon their wives for the purpose of obtaining such benefits unless they could prove that their wives contributed over one-half of their support. A four-person plurality of the Court in *Frontiero* asserted that classifications based upon gender should be declared suspect and therefore subject to strict scrutiny. They likened gender classifications to those involving race and pointed out that the United States "has had a long and unfortunate history of sex discrimination," that has been "rationalized by an attitude of 'romantic paternalism' which, in practical effect, put women, not on a pedestal, but in a cage." They also noted that many laws throughout the country were based upon "gross, stereotyped distinctions between the sexes" and that women still faced pervasive discrimination in education, in the job market, and in the political arena.

A majority of the Court, however, did not join this opinion. Although four other justices agreed that the federal statute was unconstitutional, they did not feel that it was necessary to declare gender to be a suspect classification. They preferred to follow the approach taken in *Reed* and to save for a later day the question of whether gender classifications should be strictly scrutinized. Because a majority of the Court did not join the plurality opinion, it did not have the force of law, and as of 1986, a majority of the Court had not seen fit to rule that gender is a suspect classification. However, in cases decided after *Frontiero* it became evident that a majority of the court was creating a new, intermediate level of scrutiny that would be used in cases involving gender classifications.

For some time after the Court's decision in *Frontiero,* the law concerning gender classifications remained in a state of flux. The Court struck down a provision of the Social Security Act that granted survivor's benefits to widows but not to widowers. It also invalidated a state statute that required parental support obligation for sons until they reached the age of twenty-one but for daughters only until they reached the age of eighteen. In contrast, the Court upheld a state property-tax exemption granted to widows but not widowers, and it sustained a federal regulation that required the discharge of male, but not female, naval officers who had twice failed to win promotion after nine years of service.

In 1976 the Court decided *Craig* v. *Boren* and brought a greater degree of coherence to this area of the law. *Craig* involved what may seem to be a trivial law for the occasion of announcing an important constitutional development. The law challenged in this case was a state statute that permitted the sale of 3.2 percent beer to women at age eighteen but required males to be age twenty-one. The Supreme Court found that the statute was a violation of the equal protection clause. What was most important about the Court's decision was that it expressly articulated for the first time that classifications based upon gender were to be reviewed under an intermediate level of scrutiny. Gender-based classifications, the Court stated, will be upheld only if they are shown to be substantially related to the achievement of an important state interest. Thus, in *Craig* the Court made official what had been its unspoken practice in several previous cases: the use of an intermediate level of scrutiny to evaluate classifications based upon gender.

Since its decision in *Craig* the Supreme Court has confronted a variety of laws employing gender classifications and has found many, but not all, to be unconstitutional. The Court has ruled in several cases that laws based upon overbroad generalizations about the sexes are prohibited by the equal protection clause. For instance, in *Caban* v. *Mohammed* (1979), the Court struck down a state law that granted to a mother of an illegitimate child, but not to a father of one, the right to block adoption of the child by refusing to consent to it. The argument that the law was justified because mothers have a closer relationship than fathers to their children was rejected by the Court on the ground that it was an overbroad generalization that is unacceptable as a basis for legislative distinctions.

However, the Court in *Rostker* v. *Goldberg* (1981) upheld the constitutionality of a federal statute that required men, but not women, to register for the draft. In *Rostker* the Court evidently departed from its normal practice of applying intermediate scrutiny to gender classifications, because although intermediate scrutiny is the appropriate form of review for gender classifications, minimal scrutiny is ordinarily used to review federal statutes dealing with military matters. Rather than choose one or the other form of scrutiny, the Court took the unusual step of not designating any particular level of scrutiny to be used in the case. It then went on to sustain the statute as a permissible means of achieving military preparedness. Because women were excluded from combat service, the Court thought that it was within the authority of Congress to decide that women would not be needed in the event of a draft and to therefore exempt them from registration for it.

However, the Supreme Court returned to its practice of using intermediate scrutiny to review gender classifications in *Mississippi University for Women* v. *Hogan* (1982), in which the Court held that it was an infringement of the equal protection clause for men to be denied admission to a state nursing school. The plaintiff in the case, who was a registered nurse, had been denied admission to the school's baccalaureate program solely because of his sex and had been told (in what sounded like an echo of the separate-but-equal doctrine) that he would have to attend one of the state's coeducational nursing schools to obtain his degree. The Court, noting that the single-sex admission policy reflected "archaic and stereotypic notions" about the sexes, ruled that it was unconstitutional.

Where a law is gender-neutral on its face but has an impact that is sexually disparate, the Supreme Court takes an approach that is similar to the one it takes in regard to neutral laws that have a racially disparate impact; that is, the Court will not subject the law to heightened scrutiny unless it can be shown that the law was adopted with an intent to discriminate sexually. This approach was followed by the court in *Personnel Administrator of Massachusetts* v. *Feeney* (1979), in which the Court upheld a state law that provided a lifetime preference for state civil service employment to veterans of the military service. The preference caused a severely disparate impact upon women, given that 98 percent of the state residents who were veterans were male. The lower court that had heard the case before it was appealed to the Supreme Court had found that the law worked so serious a burden upon women that the legislature must have realized that it was sexually discriminatory.

Nevertheless, the Supreme Court ruled that the law was not adopted intentionally to cause sexual discrimination and therefore would be reviewed only with minimal scrutiny. In the Court's view, the legislative intent underlying the law was to grant a preference to veterans rather than to disadvantage women, and although the legislature may have been aware of the sexually discriminatory effect the law would have, the law was adopted despite that effect and not because of it. In taking this position, the Court ignored the fact that legislation is often motivated by mutiple intentions that are not so easily separable; a more realistic view of the legislative motivation in *Feeney* might reveal that its intent was to both prefer veterans and discriminate against women.

Intermediate scrutiny is used to review the constitutionality of benign gender classifications that are directed toward reducing the disadvantages faced by women as a result of discrimination against them. These benign gender classifications are not violative of the equal protection clause so long as they truly operate to women's benefit and so long as their legislative history reveals that they were in fact adopted in order to compensate women for past discrimination. Applying this standard in *Califano* v. *Webster* (1977), the Supreme Court sustained a provision of the Social Security Act that allowed women to compute their retirement benefits by a more favorable formula than men were allowed to use. The Court stated that this form of benign gender classification was justified in light of the impor-

tant governmental objective in reducing "the disparity in economic condition between men and women caused by the long history of discrimination against women."

On the other hand, in *Orr* v. *Orr* (1979) the Court struck down a state law that authorized alimony payments for divorced wives but not for divorced husbands. The Court concluded that the law was not sufficiently related to the goal of compensating women for the effects of past discrimination because it was not based upon financial need. In striking down the law, the Court noted that even statutes purportedly designed to compensate women for past discrimination must be carefully tailored because they "carry the inherent risk of reinforcing stereotypes about the 'proper place' of women and their need for special protection."

CLASSIFICATIONS BASED UPON ILLEGITIMACY

Some laws impose unfavorable treatment on illegitimate children whose parents were not married at the time of the children's birth. The Supreme Court has said that "imposing disabilities on the illegitimate child is contrary to the basic concept of our system that legal burdens should bear some relationship to individual responsibility or wrongdoing." Nonetheless, the Court's treatment under the equal protection clause of classifications based upon illegitimacy has not always been consistent.

The Supreme Court's first encounter with an illegitimacy classification occurred in the case of *Levy* v. *Louisiana* (1968), wherein a state was held to violate the equal protection clause when it denied unacknowledged illegitimate children the right to recover damages for the wrongful death of their mother. The Court reasoned that it is invidious to discriminate against illegitimate children "when no action, conduct, or demeanor of theirs is possibly relevant to the harm that was done the mother." But three years later, in *Labine* v. *Vincent,* the Court upheld the constitutionality of a law that subordinated the inheritance rights of illegitimate children to those of other relatives of the children's parents. In sustaining the law, the Court stated that the legislature should be afforded great deference to make rules to strengthen the family as well as to regulate the disposition of property.

In subsequent cases, however, the Court changed its mind about the degree of deference that should be given to the legislature in this area and began to review illegitimacy classifications with intermediate scrutiny. In *Gomez* v. *Perez* (1973), for example, the Supreme Court ruled that it was a violation of the equal protection clause for a state to deny illegitimate children the right to support from their fathers if the same right was given to legitimate children. Again the Court pointed out that there was no reason to distinguish illegitimate and legitimate children when both were dependent upon a parent for support. In reaction to the Court's decision in *Gomez,* the state promulgated a statute allowing illegitimate children to sue for support from their fathers but requiring that the suit be brought before the child reached the age of one. This statute was held by the Court to violate the equal protection clause because it did not provide reasonable opportunity for illegitimate children to present their claims for support to a court.

OTHER CLASSIFICATIONS

In several cases decided during the 1950s and 1960s, the Supreme Court moved in the direction of ruling that classifications based upon wealth that burden the poor were suspect classifications subject to strict scrutiny under the equal protection clause. This trend was suggested by the Court's decisions striking down poll taxes that burdened the poor and laws that abridged the rights of indigent persons to equality of treatment in the criminal justice system. However, the use of strict scrutiny in these cases might be explicable by the presence of fundamental interests rather than by (or in addition to) the presence of classifications based upon wealth. Still, in the poll tax case, *Harper* v. *Virginia Board of Elections* (1966), the Court expressly stated that "lines drawn on the basis of wealth or property, like those of race, are traditionally disfavored."

This trend was reversed in 1971, beginning with the Supreme Court's decision in *James* v. *Valtierra.* This case involved a state constitutional provision barring the development of low-rent housing projects by any state agency without prior approval in a local referendum. The provision defined a low-rent housing project as any development "for persons of low income." Although the provision imposed a barrier to the development of low-income housing, the Court subjected it to only minimal scrutiny and held that it did not violate the equal protection clause. In the Court's opinion, the provision was justified because referenda enhance democratic government.

Since its decision in *James,* the Supreme Court has consistently refused to use anything but minimal scrutiny to review classifications that burden the poor. In *San Antonio Independent School District* the Court upheld a property-tax system for financing public schools under which less money would be available for students in poor school districts than for students in wealthier districts. Despite the fact that the tax system disadvantaged the poor, the court saw no reason to apply heightened scrutiny to it and stated that in no case had strict scrutiny been invoked merely because a law burdened poor persons. And in several cases involving welfare benefits, the Court has used only minimal scrutiny to evaluate the constitutionality of classifications that burden the poor. It is clear from these cases that the Court has retreated from its original position and will review classifications that burden the poor only with minimal scrutiny.

The Court has also ruled that classifications based upon age are not suspect and will be reviewed under the equal protection clause through the minimal scrutiny test. In upholding the constitutionality of mandatory retirement provisions, the Court has stated that although the aged have suffered some unfair discrimination, they have not experienced "a history of purposeful unequal treatment," nor have they "been subjected to unique disabilities on the basis of stereotyped characteristics not truly indicative of their abilities." In making this assessment, the Court may not have been entirely realistic about the degree of discrimination inflicted upon elderly persons, but the fact remains that in the view of the Supreme Court, age is not a suspect classification under the equal protection clause.

Minimal scrutiny is also used by the Supreme Court to review classifications that regulate economic or commercial interests. Since the late

THE EQUAL PROTECTION CLAUSE

1930s the Court has consistently deferred to the legislature in regulating economic and commercial activities. For example, in *New Orleans* v. *Dukes* (1976) the Court upheld a municipal regulation prohibiting pushcart vendors from a certain area unless they had been continually operating their business there for a period of at least eight years. Emphasizing that the provision was an economic regulation subject to only minimal scrutiny, the Court stated that "the judiciary may not sit as a superlegislature to judge the wisdom or desirability of legislative policy determinations made in areas that neither affect fundamental rights nor proceed along suspect lines."

Thus, it can be seen that there are several areas in which the Supreme Court is extremely deferential to legislation that is challenged as violating the equal protection clause. There is a marked difference between the Court's approach in these areas and its approach in areas that involve a suspect classification, a fundamental interest, or a classification based upon gender or illegitimacy. In the latter areas the Court employs a heightened form of scrutiny to ensure that legislation is truly nondiscriminatory.

CASES

Bradwell v. State, 16 Wallace 130 (1873)
Brown v. Board of Education, 347 U.S. 483 (1954)
Buchanan v. Warley, 245 U.S. 60 (1917)
Burton v. Wilmington Parking Authority, 365 U.S. 715 (1961)
Caban v. Mohammed, 441 U.S. 380 (1979)
Califano v. Webster, 430 U.S. 313 (1977)
Craig v. Boren, 429 U.S. 190 (1976)
Douglas v. California, 372 U.S. 353 (1963)
Eisenstadt v. Baird, 405 U.S. 438 (1972)
Foley v. Connelie, 435 U.S. 291 (1978)
Frontiero v. Richardson, 411 U.S. 677 (1973)
Fullilove v. Klutznick, 448 U.S. 448 (1980)
Goesaert v. Cleary, 335 U.S. 464 (1948)
Gomez v. Perez, 409 U.S. 535 (1973)
Griffin v. Illinois, 351 U.S. 12 (1956)
Harper v. Virginia Board of Elections, 383 U.S. 663 (1966)
Hoyt v. Florida, 368 U.S. 57 (1961)
James v. Valtierra, 402 U.S. 137 (1971)
Jones v. Helms, 452 U.S. 412 (1981)
Korematsu v. United States, 323 U.S. 214 (1944)
Kramer v. Union Free School District, 395 U.S. 621 (1969)
Labine v. Vincent, 401 U.S. 532 (1971)
Levy v. Louisiana, 391 U.S. 68 (1968)
Massachusetts Board of Retirement v. Murgia, 427 U.S. 307 (1976)

Mississippi University for Women v. Hogan, 458 U.S. 718 (1982)
Muller v. Oregon, 208 U.S. 412 (1908)
New Orleans v. Dukes, 427 U.S. 297 (1976)
Orr v. Orr, 440 U.S. 268 (1979)
Personnel Administrator of Massachusetts v. Feeney, 442 U.S. 256 (1979)
Plessy v. Ferguson, 163 U.S. 537 (1896)
Reed v. Reed, 404 U.S. 71 (1971)
Regents of the University of California v. Bakke, 438 U.S. 265 (1978)
Reynolds v. Sims, 377 U.S. 533 (1964)
Ross v. Moffitt, 417 U.S. 600 (1974)
Rostker v. Goldberg, 453 U.S. 57 (1981)
San Antonio Independent School District v. Rodriguez, 411 U.S. 1 (1973)
Shapiro v. Thompson, 394 U.S. 618 (1969)
Shelley v. Kraemer, 334 U.S. 1 (1948)
Skinner v. Oklahoma, 316 U.S. 535 (1942)
Sosna v. Iowa, 419 U.S. 393 (1975)
Strauder v. West Virginia, 100 U.S. 303 (1880)
Vance v. Bradley, 440 U.S. 93 (1979)
Washington v. Davis, 426 U.S. 229 (1976)
Williams v. Rhodes, 393 U.S. 23 (1968)
Zablocki v. Redhail, 434 U.S. 374 (1978)

BIBLIOGRAPHY

Alexander Bickel, "The Original Understanding of the Segregation Decision," in *Harvard Law Review,* 69 (1955), examines the intentions of the framers of the Fourteenth Amendment. Charles Black, "The Lawfulness of the Segregation Decision," in *Yale Law Journal,* 69 (1960), evaluates the Supreme Court's *Brown* decision. Paul Brest, "*Palmer* v. *Thompson:* An Approach to the Problem of Unconstitutional Motive," in *Supreme Court Review* (1971), analyzes the role of legislative motive in determining unjust discrimination. Jesse Choper, "Thoughts on State Action," in *Washington University Law Quarterly,* 64 (1979), discusses the state-action doctrine that defines the reach of the equal protection clause. Kenneth Clark, "The Desegregation Cases," in *Villanova Law Review,* 5 (1959), comments on the use of social science evidence in cases involving racial segregation.

John Ely, "Foreword: On Discovering Fundamental Values," in *Harvard Law Review,* 92 (1978), considers the recognition and protection of fundamental rights under the equal protection clause. Owen Fiss, "Groups and the Equal Protection Clause," in *Philosophy and Public Affairs,* 5 (1976), analyzes discriminatory statutory classifications based on group membership. John P. Frank and Robert F. Munro, "The Original Understanding of 'Equal Protection of the Laws,'" in *Columbia Law Review,* 50 (1950), provides a historical survey of the meaning of the equal protection clause. Ann E. Freedman, "Sex Equality, Sex Differences, and the Supreme Court," in *Yale Law Journal,* 92 (1983), studies discrimination based on gender.

Kent Greenawalt, "The Unresolved Problems of Reverse Discrimination," in *California Law Review,* 67 (1979), analyzes affirmative-action programs under the equal protection clause. Gerald Gunther, "Foreword: In Search of Evolving Doctrine on a Changing Court—A Model for a Newer Equal Protection," in *Harvard Law Review,* 86 (1972), examines the emergence of an intermediate level of judicial review in equal protection cases. Leo Kanowitz, "Constitutional Aspects of Sex-Based Discrimination in American Law," in *Nebraska Law Review,* 48 (1968), is a historical view and analysis of cases involving discrimination based on gender. Kenneth Karst, "Equal Citizenship Under the Fourteenth Amendment," in *Harvard Law Review,* 91 (1977), applies the equal protection clause to statutory classifications bearing upon the rights of citizenship. Richard Kluger, *Simple Justice* (1976), is an exhaustive account of the events surrounding *Brown* v. *Board of Education.*

John Nowak, Ronald Rotunda, and Nelson Young, *Constitutional Law,* 2nd ed. (1983), in chapter 16, gives an analytical overview of Supreme Court decisions involving the equal protection clause. Jeffrey Shaman, "Cracks in the Structure," in *Ohio State Law Journal,* 45 (1984), is a study of the different modes of judicial review used under the equal protection clause and an analysis of their deficiencies. Symposium, "Forum: Equal Protection and the Burger Court," in *Hastings Constitutional Law Quarterly,* 2 (1975), is a series of articles that explore the interpretation of the clause by the Burger Court. Laurence Tribe, *American Constitutional Law* (1978), in chapter 16, provides an analytical overview of Supreme Court decisions involving the equal protection clause. Joseph Tussman and Jacobus ten Broek, "The Equal Protection of the Laws," in *California Law Review,* 37 (1949), is a theoretical treatment of the meaning of equality.

[*See also* BURGER COURT AND ERA; CIVIL LIBERTIES AFTER 1937; CONSTITUTIONAL INTERPRETATION; DUE PROCESS OF LAW; FAMILY LAW; FRANCHISE; IMMIGRATION, NATURALIZATION, AND CITIZENSHIP; PRIVACY; RACIAL DISCRIMINATION AND EQUAL OPPORTUNITY; *and* SEX EQUALITY UNDER THE CONSTITUTION.]

THE EXECUTIVE AND DOMESTIC AFFAIRS

James Lare

ARTICLE II, Section 1 of the United States Constitution imposes three legal requirements on anyone seeking the presidency: "natural born" citizenship, an age of at least thirty-five, and fourteen years' residency in the United States. Other nonlegal criteria, such as government-related experience, access to campaign funds, and a popular set of political beliefs, limit those likely to be nominated by a major political party. Background factors such as race, sex, religion, and even home state have traditionally played a restrictive role, although these barriers are being surmounted one by one.

METHOD OF ELECTION

On no issue confronting it did the Constitutional Convention of 1787 spend more time or effort than on determining an appropriate method for electing the president. But it also appears that this provision is one of the few on which there was general agreement. In the *Federalist,* no. 68, Alexander Hamilton asserted that the method for electing the president was "the only part of the Constitution not condemned by its opponents."

The electoral college—actually a series of fifty-one colleges—is described in the following terms in Article II:

> Each State shall appoint, in such Manner as the Legislature thereof may direct, a Number of Electors, equal to the whole Number of Senators and Representatives to which the State may be entitled in the Congress: but no Senator or Representative, or Person holding an Office of Trust or Profit under the United States, shall be appointed an Elector.

With the method by which the electors from any state are chosen under the control of its legislature, it is predictable that an impressive variety of methods have been tried. Some of the methods were enumerated by the Supreme Court in *McPherson* v. *Blacker* (1892). In various states the electors have been chosen, the Court said,

> by the legislature itself on joint ballot; by the legislature through a concurrent vote of the two houses; by vote of the people for a general ticket; by vote of the people in districts; by choice partly by the people voting in districts and partly by the legislature; by choice by the legislature; by choice by the legislature from candidates voted for by the people in districts; and in other ways.

In the first three presidential elections, the electors were chosen by the legislature. By 1824, however, in all except six states the electors were chosen by popular vote, either by districts or by a general statewide ticket. Since the Civil War, there have only been three departures from the general-ticket, or "winner-take-all," scheme. In 1876, Colorado had just been admitted to the Union, and the legislature chose the electors; in 1892, Michigan's Democratic party–dominated legislature preferred to have the electors selected by districts, in order to retain some Democratic electors in an anticipated Republican landslide. Maine is currently the only state departing from the general-ticket system; it employs a district system for selecting half its presidential electors. In the fifty other contests, the candidate receiving a plurality of the popular vote wins all the electoral votes.

The mechanical problems created by the electoral college are generally more troubling than any bias toward certain potential "swing" voting blocs that might exercise a disproportionate balance of power under the winner-take-all system. The Constitution, for example, does not require electors to vote as the popular plurality did in the statewide election; indeed, the framers even expected the electors to vote according to their own independent judgment. Today, however, the expectation is that electors will vote for the plurality winner in their state. In fact, sixteen states have passed legislation requiring electors to vote for the nominee on whose slate they appear. The Supreme Court has declared these mandatory elector laws constitutional, but it is not certain that any corrective action can be taken against the "faithless elector" who votes for a minority candidate.

A more common and potentially troubling mechanical problem arising from the electoral college system occurs when the winner of the popular vote fails to get a majority of the electoral votes. On two occasions the decision has been thrown into the House of Representatives as provided in the Twelfth Amendment: in 1824, when Andrew Jackson won a plurality but lost to John Quincy Adams in a House contingency election, and in 1876, when Samuel J. Tilden won the popular vote but Rutherford B. Hayes was preferred by a majority of the state delegations in the House. There have been four occasions on which the winner of the popular vote failed to win the office; in addition to the two cases mentioned above, Benjamin Harrison prevailed in the electoral college in 1888 even though Grover Cleveland had won the popular vote, and in 1960, John F. Kennedy, the winner, received fewer votes than Richard M. Nixon if one subtracts from Kennedy's popular-vote total those cast for the six unpledged Alabama electors who voted for Senator Harry F. Byrd in the electoral college.

In ten additional instances a shift of only a small number of popular votes in as few as three states might have created the same inconsistency. The probability of an inconsistency between the popular and electoral college results is one in three if the popular margin in the general election is under 300,000 and one in four if the popular margin is under 1.5 million. Thus, there is a high probability that such inconsistencies will occur regularly in the future.

Despite these problems, there is considerable inertia supporting the present system. Indeed, some argue that the winner-take-all system and the requirement of a majority in the electoral college to win the presidency helps to maintain the federal system by focusing attention on particular swing or competitive states and to preserve the two-party system by reducing the rewards available to third parties. It would appear that it will take a constitutional crisis greater than any thus far experienced to prompt either the political elites or the general public to mobilize behind a major effort to reform the method of electing the president.

TERM OF OFFICE

Article II, Section 1 is very explicit in stating that the president "shall hold his office during the term of four years." And while a shift in the starting date of each four-year term, from 4 March of alternate odd years beginning with 1789 to 20 January, was provided by the Twentieth Amendment, the main controversy surrounding the president's term of office has not been when it starts but whether an incumbent should be reelected more than once and thereby serve more than two terms.

Because most of those attending the Constitutional Convention of 1787 assumed that George Washington would be the first president and that he would serve indefinitely, there was a prevailing sentiment favoring the indefinite eligibility of the incumbent for reelection. The custom limiting any individual's tenure in the office to two terms was started by Washington himself, although his decision was based almost entirely on personal preference, with no thought of creating a precedent. The two-term tradition was shattered and then institutionalized in the Twenty-second Amendment (1951) largely as a result of Franklin D. Roosevelt's having been reelected to third and fourth terms in 1940 and 1944. While the traumas of the Great Depression and a world war led the American public to turn overwhelmingly to the president in office for his third and fourth terms in the early 1940s, there was an inevitable reaction shortly after World War II, resulting in a constitutional amendment specifying that "no person shall be elected to the office of the President more than twice, and no person who has held the office of President, or acted as President, for more than two years of a term to which some other person was elected President shall be elected to the office of the President more than once." The Twenty-second Amendment is intended to settle any ambiguity concerning whether the three-term prohibition applies only to three consecutive terms. In contrast with comparable provisions of several state constitutions, this amendment imposes a permanent ineligibility on any individual who has occupied the presidency for up to two and a half terms.

SUCCESSION TO OFFICE

Until the passage of the Twenty-fifth Amendment in 1967, there were serious questions and uncertainties relating to the line of succession to the presidency and especially to the problem of the inability of a president to discharge his duties. Article II, Section 1 of the Constitution reads,

> In case of the Removal of the President from Office, or of his Death, Resignation, or Inability to discharge the Powers and Duties of the said Office, the Same shall devolve on the Vice-President, and the Congress may by Law provide for the Case of Removal, Death, Resignation or Inability, both of the President and Vice-President, declaring what Officer shall then act as President, and such Officer shall act accordingly, until the Disability be removed, or a President shall be elected.

This paragraph raises such questions as who determines disability; whether a vice-president succeeds to the duties or to the office itself; what election is referred to in the last clause, the next regular election or a special election called by the Congress; and what should occur if both offices were vacated simultaneously.

Almost all of these questions were resolved by the Twenty-fifth Amendment. It simply states, "In the case of the removal of the President from office or of his death or resignation, the Vice-President shall become President." Section 2 continues, "Whenever there is a vacancy in the office of the Vice-President, the President shall nominate a Vice-President who shall take office

upon confirmation by a majority vote of both Houses of Congress."

In less than one decade following its ratification, both of the first two sections of this amendment were tested, the latter not once but twice. When Richard Nixon resigned the presidency in August 1974, Gerald Ford, his vice-president, who had been confirmed by both houses of Congress less than a year earlier, following the resignation of Spiro Agnew, assumed the office and duties of president. Unlike Nixon, who had consulted with congressional leaders and had agreed on a "caretaker" vice-president who would not run on the national ticket in 1976, Ford, in selecting his vice-presidential nominee, did not consult with congressional leaders or the Republican National Committee but simply nominated former New York Governor Nelson Rockefeller, insisting that he wanted someone of "presidential caliber" with whom he could run on a national ticket in 1976. By taking this partisan and self-serving position, Ford aroused the congressional Democrats, who tried with some success to embarrass both Rockefeller and Ford during lengthy nomination hearings. Rockefeller was finally confirmed, although many Democrats voted against his nomination, and the Twenty-fifth Amendment functioned well under the difficult circumstances existing during the Watergate period.

Nixon had won an overwhelming electoral victory in 1972, and Ford, with advance approval by congressional leaders from both parties, provided more legitimate continuity than would have been possible if the old Succession Act of 1947 had been followed, because then the Speaker of the House, a Democrat in 1974, would have succeeded a Republican president. Clearly the requirement that a new vice-president be nominated by the one who succeeds to the presidency and confirmed by both houses of Congress is legitimate in constitutional terms, even though it may be the case, as it was in 1974, that neither had been elected by the entire American electorate.

This emphasis on constitutional rather than electoral principles in handling presidential succession has not been adhered to throughout American history. The language of Article II indicating that an acting president shall exercise the power of the office "until . . . a President shall be elected" implies the possibility of holding an interim election to resolve a succession crisis. The Succession Act of 1792 made this possibility explicit by indicating that the president pro tempore of the Senate should serve as acting president in the case of a double vacancy until an interim election could be held. The Succession Act of 1886 required that the secretary of state act as president if a double vacancy should occur "until a President shall be elected." No specific provision for an interim election was included, but the acting president was required to convene Congress within twenty days, presumably so that a special election could be requested. By the time the Succession Act of 1947 was drafted, however, the notion of holding interim presidential elections had fallen into disfavor. That post–World War II act provided that the Speaker of the House should, in the event of a double vacancy, act as president "until the expiration of the then current presidential term." Here an explicit choice had been made favoring continuity in office as opposed to the holding of special elections to fill double vacancies, and the way was thereby paved for the Twenty-fifth Amendment, which reduces the chance of a double vacancy and stresses the use of the executive and congress to ensure continuity and legitimacy without resorting to interim elections.

The Twenty-fifth Amendment also seeks to resolve many of the questions that surround both the determination of presidential disability and the ending of a state of presidential disability. Under the provisions of this amendment, if the president is disabled, the vice-president acts as president until the incumbent is able to resume the duties of his office. Section 3 of the amendment contemplates the easiest of disability cases, wherein the president on his own initiative informs the president pro tempore of the Senate and the Speaker of the House in writing that he is unable to discharge the duties of his office and subsequently communicates, again in writing, that he is able to resume his duties. Section 4 spells out procedures whereby the vice-president and either a majority of the cabinet or some other body designated by Congress may prepare a written declaration that the president is unable to discharge the duties and powers of his office. Even in this instance the president may transmit to the leaders of the two houses of Congress a written declaration that no disability exists; but if the vice-president and a majority of either the cabinet or some other body designated by Congress disagree, they may object in writing within four days, and Congress, by a two-thirds vote in both houses within twenty days after it has assembled for this purpose, must decide which official will act as president. While this procedure for resolving disagreements between the president and others concerning the existence of presidential disability seems reasonable enough and would appear to safeguard the rights of all affected parties, there are certain to be major tensions in a crisis of this kind when hours and even minutes could determine the fate of the nation and the survival of its people.

REMOVAL FROM OFFICE

Article II, Section 1 of the Constitution refers to "the removal of the President from office," including his resignation, and Section 4 indicates specifically that "the President, Vice-President and all civil Officers of the United States shall be removed from Office on Impeachment for, and Conviction of, Treason, Bribery, or other high Crimes and Misdemeanors." Article I, Section 3 indicates that "the Senate shall have the sole Power to try all Impeachments [once the articles of impeachment have been passed by the House]. When sitting for that Purpose, they [the senators] shall be on Oath or Affirmation. When the President of the United States is tried, the Chief Justice shall preside: And no Person shall be convicted without the Concurrence of two thirds of the Members present." Paragraph 7 continues, "Judgment in Cases of Impeachment shall not extend further than to removal from Office, and disqualification to hold and enjoy any Office of honor, Trust, or Profit under the United States: but the Party convicted shall, nevertheless, be liable and subject to Indictment, Trial, Judgment, and Punishment, according to Law."

Andrew Johnson is the only president who has had the House pass articles of impeachment against him and been subjected to trial and vote by the Senate. In 1868, by a single vote, Johnson was acquitted on eleven articles of impeachment, ten of which centered around his efforts to remove Secretary of War Edwin M. Stanton and replace him with General Lorenzo Thomas. The eleventh article charged, among other things, that he used unseemly language and spoke in a loud voice. The impeachment trial of Andrew Johnson was a partisan political circus. Chief Justice Salmon P. Chase, who presided, made no secret of his own desire to become president, even though the individual next in line under the 1792 succession law, Benjamin F. Wade, the president pro tempore of the Senate, refused to disqualify himself despite his obvious personal stake in the outcome of the trial.

Richard Nixon is the only other president to confront a serious threat of impeachment. But whereas Johnson's trial had focused on constitutional questions relating to his power to remove a cabinet officer, the potential case against Nixon included charges of criminal conduct by the president and his immediate subordinates. There were also a series of noncriminal charges concerning the president's failure faithfully to execute the laws of the land. Most observers of the Watergate episode concluded that Congress, and especially the House Judiciary Committee, acted with the kind of caution and care that drained all credibility from the charge that a president had been hounded from office by a partisan and vindictive Congress. But with a fixed term of office and an extremely cumbersome impeachment machinery, Nixon was able to delay his departure for more than two years while the nation was distracted and even divided by a painful series of investigations and revelations of presidential misconduct.

POWERS OF APPOINTMENT, SUPERVISION, AND REMOVAL

Article II, Section 1 of the Constitution states that "the executive Power shall be vested in a President of the United States of America." The implications of this declaration are not clear. Some clarification of what the framers expected the chief executive to do is found in Article II, Section 2, which says that the president "shall nominate, and by and with the Advice and Consent of the Senate, shall appoint Ambassadors, other public Ministers and Consuls, Judges of the supreme Court, and all other Officers of the United States, whose Appointments are not herein otherwise provided for, and which shall be established by Law."

In fact, the president today has responsibility for making approximately twenty-seven hundred appointments in the federal bureaucracy. Most of these positions are held by individuals with policymaking or policy-interpreting responsibilities. Because these officials occupying the highest echelons in executive-branch agencies serve at the pleasure of the president, they may be removed from office at his discretion. This is in contrast with the almost 3 million career civil servants employed by the United States government who, since 1883, have been selected in accordance with standards of merit established by the Office of Personnel Management.

It is clear that to lead the country, the president must first be able to direct the activities of the executive branch. This requires that the president be able to select and influence the activities of the principal policymakers. But since the enactment of the Civil Service Act in 1883, presidents have found themselves without the instruments of personnel management needed to exercise effective policy leadership. Furthermore, in his efforts to direct and manage the federal personnel system, the president is subject to powerful and continuous political pressures. These demands may have their source in a congressional committee chairperson who has a stake in a policy dispute that is influenced by a presidential appointee, in a pressure group that is concerned with the actions of an appointee, or in the federal-employee unions in a dispute over the amount of a cost-of-living pay increase. Whatever the source of pressure, a president quickly learns that most of his personnel decisions have far-reaching political implications. He frequently finds himself on the horns of a dilemma: what makes good administrative sense often makes little if any political sense, or vice versa.

The Supreme Court did, however, after sidestepping the issue for almost 140 years, finally offer a decisive opinion regarding the president's removal power in *Myers* v. *United States* (1926). Speaking for a divided Court, Chief Justice William Howard Taft upheld the removal of a first-class postmaster by direction of the president alone and struck down the provision in an 1876 act of Congress that made the president's removal power contingent upon the advice and consent of the Senate when the original appointment required Senate confirmation. In *Myers,* Taft advanced the doctrine that the president is endowed by Article II with a power of removal that, as far as "executive officers of the United States appointed by him" are concerned, is not subject to any limitation by Congress and that all such officers are intended by the Constitution to be removable at the president's will.

There are, however, certain "officers of the United States" whose decisions and discretion are not fully controllable by the president and for whose policies he is therefore not fully responsible. A major category of these officers includes those who occupy quasi-judicial positions on the multimember independent regulatory commissions. Although the president appoints the members, this appointive power is limited in several important ways. First, the period of time served by board and commission members ranges from a minimum of three years to a maximum of fourteen, and their terms are staggered, so that when a new president comes into office, he finds many regulatory agency posts filled by persons appointed by his predecessor(s). A second check on the president is that in the case of all but two of the regulatory agencies (the Federal Reserve Board and the National Labor Relations Board), no more than a simple majority of the members may be from the same political party. In sum, the independence of the regulatory agency members is encouraged, although not guaranteed, by two principal conditions: first, the lengthy, staggered terms most of them serve and, second, the fact that they do not serve at the pleasure of the president and therefore may not be removed by him arbitrarily or because of a policy disagreement.

The latter condition restricting the president's power to remove officers with quasi-judicial or quasi-legislative duties was affirmed by the Supreme Court in *Humphrey's Executor* v. *United States* (1935). Late in 1931, President Herbert Hoover reappointed William E. Humphrey to a second seven-year term as one of the five members of the Federal Trade Commission. Twice in mid-1933, newly elected President Franklin D. Roosevelt sought to obtain Humphrey's resignation on the ground that their policy views were too divergent and that the country would be better served if the commission reflected the president's views. After Humphrey refused to resign, the president notified him several weeks later than he had been removed from office. The Court held that Congress could constitutionally establish agencies that are largely independent of executive control. In the case of the Federal Trade Commission, the statute creating it had specified that commissioners could not be removed except for malfeasance, neglect of duty, or inefficiency.

The scope of the president's removal power became an issue in the 1950s when President Dwight D. Eisenhower sought to remove a member of the War Claims Commission exclusively for political reasons. This case was different from *Humphrey's Executor* in that the statute establishing the War Claims Commission did not specify the bases on which a president could remove its commissioners. The Supreme Court therefore ruled in *Wiener* v. *United States* (1958) that because this commission performed judicial rather than executive functions, the president had no authority to remove one of its members solely for political reasons.

The full extent of the president's removal power has yet to be spelled out definitively. Since the broad removal power suggested by the *Myers* opinion in 1926, the Supreme Court has weakened it not only by exempting officials with nonexecutive duties *(Humphrey)* but also by protecting employees in non-policy-sensitive positions if their performance is satisfactory (*Elrod* v. *Burns,* 1976). In sum, it would appear that only those with cabinet or subcabinet rank and the president's immediate staff are left with no claims against dismissal by the chief executive.

LOYALTY AND DISLOYALTY IN EXECUTIVE AGENCIES

Except for a few isolated pieces of legislation, the government of the United States tended to maintain an air of unconcern regarding the loyalty or prospect of disloyalty of its employees until the beginning of the cold-war period. In 1947, however, President Harry S. Truman issued Executive Order 9835, which was designed to weed out from applicant pools any potentially disloyal employees and to remove disloyal incumbents from the executive service. Until 1947, it was Congress rather than the president that seemed most concerned about the matter of employee disloyalty in the federal service. The Hatch Act (1939), for example, made it "unlawful for any person employed in any capacity by any agency of the Federal Government . . . to have membership in any political party or organization which advocates the overthrow of our constitutional form of government." Early in World War II, the House Committee on Un-American Activities was created; in 1942 it demanded that the Federal Bureau of Investigation (FBI) investigate eleven hundred allegedly "disloyal" employees, of whom only two were finally dismissed from the federal service. Four years later, President Truman, on the urging of the Civil Service Commission, created a temporary commission to make a complete investigation of the loyalty problem and to recommend an appropriate program; it included representatives of the State, War, Navy, Treasury, and Justice departments.

It was the report of this commission that led to Executive Order 9835, establishing the mechanisms and standards needed for a full-scale loyalty program. In addition to making the Civil Service Commission responsible for investigating the loyalty of applicants for the competitive service and the head of each agency responsible for appointing a three-member loyalty board to inquire into the loyalty of existing personnel, the order also defined the standard for refusal of employment and for dismissal from an executive branch agency. That standard reads, "On all the evidence, reasonable grounds exist for belief that the person involved is disloyal to the government of the United States." The order went on to identify certain activities and associations of the incumbent or applicant as evidence of disloyalty, and it concluded by stating that disloyalty could be inferred from "membership in . . . or sympathetic association with any foreign or domestic organization, association, movement, group, or combination of persons, designated by the Attorney General as totalitarian, Fascist, Communist, or subversive, or as . . . seeking to alter the form of government of the United States by unconstitutional means."

Executive Order 9835 was replaced in 1950 by the Summary Suspension Act, which empowered the head of any agency to which the act applies to suspend without pay any employee when this is deemed necessary in the interest of national security. After such investigation and review, the agency head may terminate the employment of the suspended employee, and this determination will be conclusive and final. But since the late 1950s the Supreme Court has been inclined to protect federal employees suspected of disloyalty by insisting that they have not only the right to question their accusers but also the right to due process under the Fifth Amendment.

ADMINISTRATIVE STRUCTURE AND REORGANIZATION

Although the president is the chief administrative officer in the executive branch, the authority to establish and to reorganize departments and agencies, including the Executive Office of the President, is granted to Congress under the "necessary and proper clause" found in Section 8 of Article I. Congress may, of course, delegate this responsibility to the president by law. During wartime emergencies in particular, Congress is inclined to grant the president authority to create, reorganize, and even abolish certain kinds of agencies—subject, of course, to legislative guidelines.

Although the normal vehicle for creating new administrative structures is a law passed by Congress, existing statutes sometimes provide the president with sufficient authority to create an agency without having to obtain specific statutory approval. When President Nixon wanted to establish a system of wage and price controls in 1971, existing laws permitted him to assign responsibility for those controls to the Office of Emergency Preparedness. The General Services Administration furnished the required new office space, career civil servants were transferred to the new unit from existing agencies by the Civil Service Commission, and branch offices around the country were provided by the Internal Revenue Service and the Agriculture Stabilization and Conservation Service. Within a few weeks, a new government bureau had been created; all the president had to do was appoint the top officials responsible for drafting the new policies.

Since 1939, Congress has granted presidents authority to take the initiative in proposing organizational changes throughout the executive branch. These reorganization acts normally specify that plans proposed by the president will go into effect automatically within a specific period of time, usually sixty days, if neither house of Congress passes a resolution voiding the plan. Between 1939 and 1973, 105 reorganization plans were submitted to Congress, and only 23 (less than one-fourth) were disapproved. Indeed, the last two presidents who enjoyed sweeping reorganization authority before it was allowed to lapse in 1973 had perfect reorganization "batting averages": Lyndon Johnson had all seventeen of his approved, and Richard Nixon had eight without a defeat, although his plan for revamping the entire departmental structure never received serious consideration. In 1977, with President Jimmy Carter looking forward to a major restructuring of the executive branch, the Democrat-controlled Congress provided new reorganization authority. But in contrast with earlier versions of this authority, the 1977 reorganization act did not give the president permission to create or abolish entire agencies or to terminate any statutory functions. In addition, the 1977 law permitted no omnibus plans (that is, plans for complete reorganization) of the executive branch.

When a president wants to create a new department or agency or to increase or decrease the authority of an existing one, he has to submit a legislative proposal requiring affirmative action by both houses of Congress. Because there are normally extremely close and mutually rewarding relations between congressional subcommittees and existing agencies of the executive branch, the odds that a president will get a major reorganization approved are not very good. The list of defeated restructuring proposals includes nearly every postwar administration: Truman had a "department of welfare" rejected, Kennedy lost a "department of urban affairs" proposal, and even Johnson could not persuade Congress to combine the Commerce and Labor Departments. President Nixon had an ingenious scheme to realign six existing departments into four new ones, but his arguments fell on deaf ears in Congress. Even President Carter, who succeeded in creating the Department of Energy and the Department of Education, had his proposals substantially modified by Congress, mainly to ensure that the powers of the new cabinet-level secretaries could not be used to interfere with existing linkages among Congress, interest groups, and bureaus in the executive branch. In short, Congress has not welcomed or been very receptive to bold presidential initiatives to restructure the executive branch, although it has been tolerant of considerable shuffling of units and responsibilities within the Executive Office of the President, usually by executive order. In addition, Congress has accepted with good grace and sometimes even enthusiasm the creation of all sorts of temporary units and task forces, which are normally paid for out of the "unanticipated needs" appropriations granted to the White House.

The virtues of temporary administrative units within the executive branch have prompted Congress to view favorably a "sunset" principle, whereby agencies and programs would be terminated after a specified period of operation unless the appropriate oversight committee grants a renewal charter subsequently approved by both houses of Congress. Although the sunset concept appears attractive in principle to those who have been frustrated by the longevity of bureaucratic units, it has not been embraced in practice, because those who benefit from the operation of a given unit of government prefer not to have it subjected to intensive scrutiny and the possibility of termination on a regular basis. The bill creating the Department of Energy in 1978, for example, passed the House with its own five-year sunset provision, but that stipulation was eventually dropped by the Senate.

EXECUTIVE PRIVILEGE VERSUS LEGISLATIVE PREROGATIVE

Nearly as critical to the president as the power to organize and reorganize his administrative house is his power to control information and withhold it from Congress (or the courts) when it is in his interest to do so. This claim of "executive privilege" vis-à-vis Congress has been invoked most frequently with reference to foreign relations and national-security affairs, but it has also been used in purely domestic matters, most notably with regard to information that the Nixon administration wished to withhold during the Watergate investigations.

In the nineteenth century several presidents sought to withhold information concerning diplomatic and military activities, but each of them eventually gave Congress the information it wanted or relied on laws passed by Congress as the basis for withholding it. Prior to World War II, presidential refusals to give Congress information were rare.

THE EXECUTIVE AND DOMESTIC AFFAIRS

During World War II, President Roosevelt declined to provide congressional committees with FBI files containing background information on strikers in war plants. President Truman insisted on personally determining whether or not to honor congressional requests for departmental personnel records needed for loyalty-security investigations, and President Eisenhower refused to release the records of military officers to a Senate investigation into subversive activities led by Senator Joseph R. McCarthy.

It was the Eisenhower administration that first articulated the doctrine of "executive privilege" when Attorney General Herbert Brownell used the phrase in a memorandum to a congressional subcommittee that accompanied a letter from Eisenhower to the secretary of defense, ordering senior department officials not to testify before the subcommittee. Since a majority in Congress was sympathetic to Eisenhower's attempts to prevent Senator McCarthy from using unscrupulous tactics to destroy the careers of innocent government officials, no authoritative observer seemed inclined to point out that the president was claiming a power found nowhere in the Constitution. A few years later, Attorney General William P. Rogers insisted that Eisenhower did not have to share with Congress candid advice from his assistants or to provide interdepartmental memoranda, advisory opinions, or informal working papers, on the ground that they came within the scope of executive privilege.

Since 1960, presidents have varied considerably in their use of executive privilege. Kennedy used it to hamper congressional oversight in the area of foreign policy, especially during hearings on the failure of the Bay of Pigs operation. Johnson rarely used executive privilege, relying instead on the security classification system to keep Congress from learning about his Vietnam War plans. Nixon continued this pattern of withholding from Congress information relating to the Vietnam War, and he even went so far as to appoint some of his cabinet secretaries as White House assistants so that they could legitimately invoke the executive-privilege doctrine because they acted as personal advisers to the president.

Closely related to this pattern of gradually expanding executive privilege has been the assertion of "departmental" and "agency" privilege as distinguished from presidential privilege. It has again been mainly the Defense and State departments that have sought, especially during the 1960s and 1970s, to withhold information or give summaries rather than original documents when responding to congressional inquiries. Departments have on occasion even threatened to withhold information in order to create a bargaining relationship with congressional committees, whereby the agency representatives would agree to testify in executive sessions if they were subsequently permitted to edit the hearings and committee reports to delete classified and other sensitive information.

Neither the courts nor Congress have come to grips with the extent to which a president is free to withhold information on the grounds of executive privilege. On the few occasions when the Supreme Court has addressed this issue, it has tended consistently to protect and even to strengthen the executive's right to withhold information. Even when the courts ordered President Nixon to release tapes of conversations held in his office that might bear on Watergate crimes, the ruling in *United States* v. *Nixon* (1974) was extremely narrow and therefore left the historic flexibility of the executive-privilege doctrine largely intact.

Congress has also not been very effective in challenging the claim of executive or departmental privilege. It has threatened to impound funds but has no practical means for making good on that threat. There is little Congress can do to challenge a president who claims executive privilege in national-security matters. It may, however, take rather effective budgetary action against officials who seek to claim "departmental" privilege or in other ways refuse to cooperate with committees seeking to perform their oversight function.

THE EXECUTIVE AS LEGISLATIVE LEADER

Article II, Section 3 provides the constitutional basis for the president's role as legislative leader: "He shall from time to time give to the Congress Information of the State of the Union, and recommend to their Consideration such Measures as he shall judge necessary and expedient; he may, on extraordinary Occasions, convene both Houses, or either of them." Until the turn of the twentieth century, however, the initiative in legislative matters rested largely with Congress. The strongest of the nineteenth-century presidents, Jefferson, Jackson, and Lincoln, did take a rather active role in the legislative process, but their initiatives were clearly the exception rather than the rule prior to 1900.

President Theodore Roosevelt's first term represented the first major turning point on the road toward presidential assertiveness in the legislative process. Believing that the president should be a very active force in the political arena, Roosevelt submitted a number of legislative proposals to Congress, although even he cautioned an impatient aide against "the extreme unwisdom of irritating Congress by fixing the details of a bill concerning which they are very sensitive." Woodrow Wilson carried the presidential role in the legislative process a step further by actually appearing before Congress in person to speak on behalf of his proposals.

The role of the president as initiator of legislative proposals continued under subsequent twentieth-century presidents until it reached its most fully developed expression under President Truman, who started the practice of proposing a complete, integrated legislative program at the beginning of each session of Congress. By the beginning of the Eisenhower administration in 1953, Congress had come to expect a legislative program from the president. Even the Republican leaders became critical when Eisenhower invoked his strict separation-of-powers philosophy as a rationale for not intruding on Congress with legislative proposals of his own.

This striking ascendance of the president in the legislative arena should not be interpreted to mean that Congress no longer makes any substantive contribution to the lawmaking process. It still has an important role to play, but it involves criticizing and amending presidential proposals with a view toward harmonizing them with some of the more local interests and constituencies that the members represent. Nevertheless, as Randall Ripley, a close student of Congress, has written, it is increasingly the case that the president specifies "the bulk of the legislative agenda for Congress with his various annual and specific messages. Thus, even before specific actions are taken, the President, in effect, decides what is and is not most important for Congress to consider."

At least three critical factors help to explain the emergence of the president as maker of the legislative agenda and initiator of most specific bills. First, the periods of domestic and international crisis that have dominated much of twentieth-century American history have demanded the singular kind of leadership that only the presidency can offer. Second, during these periods of war or economic crisis, the presidency has been occupied by persons whose conception of the office included vigorous leadership. Third, the problems American society has confronted have been of such complexity and sensitivity that only the information and expertise of the executive branch has been sufficient to offer constructive solutions.

The increasingly dominant role of the president in initiating legislation was enhanced very significantly by the Budget and Accounting Act of 1921, which made the president responsible for submitting an executive-branch budget to Congress each January. Before 1922 each department and agency presented its own budget estimate directly to Congress, a process that made it almost impossible for anyone to establish budget priorities or control the overall level of federal spending. Congress has taken major steps to better equip itself to deal substantively and critically with the complex issues of the modern age. It has more than doubled the size of its staff since the 1960s and has increased its ability to make a more rational and perhaps even a comprehensive assessment of each year's budget bill. In 1972, Congress passed the Technology Assessment Act, which was designed to provide it with its own independent source of expertise in analyzing policy questions with important technological features. But even these significant steps by Congress during the middle years of the twentieth century to reclaim its earlier role as initiator of legislative proposals have not lessened the steady increase in presidential leadership in this area.

THE EXECUTIVE AS INTERPRETER OF THE LAW

The theory of the separation of powers and John Locke's maxim in his *Two Treatises on Civil Government* (1690) both suggest that "the legislature may not delegate its power." But in practice the legislature has always had to grant some discretion to the executive, and therefore, in effect, the legislature delegates some of its rule-making authority to the executive. The legislature in the American context has traditionally been viewed as having the right to pass three kinds of laws that represent a delegation of powers that the legislature might have elected to exercise itself: laws giving local agencies the power of self-government; laws that will take effect after some future event has occurred and been verified by an executive agent; and laws delegating a significant amount of substantive choice to the agent who applies the laws. The shorter designations for these three kinds of delegated legislative power are self-governing legislation, contingent legislation, and skeletal legislation vesting discretion in an executive official.

The earliest judicial involvement in this matter of how the legislative responsibility of Congress might be shared with the national executive occurred in the *United States* v. *Brig Aurora* (1813). The Nonintercourse Act of 1809 was designed to control trade with Great Britain and France, and it authorized the president to implement or suspend the restrictions contained in the act, depending on the occurrence of certain events that he was to ascertain on his own or through his agents. The *Aurora* was seized by United States agents for attempting to trade contrary to the provisions of the act after it had been reinstituted through a presidential proclamation. The attorney representing the ship's owner argued that "to make the revival of a law dependent upon the presidential proclamation is to give that proclamation the force of a law. Congress cannot transfer the legislative power to the President." The Court, however, held for the exercise of presidential prerogative, asserting that it saw "no sufficient reason why the legislature should not exercise its discretion in reviving the act of 1809, either expressly or conditionally as its judgment should direct."

This precedent was followed in *Field* v. *Clark* (1891), which upheld the Tariff Act of 1890. The act had authorized the president to suspend certain provisions of the law under certain specifically described contingencies that were to be ascertained by him. In upholding this delegation of authority, the Court cited an impressive list of similar contingency provisions in other statutes and of presidential proclamations issued when the specified conditions existed. The Court concluded on the basis of both precedent and principle that the contingent provision was legitimate: "Nothing involving the expediency or just operation of . . . legislation was left to the determination of the President. . . . Legislative power was exercised when Congress declared that the suspension should take effect upon a named contingency. What the President was required to do was simply in execution of the act of Congress." Justice John Marshall Harlan's argument in *Field* turned on the alleged definiteness of the fact to be ascertained by the president. It was this unmistakable clarity of what condition Congress had in mind that precluded the president from varying the application of the will of Congress in accordance with considerations of expediency and kept his judgment and action strictly "executive." But subsequent acts of Congress in this same field of tariff application clearly went much further—authorizing the president to adjust tariff rates after determining costs of production here and abroad, and finally, in 1930, authorizing the president to raise or lower rates set by the tariff statute by as much as 50 percent.

When the contingencies that a president must consider in executing the laws become very complicated, the Congress in effect has handed over the task of rule-making to the executive. From the very beginning, for example, the courts considered the setting of railway freight charges by rate-making commissions to be the exercise of a "legislative" function by these commissions. This issue first appeared in certain state courts in the early 1880s, and the judges responded with a substantial modification of the maxim against delegated legislation. Instead of attempting to argue, as the Supreme Court would about a decade later, that the acts creating these commissions did not involve delegations of legislative power, lower courts insisted merely that they did not constitute invalid delegations, inasmuch as the power involved was of such a character that the legislature itself could not satisfactorily exercise it. Not long after, the Supreme Court began using very similar language upholding congressional delegations of authority to departmental heads to make statutory regulations, and later in 1917 it advanced an even more elastic test of what constituted legitimate delegation of legislative authority to executive agencies.

In *Buttfield* v. *Stranahan* (1904), Justice Edward D. White upheld an act authorizing the secretary of the treasury to fix "uniform standards of purity, quality, and fitness for consumption of all" teas imported into the country, because "to deny the power of Congress to delegate such a duty would, in effect, amount to declaring that the plenary power vested in Congress to regulate foreign commerce could not be efficaciously exercised." In short, Congress may delegate its legislative authority when it is necessary to do so in order to achieve the results it desires, acting within its constitutional authority.

In *United States* v. *Grimaud* (1911), Justice Joseph R. Lamar spoke for a unanimous Court in upholding regulations promulgated by the secretary of agriculture under authority conferred by Congress to control the grazing of sheep in national forests. Justice Lamar recognized that "in the nature of things it was impracticable for Congress to provide general regulations" because there were "various and varying details" of each situation that it might be called upon to evaluate and perhaps intervene. The problem of such variability reflects the increasingly complex sets of conditions that governments confront today. In the face of these complexities and changes, the Lockean aphorism that "the legislature may not delegate its power" has had to fight a losing rearguard action.

APPROPRIATION ACTS, IMPOUNDMENT POWERS, AND THE LEGISLATIVE VETO

The president becomes an interpreter of the law in a most significant way when he spends funds provided by congressional appropriations or seeks to delay or halt the spending of funds through his power of impoundment. The Constitution specifies in Article I, Section 9 that "no Money shall be drawn from the Treasury, but in Consequence of Appropriations made by Law." Because this provision is clearly intended to operate only in the executive branch, it implies that spending is primarily an executive function. Conversely, it may be read to suggest that the role of the legislature in passing appropriations laws is primarily to set limits on executive discretion in spending, a thesis that is reflected in the earliest practices of the First Congress to operate under the Constitution. The first appropriation act to reach President Washington's desk,

for example, specified "a sum not to exceed $216,000 for defraying the expense of the civil list . . . ; a sum not exceeding $137,000 for defraying the expenses of the department of war; a sum not exceeding $190,000 for discharging the warrants issued by the late board of treasury . . . ; and a sum not exceeding $96,000 for paying the pensions of invalids." Although the first three appropriation acts were limited to these same three or four general categories, beginning with the Second Congress the annual appropriation acts became increasingly detailed. By the Twenty-fourth Congress (1836), the annual appropriation act filled more than fourteen pages with minute specifications, a dramatic increase over the less than one page needed for the first acts.

It was not until the passage of the Budget and Accounting Act of 1921 that a serious effort was made to restore to the national executive responsibility for planning expenditures while leaving to Congress its power of consent and grant. This legislation gave the president considerable initiative in shaping the budget and therefore an opportunity to influence Congress as it approached the task of passing an appropriations bill. The issue of where the balance of power between the president and Congress should be in specifying the details concerning spending bills is far from settled. The Budget Control and Impoundment Act of 1974 was an effort by Congress to impose fiscal discipline on itself by establishing tentative spending limits in the form of an early budget resolution before the appropriations subcommittees attempted to sort out the urgent needs of each executive agency and each congressional district. Indeed, the problems of federal financial planning became immensely complicated in the latter half of the twentieth century by the creation of a series of fiscal "entitlement" programs through which the elderly on social security and medicare, as well as military and "civil list" pensioners, receive grants and services, including cost-of-living increases tied to the inflation rate.

Although Congress, in preparing the annual appropriation bills, is not required by the Constitution to stipulate any more than the fact that its grants be spent to promote the "general welfare," it is clear that the members are deeply interested in how the authorized spending programs will affect their constituencies, and this concern often translates into very complicated and detailed appropriation bills. In sum, Congress is free to appropriate in whatever detail it thinks desirable. By skillful use of legislative language, Congress may deprive administrators of discretion that was normally granted in more trusting periods of the nation's history.

There are, in fact, occasions when executive-branch officials act as agents of Congress, not the president. The doctrine of "ministerial duties," for example, specifies that an official perform a statutory duty without exercising any judgment or discretion. Quite literally, neither the president nor a department head has any authority to deny or control a ministerial act. In 1838, in *Kendall* v. *United States,* the Supreme Court expressed the view that it would be an "alarming doctrine" if Congress could not require of any official in the executive branch any duty it views as proper "which is not repugnant to any rights secured and protected by the constitution; and in such cases, the duty and responsibility grow out of and are subject to the control of the law, and not to the direction of the president."

It was not until the Nixon administration in the early 1970s that a president resisted the ministerial-duties doctrine with vigor. This administration sought to extend in a major way the president's authority to impound funds, a fairly routine authority to set aside funds in a budgetary reserve for savings and for contingencies that had been granted formally by Congress in the Antideficiency Act amendments of 1950. The Nixon administration's use of impoundment included the curtailment or termination of programs it simply did not want for policy reasons. During 1973 and 1974 dozens of federal court decisions forced the administration to release those funds it had impounded because of policy disagreements with Congress. To secure its prerogatives more permanently, Congress passed in 1974 the Budget Control and Impoundment Act, which strictly regulates and limits the president's power to impound funds. When the president wishes to withhold funds temporarily (a "deferral"), either house of Congress may, by itself, veto his decision. If the president wishes to terminate spending authority permanently (a "recision"), he must gain the approval of both houses of Congress within forty-five days of continuous session. The president accepted this amount of congressional involvement in administrative decisions in return for receiving a rather generous delegation of power to make policy impoundments.

In considering these delicate but almost continuous struggles between the executive and Congress over congressional intervention in administrative decisions, it is important to recognize that there is a substantial gulf between the highest level of constitutional principles (which are addressed by the White House and the Justice Department and considered by the justices when the Supreme Court is called on to arbitrate between the branches) and the operating level far below, where bureau chiefs, subcommittee chairpersons, and representatives of client groups must work out day-to-day methods of operation.

An incident early in the Carter administration described by Louis Fisher (in Heclo and Salamon) illustrates this gulf and how it is handled by those responsible for implementing policies. The newly appointed head of the Agency for International Development (AID) was told by the chairperson of a Senate appropriations subcommittee that if agency-legislative relationships were to be improved, AID would have to seek advance approval from the appropriations subcommittee having jurisdiction over foreign assistance whenever it wanted to divert economic aid to military purposes or otherwise expend funds for purposes not previously cleared with Congress. To guarantee this new clearance procedure, the AID chief drafted a letter describing it and routed it through the general counsel's office before sending it up to Capitol Hill. When the legal counsel learned from the Justice Department that such congressional participation in administrative decisions was not constitutional, the Senate subcommittee chairperson wrote the procedure into the foreign assistance appropriations bill for the next year, and President Carter signed it without expressing any reservations. At the same time, however, the president notified the secretary of state that the attorney general had doubts about the constitutionality of the clearance procedure and instructed the secretary to treat the procedure as a request for notification rather than a legally binding requirement.

Below the level of constitutional principles defended by the Justice Department, then, the secretary of state and AID could notify congressional appropriation subcommittees of their intention to reprogram appropriated funds without feeling that they had abandoned their administrative prerogatives. For the time being at least, it would appear that all parties were satisfied. The president had defended his prerogatives, the AID chief had maintained rapport with Congress by seeking approval for the clearance procedure, and the review committee continued to exercise its control over appropriations that were subject to reprogramming.

As the scope of the federal government's regulatory power expanded during the 1960s to encompass social as opposed to economic regulation—to protect the environment, the safety of workers in a factory, or consumers using a new product—Congress began to seek greater control over the regulatory agencies, especially in their rule-making role, so as to curb the costs of regulation to the industries affected and also to establish its own priorities within the regulatory field. The vehicle Congress employed in gaining the control over rule-making was the legislative veto, through which individual committees or one of the two houses reserves the power to veto particular regulations proposed by executive-branch agencies to carry out their statutory mandates. This device had been developed in the 1930s and 1940s, and by the early 1980s several hundred separate legislative veto provisions were on the books, more than half of them enacted during the preceding ten years. Beyond these individual legislative veto clauses in particular statutes, Congress had begun to consider bills that would apply the legislative veto in a blanket fashion to all regulations promulgated by executive-branch agencies as well as independent regulatory commissions.

Through the early 1980s the presidency had not been able to find an effective means for curbing this increased use of the legislative veto by Congress. President Ronald Reagan, who had campaigned on a platform that favored deregulation, was just beginning to develop some tools for undertaking regulatory management when the Supreme Court in *Immigration and Naturalization Service* v. *Chadha* (1983) offered his administration dramatic assistance by declaring that Congress could not subject to later disapproval rules it had authorized the executive to formulate in pursuit of major policy goals. This gave the president a rationale for refusing to honor

any such congressional review demands in the future. And, indeed, President Reagan cited the decision striking down the "legislative veto" a little more than a year after it was handed down when he declared that he would not honor a congressional request to return for further permission to spend money already included in an appropriation bill he had just signed.

THE EXECUTIVE AS ENFORCER OF LAWS

Under normal circumstances, laws passed by Congress and signed by the president are virtually self-enforcing. That is, law-abiding citizens and institutions that are affected by new laws and by regulations promulgated in pursuance of those laws are usually willing to abide by them once they become aware of their existence and their obligations under the law. The problem of the executive as enforcer of the law frequently begins when the president takes some action that can be questioned as being contrary to the Constitution—usually because the action threatens to abrogate an individual's constitutional rights. Wartime, quite understandably, presents the most obvious occasion when presidential actions to maintain law, order, and national security may threaten the civil liberties of individuals.

Because the Civil War was fought within the nation's borders and came rather close to its capital on several occasions, President Lincoln found it prudent to issue several orders restricting individual liberty, the most important of these being the suspension of the constitutional privilege of the writ of habeas corpus, which involves the right to be told by a civil court why one is being imprisoned. Lincoln's first habeas corpus proclamation was issued in the early weeks of the war, and it was not until 1863 that he had the benefit of an act of Congress to affirm his power to suspend the writ. Although Congress incorporated in the act several procedural devices designed to placate the courts and constitutional purists, the Habeas Corpus Act of 1863 left to the executive the setting of policy concerning arrests and imprisonments. Prisoners accused of interfering with the war effort continued to be tried by military tribunals, and they were punished or released by the War Department. The Supreme Court did confront the question of the constitutionality of Lincoln's suspension of the writ at least twice following the passage of the act of 1863 with two different outcomes.

In the first, a fiery Copperhead, Clement L. Vallandigham, was arrested, tried, and sentenced by a military commission, but managed to petition the Supreme Court that his case be tried in a civil court. The Court ruled that it had no jurisdiction because a military commission was not a "court," and the federal judiciary was limited to cases arising in courts under existing law. (*Ex parte Vallandigham*, 1864). Two years later, Lamdin Milligan, another Copperhead, was tried and condemned to hang by a military commission for making "treasonable" speeches. He invoked the writ of habeas corpus, and his appeal reached the Supreme Court, which evidently felt freer to act now that the war was over. It decided that Indiana, the state in which Milligan resided and spoke, was not in fact part of the "theater of war" and therefore the civil courts there were available to conduct his trial (*Ex parte Milligan*, 1866). The Court ruled that the writ could not be constitutionally suspended under this set of circumstances. The *Milligan* decision has become a most troubling one for those who look to presidential power to enforce laws and preserve order in time of war, just as it has become a source of hope for those seeking to protect civil liberties in times of stress. In *Milligan* the concerns of the latter clearly prevailed.

The Court was again asked to review the president's efforts to enforce law and order on the domestic front during World War II. In 1942, in *Ex parte Quirin*, it responded to the appeal of eight saboteurs, seven Germans and one American, who were arrested by the FBI and turned over to the provost marshal of the District of Columbia before they committed any acts of sabotage. After a trial was under way before a military commission appointed by the president, the defendants petitioned the Supreme Court for permission to institute habeas corpus proceedings. The Court rejected their plea, arguing that, as enemy personnel, they were never viewed as enjoying the constitutional protections of the Fifth and Sixth Amendments.

The most extreme action by a president to protect national security on the domestic front occurred shortly after the Japanese attack on Pearl Harbor, when President Roosevelt empowered the secretary of war to designate "military areas" from which "any or all persons" might be excluded to prevent espionage and sabotage; he also designated military commanders to police these areas. The War Relocation Authority was created to provide for the needs of those cleared out of the military areas. Nearly 112,000 persons, the majority of them United States citizens, were eventually removed from the West Coast and placed in ten "relocation centers" in seven western states. This relocation exercise was challenged several times, never very effectively. In *Korematsu* v. *United States* (1944), for example, a Japanese-American with United States citizenship was convicted by a district court for refusing to be relocated and for remaining in his California home. The Supreme Court once again narrowed the scope of decision dramatically by upholding the conviction on the basis of the reasoning used in earlier relocation cases—that ethnic affiliation with the enemy made Japanese-Americans on the West Coast a special threat to the war effort, even though Japan was by then in full retreat throughout the Pacific.

The Korean War provided the Supreme Court with an opportunity to define certain limits to the president's power to seize property that he believed must be appropriated to meet wartime needs. President Truman brought a very quick response from the Court when he ordered the secretary of commerce to seize and operate most of the nation's steel mills, which were threatened by a strike. The anxious president cited "the authority vested in me by the Constitution and laws of the United States," but he ignored provisions in the Taft-Hartley Act (1947) that established special procedures to be used in national labor emergencies but did not grant the president authority to seize plants. In *Youngstown Sheet and Tube Co.* v. *Sawyer* (1952) the justices argued that the president had violated legislative authority and ignored relevant statutes already on the books. Like the *Milligan* case eighty-six years earlier, *Youngstown* casts a long shadow of doubt over the president's independent power to seize property in the interests of protecting national security and prosecuting a war.

There are clearly occasions when the president does not have time to let the courts assist him in the enforcement of law and order. He must be able to call on federal marshals and on the military forces of both the federal government and the states in his efforts to ensure that the laws are faithfully executed. The president's power to employ the military in the enforcement of the laws of the United States has undergone progressive enlargement over nearly two centuries, in part because of presidential initiative and in part as a result of congressional legislation.

The earliest legislation relevant to the use of military force by the president in domestic situations is the Act of 2 May 1792, under which the famous Whiskey Rebellion was suppressed. The act considered only the "calling forth" of the state militias, but that fact should not be overemphasized, because the small regular army was at that time fully employed manning the frontier and seacoast fortifications. The important feature of this statute is its description of the conditions under which the presidential powers it confers are to be exercised: "whenever the laws of the United States shall be opposed or the execution thereof obstructed, in any state by combinations too powerful to be suppressed by the ordinary course of judicial proceedings or by the power vested in marshals." When the president is "notified" of such a situation by an associate justice or district judge of the United States, he may call forth the militia of the state involved and other states if necessary, but before unleashing them against "the insurgents," the president must first issue a proclamation commanding the rebels "to disperse and retire peaceably to their abodes."

After various extensions and expansions of this authority over the intervening years, Congress, in an act of 29 July 1861, declared "whenever by reason of unlawful obstructions, combinations, etc." it becomes impracticable, in the judgment of the president, to enforce the laws of the United States by the ordinary course of judicial proceedings, it shall be lawful for him "to call forth the militia of any or all the States, and to employ such parts of the land and naval forces of the United States as he may deem necessary to enforce the faithful execution of the laws of the United States." The earlier requirement of a proclamation is here deleted, and in a subsequent amendment in 1903 the president was authorized, when calling a state militia into national service, to issue his directive for that purpose via the governor to the militia officers. Prior to that change, the call had gone simply to the governor.

The institution of martial law may be defined as a temporary condition during which the ordinary law, administered by ordinary courts, is superseded by the will of a military commander. It would follow then that martial law, when it is proclaimed under national authority, rests ultimately on the will of the president in his capacity as commander in chief. It is important to recognize that the use of the military in the enforcement of civil law does not invariably or even usually involve martial law in the strictest sense of that concept. Soldiers are often, for example, simply placed at the disposal and direction of the civil authorities as supplementary police. At the same time, because of the discretion that the civil authorities are apt to grant the military in any emergency requiring its assistance, the distinction between a temporary employment of the military and a regime of martial law is rarely clear. For this reason the notion of martial law leads in two directions, one tending toward military government where the military replaces civil authorities and institutions almost entirely, and the other, toward situations where civil authority remains theoretically in control but is in fact dependent on direct military aid to maintain law and order. In between the two, of course, is the situation that prevailed throughout the North during the Civil War, when the privilege of habeas corpus was suspended as to certain classes of subjects, although most of the other features of martial law were not present.

THE EXECUTIVE AND SELECTED DOMESTIC POLICIES

Presidential involvement in domestic policymaking varies much more from president to president than it does in foreign affairs, and the usual pattern is for the president to be less influential in domestic matters than he is in shaping foreign policy. A number of factors account for this difference: the domestic difficulties are felt more directly by various constituencies and interest groups, Congress is better equipped and more highly motivated to formulate responses to domestic problems, and the president, except in times of extraordinary crisis, such as the Great Depression, has greater difficulty getting his way in the resolution of domestic problems. Despite these complicating features in the domestic policymaking process, virtually every modern president has had a major role in shaping the federal government's response to national economic problems such as unemployment, inflation, high interest rates, budget deficits, and trade imbalances. Since the passage of the Employment Act of 1946, the president has been obligated to provide the primary leadership in matters of economic policy. That legislation gave the president a specialized staff headed by the three-member Council of Economic Advisers to assist him in analyzing economic trends and recommending to Congress policies to help promote "maximum employment, production, and purchasing power."

Since the 1930s the president's principal problem with respect to the domestic economy has been to choose from among at least four competing economic theories that would each have the federal government use a fundamentally different approach to achieving the goals of the 1946 act. The principal approaches to economic stability and moderate but steady growth that have been in vogue during the twentieth century include the primacy of a balanced federal budget advocated by traditional conservative economists; the use of government spending and taxing powers (fiscal policy) to correct for economic fluctuations (a Keynesian approach, after the British economic theorist John Maynard Keynes); monetarism, or regulating the money supply, chiefly through the Federal Reserve System, so that it increases no faster than the actual growth rate of the economy; and "supply-side" economics, which emphasizes the need to promote savings and investment by entrepreneurs to keep production, employment, and purchasing power all at high levels. In general, it may be argued that since the 1930s, Democratic presidents have favored the fiscal approach, whereas Republican presidents have favored the monetarist approach. The balanced-budget and supply-side economic policies have not been given a real test in recent decades.

No one of these alternative approaches has been a panacea for national economic problems. Balanced budgets have been difficult to achieve because of the ease of the government's borrowing and the reluctance of elected officials to tax voters to pay for rapidly increasing and ever more costly services. Fiscal policy (government spending to stimulate greater economic activity) tends to have an inflationary bias. Monetarism

(curbing in the money supply) often leads to higher interest rates and rising unemployment. Supply-side policies tend to benefit potential investors without guaranteeing benefits to workers and consumers. Very high expenditures for national defense during the decades since the early 1940s have prevented recent presidents from testing as fully as they might any of the four approaches to national economic policy.

As with most domestic policies, economic policy is the product of multiple political and interest-group pressures, with the president—after delivering an economic message with specific policy proposals to Congress—having to settle for whatever the dominant coalition in Congress is able to get passed. Both the president and Congress are increasingly confronted with economic phenomena over which they have very limited control: the interdependence of the American economy with those of other countries, American dependence on foreign sources for raw materials and oil, and the declining productivity of the highly paid American work force relative to that of a growing number of competitors. Both the president and Congress have improved the staff support they use to provide analyses and recommendations in the economic area. Along with the Council of Economic Advisers and the Office of Management and Budget, the president is also assisted by cabinet officers and Executive Office staff members concerned with policy development, science and technology, and special trade negotiations. In the domestic policy field, macroeconomic decisions are without doubt the most critical faced by any presidential administration.

Modern presidents have also played a major role in shaping microeconomic policy, that area of economic life which focuses on specific industries or on the activities of closely related industries. The development of this area of domestic policy began at the national level with the passage of the act creating the Interstate Commerce Commission in 1887 and the Sherman Antitrust Act in 1890. Both of these statutes had as their basic purpose the preservation of fair competition in the marketplace. In the latter case in particular, it was the president—first Theodore Roosevelt and later William Howard Taft—who was responsible for giving the antitrust laws meaning. Roosevelt with his usual public fanfare and Taft with his characteristic quiet effectiveness enforced the Sherman Act to protect the marketplace from oligopoly or monopoly. Woodrow Wilson persuaded Congress to pass the Clayton Antitrust Act and to create the Federal Trade Commission in 1914; the latter agency has a broad responsibility to protect the marketplace from a number of unfair business practices. Franklin Roosevelt supported legislation establishing other regulatory commissions to oversee such varied activities as securities markets, electronic communications, commercial aviation, and labor-management relations. By the late 1940s, presidents seemed quite willing to accept this far-reaching pattern of regulation over a number of economic activities, but they differed in the degree to which they encouraged vigorous enforcement efforts.

In the late 1960s, Congress embarked on a new set of regulatory efforts designed to achieve such noneconomic goals as a cleaner environment, safe products for consumers, and greater safety in the workplace. As the economic and administrative costs of these new regulatory ventures became clearer in the 1970s, however, Gerald Ford and Jimmy Carter supported a movement toward "deregulation" that began to gain momentum in Congress. This movement, which emerged in such fields as transportation and consumer finance, gained momentum with efforts to provide regulatory relief initiated by the Reagan administration.

Given the scope of federal regulatory activity, it is unlikely that future presidents will have the option of remaining aloof from the debate over whether to expand or curtail regulatory impacts in any area of economic or social activity. At the same time, presidential management in this area of microeconomic policy is likely to focus on procedural and resource-allocation issues rather than on any sustained effort to engage in a centralized review of substantive regulations promulgated by a number of federal agencies. Only major scandals or widespread public anxiety over such issues as transport safety or contaminated medications are likely to bring the White House actively into the substantive side of current regulatory efforts, and then only when the president adheres to an activist philosophy.

The modern presidency has played a substantive, as well as a symbolic, role in promoting the cause of civil rights, particularly between the late 1950s and the mid-1960s. Until 1957 the influence of southern members of Congress with assistance from conservative northerners blocked any far-reaching efforts by the federal government to guarantee equal protection of all citizens in such areas as voting rights; access to educational, employment, and housing opportunities; and the use of public accommodations and transportation services. It was in 1957 that a southern senator who later occupied the White House, Lyndon Johnson, provided leadership for legislative attempts to give the federal government increased responsibility for ensuring all citizens equal opportunity to participate in the political, economic, and recreational life of the nation. This broad area of regulatory activity has, like economic, safety, and environmental regulation, been largely institutionalized through the operation of such agencies as the Equal Employment Opportunity Commission, the Departments of Education and Labor, and the Civil Rights Division of the Justice Department. But, as in most other areas of domestic policy, it is presidential initiatives through public statements and the issuing of executive orders that mobilize energy and resources to address the remaining instances of discrimination and segregation in American society.

By the 1980s the problems of civil rights enforcement were primarily a matter of fine-tuning the effects of legislation and agencies already in operation. Activist presidents, whether liberal or conservative, are more likely than passive chief executives to enter into such equal-rights controversies as affirmative action and comparable worth. It is clear, however, that when influential or even simply vocal segments of the body politic become aroused on domestic issues such as civil rights, it is difficult for a modern president to remain on the sidelines. The expectation of the American public, for better or worse, is that the president can and should be involved in settling virtually every major public dispute and resolving every significant public problem. This expectation often places an impossible burden on a single official, notwithstanding the massive institutionalization of his office in the mid-twentieth century, but this popular focus on the chief executive is also a powerful unifying force in an otherwise strikingly diverse and at times seriously fragmented society.

THE EXECUTIVE AND DOMESTIC AFFAIRS

CASES

Buttfield v. Stranahan, 192 U.S. 470 (1904)
Elrod v. Burns, 427 U.S. 347 (1976)
Field v. Clark, 143 U.S. 649 (1891)
Humphrey's Executor v. United States, 295 U.S. 602 (1935)
Immigration and Naturalization Service v. Chadha, 462 U.S. 919 (1983)
Kendall v. United States, 12 Peters 524 (1838)
Korematsu v. United States, 323 U.S. 214 (1944)
McPherson v. Blacker, 146 U.S. 1 (1892)
Ex parte Milligan, 4 Wallace 2 (1866)
Myers v. United States, 272 U.S. 52 (1926)
Ex parte Quirin, 317 U.S. 1 (1942)
United States v. Brig Aurora, 7 Cranch 382 (1813)
United States v. Grimaud, 220 U.S. 506 (1911)
United States v. Nixon, 418 U.S. 683 (1974)
Ex parte Vallandigham, 1 Wallace 243 (1864)
Wiener v. United States, 357 U.S. 349 (1958)
Youngstown Sheet and Tube Co. v. Sawyer, 343 U.S. 579 (1952)

BIBLIOGRAPHY

Harold M. Barger, *The Impossible Presidency* (1984), suggests that popular expectations have outdistanced the capacity of the office to respond. James M. Burns, *The Power to Lead: The Crisis of the American Presidency* (1984), provides an analysis emphasizing that the institutional setting in which the presidency must operate contributes to the difficulties of the office. Edwin S. Corwin, *The President: Office and Powers, 1787–1984,* 5th ed. (1984), is the standard work on the constitutional and judicial bases of the office. Robert E. Di Clerico, *The American President,* 2nd ed. (1983), includes some of the newer perspectives on the presidency, including the role of the press, leadership, White House decision-making, and presidential personality; and, as ed., *Analyzing the Presidency* (1985), is a collection of essays on aspects of the office.

George C. Edwards III and Stephen J. Wayne, eds., *Studying the Presidency* (1983), offers guidance on approaches to analyzing the office. Hugh Heclo and Lester M. Salamon, eds., *The Illusion of Presidential Government* (1981), is a collection of rather sophisticated essays on aspects of presidential management in such areas as budgeting, personnel, federal regulation, macroeconomic policy, and national security. Emmet J. Hughes, *The Living Presidency* (1973), is a very realistic and insightful view of the office by one who served in the Eisenhower administration. Louis W. Koenig, *The Chief Executive,* 4th ed. (1981), remains one of the best-organized and most comprehensive texts on the presidency. Richard E. Neustadt, *Presidential Power* (1980), became an immediate classic when it was interpreted as a guidebook for John F. Kennedy when he was elected.

Richard M. Pious, *The American Presidency* (1979), asks whether presidential power is a poison or a positive instrument and concludes that we can find a better balance between presidential leadership and collaborative government. George Reedy, *The Twilight of the Presidency* (1970), suggests that modern presidents are increasingly isolated from real public concerns by their "palace guards." Randall Ripley, *Congress: Process and Policy* (1975), is a most useful compendium of data concerning the ways in which the legislative and executive branches interact in the making of public policy. Clinton L. Rossiter, *The American Presidency,* 2nd ed. (1960), was the first of the post–World War II classics examining the presidency. Arthur Schlesinger, Jr., *The Imperial Presidency* (1973), argues that presidential power and influence is increasingly unchecked by Congress, interest groups, or other representative bodies. Richard A. Watson and Norman C. Thomas, *The Politics of the Presidency* (1983), is a primarily political interpretation of the office, with a distinctive thesis. [*See also* ADMINISTRATIVE AGENCIES; ADMINISTRATIVE LAW; CONGRESS; EXECUTIVE AND FOREIGN AFFAIRS; MILITARY LAW; *and* RACIAL DISCRIMINATION AND EQUAL OPPORTUNITY.]

THE EXECUTIVE
AND FOREIGN AFFAIRS

Louis Henkin

"THE transaction of business with foreign nations," Thomas Jefferson wrote, "is *Executive altogether*" (emphasis his). One hundred and fifty years later, the Supreme Court of the United States referred, as to an established, incontrovertible fact, to the "very delicate, plenary and exclusive power of the President as the sole organ of the federal government in the field of international relations" (*United States* v. *Curtiss-Wright Export Corp.,* 1936).

A plenary and exclusive executive power in international relations is not easy to find in the United States Constitution. Yet, without firm support in constitutional text, the presidency has grown in two hundred years to become what is probably the most powerful legitimate office in the world, and control of foreign affairs is a large part of that power. With time, constitutional principle has grown to reflect and support historical practice.

Presidential authority in foreign affairs, however, is not unlimited. It is subject to important qualifications and restraints built into the constitutional framework. Large areas of authority that presidents have claimed have not gone uncontested. Beginning with James Madison's challenge to Alexander Hamilton's defense of President Washington's Neutrality Proclamation, constitutional text has been invoked to support congressional claims to substantial exclusive powers in foreign affairs and to a large concurrent authority with the president, with Congress dominating in case of conflict. In the 1970s, when the national malaise over the Vietnam War and the Watergate affair led to recriminations against presidents and the presidency, Congress asserted authority more widely and with increasing vigor.

The competing claims of president and Congress remain largely unresolved, in principle and in practice. The courts have said little. The scope of executive authority in foreign affairs and its relation to the powers of Congress are the major unresolved and perhaps intractable issues of separation of powers in constitutional jurisprudence and in national politics.

The United States Constitution speaks of "the President." In fact, the president is the presidency, which in turn has become the executive branch, consisting now of millions of officials and employees, of whom tens of thousands in the Department of State and the Foreign Service are directly involved in foreign relations and many more of which in the Departments of Defense, Commerce, Justice, and others impinge on foreign affairs in important ways. In constitutional theory, they are all "the President," though occasionally that theory recognizes the bureaucratic realities of the foreign-policy process.

THE CONSTITUTIONAL BLUEPRINT

Although the words *foreign affairs* are not in the United States Constitution, it is clear that United States relations with other states were to be the sole responsibility of the national government. The distribution of that authority among the branches of that government has been less clear. The powers of the president in particular seem few and meager.

Article II contains all that the Constitution says about presidential power. Under its terms, the foreign-affairs powers of the president appear to consist only of power to appoint ambassadors, with the advice and consent of the Senate, and power to make treaties, also subject to such advice and consent with the proviso that two-thirds of the senators present must concur (Article II, Section 2). The president also has authority to receive ambassadors (Article II, Section 3). Other general powers conferred on him may also have significance for foreign relations. The president shall be commander in chief of the armed forces (Article II, Section 2). He shall take care that the laws be faithfully executed (Article II, Section 3), which includes laws relating to American foreign relations. These explicit constitutional provisions hardly seem sufficient to support the powerful presidency of the end of the twentieth century.

There have been views on presidential power that support extensive executive authority in foreign and domestic affairs beyond what the Constitution explicitly provides. In particular, Theodore Roosevelt contended that every executive officer was a "steward of the people," with authority to do whatever was in the people's interest, and that the president could do anything that the public interest required so long as it was not forbidden by the Constitution or the laws. That view, however, was rejected as a general principle by Roosevelt's successor, William Howard Taft, and has not commended itself to many. Although it may not be an inaccurate description of the views that presidents generally hold of their authority in foreign affairs, it is at best a conclusion and has to be supported by reference to accepted constitutional sources.

Constitutional reticence as to presidential power has inspired imaginative constitutional construction. Alexander Hamilton argued that the United States Constitution, in providing that "the executive Power shall be vested in a President of the United States of America," conferred upon the president the executive power, all executive power. Principal forms of executive power —authority to make treaties and to appoint and receive ambassadors, and the command of the armed forces—are expressly enumerated, but the rest of the executive power is conferred upon the president by the general grant. That, according to Montesquieu and others, includes the control of foreign relations. According to the United States Constitution, the president's executive power is indeed subject to express limitations and qualifications: the need for Senate consent to appointments and treaties; and the express allocation of some executive authority to Congress, such as the powers to declare war, to regulate commerce with foreign nations, and to appropriate money. But whatever foreign-affairs powers are not otherwise allocated or limited are within the executive power of the president. All limitations and qualifications on that general grant are to be strictly construed.

A different basis for supplementing the express allocations of authority to the president builds on the *Curtiss-Wright* doctrine. In that case, the Supreme Court expounded that as regards foreign affairs, the federal government has all the powers inherent in the nationhood and sovereignty of the United States, whether or not such powers are enumerated in the Constitution. Those unlisted powers are, as a matter of course, exercised for the United States by the political branches of the national government. In addition to enumerated powers, then, the president exercises those powers inherent in the nationhood of the United States that are "executive" in character, and Congress those that are "legislative." It would remain to determine which powers inherent in sovereignty are executive in character or have executive dimensions.

Hamilton's view that the executive-power clause is a "grant in bulk" of executive power, including the conduct of foreign relations, has never been accepted by the Supreme Court (though it has not been rejected either). The extraconstitutional source of national power in foreign affairs suggested by *Curtiss-Wright* also has not been enthusiastically embraced. Both theories, moreover, carry the implication that the foreign and the domestic domains are discrete, and assume that they can be readily defined; but while some elements in national policy can be readily classified as foreign or domestic, others may as easily be considered domestic as foreign or may partake sufficiently of each to belong in both classes.

Avoiding such special doctrines, some courts and commentators have invoked accepted modes of construing the Constitution to infer additional presidential powers from those expressed. Some of the extrapolations that have been proposed are less plausible than others; and sometimes it is as reasonable to conclude that a particular power claimed by the president belongs rather to Congress, as implied in one of its express powers. But it is not extravagant to conclude that the president's power to appoint ambassadors and his authority to receive foreign ambassadors imply the power to recognize foreign states and governments, to maintain or terminate diplomatic relations, and to accord or deny diplomatic privileges, immunities, or courtesies. It is a small additional step to accept the view that the president is "sole organ" in foreign relations, a characterization expressed by Representative John Marshall before he became chief justice of the United States and adopted by the Supreme Court in *Curtiss-Wright.*

TWO HUNDRED YEARS AS SOLE ORGAN

The president's listed powers—the treaty power, the power to appoint ambassadors, the authority as commander in chief of the armed forces—have been important building blocks of his plenary power in foreign affairs. No less important has been the development of his role as sole organ. In its primary meaning and its principal implications, that presidential role was not doubted even before Marshall gave it a name. Since then, it has been firmly established and is beyond question. Today Congress and congressional committees are "lobbied" by representatives of foreign governments, who in turn monitor what Congress does and says, including much that often is intended for, if not addressed primarily to, one or more foreign governments. But only the president speaks officially for the United States; only the president communicates officially with other states.

When Marshall described the president as the sole organ of communication he did not necessarily imply that the president also determines what shall be communicated. From the beginning, however, control of the means of communication governed the message. Ambassadors were appointed by the president and reported to him, giving the president a monopoly of information and acknowledged expertise. Through them, the president was the eyes, ears, and voice of the United States. Diplomacy, moreover, had the tradition, and engendered the habits, of secrecy, and it secrets were not to be shared lightly with the public or even its representatives in Congress.

The president (and the executive branch) conducts United States foreign relations, which is sometimes distinguished from "making foreign policy." But conducting foreign relations itself makes policy, for it communicates attitudes and intentions and inevitably leads to understandings and commitments as the president acts and makes claims on behalf of the United States and responds to the actions and claims of others. From the Monroe Doctrine (and earlier) to contemporary presidential doctrines, presidents have also explicitly declared the interests and proclaimed the intentions of the United States.

Foreign affairs, moreover, do not consist only, or even principally, of major doctrines or declarations or of treaties made or wars declared: they are a continuing process, and only the president works at foreign relations daily. That has caused power to flow to the president from the beginning. The president was always in session. Congress was not, and could not be readily brought into session, especially given the means of communication and transportation in the early years of the Republic. Congress, moreover, could act only as a parliamentary body, only formally; the myriad of informal, small actions and reactions, abstentions and omissions, which are the stuff of United States foreign policy could be determined and executed only by the president, his Department of State, his ambassadors. Even scrupulous, non-self-aggrandizing, nonimperial George Washington made foreign policy regularly, privately, informally; it was only the most dramatic and best-known instance when, without Congress, he sent the misbehaving French minister home. Congress (or the Senate alone) was constitutionally necessary when national policy required a treaty or an appropriation of funds, but such formal participation was not often needed.

Without information and continuing participation, Congress did not monitor, and was not equipped to monitor, presidential foreign policy even in the days when it was less complex; Congress did not develop expertise, and it acquired the habit of deferring to that of the executive. Congress also began to delegate to the president large portions of its own authority, often retaining little control and exercising little oversight. Whether the president claimed to act under his own or under delegated authority, Congress did not often bestir itself to disown what the president had done or even to question his right to do it. Sometimes, when issues of authority arose, they became enmeshed in partisan dispute, the president's party in Congress ordinarily defending his authority, with the opposition's strictures being seen, and dismissed, as partisan rather than principled—that is, constitutional. In time, the issue ceased to be whether the president had authority to act and became only a question of the limits on his authority. The issue was not whether the president could act when Congress was silent but whether he could act contrary to its expressed wishes; whether Congress could direct, control, or supersede his decisions; and whether Congress was constitutionally free not to implement presidential policies.

Perhaps presidential authority in foreign affairs has grown steadily because it seemed necessary or efficient. The result has been that although Hamilton's interpretation of the executive-power clause as a plenary grant of foreign affairs power has never been accepted, presidents have acted as though it had been, and Congress has largely acquiesced. Later, as United States foreign policy became more complex, especially as it came to involve high expenditures and frequent uses of the armed forces, sometimes involving full-scale hostilities and war, Congress was forced into the process, though often only to withdraw again.

In the 1970s, however, the Watergate and Vietnam issues weakened the presidency and gave Congress new incentive and impetus to claim, or reclaim, larger authority and a larger role in the foreign-policy process. Congress expanded its staff and developed its own experts and expertise and some independent sources of information. It intensified oversight of executive activity—particularly what was done pursuant to congressional delegation—by committee hearings and by legislative veto. It rejected presidential pretension to authority to impound and not spend money appropriated by Congress. It adopted resolutions declaring limits on presidential powers to commit the United States by executive agreement or to engage the armed forces in hostilities.

The success of these measures in containing presidential initiative has been spotty, often depending on the popularity of the particular president and the success of a particular presidential venture. The courts—when they did not abstain —have generally legitimated the president's claims. The president's authority to conclude executive agreements to settle international claims

was upheld by the Supreme Court in 1981 in the Iranian hostages case *(Dames & Moore* v. *Regan),* largely because Congress had long conceded that authority to him. The legislative veto as a means of containing executive authority generally was invalidated in 1983, though the impact of that decision on the modes of congressional delegation of authority to the president and the consequences for congressional-executive relations in foreign affairs generally are yet to unfold.

It is not unwarranted to conclude that in addition to his authority under his explicit, specific powers, the president is the sole organ of the United States in its relations with other nations and that this role or function is a source of constitutional power and authority, often referred to as the president's foreign-affairs power. It is a general power in foreign affairs, not unlike that claimed by Hamilton, and casts on those who challenge a particular exercise of executive authority the burden of showing, by constitutional construction, that it is prohibited or qualified expressly or by implication—for example, because it is within a power given to Congress exclusively.

EXECUTIVE FOREIGN-AFFAIRS POWERS

The president acts for the United States in its relations with other states. He has sole authority to recognize states and governments and to maintain or disrupt diplomatic relations. The courts will give effect to his decisions and the implications of those decisions, for example, by following his suggestions of immunity for foreign heads of state or their public vessels, by opening the courts to suits of recognized governments only, or by giving effect to the acts of state of recognized governments, but not of unrecognized governments. The president also recognizes (or refuses to recognize) acquisitions of territory by other states. He can negotiate at will. He has authority to make claims for the United States against other states, on its own behalf or on behalf of United States citizens, and to respond to claims against the United States by others. He acts for the United States in the mysterious process by which states make customary international law. He can stand for the United

States at its borders, inviting or denying entry of persons, goods, vessels, or undersea cables. He expresses attitudes and intentions, even some that may require congressional action to fulfill, drawing on large delegations of authority or confident that Congress will not lightly repudiate his commitments. And he can make important, legally binding agreements with other countries on his own authority, without the advice and consent of the Senate or the approval of both houses of Congress. The president determines the United States position in relation to other states as to the meaning of international agreements or other international legal obligations. Within the United States, such executive interpretations and determinations are given great weight by Congress and by the courts.

The foreign-affairs power of the president is intrinsically an external power, to act for the United States in relation to other states. But many presidential acts have important domestic consequences and sometimes have the effect of law. Before Congress legislated on the subject, it was held that the president may authorize wiretaps in the United States without a judicial warrant for the purpose of gathering foreign intelligence, as in *United States* v. *Butenko* (1974). Treaties and executive agreements are law of the land. Presidential decisions to grant or to deny immunities to foreign governments are given effect as law. Thus, before sovereign immunity was regulated by act of Congress, the Supreme Court held that when the executive branch indicates to a court that a vessel owned by a foreign government is entitled to sovereign immunity, that declaration "must be accepted by the courts as a conclusive determination by the political arm of the Government that the continued retention of the vessel interferes with the proper conduct of our foreign relations" (*Ex parte Peru*, 1943). Similarly, when the executive branch concluded "that it is the national policy" not to extend immunity, "it is the duty of the courts, in a matter so intimately associated with our foreign policy and which may profoundly affect it, not to enlarge an immunity to an extent which the government . . . has not seen fit to recognize" (*Mexico* v. *Hoffman*, 1945).

A similar power in the president to "make law" in the United States was recognized by some judges in cases involving the somewhat analogous act of state doctrine. By that doctrine,

courts refrain from sitting in judgment on the validity of an act of a foreign state performed in its own territory, such as an expropriation of property (*Banco Nacional de Cuba* v. *Sabbatino*, 1964). But, it was suggested, the courts would, or may, examine the validity of such an act of a foreign state if the executive branch, by means of what came to be known as a "Bernstein letter," informed the court that it saw no foreign-policy reason for the court to refrain from judgment in the particular case. In *First National City Bank* v. *Banco Nacional de Cuba* (1972) the Supreme Court's decision coincided with the result favored by the executive branch, but three of the five justices in the majority decided as they did on the ground that the courts should consider the validity of the act of a foreign state when the executive wrote that it had no objection. (The other two justices in the majority and the four dissenting justices thought that the courts were not bound by executive views in such cases.) When Congress legislated that the act of state doctrine shall not be applied in certain cases, it especially instructed the courts to continue to apply the doctrine if the president requested them to do so.

POWER TO APPOINT AMBASSADORS

The president has power to appoint ambassadors and other public ministers and consuls, with the advice and consent of the Senate, and he can fill other offices created by Congress without Senate approval unless Congress requires it. Presidents have interpreted the requirement of Senate consent to apply only to appointments of diplomats on regular, permanent assignment, and presidents have on innumerable occasions appointed agents for ad hoc foreign-affairs assignments without seeking Senate consent, sometimes giving them the personal rank of ambassador. The Senate has not objected strongly.

The president's power to appoint diplomatic personnel is an aspect of his general power to appoint. The president appoints; Congress cannot appoint. Congress can regulate the offices it creates, including those in the president's foreign-service establishment, but it cannot in the guise of creating or regulating offices usurp the appointment power—for example, by prescribing qualifications so precise and detailed as virtu-

1078

ally to identify the person to be appointed. Neither can Congress exclude persons by name or specific designation, which would be tantamount to a bill of attainder, a legislative conviction and punishment without trial, which is forbidden by the Constitution (Article I, Section 9).

INTERNATIONAL AGREEMENTS

The president "shall have Power, by and with the Advice and Consent of the Senate, to make Treaties, provided two thirds of the Senators present concur" (Article II, Section 2). The power to make treaties implies the power to negotiate them. It is the president who decides whether to negotiate a treaty, with which states, on which subjects, and to what effect. He may seek the Senate's advice along the way, and the Senate may offer advice unsought, but formal Senate advice, except such as might be incidental to its consent to a treaty already concluded, is only advisory and has not been sought as a regular matter since the early days of the Republic. As a result of several unhappy incidents culminating in President Woodrow Wilson's disastrous experiences with the Treaty of Versailles, the executive branch has improved informal consultation with Senate members and committees, and has sometimes included senators in delegations negotiating important treaties. Informal coordination has served to reduce the likelihood of Senate rejection of a treaty; but a number have languished on the Senate shelf, such as the Genocide Convention, introduced in the late 1940s but not given Senate consent until 1986.

Having negotiated a treaty, the president requires the consent of the Senate to bring the treaty into effect for the United States. The Senate may give its consent subject to conditions. If the condition is a change in the treaty, the president can make the treaty only with that change. If the Senate gives consent on the basis of an understanding of what a provision means, the president can make the treaty for the United States only on that understanding. Conditions related to the treaty's implementation in the United States are also binding on the president.

The Constitution does not define "treaty" and presumably uses that term as it is used in international relations and international law. The president, then, has authority to make for the United States any agreement that any other state may make under international law. This grant to the president is independent of the powers of Congress. Although war is declared by Congress, the president can make peace by treaty. The president may make a treaty on subjects that are also subject to legislation by Congress, such as international trade. And it is established that treaties and statutes are equal in status in United States law, and in case of conflict the most recent is to be given effect by the courts. The president may also make treaties on subjects that apart from treaty are left to the states and are not within the enumerated powers of Congress (*Missouri* v. *Holland,* 1920). Principles of federalism limit the treaty power only in small, hypothetical respects: for example, it is accepted that the United States cannot, by treaty, cede territory of a state in the Union to a foreign country without the state's consent.

Treaties are the supreme law of the land, and courts will give a treaty effect as law without awaiting implementation by Congress. Some treaties, however, are interpreted as implying only a promise by the United States to take measures. In such cases, the treaty itself is non-self-executing and is not treated as law, and the courts will give it effect only when it is implemented by Congress.

It is now settled that a treaty of the United States is subject to the limitations of the Bill of Rights and other provisions of the Constitution. A treaty, or a provision in a treaty, that violates a constitutional prohibition cannot be enforced in the United States; if it did, the United States would have to default on its international undertaking. To date, no provision in a United States treaty has been held unconstitutional by the Supreme Court.

Under international law, the United States may terminate a treaty when the right to do so is provided in the treaty. It may sometimes terminate a treaty also because of some invalidating circumstances (such as fraud, error, or duress against the agents who negotiated for the United States), because of a significant change of circumstances, or because of a material breach by the other party. Also, the United States, like any other state, may decide to denounce or violate a treaty and pay damages or suffer other international consequences. The Constitution does not address the authority of the United States to terminate a treaty in any of these circumstances, but it is inconceivable that the framers intended to deny the federal government authority to do so; the question is who can act for the United States.

Although the subject has been in controversy —notably in 1978–1979, in connection with President Jimmy Carter's termination of the Mutual Defense Treaty with the Republic of China (Taiwan)—the prevailing view is that the president has power to terminate treaties for the United States in all the circumstances indicated, without the consent of the Senate or the Congress as a whole. Some have derived the president's authority to terminate treaties from his power to make them, arguing that the Senate's advice and consent is required only when obligations are assumed for the United States, not when they are shed. It may be easier to find the president's power to terminate a treaty in his general power to act for the United States in relation to other nations under international law.

The Constitution does not mention federal authority to make agreements other than treaties, but the president has concluded many such agreements in different forms. The president has made some agreements pursuant to an earlier treaty, where that treaty plausibly contemplated such ancillary agreements; the Senate's consent to the original treaty is presumed to apply also to the subsequent agreements. The president has also made numerous congressional-executive agreements, agreements authorized by statute or resolution of Congress or which Congress approved after they were concluded. Such agreements, drawing on the joint authority of the president and Congress, have the full political authority of the United States. It is accepted that this method can be used in any case as an alternative to the treaty process.

At one time it was assumed that the congressional-executive agreement would replace the treaty. The congressional-executive agreement not only avoided the need for a two-thirds vote in the Senate but also gave the House of Representatives, the more representative body, the role it had long sought and simplified the legislative process by allowing the simultaneous enactment of any implementing legislation that might be required. But the Senate has been unwilling to give up its special prerogative, often resisting any executive inclinations to transmit an agree-

ment for congressional approval by joint resolution. However, while the treaty process remains a mainstay for making international agreements, some kinds of agreements are commonly concluded as congressional-executive agreements, notably those regulating trade, perhaps in deference to the special provision in the Constitution that all bills for raising revenue (which includes tariffs) shall originate in the House of Representatives (Article I, Section 7).

From the beginning of the Republic, presidents have also made international agreements on their own authority. Informal understandings, including some that may amount to binding agreements under international law, are an inevitable product of diplomatic relations with another country. But presidents have also made more explicit agreements, formal or informal, oral or written. That the president has authority to make some executive agreements has always been conceded. Agreements to recognize and establish diplomatic relations with another government and more-elaborate agreements concomitant with, or incidental to, such recognition, as in the case of the Soviet Union, have been made by the president without objection by the Senate, and their validity has been upheld by the Supreme Court (*United States* v. *Belmont,* 1937). It is established that the president can make agreements settling international claims by or against the United States, if only because the president has long made such agreements, and Congress has not challenged, and has indeed accepted, that authority (*Dames & Moore* v. *Regan).* No one has seriously challenged armistice or other military agreements by the president as commander in chief, such as those terminating hostilities in World War I, in Korea, and in Vietnam. But presidents have also made executive agreements on a range of other foreign-affairs subjects, some of substantial importance and formality, and the president's authority to do so without Senate consent (or approval by joint resolution of Congress) has often been challenged, though not in court.

It is clear that the president has authority to make some sole agreements. It is clear that other agreements are beyond his sole authority and require the consent of the Senate or the approval of Congress. But no one has provided the principle that would define the limits of sole presidential authority. A Senate resolution has declared that the president cannot commit the United States to expend money or to deploy its armed forces. Presumably, agreements of sufficient importance, dignity, and formality are beyond the president's sole authority, but such a line is hardly self-defining, and some important agreements have been made by the president and not objected to by the Senate, perhaps because it was thought desirable to keep them secret.

GENERAL POWERS OF THE PRESIDENT

To the president's foreign-affairs powers may be added other general authority conferred upon him. "He shall take Care that the Laws be faithfully executed" (Article II, Section 3). The take-care clause gives the president the duty, and therefore the necessary authority, to enforce federal statutes (including those relating to foreign affairs) and treaties of the United States, both of which are expressly declared to be "supreme Law of the Land" and binding on the states as well (Article VI).

Other international agreements within the president's constitutional power or made by authority delegated to him by Congress are also supreme law of the land. Customary international law is also law of the United States, supreme to state law, which the president has the duty and authority to execute. However, the take-care clause does not imply any authority in the president to enforce international law against foreign states acting outside the United States, because his authority is to enforce United States law, and in those circumstances international law is not being applied as United States law. Any authority the president may have to invoke international law in those circumstances must derive from his general authority as representative of the United States in international affairs.

The president has also derived foreign-affairs power from his designation as commander in chief of the armed forces. Presidents have seen it as within their authority to use the forces under their command to implement their treaties and to pursue other foreign-policy interests of the United States as they perceive them. As com-

manders in chief, presidents have also made important executive agreements with other countries, such as military-base agreements or other cooperative defense arrangements.

LIMITATIONS ON EXECUTIVE POWER

The luxuriant growth of presidential powers over two hundred years may support a description of them as plenary, but they are not unlimited, and they are not exclusive. They are qualified by the explicit veto that the United States Senate can exercise over the president's appointments and his treaties. They are limited by implication by express allocations of some foreign-affairs powers to Congress. (They are limited, too—in common with other exercises of federal authority—by the Bill of Rights and other constitutional safeguards for the individual.)

Some authority allocated to Congress by the Constitution is clearly exclusive. The power of Congress to declare war is the power to decide to take the country into war; no president has claimed the power to initiate war against a foreign country on his own authority. It has been argued, indeed, that the president may not exercise any of his powers in such a way as to risk bringing the country into war. Similarly, the constitutional provision that "No Money shall be drawn from the Treasury, but in Consequence of Appropriations made by Law" (Article I, Section 9) is an exclusive grant to Congress of the power to appropriate money; with the possible exception of President Abraham Lincoln (whose actions were later ratified by Congress), no president has claimed authority to draw money from the United States Treasury on his own authority, even for foreign-policy purposes.

In general, the president's powers are limited also by the implications of the constitutional distinction between executive and legislative power. The power to make law in the United States is lodged in Congress. The president does not make law in the ordinary sense. He cannot ordinarily prescribe or forbid conduct by persons or determine their status, rights, interests, or relations with respect to other persons or things in the United States. Surely only Congress, not the president, can enact criminal law and render persons subject to the criminal process and to criminal punishment.

The Supreme Court has held that the president cannot extradite a person to a foreign country except pursuant to an act of Congress or a treaty (*Valentine* v. *United States ex rel. Neidecker*, 1936). A request for extradition is an international act addressed to the executive. (It was in connection with such a request that Marshall pronounced the president "sole organ" authorized to act for the United States.) Extradition, moreover, is not part of the criminal law and process of the United States. But extradition requires the arrest of a person and his forcible detention and transfer to another country, and the Court apparently considered it a deprivation of liberty that requires the authority and safeguards of the processes of legislation or at least of a treaty.

CONCURRENT AUTHORITY OF PRESIDENT AND CONGRESS

Important powers of Congress are exclusive, and denied to the president, even as the principal presidential powers are exclusively his and not for Congress to exercise. But clearly some of the powers of the president and Congress overlap. Even Hamilton's argument for large executive power did not claim that presidential power was necessarily exclusive of Congress. In a famous passage, Justice Robert Jackson said, "There is a zone of twilight in which he [the president] and Congress may have concurrent authority, or in which its distribution is uncertain" (*Youngstown Sheet and Tube Co.* v. *Sawyer*, 1952). Jackson did not define its contours or content, or offer any guidance as to how competing exercises of such concurrent authority might be accommodated or which branch shall prevail in case of conflict.

Overlapping powers and a twilight zone of concurrent authority are characteristic of foreign affairs in particular. Congress is expressly given power to regulate commerce with foreign nations, but the president can do so also by treaty and to some extent even by sole executive agreement. And since it is established that commerce includes intercourse generally, Congress for its part might claim authority to regulate not only trade but much else that goes on between the United States and other nations and that is within the president's foreign-affairs powers. The president's power as commander in chief overlaps that of Congress to make rules for the government and regulation of the armed forces. No one can disentangle the powers of the two branches to act during war toward the enemy, toward neutrals, or toward foreign nationals.

For the reasons generally favoring executive initiative, presidents have successfully claimed to duplicate powers of Congress more often than Congress has been able to act in what is indubitably the president's domain, though exactly how much congressional power presidents could exercise on their own authority is difficult to determine, since they exercise so much by delegation from Congress. When the president acts and Congress is silent, there is often a justifiable presumption that Congress has acquiesced in, or even approved, what the president has done; if so, the action is supported by the constitutional power of both branches. A president's failure to veto congressional legislation or to protest other congressional initiatives might also signify agreement that Congress has constitutional authority for a particular action.

Overlapping or concurrent jurisdiction has been exercised frequently by either or both branches. The president and Congress have each asserted sovereign powers for the United States: President Harry Truman claimed for the United States exclusive rights to its continental shelf, and Congress declared United States sovereignty to its air space and a two-hundred-mile exclusive fishing zone. In a number of instances, Congress asserted authority where earlier there had been only executive (or judicial) action, as on sovereign immunity or the act of state doctrine; neither the courts nor the executive have questioned the authority of Congress to act or the validity of its particular enactments. Presidents have made armistice agreements that effectively brought an end to hostilities; Congress has by resolution declared an end to war; and presidents have made treaties of peace. The Supreme Court held that presidential courts in occupied Germany after World War II could exercise jurisdiction over an American civilian for whom Congress had in effect provided trial by court-martial (*Madsen* v. *Kinsella*, 1952). Inevitably, however, concurrent or overlapping jurisdiction may lead to inconsistent actions, raising questions as to which should prevail as a matter of law. Congress has sometimes also purported to legislate limitations on executive action, which presidents have challenged.

In a number of instances, there have been inconsistencies between an act of Congress and a treaty provision, sometimes purposefully, sometimes perhaps inadvertently. The courts have sought to reconcile statute and treaty by interpretation, but where that was not possible, they established the principle that since the two have equal status as law, the one enacted later in time should prevail and be given effect. If a later statutory provision is given effect as domestic law, the United States is thereby put in default of its international obligation.

Neither branch has questioned the authority of the other in such cases, it being accepted that the possibility of such inconsistency is built into the allocation of lawmaking and treatymaking to different hands. In some other cases, too, the authority of each branch to act is not questioned, nor is the consequence of inconsistent actions. That the area of concurrent power seems to involve largely presidential pretensions where congressional authority is clear would suggest that Congress should usually prevail in case of conflict, no matter which branch acted first. So, surely, the president is bound to follow congressional directives in regard to neutrality or foreign intelligence surveillance. Even where the president's authority is clear and perhaps primary, his acts will bow before an act of Congress for purposes of domestic law: the president is bound by, and the courts will give effect to, congressional legislation modifying the act of state doctrine or regulating the extradition of inhabitants of the United States or the admission of foreign forces, perhaps even diplomatic immunities (for example, *Banco Nacional de Cuba* v. *Farr*, 1968; the Foreign Sovereign Immunities Act of 1976; and the Foreign Intelligence Surveillance Act of 1978).

The cases cited above, which recognized presidential power to determine sovereign immunity, were decided during a time in constitutional history when the courts were most deferential to the federal government in general, including the executive; they did not involve an issue between president and Congress. In 1976, Congress, with executive approval, enacted the Foreign Sovereign Immunities Act to regulate sovereign im-

munity, remove the executive branch from the process, and leave claims of immunity to be determined by the courts. But whether that statute purported to terminate the president's authority to indicate immunity, whether it did so for all cases, and whether Congress could constitutionally deny that power to the president has not been resolved. It has been suggested that in the face of the act of Congress, the president in effect recognized such immunity for the government of Iran in the hostage settlement agreement.

Conflict between the president and Congress has been recurrent and unresolved in two areas. Congress (the Senate in particular) has challenged the president's claim of large authority to make sole executive agreements. But the Senate has no formal means to compel the president to seek its consent to a particular agreement on the ground that it is properly a treaty and therefore he has no authority to make it without Senate consent; and informal political pressures have often not availed. Numerous proposals to define the scope of the president's authority by constitutional amendment or by resolution of Congress have not been adopted, perhaps because it proved too difficult to articulate an effective distinction between agreements for which the president needed Senate consent and those which he could make on his own authority. In 1969 the Senate adopted the National Commitments Resolution, which expressed the sense of the Senate that the president did not have sole authority to use the armed forces of the United States on foreign territory or to promise to assist a foreign country by the use of the armed forces or financial resources of the United States. Presidents appear not to have accepted that limitation. Congress did adopt the Case Act of 1972 to require the executive branch to transmit to Congress or, in confidence, to congressional committees the texts of any agreements made on presidential authority alone.

There has been no definition either of the respective powers of the president and Congress during war and no resolution of the recurrent tensions between the two branches over the deployment and use of the armed forces abroad by the president without congressional authorization. The Constitution confers on Congress the power to tax to provide for the common defense, to declare war, to raise and support armed forces, and to make rules for their governance

(Article I, Section 8). It is accepted that the power of Congress to declare war is the power to make war and to wage war successfully. It is for Congress to decide whether the United States shall go to war. The Constitution also declares that the president shall be commander in chief of the armed forces. In the *Federalist Papers,* no. 69, Alexander Hamilton (later a leading proponent of large presidential power) depreciated the significance of the commander-in-chief clause:

> It would amount to nothing more than the Supreme command and direction of the military and naval forces, as first general and admiral of the Confederacy; while that of the British king extends to the declaring of war and to the raising and regulating of fleets and armies,—all which, by the Constitution under consideration, would appertain to the legislature.

Taking a similar view, some have read the constitutional blueprint as meaning that the president was to command the forces in wars declared by Congress and perhaps on other missions or for other purposes indicated by Congress, presumably under general guidelines laid down by Congress. However, presidents have generally asserted substantial independence from Congress in the exercise of their command, and have seen the command as a source of independent constitutional power.

During war, Congress has in fact generally given the president free rein and has ratified or acknowledged what he and his generals deemed desirable. During World War II, President Franklin Roosevelt threatened to act unilaterally to repeal a provision of congressional emergency economic legislation unless Congress did so; Congress did. The president exercised authority to relocate and even confine citizens of Japanese ancestry, and Congress ratified that action and confirmed that authority. During the Civil War, World War II, and the Korean War, congressional committees exercised some oversight of the conduct of the war, but there was no attempt by Congress to involve itself in military strategy or the conduct of campaigns. During the Vietnam War, there were attempts in Congress to legislate limitations to hostilities and later to end them, but no limitations were formally adopted until the president ceased to object, and

an end to hostilities came only after the president had approved a cease-fire agreement.

There is no basis in constitutional jurisprudence on which to resolve with confidence conflicting assertions of authority between Congress and president as to the conduct of war. In principle, it might be argued that just as the issue of war or peace is for Congress, so are major issues as to the kind of war to be waged. It has been suggested that tactical decisions are for the president but strategic ones and large political questions are for Congress. Congress can decide whether war shall be total or limited and whether or not it shall be extended to additional countries. By now, Congress ought to be able to decide whether the United States shall use nuclear weapons; at least, the president ought not be able to use them if Congress has forbidden it. But Congress has not legislated such distinctions, and presidents surely have not accepted them, nor have the courts addressed them.

The advent of nuclear weapons has raised constitutional issues between president and Congress apart from declared wars, issues that the framers of the Constitution could not have conceived of and that constitutional text and interpretation provide little help in resolving. It is accepted by even the strongest champions of congressional authority that though the power to decide for war is in Congress, when war is imposed on the United States by invasion, the president has the duty and the authority to defend the country. Presumably, time would be of the essence, and congressional authorization to the president to defend the country is assumed, at least until Congress convenes and addresses the situation. Similarly, in case of a nuclear attack on the United States, the president, it has been assumed, has constitutional authority to launch, or Congress would be presumed to have authorized, a second strike against an attacking enemy to prevent or deter it from further attack. The question remains whether the president also has authority to launch a preemptive first strike if he believes an enemy attack might be impending. Such assumptions and issues have fortunately been theoretical and academic, but there is no indication that either Congress or the executive branch has seriously addressed them in their contingency planning. Surely, Congress has not seen fit to legislate, either to confirm or to delegate authority to the president, or to establish institutions and procedures to regulate or guide that authority.

Not at all academic have been the recurrent issues between president and Congress as to his authority to deploy the armed forces of the United States, sometimes to engage in hostilities, where Congress has not declared war or otherwise granted the president authority. In several hundred instances (the number depending on definition and the principle of inclusion), the president has ordered the armed forces to enter foreign territory or foreign waters or to take action on the high seas, on missions varying in national purpose and degrees of engagement and danger. In the Cuban missile crisis (1962), President John Kennedy instituted a blockade that was provocative and that many think created a serious danger of war. Presidents have asserted independent authority to deploy the armed forces for foreign-policy purposes short of war: the president as commander in chief, it is claimed, can properly use the forces under his command to execute the powers and policies of the president as sole organ so long as he does not initiate full-scale war. Presidents have claimed constitutional authority to take measures, including the use of force, to protect the lives of United States citizens abroad, beyond any authority conferred upon them by Congress.

Disputes between presidents and their congressional critics have recurred throughout United States history, but they came to a head in the wake of the Vietnam War. The Vietnam War was not waged without congressional authorization: the Tonkin Gulf Resolution of 1964 clearly authorized the use of the armed forces of the United States, even if those who enacted it did not perhaps appreciate how many armed forces the president would send, for how long, and in how intensive a war. In 1972–1973, however, unhappiness over the war and a sense that Congress had been misled or had acted improvidently impelled Congress to attempt to regulate introduction by the president of United States armed forces "into hostilities, or into situations where imminent involvement in hostilities is clearly indicated by the circumstances."

As enacted over the president's veto, the War Powers Resolution purported first to define the constitutional powers of the president:

The constitutional powers of the President as Commander-in-Chief to introduce United States Armed Forces into hostilities, or into situations where imminent involvement in hostilities is clearly indicated by the circumstances, are exercised only pursuant to (1) a declaration of war, (2) specific statutory authorization, or (3) a national emergency created by attack upon the United States, its territories or possessions, or its armed forces.

In addition the resolution provided (1) that the president consult with Congress "in every possible instance" before introducing armed forces into hostilities or into situations of imminent involvement in hostilities and regularly thereafter while they were so involved; (2) that the president report to Congress when armed forces are introduced into hostilities or into situations of imminent involvement, when they are introduced into foreign territory while equipped for combat, or when the numbers of United States forces equipped for combat in foreign territory are substantially enlarged; (3) that the president terminate such involvement after sixty days (or after thirty days more if the president certifies necessity); and (4) that at any time, Congress may direct the president to terminate hostilities by concurrent resolution (that is, without being subject to presidential veto).

In vetoing the resolution, and since then, presidents and their spokesmen have challenged its constitutionality, but there has been no attempt to articulate with precision the scope of presidential power as the executive branch sees it. While no president has claimed the constitutional power to make war on his own authority, presidents have in effect claimed the right to use the armed forces where necessary for national purposes, even if it involved their engagement in hostilities, so long as these were "short of war." On this view, the resolution was in error in its definition of the president's authority under the Constitution: the president may introduce forces into hostilities not only in case of attack on the United States or on its armed forces but also to further other national interests so long as he did not put the country into full-scale war. Therefore, the other provisions of the resolution were invalid, because they purported to regulate what was in the president's constitutional authority to do as he sees fit; Congress could not demand consultation or reporting, or direct the president to terminate hostilities, in circumstances that did not involve "war" as constitutionally defined. In addition, the provision requiring termination of hostilities upon the adoption of a concurrent resolution by both houses of Congress has been deemed nullified by the Supreme Court's invalidation of such legislative vetoes generally (*Immigration and Naturalization Service* v. *Chadha*, 1983).

The constitutional issues remain unresolved. Though the term *hostilities* has not been further defined, members of Congress have claimed, and presidents have sometimes conceded, that armed forces have been sent into hostilities. There has been no instance of "consultation with Congress," which would seem to require consultation with both houses, more or less formally, not merely with committees or with selected members. There has been some voluntary reporting in some but not in all cases. In 1983, Congress authorized the president to send troops to Lebanon for defined purposes and a limited term, which the president accepted, and some have interpreted his action as an acceptance of the authority of Congress as reflected in the War Powers Resolution.

CONFLICT AND COOPERATION

Executive power in foreign affairs has had to take account of issues of separation of powers generally. The principle of separation is theoretically applicable to foreign affairs as elsewhere, but the large area of concurrent jurisdiction gives that principle a very different look.

Limitations on delegation, notably by Congress to the president, apply in theory to foreign affairs, but the Supreme Court has held that in foreign affairs much more may be delegated by Congress in view of the large responsibility and authority of the president in that domain (*Curtiss Wright*). Presidents once claimed authority to impound or defer spending funds appropriated by Congress, but such claims seem no longer to be made even in respect to foreign affairs, where they used to be made with special vigor in view of the president's foreign-affairs responsibility. Efforts by Congress to entrench on the president's power to appoint officials have been invalidated in domestic affairs (*Buckley* v. *Valeo*,

1976) and would be invalid as well in foreign affairs. The efforts of Congress to exercise a legislative veto have also been invalidated generally (*Chadha*) and would presumably be invalid as well in legislation affecting foreign relations. A different kind of conflict, between the president's claim to executive privilege for documents or testimony and Congress' assertion of a need and a right to know, continues to recur and has never been resolved. In foreign affairs, the president's privilege weighs more than in domestic matters when he claims the needs of diplomatic confidentiality and of demands of secrecy by foreign governments, but whether it outweighs the congressional need to know is uncertain.

IMPLEMENTATION OF EXECUTIVE POWER

Most exercises of executive power require appropriation of funds. Some can be made effective only by legislation. Often criminal laws are necessary to induce or enforce compliance. The president cannot take money from the Treasury without congressional appropriation (Article I, Section 9), and only Congress can enact criminal laws in the United States.

Congress has the constitutional authority to appropriate such funds or enact such laws, as "necessary and proper" to carry out the powers of the president (Article I, Section 8). It is also accepted that Congress is "constitutionally obligated" to do so. The separation and independence of the branches of government would be vitiated if Congress were free to nullify presidential power by making it impossible for him to function. Thus, if the president recognizes a foreign government and appoints an ambassador to that country (with the consent of the Senate), Congress is not free to refuse to appropriate money for the mission or for the ambassador's salary (just as it is not free to refuse to appropriate funds for the president's own salary). If the president makes a treaty (with the advice and consent of the Senate), Congress is constitutionally obligated to enact the laws and appropriate the funds to carry out United States obligations under the treaty. Although such a constitutional obligation is not enforceable in court, Congress has in fact recognized and honored such obliga-

THE EXECUTIVE AND FOREIGN AFFAIRS

tions since the beginning of the nation's history. Congress is not bound by the president's judgment as to what law or how much money is needed. And Congress is not obligated to appropriate or legislate to carry out an action that in its view is beyond the president's constitutional power, unless the courts uphold its constitutionality.

A different question arises when the president proposes financial assistance to a foreign government. Foreign aid has been a staple of United States foreign policy since the end of World War II, and presidents have often urged such aid as vital to United States interests. Occasionally, on the other hand, Congress has favored aid to a particular country while the president opposed it or urged less aid. In such cases, presidents sometimes claim the right to control, if not dictate, foreign aid, but in constitutional terms foreign aid is an exercise of the "spending power," the power to provide for the general welfare, an express power of Congress (Article I, Section 8). However important such financial assistance may be to the president's foreign policy, it is Congress that has the constitutional authority and responsibility.

EXECUTIVE POWER IN THE COURTS

Some of the issues of executive power in foreign affairs have not been resolved by the courts; some may never be. The federal courts are forbidden to issue advisory opinions; they can only decide "cases" or "controversies" (Article III, Section 2). That concept includes a requirement that a plaintiff have standing to bring a suit and that the controversy be "ripe" for adjudication; additional requirements for standing and ripeness have been added by the courts not as constitutionally required but as "prudential" for the proper exercise of the judicial function. A number of foreign-affairs issues cannot easily come to court because there is no plaintiff with the necessary standing—that is, with a sufficient personal interest in the outcome. Issues between Congress and the president cannot ordinarily be brought by one branch against the other, because their interests are deemed to be not "personal," but only political. Individual members of Congress have been accorded standing in the lower courts but only in limited circumstances, where the individual member claimed to be vindicating the integrity of his or her vote, but the Supreme Court has yet to address the propriety and scope of a congressional member's standing.

The courts have interpreted federal statutes as conferring large authority on the executive branch in matters relating to foreign affairs, except sometimes when a constitutional right is implicated. In principle, executive power in foreign affairs, like other federal power, is subject to constitutional limitations, but the courts have been reluctant to intervene to frustrate executive action in foreign affairs, sometimes even when individual rights are implicated. Matters relating to the conduct of foreign relations "are so exclusively entrusted to the political branches of governments as to be largely immune from judicial inquiry or interference" (*Harisiades* v. *Shaughnessy,* 1952). In almost all cases that "classical deference" is to the executive. A principal tool to that end has been the doctrine that certain issues, even constitutional issues, are not justiciable, because they are "political questions," and high on any list of such political questions have been a number of foreign-affairs issues (*Baker* v. *Carr,* 1962).

In *Goldwater* v. *Carter* (1979), four justices of the Supreme Court declared that whether the president can terminate the defense treaty with Taiwan on his own authority is an issue between Congress and the president that involved foreign affairs, as to which the Constitution gave little guidance and in which the courts should not intervene. They distinguished cases where private interests were affected. In the case before them, Justice William Rehnquist said, "We are asked to settle a dispute between coequal branches of our Government, each of which has resources available to protect and assert its interests."

However, Justice William Brennan, the author of the contemporary restatement of the political-question doctrine, wrote that Justice Rehnquist's opinion

profoundly misapprehends the political-question principle as it applies to matters of foreign relations. Properly understood, the political-question doctrine restrains courts from reviewing an exercise of foreign policy judgment by the coordinate political branch to which authority to make that judgment has been 'constitutional[ly] commit[ted].' . . . But the doctrine does not pertain when a court is faced with the *antecedent* question whether a particular branch has been constitutionally designated as the repository of political decisionmaking power.

SUMMARY

The United States Constitution of 1787 was a mosaic of hard-won compromises, and much was compromised by omission and postponement. There was an inclination also to mute the radical transformations that the Constitution would effect—the new central government supreme to the sovereign states, a parliament responsible in substantial measure to the people (rather than the states), an independent executive. Doubtless, some issues were not foreseen.

The constitutional blueprint was framed two hundred years ago, reflecting ancestral values, assumptions, and expectations. In the intervening centuries, the United States bridged a continent and became an empire and a superpower. It also became, finally, a democracy, with authentic universal suffrage. Yet, the eighteenth-century system for conducting foreign relations has not been amended at all. Amazingly, it continues to work, adjusting itself to new circumstances and needs. It will work better if president and Congress join to reexamine their constitutional relationship and establish a new mode and new procedures to achieve a foreign policy for the nuclear age that is both democratic and more effective.

CASES

Baker v. Carr, 369 U.S. 186 (1962)
Banco Nacional de Cuba v. Farr, 243 F. Supp. 957 (S.D.N.Y. 1965) aff'd, 383 F.2d 166 (2d Cir. 1967), cert. denied, 390 U.S. 956 (1968)
Banco Nacional de Cuba v. Sabbatino, 376 U.S. 398 (1964)
Buckley v. Valeo, 424 U.S. 1936 (1976)
Dames & Moore v. Regan, 453 U.S. 654 (1981)
First National City Bank v. Banco Nacional de Cuba, 406 U.S. 759 (1972)
Goldwater v. Carter, 444 U.S. 996 (1979)
Haig v. Agee, 453 U.S. 280 (1981)
Harisiades v. Shaughnessy, 342 U.S. 580 (1952)
Immigration and Naturalization Service v. Chadha, 462 U.S. 919 (1983)
Kent v. Dulles, 357 U.S. 116 (1958)
Madsen v. Kinsella, 343 U.S. 341 (1952)
Mexico v. Hoffman, 324 U.S. 30 (1945)
Missouri v. Holland, 252 U.S. 416 (1920)
Ex parte Peru, 318 U.S. 578 (1943)
United States v. Belmont, 301 U.S. 324 (1937)
United States v. Butenko, 494 F.2d 593 (3d Cir. 1974), cert. denied, 419 U.S. 881 (1974)
United States v. Curtiss-Wright Export Corp., 299 U.S. 304 (1936)
Valentine v. United States ex rel. Neidecker, 299 U.S. 5 (1936)
Youngstown Sheet and Tube Co. v. Sawyer, 343 U.S. 579 (1952)

BIBLIOGRAPHY

Daniel Cheever and H. Field Haviland, *American Foreign Policy and the Separation of Powers* (1952). Edward S. Corwin, *The President's Control of Foreign Relations* (1917); *The President: Office and Powers,* 4th ed. (1957). John C. Hamilton, ed., *The Works of Alexander Hamilton* (1851), vol. 7 (The Letters of Pacificus). Louis Henkin, *Foreign Affairs and the Constitution* (1972). Gaillard Hunt, ed., *The Writings of James Madison* (1906) vol. 6 (The Letters of Helvidius).

Wallace McClure, *International Executive Agreements* (1941). Richard M. Pious, *The American Presidency* (1979). Arthur M. Schlesinger, Jr., *The Imperial Presidency* (1973). Abraham D. Sofaer, *War, Foreign Affairs and Constitutional Power* (1976). Quincy Wright, *The Control of American Foreign Relations* (1922).

[*See also* Burger Court and Era; Congress; Executive and Domestic Affairs; International Economic Law; International Human Rights Law; Military Law; Racial Discrimination and Equal Opportunity; Stone and Vinson Courts and Eras; *and* Supreme Court of the United States.]

FEDERALISM

Tony Freyer

THE courts hold a vital place in the federal system established under the Constitution. From the colonial, revolutionary, and Confederation experience, the framers of the Constitution learned that a division of sovereign authority between state and national governments suited well the American Republic. The benefits gained from divided sovereignty did not, however, eradicate tension within the federal system. Eventually, significant responsibility for resolving these conflicts was left to the judiciary, particularly the United States Supreme Court.

The courts' role in American federalism encompassed both the formal doctrines of constitutional law and a rich interplay of political and social interests. Throughout the nation's history, judges have worked to balance local and federal control as well as individual and states' rights. From 1789 to the Civil War, a system of dual federalism emerged in which state sovereignty predominated. Beginning with Reconstruction and the passage of the Thirteenth, Fourteenth, and Fifteenth Amendments, dual federalism underwent a gradual transformation in which federal authority increased while state power remained comparatively undiminished. The Great Depression destroyed this system, fostering the rise of a new order known as cooperative federalism, in which the federal government dominated. By the end of the twentieth century new stresses had developed, but the balancing function of the courts had not diminished.

THE REVOLUTIONARY HERITAGE

Broad experience shaped the framers' formulation of the role of the judiciary in the federal system under the Constitution. The British crown's charters, upon which the establishment of the American colonies so much depended, guaranteed the rights of Englishmen, symbolized by Magna Charta. Along with a general recognition of vaguely defined legislative and executive powers, the charters contained judicial provisions designed to uphold such rights as trial by jury, general principles of due process, and the common law. Because each colony developed its legal institutions and a local common law that was subject to its particular needs, there was considerable diversity between colonies as well as between America and the mother country. The Privy Council's sporadic review of American court decisions and legislative acts did not significantly diminish these differences. Thus, a distinction between central and local authority, separation of powers, individual rights enshrined in written fundamental law, an independent judiciary, and judicial review were all part of the heritage bequeathed to the Founding Fathers in 1787. Yet, the disparities inherent in this experience made its use problematic.

Disagreement over the nature of fundamental law contributed to the movement for independence. The English constitution was an amalgam of traditions and practices that had evolved throughout the country's history. The principle that Parliament was supreme was basic to this view of the constitution. Parliamentary supremacy meant that that there was no law higher than that passed by Parliament. In the years prior to the Declaration of Independence, Americans gradually developed constitutional ideas that rejected the English position. The patriots recognized a distinction between a constitution agreed to by a sovereign people and the government that such a constitution established. "A constitution is a thing *antecedent* to a government," said

Thomas Paine in language that represented the views of many Americans, "and a government is only the creature of a constitution. The constitution of a country is not the act of its government, but the people constituting a government." According to the American revolutionaries, then, a constitution was a higher law to which they held the acts of government accountable, and a governmental action contrary to a constitution was void. This was so because no provision could be allowed that violated popular sovereignty—the supremacy of the people—as expressed in the formulation of the fundamental law. By 1776 the colonies and the mother country were unable to resolve these opposing views; consequently, the Americans demanded independence, and a bloody war ensued.

Victory in 1783 brought home to Americans the full implications of their revolutionary arguments and actions. Ironically, the very principles that were central to the struggle against English authority jeopardized the New Republic. The principle of popular sovereignty underlying the state constitutions ratified after the Massachusetts Constitution of 1780 fostered the dominance of state legislatures. Although these constitutions gave formal recognition to separation of powers, the realities of local politics resulted in legislative supremacy. And because this condition followed from the people's action in creating their fundamental law, the principle of higher law seemed to sanction the legislature's power. A further consequence was the triumph of state over national authority. In keeping with the Americans' struggle against centralized British authority, the Articles of Confederation established a national government, but its power and very existence depended upon and was circumscribed by the states. Constitutional ideas and practical politics thus combined to weaken the bonds of national loyalty and to reinforce state sovereignty.

But, by 1787, abuses of state power fostered the movement for constitutional revision. Many advocates of change were nationalists who believed that state paper-money measures and debtor-creditor laws threatened individual rights and the nation's welfare. Moreover, impotence in foreign affairs, domestic unrest, and interstate rivalries and tensions prompted even some proponents of state sovereignty to support the revisionist effort. Both groups shared a concern that the revolutionary experiment in republican government was about to fail. Yet, opponents of this movement feared that a more vigorous national government might be given the sort of unrestrained power exercised by state legislatures, which threatened local control and the factions it represented.

Central to this struggle was the nature of sovereignty. Since Aristotle, sovereignty had been viewed as unitary and indivisible. According to this conception, a division of authority between equally sovereign entities was impossible. Thus, the ultimate center of power had to be lodged in one place—as with the king in a monarchy or with the member states in a confederation. Moreover, this perception of sovereignty had critical implications for republics because it was assumed that popular rule could exist only within small territorial units. In part, this principle arose out of a belief that the people's representatives should keep close to their constituents' needs and interests; only in this way could individual liberty and civic virtue be preserved. This logic resulted in the belief that the locus of sovereignty was indeed the people but they had delegated administrative authority to the legislature, which could govern effectively only over a limited territory. Out of deference to this theory, state sovereignty had superseded national sovereignty under the Articles of Confederation.

For these political and theoretical problems the Constitutional Convention of 1787 in Philadelphia provided revolutionary solutions. Central to the framers' work was a new conception of sovereignty applied within a federal system. James Madison wrote to George Washington prior to the convention that it was essential to strike a balance between state and national power. "Conceiving that an individual independence of the States is utterly irreconcilable with their aggregate sovereignty; and that a consolidation of the whole into one simple republic would be as inexpedient as it is unattainable, I have sought for some middle ground." In their search for the proper balance, Madison and his colleagues in Philadelphia repudiated the theory of unitary sovereignty and small republics. Like virtually all Americans, the framers believed that the people were the basis of republican government. For the purposes of creating a constitution, however, the people represented by their chosen delegates in special constitutional conventions constituted a national whole. And in this national capacity the people, as the ultimate sovereigns, could divide governmental authority, giving certain powers to a national government and other powers to the states. At the same time, the people could impose upon both governments limitations that would preserve liberty. In this way national and state authority could govern the same territory by exercising only those powers assigned to each.

The new system was, said Madison later, "a novelty and a compound." The Constitution created two distinct spheres of authority in which the national government exerted "complete and compulsive operation" upon individual Americans under its jurisdiction and the states retained their sovereignty within their constitutionally defined sphere. The formal structure of this "compound" embodied a central government composed of a legislature, executive, and judiciary. This government could tax and appropriate money, declare war, raise armies, and command state militias. It could also make laws "necessary and proper" for carrying into execution the powers given it under the Constitution, but the very "enumeration" of these powers was considered a limitation of their scope. The Constitution imposed limits, too, on the states' authority; the states could not violate contract rights, interfere with the writ of habeas corpus, pass ex post facto laws, emit bills of credit, or violate private rights in other ways. The fundamental law indirectly sanctioned slavery, guaranteed the states a republican form of government, and made national laws or treaties passed under the Constitution the supreme law of the land. There was, of course, no bill of rights.

The national judiciary held a significant place in this new federal system. The framers demonstrated their commitment to separation of powers in Article III, which established a Supreme Court and gave Congress the power to create lower federal tribunals. Tenure based upon good behavior and executive appointment with the advice and consent of the Senate significantly insulated federal judges from popular pressures and the interference of other branches of government. Article III also established the jurisdiction of the federal judiciary, which, although limited, was important, particularly in conjunction with Article VI of the Constitution. Article

VI made the Constitution and federal laws made "in Pursuance thereof" the "supreme Law of the Land"; subordinate in authority were state constitutions and state laws. Furthermore, Article VI bound state judges to this hierarchy of authority, and if a conflict between federal and state law arose, federal law was supreme. Taken together, the two provisions established the national courts, especially the Supreme Court, as a supervisory authority within the federal system. But although the English heritage, colonial experience, and a congressional judicial committee under the articles provided precedent for such a role, its precise scope and function was unclear.

The meaning and character of the Constitution was central to the struggle over ratification. Adhering to the precepts of traditional republicanism, the Antifederalists claimed that the national government was in fact an engine of centralized aristocratic power that would obliterate the states, corrupt civic virtue, and destroy liberty. They based their argument upon a unitary theory of sovereignty and the small-republic idea. Although many of the Antifederalists acknowledged the need for reform—many, for example, admitted the value of national courts with limited jurisdiction—they nonetheless condemned the work of the Philadelphia convention as having gone too far. The Federalists responded to these attacks, particularly in the famous *Federalist Papers,* by articulating their novel conception of popular sovereignty, compound government, enumerated powers, and large republics.

The Federalists accepted their opponents' demand for a bill of rights, and the Constitution was ratified as the nation's fundamental law. The nationalists' triumph had profound implications for federalism and its relationship to the courts. The novel principle of divided sovereignty was no mere abstraction: it was the very foundation of power. Yet, neither the ratification struggle nor the Constitution itself prescribed unequivocally the precise sphere of authority of either the state or federal government. Indeed, Madison's *Federalist Paper* no. 10 argued that the proper limits of power would emerge from the clash of factions. It was apparent that the framers expected that by maintaining a supervisory role, the judiciary would mitigate this conflict. But despite precedents from the English past, the nation's colonial heritage, and the Confederation period, there was little agreement upon the scope of judicial power. Thus, the framers' tying of the issue of sovereignty to the struggle of interests meant potentially that narrow political disputes could become controversies over the very existence of the Union. And in such confrontations the courts might represent both a source of conflict and a factor in its resolution.

THE EMERGENCE OF DUAL FEDERALISM

Tension characterized the evolution of federalism prior to the firing on Fort Sumter. Yet the scope of federal-state relations also reflected social and economic realities that encouraged local over national control. From this interplay of conflict and stability emerged a governmental system known as dual federalism. According to this principle, the national government could not exceed its enumerated powers and could constitutionally promote only a few specific policies; the state and federal governments existed within distinct, separate, and equal spheres; and competition, rather than cooperation, governed the relationship between these two spheres.

As the Founding Fathers intended, the judiciary occupied a central but not undisputed place in this system. Pursuant to Article III, the First Congress established the organization, process, and jurisdiction of the national courts in the Federal Judiciary Act of 1789. The chief purposes of federal jurisdiction were to provide the national government a means to enforce its authority directly upon individuals and to give nonresidents of the states a forum removed from local prejudices. The Supreme Court, of course, exercised appellate jurisdiction over the lower federal courts. More significant perhaps, Section 25 of the Judiciary Act provided for appeals from state tribunals of last resort to the federal Supreme Court. But even though Section 25 gave federal judges the authority to enforce the supremacy clause of Article VI, the actual scope of the review power was left unclear. Similarly, under Section 34 of the act, state law bound federal courts in all cases where it applied. The clause did not specify, however, how far it controlled national judges where other sources of law might apply to those same cases. The Judiciary Act thus brought the nationalizing influence of federal jurisdiction to the local level, but this influence was both circumscribed and unsettled.

The conspicuous but limited authority of the federal government compounded the uncertainty surrounding the judiciary's power. The administrative establishment, the regular army, and the taxes of the central government left untouched all but a tiny proportion of the private sector's resources. Although monetary and currency policy (especially during the existence of the Bank of the United States), internal improvements, and the distribution of public lands had important impact, they did not significantly diminish the autonomy of the states. Federal enforcement of the Constitution's fugitive-slave clause did not become a major issue until the 1840s; then it aroused controversy not because of too much federal interference but because of too little. Similarly, through the Corps of Engineers, coastal and waterway regulations, the patent office, federal court and Indian agents, customs officials, boiler inspectors on riverboats, land officers, and postmasters, the federal government maintained a presence, but not an overbearing one.

By contrast, the states occupied a prominent and ultimately obtrusive place in the federal structure. Unlike the federal government, in which the actual exercise of authority was comparatively confined, the states in many ways perpetuated the broad-gauged intrusive role characteristic of the Confederation period. The states controlled labor conditions and race relations, including slavery. They maintained almost total control over the electoral process and apportionment, education, property rights, criminal and family law, civil rights, and local government. After President Andrew Jackson's veto of the recharter of the Bank of the United States in the 1830s, responsibility for banking, monetary policy, and commercial credit generally shifted to the states. Despite some federal assistance, the states also dominated transportation policy.

The power of the states resulted in significant confrontations with the national government that only indirectly involved the judiciary. A theoretical justification for state resistance emerged within a decade of the founding of the Republic during the controversy over the Alien and Sedition Acts. In the Virginia and Kentucky Resolutions, Madison and Thomas Jefferson claimed that the states possessed the power to judge the constitutionality of national laws. As the confrontation persisted, Jefferson advanced the more extreme proposition that state authorities could nullify federal measures that they considered unconstitutional. Although initially public officials throughout the nation rejected such strong language, New England resorted to similar reasoning during the War of 1812 and generally succeeded in avoiding compliance with national calls for taxes and the mobilization of the militia. By contrast, when South Carolina used John C. Calhoun's interpretation of the Virginia and Kentucky Resolutions in an attempt to nullify the tariff, federal power triumphed under President Andrew Jackson's leadership.

The courts were also often involved in clashes in which the limits of state and federal power were at issue. In *Chisholm* v. *Georgia* (1793), South Carolina executors of British creditors sued Georgia in the United States Supreme Court for property the state had seized. The state denied the Court's jurisdiction and refused to execute the Court's order favoring the creditors. Then Congress initiated action that in 1798 resulted in passage of the Eleventh Amendment, which denied the federal courts jurisdiction over private suits against states. Although this was the only instance in American history in which federal jurisdiction was circumscribed by a constitutional amendment, it represented a significant symbolic victory for state sovereignty.

The Supreme Court under Chief Justice John Marshall took a nationalistic stance in deciding such conflicts. Perhaps the Marshall Court's fullest application of the national supremacy doctrine was *McCulloch* v. *Maryland* (1819). Maryland sought to exclude the Bank of the United States from operating within the state, imposing a tax on its Baltimore branch. The bank challenged the tax in the local courts; when it lost there, it appealed to the United States Supreme Court. In a unanimous decision the Marshall Court sustained the constitutional authority of Congress to charter the bank and to manage it without state interference, rejected the state's power to tax it, and found the Maryland law unconstitutional. The chief justice acknowledged that state and federal sovereignty were divided into separate and distinct spheres. Nevertheless, national sovereignty rested not upon the states but upon the consent of the people, who had ratified the Constitution. Thus, the national government, "though limited in its powers," the Court said, was "supreme within its sphere of action."

The Marshall Court maintained this nationalistic spirit in many of its decisions. When Virginia challenged as a violation of state sovereignty the right to appeal from state to federal tribunals under Section 25 of the Judiciary Act, the Court in *Martin* v. *Hunter's Lessee* (1816) and *Cohens* v. *Virginia* (1821) forcefully upheld national judicial authority. Congress indirectly affirmed these decisions when efforts to repeal Section 25 failed. Similarly, the Marshall Court overruled as an unconstitutional violation of the commerce clause and federal law New York's effort to maintain Robert Fulton's steamboat monopoly in *Gibbons* v. *Ogden* (1824). Because it facilitated the development of steamboat construction, the decision received acclaim throughout the nation.

But, in other cases, faithful to dual federalism, the Court struck a balance in federal-state relations. Although recognizing important qualifications in contract clause cases such as *Fletcher* v. *Peck* (1810), where Georgia's repudiation of contractual rights was found to be unconstitutional, the Court nonetheless sustained extensive state control over debtor-creditor relations and insolvency. Moreover, in *Cherokee Nation* v. *Georgia* (1831) and *Worcester* v. *Georgia* (1832), President Jackson supported state interests over the Court's attempted protection of Indian rights. And just five years after *Gibbons* the Marshall Court, in *Willson* v. *Black Bird Creek Marsh Co.* (1829), sanctioned state power over commerce as long as Congress had not preempted the field. The Court also kept its nationalism within bounds by sanctioning a relatively limited admiralty jurisdiction; by holding in *Barron* v. *Baltimore* (1833) that the Bill of Rights applied only to the federal government, not to the states; by denying to federal tribunals (after some vacillation) any criminal common-law jurisdiction; and by deciding in *Dartmouth College* v. *Woodward* (1819) that it could not be presumed that a state had surrendered its regulatory authority in corporate charters unless expressly provided for by the legislature. In deciding the important question of whether state law bound federal judges in commercial credit litigation under Section 34 of the Judiciary Act, the Marshall Court used procedural technicalities to circumvent state decisions but declined to establish a clear doctrinal basis for doing so. Thus, the undeniable nationalism of the Marshall Court did not subvert the equally powerful claims of state sovereignty.

The Supreme Court under Chief Justice Roger B. Taney refined and extended both federal and state sovereignty. In a series of important commerce clause cases, a majority of Jacksonian justices elaborated upon Marshall Court principles. The Court hammered out the doctrine of "concurrent powers," which permitted ample state authority as long as Congress did not act. The culmination of these decisions was *Cooley* v. *Board of Wardens* (1851), in which the high tribunal sustained a Pennsylvania law regulating pilotage in Philadelphia Harbor. The Taney Court was more nationalistic in construing Section 34 in *Swift* v. *Tyson* (1842); going beyond an ad hoc approach pursued by Marshall, it held that in certain commercial litigation, federal judges were free to determine for themselves the rule of decision, regardless of state law. At the same time, however, *Swift* affirmed the need to follow state law where it did apply. The Court struck a balance between state and federal power in other ways: in its admiralty opinions it was actually more nationalistic than the Marshall Court; but on questions involving the exercise of state eminent-domain power it upheld virtually unlimited state authority. And in *Luther* v. *Borden* (1849) the Court refused to consider whether Rhode Island's government was republican under the guarantee clause of the Constitution by declaring that the matter was a "political question" beyond the reach of judicial authority.

In cases involving Article I, Section 10 (the contract clause), the Court further developed dual federalism. When the Massachusetts legislature authorized the construction of a bridge over the Charles River, a company already operating there under an old charter claimed that the inevitable competition violated property rights guaranteed by the contract clause of the Constitution. Taney, however, in *Charles River Bridge* v. *Warren Bridge* (1837), upheld the legislature's authority to charter the new bridge as within the "portion of that power over their own internal police and improvement, which is so necessary to their well being and prosperity." But the Taney Court recognized limits to state sovereignty in

Bronson v. *Kinzie* (1843), a case involving two Illinois laws that restricted foreclosure sales and contained other provisions favorable to debtors. The Court declared the statutes to be an unconstitutional violation of Article I, Section 10. Moreover, the Court in *Gelpcke* v. *Dubuque* (1864) tied the federal judge's independent judgment under Section 34 to the contract clause. In Iowa and many other midwestern and southern states, state supreme courts applied state constitutional provisions to allow local communities to repudiate municipal debts based on bonds. Creditors, mostly railroads and foreign investors, sued local governments for recovery on the bonds. The Court, following the *Swift* decision, established in *Gelpcke* the doctrine that federal tribunals are free to ignore state court precedents in order to defend creditor rights protected by the contract clause.

Thus, consistent with the framers' intent, the federal judiciary worked out the constitutional limits of federal and state power. But when this role became entangled in the issue of slavery, the implications were ominous. Under both Marshall and Taney the federal judiciary had sustained the sovereignty of the state and national governments in their respective spheres. Yet, as a practical matter, federal power was quite limited, with the states possessing much greater real authority. As the nation's population spread west into new territories, free labor gradually superseded slave labor, even though the slave states maintained a balance in the Senate and southerners dominated the presidency. Increased competition between the two labor systems by the 1840s enflamed the issue of whether the Constitution guaranteed the South the right to extend slavery into the territories. Both proslavery and antislavery forces conceived of their opponents' position as a threat to liberty, although only the abolitionists defended the liberty of the slaves.

Northern liberty laws challenged the constitutional status of slavery outside the South. For decades before the Civil War, the right of northern public officials to interpose the state's authority between its citizens and the federal government was an intractable issue. Northern and western states enforced this right through "personal-liberty laws," which affirmed for blacks as well as whites such basic constitutional rights as the writ of habeas corpus, jury trial, and other principles of due process. These laws challenged the slaveholders' claim that slaves were property, possessing the same constitutional protection from interference as all forms of property and lacking rights adhering to citizenship. This meant that slaves remained slaves when they escaped or were taken into free states or territories. By extending constitutional rights to blacks, the personal-liberty laws threatened southerners' ability to control sojourner and fugitive slaves. At the same time, these statutes angered the South because they conferred upon free blacks rights that southern laws denied.

In the 1850s the conflict over the personal-liberty laws and slavery in the territories came to the Supreme Court for resolution. Taney and a divided Court in *Dred Scott* v. *Sandford* (1857) sustained the southern states' power by declaring unconstitutional the right of Congress to exclude slavery from the territories. Moreover, as far as the federal government was concerned, Taney said, blacks, whether slave or free, possessed "no rights" that "white men" were "bound to respect." Shortly after the *Dred Scott* decision, the Court confronted a direct challenge to federal authority from Wisconsin. Pursuant to the state's personal-liberty law, Wisconsin officials defied a federal court order in a case that involved a fugitive slave. Even after the United States Supreme Court struck down the Wisconsin law in *Ableman* v. *Booth* (1859), state resistance in Wisconsin and throughout the North persisted. And as in *Dred Scott* itself, the Court's action merely exacerbated the larger sectional conflict. Northern opposition to both decisions lent credence to the extremists' arguments that the South's constitutional rights could not be preserved within the Union. In Congress and the northern states, Republicans tenaciously affirmed local control of constitutional rights, despite federal and southern assertions to the contrary. Entwined as it was with the status of slavery in the territories, the controversy over the personal-liberty laws thus aggravated a confrontation that contributed to bringing about the nation's greatest tragedy.

The secessionist arguments of 1860 fundamentally challenged the American federal system and resulted in the Civil War. At stake on the battlefield was the constitutional meaning of both national and state sovereignty, and individual and states' rights. The end of bloodshed at Appomattox brought about the triumph of national supremacy as an abstract principle, but the nation's subsequent failure to sustain the freedmen's liberty revealed the limits of victory.

THE TRANSFORMATION OF DUAL FEDERALISM

During Reconstruction the Republican party pursued peace with a firm commitment to both national sovereignty and states' rights. The Supreme Court reflected both these concerns in asserting in *Texas* v. *White* (1869), "The Constitution, in all its provisions, looks to an indestructible Union composed of indestructible States." Yet, unquestionably the most important change in the nation's fundamental law were three constitutional amendments, the so-called Civil War Amendments. In order to end the Constitution's indirect sanction of slavery and to give the fullest possible scope to President Abraham Lincoln's emancipation policy, the Thirteenth Amendment abolished slavery. Through its privileges-and-immunities, equal protection, and due process clauses, the Fourteenth Amendment voided Taney's holding in the *Dred Scott* case that blacks possessed virtually no constitutional rights. The Fifteenth Amendment carried this principle further by establishing that neither race nor a previous condition of servitude should abridge a citizen's right to vote. Along with civil rights legislation and increased federal court jurisdiction, these Reconstruction measures seemed to guarantee legal and political equality for blacks. However, by 1877, when Reconstruction ended, political exigencies involving the Republican and Democratic parties and the rise of such brutal groups as the Ku Klux Klan had destroyed such hopes.

No institution did more to undercut Reconstruction's support of equality under law than the United States Supreme Court. True, when it appeared that the Court might consider the validity of certain Reconstruction measures in *Ex parte McCardle* (1868), Congress withdrew federal jurisdiction over the case, and the justices sustained this diminution of authority. But as the Republicans and the North steadily withdrew their support for the freedman's rights, the Court followed suit. In the *Slaughterhouse Cases* (1874) the justices affirmed the principle that the

Fourteenth Amendment was intended to protect black rights. Nonetheless, they then virtually emasculated the amendment's protective guaranties through narrow construction. The rights flowing from national citizenship were few, the Court held, whereas most of the citizen's liberties were protected by state action. Under this interpretation, the Court eventually said, the Fourteenth Amendment authorized federal measures only against state action that specifically denied rights. During the twentieth century the Court began to hold that provisions of the Bill of Rights were incorporated into the due process clause of the Fourteenth Amendment, which gradually reduced the significance of the state-action principle. But, despite the eventual change brought about by the incorporation doctrine, state action effectively restricted the power of the federal government to protect civil rights during most of the century following Reconstruction. Moreover, the Court held that neither the Thirteenth nor Fifteenth Amendments permitted federal legislation on behalf of blacks unless racial hostility was explicitly proved, something that was found difficult to do.

By the end of the century the Court's retreat from constitutional guaranties of equal justice was pronounced. In the *Civil Rights Cases* of 1883 the justices overturned the Civil Rights Act of 1875 because it dealt with private, rather than state-imposed, discrimination in public accommodations. The highest tribunal held further that the denial of equal access to public accommodations did not constitute "badges or incidents" of slavery under the Thirteenth Amendment. Similarly, when the federal government indicted a Kentucky voting official for refusing to count a black's vote in a state election, the Court struck down the federal statute upon which the indictment was based, holding in *United States* v. *Reese* (1876) that the Fifteenth Amendment did not confer the right to vote on anyone. Under the amendment, the Court said, the states retained primary control of the suffrage unless clear proof existed that race was a factor in disfranchisement. Although initially the Court more vigorously defended voting rights in national elections in *Ex parte Yarbrough* (1884), the case had relatively little impact after 1898 when the justices sustained state-mandated literacy tests in *Williams* v. *Mississippi*. Massive exclusions of blacks from elections thereby resulted.

The culmination of this retreat occurred in *Plessy* v. *Ferguson* (1896). On the basis of the separate-but-equal doctrine, the Court upheld a Louisiana law that established formal racial classifications—something it had previously refused to do—in railway coaches as long as "equal" facilities were provided. The doctrine encouraged state-enforced separation based on race to spread throughout southern society. And because blacks had been stripped of political and legal rights, they lacked the power to bring about even the enforcement of the equal-facilities provision of the *Plessy* doctrine. Consequently, under the system of dual federalism that emerged after Reconstruction, blacks became second-class citizens.

In other ways, the Court refused to curb state authority over individual rights. It found an Illinois law that excluded qualified women from practicing law not to be an unconstitutional violation of the privileges-and-immunities clause of the Fourteenth Amendment, in *Bradwell* v. *Illinois* (1873). Similarly, the Court held in *Minor* v. *Happersett* (1875) that the Fourteenth Amendment did not confer the right to vote on women and that the state could therefore exclude them from voting if it chose to do so. Moreover, the Court affirmed that the Eighth Amendment's barring of "cruel and unusual punishment" was inapplicable to the states in *O'Neil* v. *Vermont* (1892), where a citizen received a fifty-four-year prison term for violating Vermont's prohibition law. Similarly, in *Hurtado* v. *California* (1884), the justices held that the Fifth Amendment of the Bill of Rights did not prohibit through the Fourteenth Amendment a murder indictment under California law. Thus, an early attempt to establish the idea of incorporation failed.

The failure to protect civil rights, however, encouraged the willingness to defend and foster economic liberty. The judiciary sought to strike a balance between federal and local control of the nation's economic order. The enlarged jurisdiction of the federal courts opened them to growing numbers of business litigants, particularly corporations. In *Munn* v. *Illinois* (1877) one of the Midwest's largest warehouses challenged state regulation of its business. The Court sustained Illinois on the grounds that the state's police powers—recognized in such cases as *Willson* and *Charles River Bridge*—sanctioned control of enterprises "affected with the public interest."

Two decades later, the Court upheld on the basis of the police power a Utah law proscribing an eight-hour limit on work in the mining industry. Thus, national tribunals used the police power and other doctrines to favor state authority over business.

By contrast, in *Wabash, St. Louis and Pacific Railway* v. *Illinois* (1886) the Court overturned state regulation of interstate railroads, holding that only Congress properly possessed such power. The next year, partially in response to this decision, Congress enacted the Interstate Commerce Act, which created the nation's first federal regulatory agency, the Interstate Commerce Commission (ICC). At the same time, federal judges applied the *Swift* and *Gelpcke* precedents to fashion a federal common law that helped protect the interests of national corporate enterprise. Moreover, in *Pensacola Telegraph Co.* v. *Western Union Telegraph Co.* (1877) the Court upheld congressional power over such new technologies as the telegraph. And in *Allgeyer* v. *Louisiana* (1897) the Court struck down a state provision protecting workers in their bargaining with employers as a violation of so-called liberty of contract protected by the due process clause of the Fourteenth Amendment.

The Court also scrutinized carefully the centralizing influence of federal authority. During the 1890s the justices interpreted in limited ways the power of the ICC. In *Interstate Commerce Commission* v. *Cincinnati, New Orleans and Texas Pacific Railway* (1897) the Court held that the ICC had no authority to set railroad rates unless Congress specifically granted the power, which it had not. It also circumscribed the ICC's investigatory and fact-finding role in *Interstate Commerce Commission* v. *Alabama Midland Railway* (1897), but it did allow regulatory authority over certain forms of rate competition. In *United States* v. *Trans-Missouri Freight Assn.* (1897) the Court further weakened the ICC by holding that its approval of interstate railroads' rate agreements, which stabilized prices but also prevented competition, violated the Sherman Antitrust Act (passed in 1890 to establish federal supervision of anticompetitive business agreements). In other antitrust cases, the Court sustained federal intervention that favored competition. *United States* v. *Joint-Traffic Assn.* (1898) involved thirty-one railroads running between Chicago and the East Coast which had joined together to fix rates; the justices divided 5–4 but found the price-fixing agreement in violation of the Sherman Act. Where, however, the government prosecuted small, unincorporated midwestern livestock dealers in *Hopkins* v. *United States* (1898), the Court upheld their noncompetitive price agreements under the Sherman Act. By contrast, in *United States* v. *E. C. Knight Co.* (1895) the justices sustained a state-sanctioned corporate structure that permitted one Pennsylvania company to dominate the nation's sugar production.

After the turn of the century, governmental administrative authority gradually increased. The Progressive Era's commitment to bureaucratization and professionalization of government in part facilitated this trend. On both the state and federal levels there developed a greater emphasis upon civil service merit systems and reliance upon experts. These technocrats established an administrative process that cut across formal divisions of federal, state, and local authority and transcended traditional political boundaries. Some progressives also won franchise restrictions that institutionalized so-called Jim Crow racial segregation and undercut the voting strength of ethnic groups and the poor. Thus, as the dependence on administrators grew, an erosion of democracy coincided with the slow emergence of big governments.

The federal government contributed to this change, although state authority remained ample. By delegating authority to administrative bodies, Congress enlarged national control over food, drugs, merchant seamen's working conditions, labor-management relations in the railroad industry, farm credit, and, perhaps most significantly, currency and credit (through the new Federal Reserve system). Other important manifestations of greater federal power were Prohibition, the income tax, and child-labor laws. Another result of administrative centralization was increased intergovernmental cooperation. Under the Agricultural Experiment Stations Act of 1887, the national government began giving cash grants to states. The Newlands Act of 1902 established for the first time a revolving fund that was made independent of the regular congressional budgeting process. As the amount of money for intergovernmental programs grew, the federal government established tighter regulations governing its use by the states. Most state officials were willing to accept restrictions upon state authority in return for federal funds. But when Congress passed the controversial Sheppard-Towner Maternity Act of 1921, which prescribed standards for the first major social program in the states, a challenge arose from Massachusetts. The Supreme Court, however, did not question the principle of intergovernmental funding itself—and the federal administrative rules governing its expenditure—for infant and maternity care in *Massachusetts* v. *Mellon* (1923). Although the Court decided *Mellon* on narrow jurisdictional grounds, the result was to sanction a significant enlargement of federal power based on intergovernmental spending. Yet, state power and local control remained conspicuous. Even though funding for intergovernmental projects steadily increased, as late as 1927 it nonetheless constituted less than 2 percent of state revenues.

Meanwhile, the federal judiciary was doing little to limit local control of individual rights. In the South, state authorities used their power to oppress blacks. Some states, for instance, passed laws giving local governments and individual white southerners the power to control labor, entrapping many blacks in a labor system that was virtually inescapable. The Court invalidated these measures in *Bailey* v. *Alabama* (1910), but the practice persisted as local custom. Similarly, in response to litigation sponsored by the National Association for the Advancement of Colored People, the Court in *Guinn* v. *United States* (1915) struck down state "grandfather laws," which had disenfranchised blacks by extending the franchise only to those citizens whose ancestors could vote in 1866; but the number of blacks actually voting continued to be small. In *Buchanan* v. *Warley* (1917) the justices held unconstitutional municipal ordinances that enforced racial segregation in residential areas. Yet, because they were circumvented, none of these decisions significantly diminished segregation or fostered racial justice. Moreover, where states punished freedom of expression during World War I and the 1920s, the Court sustained state action by refusing to hold that the First Amendment barred it through the Fourteenth Amendment. *Gilbert* v. *Minnesota* (1920) upheld a state law allowing prosecution of speech that sought to discourage enlistment in the military. And although it admitted that under the Fourteenth Amendment the First Amendment might restrict

state power in some instances, the Court nonetheless affirmed a New York law punishing the expression of certain controversial ideas in *Gitlow* v. *New York* (1925).

By contrast, where the regulation of economic liberty was at issue during the early twentieth century, the Supreme Court sought to balance federal and state authority. Relying upon the freedom-of-contract doctrine of the due process clause of the Fourteenth Amendment, the Court in *Lochner* v. *New York* (1905) overturned a New York law restricting the hours of bakery workers to no more than ten per day and sixty per week. In *Coppage* v. *Kansas* (1915) the justices struck down on the same grounds a Kansas law that prohibited "yellow dog" contracts, which allowed employers to require a worker, as a condition of employment, to promise not to join a labor union. The Court in *Adair* v. *United States* (1908) struck down the Erdman Act of 1898, which outlawed the dismissal of employees of interstate transportation companies for membership in a labor union. State efforts to protect labor unions also received a setback in *Truax* v. *Corrigan* (1921) when the Court overturned as a violation of the Fourteenth Amendment's due process clause an Arizona law prohibiting state tribunals from granting injunctions against picketing. But in *Muller* v. *Oregon* (1908) the Court sustained as a legitimate exercise of the police power an Oregon law limiting the hours of work of women in factories and laundries. Similarly, the Court upheld state eight-hour laws for public-works employees in *Atkin* v. *Kansas* (1903).

In other cases, the Court further struck a balance in favor of state power. It held as constitutional state laws regulating child labor in *Sturges & Burn Manufacturing Co.* v. *Beauchamp* (1913); however, it invalidated federal child labor laws twice, in *Hammer* v. *Dagenhart* (1918) and *Bailey* v. *Drexel Furniture Co.* (1922). State use of the police power to pass minimum-wage legislation also received indirect approval when the Court split 4–4 on the constitutionality of such measures in *Stettler* v. *O'Hara* (1916).

The federal judiciary also scrutinized carefully the increased power of the federal government over big business. After the turn of the century, the Court supported the Justice Department's prosecution of several corporate giants. The justices upheld as violations of the Sherman Act the breakup of a huge railroad combination in

Northern Securities Co. v. *United States* (1904), the consolidated meat-packing business in *Swift and Co.* v. *United States* (1905), and a monopolistic oil firm in *Standard Oil Co.* v. *United States* (1911). Yet, by the 1920s its support for trust-busting had flagged. In *United States* v. *United States Steel* (1920) the Court rejected the government's attempt to dissolve the nation's biggest steel producer on the ground that United States Steel did not constitute an unreasonable violation of the Sherman Act. After some vacillation the Court also overruled federal prosecution of another form of cooperation among large firms known as trade associations, in *Maple Flooring Manufacturers' Assn.* v. *United States* (1925). But when the nation experienced unprecedented economic dislocation in 1929, the Court's willingness to support extensive federal intervention in society became problematic.

THE EMERGENCE OF COOPERATIVE FEDERALISM

Under the shock of the Great Depression, dual federalism collapsed. In its place arose a new relationship between federal and state governments in which state power remained important but federal authority became paramount. Beginning in the 1930s the promise of national supremacy that had triumphed in the Civil War was finally fulfilled. Although the new system continued to evolve throughout the remainder of the twentieth century, the term that perhaps best describes its essential character is *cooperative federalism.* Like the doctrine it superseded, cooperative federalism possessed several basic elements. First, federal policymaking replaced state and local action on a scale unprecedented in peacetime. Second, a revolution in constitutional doctrines governing states' rights, due process, and the tax and commerce power received the sanction of the Supreme Court (after considerable resistance from a narrow majority of justices prior to 1936–1937 resulted in a dramatic shift). Third, a large federal bureaucracy whose taxing, spending, and employment consumed an ever-growing percentage of the nation's income apparently became permanent. Fourth, corresponding to the concomitant expansion of intergovernmental grant programs, state and federal bureaucratic power increasingly inter-meshed. Fifth, through a remarkable proliferation of federal regulatory agencies and executive offices, an enormous expansion of presidential power took place.

President Franklin D. Roosevelt's New Deal established the general structure of cooperative federalism. As Congress delegated authority to the president, national power superseded state power to such an extent that the federal government became America's general manager. The production and prices of agriculture's primary crops came under federal control. First through the National Recovery Administration and then through other bureaucratic agencies, industry also was subject to greater centralized direction. With the Wagner Act of 1935 and the initiation of minimum-wage standards, the federal government established a leading role in labor-management relations. Also beginning in 1935, Congress created the social security and unemployment-compensation systems, the administration of which was shared by state and federal officials. Moreover, the federal government promoted regional development with the Tennessee Valley Authority (TVA) and, through public-works projects, enlarged its conservation and reclamation activities. Congress further increased national authority in the area of intergovernmental programs by extending the conditions governing the states' acceptance of grants. In addition, social security, public housing, fish and wildlife conservation, highway construction, aid to dependent children and the elderly, and the allocation of farm produce to the disadvantaged were new grant programs that Congress initiated.

A measure of the New Deal's innovativeness was its initial reception by the Supreme Court. Of the New Deal legislation that the Court reviewed, during a sixteen-month period between 1935 and 1936, it struck down eight acts out of ten. Among the acts overturned were those establishing federal regulation of industrial and agricultural sectors—the National Industrial Recovery Act and the Agricultural Adjustment Act. A unanimous Court in *Schechter Poultry Corp.* v. *United States* (1935) found the former unconstitutional because Congress had delegated much more authority to the president to manage industrial relations than had ever been claimed under the commerce power in peacetime. By 6–3, in *United States* v. *Butler* (1936) the Court also invalidated as an unlawful use of the taxing power that portion of the latter act which taxed stages of production. The justices then held that the section allocating subsidies to the states was an unconstitutional violation of the Tenth Amendment. The New Deal's one major victory was *Ashwander* v. *Tennessee Valley Authority* (1936), wherein the Court upheld the federal government's production and sale of electric power.

Internal and external pressures, however, brought about a dramatic reversal in the Court's stance. During 1936–1937 the Roosevelt administration proposed its Court-packing plan, which provided for a significant increase in the number of justices. At the same time, a realignment occurred within the Court in favor of the New Deal. Roosevelt's plan was defeated, but early in 1937 the Court retreated from its hard line and upheld on the basis of the commerce power the National Labor Relations Act in *National Labor Relations Board* v. *Jones & Laughlin Steel Corporation.* Chief Justice Charles Evans Hughes and Justice Owen Roberts, who had until then voted with the conservatives, switched to support those favoring the New Deal. They made the dramatic shift because they realized that the severity of economic collapse required a broader construction of the Constitution. The new majority also reduced its *Butler* opinion to virtually a dead letter in *Wickard* v. *Filburn* (1942), sustaining a revised Agricultural Adjustment Act. The Social Security Act was held to be constitutional under the taxing power in *Stewart Machine Co.* v. *Davis* (1937). In these and other cases the Court increasingly deferred to Congress on an ever-growing number of policy matters. Consequently, the Fourteenth Amendment's due process clause no longer stood as the bulwark of economic liberty, and states' rights no longer barred federal action under the commerce power. Moreover, in *Erie Railroad* v. *Tompkins* (1938) the Court, after nearly a century of precedent, overruled the *Swift* doctrine, holding that in all cases but those presenting federal or constitutional questions, state law must govern federal judges. Strictly speaking, *Erie* was not an example of increased nationalization. But the overruling of the long-established *Swift* doctrine was indicative of the new activism that the Court practiced to enlarge federal authority.

But the Court also began balancing its self-restraint with judicial activism in cases involving civil liberties. During the nineteenth century the Supreme Court had denied that the Bill of Rights applied to the states, even after passage of the Fourteenth Amendment provided the constitutional means to impose national civil rights provisions upon state and local authorities. As the Court retreated from its defense of economic liberty after 1937, however, it manifested greater concern for civil rights. In *Palko* v. *Connecticut* (1937) the Court admitted that through a "process of absorption" certain principles inherent in the Bill of Rights had become part of the due process clause of the Fourteenth Amendment. The Court did not attempt to specify which rights were incorporated and rejected the general idea advocated by Justice Hugo L. Black that Bill of Rights guaranties per se were part of the due process clause. Yet, it did hold that the First Amendment freedoms were so vital to "ordered liberty" that they existed on a "different plane of social and moral values." This established the preferred-freedoms doctrine, which the Court could use if it chose to do so to protect individual rights from state interference. Similarly, the Court delt a blow to segregation and the separate-but-equal doctrine in *Missouri ex rel. Gaines* v. *Canada* (1938). Here the Court held that Missouri's refusal to admit a black man to its law school, even though it provided funds for him to acquire a legal education out of state, was not equal under the separate-but-equal doctrine.

Within these limits, cooperative federalism evolved during the postwar era. From the 1940s to the 1960s, Democratic and Republican administrations extended federal authority. Under Presidents Dwight D. Eisenhower, John F. Kennedy, and Lyndon B. Johnson, Congress broadened social security programs, increased federal highway spending, and, beginning with the National Defense Education Act of 1958, injected the federal government on an unprecedented scale into what traditionally had been the state and locally controlled field of education. Johnson's War on Poverty and Court-prompted civil rights measures of the mid-1960s brought about still greater centralization.

During these same years judicial activism and self-restraint remained in constant tension. During the 1940s and early 1950s, federal tribunals deferred to federal and state coercive authority

FEDERALISM

in such controversial and ultimately ill-founded cases as the wartime internment of the Japanese and the cold-war attacks upon freedom of association and speech arising from the fear of Communism. But by the mid-1950s, judicial activism reached new heights under Chief Justice Earl Warren. In *Yates* v. *United States* (1957) the Court repudiated its position in regard to the federal government's power to prosecute minor Communists for advocating radical ideas. Mere advocacy, without concrete acts of violence or conspiracy, were protected by the First Amendment, the justices held. *Pennsylvania* v. *Nelson* (1956) also indirectly imposed a similar standard on the states by holding that the issue was within federal jurisdiction alone and therefore not subject to state action. The Court also attempted, through the incorporation doctrine of the Fourteenth Amendment, to impose uniform criminal-procedure guaranties of the Bill of Rights on local law enforcement officials. Beginning in *Baker* v. *Carr* (1962), the Court also enlarged the meaning of democracy in legislative reapportionment cases by moving toward the principle of "one man, one vote."

This tension was evident even in the area of racial justice. As the Court attacked the South's system of racial segregation, it nonetheless maintained a respect for federalism. In the revolutionary decision of *Brown* v. *Board of Education* (1954) the Court virtually overturned the separate-but-equal doctrine as it applied to public education. Sensitive to the difficulties that would inevitably arise from enforcing racial justice in the states, the Court ordered desegregation to proceed "with all deliberate speed" rather than immediately. Consequently, the ideal of equal justice was compromised. The precise connection between the Court's gradualistic approach and the limited degree of integration that existed in education and other areas of society by the 1980s remained problematic. But as the struggle for integration moved from the massive resistance begun in Little Rock in 1957, to the federal civil rights legislation of the 1960s, to the complexities of reverse discrimination, busing, and "white flight" of the 1970s and 1980s, it became apparent that the essence of the Court's policy was moderation. Although the justices embraced activism to begin the revolution, in its long-term implementation they exercised restraint.

The erosion of postwar prosperity imposed new pressures on the federal system. By the 1970s and 1980s, inflation, the nation's weakened status in international relations, and the rise of information technology intensified political and economic competition for resources. Economic contraction forced federal and state officials to reconsider policy priorities. In an effort to shift funding from federal to state budgets, Republican administrations pushed through significant reductions in government programs. And federal-state tensions persisted in policy areas involving federal regulations on water quality, air pollution, government lands, and offshore oil.

Yet, despite political rhetoric that advocated the contrary, there was no break in the growth of federal power. During the 1980s, in spite of reductions in many social programs—especially those serving the poor and dispossessed—certain entitlement payments for such programs as social security and subsidies for tobacco and sugar steadily increased. There was also a massive expansion of spending for military and defense purposes. These expenditures brought about an unprecedented federal budget deficit that further extended federal influence over the nation's financial structure.

Under Chief Justice Warren Burger's leadership, judicial lawmaking reflected these tensions. In cases involving federal authority over state employment practices, the Court reached opposing results. The Burger Court gave states' rights a boost in *National League of Cities* v. *Usery* (1976) when it overruled a 1968 decision and held that Congress had gone beyond its constitutional limits in imposing wage-and-hour standards on state and local government employees. But in *Garcia* v. *San Antonio Metropolitan Transit Authority* (1985) the Court upheld federal minimum-wage and overtime requirements for public mass-transit employees. Similarly, the Court reversed itself to sustain states' rights over riverbed land in *Oregon* v. *Corvallis Sand and Gravel Co.* (1977). It overturned, however, in *Metropolitan Life Insurance Co.* v. *Ward* (1985), an Alabama law that taxed out-of-state insurance companies at a higher rate than state insurance firms.

Perhaps the single most difficult area for the Burger Court was race relations. The civil rights acts of the mid-1960s gave the federal government coercive authority to enforce integration. The Court sustained this power in *Swann* v. *Charlotte-Mecklenburg Board of Education* (1971), which established particular criteria, including limited busing where necessary, to measure whether a school desegregation plan in fact worked. When, however, the issue arose of using this authority in northern and western cities, the Court reached divergent opinions in cases involving Denver, Detroit, and Indianapolis. Similarly, when state officials established a policy favoring racial quotas in admission to a University of California medical school, the Court struck the plan down as a denial of an unsuccessful white applicant's equal-protection rights in *University of California Regents* v. *Bakke* (1978). But where a similar policy was applied in a preferential employment plan in private industry, it was sustained by the Court in *United Steelworkers of America* v. *Weber* (1979). This balancing act in racial cases continued into the 1980s.

The Burger Court also dealt with federal-state issues and individual rights in nonrace cases. In a wholesale reversal of nineteenth-century precedents, the justices protected women's rights in such cases as *Reed* v. *Reed* (1971). Here the Court found an Idaho law that specifically favored men over women in the administration of an estranged couple's deceased child's estate to be a violation of the equal protection clause of the Fourteenth Amendment. Moreover, in *Roe* v. *Wade* (1973) the Court struck down a Texas statute that made abortion a crime, on the ground that the statute violated a woman's right to privacy under the Fourteenth Amendment.

CONCLUSION

To resolve the tensions inherent in the system of divided sovereignty established under the Constitution, the framers relied significantly upon the judiciary. From the nation's earliest days the courts, particularly the Supreme Court, sought to strike a balance between individual rights and governmental authority and between state and federal power. In the fundamental transition from dual to cooperative federalism that encompassed this struggle, there were always winners and losers. At different times, constitutional doctrines governing federal-state relations sanctioned such extremes as Jacksonian

democracy and slavery, progressive voting reforms and segregation, and increased economic opportunity for big business and diminished protection for workers. Yet, the courts also provided abolitionists, civil libertarians, and other activists with the institutional means to fight for minority and individual rights. But humanitarian interest groups were not alone in using the courts to influence public policy. The antislavery (in contrast to the abolitionist) crusade against the expansion of slavery into the territories, like the complicated struggles in the twentieth century that shaped the allocation of grants-in-aid and federal budgetary priorities in general, reflected the interplay of democratic politics, the judiciary, and federalism. Thus, if conflicts within the federal system have imperiled individual liberty, the courts have nevertheless possessed a remedy for the system's weaknesses.

CASES

Ableman v. Booth, 18 Howard 479 (1859)
Adair v. United States, 208 U.S. 161 (1908)
Allgeyer v. Louisiana, 165 U.S. 378 (1897)
Ashwander v. Tennessee Valley Authority, 297 U.S. 288 (1936)
Atkin v. Kansas, 191 U.S. 207 (1903)
Bailey v. Alabama, 219 U.S. 219 (1910)
Bailey v. Drexel Furniture Co., 259 U.S. 20 (1922)
Baker v. Carr, 369 U.S. 186 (1962)
Barron v. Baltimore, 7 Peters 243 (1833)
Bradwell v. Illinois, 16 Wallace 130 (1873)
Bronson v. Kinzie, 7 Howard 311 (1843)
Brown v. Board of Education, 349 U.S. 294 (1954)
Buchanan v. Warley, 245 U.S. 60 (1917)
Charles River Bridge v. Warren Bridge, 11 Peters 420 (1837)
Cherokee Nation v. Georgia, 5 Peters 1 (1831)
Chisholm v. Georgia, 2 Dallas 419 (1793)
Civil Rights Cases, 109 U.S. 3 (1883)
Cohens v. Virginia, 6 Wheaton 264 (1821)
Cooley v. Board of Wardens, 12 Howard 299 (1851)
Coppage v. Kansas, 235 U.S. 1 (1915)
Dartmouth College v. Woodward, 4 Wheaton 518 (1819)
Dred Scott v. Sandford, 19 Howard 393 (1857)
Erie Railroad v. Tompkins, 304 U.S. 64 (1938)
Fletcher v. Peck, 6 Cranch 87 (1810)
Garcia v. San Antonio Metropolitan Transit Authority, 105 S.Ct. 1005 (1985)
Gelpcke v. Dubuque, 1 Wallace 175 (1864)
Gibbons v. Ogden, 9 Wheaton 1 (1824)
Gilbert v. Minnesota, 254 U.S. 325 (1920)
Gitlow v. New York, 268 U.S. 652 (1925)
Guinn v. United States, 238 U.S. 347 (1915)
Hammer v. Dagenhart, 247 U.S. 251 (1918)

Hopkins v. United States, 171 U.S. 578 (1898)

Hurtado v. California, 110 U.S. 516 (1884)

Interstate Commerce Commission v. Alabama Midland Railway, 168 U.S. 144 (1897)

Interstate Commerce Commission v. Cincinnati, New Orleans and Texas Pacific Railway, 167 U.S. 479 (1897)

Lochner v. New York, 198 U.S. 45 (1905)

Luther v. Borden, 7 Howard 1 (1849)

Ex parte McCardle, 6 Wallace 318 (1868)

McCulloch v. Maryland, 4 Wheaton 316 (1819)

Maple Flooring Manufacturers' Assn. v. United States, 268 U.S. 563 (1925)

Martin v. Hunter's Lessee, 1 Wheaton 304 (1816)

Massachusetts v. Mellon, 262 U.S. 447 (1923)

Metropolitan Life Insurance Co. v. Ward, 105 S.Ct. 1676 (1985)

Minor v. Happersett, 21 Wallace 162 (1875)

Missouri ex rel. Gaines v. Canada, 305 U.S. 337 (1938)

Muller v. Oregon, 208 U.S. 412 (1908)

Munn v. Illinois, 94 U.S. 113 (1877)

National Labor Relations Board v. Jones & Laughlin Steel Corp., 301 U.S. 1 (1937)

National League of Cities v. Usery, 426 U.S. 833 (1976)

Northern Securities Co. v. United States, 193 U.S. 197 (1904)

O'Neil v. Vermont, 144 U.S. 323 (1892)

Oregon ex rel. State Land Board v. Corvallis Sand and Gravel Co., 429 U.S. 363 (1977)

Palko v. Connecticut, 302 U.S. 319 (1937)

Pennsylvania v. Nelson, 350 U.S. 497 (1956)

Pensacola Telegraph Co. v. Western Union Telegraph Co., 96 U.S. 1 (1877)

Plessy v. Ferguson, 163 U.S. 537 (1896)

Reed v. Reed, 404 U.S. 71 (1971)

Roe v. Wade, 410 U.S. 113 (1973)

Schechter Poultry Corp. v. United States, 295 U.S. 495 (1935)

Slaughterhouse Cases, 10 Wallace 273 (1874)

Standard Oil Co. v. United States, 221 U.S. 1 (1911)

Stettler v. O'Hara, 243 U.S. 629 (1916)

Stewart Machine Co. v. Davis, 301 U.S. 548 (1937)

Sturges & Burn Manufacturing Co. v. Beauchamp, 321 U.S. 320 (1913)

Swann v. Charlotte-Mecklenburg Board of Education, 402 U.S. 1 (1971)

Swift v. Tyson, 16 Peters 1 (1842)

Swift and Co. v. United States, 196 U.S. 375 (1905)

Texas v. White, 7 Wallace 700 (1869)

Truax v. Corrigan, 257 U.S. 312 (1921)

University of California Regents v. Bakke, 438 U.S. 265 (1978)

United States v. Butler, 297 U.S. 1 (1936)

United States v. E. C. Knight Co., 156 U.S. 1 (1895)

United States v. Joint-Traffic Assn., 171 U.S. 505 (1898)

United States v. Reese, 92 U.S. 214 (1876)

United States v. Trans-Missouri Freight Assn., 166 U.S. 290 (1897)

United States v. United States Steel, 251 U.S. 417 (1920)

United Steelworkers of America v. Weber, 443 U.S. 193 (1979)

Wabash, St. Louis and Pacific Railway v. Illinois, 118 U.S. 557 (1886)

Wickard v. Filburn, 317 U.S. 111 (1942)

Williams v. Mississippi, 170 U.S. 213 (1898)

Willson v. Black Bird Creek Marsh Co., 2 Peters 245 (1829)

Worcester v. Georgia, 6 Peters 515 (1832)

Ex parte Yarbrough, 110 U.S. 651 (1884)

Yates v. United States, 354 U.S. 298 (1957)

BIBLIOGRAPHY

Maurice G. Baxter, *The Steamboat Monopoly: Gibbons v. Ogden, 1824* (1972), provides a useful account of the evolution of the Constitution's commerce clause as it relates to the federal system during the pre–Civil War years. Vincent Blasi, ed., *The Burger Court: The Counter-Revolution That Wasn't* (1983), treats developments in constitutional law during the years following the départure of Chief Justice Earl Warren and contains many insights pertinent to the status of federalism in the 1970s and early 1980s. William J. Brennan, Jr., "State Court Decisions and the Supreme Court" and the reply by the Conference of State Chief Justices in "The Supreme Court and the States: A Critique," both in Robert Scigliano, ed., *The Courts: A Reader in the Judicial Process* (1962), give divergent views of the role of the United States Supreme Court in the federal system, particularly as it pertains to state judicial power.

Martin Diamond, "What the Framers Meant by Federalism," in Robert A. Godwin, ed., *A Nation of States: Essays on the American Federal System* (1963), incisively analyzes the ways in which the Federalists transformed the theoretical meaning of federalism, so essential to understanding the role of the judiciary in American federalism. Tony Freyer, *Forums of Order: The Federal Courts and Business in American History* (1979), discusses the relationship between federal and state courts as it relates to economic development; *Harmony and Dissonance: The Swift and Erie Cases in American Federalism* (1981), examines that relationship as a component of the federal system; and two studies, *The Little Rock Crisis* (1984) and "Law and the Antebellum Southern Economy: An Interpretation," in David J. Bodenhamer and James W. Ely, Jr., eds., *Ambivalent Legacy: A Legal History of the South* (1984), discuss the significance of regionalism in the development of federal-state relations and the courts at different times in the nation's history. Lawrence M. Friedman, *American Law* (1984) and *A History of American Law* (1973), discuss numerous ways in which the judiciary has shaped and been shaped by federalism.

Thomas K. McCraw, *Prophets of Regulation* (1984), has much to say about business-government relations, bureaucracy, and administrative policy that is invaluable in explaining the working realities of the federal system, although federalism is not his central theme. Forrest McDonald, *E Pluribus Unum: The Formation of the American Republic, 1776–1790* (1965), eloquently treats the respective influences of the colonial experience, the Revolution, and the Confederation era upon the federal system that emerged in the Constitution.

Harry N. Scheiber, *The Condition of American Federalism: An Historian's View* (1966); "Federalism and the American Economic Order, 1789–1910," in *Law and Society Review*, 10 (1975); "American Federalism and the Diffusion of Power: Historical and Contemporary Perspectives," in *University of Toledo Law Review*, 9 (1977–1978); and "Federalism, the

Southern Regional Economy, and Public Policy Since 1965,'' in Bodenhamer and Ely, eds., *Ambivalent Legacy* (1984), are by the leading historian of federalism. Herbert J. Storing, *What the Anti-Federalists Were For* (1982), and, with Murry Dry and Herbert J. Story, eds., *The Complete Anti-Federalist* (7 vols., 1982), treats sympathetically yet critically the works of the opponents of the Constitution. Gordon Wood, *The Creation of the American Republic, 1776–1787* (1969), presents well the interplay of ideas and institutions as they relate to federalism and the courts.

[*See also* ARTICLES OF CONFEDERATION; COLONIAL LAW AND JUSTICE; COMMERCE CLAUSE; COURTS AND CONSTITUTIONAL-ISM; DUE PROCESS OF LAW; FRAMING THE CONSTITUTION; *and* MARSHALL COURT AND ERA.]

THE FRANCHISE

Gayle Binion

PERHAPS the most fundamental right in a democracy is the right to vote. In a large modern political system, elections are the means by which the people—or at least the greater part thereof—select their leaders and express their policy preferences. Without elections and an open political process, how are we to know what the majority wants and in what direction and under whose leadership the society should move. Thus, the right to vote and the democratic electoral process of which it is a part are critical elements in any system of popular self-government.

WHO SHALL VOTE?

Under the United States Constitution prior to the passage of the Thirteenth, Fourteenth, and Fifteenth Amendments (the Civil War Amendments), qualifications for voting were almost exclusively a matter of state law. The original Constitution set no qualifications for voting in state elections and included only a few basic rules for enfranchisement in federal elections. Under Article I, Section 2 of the Constitution, each state must use the same voting qualifications for participation in elections for the United States House of Representatives as it uses for the "most numerous branch" of its own legislature. House members must therefore be popularly elected; but the Constitution left the definition of *popular* to states' own electoral laws. The selection of United States senators (under Article I, Section 3) was entrusted not to the citizenry but rather to the legislatures of the states. This was changed by the Seventeenth Amendment to the Constitution, ratified in 1913, which requires the popular election of United States senators. With respect to presidential elections, Article II,

Section 1 of the Constitution allows the states' legislatures to determine the manner in which to select the presidential electors for the electoral college. This provision has never been formally changed, but state legislative actions have resulted in popular election of the electors who choose the president of the United States. Finally, the residents of the District of Columbia, long excluded from the federal electoral process, were granted the right to vote for presidential electors by the Twenty-third Amendment, ratified in 1961.

Because states retained nearly complete authority over the franchise under the Constitution, there were naturally variations among them with respect to their rules on voter eligibility. But the franchise in the eighteenth and early nineteenth centuries was given almost exclusively to propertied white males over twenty-one years of age. Over time, however, the combined effect of constitutional amendments, Supreme Court case law, and movements for democratization has been the extension of the franchise far beyond those eligible during the early years of the Republic. Legal restrictions on eligibility for voting have been lessened, and they have also become quite similar from state to state. Although states may still disenfranchise noncitizens, convicted felons, those under eighteen years of age, and those who are deemed mentally incompetent, most of the other restrictions involving age, gender, residency, property ownership, and race have either been abolished or have become minimal. And the significant expansion in federal protections for the right actually to cast a ballot have been accompanied by a parallel concern for the right to a vote of equal weight.

Gender. Women were not protected by the federal Constitution in their right to vote until the passage of the Nineteenth Amendment in

1920. This amendment forbids the United States or any state from denying the franchise on the basis of sex. Although the Nineteenth Amendment protects the franchise, its passage did not signal the start of women's suffrage in this country. By the time that this amendment was ratified, more than half of the states, through referenda or legislative action, had already enfranchised women. Interestingly enough, nearly all of these state actions had occurred during the decade just prior to the ratification of the Nineteenth Amendment. In fact, before the turn of the twentieth century, only Wyoming, Colorado, Utah, and Idaho—pioneer states—had given women the vote. (New Jersey had enfranchised women in its original constitution, but this was repealed by that state's constitution of 1807.)

Ratification of the Nineteenth Amendment had proved necessary for the suffrage movement because neither the political process nor constitutional litigation had been successful. Although there were victories for women's suffrage in more than thirty states before the ratification of the amendment, in the South and in many industrial states, bills and referenda had been defeated. And the Supreme Court in 1874 had rejected the argument that the Fourteenth Amendment, ratified in 1868, protected the right of women to vote. In *Minor* v. *Happersett* the plaintiff claimed that Missouri had violated the "privileges and immunities" clause of the Fourteenth Amendment by denying her the right to vote on the basis of her sex. The Fourteenth Amendment declares that persons born or naturalized in the United States are citizens of the United States and of the state in which they reside. Mrs. Minor argued that a privilege and immunity of a United States citizen was the right to vote. The Supreme Court, however, concluded that suffrage was not identical to citizenship and that the states could therefore disenfranchise female citizens. This proposition, as it affected women, was essentially overruled by the passage of the Nineteenth Amendment, forty-five years later.

Age. Historically, most states set the minimum age for voting at twenty-one. Notable exceptions to this are Georgia and Kentucky, which lowered their voting ages to eighteen in 1944 and 1956, respectively; Alaska, which enfranchised nineteen-year-olds; and Hawaii, which set its minimum age for voting at twenty. In 1970, however,

Congress attempted to preempt relevant state laws and, under Section 302 of the Voting Rights Act amendments, prohibited the states from denying the franchise in any election to persons over eighteen years of age. Congress based this law on its authority under Section 5 of the Fourteenth Amendment, which empowers Congress by legislation to carry out the foregoing provisions of the amendment. Because Congress concluded that denying the vote to those between eighteen and twenty-one years of age denied them the "equal protection of the laws," which states are prohibited from doing under Section 1 of the amendment, it took this "corrective" action. The federal law applied to all elections, state and federal. Two states, Oregon and Arizona, challenged the constitutionality of the law, and in a rare instance of the Supreme Court's exercise of original jurisdiction, a decision was reached within a few months of the law's passage.

The plaintiff states argued essentially that Congress did not have the power to interfere with the autonomy of the states to control the franchise either under Article I, Section 4 with respect to federal elections (for which Congress may regulate "Times, Places and Manner") or under the Fourteenth Amendment's equal protection and enforcement clauses with respect to state or federal elections. Oregon and Arizona won a partial, some might say Pyrrhic, victory in *Oregon* v. *Mitchell* (1970). The decision of the Court in the case was complex and the result of an unusual voting coalition. By a 5–4 vote, the Court upheld the congressional act with respect to federal elections (under Article I, Section 4) but rejected the argument that the Fourteenth Amendment provided a basis for Congress to regulate the voting age generally. This bifurcation of congressional power between federal and state elections was a conclusion that was subscribed to only by Justice Hugo L. Black. How then did it become the decision of the nine-member body? Four justices thought that Congress could, under the Fourteenth Amendment, lower the voting age in all elections; four thought that neither Article I, Section 4 nor the Fourteenth Amendment provided any congressional authority over the age of enfranchisment. Justice Black found such authority only in Article I and therefore only as it affected federal elections. With respect to federal elections he was joined by the

THE FRANCHISE

four justices who found congressional power over both types of elections, and with respect to state elections he was joined by the four justices who found congressional power over neither type of election.

The victory for states' rights was therefore only partial and understandably short-lived. The ruling of the Court meant that states had to enfranchise eighteen-year-olds in presidential and congressional elections. Those states wishing to retain a higher minimum voting age for state elections would have been forced to conduct two separate electoral processes, one for federal offices and another for state and local contests. The fact that this was clearly not practical or economically feasible was recognized and became a strong factor in the immediate passage by Congress, and ratification by the states, of the Twenty-sixth Amendment to the Constitution, which grants the suffrage to eighteen-year-old citizens in all elections. What Congress could not do entirely through legislation was accomplished with unprecedented speed through the constitutional amendment process.

Property Ownership. In the early years of the Republic, all of the states' constitutions limited the franchise to real-property-owning taxpayers. A belief in the "stake in society" concept of responsible citizenship coupled with the property owners' strong fear that those without property, if enfranchised, would endanger their holdings, supported this then ubiquitous electoral qualification. By the mid nineteenth century, however, such restrictions had virtually disappeared as a result of both efforts of Jacksonian democrats to broaden democracy and the interest of many other politicians in appealing to the propertyless as a source of electoral support. Despite this democratization process, however, property-ownership qualifications have not entirely disappeared from the states' electoral systems. Although such qualifications may not be imposed on electors in general or broad-purpose governmental units, many single-purpose or limited-function jurisdictions continue to impose such restrictions. This is because since the mid-1960s the Supreme Court has scrutinized property-holding limitations on the franchise and has developed these guidelines under the equal protection clause of the Fourteenth Amendment. The Court has rejected such schemes in cases involving bond elections and school-district

elections but has more recently upheld them in cases involving water storage and agriculture and power districts. The different outcomes of these cases reflect the Court's conception of where a limited public interest exists and its application of a different standard of review under the equal protection clause to the "special district" cases.

In the three major bond-election cases, *Cipriano* v. *City of Houma* (1969), *Phoenix* v. *Kolodziejski* (1970), and *Hill* v. *Stone* (1975), the Court ruled unconstitutional provisions limiting the vote to those holding real property. Although the state maintained that the financial interest of these individuals in the ballot issue was clearly greater than that of the general population, the Supreme Court held that the public at large clearly had an interest in the policy ramifications of decisions on municipal bond questions. In these cases, the Court applied the test commonly used for unequal restrictions on fundamental rights (such as voting) under the equal protection clause: the state must demonstrate that it has a "compelling interest" in the unequal restrictions on the right in question. In each of the bond-election cases, the Court concluded that the state had not satisfied this strict standard of review and consequently had not justified its property-ownership qualifications for voting in the bond elections.

Similarly, in *Kramer* v. *Union Free School District* (1969) the Court had declared violative of the equal protection clause a New York law limiting the franchise in certain school districts' elections. Under the challenged law, only owners and lessees of taxable real property, their spouses, and the parents and guardians of children in the public schools were enfranchised. The Supreme Court determined that the state had not demonstrated a compelling need to limit the vote and that many disenfranchised citizens had an interest in educational policy.

The Court in *Kramer* left open the possibility that a less than universal adult suffrage might be justified in some elections where there was an identifiable group with a "primary interest," and in two subsequent cases upheld property-ownership qualifications for voting in limited-function special-district elections. But the Court's decisions in *Salyer Land Co.* v. *Tulare Lake Basin Water Storage District* (1973) and *Ball* v. *James* (1981), which upheld these restrictions, did not determine that the states had a compelling need to limit the franchise. Instead, the Court held that in such limited-function districts (in these cases, a water-storage district and an agricultural-improvement and power district, respectively), restricting the franchise and apportioning it according to one's land holdings was "reasonable." In sum, the Court was able to resolve these special-district cases differently by applying a lower standard of review than it had in previous cases. The property-ownership qualification had to be only reasonably related to a governmental goal or interest; the governmental need did not have to be compelling. Although the Court stressed the limited purposes of the special districts in question, critics of these decisions have suggested not only that the Court should apply the same level of scrutiny to all voting cases but also that many who are not property owners have an interest in the policies of such special districts, especially as such policies affect resources and the environment.

Residency. Like property-ownership qualifications for the franchise, residency requirements have long been justified on the assumption that residents have a greater stake in, and concern for, the community. Banning recent arrivals and transients from voting has been further predicated on the belief that a person needs to live in a jurisdiction for a particular period of time in order to be a knowledgeable and therefore intelligent voter. Although these propositions do reflect a fundamental axiom of democracy—that is, that public decisions ought to be made by those who are both capable of making them and are affected by them—serious constitutional questions have been raised about the residency policies of some states and counties. These policies have involved two types of residency restrictions: against those with insufficient duration residency and against those who, despite their physical presence, are thought to be transients. In both types of cases, Congress and the Supreme Court have each limited the states' discretion. Durational residency requirements for new arrivals have been limited to the time necessary to meet the administrative needs of the states and to prevent fraud, and "irrebuttable presumptions" about the nonresidency of certain classes of people have been prohibited.

Until minimum residency requirements came under constitutional attack, about half of the states had minimum residency requirements of one year, and most of the rest applied a standard of six months. Most further disenfranchised those who, despite meeting the state's residency requirement, moved to a new county or precinct within one to six months before an election. These restrictions were thought to ensure knowledgeable voting and to facilitate reliable electoral record keeping. But their legitimacy was called into question during the 1960s in the wake of three developments. The first was a recognition that because modern mass communications made information on public issues readily available to new voters, new arrivals could learn about the issues in a relatively short time. Second, it became apparent that state record-keeping systems were, or could be, modernized to minimize the time necessary to update them and to prevent electoral fraud. Finally, census and research data demonstrated that more than 5 million otherwise eligible voters were disenfranchised by durational residency requirements.

Congress took note of these factors and in its 1970 Voting Rights Act amendments included Section 202, which protects the right to vote in presidential elections. Voters who move more than thirty days prior to an election must be permitted to register at their new residence. Those who move within thirty days of a presidential election must be permitted to vote by absentee ballot at their previous address. In *Oregon* v. *Mitchell,* the case that also upheld the eighteen-year-old vote for federal (but not state) elections, the Supreme Court upheld Congress's power over durational residency requirements in presidential elections. But the 1970 amendments did not affect residency requirements for congressional or state and local races. These were to be restricted by Court decisions under the equal protection clause of the Fourteenth Amendment.

Numerous cases were litigated in the federal district courts on durational residency requirements for state and local elections. These courts were divided on whether such policies violated the equal protection clause. It therefore fell to the Supreme Court to resolve inconsistencies among the subordinate courts' rulings. In 1972 the Court did so in *Dunn* v. *Blumstein.* Applying the strict test for violations of the equal protection clause, the Court concluded that the state could not demonstrate that laws requiring residency of one year in the state and thirty days in the county were "necessary to promote a compelling governmental interest." The Court's decision rested not only on the unequal denial of the right to vote but also on the law's punitive effects on the right of interstate travel and migration, rights protected under the privileges-and-immunities clause of the Fourteenth Amendment. By judicial mandate, therefore, *Dunn* applied to other elections the limitations on state power to enforce residency laws that Congress had applied with respect to presidential elections. The Court did not set a thirty-day preelection cutoff for registration, but it did suggest in *Dunn* that that would seem a reasonable length of time to allow the state to meet legitimate needs, including the prevention of fraud. The Court set no firm rule, however, and it has subsequently upheld closures of voter registration fifty days before election day. In *Burns* v. *Fortson* (1973) and *Marston* v. *Lewis* (1973) the Court concluded that Georgia and Arizona, respectively, had demonstrated their need for fifty days of administrative lead time. The Court in *Burns* cautioned, however, that "the 50-day registration period approaches the outer constitutional limits in this area." States are therefore no longer likely to attempt to impose longer durational residency requirements on new voters, because of the burdens they face in demonstrating their need to do so.

In addition to durational residency requirements for all voters, states have also traditionally defined certain categories of persons as ineligible for electoral residency. Despite meeting the durational residency requirements, members of the armed forces and residents of other federal enclaves, as well as students living away from their parents, were in many states unable to register to vote in their actual places of domicile. These states simply operated on the "irrebuttable presumption" that such people were inherently transient. Like the durational residency requirement, these restrictions on the granting of the franchise were minimized by congressional and judicial action during the 1960s and 1970s.

Beginning with *Carrington* v. *Rash* (1965), the Supreme Court has required that the states provide the same opportunity to all people to demonstrate their actual residency and intention to remain in the community. The *Carrington* case challenged Texas' prohibition on voting by members of the military stationed therein, and the Court concluded that wearing a United States uniform cannot be "a badge of disenfranchisement." Three years after the *Carrington* case, Congress changed relevant federal legislation from presuming that members of the military continued to reside in their states of origin, to facilitating their acquiring residency in the states in which they are stationed. Shortly thereafter, in *Evans* v. *Cornman* (1970), the Supreme Court applied a rationale similar to that in *Carrington* to a Maryland law disenfranchising residents of a federal enclave, the National Institutes of Health (NIH). Because the Court found that "residents of the NIH grounds are just as interested in and connected with electoral decisions . . . as are their neighbors who live off the enclave," it concluded that Maryland's policy violated the equal protection clause.

Finally, another controversy involving transiency centered on state policies designed to prevent college students from voting at their college (apartment or dormitory) residences. Many states feared the potential bloc voting strength of students in college communities and, despite the ratification of the Twenty-sixth Amendment, were slow to conform to the new constitutional mandate. Many courts in the United States have, under the amendment and relevant federal statutory law, enjoined states from discriminating against student registrants or applying to them any standards or practices not applied to all voters. In *Symm* v. *United States* (1979) the Supreme Court summarily upheld one such injunction, and states have slowly complied with the constitutional protections afforded equally to all citizens over eighteen years of age.

RACE AND THE FRANCHISE

By far the most significant volume of litigation over voting rights in the United States has involved the voting rights of blacks. Since the Civil War, the emancipation of the slaves, and the passage of the Thirteenth, Fourteenth, and Fifteenth Amendments, there has been considerable controversy over the practices of the states, almost exclusively the southern states, designed to prevent blacks from voting or attaining political power. Although problems still remain with respect to the black franchise, a century of judicial decision-making and more recent congressional and executive actions have controlled the most egregious of these practices.

The critical foundations for federal protections of voting rights for blacks are found in the Thirteenth, Fourteenth, and Fifteenth Amendments because they not only specifically protect the franchise but also fundamentally redefine American citizenship. The Thirteenth Amendment outlawed slavery, and the Fourteenth Amendment made the federal government the source of United States citizenship and required that the states respect the "privileges and immunities" of this citizenship. Also relevant to voting rights in the Fourteenth Amendment are the equal protection and representation clauses. Under the latter (never enforced) clause, states denying the vote on the basis of race were to have their seats in the United States House of Representatives reduced proportionally. Under the equal protection clause, as interpreted by the judiciary, states are prohibited from discriminating in the granting of the franchise, although, as the Court said very early on in *Minor* v. *Happersett* (1874), the Fourteenth Amendment does not of itself grant the franchise to anyone. The Fifteenth Amendment, ratified in 1870, specifically protects the voting rights of American citizens from discrimination on the basis of "race, color, or previous condition of servitude."

Because states could no longer legally prohibit blacks from voting after the passage of the Fourteenth and Fifteenth Amendments, other mechanisms of disenfranchisement developed quickly. Although it may be argued that physical, social, and economic intimidation—which remained virtually untouched until after the passage of the 1965 Voting Rights Act—were the most effective means of discrimination, states developed more-formalized methods of "legal" disenfranchisement. Prominent among these were the literacy test, the poll tax, and the white primary.

It has already been demonstrated that the Fourteenth Amendment has been an important constitutional foundation for judicial decisions restricting age and residency requirements in the granting of the franchise. The Fourteenth and Fifteenth Amendments, and the congressional acts passed in pursuance of these amendments, have proved to be critical vehicles for lessening racial discrimination in voting. In the case of literacy tests and poll taxes, although the Supreme Court issued some very important decisions, it basically awaited the lead of the executive and legislative branches or deferred to their authority. In the case of the white primary, however—a practice far less subtle in its discriminatory design—the Court acted more readily on its own independent authority to interpret and apply the Fourteenth and Fifteenth Amendments.

Literacy Tests. Ironically, although other states had various types of literacy requirements during the nineteenth century, no southern state had such requirements until 1890, and then all of the states with the largest black populations began to institute them. Literacy may be valued in a voter because it is suggestive of a more intelligent use of the franchise; however, the adoption of literacy and "interpretation" tests by the southern states quite clearly had the purpose and effect of denying the vote to blacks. Several features of literacy tests were especially pernicious in their racial purposes and consequences: "grandfather" clauses, exceptions for property holders and those of "good moral character," and entirely discretionary administration by local voter registrars.

The grandfather clause exempted from literacy tests all new voters whose grandfathers had voted (generally) before blacks were legally entitled to do so. This exemption from literacy tests, available to white registrants, was clearly and intentionally unavailable to blacks. The grandfather clause was also not even remotely related to the states' interest in a literate electorate. Therefore, in 1915, in *Guinn* v. *United States,* the Supreme Court declared this practice unconstitutional. But the literacy test, other questionable exemptions, and the often arbitrary application of the test remained intact in many states until the mid-1960s.

In 1959 the Supreme Court rejected a "frontal attack" on literacy tests in *Lassiter* v. *Northhampton County Board of Elections.* The case was brought by a black citizen who challenged the constitutionality of North Carolina's literacy test. The Court, in a unanimous opinion written by Justice William O. Douglas, held that there was no evidence presented of unequal application of the test on a racial basis. But such evidence was soon to be gathered, and such practices documented with aggregate statistics, by both the United States Department of Justice and by Congress. On the basis of such evidence, the Department of Justice brought suit against Louisiana and Mississippi under the Fourteenth and Fifteenth Amendments and federal enforcement legislation.

In two related decisions in 1965, the Supreme Court upheld both the authority of the federal government to bring suit and a finding of excessive and racially discriminatory discretion in the administration of the literacy tests challenged. The Court did not hold, however, that literacy tests were per se unconstitutional. Yet, by this time, spurred by the civil rights movement, Congress had already begun to act against literacy tests as well as other roadblocks to the effective enfranchisement of blacks. The 1964 Civil Rights Act, although it dealt largely with open accommodations and employment discrimination, contained an important voting provision. For the purpose of federal elections, citizens with six years of formal education were presumed to be literate, and states were further restricted to administering only those literacy tests which were conducted entirely in writing. These were important steps, but they governed only federal elections.

The passage of the Voting Rights Act in 1965 signaled the beginning of the end of all literacy tests for voting in the United States. Under the original provisions of the law, states with exceptionally low voter registration or turnout (as defined by the statute) were prohibited from using any such registration devices. And the law further presumed literacy for those educated in American schools where the primary language was other than English.

In *South Carolina* v. *Katzenbach* (1966) and *Katzenbach* v. *Morgan* (1966), respectively, the Supreme Court upheld Congress's power to pass such legislation under the Fourteenth and Fifteenth Amendments. In the 1970 amendments to the act, Congress extended the ban on literacy tests to the entire country, and on two subsequent occasions it has renewed the ban. Given the presumption of nearly universal literacy in the United States, it is unlikely that literacy tests will ever again be permitted or justified.

Poll Taxes. As with literacy tests, poll taxes, which are presumably neutral on their face, were often designed to disenfranchise, or resulted in the disenfranchisement of, blacks. And, as with

the history of literacy tests, their ultimate eradication was initially the result of the efforts of the legislative and executive branches, with the judiciary then buttressing these efforts.

In 1787, only New Hampshire required the payment of a poll tax, but in the nineteenth century many states adopted this fee in lieu of the previous requirement of "taxpayer" status in order to vote. This was thought to be a democratizing change insofar as many who could afford the relatively small levy of a poll tax were not otherwise "taxpayers" (generally defined as owning and paying taxes on real property). By the Reconstruction era, however, the role of the poll tax had changed again and had become a means of preventing blacks from voting. Blacks were poorer than the white population and hence more burdened by the tax; it was one more impediment to their registration as voters.

In *Breedlove* v. *Suttles* (1937) the Supreme Court upheld Georgia's poll-tax provision even as it affected federal elections. The Court rejected challenges based on the Fourteenth, Fifteenth, and Nineteenth Amendments (women were exempt from the poll tax) and deemed such taxes to be legitimate revenue measures. It was to be nearly thirty years after the *Breedlove* ruling before an effective political and legal assault was launched against the poll tax. It must be noted, however, that despite the Court's endorsement in *Breedlove,* poll taxes had become a distinct oddity in mid-twentieth-century America. In fact, they remained an obstacle to the franchise in only five southern states. But eradicating these policies in five states and their (arguably relatively small) contribution to the disenfranchisement of blacks took a constitutional amendment, a federal statute, and a major constitutional decision by the United States Supreme Court. Interestingly enough, this was all accomplished within a two-year period.

In 1964 Congress passed, and the states ratified, the Twenty-fourth Amendment to the Constitution, which prohibits the imposition of poll taxes in federal elections. In *Harman* v. *Forssenius* (1965) the Court gave a broad interpretation to this amendment and prohibited the state of Virginia from requiring a burdensome preregistration procedure in lieu of the payment of a poll tax in a federal election. In the same year, in a compromise version of the Voting Rights Act, Congress empowered the United States attorney general to seek judicial injunctions against poll taxes in state and local elections if these taxes were shown to impede the full exercise of the franchise. Although Congress did not go so far as to render all poll taxes (not covered by the Twenty-fourth Amendment) illegal under the act, the Supreme Court was soon to do so directly under the Constitution. In *Harper* v. *Virginia Board of Elections* (1966) the Court declared poll taxes a violation of the equal protection clause of the Fourteenth Amendment. The Court, while mindful of the racial significance and symbolism of these taxes, focused its decision on the inherent irrationality of conditioning the right to vote on the ability to pay. Through this decision and the congressional actions that preceded it, poll taxes—for a century a factor in the disenfranchisment of blacks—became over a two-year period a relic of history.

White Primaries. Perhaps the most "creative" response to the threat of blacks voting in the South was the white primary. Faced with the fact that official prohibitions on blacks voting in state or federal elections violated the Fourteenth and Fifteenth Amendments, certain states turned to the primary election process. A 1921 decision of the Supreme Court that did not involve racial issues had suggested a lack of federal authority over the primary election process. Texas soon passed a law prohibiting blacks from voting in Democratic party primaries. In the one-party South, the primaries represented the real electoral contests; general elections merely ratified the choices made in the Democratic primaries. Prohibiting blacks from participating in these primaries was therefore tantamount to total disenfranchisement.

The Texas prohibition was successfully challenged in *Nixon* v. *Herndon* (1927), in which Justice Oliver Wendell Holmes found that the state law violated the equal protection clause. Texas' response to this ruling was to repeal the law in question but to pass another that allowed the executive committee of the party to set its own rules for membership and for voting in primaries. The party again barred blacks from voting in the primaries but claimed that it was acting as a private group. The Fourteenth Amendment, which prohibits only states from denying the "equal protection of the laws" (constitutional rights in general are rights against government only and not private parties), was nevertheless found applicable in *Nixon* v. *Condon* (1932). The Court reasoned that the executive committee of the party had acted under the authority of the state legislature and therefore the "state action" requirement of the Fourteenth Amendment had been met. But the Court's decision in *Grovey* v. *Townsend* (1935) allowed parties to bar blacks from voting in the primary if this action was not actually "authorized" by the state legislature.

It was not until 1941 that the Supreme Court began to see primary elections as an integral part of the larger electoral process, and it was 1944 before this view was applied to racial exclusion from the process. In *Smith* v. *Allwright* (again a Texas case in which blacks were denied the primary ballot), the Court began to treat political parties and their primary elections as inherently governmental in character. One no longer had to show that state officials were involved in the party's discriminatory actions for the Fourteenth Amendment to apply. The actions of party officials were themselves equivalent to acts of government. This orientation led the Court to strike down, in *Terry* v. *Adams* (1953), the final attempt of Texas Democrats to preserve the white primary process. A "private" all-white club called the Jaybirds held a "primary," and the winners became the ballot choices of the local Democratic party. The Supreme Court held that any electoral practice with the purpose or effect of disenfranchising blacks was in violation of the Fifteenth Amendment. The discriminatory nature of the white-only primary was always apparent, but it took twenty-five years of litigation to end the practice.

THE 1965 VOTING RIGHTS ACT

Civil rights activists and legal scholars are in agreement that the most effective piece of federal civil rights legislation ever enacted is the 1965 Voting Rights Act (amended in 1970, 1975, and 1982). Although earlier voting rights laws (1957 and 1960) and court decisions laid important legal foundations and developed constitutional principles of equality, it was not until the passage of the 1965 act that there existed the machinery for transforming racist electoral and political systems.

The Voting Rights Act has many provisions, but among its most important are the suspension of "tests and devices" and the assignment of federal registrars and election observers in covered jurisdictions. Covered jurisdictions include counties in which fewer than 50 percent of the adult population was either registered to vote or actually voted in the 1964 presidential election; later presidential elections have been used as the basis for this determination in subsequent amendments to the act. (As already noted, the suspension of literacy tests has applied nationally since 1970.) The assignment of federal registrars and observers proved to be an enormously important means of counteracting the various forms of intimidation encountered by blacks who attempted to register or to vote in the South. The protection for the black voter was in an immediate and practical sense provided by the federal government; he or she did not bear the burden of seeking redress. This day-to-day, on-the-spot administrative commitment of federal agents was critical to the success of the law.

The effects of this part of the law were almost immediately apparent. One million new black voters were registered in the South between 1964 and 1972. This same time period witnessed the increase in black elected officials from fewer than one hundred to more than one thousand. Certain southern states claimed that these provisions of the law were discriminatory and unconstitutional, but the Supreme Court upheld them in *South Carolina* v. *Katzenbach.*

One of the major complaints against the act was the so-called trigger provision. States or counties in which fewer than 50 percent of potential voters were registered or actually voted in the November 1964 elections were automatically covered and, in a sense, presumed to have discriminated against black voters. "Bailing out" of this coverage could be done only if the jurisdiction in question proved to a federal district-court judge that it had had "clean hands" for at least the previous five years. (In subsequent amendments to the act, later trigger election dates were employed, and many new jurisdictions outside of the South—including, for example, Bronx, New York—came under the act's coverage. And in later judicial decisions, the trigger and bail-out facets of the law have continued to withstand assault.)

The suspension of tests and the provision of federal registrars and observers formed the critical core of the 1965 act, but other sections of the law have also been enormously important, as well as controversial. The 1975 amendments to the act (partially modified in 1982) require the availability of foreign-language ballots and voting materials wherever a language minority is more than 5 percent of the voting-age population. It might be suggested that this provision enfranchises a more knowledgeable electorate insofar as a voter can more fully understand the issues in his or her native language. Reactions to the provision have been negative, however, both from local governments (which must bear the costs associated with foreign-language ballots) and from those who think it unpatriotic to vote and not to speak English. This section of the act has been a target for those campaigning for a constitutional amendment to make English the official language of the United States.

Perhaps most important in the long run, and the focus of nearly all of the litigation under the Voting Rights Act, has been Section 5. Under this section, covered jurisdictions are prohibited from changing their electoral systems without the prior approval of the United States attorney general or the United States District Court for the District of Columbia. The attorney general or the court (the latter is almost never used because it is time-consuming and expensive) must determine that the proposed electoral change does not have the purpose and will not have the effect of discriminating against black voters.

Several features of Section 5 of the law have made it quite powerful as a weapon against discrimination. First, it is prophylactic: it prevents covered jurisdictions from instituting new, possibly racially biased electoral policies until they are screened by the Justice Department. It therefore prevents the substitution of new modes of discrimination for the old. Second, the burden is on the state to demonstrate that the new law will not discriminate; the attorney general need not prove that it will. Third, Section 5 prohibits discrimination in both intent and effect; either is sufficient to render a proposed law unenforceable. This aspect of the act has come to be very important because in *Mobile* v. *Bolden* (1980) the Supreme Court held that in a challenge to an electoral scheme under the Fifteenth Amendment, the plaintiff must demonstrate racist intent. Under Section 5 (and, since the passage of the 1982 Amendments to the Voting Rights Act, under the act more generally), racially unequal consequences of electoral processes may themselves be illegal. Finally, the language in Section 5 is much broader than that in other sections of the law insofar as it goes well beyond the acts of registration and voting and covers changes in entire electoral systems in the covered jurisdictions. Section 5 covers "standards," "practices," and "procedures" with respect to voting. This has allowed the attorney general to scrutinize, among other things, municipal boundary changes as well as reapportionment plans. (Although it is beyond the scope of this essay, it should also be noted that Section 5 serves as a tool to protect black candidates for public office from changes in rules governing candidacies that could be detrimental to them.)

Boundary Changes and Section 5. While the vast majority of municipal boundary changes are probably undertaken for sound fiscal or governmental reasons, others have been motivated by, and/or have resulted in, a serious diminution of black political power. The most notorious example of this phenomenon occurred in 1957 when the Alabama legislature redrew the boundaries of the city of Tuskegee. By creating a twenty-eight-sided city, it managed to exclude from the city limits all but four or five of Tuskegee's black voters. In *Gomillion* v. *Lightfoot* (1960) the Supreme Court held that this action violated the Fifteenth Amendment. Although blacks were not technically denied the right to vote per se, they were deprived of the franchise within Tuskegee. This case arose several years before the passage of the 1965 Voting Rights Act, but it set an important precedent with respect to racial gerrymandering that has influenced the enforcement of Section 5. Because all boundary-change practices in covered jurisdictions must be submitted to the attorney general before they take effect, incidents such as the one in Tuskegee are less likely to occur.

Compliance with Section 5 has not been universal, and according to some critics, the attorney general has not always been firm enough in raising objections to the proposed boundary alterations. On the other hand, under Section 5 the attorney general has sometimes been able to accomplish more for black political power through negotiation than through simple enforcement of the law. A few examples will suffice.

Tales of noncompliance with the preclearance requirements of Section 5 are numerous. In 1966, Mississippi passed a law facilitating the consolidation of majority-black counties with neighboring white counties, thereby diluting the emerging electoral power of blacks. Three years later, after litigation, a court finally ordered the state to submit this law for federal approval. A similar boundary-change action occurred in Richmond, Virginia, where in 1969 it was forecast that blacks would take electoral control in the next municipal elections. Richmond proceeded to annex, with unprecedented speed, a section of white, suburban Chesterfield County. This reduced Richmond's black population from 52 percent to 42 percent. Richmond did not voluntarily submit this boundary change to the attorney general for preclearance. After the city was forced to do so by a federal judge, the attorney general objected to the plan but later reached a compromise. The city was permitted to keep its annexed territory, but it had to conduct elections on a ward, rather than at-large, basis. This would maximize black political strength, which was concentrated in particular geographical areas of Richmond. In *Richmond* v. *United States* (1975) the Supreme Court essentially endorsed the city's action, because although the annexation was initially racially motivated, it had come to provide other civil benefits. The Court was of course influenced by the attorney general's withdrawal of his objection in return for the ward-based elections. Civil rights activists continued to view Richmond's boundary change as not only in violation of the Fourteenth and Fifteenth Amendments but also as contrary to the proscriptions of the Voting Rights Act.

In contrast with the widely criticized handling of the Richmond case, the actions of the attorney general in an annexation in McComb, Mississippi, resulted in changes in the city's proposed political boundaries to include blacks who desired the municipal services that McComb could provide. Similarly, the attorney general was also able to "persuade" Pearl, Mississippi, which was seeking to incorporate as a city, to change its proposed boundaries to include more blacks. In each of these cases the attorney general was able to secure more favorable electoral conditions for potential black voters in return for lifting objections to the proposed boundary actions.

Reapportionment and Section 5. The second area in which Section 5 preclearance has affected the translation of the black vote into political power is reapportionment. Whereas boundary-change actions involve a geographical redefinition of who is part of a political community, such as a city or town, reapportionment involves the redrawing of the boundaries of legislative electoral districts, such as those for city council, state legislature, or the United States House of Representatives. Although the following discussion of reapportionment suggests the standards generally applicable to legislative district-drawing, Section 5 allows for stricter monitoring of these changes in districts with a history of presumed racial discrimination. This power has proved to be important with respect to both the "undrawing" of districts (into at-large electoral systems) and the selection of new district boundaries in single-member districts.

A not uncommon method of selecting members of city councils, county boards of supervisors, and officials of special-function districts, such as school districts, is at-large elections. Under this system all members of the legislative body are elected on a citywide, countywide, or districtwide basis. Courts have generally upheld such electoral arrangements as not in any way an abridgment of the right to vote; all members of the political community can vote and vote equally for the candidates for all seats. But such systems clearly do have the effect of minimizing black political power both with respect to the electoral strength of black voters and with respect to the electability of black candidates. If black residents were dispersed evenly throughout a jurisdiction, or if there were no racial polarization, at-large elections would not be racially problematic; however, black voters are generally concentrated in certain sections of cities and counties. A fair district-based representational scheme can translate that concentration into electoral power over some seats on the governmental body, but at-large systems dilute that voting strength and make it unlikely that even a sizable minority group can seriously influence the election of any of the decision-makers. A further ramification of the at-large electoral process is that the officials who are elected under it may feel no affiliation with, or electoral obligation to, the minority community and may pay little attention to the needs of this group.

The Supreme Court has not, however, found such effects of at-large voting systems to be a violation of either the Fourteenth or Fifteenth Amendments. Operating on the premise that no group has a constitutional right to representation proportional to its numbers, the Court has held that at-large electoral systems that prevent black communities from exercising political power are unconstitutional only if they are adopted or retained for this purpose. In brief, discriminatory intent must be demonstrated in order to challenge such a system successfully. Unequal effects are not themselves unconstitutional.

In two challenges to at-large systems the Court has reached opposite conclusions about the intent despite nearly identical data and arguments. In *Mobile* v. *Bolden* the Court held that there was no evidence of discriminatory intent in the at-large system; two years later, it found such intent in a similar case from Burke County, Georgia (*Rogers* v. *Lodge*, 1982). Most critics were surprised at the Court's ability to differentiate between these cases, as both involved systems in effect since 1911 under which no black had ever held elective office, despite the presence of sizable black populations in both communities. But it is most important to note, with respect to the significance of Section 5 of the Voting Rights Act, that it is applicable only to electoral-system changes instituted since 1964. The attorney general therefore could not challenge the at-large electoral systems of either Mobile, Alabama, or Burke County, Georgia, under Section 5, but he can prevent shifts to such systems in other places. And the attorney general need not allege a nefarious motive; a projection of discriminatory effects is sufficient to warrant a Section 5 objection.

In 1966, Mississippi passed a law to facilitate the shift in county electoral systems from district-based to at-large. The attorney general lodged an objection to this law, and in *Allen* v. *State Board of Elections* (1969) the Supreme Court specifically held that a change to an at-large electoral system is a change in a "standard, practice or procedure with respect to voting" that must be precleared by the attorney general. Although it was apparent that the changes challenged in *Allen* and related cases were designed to minimize the electoral strength of newly enfranchised black voters, what is potentially most important about a Section 5 objection is that in contrast with the Supreme Court's constitutional pronouncement in *Mobile* and *Rogers*, no racially discriminatory motive need be shown. Section 5 is therefore considerably more protective of black voting power than is the Constitution as interpreted by the majority of the contemporary Court members. The attorney general may prohibit a change to an at-large electoral process unless the state demonstrates that the change has neither the purpose nor the effect of diminishing black electoral strength.

As in the case of changes to at-large elections, changes in the boundaries for legislative districts in covered jurisdictions are also under the purview of the attorney general. In 1973, in *Georgia* v. *United States,* the Supreme Court ruled that new legislative districts devised and adopted by the legislature could not be used until the attorney general (or the United States District Court for the District of Columbia) had approved the changes. Because legislatures at all levels must reapportion periodically to meet the Court's standards for population equality under *Reynolds* v. *Sims* (1964; discussed below), the attorney general has significant authority to pressure jurisdictions to select district boundaries that will maximize the possibility of fair political representation for minorities. Electoral districts must be relatively equal in population, and there are many ways to accomplish this and many different places in which to draw the lines. In *United Jewish Organizations* v. *Carey* (1977) the Supreme Court endorsed the principle that reapportionment plans (in this case, those of the New York state legislature) in covered jurisdictions must take race into account when drawing boundary lines. This is to prevent retrogression—that is, a reduction in the electoral power of minority voters from that existing under the preceding apportionment.

There are, however, three limitations imposed by the Supreme Court on the attorney general's authority to object to reapportionment plans in covered jurisdictions. The first restriction is that only those reapportionments which were adopted by legislative bodies are subject to preclearance. In *East Carroll Parish School Board* v. *Marshall* (1976) the Supreme Court clarified that judicially ordered reapportionments are exempt from Section 5 coverage. Also in 1976, in *Beer* v. *United States,* the Court set two additional limitations on the power of the attorney general. The city of New Orleans sought and received a judicial declaratory judgment that its apportionment plan for its city council did not violate the Voting Rights Act. The attorney general had sought to force the city to drop the at-large seats that constituted part of the plan and to redraw district boundaries so as to increase the relative electoral power of black voters. The Court ruled, however, that preexisting features of a reapportionment plan are not "changes" within the meaning of Section 5 and are therefore exempt from preclearance. Because the preceding apportionment scheme in New Orleans included the at-large seats, this was not itself a "change." Finally, the Court ruled that the substantive powers of the attorney general to object to the "new" features of the proposed plan extended only so far as to prevent retrogression. All that the attorney general may require is that the proposed plan not further minimize black electoral power. As long as the new apportionment schemes do not worsen the electoral situation of black voters, Section 5 is satisfied. The attorney general cannot demand that black political power be brought into relative parity with blacks' numbers or that existing underrepresentation be in any sense improved upon.

For millions of black Americans, the 1965 Voting Rights Act has been extremely important in translating the legal right to vote into an actual ability to vote. The end of literacy tests and various forms of intimidation have given many the confidence to exercise the franchise that was legally protected shortly after the Civil War. Section 5 has proved important insofar as the attorney general is empowered to prevent electoral changes that will diminish black political power; however, more recent decisions have made the attorney general powerless to force covered jurisdictions to improve the electoral position of blacks.

REAPPORTIONMENT

Chief Justice Earl Warren reflected at the time of his retirement, "I think the reapportionment not only of state legislatures, but of representative government in this country, is perhaps the most important issue we have had before the Supreme Court" (quoted in Spaeth and Rohde, 178). During the 1960s, the decade in which the Court expanded the access to the ballot for many effectively disfranchised citizens, the Court also began to define the right not just to vote, but to an equal vote.

The obvious target was malapportioned legislatures. Population shifts from rural to urban areas had not been accompanied by equivalent redistricting to render each legislative district relatively equal in population and each voter relatively equal in electoral power. Some states simply ignored their own state constitutional mandates to reapportion every ten years. In other states, legislative districts were redrawn but with the goal of protecting the electability of those already in the legislature. And in still other states, the law did not even use population equality as the basis for districting. The result was that as more and more people moved to the cities, the states' legislatures became less and less reflective of the geographical distribution of the populace. Rural areas, and consequently rural concerns, were overrepresented in the state capitols; urban areas and interests were underrepresented.

Until 1962, however, this was not thought to be an issue that was subject to resolution in the federal courts. This is because in 1946, in *Colegrove* v. *Green,* the Supreme Court had relied on a then century-old precedent on the nonjusticiability of the "guaranty clause." Justice Felix Frankfurter argued that Article IV, Section 4 of the Constitution, which guarantees to each state "a Republican Form of Government," was the only possible basis for a suit against legislative malapportionment and that that clause was not subject to judicial interpretation. The Court suggested that recourse could be had only through the states' legislatures. The legislatures, however, were the source of the problem, and consequently they were not an effective forum for relief.

In 1962, in *Baker* v. *Carr,* the Supreme Court held that malapportionment was justiciable under the equal protection clause. It did not reach the merits of the case—that is, it did not decide that the equal protection clause was actually violated, only that federal courts could decide the question. It was two years later, amid much legal controversy and significant political backlash, that the Court reached the substantive issue. In numerous decisions during the 1963–1964 term of the Court, the districting of the state legislatures of Alabama, New York, Maryland, Virginia, Delaware, and Colorado were found in violation of the equal protection clause. The famous principle of "one person, one vote" from *Reynolds* was then applied to the dozens of

similar cases heard by the Court over the following decade. The Court's message was at first simple: population must be the basis for legislative representation—not cows, acreage, county lines, or the electoral self-interest of legislators. And the dictum was equally applicable to both houses of the states' legislatures. (Only Nebraska has a unicameral legislature.) In *Lucas* v. *Forty-fourth General Assembly of Colorado* (1964) the Supreme Court declared unconstitutional a 1962 state constitutional amendment putting one house of the legislature on a districting basis involving criteria other than population. The Court rejected an analogy to the United States Congress according to which the lower house is apportioned to the states on the basis of population but the upper chamber represents each state equally, regardless of population. To the Supreme Court, the "great compromise" that provided this arrangement was an act of political necessity to form the union and not an act of political virtue. In the Court's view, it was neither relevant to the states' representational systems nor a model to emulate.

The Court answered two important questions in *Reynolds* and *Lucas,* but two other conceptual questions remained. Would the decision govern all types of legislative bodies? How equal would the populations have to be in the different districts? The former question had been answered in part by the Court's disposition of *Wesberry* v. *Sanders* (1964). Challenged in *Wesberry* was the constitutionality of Georgia's apportionment of its congressional delegation. The Court held that the command of Article I, Section 2 that the House of Representatives be elected "by the People" meant that as nearly as practicable, each person's vote should count equally. In subsequent cases before the Court, congressional districting has been subjected to a much more demanding "as nearly as practicable" standard than have the states' legislatures.

Equality in apportionment has not been limited to state legislatures and congressional districts; the Court has also applied this constitutional mandate to all general-function local governments and school districts. Exempt from the one-person, one-vote requirement are some special-function districts; judicial, executive, and administrative positions; and those decision-making bodies not directly selected by the public. Thus, although the Court has ordered county boards of supervisors, city councils, and school districts to conduct elections in districts of equal population, it has not applied the same standard to judicial districts, water-storage districts, and district-based appointments made by legislative bodies. Moreover, under *Dusch* v. *Davis* (1967), states are permitted to require officials elected at large to be residents of districts with unequal populations.

The Supreme Court met with much criticism from both politicians and constitutional lawyers who objected to the manner of the Court's disposition of the reapportionment cases. Some thought that the Court applied the population-equality doctrine too broadly; others objected to the Court's exemption of certain governmental bodies and offices. All, however, recognized the difficulty inherent in the Court's determining, in any case, whether the population equality doctrine has been satisfied as nearly as practicable. Yet, the experience of the courts during more than two decades of reapportionment litigation suggests that mathematical niceties are not as problematic as many critics had feared. Reapportionment, like constitutional law, has not been an exact science.

In 1967, in cases challenging the apportionment plans for the lower houses of the Florida and Texas legislatures, the Supreme Court rejected unnecessarily large population differences between the smallest and largest electoral districts. It found unconstitutional maximum population deviations in the states' legislative districts of approximately 40 percent and 30 percent, respectively. In more recent cases, however, the Court has suggested that although the state must always bear the burden of justifying substantial variations in population, minor variations among districts need not be justified.

The level of population variance that is allowed by the Court appears to be largely a function of the level of government involved. Local governmental bodies of a town, city, or county have the most flexibility in their apportioning. The Court assumes that other considerations besides population may reasonably influence the selection of such districts' boundaries. States' legislatures are somewhat more restricted in their freedom to deviate from strict population equality in districting. *Mahan* v. *Howell* (1973) suggested that a 10 percent variance at this level of government would be as-sumed to be population equality as nearly as practicable. For larger variations, the state would have to demonstrate need. Finally, the least local level of legislature, the United States House of Representatives, must be apportioned in closer accord with population equality than must any other body. The standard that has been applied to congressional districts is whether population deviations can be avoided. The Court has consequently rejected population deviations as low as 4 percent and 5 percent in states' congressional districting and has suggested that no other political values but population equality are germane at this level.

Justice Frankfurter warned the Court to stay out of reapportionment and thereby avoid "the political thicket." Reapportionment has indeed been controversial, time-consuming, and not altogether satisfactory from almost any point of view. But if the right to vote were not accompanied by a right to an equal vote, it would indeed be a superficial guarantee.

CONCLUSION

The franchise has expanded significantly since the early days of the Republic, from being limited to an electorate composed almost entirely of propertied white males over the age of twenty-one, to nearly universal adult suffrage as a legal principle. The process by which this expansion occurred involved the complex interaction of social, political, and judicial institutions. Although barriers to the franchise began to disappear in the nineteenth and early twentieth centuries with respect to property ownership and gender, respectively, the major voting rights developments occurred in the 1960s. During the 1960s and early 1970s the actions of the judicial, legislative, and executive branches significantly altered the shape of the eligible American electorate. These major developments included the enfranchisement of eighteen-year-olds, the end of poll taxes and literacy tests, the virtual disappearance of residency requirements, and the advent of the one-person, one-vote dictum of reapportionment. And finally, in addition to these legal principles, the first federal administrative commitment to racial equality in voting came with the implementation of the 1965 Voting Rights Act.

THE FRANCHISE

CASES

Allen v. State Board of Elections, 393 U.S. 544 (1969)
Baker v. Carr, 369 U.S. 186 (1962)
Ball v. James, 451 U.S. 355 (1981)
Beer v. United States, 425 U.S. 130 (1976)
Breedlove v. Suttles, 302 U.S. 277 (1937)
Burns v. Fortson, 410 U.S. 686 (1973)
Carrington v. Rash, 380 U.S. 89 (1965)
Cipriano v. City of Houma, 395 U.S. 701 (1969)
Colegrove v. Green, 328 U.S. 549 (1946)
Dunn v. Blumstein, 405 U.S. 330 (1972)
Dusch v. Davis, 387 U.S. 112 (1967)
East Carroll Parish School Board v. Marshall, 424 U.S. 636 (1976)
Evans v. Cornman, 398 U.S. 419 (1970)
Georgia v. United States, 411 U.S. 526 (1973)
Gomillion v. Lightfoot, 364 U.S. 339 (1960)
Grovey v. Townsend, 295 U.S. 45 (1935)
Guinn v. United States, 238 U.S. 347 (1915)
Harman v. Forssenius, 380 U.S. 528 (1965)
Harper v. Virginia Board of Elections, 383 U.S. 663 (1966)
Hill v. Stone, 421 U.S. 289 (1975)
Katzenbach v. Morgan, 384 U.S. 641 (1966)
Kramer v. Union Free School District, 395 U.S. 621 (1969)
Lassiter v. Northhampton County Board of Elections, 360 U.S. 45 (1959)
Lucas v. Forty-fourth General Assembly of Colorado, 377 U.S. 713 (1964)
Mahan v. Howell, 410 U.S. 315 (1973)
Marston v. Lewis, 410 U.S. 679 (1973)
Minor v. Happersett, 21 Wallace 162 (1874)
Mobile v. Bolden, 446 U.S. 55 (1980)
Nixon v. Condon, 286 U.S. 73 (1932)
Nixon v. Herndon, 273 U.S. 536 (1927)
Oregon v. Mitchell, 400 U.S. 112 (1970)
Phoenix v. Kolodziejski, 399 U.S. 204 (1970)
Reynolds v. Sims, 377 U.S. 533 (1964)
Richmond v. United States, 422 U.S. 358 (1975)
Rogers v. Lodge, 458 U.S. 613 (1982)
Salyer Land Co. v. Tulare Lake Basin Water Storage District, 410 U.S. 719 (1973)
Smith v. Allwright, 321 U.S. 649 (1944)
South Carolina v. Katzenbach, 383 U.S. 301 (1966)
Symm v. United States, 439 U.S. 1105 (1979)
Terry v. Adams, 345 U.S. 461 (1953)
United Jewish Organizations v. Carey, 430 U.S. 144 (1977)
Wesberry v. Sanders, 376 U.S. 1 (1964)

BIBLIOGRAPHY

Gordon E. Baker, *The Reapportionment Revolution* (1966), offers an insightful analysis of reapportionment under the American constitutional system. Charles S. Bullock III and Charles Lamb, *Implementation of Civil Rights Policy* (1984), provides in Chapter 2 an interesting analysis of the implementation and impact of the 1965 Voting Rights Act. Richard Claude, *The Supreme Court and the Electoral Process* (1970), is an excellent and comprehensive history of the Supreme Court's disposition of many different kinds of cases on voting rights. Barbara Deckard, *The Women's Movement: Political, Socioeconomic, and Psychological Issues* (1975), gives in Chapter 10 an excellent analysis of women's suffrage in the United States, with attention to the interaction of law and politics. Robert Dixon, Jr., *Democratic Representation: Reapportionment in Law and Politics* (1968), assesses reapportionment as a legal and political phenomenon.

C. Herman Pritchett, *Constitutional Civil Liberties* (1984), provides in Chapter 13 an interesting and useful analytical summary of the major constitutional cases on the right to vote. Alan Reitman and Robert Davidson, *The Election Process: Voting Laws and Procedures* (1972), offers a useful manual on voting rights that inventories the laws and policies of the various states. Harold Spaeth and David Rohde, *Supreme Court Decision Making* (1976), is a good introduction to the decision-making processes of the Supreme Court. Laurence Tribe, *American Constitutional Law* (1978), is a very good overview of the right of political participation under the American constitutional system.

[See also CONSTITUTIONAL INTERPRETATION; EQUAL PROTECTION CLAUSE; PRIVILEGES AND IMMUNITIES; and WARREN COURT AND ERA.]

FREE SPEECH AND EXPRESSION

David S. Bogen

"ONGRESS shall make no law . . . abridging the freedom of speech, or of the press." This guaranty of freedom of expression in the First Amendment is both broader and narrower than it appears. The language refers only to Congress, but it affects the executive and judicial branches of government as well. The sweeping command that Congress make "no law," however, applies only to "abridging the freedom of speech, or of the press," and many laws that affect speech but do not "abridge" it directly have been upheld. The First Amendment's meaning is the product not only of its language but also of its history, philosophy, and experience.

Unlike the other amendments in the Bill of Rights, which are stated as rights of the individual, the First Amendment is framed as a restriction on the legislature. James Madison's initial proposal for an amendment was drafted as a right of the individual, and the amendment passed by the House continued to use the form of an individual right. In the Senate, however, the provisions on speech were consolidated with the proposed amendment on religion, and this changed the form of the amendment into a restriction on Congress.

The Constitution gives federal courts power to hear disputes between citizens of different states. In exercising this power, a federal court might be asked to enforce an agreement to pay money to a church. Congress feared this might be held an "establishment" of religion. They resolved this problem by framing the prohibition on establishment of religion to apply only to Congress. Thus, a federal court could require payments to churches based on private agreements or state law but not based on any federal policy of church support.

Applying the same principle to free speech,

the First Amendment forbids abridgment of freedom of speech pursuant to federal law (as the Congress enacts it, the judiciary applies it, or the executive enforces it), but it does not forbid abridgment by the states, even if a federal institution is called upon to apply the state law. This distinction lost its significance in the twentieth century when the Supreme Court determined that the due process clause of the Fourteenth Amendment forbids the states from abridging freedom of speech or press. Thus, today every institution of government at every level is forbidden to abridge the freedom of speech or of the press.

The most controversial issue in interpreting the language of the First Amendment is what constitutes an abridgment of "the freedom of" speech or the press. *Freedom* refers to the absence of some restriction, but not necessarily all restrictions. A "free" individual may be one who is not a slave, who is not in jail, who is not married, who does not presently have a job, or who does not conform to social conventions; but it would be an unusual use of the adjective to mean a person not subject to any law. If *freedom of speech* refers to the absence of a particular kind of restriction on speech, language alone does not reveal what kind of restriction is barred. It is necessary to look at the history of the amendment to begin to obtain a context for the phrase. That history then provides a point of departure for a variety of views on freedom.

HISTORICAL BACKGROUND

In the *Federalist Papers*, no. 84, Alexander Hamilton defended the omission from the original Constitution of a clause on freedom of the press by arguing that it was unnecessary. "Why," wrote Hamilton, "should it be said that the liberty of the press shall not be restrained, when no power is given by which restrictions may be imposed?" He even argued that a provision on liberty of the press might dangerously expand congressional power by permitting the inference that Congress had legislative powers beyond those granted in the document. Finally, he insisted that such a provision would be useless:

> What is the liberty of the press? Who can give it any definition which would not leave the utmost latitude for evasion? I hold it to be impracticable; and from this I infer that its security, whatever fine declarations may be inserted in any constitution respecting it, must altogether depend on public opinion, and on the general spirit of the people and of the government.

Although the Constitution was ratified without a guaranty of free expression, public opinion demanded amendment. A coauthor of the *Federalist Papers,* James Madison, was persuaded to draft amendments to protect individual liberties. Madison opened the debate in the First Congress on proposed amendments by addressing the arguments that they were unnecessary and useless. To the objection that guaranties of basic rights were superfluous because Congress was granted no power to abridge them, Madison replied, "Now may not laws be considered necessary and proper by Congress, (for it is for them to judge of the necessity and propriety to accomplish those special purposes which they may have in contemplation) which laws in themselves are neither necessary nor proper?" (*Annals of Congress,* 438). In this light, the First Amendment was necessary to hold Congress within the bounds of the legitimate scope for government action. It reflected the common understanding that the states had the basic responsibilities of government and the powers of the federal government were limited, but Madison's comments do not help substantially to fix those limits.

If the legislature defined its own limits, Hamilton's dismissal of a constitutional guaranty as useless would be accurate. Madison pointed out, however, that the courts would check the legislature's errors:

> Independent tribunals of justice will consider themselves in a peculiar manner the guardians of those rights; they will be an impenetrable bulwark against every assumption of power in the Legislative or Executive; they will be naturally led to resist every encroachment upon rights expressly stipulated for in the Constitution by the declaration of rights.
>
> (*Annals of Congress,* 439)

Yet, Hamilton was right about the difficulty of definition. Speeches in Congress that proposed the amendment and the state legislatures that ratified it and contemporary writings that mentioned free speech offered the courts little help in giving content to the right. Neither Hamilton nor anyone else involved in the drafting and ratification of either the original Constitution or the First Amendment argued that a prohibition on abridgment of the freedom of speech or of the press might prevent the government from enacting useful laws. They were aware that speech can be harmful. They supported state laws that provided remedies for libel, deceit, solicitation of crimes, and other harmful communications.

Nevertheless, everyone agreed that the freedom of speech and of the press was an unalloyed good. There are two explanations for this apparent paradox. One is that state governments could deal adequately with harmful speech and no federal power was needed. Consequently, Congress could safely be forbidden from passing any law limiting expression. The other explanation is that the framers distinguished the freedom of speech from abuses of speech. Government may punish abuses of the privilege of speaking and writing; it may not punish instances of speech and writing that are not abuses. Thus, the First Amendment's language was virtually a syllogism: Congress shall make no law abridging speech and press that should not be abridged. No one can disagree with the sentiment, yet it can be criticized as a constitutional command. It ignores differences of opinion over what speech is an abuse. The speaker typically considers his activity an exercise of freedom, while the opponent considers the same activity an abuse of freedom of speech. There are also institutional difficulties in dealing with abuses of speech without impairing its freedom. None of these problems were discussed during the process of adopting the amendment.

The participants in the drafting and ratification of the First Amendment discussed freedom of speech and press as natural rights. For example, in his notes for the speech introducing the proposed amendments that he had drafted, Madison indicated that freedom of speech was to be characterized as a natural right to be retained by the people when powers were given to the legislature. In a state of nature before governments were formed, people had the power to speak and to write. The purpose of government, according to the philosophy of the Declaration of Independence, is to secure certain "unalienable rights," including the rights of life, liberty, and the pursuit of happiness. Restrictions on natural rights such as speech could be justified only if necessary to secure the rights of others. But government always claims that its restrictions on speech are necessary to protect members of society from harm. Thus, a natural-rights theory alone does not help to fix the limits of government power.

Special protection for "freedom of speech or of the press" implies a common understanding of the legitimate and illegitimate functions of government, but no one stated it in the Constitution. It is not clear there was agreement. Some men who voted for the amendment in Congress or in the state legislatures ratifying the amendment may have focused on statements made during the debates on the Constitution by supporters of ratification who said that an amendment to protect freedom of speech was unnecessary because the federal government had no power to deny freedom of speech. Those statements could lead to the conclusion that in the context of a restriction on Congress, "freedom of speech" meant that the federal government had no power over expression. But Madison also sought—unsuccessfully—to obtain an amendment to prevent the states from infringing the freedom of speech or press. Men who considered the freedom of speech or press outside the context of federalism probably viewed the language as a statement of a principle derived from England. That principle was still in the process of development and could be given several meanings.

In England power struggles between various groups had resulted in a variety of speech-protective rules. When such expedients proved satisfactory, the protection they offered speech came to be appreciated as part of "the freedom of speech" or "the freedom of the press." Further, government opponents, such as later American revolutionaries, claimed that their criticism was useful to society and should also be protected. By the time the First Amendment was drafted, the common understanding of the freedom of speech and press in America had been extended beyond the natural-rights platitude that speech should not be restricted if it was not harmful. That understanding had at least advanced to the specific propositions that honest, accurate criticism of government was an exercise of free speech and that a system of prior censorship for all printed matter abridged freedom of the press.

The freedom of the press meant at a minimum the absence of a system of prior restraint. The Licensing Act in England failed to suppress objectionable works, which were simply printed in secret without a license. Official censors were prone to accept bribes, and the main effect of the requirement that all books be submitted to a censor before publication was to delay the printing of totally unobjectionable material and drive up the costs of books and pamphlets. These practical objections led to the end of the system in 1694. Within a century, the fact of abolition became a principle. Thus, William Blackstone wrote in his *Commentaries on the Laws of England*,

> The liberty of the press is indeed essential to the nature of a free state: but this consists in laying no *previous* restraints upon publication, and not in freedom from censure for criminal matter when published. Every free man has an undoubted right to lay what sentiments he pleases before the public; to forbid this is to destroy the freedom of the press; but if he publishes what is improper, mischievous, or illegal, he must take the consequences of his own temerity.

After the American Revolution, almost all of the states included a provision on the freedom of the press in their declarations of rights or state constitutions. When Antifederalists attacked the federal Constitution for failure to secure the freedom of the press, several of the Constitution's supporters replied in a manner that showed they understood the term to mean no more than the absence of prior restraint. For example, Hugh Williamson wrote in his *Remarks on the New Plan of Government,*

> There was a time in England, when neither book, pamphlet, nor paper could be published without a license from government. That re-

straint was finally removed in the year 1694 and, by such removal, their press became perfectly free, for it is not under the restraint of any license. Certainly the new government can have no power to impose restraints.

(Schwartz, vol. 1, 551)

At least some contemporaries understood "the freedom of the press" in a broader sense. The members of the convention to ratify the Constitution in New York proposed a new amendment that stated, "Freedom of the Press ought not to be violated or restrained." The disjunctive wording indicates that something other than restraint could violate the freedom of the press. A minority report at the Maryland ratification convention proposed an amendment that stated "that the freedom of the press be inviolably preserved." The report noted, "In prosecutions in the federal courts for libels, the constitutional preservation of this great and fundamental right may prove invaluable." For these men, the substantive and procedural common-law rights of defendants in libel trials were part of the freedom of the press.

Even if "the freedom of the press" meant only the absence of a system of prior restraints, the First Amendment went beyond it to protect "the freedom of speech." State constitutions had no similar provision. Only Pennsylvania and Vermont mentioned freedom of speech in their declarations of rights, and they did so only as a preamble to a specific provision securing the freedom of the press. Freedom of speech in natural-rights theory includes all expression, but there is some historical support for giving the term a limited political focus. In ancient Greece, the "freedom of speech" referred to the right of a citizen to speak in the legislative assembly. Prior to the American Revolution, the only mention of freedom of speech in colonial charters referred to legislative privilege. Freedom of speech as a protection of legislatures against executive power was considered an important principle in England and in the colonies. This right did not protect the legislator from punishment at the hands of his fellow legislators, but they were reluctant to invoke sanctions, and no other body could punish the legislator.

After the Revolution, both state and federal constitutions provided for legislative immunity. The impact of that principle on contemporary conceptions of freedom of speech is not unambiguous. It was even used prior to the Revolution to punish persons who criticized the legislature. Nevertheless, by the time of the Constitution, there was a recognition of the importance of open debate to the democratic process.

Another strand of development for free speech was the position taken by members of the government opposition that their criticism should be protected. John Peter Zenger became a symbol of free speech in America when his counsel successfully convinced the jury to override the Court's instructions and find Zenger not guilty of libel because his statements were true. The fame of the case was spread by James Alexander's *Brief Narrative of the Case and Tryal of John Peter Zenger, Printer of the New York Weekly Journal* (1736).

One of the most familiar discussions of freedom of speech was contained in *Cato's Letters*, written by John Trenchard and Thomas Gordon as a series of newspaper articles in England and often republished in America prior to the Revolution. *Cato's Letters* initially spoke of freedom of speech in natural-right terms as "the Right of every Man, as far as by it he does not hurt and controul the Right of another, and this is the only Check which it ought to suffer, the only Bounds which it ought to know" (no. 15). But a later article made clear that some speech that might be considered harmful by those in power should never be considered an impairment of the rights of others. "The exposing therefore of publick Wickedness, as it is a Duty which every Man owes to Truth and his Country, can never be a Libel in the Nature of Things" (no. 32).

The limited role envisioned for the federal government, the natural-rights theory that held expression should not be suppressed unless necessary for the proper functioning of government, the abolition of prior restraints, legislative immunity, and the duty to criticize government were all relevant to individual perceptions of the First Amendment. Divisions of opinion and differences of emphasis did not surface until the debates over the Alien and Sedition Acts of 1798. Federalists admitted that the government has no legitimate purpose in punishing truthful criticisms of its operation, but they insisted that false accusations were abuses of speech and sought to punish malicious statements that brought the government into disrepute, permitting truth to be pleaded as a defense. The sponsors of the Alien and Sedition Acts viewed the First Amendment as constitutionalizing English law on speech. Their political opponents, led by Thomas Jefferson and Madison, contended that the law interfered with the right to criticize government freely. Sedition Act opponents protested that the First Amendment reflected concern over federal power and was intended to make it clear that the federal government had no legitimate interest in regulating any speech, whether true or false, since the states could deal with libel and other harmful speech. History furnished ammunition for both positions.

This partisan political controversy demonstrated that there was no consensus over the application of the First Amendment. Although the controversy never reached the Supreme Court, all the Supreme Court justices who passed on the issue in their capacity as members of the circuit courts upheld the law. On the other hand, Jefferson pardoned all those imprisoned under the law when he became president, and the law was allowed to lapse.

MILL'S THEORY

The next major step in the development of freedom of speech and press was the publication of *On Liberty* in 1859 by the English philosopher John Stuart Mill. Mill attempted to apply his utilitarian philosophy to the treatment of expression by government. He was not construing the American Constitution, but the language of the First Amendment made the English philosopher's reflections relevant to American constitutional limits. He argued that the control of the expression of opinion is not a legitimate power of government.

Mill's essay focused attention on the problems of permitting any body, whether executive, legislative, or judicial, to decide whether particular expressions should be suppressed. This struck a resonant chord in America, where the Sedition Act prosecutions had been so politically controversial. Mill wrote,

> First, if any opinion is compelled to silence, that opinion may, for aught we can certainly know, be true. To deny this is to assume our own infallibility.
>
> Secondly, though the silenced opinion be an

error, it may, and very commonly does, contain a portion of the truth; and since the general or prevailing opinion on any subject is rarely or never the whole truth, it is only by the collision of adverse opinions that the remainder of the truth has any chance of being supplied.

> Thirdly, even if the received opinion be not only true, but the whole truth; unless it is suffered to be, and actually is, vigorously and earnestly contested, it will, by most of those who receive it, be held in the manner of a prejudice, with little comprehension or feeling of its rational grounds. And not only this, but, fourthly, the meaning of the doctrine itself will be in danger of being lost or enfeebled, and deprived of its vital effect on the character and conduct: the dogma becoming a mere formal profession, inefficacious for good, but cumbering the ground and preventing the growth of any real and heartfelt conviction from reason and personal experience.

This argument does not assume that truth will always prevail over falsehood in an open debate, nor does it deny that allowing the expression of certain ideas may lead to immoral and noxious events. It merely asserts that open debate is a better process than permitting restraints. "There is the same need of an infallible judge of opinions to decide an opinion to be noxious as to decide it to be false, unless the opinion condemned has full opportunity of defending itself," wrote Mill.

Mill's argument is not conclusive. When he points to the benefits to truth of permitting false statements to be made, he neglects the harms that such statements may produce. Once it is acknowledged that sometimes falsehoods are believed over truth and that false opinions can lead to terrible results, it can be argued that suppression of some ideas would be beneficial to society. Even if the body suppressing ideas is not infallible and may err in judging which ideas are more harmful than beneficial, the harm from those errors may still be less than the harm from allowing all ideas to be expressed.

HOLMES, BRANDEIS, AND MEIKLEJOHN

Sixty years after Mill set forth his ideas on freedom of speech, Justice Oliver Wendell Holmes, Jr., recognized that the argument was only a hypothesis, yet he embraced it as the basis for the First Amendment. In 1919 he and Justice Louis D. Brandeis dissented in *Abrams* v. *United States* from a decision upholding the conviction for obstruction of the war effort against Germany of individuals who distributed leaflets calling for stopping production of war materials that might be used against the Russian revolution. Holmes wrote,

> To allow opposition by speech seems to indicate that you think the speech impotent, as when a man says that he has squared the circle, or that you do not care whole-heartedly for the result, or that you doubt either your power or your premises. But when men have realized that time has upset many fighting faiths, they may come to believe even more than they believe the very foundations of their own conduct that the ultimate good desired is better reached by free trade in ideas,—that the best test of truth is the power of the thought to get itself accepted in the competition of the market; and that truth is the only ground upon which their wishes safely can be carried out. That, at any rate, is the theory of our Constitution. It is an experiment, as all life is an experiment.

The experiment did not require allowing all ideas to be expressed. Even Mill wrote that "opinions lose their immunity when the circumstances in which they are expressed are such as to constitute their expression a positive instigation to some mischievous act." Several months before his dissent in *Abrams,* in an opinion for the Court in *Schenck* v. *United States* (1919) upholding the conviction of persons who distributed draft-resistance leaflets to draftees, Justice Holmes had suggested a standard for determining when speech could be suppressed: "The question in every case is whether the words used are used in such circumstances and are of such a nature as to create a clear and present danger that they will bring about the substantive evils that Congress has a right to prevent." The "clear and present danger" test was derived from Holmes's speculations on the law of criminal attempt. It was designed to mark the boundary between the illegitimate punishment of expression and the legitimate concerns of society over illegal conduct.

Freedom of speech and expression took two more steps in *Gitlow* v. *New York* (1925). The majority of the Court upheld the conviction of Benjamin Gitlow for advocating criminal anarchy, but in the process, they assumed that freedom of speech and of the press "are among the fundamental personal rights and 'liberties' protected by the due process clause of the Fourteenth Amendment from impairment by the states." This application of guaranties of free speech and press to the states greatly expanded the kinds of issues to reach the court, for the states traditionally had been left to deal with harms posed by speech subject only to the restraints of state constitutional provisions. The extension had little immediate impact, for the Supreme Court was still willing to uphold restraints on any speech that had a tendency to hinder or impede government in the performance of its duties (the "bad tendency" test).

Holmes's dissent in *Gitlow,* in which Brandeis joined, recognized that any criticism of government might tend to impede its performance. He insisted on a higher standard of protection for speech:

> Eloquence may set fire to reason. But whatever may be thought of the redundant discourse before us, it had no chance of starting a present conflagration. If, in the long run, the beliefs expressed in proletarian dictatorship are destined to be accepted by the dominant forces of the community, the only meaning of free speech is that they should be given their chance and have their way.

Two years later, in a concurring opinion in *Whitney* v. *California,* in which Holmes joined, Justice Brandeis drew together the marketplace metaphor of the *Abrams* dissent, the hints at democratic theory from the *Gitlow* dissent, and his own ideas on the importance of free speech to the individual and to the working of government:

> Those who won our independence believed that the final end of the State was to make men free to develop their faculties; and that in its government the deliberative forces should prevail over the arbitrary. They valued liberty both as an end and as a means. They believed liberty to be the secret of happiness and courage to be the secret of liberty. They believed that freedom to think as you will and to speak as you think are means indispensable to the discovery and spread of political truth; that without free speech and assembly discussion would be futile; that with them, discussion affords ordinarily adequate protection against the dissemination of noxious doctrine; that the greatest menace to freedom is an

inert people; that public discussion is a political duty; and that this should be a fundamental principle of American government. They recognized the risks to which all human institutions are subject. But they knew that order cannot be secured merely through fear of punishment for its infraction; that it is hazardous to discourage thought, hope and imagination; that fear breeds repression; that repression breeds hate; that hate menaces stable government; that the path of safety lies in the opportunity to discuss freely supposed grievances and proposed remedies; and that the fitting remedy for evil counsels is good ones.

Whether Brandeis accurately described the beliefs of the framers may be debated, but he did make a powerful case for confining government restrictions of speech. The eloquence of Holmes and Brandeis ultimately persuaded the Court to adopt the clear-and-present-danger test for restriction of speech critical of the government. Although it was a significant advance over the bad-tendency test of *Gitlow*, the clear-and-present-danger standard provided insufficient protection against strong national passion and paranoia. In the hands of the Court during the cold-war period from the late 1940s to the early 1950s, the test proved rather flexible.

In the early 1950s the Communist Party of America was considered a clear and present danger to the nation, and the prosecution of its leaders was upheld in *Dennis* v. *United States* (1951). These prosecutions and the growth of institutions such as the House Un-American Activities Committee provoked a response by the philosopher Alexander Meiklejohn, whose work added another dimension to conceptions of free speech.

Meiklejohn argued that unrestrained political discussion was the premise of democratic government:

> Just so far as, at any point, the citizens who are to decide an issue are denied acquaintance with information or opinion or doubt or disbelief or criticism which is relevant to that issue, just so far the result must be ill-considered, ill-balanced planning for the general good. *It is that mutilation of the thinking process of the community against which the First Amendment of the Constitution is directed.* The principle of the freedom of speech springs from the necessities of the program of self-government. It is not a Law of Nature or of Reason in the abstract. It is a deduction from the basic American agreement that public issues shall be decided by universal suffrage.
>
> (p. 27; emphasis in original)

Meiklejohn's position became more attractive as fear of domestic subversion faded and Senator Joseph McCarthy fell from power. The morality of American government came under sharp criticism over its actions regarding civil rights and the war in Vietnam. Amid the emotional turmoil of these popular protests, the Court came to recognize that even advocacy of illegal acts was intimately tied to the depth of feeling over the behavior of government.

In *Brandenburg* v. *Ohio* (1969) the Court said, "The constitutional guarantees of free speech and free press do not permit a State to forbid or proscribe advocacy of the use of force or of law violation except where such advocacy is directed to inciting or producing imminent lawless action and is likely to incite or produce such action." In *National Association for the Advancement of Colored People* v. *Claiborne Hardware Co.* (1982), Justice John Paul Stevens placed a further gloss on the standard announced in *Brandenburg:* "Strong and effective extemporaneous rhetoric cannot be nicely channeled in purely dulcet phrases. An advocate must be free to stimulate his audience with spontaneous and emotional appeals for unity and action in a common cause. When such appeals do not incite lawless action, they must be regarded as protected speech."

The *Brandenburg* variation on the clear-and-present-danger test provides a clear standard for limiting government power to deal with political criticism. Criticism of government and proposals for change cannot be restrained unless they involve direct incitement to illegal acts and are likely to incite such acts. Indeed, if no illegal acts follow the speech, it is likely to be regarded as protected political rhetoric. In this respect, the "experiment" of which Holmes spoke has been a bold one, but the overreaction to political dissent throughout American history has demonstrated the need for a stringent standard to protect dissenters.

DYNAMICS OF LIMITATIONS ON SPEECH

Thomas Emerson described the forces that lead to the suppression of ideas in *Toward a Gen-*

FREE SPEECH AND EXPRESSION

eral Theory of the First Amendment. First, he described the interests in suppression. There is a strong human desire to suppress deviant opinions, and persons who challenge orthodox beliefs often do so with such intensity that they violate conventional norms and thus compound the anxiety and hostility of the orthodox. Further, immediate short-term interests, such as the perpetuation of the status quo, have a more compelling pull than do long-term interests of society, such as freedom of speech.

Second, effective limitations tend to affect more expression than actually poses the harm to be protected against. This is because limitations on expression tend to be attempts to prevent the possibility of harm occurring as a result of the speech rather than a punishment after the harm has taken place. Further, the varieties and subtleties of communication make it difficult to frame limitations in definite and precise terms.

Third, the apparatus of administering and enforcing limits on speech threaten to discourage more speech than the law is intended to reach. Persons assigned to the task have an interest in success in restricting expression, and the techniques of enforcement tend to exercise a repressive influence on expression. The mere existence of an enforcement apparatus may discourage speech even though that speech could not in fact be successfully restrained.

Fourth, the objectives of limitation are readily subject to distortion. It is often hard to separate the undesirable conduct of persons expressing unwanted ideas from the ideas themselves. Thus, limits on behavior may be used as means to suppress ideas.

The evolution of First Amendment standards from "bad tendency" through "clear and present danger" to the *Brandenburg* standards for punishment of speech that urges opposition to government responded to the type of problems Emerson discussed as they are revealed in American history. While standards tightened to protect expression in this narrow area, the Court also broadened the scope of application for free-speech guaranties.

EXPANSION OF FREEDOM OF SPEECH

The extension of freedom of speech and press to state governments raised problems not considered when the First Amendment was adopted.

The Fourteenth Amendment was understood to prevent states from punishing critics of slavery, but no greater thought was given to the effect that freedom of speech might have on existing state laws. State governments traditionally dealt with harms that speech causes individuals. The bold stand Jefferson and Madison took for an absolute bar to federal restraints on expression was possible because they understood that the states were free to deal with "abuses."

In the twentieth century, Justices Hugo Black and William O. Douglas have insisted that the guaranty of free speech in the First Amendment and its incorporation against the states by the Fourteenth Amendment extend an absolute bar to any restrictions on the content of expression. The rest of the Court has never accepted this view. Indeed, in *Chaplinsky* v. *New Hampshire* (1942) the Court announced that certain areas of expression traditionally dealt with by the states were not protected by the Constitution:

> These include the lewd and obscene, the profane, the libelous, and the insulting or "fighting" words—those which by their very utterance inflict injury or tend to incite an immediate breach of the peace. It has been well observed that such utterances are no essential part of any exposition of ideas, and are of such slight social value as a step to truth that any benefit that may be derived from them is clearly outweighed by the social interest in order and morality.

In other cases, the Court had also found speech that proposed a commercial transaction was outside constitutional protection.

The position that insults, obscenity, libel, and commercial speech are abuses of speech not protected by the freedom of speech began to break down in the 1950s. In each case, the application of the guaranty of freedom of speech to previously excluded categories of expression was triggered by developments that demonstrated that restraints on such expression affected the political process. Consideration of these cases led to an appreciation of values of speech beyond the political process.

Chaplinsky itself should have demonstrated the threat to criticism of government that is posed by punishing insults. Chaplinsky, a Jehovah's Witness, was convicted of calling a city marshal a "racketeer" and a "damned Fascist" when the marshal prevented him from preaching on a street corner. State and local laws had traditionally provided remedies for persons insulted, in part to forestall violence. It provided an alternative to the duel or other violent responses to a verbal attack. Yet, no case involving a purely personal insult to a private individual came before the Supreme Court. Instead, in every case heard by the Court since *Chaplinsky*, the insult has been directed at a public official or public institution as part of a complaint about official behavior. Mill had foreseen the problem a century earlier:

> With regard to what is commonly meant by intemperate discussion, namely invective, sarcasm, personality, and the like, the denunciation of these weapons would deserve more sympathy if it were ever proposed to interdict them equally to both sides; but it is only desired to restrain the employment of them against the prevailing opinion; against the unprevailing they may not only be used without general disapproval, but will be likely to obtain for him who uses them the praise of honest zeal and righteous indignation.

Some scholars, such as Franklyn Haiman, would prevent government from punishing even private insults. He points out that the harm the government wishes to prevent is a result of the mental processes of the addressee. He concludes that such harm is inextricably linked to the communication of ideas.

The Court, however, considered face-to-face personal insults as the verbal equivalent of physical attack. They are uttered to harm, not to inform. Yet, the potential for suppressing criticism by punishing insults is now recognized. The Court has dealt with the problem indirectly. Beginning soon after its decision in *Chaplinsky*, the Supreme Court reversed convictions for "fighting words" in all but one case. Each time it held that the statute under which the conviction was obtained was overbroad because it could be used to punish speakers whose ideas were thought to be offensive.

The Court was divided over appropriate limits for more narrowly drafted laws in this area. Chief Justice Warren Burger, Justice Harry Blackmun, and Justice William Rehnquist considered personal insults as punishable even if directed at public officials. Other justices would protect insults unless uttered with the intent of provoking violence and would recognize that police officers should be trained to resist provocation. Justice Powell, who often held a crucial vote in such cases, would also have permitted restraint of "scurrilous language calculated to offend the sensibilities of an unwilling audience" (*Rosenfeld* v. *New Jersey*, 1972).

A second category of speech that had been traditionally regulated by state law and excluded from the protection of free speech under *Chaplinsky* is libel. Under the common law, statements that injured an individual's reputation were actionable unless the speaker could show they were true and were published from good motives. Opinions (other than personal insults) were privileged, and honestly mistaken statements in public proceedings were not actionable.

Until 1964 there was no serious challenge to the constitutionality of common-law libel. In that year, however, a case arising out of the civil rights movement demonstrated the capacity of common-law libel rules to choke political criticism. An advertisement in the *New York Times* that appealed for funds for civil rights work in the South contained a number of factually inaccurate statements. The points made were valid, but the events illustrating them were exaggerated. The commissioner of public affairs in Montgomery, Alabama, claimed that the statements referred to the police there and libeled him as the supervisor of the police. He obtained a verdict for $500,000 from an Alabama jury although only four hundred copies of the paper were circulated in the state. In the context of that case, it was apparent that the libel verdict was a means to suppress opposition to segregation in Montgomery.

In *New York Times* v. *Sullivan*, the Supreme Court responded that "libel can claim no talismanic immunity from constitutional limitations. It must be measured by standards that satisfy the First Amendment." The Court noted that traditional libel law deterred criticism of official conduct "even though it is believed to be true and even though it is in fact true, because of doubt whether it can be proved in court or fear of the expense of having to do so." The Court concluded, "The constitutional guarantees require, we think, a federal rule that prohibits a public official from recovering damages for a defamatory falsehood relating to his official conduct unless he proves that the statement was made with "actual malice"—that is, with knowledge that it was false or with reckless disregard of whether it was false or not."

Justices Black and Douglas wanted the Court to go even further. They argued that the First Amendment should bar any recovery for libel. If there are any grounds upon which a suit for libel may be maintained, a jury could err in determining whether a statement is true, and speakers may be deterred from expression by the costs of defending a libel suit. The majority thought these risks minimal under the actual-malice standard in light of the harms caused. They insisted that "calculated falsehood" deserved no protection. It causes injury without making a significant contribution to the search for truth, or the functioning of the democratic process.

The requirement of actual malice for libel actions by public officials has been extended to "public figures." Some individuals are so well known that they have ready access to the media and may use that access to influence public policy. In *Curtis Publishing Co.* v. *Butts* (1967), Chief Justice Earl Warren wrote, "Our citizenry has a legitimate and substantial interest in the conduct of such persons, and freedom of the press to engage in uninhibited debate about their involvement in public issues and events is as crucial as it is in the case of 'public officials.' " The Court has been careful to note that public interest in an individual does not make that person a public figure. If it did, the media could make anyone a public figure by writing about them. In a series of cases, the Supreme Court has held that an attorney, a society matron, a researcher receiving a federal grant, and a person convicted of contempt of court for failure to obey a subpoena were not public figures. The status appears to be reserved for persons who seek public attention to promote their views on public issues and for celebrities, predominantly in the entertainment world, who have broad public recognition.

Over the dissent of Justice Byron White, the Court has offered some protection for false statements about private individuals. In *Gertz* v. *Robert Welch, Inc.* (1974) the Court held that media are liable for false statements about a private individual only if they have acted negligently in making their report, and it limited that liability to actual damages unless actual malice is shown. Justice Powell, for the majority, said that strict liability would be too onerous on the media and would dampen reporting. If the statement does

not involve a matter of public concern, the plaintiff is not required to show actual malice in order to recover presumed or punitive damages. Indeed, the Court has not yet determined whether a private individual must show that the defendant was negligent, in order to recover for false statements on a matter that is not of public concern.

A third category of speech initially deemed unprotected in *Chaplinsky* is obscenity. In its decision in *Roth* v. *United States* (1957), the Court said, "Implicit in the history of the First Amendment is the rejection of obscenity as utterly without redeeming social importance." But the 1950s were an important period of change for public attitudes on sexual matters. Public discussion of private sexual behavior was triggered by the works of Dr. Alfred Kinsey. Only two years after its decision in *Roth,* the Court overturned the denial of license to distribute a film version of D. H. Lawrence's *Lady Chatterley's Lover.* The basis for the denial had been that the film portrayed adultery as desirable behavior. In *Kingsley International Pictures Corp.* v. *Regents* (1959), Justice Potter Stewart wrote, "The First Amendment's basic guarantee is of freedom to advocate ideas. The State, quite simply, has thus struck at the very heart of constitutionally protected liberty."

During the 1950s a small group of individuals self-consciously challenged the values and lifestyles of the majority. The writers and poets of the "beat generation" were joined by mainstream intellectuals like John Kenneth Galbraith in questioning the moral fiber of the nation. In the succeeding decades the challenge focused on specific policies on civil rights and the war in Vietnam. The strength of challenges to political morality tended to legitimate other challenges to morality, and it became harder to defend the separation of obscenity from political discussion.

Judicial opinions during these years followed an unsteady course marked by increasing toleration of sexually explicit materials. Nevertheless, the Court never removed all limits on obscenity, upholding the proscription of materials sold or distributed for the sole purpose of arousing the libido. The line between freedom of speech and unprotected obscenity was finally established in *Miller* v. *California* (1973), wherein a majority held obscenity regulation was permissible for works that depict or describe sexual conduct:

That conduct must be specifically defined by the applicable state law, as written or authoritatively construed. A state offense must also be limited to works which, taken as a whole, appeal to the prurient interest in sex, which portray sexual conduct in a patently offensive way, and which, taken as a whole, do not have serious literary, artistic, political, or scientific value.

Dissenters, led by Justice William Brennan, urged that the standard was too vague. They contended there was insufficient proof that obscenity led to illegal conduct and that government should not regulate expression to affect morality. The majority insisted that its standard protected all works of serious literary, artistic, political, or scientific value, but "the public portrayal of hard-core sexual conduct for its own sake, and for the ensuing commercial gain, is a different matter." Under present standards, nudity cannot be proscribed in materials sold to adults if sexual conduct is not depicted therein. This state of the law draws fire from those who believe that such materials injure women by portraying them as sex objects and demeaning their humanity. The controversy is likely to continue for many years between those who perceive the suppression of obscenity as a threat to expression because it is an attempt to prevent people from holding particular views about sexual relations and those who argue that obscenity is an appeal to the libido, not to reason, and is therefore not expression at all.

Finally, the Court for many years considered speech proposing a commercial transaction to be outside the protection of the Constitution. It treated such speech as subject to the same degree of regulation as the transaction itself, considering the commercial realm as being far removed from the political concerns that lay in the forefront of justifications for protecting speech. In 1975 it was forced to reexamine these assumptions. Jeffrey Bigelow was convicted for publishing an ad for a New York abortion referral agency in his newspaper. The statute under which he was convicted prohibited anyone from encouraging another to have an abortion, and it was apparent that the state policy was not limited to concerns over commerce but was directed at suppressing all discussion of this volatile issue. Bigelow's conviction was overturned in *Bigelow* v. *Virginia* (1975), wherein the Court abandoned its earlier approach and asserted, "A court may not escape the task of assessing the First Amendment interest at stake and weighing it against the public interest allegedly served by the regulation."

In a number of subsequent cases the Court found that particular restrictions on commercial speech did not protect consumers but, rather, suppressed accurate and useful information. It struck down prohibitions on advertising the price of drugs, the services of lawyers, and contraceptives. Laws restricting commercial speech in the interest of the consumer remain valid. Thus, in *Central Hudson Gas and Electric Corp.* v. *Public Service Commission* (1980), the Court said that commercial speech will not be protected by the First Amendment unless it concerns lawful activity and is not misleading. Even accurate commercial speech that proposes lawful activity may be regulated in circumstances where political speech could not be banned. Restrictions on the time, place, and manner of advertising will not suppress the speech, because the profit motive assures that the seller will use alternatives to tell the public of his wares. Further, a narrow majority appears to believe that government should be able to prevent advertising from creating an appetite for goods or services that create social problems. Thus, in *Central Hudson*, the majority said a state may conserve energy by restricting advertisements for goods that promote energy consumption, although the state does not restrict the purchase of such goods. A substantial minority on the Court contend that the government must satisfy its interest by regulation of the commercial transaction and not by affecting speech.

Until 1950, discussion of freedom of speech and expression in the Court and in scholarly debate focused on its role in the political process. Individual speech needed protection from government restriction as a means to social ends—Mill's concern for the advance of truth, Meiklejohn's for the proper operation of democracy, and Brandeis' argument in favor of stability in government. Justice Brandeis had also stated in *Whitney* that "the final end of the state was to make men free to develop their faculties" and that liberty was to be valued as an end as well as a means, but this portion of his thought was not taken up during the first half of the twentieth century.

As the protection of the guaranty of freedom of speech was extended to offensive language, libel, obscenity, and commercial speech, both the Court and scholars paid increased attention to the individual. Those categories of speech had been considered unprotected, in part because they involved personal rather than public concerns. The Court had determined that the state could deal with the injury that such speech inflicted, because there was little social value in permitting it. The extension of constitutional protection stemmed from the realization that the state sometimes acts to censor ideas that are of public concern. However, the application of the First Amendment to speech that had been viewed as without social value stimulated a reconsideration of the value of permitting such speech.

Meiklejohn focused on the need for unrestrained debate to make political decisions: the same debate is crucial for individual decisions. Personal choices of occupation, friends, and lifestyle are as important to the individual as the behavior of government is. Suppression of ideas and opinions on these matters skew personal choice just as suppression of political discussion alters the political process. Further, articulation of our opinions and beliefs is a way in which we express our identity. The natural-rights roots of the First Amendment provide historical footing for this concern with the individual, although they also support justifications for imposing limits. Critics of the concept of personal autonomy as a core value of the First Amendment often contend that it is not helpful in applying the Constitution to concrete cases where personal autonomy conflicts with social interests. Everything that we do, not just what we say, is a manifestation of our individuality, but this does not prevent government from regulating our behavior. Yet, protection of communicative expression from government restriction serves to advance personal autonomy.

BALANCING INTERESTS AND ABSOLUTISM

The wide variety of philosophical justifications for restricting government power over expression, the differing perspectives on the intent of the framers of the First Amendment reflected in the controversy over the Alien and Sedition Acts, and the changing position of the Supreme Court on the application of the constitutional guaranty furnish support for an enormous range of views on freedom of speech and expression. In *Free Speech: A Philosophical Enquiry,* Frederick Schauer argued that freedom of speech requires a balancing of interests. In any conflict between expression and an interest asserted by government, the government must provide a greater justification for speech restriction than it would need to justify other types of restrictions. The point at which the balance should be struck depends on careful analysis of the values that allowance of this particular speech would serve. Each of the various justifications for restricting government power must be considered in evaluating the weight of the speech interest, and institutional problems of decision-making may lead to the use of categories to assign weights in the balancing process.

In *The System of Freedom of Expression,* Emerson attacked balancing speech values against social harms as insufficiently resistant to the dynamics of speech limitation. He proposed a distinction between "expression" and "conduct" as the best means of vindicating the values of free speech. His critics argued that the categories of expression (which may not be regulated) and conduct (which may be restricted) ultimately collapse and can be easily manipulated to serve the values of the decision-maker. After all, communication necessarily involves conduct (speaking, writing, gesturing), and even Emerson would punish some criminal solicitation as conduct.

Another view is that the guaranty prevents the government from acting against a communication because it finds the idea expressed distasteful or fears that society would be harmed if others agreed with it. It is not a legitimate function of government to decide what ideas are true or false, good or bad, for such decisions are left to each individual. Nevertheless, government may pass laws affecting communication to vindicate its legitimate interests. The ban on restrictions to suppress ideas is absolute, but its application requires interests to be balanced when other grounds of restriction are set forth.

THE METHODOLOGY OF THE COURT

Under the present doctrine of the Court, there is no idea that cannot be expressed in some context or other. Statements regulated as commercial speech are protected when made by disinterested persons; defamatory statements that are actionable when made negligently are immune from sanctions when the speaker is not negligent; hard-core pornography takes on the mantle of the Constitution for use by research scientists; and insults condemned by law when used to injure can be freely used about a person who is not there. It is the context of speech that renders it subject to regulation and not its content alone.

Where communicative conduct is regulated, the Supreme Court measures it by the standard announced in *United States* v. *O'Brien* (1968):

> We think it clear that a government regulation is sufficiently justified if it is within the constitutional power of the Government; if it furthers an important or substantial governmental interest; if the governmental interest is unrelated to the suppression of free expression; and if the incidental restriction on alleged First Amendment freedoms is no greater than is essential to the furtherance of that interest.

This four-step test begins where debate on the First Amendment began—with the proposition that the natural right of expression cannot be limited by government unless the government is acting within the scope of the power granted by its constitutive document. The second step requires government to show that the regulation furthers an important or substantial interest. Given the value of expression, restriction for trivial reasons demonstrates either that the government is ignoring the value of free speech in its decision or that it is in fact using a trivial justification to mask its true intent to suppress ideas. The third step demands a showing that the regulation furthers a government interest unrelated to the suppression of free expression. In other words, the government cannot justify regulations of speech by any asserted interest in what individuals think and believe. Yet, government can justify regulations that have the effect of diminishing the flow of ideas, by reference to legitimate government purposes. Emerson's analysis of the dynamics of limitation demonstrates that the third step will not suffice to prevent the suppression of ideas. Thus, the critical step in the Court's protection of free speech is its fourth step—that the incidental restriction on

speech is no greater than is essential to the furtherance of the substantial government interest unrelated to suppression of ideas. Most litigation today revolves around contentions that the regulation is not essential to the government interest. The Supreme Court resorts to an arsenal of subsidiary doctrines to test whether the regulation is essential.

These ancillary doctrines include the presumption against prior restraints, the avoidance of unnecessary constitutional decisions, preemption, overbreadth, vagueness, and equal protection. The absence of prior restraint was the original core of freedom of the press. Any requirement that printed material be submitted to a third party for approval before publication places a burden on even unobjectionable works. Nevertheless, the Supreme Court has permitted systems for prior approval in limited circumstances. Simultaneous claims by different groups to use the same location at the same time for speech purposes could result in a chaos where nothing can be understood. Thus, permit systems for the allocation of use of public places have been upheld as methods to further expression. Such permit systems will be carefully scrutinized by the Court, however, to assure they do not allow the administrator to grant or deny permits on the basis of the conformity of the speech to the administrator's own ideas.

The Court has said that there is a presumption against prior restraints. Normally, the threat of subsequent punishment will be an adequate deterrent to harmful speech. Where a prior restraint is not essential to protect the government's legitimate interest, it is unconstitutional. Nevertheless, a divided Court has upheld some forms of prior-review systems. For example, it permitted the Central Intelligence Agency to require its agents to submit their public writings on intelligence operations to the agency for review to assure that they do not reveal secret information that the agent obtained through his official position. The Court also permitted military commanders to institute an approval system for speech on the base as necessary to protect military discipline and avoid political entanglement.

A second technique for protecting speech is narrow construction to avoid conflict with speech values. This is a common technique used by the Court to avoid confrontation with the legislature over any constitutional value, but it takes on special force with respect to laws that might be interpreted to affect expression. Although the Court will uphold incidental restrictions on speech that are essential to further legitimate nonspeech interests, it must first be assured that the legislature has found it necessary to restrict speech to further that interest. Thus, whenever a statute is capable of more than one interpretation, the Court will prefer the interpretation that places the least burden on speech. If Congress prefers the more restrictive application, it must make it clear. Similarly, the Court will often construe general grants of power to an administrative agency narrowly and will invalidate the agency action restricting expression as beyond its delegated power. Again, if Congress wishes the administrative agency to impose speech-restrictive regulations, it must make it explicit in the statute that establishes the agency's authority.

Federal preemption is another technique used by the Court to protect speech. Federal laws may be interpreted to forbid any state law regulating speech within the scope of the federal concern.

Perhaps the most important technique for protecting speech interests against the government is the doctrine of overbreadth. Under the *O'Brien* tests, a statute cannot validly be enforced to the extent its effect on speech is not essential to vindicate the government's legitimate interests. Nevertheless, the existence of the overbroad statute will discourage the protected speech because prospective speakers will keep silent rather than face the risk and expense of litigating their rights.

The chilling effect of overbroad regulation has led the Court to permit persons to challenge the constitutionality of statutes even though their conduct is properly subject to regulation. A statute that is unconstitutionally overbroad cannot apply to anyone, and the government must enact a new law more carefully tailored to its legitimate purposes in order to vindicate those interests. This presents a serious problem for criminal law, since the Constitution also forbids ex post facto (that is, retroactive) laws. If the only statute applicable to injurious conduct by an individual is held unconstitutional because it also applies to protected speech, that individual will escape all punishment. In view of this result, the Court will strike down statutes for overbreadth only where the overbreadth is substantial when

"judged in relation to the statute's plainly legitimate sweep."

Where a regulation does not pose the problem of ex post facto applications, the Court may be far more stringent in applying overbreadth. For example, civil disability schemes that deny public employment or professional licenses to persons on the grounds of specified speech or associational activity may be struck down without danger to the legitimate interests of the state. The hiring or licensing body can immediately establish proper criteria that will still serve to exclude those persons who can legitimately be excluded. A strict application of overbreadth theory here is responsive to Emerson's point that speech limitations tend to be overbroad in order to assure that they are totally effective in reaching harmful activities. The government may argue that it is justified in excluding Communists from employment in defense facilities, because the possibility of sabotage to defense efforts is greater from Communists than from non-Communists. Such a law was struck down for overbreadth in *United States* v. *Robel* (1967), wherein the Court pointed out that only persons who seek violent overthrow pose the danger of sabotage and that membership alone does not mean an individual shares all the aims of an organization or would act to further those aims. Robel, although working in a defense facility, did not hold a sensitive job or have access to particularly sensitive materials. The majority concluded that the statute could be more narrowly tailored to prevent potential saboteurs without infringing so severely on association.

In fact, the more narrowly drawn regulation would probably not be quite as effective in preventing persons who would abuse their position from getting the job. The percentage of persons who would use their position to harm the government is likely to be higher in a group drawn from the Communist party than in a random population sample. Further, it may be difficult to prove that a specific individual member of the party does have knowledge of its illegal goals and intends to further them. Thus, the overbroad statute may have some incremental security effect. On the other hand, it operates to deprive many people of employment when there is little likelihood they would be unsatisfactory. In determining that the statute in *Robel* was overbroad, the Court actually was finding that the incremental security interest was trivial in comparison with the impact on speech.

A closely related doctrine finds the Court striking down statutes for vagueness. The Court may use its power to interpret federal statutes to eliminate any infirmities in statutory language, but it does not have the ultimate authority to construe state law. The vague statute always poses due process issues, for the defendant may argue that it did not provide fair warning that his activity was proscribed. First Amendment concerns point to an additional problem. The vagueness in a statute may extend to areas that are constitutionally protected because it is not essential to restrict them to serve the interests of the state that are unrelated to the suppression of free expression. Like the overbroad statute, the vague statute will discourage expression within the protected area. This suggests that relaxed standing rules should be applied. On the other hand, the vague statute may be saved for later use by a limiting construction that eliminates the vagueness and avoids overbreadth. Thus, in *Young* v. *American Mini Theatres* (1976), wherein a zoning regulation affecting distribution of sexually explicit materials was challenged, the Court rejected arguments based on vagueness and stated, "If the statute's deterrent effect on legitimate expression is not 'both real and substantial,' and if the statute is 'readily subject to a narrowing construction by the state courts,' . . . the litigant is not permitted to assert the rights of third parties."

Beginning in 1969, the Court added yet another doctrine designed to assure that regulations go no further than is essential to further the legitimate state interest. Overbreadth and vagueness doctrines are used to invalidate laws that affect speech that cannot be justifiably regulated to satisfy the purported government interest. The Court is now beginning to use equal protection to measure statutes that prohibit speech activities that could be regulated for legitimate reasons yet exempt other speech activities that are subject to the same objection. This discrimination suggests that the real end of the law is to suppress the ideas of the nonexempt speech, for the exemption of particular speech indicates that the purported legitimate interest was not sufficiently strong.

Armed with these ancillary doctrines, the Court now examines every law challenged as restrictive of speech both for the legitimacy of the governmental interest asserted and the need for the speech restriction to further that interest. For example, the Court has found that the government has a legitimate interest in protecting the public from injuries inflicted by the means used to communicate (for example, excessive noise, obstruction of public passageways) or by acts linked to the speech (for example, illegal behavior, commercial sales). It has an interest in efficient performance of its tasks and can exclude from employment persons whose speech is inconsistent with proper job performance (for example, insubordination, partisanship within civil service) or is evidence of unfitness for the job (for example, advocacy of violent revolution against the existing government by an employee in a defense plant). It can preserve secrecy in limited circumstances to prevent damage to discussion within government (for example, executive privilege) or the use of information as a basis to commit harmful acts (for example, national defense secrets).

The list of legitimate government concerns is virtually endless, and one may be found as a pretext to support most laws intended to suppress ideas. Nevertheless, the Court occasionally has found asserted interests illegitimate. Although it found that the prevention of bribery and the appearance of corruption justifies limits on contributions to political campaigns, it held in *Buckley* v. *Valeo* (1976) that limits on expenditures were invalid because government has no legitimate interest in restricting the circulation of ideas. Far more frequently, the Supreme Court has used the ancillary First Amendment doctrines to invalidate laws, holding that the asserted interest of government may be vindicated by means less restrictive of speech.

THE FUTURE OF FREEDOM OF SPEECH

Freedom of speech has at its core an abiding suspicion of government decisions on expression. The principle was in the process of development when it was placed in the Constitution, it has developed further in the intervening centuries, and there is no reason to believe that the development has stopped. There is an emerging right to gather information that has been asserted in media demands for access to trials despite the parties' desire to keep the proceedings closed, for access to prisons despite prison authorities' desire to exclude the public, for travel to countries declared off limits, and for travel in the United States by speakers from foreign lands, as well as claims to a privilege to keep sources confidential. While media seek access to information, private individuals seek access to the modern means of mass communication—radio, television, and cable.

Questions on the role of government in sponsoring speech may also shape our views on freedom of expression. These issues point toward a possible affirmative role for government in providing information and conflicting views to the public. Any movement from the traditional freedom from restriction to an affirmative freedom to obtain views raises difficult issues, for it expands the role of the Supreme Court in supervising expression but compels the question of whether the judiciary may itself be a suspect institution for determining what views must be raised. Media claims to special treatment because of their function in the dissemination of views and opinions raise problems of a potential slighting of the rights of private individuals and the imposition of legally enforceable responsibilities to accompany the rights of the press. Each generation must consider anew the problems of maintaining an open society with respect for each individual. The past suggests that we can keep freedom of expression a vital part of the world of computers and cable television, but it also reveals that it will not be an easy task.

CASES

Abrams v. United States, 250 U.S. 616 (1919)
Bigelow v. Virginia, 421 U.S. 809 (1975)
Brandenburg v. Ohio, 395 U.S. 444 (1969)
Buckley v. Valeo, 424 U.S. 1 (1976)
Central Hudson Gas and Electric Corp. v. Public Service Commission, 447 U.S. 557 (1980)
Chaplinsky v. New Hampshire, 315 U.S. 568 (1942)
Curtis Publishing Co. v. Butts, 388 U.S. 130 (1967)
Dennis v. United States, 341 U.S. 494 (1951)
Gertz v. Robert Welch, Inc., 418 U.S. 323 (1974)
Gitlow v. New York, 268 U.S. 652 (1925)
Kingsley International Pictures Corp. v. Regents, 360 U.S. 684 (1959)
Miller v. California, 413 U.S. 15 (1973)

National Association for the Advancement of Colored People v. Claiborne Hardware Co., 458 U.S. 886 (1982)
New York Times v. Sullivan, 376 U.S. 254 (1964)
Rosenfeld v. New Jersey, 408 U.S. 901 (1972)
Roth v. United States, 354 U.S. 476 (1957)
Schenck v. United States, 249 U.S. 47 (1919)
United States v. O'Brien, 391 U.S. 367 (1968)
United States v. Robel, 389 U.S. 258 (1967)
Whitney v. California, 274 U.S. 357 (1927)
Young v. American Mini Theatres, 427 U.S. 50 (1976)

BIBLIOGRAPHY

Annals of Congress, vol. 1, edited by Joseph Gales (1834), contains much on the debate surrounding the First Amendment. Jerome Barron, *Freedom of the Press for Whom? The Right of Access to Mass Media* (1973), which sets forth highly controversial arguments, is by the foremost advocate for a legal right of access to privately owned mass media. David S. Bogen, *Bulwark of Liberty: The Court and the First Amendment* (1984), states the principle that the First Amendment forbids government from acting for the purpose of suppressing ideas, and analyzes the decisions of the Supreme Court as attempts to enforce that principle. Zechariah Chafee, Jr., *Free Speech in the United States* (1941), traces free-speech issues, particularly during World War I and its aftermath, focusing on the problems of protecting political opposition.

Thomas I. Emerson, *Toward a General Theory of the First Amendment* (1966), the forerunner of the full development of Emerson's standard for protecting expression, contains a fuller presentation of the values and functions of free expression and is the classic discussion of the dynamics of limitation; and *The System of Freedom of Expression* (1970), shows the distinction between expression and action, the key to his theory of protecting expression, and develops and applies it across a broad range of issues. Franklyn S. Haiman, *Speech and Law in a Free Society* (1981), discusses resolutions for a wide variety of problems by applying his own value premises and is a good example of the application of modern concerns for promoting the autonomy of the individual. Harry Kalven, *The Negro and the First Amendment* (1966), discusses the impact of the civil rights movement on libel, association, and demonstrations and contains an excellent discussion of the problems of the public forum.

Leonard W. Levy, *Emergence of a Free Press* (1985), a revised and enlarged version of his classic study of free speech, *Legacy of Suppression,* which is the finest history of English and colonial thought on freedom of expression, contends that the framers of the amendment understood it narrowly as the absence of prior restraints and that libertarian theory emerged later in the crucible of the Alien and Sedition Acts experience. Alexander Meiklejohn, *Political Freedom* (1960), a revision of his *Free Speech and Its Relation to Self-Government* (1948), argues that freedom of speech is a consequence of the principle of self-government and attempts to narrow the area of protected speech to political discussion in order to increase the degree of protection given that speech. John Stuart Mill, *On Liberty* (1859), in Chapter 2, contributes the most important reflection in the English language on the relationship between government and expression. Melville B. Nimmer, *Nimmer on Freedom of Speech: A Treatise on the Theory of the First Amendment* (1984), presents views on the First Amendment, particularly in its analysis of "anti-speech" interests asserted to justify speech restrictions, and explores the viability of several proposals for new directions for freedom of speech. Ithiel de Sola Pool, *Technologies of Freedom* (1983), which confronts vital questions for the future where communications systems embrace new technologies that are extensively regulated as business ventures, may be more valuable for its identification of the issues than as a resolution of all the problems.

Frederick Schauer, *Free Speech: A Philosophical Enquiry* (1982), superbly dissects the philosophical bases for freedom of speech, exploring the strengths and weaknesses of each justification, including the degree to which justifications for protecting speech are distinct from other philosophical principles. Benno Schmidt, Jr., *Freedom of the Press vs. Public Access* (1976), carefully explores public-access issues raised by Barron and shows there are no easy answers to the problems of preserving the free flow of ideas in the modern world. Bernard Schwartz, *The Bill of Rights: A Documentary History*, vols. 1 and 2 (1971), provides an invaluable collection of the documents bearing on the formation of the Bill of Rights from early colonial charters through the constitutional ratification debates and the congressional debates on the amendments. Fredrick S. Siebert, *Freedom of the Press in England, 1476–1776* (1936), presents a good, readable history of the development of the press and licensing system in England through the controversies with John Wilkes near the beginning of the American Revolution. James Morton Smith, *Freedom's Fetters: The Alien and Sedition Laws and American Civil Liberties* (1956), engrossingly recounts the most crucial incidents in the development of American thought on freedom of expression.

John Trenchard and Thomas Gordon, *Cato's Letters: or, Essays on Liberty, Civil and Religious* (1755), the most popular source for political ideas in the colonial period, focuses on freedom of speech as the right to expose mismanagement of the government in nos. 15, 32, and 101. William W. Van Alstyne, *Interpretations of the First Amendment* (1984), includes a graphic review of the free-speech clause that may be a helpful way for viewing the issues of freedom of expression, as well as thoughtful consideration of new proposals for special treatment of the press and the problems of broadcast regulation. Mark Yudof, *When Government Speaks: Politics, Law, and Government Expression in America* (1983), thoughtfully addresses the activity of government in trying to shape the values of society through indoctrination as an issue of freedom of expression.

[*See also* Constitutional Interpretation *and* Law and Morality.]

IMMIGRATION, NATURALIZATION, AND CITIZENSHIP

William J. Daniels

THE United States of America is a nation created and shaped by voluntary and involuntary immigrants. It has accepted and absorbed more immigrants than any other nation in history. From the earliest settlers to the most recent refugees and undocumented aliens. America has been perceived by potential immigrants as a land of opportunity where an improvement in one's religious, social, political, or economic condition could be achieved.

Immigrants to America have been inducted and assimilated into its political and social cultures. The process of naturalization initially was in the hands of the respective state governments and required only a perfunctory pledge of loyalty. It is now under the full control of the federal government, and the standards for admission into the political community have become more exacting and demanding. The federal government now determines legislatively how many persons enter the country (undocumented aliens notwithstanding), the characteristics and qualifications they must possess, the purposes and conditions to be satisfied, and the standards of behavior deemed appropriate during temporary visits or probationary residency pending citizenship proceedings.

The American experiences with immigration, naturalization, and citizenship bear the personal imprint of historical trends and continue to be shaped by current conditions and evolving political pressures. Patterns of immigration have altered in reaction to political events external to the United States and to domestic concerns about the proper characteristics and attributes for assimilable immigrants. The standards for naturalization have become ever more sensitive to an alien's professed political beliefs and actual political behavior. The nature and availability of citizenship, the rights associated with the status of citizen, and the meaning of citizenship within the political and governmental setting have taken on new meanings with the passage of time.

Citizenship has been made available to greater numbers of persons and the range of rights associated with the status has increased. However, it would appear that the ideal of altruism previously associated with citizenship has been narrowed dramatically.

CITIZENSHIP IN THE COLONIAL PERIOD

During the period prior to 1775 a consensus existed between the relevant parties in England (namely, the crown, Parliament, and the Board of Trade) and the American colonies that the need for labor in the New World was of paramount importance. There was less than full agreement as to how this need would be satisfied. The British government seized the opportunity to unload convicted felons and did not generally support requests by the colonists for an open immigration policy. The crown's refusal to recognize general acts of naturalization and its efforts to restrict westward settlement would be among the grievances listed in the Declaration of Independence.

For the colonies the acute need for labor brought about the practice of advertising opportunities available in the New World. By 1700, nearly all the colonies were employing some means to increase immigration. Perhaps the most extensive advertising drive of the period was initiated by William Penn of Pennsylvania, who went so far as to go to Europe to conduct and coordinate recruitment efforts. Penn distributed hundreds of pamphlets that announced the advantages of Pennsylvania, including the right to vote for all males, the existence of a humane penal code, and the absence of any military obligation. The southern colonies had a more difficult time attracting new blood, because of the climate, sparse population, and the absence of free land and large-scale industry.

Common among the inducements to attract immigrants was the practice of making land grants to entrepreneurs who brought in immigrants. For the immigrants the advantage was exemption from certain forms of taxation for limited periods of time. The prospect of attracting immigrants was a primary consideration in formulating laws of immigration by the colonies. For example, customs of naturalization permitted newcomers to secure land without transfer restrictions upon arrival.

The implementation of the liberal policies stopped short of admitting any and all newcomers. Some were not welcome. Exclusionary laws were enacted by Virginia and Maryland in the late 1600s to restrict the transportation of the unwanted felons from England. Parliament overruled these restrictions. The Puritans limited their recruitment to members of their own church. Some colonies specified that only Protestants were wanted.

The practice of indentured servitude was pioneered by the Virginia Company. The shortage of labor in the colonies was instrumental in the development of this form of contract labor to recruit immigrants, usually called free-willers or redemptioners. The immigrant would be bound to indenture or a contract for labor for a period of four to seven years and, in return, could receive one or more of the following: free passage, clothing, tools, a gun, a year's provisions, a house, or a share of the crops produced by the redemptioner. In the seventeenth century the Virginia Company brought, primarily from England and Germany, an average of fifteen hundred bonded laborers each year to Chesapeake Bay. During this period indentured servants were more numerous than slaves in all of the colonies; during the eighteenth century they continued to outnumber slaves in the middle colonies.

The colonial governments granted naturalization or deeds of "denization" to German and Irish immigrants upon arrival. Subsequently, such deeds were issued to aliens from England.

A naturalized person would then have civil rights and the right to hold property prior to full British citizenship. However, some colonies did not honor the deeds of denization, and the deeds were not binding upon the imperial government. In 1740, Parliament made immigration more attractive when it permitted all aliens in the colonies to become fully naturalized British subjects as soon as a continuous seven-year period of residency was accomplished.

Several aspects of immigration had a continuous influence during the colonial period. The search for jobs and the need for labor were primary motivations for immigration to the New World; the recruitment of immigrants was primarily the responsibility of local colonies and entrepreneurs; and jurisdiction over matters of immigration and settlement (enforcing contracts of indenture, for example) were left to local and, subsequently, colonial governments. This jurisdictional control would remain essentially in place until after the Civil War.

THE ARTICLES OF CONFEDERATION

The Articles of Confederation, effective as of 1 March 1781, established a framework of government for the thirteen "United States of America." The concept of citizenship is inherent in this document but not prominent. The words *citizens* and *foreigners* are used only once each and then indirectly. The clause in which *citizens* appears notes that "free inhabitants" of the states shall be entitled to all privileges and immunities of "free citizens" in the several states. By the same token, the word *foreigners* was utilized in a passage that restricted the power of the Confederation with respect to commerce—namely, that the legislative power of the United States shall not be used to enter into treaties that would restrain the respective states from imposing imposts and duties on "foreigners."

Indians, by implication, were not considered citizens. They were mentioned twice, once in terms of war powers and again with respect to regulating trade. The states were prohibited, with some exceptions, from individually engaging in war; one exception was if a state had "received certain advice of a resolution being formed by some nation of Indians to invade such state" and the state believed the threat to be imminent. A second reference was that the

United States in Congress was given the power to manage "all affairs with the Indians," provided that the Indians were "not members of any of the states."

Thus, the government of the United States was launched. The separation between the new government and the king had been established; citizenship was not expressly defined. The term *free citizens* was used in conjunction with the clause "free inhabitants" in the several states; the notion of "liberties" was applied to individual states; Indians were implicitly excluded from membership in the newly created governmental entity; and "foreigners" within the context of the Articles of Confederation was a reference to "foreign" states in matters of trade and commerce.

THE CONSTITUTION AND THE BILL OF RIGHTS

The Constitution of the United States was the product of the Philadelphia Convention of 1787, which ostensibly met to revise the Articles of Confederation. The outcome, however, was that the convention drafted a new document, which went into effect two years later.

Deliberations at the convention reflected a range of opinion regarding immigrants: that immigrants should not be discriminated against, for they could make valuable contributions to the new nation; that America should be ruled by Americans and not foreigners; and that foreigners from countries with despotic governments might not have a commitment to the democratic principles expressed in the new constitutional democracy. But this debate concluded merely with a provision in the Constitution in which power is delegated to the Congress (Article I, Section 8) "to establish a uniform Rule of Naturalization." Consistent with this authority, Congress passed general legislation (1790) concerning the naturalization of aliens. Any free white person who could establish in any common-law court of record in any state that a two-year residency "within the limits and under the jurisdiction of the United States" had been completed could acquire American citizenship.

The Constitution is devoid of any discussion of the nature of citizenship. The term *citizen* or *citizens* can be found only four times in the document: once (Article IV) in which it is noted that "the Citizens of each State shall be entitled to all Privileges and Immunities of Citizens in the several states," and on three separate occasions that relate the qualifications to hold national governmental office. The clause embodying qualifications to be president is the only instance in which the document makes a distinction between a natural-born citizen and a naturalized citizen.

The framers were distrustful that foreign powers might attempt to use "status" to unduly influence, flatter, bribe, or perhaps corrupt public officials. Hence, there are two provisions in the Constitution that reject explicitly the idea of royalty or nobility. The federal government is denied the power in Article I, Section 9 to grant any title of nobility, nor may any public official accept any title; in the following section, the authority of the state governments is limited similarly.

Two years after the ratification of the Constitution, the first ten amendments—the Bill of Rights—were approved in response to a general demand that the new Constitution lacked certain fundamental rights and specific guarantees. In fact, there had been an understanding that the first order of business for Congress would be the formulation of some basic rights.

Many of the first ten amendments could be classified as negative rights in the sense that they specify limitations on the power or authority of the national government. It should be noted that rights secured to the individual by the Fifth or by the Sixth Amendments are not, according to the Supreme Court, privileges and immunities granted and belonging to the individual as a citizen of the United States. They are secured to all persons as against the federal government entirely irrespective of such citizenship (*Maxwell* v. *Dow*, 1900). Further, the Court held that the Fourteenth Amendment applies to all persons, not just citizens (*Yick Wo* v. *Hopkins*, 1886). Nowhere does the Constitution say that only citizens shall enjoy the rights and protections specified; rather, they belong to "people," "owners," "persons," and the "accused."

THE NEW NATION

A bitter division of opinion about immigration surfaced not long after the new government got settled. As immigrants became involved in the political struggles of the times—in political parties and in sectional disputes, for example—some Federalists began to question the immigration policies in force at the time. The Irish formed an alliance, especially in New England, with the Democratic-Republicans, and most Federalists became convinced that restrictions should be placed on the enfranchisement of immigrants.

Many radical Irish newcomers had been critical of the foreign policy of the Federalist party, especially the party's reaction to the XYZ affair (1798), which involved a French attempt to extort money from an American diplomatic commission to France. A sufficient number of Federalists concluded that the criticism was disloyal. Consequently, the Federalist party secured the passage of four pieces of legislation, collectively called the Alien and Sedition Acts (1798), designed to harass immigrants who might have been drawn to the rival political party.

Although unsuccessful, the first attempt to deprive the opposition Democratic-Republican party of its supply of foreign-born voters was a proposal to levy a tax of $20 on certificates of naturalization ostensibly to debar citizenship to vicious and disorganizing characters. The tax was rejected, but Congress adopted a revised act of naturalization.

The Naturalization Act (1798) raised the residency requirement for citizenship from five to fourteen years. However, this measure was repealed in 1802 and the five-year period of residency was reinstated following a Republican election victory in 1800. This action was followed by the passage of two legislative measures that gave extraordinary powers to the president, The Alien Act and the Alien Enemies Act (both 1798). The Alien Act gave power to the president to seize and deport resident aliens suspected of engaging in subversive activities or being dangerous "to the peace and safety of the United States." The Alien Enemies Act, passed two weeks later, was designed to enable the president in times of war to deal with enemy aliens. Although the legislation existed for two years, it never became operative, because war with France failed to materialize.

The Sedition Act followed the Alien Enemies Act by a week (and also was in effect for two years) and is usually considered the most notorious of the several acts. It was not exclusively an anti-immigrant act but was designed in part to affect foreign-born journalists and pamphleteers. The Federalists wished to silence criticism of the government; to bring their objective within the spirit of the First Amendment, they proposed legislation that made it a crime to publish false or scandalous information about the government.

The federal government did little in the way of supervising immigration during the first half of the nineteenth century. In 1820 the Department of State at least began to count immigrants. The need for manpower remained unabated. Urban industrialization and the expanding frontier encouraged states to continue to advertise for newcomers and to establish immigration offices. Hence, state governments were the primary actors in promoting and controlling immigration. The authority of the state to regulate, admit, or reject immigrants was legitimized by a decision of the United States Supreme Court in *Mayor of New York* v. *Miln* (1837). Challenged in this case, as an obstruction to interstate and foreign commerce, was a New York State regulation that required the screening of immigrants entering the state. The Court held that the authority of the state to act in this manner was derived legitimately from its police power. In this regard the Court treated the issue as one involving health and morals: "We think it as competent for a state to provide precautionary measures against the moral pestilence of paupers, vagabonds, and possible convicts . . . as it is to guard against . . . physical pestilence."

During the second half of the nineteenth century, there were several significant developments regarding the definition of citizenship and concerning federal regulation of immigration. Primary roles were played by the Congress and the Supreme Court. The decision by the Supreme Court in *Dred Scott* v. *Sandford* (1857) served to exclude from citizenship all blacks, whether slave or free.

Dred Scott, a slave in the state of Missouri, had been taken by his owner into Illinois and the Louisiana Territory. Slavery was prohibited in these areas by, respectively, the Northwest Ordinance of 1787 and the Missouri Compromise of 1820. Scott argued essentially that his residence on free soil had made him a free person. The Court did not agree with this contention, and all nine justices wrote opinions. The gist of their arguments was that Dred Scott could not sue in federal courts because he was not a citizen. Blacks, the Court reasoned, were not included by the framers in the category of "citizen" in the United States Constitution and could therefore claim none of the rights and privileges secured by that document to citizens of the United States. Thus, involuntary servitude was legitimized because owners were given absolute authority over their property. Moreover, by application, state citizenship was determined to be the source of federal citizenship; furthermore, the state had no power to confer national citizenship by making persons citizens of the state.

The Thirteenth Amendment to the Constitution (1865) stipulated that "neither slavery nor involuntary servitude . . . shall exist within the United States," thereby abolishing the peculiar institution of slavery. However, in view of the holding of the Court in *Dred Scott*—namely, that blacks remained subject to the authority of their owners, whether emancipated or not, and could not become citizens of the United States—it became necessary to remove blacks from the personal attachment of their property.

The Fourteenth Amendment accomplished this objective by reversing the holding of the Court in the *Dred Scott* decision. The amendment consists of five sections, only the first of which has applicability to the matter of citizenship. The first sentence sets forth for the first time the terms of national citizenship: "All persons born or naturalized in the United States, and subject to the jurisdiction thereof, are citizens of the United States and of the State wherein they reside." Persons born in the United States become citizens because they are born on American soil or by reason of the principle of "jus soli" (nationality determined by place of birth), provided they are subject to the authority of the United States. The jurisdiction proviso excludes, for example, children born to foreign diplomats and, for reasons to be discussed later, Indians. Congress is not prohibited from conferring citizenship by reason of blood relationship, or "jus sanguinis," by allowing, for example, the children of citizens born outside the United States to become citizens "from birth." A naturalized citizen, by this amendment, is a citizen of equal status to those born in the United States. Clearly, it was also the intent of this amendment that national citizenship have precedence over state citizenship.

Three interesting developments occurred in 1864. First, Congress created the Bureau of Immigration. Second, Congress for the first time got involved in the area of contract labor by passing the Contract Labor Law, which authorized the financing of transportation of immigrant workers by employers and binding their service in advance. This measure was repealed four years later. And finally, the Republican party wrote a plank in its platform for the election of 1864 and two successive campaigns that urged the federal government to develop a stronger immigration policy.

Shortly thereafter, the Supreme Court provided the authority for a more forceful federal presence in the matter of immigration policy. In an opinion that overruled its previous findings in *Miln*, the Court in *Henderson* v. *Mayor of New York* (1876) held that Congress had the exclusive power to regulate immigration under the commerce clause (Article I, Section 8) and that all state laws were therefore an unconstitutional usurpation of the exclusive power of Congress to regulate foreign commerce.

Congress followed with statutes that brought immigration under direct control of the national government and enacted legislation that gave the power to the government to set standards and to exclude from entry those who failed to meet those standards. It passed the first comprehensive federal immigration law in August 1882. The main feature of this measure was an imposition of a head tax of 50 cents on each alien entering the country. Authority was delegated to the Department of the Treasury to enforce the statute; however, the legislation provided that funds generated would be provided to the states. The states would then use the funds to enforce the exclusions specified in the legislation—namely, lunatics, idiots, convicts, and incapacitated persons who might become public charges.

Also, the Chinese Exclusion Act of 1882 barred Chinese immigrants from entry into the United States. The Chinese were not treated as welcome immigrants, especially in California and particularly by organized labor. Throughout the 1850s and 1860s they were sporadically subjected to mass violence, which intensified during the depression of the 1870s. There was a widespread belief that they threatened free labor because they were a servile class with vicious customs.

A most significant feature of this legislation is that it initiated a restrictive device; for the first time federal legislation barred a specific group of immigrants from becoming citizens because of race. All foreign-born Chinese were precluded from American citizenship by reason of the Naturalization Act of 1790, which limited naturalized citizenship to "free white persons." It was now clear that the federal government could, and would, exercise its authority to restrict from entry into the country specific unwanted "racial" groups.

This legislation was to be a precursor of many measures that would curb immigration. At the turn of the century, as an example of actions taken, organized labor in San Francisco formed the Japanese and Korean Exclusion League (1905) to deal with what was considered to be immoral, subversive, and servile elements that posed a threat to living standards of the American worker. At the beginning of the 1906 school year, segregated educational facilities were provided for the Japanese in the San Francisco public schools. The international reaction was an embarrassment to the United States. Subsequently, President Theodore Roosevelt intervened and the city agreed to withdraw its program of segregated education if Japan would restrict the flow of Japanese immigrants to the area. The result was the so-called gentleman's agreement of 1907–1908 between the governments of Japan and 'the United States whereby the Japanese government began to deny passports to laborers who desired to travel directly to the United States.

However, the California legislature took additional restrictive action against the Japanese by denying them ownership of agricultural land. The state Alien Land Law (1913) denied the ownership of land to "yellow" Japanese aliens in a manner similar to the federal legislation that made the Chinese ineligible for naturalized citizenship.

The 1882 legislation was succeeded by the Foran Act (1885), which was aimed at denying admission to unskilled laborers, and an act in 1888 that provided that alien contract laborers could be deported within one year of entry. Congress assumed full control of immigration in 1891 by creating the institutional predecessor to the Immigration and Naturalization Service (INS).

The 1891 legislation added to the 1882 list of those to be denied entry—namely, paupers, polygamists, and persons suffering from loathsome and contagious diseases. Means for deporting aliens entering illegally or those who became public charges within a year of arrival were provided. The matter of contract labor was again addressed by making it illegal for employers to advertise abroad for workers and making it illegal for laborers to enter the country in response to illegal advertisements.

The list of persons to be excluded from admission was lengthened in 1903 and again in 1907. Added to the list were epileptics, prostitutes, professional beggars, and persons believing in the overthrow of the government by force or violence. In 1907 the list was further extended to include imbeciles, those suffering from tuberculosis, and those who had committed a crime involving "moral turpitude."

At the behest of restrictionists wishing to curb the flow, Congress appointed a commission in 1907 to examine the issue of immigration. The Dillingham Commission, named after Senator William P. Dillingham of Vermont, issued a report of more than forty volumes in 1910, noting that the nature and character of immigration had changed. Its review of the geographical origins for three waves of immigrants toward the end of the nineteenth century asserted that the immigrants who arrived between 1890 and 1914, primarily from southern and eastern Europe, were not equal to those who preceded them. They were, according to the report, transients who were not family-oriented and who were largely unskilled laborers and avoided agriculture; moreover, they did not attempt to assimilate and congregated apart from the old immigrants in the industrial centers in the East and Middle West. In short, the Dillingham Commission concluded that the new immigrants were racially inferior to the previous immigrants and the material in the report was designed to support arguments for restricting their entry.

WORLD WAR I AND IMMIGRATION POLICY

On the eve of American entry into World War I, Wilson's veto was overridden and the Comprehensive Immigration Law of 1917, based on the findings of the Dillingham Commission report, was passed. The act included a literacy-test provision that excluded aliens sixteen years or older who were unable to read a short passage in English or some other language. The requirement was not applied to the immediate family members of admitted aliens or those fleeing religious persecution.

Furthermore, the Immigration Law of 1917 codified existing immigration law, doubled the head tax to $8, and extended the list of persons to be excluded to chronic alcoholics, vagrants, and "persons of constitutional psychopathic inferiority." Moreover, virtually all Asian immigrants were to be denied by a provision in the act.

During World War I, the emphasis was on the Americanization of the immigrant in an effort to promote national homogeneity and national unity. Following the armistice of 1918, fears were transferred from wartime enemies to alien radicals and revolutionaries. The newly formed American Communist parties, other radical organizations, and the Russian Revolution had produced a "Red scare." Immigrant workers had been prominent in the textile strikes and steel strike during the spring and summer of 1919. Thousands of alien radicals were seized in 1919, and hundreds were deported to Russia in December of that year.

A new agitation for restricting immigration surfaced during the isolationist mood following the war. Three dominant views contributed to the anti-immigrant sentiment: fear of international threats and conspiracies, blatant racism, and concern about the economic threat posed by immigrants. The legislative response by the Congress was the Per Centum Limit Act (the Quota Law or Johnson Act) of 1921, which created restrictions on the basis of nationality. The provisions placed a limit on the number of immigrants to 3 percent of the number of people born in a country and residing in the United States as recorded in the last available census. Quotas were established for Australia, New Zealand, and countries in Africa, Europe, and the Near East. The restrictive formula provided in the act ensured that approximately 60 percent of the nearly 360,000 immigrants each year subsequently would come from northern and western Europe. Southern and eastern European immigration ultimately was reduced to less than one-quarter of the number of immigrants that came prior to the war.

Free immigration was allowed to countries in the western hemisphere. During the decade 1920–1930, nearly 1 million Canadians crossed the border into the United States, but in the following decade, only about one hundred thousand entered. The exemption for Mexico was explained in one of two ways: as a concession to southwestern farmers who depended on cheap Mexican labor and as a natural domestic response to draw closer to a neighbor in an atmosphere of international isolationism. Asian immigration remained subject to the 1917 exclusions. A principle of special preferences and a new class or "nonquota" category were introduced in the 1921 legislation. For example, preferences were given to wives of citizens of the United States, and aliens returning to the United States were not included in the quota count. Pressure for restriction continued; the response from Congress was a measure intended to control the flow of arriving immigrants and to stabilize the composition of the population of the United States.

After 1927, the quota system was replaced with the "national-origins principle." All immigrants were required to secure a visa from the country of origin. Under the new system, a total of 150,000 visas (a further reduction) would be allocated in proportion to the national origins of the total white population of 1920. The imposition of the visa requirement authorized initial screening and permitted the selection of preferred immigrants. The principle underlying this legislation and its discriminatory implementation was that it would more sharply curtail the influence of southern and eastern European immigration. For example, Americans were not classified by the United States census by descent beyond the second generation. So, in reviewing the names in the population for purposes of establishing national origins, the tendency was to assume that a name such as Smith was of British origin. Allowances were not made for the fact that this name could belong to a long-term black resident or be a variation of the German name Schmidt. As a result, 57 percent of the annual quota was given to Great Britain.

From the implementation of the national-origins principle, until most restrictions were lifted in 1965, the bulk of immigration legislation focused on national-security concerns. The Alien Registration Act of 1940, for the first time, required that nonimmigrants procure visas and that they be registered and fingerprinted. The class of deportable aliens was expanded to include smugglers, those abetting illegal entry, and those carrying weapons illegally. It is also significant that the INS was moved to an organization with an enforcement focus, the Department of Justice, after seven years in the Department of Labor. The Smith Act of 1940 authorized the refusal of visas to persons deemed a potential threat to "the public safety" and permitted the president to deport any alien "in the interest of the United States."

THE COLD WAR AND AFTER

The cold war was the motivating force for restrictionists to argue for a reevaluation, recodification, and updating of immigration law in light of the perceived threats posed by the emerging Communist party. The result of a recodification of immigration law was the Immigration and Nationality Act (McCarran-Walter Act) of 1952, which focused on an immigrant's political ideology as grounds upon which to make judgments about suitability. The law was designed especially to restrict the entry of Communists but also extended to drug addicts and those convicted of two or more offenses (even without the previous moral-turpitude stipulations). Also included in this legislation were provisions that allowed for expulsion of an alien on the basis of confidential information without a hearing. The national-origins principle for fixing quotas was retained in the recodified legislation. Of the total annual quota, 85 percent was now assigned to countries of northern and western Europe.

Immigrants from colonies of European nations could no longer qualify for admissions on the unused quota portion of the mother country; each colonial territory was assigned a specific quota. For example, there were approximately one hundred thousand immigrants from the British West Indies during the first three decades at the turn of the century. The allocation of a tiny quota was instrumental in redirecting the flow of West Indian immigrants to London, Birmingham, and other British industrial cities. The act

gave first preference to those with special skills deemed to be of value to the United States. Priority was afforded to close relatives of citizens of the United States or lawfully admitted aliens, and the category of aliens ineligible for citizenship was abolished. This last provision eliminated the practice of excluding Asians and banning their naturalization, although the quotas assigned Asian countries were quite small.

The 1952 Immigration and Nationality Act, passed over the veto of President Harry S. Truman, proved to be quite unpopular. It certainly was inconsistent with the temper of the 1960s quest for civil rights and efforts of the United States to establish friendly relations with the emerging independent nations of Africa and Asia. The act was amended by the Hart-Celler Act of 1965, which took effect in 1968. Some of the amendments were liberalizing, and others were not. The national-origins quota system and restrictions on the Asia-Pacific Triangle were abolished. Thus, immigrants from Asian and southern and eastern Europe would no longer be restricted from entry or subjected to severe limitations. The act was restricting with respect to the placement of numerical limits on countries of the western hemisphere, reflecting in part a concern with increasing levels of immigration from Latin America.

A ceiling of 170,000 visas was set for eastern hemisphere countries subject to numerical limitation, and a total of 120,000 was set for western hemisphere countries subject to numerical limitation. These numbers were combined into a worldwide total in 1980 when legislation was passed to accommodate the increasing number of refugees. A limit of 20,000 visas per country was established for eastern hemisphere countries, regardless of size, but the principle of "first come, first served" would apply to all western hemisphere countries subject to numerical limitation. Further, the 1965 amendments retained some nonquota admissions; however, within the specified limitations for each country, a preference was established for the allocation of visas. Six rank-ordered categories of preference were established and an allotment of visas was applied to each. For example, the first preference category provided that 20 percent of the visas would be assigned to unmarried adult children of citizens of the United States. Finally, there was a catch-all nonpreference category to accommodate any unassigned visas from the six ordered categories. Here immigrants not related to persons already in the country could be admitted if they could certify that American workers were not available for the jobs they wanted and that their presence would not depress wages or have an unfavorable impact on working conditions.

Two emerging problems were not addressed adequately by the 1965 amendments. First, restrictions on western hemisphere residents contributed to an increase in the number of illegal immigrants from Mexico and other Latin American countries. Second, it was found that the matter of refugees would require further attention.

Current issues that relate to the nature, pattern, and extent of immigration from Mexico to the United States have their bases in the particular historical relationship between the two countries. In the mid-1980s, a substantial number of aliens from Mexico who had not entered the country legally resided in the United States. Estimates of the number of undocumented aliens range between 1 million and 8 million.

At the turn of the century, immigration in large numbers from Mexico to the United States began. The surge lasted for thirty years as a consequence of political instability in Mexico. Also, the dramatic expansion of American agriculture created a demand for cheap, unskilled, and migratory labor in the Southwest. Immigration from Mexico increased to meet the demand.

By the beginning of World War II, Mexican laborers had become the prime labor force for cultivating, harvesting, and packing citrus fruits, vegetables, cotton, and sugarcane crops in the Southwest. The Great Depression curtailed, but did not end, Mexican immigration, and beginning in 1942 the government of the United States began actively to recruit Mexicans for seasonal work (the Bracero Program). The program was designed to fill temporarily the void left by American workers who had gone to war.

For two decades after the war, more than 1.3 million Mexican nationals became resident aliens in the United States. Illegal immigration continued to increase: employment opportunities in Mexico were bleak because of the slow growth of the Mexican economy and the rapid increase in the population; the standard of living was considerably higher in the United States,

and its border was easily crossed; and once in the United States, an undocumented alien could easily blend in with other Mexican workers. The Bracero Program was terminated in 1964, and workers were thereby denied opportunities for legal employment. Illegal immigration continued to mushroom: the INS reported that it annually deports more than half a million persons, most of whom are Mexican farm workers and other unskilled laborers.

The flagrant disregard for the legal status of the border of the United States by persons who cross illegally has created a state of lawlessness. Furthermore, it is claimed that undocumented aliens are taking jobs needed by American citizens and legally resident aliens. A contrary position, however, is that undocumented aliens constitute a useful and necessary supply of unskilled labor to perform work that no one else wants to do.

Recognizing that the large number of undocumented aliens crossing the Mexican border poses a significant and increasing problem, Congress passed the sweeping Immigration Reform Bill of 1986 to address many of the dominant concerns. First, the law recognized the need to eliminate the pull of employment opportunities and contains a new system of penalties against employers who are convicted of failing to examine credentials of newly hired people or knowingly hiring or recruiting aliens not authorized to work in the United States. A second key provision of the legislation dealt with the potentially explosive deportation issue by allowing for the assignment of temporary resident status to undocumented aliens who have resided continuously in the United States since before 1 January 1982. The third feature of the immigration law is a number of measures, similiar to the Bracero Program, to ensure that growers have sufficient workers for the timely harvest of crops. This is accomplished primarily by expanding and revising existing temporary foreign worker and resident status statutory provisions.

Another glaring problem that surfaced following the 1965 amendments was that provisions had not been made to accommodate the increasing numbers of refugees seeking admission to the United States, especially Cubans. The approach to victims of persecution prior to the twentieth century was to admit them in the general flow of immigrants, but there was no governmental assistance to refugees as such. The experience of the first two-thirds of the century can best be characterized as ad hoc attempts to respond to specific situations.

The insensitivity of the policies of the United States toward refugees was evident during World War II when boatloads of fleeing Jewish refugees were turned away and forced to return to what was known to be certain death in Hitler's Germany. By the end of the war, for a period extending back to the Depression, fewer than 250,000 refugees had been admitted as immigrants. During this period of extensive worldwide refugee movement, the United States was distinguished as having received its fewest number of immigrants since the 1800s.

The decade extending from the conclusion of the war found a substantial increase in the number of refugees and corresponding measures by the government aimed at accommodating immigration. An executive order by President Harry S. Truman in 1945 that provided that displaced persons be given priority and be admitted under the regular quota system was the first of several consecutive actions by the government. However, since most of the persons to be served were from countries with low quotas, in the first two and one-half years only 41,000 refugees were able to enter under this order. Congress followed with the War Brides Act of 1945 (with an extension in 1947) and the first Displaced Persons Act in 1948.

The war-brides measures permitted the admission of approximately 120,000 alien wives and children of American soldiers. The Displaced Persons Act allowed for the two-year accommodation of immigrants from Poland, Germany, Latvia, Russia, and Yugoslavia, provided that their admission be charged to the quotas of their country of origin, or "mortgaged." The formula called for a maximum of 50 percent of any quota to be mortgaged annually for as many years as was necessary to pay back for the admission of the displaced persons. The 1950 amendment to the act liberalized the terms of admission and set a new two-year ceiling of 415,000. The mortgaging principle was retained until 1953, when it was abandoned by the Refugee Relief Act.

Authorization was then given for 214,000 refugees to be admitted on a nonquota basis during

a forty-one-month period. About 5,000 Hungarian "freedom fighters" were granted visas in 1956 under the provisions of the act, which was due to expire at the end of the year. Thus, the act narrowly circumscribed the ability of the United States to help the nearly 200,000 Hungarians who fled their country after the revolution. President Dwight D. Eisenhower invited 30,000 additional refugees to come on parole (that is, without an immigrant visa).

Most of the refugees during the years 1961–1979 were admitted under the parole authority of the president, consistent with the permanent power provided to the office by the Fair-Share Refugee Act of 1960. The Department of Justice under this law was permitted to parole into the United States refugees who fled Communist or Middle East countries. A permanent program for the admission of alien orphans was established on a nonquota basis, and the 2,000-visa limitation was lifted from Asia the following year. Refugee policy was becoming ever more an extension of the foreign policy of the United States.

The Vietnam War and its aftermath was responsible for a surge of refugees from Vietnam, Cambodia, and Laos during the later 1970s and early 1980s. Funds were appropriated to help more than 200,000 Indochinese refugees in 1975; by 1985, nearly 400,000 Southeast Asians had been admitted to the United States. During and extending from the same period, thousands of Jewish refugees were immigrating from Russia.

The Refugee Act of 1980, reflecting the experience with refugees from Southeast Asia, raised the annual ceiling on immigrants from 290,000 to 320,000, with 50,000 visas of this total for refugees. Mass admittances under the parole authority of the president were disallowed, but the president was permitted to determine who qualifies as refugees and to admit persons beyond the 50,000 limit in consultation with Congress.

A refugee, defined following World War II as a person fleeing Communist domination or fleeing a country in the Middle East, was redefined. To qualify as a refugee under the 1980 act, it was necessary for a person to be afraid or unwilling to return to his or her country of origin because of a well founded fear of persecution based on race, religion, social class, or political opinion.

IMMIGRATION, NATURALIZATION, AND CITIZENSHIP

The procedures established for the assimilation of refugees and the new definition were tested by, respectively, the Cuban "freedom flotilla" and the Haitian "boat people" during the early 1980s. The previous experience had been with refugees already in the country of first asylum and away from the shores of the United States. From the accession to power of Fidel Castro in Cuba in 1959 until the boatlift in 1980, nearly 600,000 Cubans immigrated to the United States, but it was the 125,000 who came to the country in boats and made America the first country of asylum that sorely tested the ability to adjust and assimilate refugees. The machinery gradually, but not flawlessly, processed the Cuban refugees because they were viewed as fleeing Communist domination.

The Haitians, who also came in boats, provided a test for acquiring the status of refugee. The Haitians claimed they were refugees from poverty, a classification not covered in the refugee definition. However, they claimed that once they had left Haiti they could not return, because they would be subject to political persecution, a classification covered in the refugee definition, given the conditions under which they had left. The government did not accept their fear of persecution as sufficient; it was concluded that the Haitian boat people were not refugees but economic immigrants and that any persecution was not their reason for leaving but a consequence of their leaving.

Hence, the reception accorded the Haitians was not warm; they were detained in large relocation camps, ended up in court, and were deported. President Ronald Reagan issued an executive order in September 1981 that authorized the Coast Guard to stop boats leaving Haiti, question those aboard, and turn them around if a conclusion was reached that the immigration laws of the United States might be broken. Assurances were offered by governmental officials that those fleeing political persecution would not be turned around, but several civil rights organizations contended that a predetermined decision had been made not to grant refugee status to persons not fleeing a country viewed by the United States as within the domination of Communism.

In 1985 it was estimated that the worldwide refugee population was approximately 16 million. It is clear that the policy of the United States as written and administered is sympathetic to anyone fleeing Communism. However, some observers, using Haiti and Chile as examples, contend that the policy of the United States is hazy, if not hostile, when it comes to according refugee status to those fleeing right-wing dictatorships.

NATURALIZATION

Naturalization is a process by which a person acquires citizenship after birth. Specifically, naturalization involves a set of standards with accompanying procedures established by law that specify eligibility qualifications to be a candidate for naturalization and the requirements an alien must meet successfully to be admitted to citizenship. When a person has been made a citizen in the naturalization court, a "naturalization paper" is issued. A "citizenship paper" shows that citizenship was granted automatically upon the naturalization of a child's parents. A "certificate of citizenship" confirms that a person is a citizen, for example, if born in a foreign country of one or two citizens of the United States.

The national government created by the Articles of Confederation and the Constitution of the United States left virtually undisturbed the power and authority of the state governments with respect to naturalization. The primary concern at the time was the removal of the disabilities of foreign birth. Acting under the authority to enact uniform laws of naturalization, the first naturalization law was passed in 1790; it gave jurisdiction to any common-law court of record. The limited requirements for citizenship were that applicants be free, white, and reside within the limits and under the jurisdiction of the United States for a period of two years. The residency requirement was raised to five years (1795), increased to fourteen (1798), and then returned to five (1801). It has since remained at five years.

An 1802 federal law of naturalization would govern the process of naturalization for more than one hundred years. The new law retained racial and court-jurisdiction provisions but added three additional requirements: a one-year residency in the state in which one applied, a declaration of intention to become a citizen at least three years prior to naturalization, and an oath to uphold the Constitution of the United

States and to renounce allegiance to any foreign sovereign. Common-law practice followed at the time provided that a wife and children under twenty-one became citizens at the time of the naturalization of the husband.

The new category "aliens ineligible for citizenship" was made applicable to all Chinese in 1882. This was the first occasion on which national origin was used to deny access to citizenship. However, the reasons used for exclusion from citizenship were increased incrementally after 1891, when the federal government assumed full control over immigration policy. Congress has legislated nine categories that circumscribe characteristics or behavior that, as implemented, served to exclude from the United States a total of 628,884 persons during the period 1892–1978. The percentage that each category for exclusion has contributed to this total over the period of eighty-six years are as follows: likely to become a public charge, 34.9 percent; attempted entry without proper documents, 30 percent; mental or physical defect, 13.2 percent; contract laborer, 7 percent; stowaway, 2.2 percent; unable to read, 2.2 percent; criminal, 2 percent; immoral, 1.3 percent; subversive, .2 percent; and miscellaneous, 7 percent.

The expansion of the United States beyond the bounds of the forty-eight contiguous states was responsible for a variant of traditional notions of naturalization. Alaska, purchased in 1867, and Hawaii, annexed in 1898, provide examples of collective naturalization at the time of statehood. Congress made these possessions "incorporated territories" and subjected them to the Constitution of the United States. Thus, by law, their populations were collectively naturalized as citizens when those territories both became states in 1959.

Collective naturalization has been applied to inhabitants of territories that have not been granted statehood; two such instances are Guam and the United States Virgin Islands. Acquired in 1898, Guam was an unincorporated territory of the United States until an organic act of Congress in 1950 conferred citizenship on its inhabitants. The Virgin Islands were purchased from Denmark in 1917, and Congress granted the inhabitants citizenship ten years later.

The Philippine Islands and Puerto Rico were both acquired by cession in 1898, and for a time the status of their inhabitants was similar. The Supreme Court held that these areas were "appurtenant thereto as a possession" and had not been incorporated by the United States. Given this association, it was reasoned that the status of inhabitants could not be aliens and they were not citizens. The designation "national" was devised to cover this situation. A national is a noncitizen who owes loyalty to the government of the United States and who is entitled to the protection of its laws. Nationals are permitted to enter and leave the United States at will. The inhabitants of the Philippine Islands retained the status of nationals under the colonial rule of the United States until 1946, when the islands achieved independence and nationhood. The inhabitants of Puerto Rico were granted citizenship by the Jones Act in 1917.

The Immigration Law of 1906 codified naturalization proceedings and outlined three distinct phases (referred to as "papers"). The declaration of an intention to become a citizen constitutes "first papers" and must be filed no less than two years and no more than seven years before a petition is filed. The next step involves filing the petition for naturalization, or "second papers," under the applicant's signature. A ninety-day waiting period is specified to allow time for an investigation. Finally, a hearing on the petition, or "final papers," is held to determine if the certificate of naturalization is to be denied or granted and citizenship conferred.

The current standards that apply to determine who becomes a citizen include requirements that an applicant for naturalization (1) enter the United States lawfully and apply for entry for permanent residence as an immigrant; (2) be at least eighteen years old; (3) file a declaration of intention; (4) have a five-year period of continuous residence before applying for naturalization with the last six months in the district where the naturalization court is located; (5) have knowledge and understanding of the history of the United States and its form of government; (6) attach oneself to the principles of American government; (7) demonstrate an ability to write and speak the English language; (8) not be a member of a Communist organization, not be connected with (inside or outside of the United States) or advocate Communism or any other subversive doctrine, and not be a member of any other subversive or totalitarian organization for a period of ten years prior to the application for naturalization; (9) show evidence of good moral character by successfully passing an examination for fitness for citizenship; (10) take an oath of allegiance to the United States; (11) renounce allegiance to one's former country and any foreign title; (12) promise to obey the laws of the United States and defend its Constitution and laws; and (13) promise to bear arms or fight for the United States or perform other types of service in the armed services when asked to do so.

THE RIGHTS OF CITIZENSHIP: BLACKS AND NATIVE AMERICANS

A fundamental assumption implicit in the Constitution is that federal citizenship be derived from state citizenship. It further assumes that citizenship in the United States, once confirmed, be uniform. In reality, the precise relationship between federal citizenship and state citizenship was not worked out. This matter would present itself later for resolution in the conflict between the North and the South—especially regarding the peculiar institution of slavery.

The process of sorting out the distinction between federal and state citizenship began in earnest when states in the South began to challenge the assumption that federal citizenship flowed from state citizenship. The problem as seen by southerners was that nonslave states began to admit free blacks to citizenship. This practice was consistent with the Missouri Compromise of 1820, but southerners desired to maintain full control over all local blacks. It was imperative in their view to admit to no rights or any measure of citizenship even to free blacks. The holding of the Supreme Court in *Dred Scott* amply satisfied the concerns of those who wanted to deny rights associated with citizenship. Chief Justice Roger B. Taney wrote for the Court in *Dred Scott* that blacks are "beings of an inferior order, and altogether unfit to associate with the white race, either in social or political relations; and so far inferior, that they had no rights which the white man was bound to respect."

The Fourteenth Amendment was intended by its framers to fill the void left by the *Dred Scott*

opinion and to provide citizenship status with the accompanying political and legal rights to newly freed blacks. Unfortunately, the first interpretation of this amendment by the Supreme Court, in the *Slaughterhouse Cases* (1873), produced an extremely narrow reading of one of its provisions: "No State shall make or enforce any law which shall abridge the privileges or immunities of citizens of the United States."

On the surface, the case had nothing to do with the rights of blacks. The litigants were employees in several slaughterhouses who argued that they had been deprived of their privileges and immunities (jobs) because of a state contract with other slaughterhouses. The Court ruled that the amendment provision referred to citizenship in the United States, conferred no new privileges, immunities, or rights and merely served as a federal guarantee against state abridgment of existing rights. The Fourteenth Amendment, the Court argued, was designed to safeguard those privileges and immunities fixed by state law or those broadly articulated by the Constitution. The problem for blacks was that most of the difficulties they faced were under the color of state law.

At this phase in the litigation of the Fourteenth Amendment, dual citizenship (federal and state) had been clearly established, state citizenship was derived from federal citizenship, there could be no state citizenship without federal citizenship, and state citizenship could not be deprived by the states. However, the rights related to national citizenship remained vague and ill defined.

It was not until the Supreme Court decision in *Brown* v. *Board of Education* (1954) that consequent legal barriers were challenged successfully in courts and in legislative bodies at the federal and state level. For blacks, the condition of their forced immigration, the peculiar institution of slavery, and racial hatred and discrimination has had a lasting negative impact on their acceptance as full members of American society, with all of the rights and privileges associated with full citizenship.

The experiences of black Americans presented questions about the definition and application of the rights of citizenship. Similarly, the citizenship status of American Indians has been in a perpetual state of flux and continues to be ambiguous. Issues and conflicts pertaining to the civil status of Indians in America are associated with questions of recognition, status, and allegiance of Native Americans as well as sovereignty and jurisdiction of tribes.

Tribal Indians on the North American continent unofficially became involved with two governments when the United States and Canada established an international border between the two countries with the Treaty of Paris of 1783. The boundary dissected the homelands of several tribes; the tribes were not consulted, and neither their status nor their relationship with respect to the border was a part of the treaty.

The government of the United States recognized seven Indian nations as independent tribal sovereigns and established the Saint Regis Mohawk Reservation with a treaty in 1796. Prior to 1871, when Congress declared that no additional treaties with Indian tribes would be negotiated, a total of 389 treaties had been signed and ratified that established tribes of Indians as sovereign nations. Consistent with this status, citizens of the United States were required by the government to obtain a passport before entering Indian territory. This relationship was altered over the years by a number of interactions with the federal government, each of which tended to diminish the civil status of the Indian.

Beginning about 1815, the policy of the federal government supported the removal of Indians from their traditional territories to isolated reserved areas that were administered as trusts by the government. Between 1830 and 1840 more than sixty thousand were forced to move to the newly established Indian Territory (in what later became Oklahoma), which was already in use by other Native Americans.

Forced assimilation was the primary motivation behind the Dawes Act (1887). The act provided for grants of citizenship to individual Indians who left the tribe for civil society. It also authorized the breakup of tribal lands into individual units of 40–160 acres and encouraged Indians to be farmers. Essentially, the result of this land policy was the large-scale sale and transfer of lands to whites; 63 million acres of land owned by Indians had been reduced to 19 million acres by the time the Dawes Act was overturned in 1934 by the Indian Reorganization (Wheeler-Howard) Act.

The Citizenship Act of 1924 extended citizenship to all noncitizen Indians who were born within the territorial limits of the United States. This act conveyed an individual status on the Indian and thus added another loyalty that served to diminish the attachment of the Indian to the tribe. This same year, the Immigration Act specified that aliens ineligible for citizenship could not be admitted as aliens. Together these two acts served to deny entrance to Canadian-born Indians as immigrants, even though of the same tribe as their American-born counterparts, because they could not become citizens—and once in the country could be deported. Subsequently, courts ruled that the right to free passage across the border of the United States was guaranteed to Canadian-born Indians by provisions of Jay's Treaty and that Indians born in Canada are not subject to deportation of any kind.

The Immigration and Nationality Act of 1952 continued to permit entry to the United States by Indians born in Canada but converted the previous political right to a racially derived right with this language: "but such right shall extend only to persons who shall possess at least 50 percentum of blood of the American Indian race."

The matter of citizenship and attachment is especially significant and not particularly easy for the American Indian, given a unique social and political situation. The Indian has a tribal identification and a band or clan (and perhaps reservation) identification and is also a citizen of the United States and the state wherein there is residence. There are rights, duties, and obligations that correspond to each of these attachments.

The myriad complex associations of the Native American with the government of the United States have been resolved on an issue-by-issue basis. Indian tribes are viewed as domestic dependent nations but unrestrained by the Bill of Rights and the Fourteenth Amendment (even though the Civil Rights Act of 1968 did impose some restraints similar to the protections found in these documents on the tribal governments). Thus, tribes are viewed as having inherent power to govern themselves and their own people. Where outside law is applicable, tribal law tends to take precedence over state law, and nonreservation Indians are entitled to be treated the same as other citizens. None of the restrictions that apply to aliens are imposed on Indians (including all registrations and visa requirements), and they may not be deported.

THE RIGHTS OF ALIENS

The alien is neither a citizen nor a national and, if not an expatriate, owes allegiance to a foreign power. Aliens have no right to live in the United States; they are admitted under legislation passed by Congress, which has the authority to regulate their behavior. However, most of the provisions of the Bill of Rights apply to aliens; in addition, they are considered "persons" within the meaning of the Fourteenth Amendment and are also protected by its terms. That is, there is to be no arbitrary discrimination against aliens, though "alienage" is not a suspect classification in terms of state and federal laws and regulations.

There are certain rights and privileges reserved for citizens and restricted to aliens. In some states, aliens may not engage in certain professions, may not own firearms, may not hold government employment, and may be restricted with respect to certain real estate transactions. Aliens must, on the other hand, pay taxes and, in accord with appropriate treaty provisions, may be asked to serve in the armed services.

The alien lives under the continuing possibility of deportation. Since 1892, Congress has determined that a variety of activities are harmful and incompatible with continued residence in the United States. Specified transgressions have been legislated to be sufficient for the expulsion of aliens. During the sixty-nine years between 1908 and 1978, a total of 769,686 aliens were deported in accordance with twelve categorical reasons for expulsion, including subversive, criminal, or immoral behavior; violation of narcotic laws; and mental or physical defects. Approximately one-third of the total number of aliens expelled during this entire period were deported between the mid-1960s and the mid-1980s and for one of three reasons: failing to maintain or comply with conditions of nonimmigrant status, entering without documents, or entering without inspection or by false statements.

In 1913, the Supreme Court held that a deportation hearing was not part of the criminal justice process and deportable aliens are therefore not afforded Fifth and Sixth Amendment protections provided defendants in criminal proceedings (*Luria* v. *United States*, 1913). Since deportation proceedings are administrative and not criminal, during the initial stages, aliens may be arrested and detained without a warrant. Generally speaking, the substantive rights and opportunities for judicial review are narrow for aliens in matters of deportation.

NATURALIZED CITIZENS

The alien seeking citizenship is required to satisfy the previously specified conditions of naturalization to be accepted into membership, but both the naturalized citizen and the native-born citizen acquire their citizenship by virtue of the first sentence of the Fourteenth Amendment. However, certain violations of the preconditions leading to naturalization can serve as justification for denaturalization. The naturalized citizen may well have citizenship annulled if proof is found of fraud or willful misrepresentation in the process of naturalization. Legislation does allow for denaturalization of naturalized citizens who violate subsequently the terms of naturalization, including, for example, although never invoked, becoming a member of, or affiliated with, a proscribed subversive organization within five years of naturalization.

Children who receive citizenship by reason of the principle of jus sanguinis will find an additional requirement of residency in order to retain citizenship status. Normally, a five-year period of continuous residency is required between the ages of fourteen and twenty-eight years (*Rogers* v. *Beller*, 1971). Frequently, these children may have dual citizenship in two countries, especially if the foreign country in which the child was born recognizes citizenship by virtue of this birth within its borders and jurisdiction.

EXPATRIATION

Expatriation is the term used to describe the relinquishment of citizenship. Congress has declared that citizens of the United States have the right to change allegiance at will. This right is not available to citizens in countries within the Soviet bloc, where one needs the permission of the government to make such a change. The motivation for the move by Congress is said to be justification for the large numbers of immigrants coming to the United States.

Congress has passed several statutory laws of expatriation. The assumption of these laws is that a citizen should be aware of, and must be willing to accept, the consequences of acting in a manner prohibited by law. Several of the laws of expatriation that would have deprived Americans of their citizenship have been voided by the United States Supreme Court, including: voting in a foreign election, avoiding military service by fleeing the country, successful wartime desertion, or serving in a foreign military without consent. The statutes were struck down because the Court observed that participation in the proscribed activities did not necessarily indicate an intention by a citizen to renounce citizenship.

The decisions and opinions of the Supreme Court suggest that only an affirmative action of renunciation is acceptable. This can be done at home only in times of war or in a foreign country before a diplomatic officer. Affirmative acts would include being naturalized as a citizen in a foreign country or taking an oath of allegiance to another government.

It is clear that politics defines citizenship and that governments have an exclusive right to confer citizenship. First and foremost, citizenship is a status conferred on individuals, but it also calls attention to the larger group of which the individual is a part. In this way citizenship involves a form of political association drawn in part from the classical ideal of working together for the public good. And citizenship is a legal status that is the foundation of rights and therefore involves access to rights. J. Roland Pennock observed that as a citizen, one "has a right to have rights enforced as a matter of right."

CASES

Brown v. Board of Education, 347 U.S. 483 (1954)
Dred Scott v. Sandford, 19 Howard 393 (1857)
Henderson v. Mayor of New York, 92 U.S. 259 (1876)
Luria v. United States, 231 U.S. 9 (1913)
Maxwell v. Dow, 176 U.S. 581 (1900)
Mayor of New York v. Miln, 11 Peters 102 (1837)
Rogers v. Beller, 401 U.S. 815 (1971)
Slaughterhouse Cases, 16 Wallace 36 (1873)
Yick Wo v. Hopkins, 118 U.S. 356 (1886)

BIBLIOGRAPHY

Walter R. Agard, *What Democracy Meant to the Greeks* (1942), studies the human values sought and realized by Greek democracy. Pastora San Juan Cafferty and Barry Chiswick, *The Dilemma of American Immigration: Beyond the Golden Door* (1983), examines the past two hundred years of immigration and refugee policies in view of concerns about present immigration from Mexico and Central America.

Richard Dagger, "Metropolis, Memory, and Citizenship," in *American Journal of Political Science*, 25 (1981), argues for the reformation of American cities so that they may again have civic memory and become the true home of citizenship. Ralf Dahrendorf, "Citizenship and Beyond: The Social Dynamics of an Idea," in *Social Research* 41 (1974), discusses how the expansion of citizenship has changed society. It is concluded that the dynamics of citizenship now defeats the purpose it set in motion, namely, creating societies that offer the greatest good to the greatest number. John K. Davies, "Athenian Citizenship," in *Classical Journal*, 73 (1977–1978), discusses the public and private advantages of citizenship.

Richard A. Easterlin and David Ward, *Immigration: Dimensions of Ethnicity* (1982), synthesizes major contributions from doctoral dissertations to the study of immigration during the years 1962–1972. Richard Flathman, "Citizenship and Authority: A Chastened View of Citizenship," in *APSA News* (1981), discusses the role and status of citizenship as the distinctive feature of political society. Maldwyn Jones, *American Immigration* (1960), explains how American history has been shaped by forces external to its shores. Richard Kluger, *Simple Justice: The History of Brown v. Board of Education* (1975), gives an outstanding historical treatment of the century-long struggle by blacks against racial hatred, discrimination, and segregation.

T. H. Marshall, *Class, Citizenship and Social Development* (1965), examines the relationship between citizenship rights and social class. Donald B. Murdock, "The Case for Native American Tribal Citizenship," in *Indian Historian*, 8 (1975), discusses the negative impact of multiple loyalties upon Native Americans. John E. Nowak et al., eds., *Handbook on Constitutional Law* (1978), contains a chapter on naturalization and citizenship, with sections on administration of immigration, acquisition of citizenship, voluntary and involuntary expatriation, and deportation. Sharon O'Brien, "Final Report on the Relationship of Federal Indian and Immigration Law" (1980). Jack W. Peltason, *Understanding the Constitution*, 10th ed. (1985), provides an excellent treatment of the Fourteenth Amendment and citizenship. J. Roland Pennock, "Rights and Citizenship," in *APSA News* (1981), classifies and discusses a range of rights derived from citizenship, including fundamental, moral, natural, and human rights.

Adrian N. Sherwin-White, *The Roman Citizenship* (1973), reviews some modern theories that relate to the essential characteristics of Roman citizenship. Michael Smith, "Tribal Sovereignty and the 1968 Indian Bill of Rights," in *Civil Rights Digest*, 3 (1970), gives a brief treatment of the legal rights of Indians with respect to the intersection of federal legislation and statutes. Philip Taylor, *The Distant Magnet: European Immigration to the U.S.A.* (1971), presents a study of 35 million Europeans who immigrated to the United States between 1830 and 1930. Stephan Thernstrom, ed., *Harvard Encyclopedia of American Ethnic Groups* (1980), offers a comprehensive review of the major developments in immigration as classified within five peak periods. Joseph Wambaugh, *Lines and Shadows* (1984), gives a moving account of the victimization of undocumented aliens at the southern borders of the United States.

Frederick Whelan, "Citizenship and the Right to Leave," in *American Political Science Review,* 75 (1981), attempts to show that the Universal Declaration of Human Rights is historically grounded and plausible.

[*See also* ARTICLES OF CONFEDERATION; EQUAL PROTECTION CLAUSE; PRIVILEGES AND IMMUNITIES; *and* RACIAL DISCRIMINATION AND EQUAL OPPORTUNITY.]

JUDICIAL REVIEW

Arthur S. Miller

ALTHOUGH not limited today to the United States, judicial review is the unique American contribution to the art of governance. It has no historical counterpart, and other modern nations have not carried the process nearly as far as has the United States. Often considered the principal means of resolving disputes over constitutional boundaries, in recent years judicial review has taken on a significant new dimension—that of judges filling in the interstices of statutes written in general terms or giving meaning to ambiguous statutory terms. In both roles, judges have a significant policymaking function; by no means are they passionless recipients of data presented by litigants. Justice Robert H. Jackson once wrote, "The political nature of judicial review generally is either unrecognized or ignored. But it is that which gives significance to constitutional litigation and which makes it transcend mere legal proceedings" (p. 311).

Although some mention will be made of other courts, this essay discusses judicial review principally as exercised by the Supreme Court of the United States. The Supreme Court may, and does, propose, but other courts (and administrators) may, and do, dispose. In this respect, there are lower-court and administrative checks on Supreme Court power. Because most law cases begin and end at the trial level, with the Supreme Court ruling definitively on only 150–200 out of the more than 4,000 cases filed each year, trial-court rulings become a significant aspect of judicial review. The Supreme Court interprets the Constitution and statutes, but lower courts, both federal and state, and administrators interpret the Court.

No commonly accepted definition of judicial review exists. To add focus to the ensuing discussion, judicial review is here defined as a process by which lawyer-judges, sitting as official organs of the state, determine the constitutional validity of actions of other governmental officers, at all levels and in all departments, and construe statutory language. This definition is based upon the following assumptions: courts are part of the governing coalition of the nation; in interpreting both the Constitution and statutes, judges cannot avoid being lawmakers; and to some extent, all judges bring their personal philosophies to the judging process, and these philosophies guide their determinations. Each of these assumptions is to some extent controversial, but the intellectual disputes over them are less over their validity than over the legitimacy of judicial review itself or the desirability of what is judicially decided—the results reached rather than the process. Leonard Levy wrote, "Much of the literature on the Supreme Court reflects the principle of the gored ox. Attitudes toward the Court quite often depend on whether its decisions are agreeable" (p. 1).

Judicial review was an inevitable consequence of the coincidence of three historical factors: a new nation with a written constitution; a federal system (that is, with the powers of government divided between those allocated to the national government and those retained by, or denied to, the states); and a tradition of judge-made law in both Great Britain and the American colonies. A written constitution requires, at least in most instances, one body to give ultimate meaning to its terms, and a federal system needs an umpire to settle the unavoidable conflicts that arise between local and national powers. However much disliked—and often they have been and are—judges have lent a sense of continuity to the American experience.

In the United States the Supreme Court, not without stout opposition, assumed the roles of determining the limits of constitutional powers generally and of arbitrating the federal system. The latter is perhaps the more important. Justice Oliver Wendell Holmes once asserted that he did not believe the United States would be seriously damaged if the Supreme Court lost its power to invalidate congressional statutes, but the nation would be imperiled if the Court could not determine the validity of the laws of the several states. It is worth mentioning that most constitutional questions that the Supreme Court decides today derive from actions of state, rather than national, governmental officers. The contrary is true for statutes, with the Court sitting as a supreme tribunal of interpretation of the growing number of federal statutes.

THE CONSTITUTION AND JUDICIAL POWERS

Although the question of judicial review was debated in the Constitutional Convention of 1787, no provision was made for it in the Constitution. At best, the evidence is inconclusive as to whether the framers assumed the general propriety of judicial review, however much they may have disagreed on details.

What can be said with certainty is that the idea was far from unknown in pre-1787 America. Some trace its beginning to England and Sir Edward Coke's famous, albeit questionable, statement in *Bonham's Case* (1610): "When an act of parliament is against common right and reason, or repugnant, or impossible to be performed, the common law will controul it, and adjudge such act to be void." The actual intent of Coke's decision, however, is still debated in Great Britain (although modern versions may still be found in cases where British judges rely on "natural justice" in deciding cases).

Relatively little attention was paid to the powers of the judiciary in the *Federalist Papers,* the essays by Alexander Hamilton, James Madison, and John Jay that were designed to sway public opinion in favor of the new constitution. Of the eighty-five papers, the final six, all written by Hamilton, deal in part with the courts. *Federalist* no. 78 is the most important; in it Hamilton seems to go out of his way to allay fears of an all-powerful judiciary:

> Whoever attentively considers the different departments of power must perceive that, in a government in which they are separated from each other, the judiciary, from the nature of its functions, will always be the least dangerous to the political rights of the Constitution; because it will be least in a capacity to annoy or injure them. The executive not only dispenses the honors but holds the sword of the community. The legislature not only commands the purse, but prescribes the rules by which the duties and rights of every citizen are to be regulated. The judiciary, on the contrary, has no influence over either the sword or purse; no direction either of the strength or of the wealth of the society; and can take no active resolution whatever. It may truly be said to have neither FORCE nor WILL, but merely judgment; and must ultimately depend upon the aid of the executive arm even for the efficacy of its judgments.

Hamilton either did not foresee the ways in which the powers of the judiciary would develop or was disingenuous in some of that statement—or both, which is likely.

However much serious scholars may disagree about particular decisions, all acknowledge today that judges have more than mere "judgment" and that they often exercise "will," if not "force." Although it has been asserted that judicial review was not imposed by the Court on an unwilling people, it is also fair to say that had the framers foreseen what the Supreme Court and judicial review were to become two centuries later, they probably would have taken steps to ensure that judicial power could not be—as it has been—aggrandized.

As in all its litigable provisions, the Constitution speaks in general, even vague, terms about the judiciary. Article III, Section 2 states in part,

> The judicial Power shall extend to all Cases, in Law and Equity, arising under this Constitution, the Laws of the United States, and Treaties made, or which shall be made, under their Authority;—to all Cases affecting Ambassadors, other public Ministers and Consuls;—to all Cases of admiralty and maritime Jurisdiction;—to Controversies in which the United States shall be a party;—to Controversies between two or more States;—between a State and Citizens of different States;—between Citizens of the same State claiming Lands under Grants of different States, and between a State, or the citizens thereof, and foreign States, Citizens or Subjects.

> In all Cases affecting Ambassadors, other public Ministers and Consuls, and those in

which a State shall be a Party, the supreme Court shall have original jurisdiction. In all other Cases before mentioned, the supreme Court shall have appellate Jurisdiction, both as to Law and Fact, with such Exceptions, and under such Regulations as the Congress shall make.

Two aspects of Article III merit mention. First, the framers wanted to create an independent judiciary; that is the substance of Section 1. But they also wished to check judicial power—hence, the provision in the second clause of Section 2 concerning Congress's power to regulate the appellate jurisdiction of the Supreme Court. Because all but a handful of the cases that the Court decides come to it by some form of appeal, this clause is—at least it could be, for its exact meaning is yet to be determined—an important limitation on the High Bench. Furthermore, by not mentioning judicial review, the framers at least implicitly rejected the idea, advanced in the Convention of 1787, that the Supreme Court should act as a "council of revision" of congressional enactments. Two centuries later, a perhaps persuasive case can be made for the Court's having become a type of de facto "council," not in the original sense of having prior scrutiny of statutes but by virtue of the fact that the Court's decisions on the meanings to be given statutory language are often difficult for Congress to alter.

The only other important constitutional provision concerning the judiciary, and then only inferentially, is in the second clause of Article VI:

This Constitution, and the Laws of the United States which shall be made in Pursuance thereof; and all Treaties made, or which shall be made, under the Authority of the United States, shall be the supreme Law of the Land; and the Judges in every State shall be bound thereby, any Thing in the Constitution or Laws of any State to the Contrary notwithstanding.

This, in brief, is a constitutional provision for the principle of federal supremacy, a principle that has had great significance for the legal relationships within the federal system.

The spare terms of the Constitution concerning the courts obviously pose more questions than they provide answers for. Perhaps most significant among those questions is how Article III is to be executed. Only when Congress, on 24 September 1789, passed "An Act to establish the Judicial Courts of the United States" was flesh put on the bare constitutional bones. The powers that federal courts, particularly the Supreme Court, exercise today are thus the result of a combination of ambiguous constitutional provisions and the greater specificity of the Judiciary Act of 1789. That statute is one of the most important ever enacted by Congress—so much so that it should be viewed as at least a quasi-constitutional pronouncement.

For present purposes, Section 25 of the Judiciary Act is the most significant. It provided for Supreme Court review of final judgments or decrees "in the highest court of law or equity of a State in which a decision in the suit could be had," in three situations:

where is drawn in question the validity of a treaty or statute of, or an authority exercised under the United States, and the decision is against their validity; or where is drawn in question the validity of a statute of, or an authority exercised under, any State, on the ground of their being repugnant to the constitution, treaties, or laws of the United States, and the decision is in favor of such validity; or where is drawn in question the construction of any clause of the constitution, or of a treaty, or statute of, or commission held under, the United States, and the decision is against the title, right, privilege or exemption specially set up or claimed [thereunder].

Although subsequent statutes amended the Judiciary Act of 1789, its principal thrust has remained intact. The importance of the statute, considered together with the constitutional provisions, cannot be overestimated—particularly when one realizes that it is the judiciary itself that gives ultimate meaning to what the constitutional framers (and Congress) intended. In that sense, judges are permitted to judge their own causes.

THE EXPERIENCE OF JUDICIAL REVIEW

Although judicial review is taken for granted today, with little dissent except over specific decisions, it is indeed extraordinary for one organ of the state to sit in judgment on acts of other organs of the governing apparatus of the state. That this is tolerated is best explained by the fact that as a part of the governing coalition of the nation, the judiciary cannot long be out of phase with the other parts of the coalition. Supreme Court justices assert the power to say what the law is, but their power is attenuated in fact. There is only a superficial validity to Justice Jackson's well known comment about the Supreme Court: "We are not final because we are infallible, but we are infallible only because we are final" (*Brown* v. *Allen,* 1953). Finality is not the language of politics, and the Court cannot avoid being deeply immersed in the political process.

Judicial review is therefore politics carried on under another name and in different forums. As lawmakers, the courts are targets of pressure-group tactics. This is seen, to mention the outstanding example, in the way in which black Americans employed the judiciary in the 1940s, 1950s, and 1960s as a means of enhancing their status. If they were to work "within the system," they had to seek a judicial remedy because the avowedly political branches of government completely failed to comply with the spirit and promise of the Constitution's guarantee of equal protection under the laws.

Americans are notoriously litigious—much more so than people in other nations—and they have made judicial review the linchpin of the American legal order. Other means of dispute settlement are, of course, available and are used, but the ultimate resort is to invocation of the state's judicial arm. In addition, this means that Supreme Court decisions on the affirmative powers of government—as distinguished from the negative limitations on government—serve to lend constitutional legitimacy to those powers.

In the last analysis, judicial review is what the Supreme Court says it is. It is important to realize that although the process began slowly and has been highly discontinuous, in that different issues are prominent in different periods of time, the years since 1789 have seen a steady aggrandizement of power in the judiciary. In the 1830s, Alexis de Tocqueville asserted in his classic *Democracy in America* that almost all political questions in the nation are sooner or later presented to the courts as judicial questions—a statement that was not completely accurate when made and is only apparently true today. Many political

questions simply did not receive judicial cognizance in the nineteenth century—for example, the question of the exploitation of the nation's resources in accordance with principles early stated by Hamilton in such influential state papers as his *Report on Manufactures* (1791).

In recent decades, for reasons not yet fully studied or understood, the Supreme Court has carved out larger areas of judicial concern, as in the belated enforcement of the Bill of Rights and the Civil War Amendments. Even so, much that is political today does not become judicial, either because the justices eschew ruling because they observe a number of self-imposed restrictions or because the pervasiveness and complexity of government make it difficult and often counterproductive to trigger the judicial process. In a society characterized by rapid and continuing social change, the delays inherent in the judicial system militate against even greater use of courts. Of course, some benefit from delay and readily resort to the judiciary, as is clear from the numerous appeals filed by the more than 1,450 men and women who were on Death Row in 1984 awaiting execution.

Moreover, a tension has always existed in the United States between the idea of popular sovereignty (the view that ultimate power rests in the people) and of a Constitution that in certain designated instances places limits on the power of the people. Majoritarianism thus conflicts with the purportedly immutable principles of limited government. President Abraham Lincoln, among others, drew attention to these tensions when in his first inaugural address he criticized the Supreme Court, which had assumed the task of reconciling the disputes emanating from two apparently irreconcilable polar opposites:

> The candid citizen must confess that if the policy of the government upon vital questions affecting the whole people is to be irrevocably fixed by decisions of the Supreme Court, the instant they are made in ordinary litigation between parties in personal actions the people will have ceased to be their own rulers, having to that extent practically resigned the government into the hands of that eminent tribunal.

In the end, judges making constitutional (and other) decisions are not passive instruments of objective justice. Their rulings, as Theodore

Roosevelt remarked to the dismay of many conservatives, depend upon their economic and social philosophies. All serious students of the judicial process concede the point—as do presidents when they are filling Supreme Court vacancies. They search for men and women whose political philosophies parallel their own. However much judges may strive to be invincibly disinterested, they are, like all people, prisoners of their heredity and their environment. There is a pervasive myth of neutrality in constitutional decision-making. In the words of Judge Learned Hand,

> [Judges] do not, indeed may not, say that taking all things into consideration, the [governmental act] is too strong for the judicial stomach. On the contrary, they wrap their veto in a protective veil of adjectives such as "arbitrary," "artificial," "normal," "reasonable," "inherent," "fundamental," or "essential," whose office usually, though quite innocently, is to disguise what they are doing and impute it to a derivation far more impressive than their personal preferences, which are all that in fact lie behind the decision.
> (p. 70)

Judges, it must be stressed, are hardly as innocent as Hand stated. Holmes once commented that judges tend to be naive, unsophisticated people who needed a touch of Mephistopheles. One wonders what company he and Hand kept. Judges are generally hard-nosed realists, fully aware of what they are doing.

In the American system judges are not self-starters. They must await the accident of litigation before making decisions. The astonishing consequence is that portentous problems of public policy are made into legal-constitutional questions by fortuitous litigation. Yet, the fact that judges are not self-starters emphatically does not mean that they are fettered by what lawyers present to them in their briefs and oral argument. Supreme Court justices routinely do independent research into the legal issues involved in a case—not personally, it should be noted, but through their law clerks. Moreover, they make extensive use of "judicial notice," by which that which is said to be "common knowledge" becomes a part of the information considered by the Court. Both independent research and judicial notice are discretionary, although

limits supposedly, but not actually, exist on use of the latter. In *Roe* v. *Wade* (1973), for example, Justice Harry Blackmun, writing for the majority in the decision validating consensual abortions, cited numerous medical data not presented to the Court by the lawyers. Chief Justice Warren Burger, in a concurring opinion, observed that Blackmun had taken judicial notice to its outermost limits (which he did not define) but had not gone beyond them.

Acceptance of judicial review by the populace apparently rests on a myth of judicial independence and a belief in the sovereignty of the "rule of law." The idea of an independent judiciary "is simply an elaborate rationalization for the substitution of coercion for consent. . . . The myth of judicial independence is designed to mollify the loser" (Shapiro, 1981, 65). The myth thus has a functional utility. The same may be said for the conventional notion of the rule of law, which purportedly binds even the sovereign. A "government of laws and not of men," as the shibboleth goes, is an ideal construct, often far from the actuality. It, too, is a myth, one that serves to hide the realities of the exercise of power.

THE MECHANICS OF JUDICIAL REVIEW

The institution of judicial review has several distinct characteristics. Initially at least, it is adversarial. The cases that the Supreme Court accepts for decision "on the merits"—about one out of twenty-five of the four thousand to five thousand that are filed each year—are chosen not because of the litigants but in the interests of development of the law. Litigants are important because only they can start the process. Once the Court takes a case for full-dress examination, the litigants usually fade into the background, as the justices routinely promulgate general rules in specific decisions. Although it is logically impossible to infer a general principle from one particular, the practice is accepted by bench, bar, and professoriat alike. Here again the justices have discretion: they can, and sometimes do, limit the effect of a decision to the facts and the particular litigants before them. But the usual practice is to state a general rule—which makes the Supreme Court a de facto third (and at times apparently the highest) legislative chamber. This is true even though, as a matter of technical law, only the parties before the Court are bound by the decision. In sum, most Supreme Court decisions on constitutional questions are essentially "class actions," with an individual or small group suing on behalf of himself or itself and "all others similarly situated." For example, *Brown* v. *Board of Education* (1954), the school desgregation case, was a class action brought by Linda Brown for herself and all other black schoolchildren who were kept in racially separated schools.

Yet, the adversary system is flawed. For instance, it is assumed that lawyers are of approximately equal competence. They are not: a wide disparity in ability may be seen in the legal profession. For that matter, the level of advocacy before the Supreme Court is often depressingly low. Furthermore, the flow of information to the Court is faulty, in that much information relevant to a case is not presented by counsel for the litigants. This leads, as previously noted, to independent research and use of judicial notice—and also to participation of "friends of the court" *(amici curiae)*, individuals or groups who do not have a direct interest in a case but are thought to be able to be of help in sorting out the complexities of the case. Even then, the justices frequently issue rulings in cases where considerable relevant information simply is not available—particularly on the social consequences of decisions. Moreover, judges are often narrow-minded lawyers whose background gives them little experience in dealing with significant governmental affairs.

All but a few cases come to the Supreme Court from some other court. Within the national government there is a three-tiered system of courts: the district (trial) courts, the courts of appeal, and the Supreme Court. In addition, there are some specialized courts, such as the Temporary Emergency Court of Appeals (dealing mainly with energy problems) and the Foreign Intelligence Surveillance Court (a highly secret body that passes on requests for eavesdropping for foreign intelligence purposes). The federal Supreme Court also reviews decisions of state supreme courts but only when federal questions are involved. Justice Felix Frankfurter once remarked that the Supreme Court is not a super legal-aid bureau. A federal question is one that concerns litigation in which the Constitution, a congressional statute, or a treaty is at issue.

Americans thus are governed by two sets of courts and have recourse to two constitutions—national and state—when their rights are concerned. (State courts must decide federal constitutional questions when properly presented by a litigant.)

Litigants who lose in a lower federal or a state court have two principal avenues to the Supreme Court—appeal and writ of certiorari. (A third route, certification, is seldom used, and then not by a litigant but by a court of appeals that considers some issue so important that the Supreme Court should decide it at once. The Court may at its discretion send it back to the court of appeals to get the benefit of that tribunal's reasoning.) *Appeal* is a word of art, theoretically meaning that the Supreme Court must rule on the merits—that is, give the case the complete treatment of briefs and oral argument. Generally, this avenue is limited to instances in which a federal action has been declared unconstitutional in the lower court. In practice, the Court handles an appeal much the same as a petition for certiorari (what lawyers call "cert"). Such a petition is a request that the record of the proceedings in the lower court be transmitted to the Supreme Court for its review. Most cases come to the Court through the cert process. And the great majority are summarily denied, with no reason given for denial (although on occasion a justice will write a dissent to a denial). For cert to be granted, the "rule of four" applies: four Justices must agree that the case merits full-dress treatment. Whatever the avenue followed, only 150–200 cases receive consideration on the merits each year. (In theory, denial of cert means neither approval nor disapproval of the decision below, although many nonlawyers believe to the contrary. The same applies to appeals that are dismissed, often "for want of a substantial federal question," although some argue that such dismissals are rulings on the merits.)

Opinions are routinely written on cases decided on the merits. Increasingly in recent years, opinions are written by several justices, which makes it difficult and at times impossible for lawyers to determine the exact meaning of the decision. Most opinions are signed by the justices who wrote them, although "per curiam" (unsigned) opinions are issued from time to time. The office of the opinion is supposedly to explain the reasoning that led to the conclusion.

Often, however, opinions are more rationalizations than explanations, and at times the "reasoning" is circular, with the justice restating the question being decided and using it as a reason for the decision. The methodology of judicial reasoning is one of the more controversial aspects of judicial review. Although most observers agree that opinions should be "principled," it is fair to say that there is a high degree of disagreement over the meaning of that word.

It is clear that judges consider the social consequences of their decisions; that is, they attempt, however imperfectly (because the relevant information is not always available), to forecast the impact of a given decision on the social order. They thus tend to be forward-looking rather than applying, as the myth would have it, the law as it has been received and understood. This means that judges are "result-oriented" to some degree. *Result-orientation* is a Frankfurter neologism; it is a term of opprobrium in some circles, used to castigate some judges, such as Chief Justice Earl Warren, for paying what some commentators believe is excessive attention to who the litigants are rather than to "the law."

Judicial review is instrumental. Judge Benjamin Cardozo once correctly remarked that the teleological conception of the judge's function must always be in his or her mind. Judicial review thus is purposive, with the justices seeking to further their personal value preferences. This may be seen in the way in which judicial review has evolved since 1789.

HISTORICAL DEVELOPMENT

Judicial review was the first major constitutional silence filled by judicial decree. Always controversial, it has now achieved legitimacy simply because almost two centuries of practice have solidified the claim of lawyer-judges on the highest tribunal to be a constituent part of the governing process. Those two hundred years may usefully be divided into several segments: the establishment of the authority of the courts to rule; the period to the end of the Civil War, when considerations of nationalism and localism were high on the Supreme Court's agenda; the three-quarters of a century leading up to 1937, during which protection of corporate capitalism was the ultimate judicial goal; and the period since 1937, during which several developments may be seen, including the protection of human rights and liberties for the first time in American history, the Supreme Court's "abdication" as czar of national economic policy, and the approval of aspects of the emergent "national security state." The dates, of course, are approximate; the Supreme Court has never announced sharp shifts in doctrine in so many words. Only hindsight enables one to perceive patterns of development. Moreover, there were, and are, aberrations in each period.

By no means was it clear in 1789 that the Supreme Court or any other organ of government would have the authority to say what the law is with respect to the Constitution. The Court had so little prestige that John Jay declined reappointment as chief justice to be governor of New York. Jay told President John Adams that he doubted that the Court would ever acquire enough energy, weight, and dignity to be important in the governing structure. Perhaps because judges were aware both that inherent limitations to their power existed and that there was an endemic dislike of the judiciary, the edifice of judicial review was constructed slowly. These fears were verified for many when *Chisholm v. Georgia* (1793) was decided: a furor erupted when the Court held that a citizen of South Carolina could sue Georgia in federal court. For the first, but not the last, time, a Supreme Court decision was reversed by constitutional amendment (the Eleventh, in 1798).

Chisholm is an early example of the interplay of politics and law in the judicial process. The members of the Supreme Court were to a man ardent Federalists; they believed in a strong central government at the expense of state "sovereignty," and they saw in the courts one means of furthering that goal. By erring politically in *Chisholm*, they learned a hard lesson—that they had to proceed circumspectly. When Adams named John Marshall, as canny a politician as ever sat on the High Bench, to be chief justice, he chose a man thoroughly wedded to Hamiltonian principles of nationalism. Marshall knew that caution was the best strategy. Thomas Jefferson had won the 1800 presidential election, and he and his party had a fervent desire to undo what they considered to be outrages by Federalist judges.

JUDICIAL REVIEW

Marshall took office in 1801 and served for thirty-four years. By 1803 he felt confident enough to seize upon an otherwise trivial dispute—whether William Marbury was entitled to his commission as a justice of the peace in the District of Columbia—to assert judicial preeminence in constitutional interpretations. Adams had appointed Marbury at the last moment but failed to deliver his commission; Jefferson and Secretary of State James Madison refused to do so. Marbury then asked the Supreme Court to order Madison to hand it over. The result was the famous decision in *Marbury* v. *Madison* (1803). Marbury relied on a part of the Judiciary Act of 1789 that seemed to permit the Court to issue such orders as part of its "original" jurisdiction. Marshall was confronted with a dilemma. If he ordered Madison to deliver the commission, Jefferson and Madison doubtless would refuse, and the Court would suffer a grievous blow. But if he did not sustain Marbury's claim, he would give aid and comfort to his political enemies, who were determined to purge the federal judiciary of Federalist judges.

Marshall's decision in *Marbury* was Solomonic: he gave a little to both parties and then, with a remarkable display of political shrewdness, lofted the banner of judicial supremacy. After conceding that the commission was being illegally withheld, he went on to say that even so, Marbury did not have a remedy in the Supreme Court. The reason for this was that Congress cannot constitutionally enlarge upon the original jurisdiction of the Supreme Court. Congress's attempt to allow the Court to issue mandatory writs had failed because such a power was not listed in Article III; it was therefore void.

In an opinion that is a masterpiece of judicial casuistry, Marshall began to construct the foundation of judicial review under the Constitution. The nominal victory of Jefferson—he now could appoint the person of his choice to the office—was far overshadowed by the astute Marshall's willingness to absorb a minor "defeat," all the while keeping his eye on his long-term objectives: to increase judicial power in general and simultaneously diminish the constitutional powers of the several states.

Jefferson, however, was not appeased; he and his party soon began a process of impeachment of Federalist judges. Choosing their targets carefully, they began with the hopelessly insane District Judge John Pickering of New Hampshire. Successful there, they chose as their next target the savage and vindictive Justice Samuel Chase of the Supreme Court. The House of Representatives impeached him, but the Senate refused to convict. The idea of an independent judiciary was saved, at least in theory, although independence from the governing coalition of the nation has always been more apparent than real. But the episode so alarmed Marshall that he wrote an amazing letter to a friend, proposing to give Congress appellate jurisdiction over Supreme Court decisions as an alternative to impeachment. Chase's acquittal obviated the need for this alternative. Marshall, however, paid a small price for (theoretical) judicial independence: for a time he ruled cautiously, thus giving the Jeffersonians no overt cause for complaint. By voluntarily giving up some power, Marshall paradoxically gained more power for the Supreme Court.

The chief justice bided his time, awaiting an opportunity to realize his twin goals of judicial supremacy and diminution of state power. It came in 1810, when for the first time the Court declared a state law unconstitutional. The case, *Fletcher* v. *Peck*, dealt with the so-called Yazoo land fraud. The Georgia legislature had sold most of what is now Alabama and Mississippi at about one cent an acre. It soon became known that the legislators had been bribed, and a subsequent legislature canceled the grant. In the meantime, much of the land had been sold to allegedly innocent third parties. Was the rescission of the grant valid? The answer from the Supreme Court: No. In a classic example of scrambled judicial rhetoric, Marshall did not seem to know why the cancellation was invalid, only that it was. His turgid opinion concludes that the "state of Georgia was restrained, either by general principles, which are common to our free institutions, or by the particular provisions of the Constitution" from rescinding the fraudulent grant. Justice William Johnson went even further. In the only instance in which a Supreme Court justice asserted that the writ of the Court could run against the Supreme Being, he said that the rescinding law was invalid on "the reason and nature of things: a principle which will impose laws even on the Deity."

John Marshall in effect rewrote the contract clause of the Constitution in *Fletcher* by first calling the legislative grant a contract and, more important, holding that a state is bound by its own contracts, thus chipping away at the foundation of state sovereignty. *Marbury* and *Fletcher* laid the foundation for the development of judicial review. But it was not merely review for the sake of review: Marshall had in mind the larger goal of constructing the legal basis for making the national government supreme.

Several decisions are especially noteworthy in what was to become the second important historical period: *Martin* v. *Hunter's Lessee* (1816), *Cohens* v. *Virginia* (1821), *McCulloch* v. *Maryland* (1819), and *Gibbons* v. *Ogden* (1824). Together with *Marbury* and *Fletcher,* these decisions are the pillars of national supremacy. To the extent that law can alter human affairs, itself a difficult and complex question, they helped to make a united state out of the United States. In addition, during this second period Chief Justice Marshall went far toward making "vested rights"—the protection of property rights—the basic doctrine of American constitutional law.

The meaning to be given to Section 25 of the Judiciary Act of 1789 was the focus of judicial attention in *Martin* and *Cohens.* Could the Supreme Court review decisions of state supreme courts in civil matters *(Martin)* and in criminal law cases *(Cohens)* when a federal question was involved in the litigation? The Court answered both questions in the affirmative. Again a furor erupted. A truly basic question of American federalism was at issue: Who was to have the ultimate word in such problems—state supreme courts or the Supreme Court of the United States? Attacking neither the Constitution itself nor the Judiciary Act, Virginia insisted in both cases that its highest court was as capable of interpreting the Constitution and statutes as the United States Supreme Court—a point that Justice Joseph Story cheerfully conceded in *Martin.* (Story wrote the opinion because Marshall had disqualified himself.) But Story knew that how the question of ultimate power was resolved would be crucial to the formation of American nationalism. If each state could say what the Constitution meant, the result would be a balkanized United States. Story and Marshall prevailed, not without difficulty, and the law is clear today. Judge Spencer Roane of Virginia, among others, waxed apoplectic at the decision in *Cohens;* he called it monstrous, unexampled, and

motivated by a grasping for power that history had taught corrupts all who wield it.

Martin and *Cohens* thus settled the questions of judicial supremacy and national supremacy, with the Supreme Court acting as a vital part of the federal government. The other legs of the four-legged stool are *McCulloch* and *Gibbons,* which dealt not with judicial power as such but with the range and nature of congressional powers. *McCulloch's* significance cannot be overestimated, both for its specific holding—that Congress had the implied power to create a national bank free from the taxing power of the state of Maryland—and for Marshall's theory of constitutional interpretation.

The shrewd chief justice varied his methodology to suit the case before him. In *Marbury,* for example, he treated the Constitution as a simple legal instrument, such as a contract or a will, and refused to add to Article III's listing of the original jurisdiction of the Court. Because the framers had not given the Court the power to issue mandatory writs, Congress could not do so by statute. Had Marshall employed his *McCulloch* technique, by which he read the Constitution expansively (saying that the justices should never forget that they were expounding a constitution), the result in *Marbury* would likely have been different. But that would not have suited Marshall's long-range goals. In 1819, Marshall considered the Constitution to be something far greater than a simple legal document: it was an instrument designed for the ages and to deal with the various crises in human affairs. This neat bit of intellectual footwork makes *McCulloch* the most important decision in American history insofar as constitutional interpretation is concerned. It paved the way for later expansive readings of the document. The larger point is truly significant: there is no one way to interpret the Constitution. The method chosen in any given case, as in the result reached, depends upon the personal preferences of the justices.

Gibbons is the other leg of the stool of judicial monopoly on constitutional interpretation and for national supremacy. Congress has express power "to regulate Commerce . . . among the several States." As usual, the phrase was not defined by the framers. *Gibbons* provided a prime opportunity for the Court (and Marshall) to say what the phrase meant. At issue was a monopoly granted by New York for steamboat navigation in the waters of New York. Did that grant unconstitutionally infringe upon the congressional power over commerce? In a decision that is cited to this day, Marshall first defined *commerce* (following his *McCulloch* lead, quite expansively) and then said that the congressional power was plenary. But with characteristic casuistry he did not go the full mile and invalidate the New York statute because it was at odds with the constitutional commerce clause; rather, he determined that New York's action conflicted with a federal coastal licensing statute. He thus achieved long-lasting results while cleverly sidestepping the area of greatest controversy—the nature and reach of the federal power over commerce. Not until 1851 did the Court, this time under Chief Justice Roger B. Taney, finally rule that the commerce power by itself could prevail over state laws even in the absence of federal action.

Marshall's contributions to the establishment of judicial review and national supremacy were so firmly embedded in the law and in the mores of the people that they have remained viable to this day. If success is a criterion of greatness, then John Marshall must be given the mantle of the greatest chief justice.

When President Andrew Jackson named Taney to succeed Marshall, some thought that the clock would be turned back and that the Supreme Court would begin to follow Jeffersonian principles. But that was not to be. If anything, judicial review became even more secure in the public mind. Marshallian principles were in general still followed. Marshall's strong edifice of judicial review even survived Taney's dreadful decision in *Dred Scott* v. *Sandford* (1857), declaring void the Missouri Compromise, only the second federal statute to meet that end. Taney denied blacks the right to citizenship and Congress the power to control slavery in the territories, relying on what he said were the intentions of the framers.

The Taney Court, spanning the years 1836–1865, consolidated principles first enunciated by the Marshall Court. But it failed miserably in coping with the slavery question, as did the other branches of government, state and national. Only a sanguinary war would determine, seemingly permanently, that the United States was both one nation indivisible (Lincoln's primary goal) and a nation in which the "peculiar institution" of slavery was outlawed. The Taney

Court's judicial failure meant that the very idea of judicial review, for a time at least, hung in the balance.

Judicial review was saved by a strategic judicial retreat during the Civil War, with the Court validating some of President Lincoln's extraconstitutional actions taken at the beginning of the war. Again, the paradox: the Court relinquished power only soon to become more powerful. The landmark decision came in the *Prize Cases* (1863), in which Lincoln's order to blockade Southern ports in the early part of the war was challenged. For the first time, the Court considered what John Locke called the "executive prerogative," or reason of state. Does the president have inherent power to take action he considers necessary in times of emergency? As the Supreme Court has often done in times of national emergency as perceived by the executive, it in effect became an arm of the executive and constitutionalized the prerogative. Said Justice Robert C. Grier in the *Prize Cases:*

> Whether the President in fulfilling his duties, as Commander-in-Chief, in suppressing an insurrection, has met with such armed hostile resistance, and a civil war of such alarming proportions as will compel him to accord to them the character of belligerents, is a question to be decided *by him,* and this Court must be governed by the decisions and acts of the political department of the Government to which this power was entrusted. "He must determine what degree of force the crisis demands."
>
> (emphasis in original)

With that decision the Court either neatly amended the Constitution—if for no other reason than that the Constitution probably would not have been ratified had the thirteen original states thought they were not free to leave the Union—or, at the very least, added constitutional reason of state to what the framers wrote. (The prerogative or reason of state is the principle that those responsible for the survival of the state can take actions to save it, even in the absence of permissive legislation—or, indeed, even if such action is against the law.)

Far from being an aberration, the *Prize Cases* set a precedent for numerous extraordinary, even extraconstitutional, actions by subsequent presidents. The outstanding example is *Kore-*

matsu v. *United States* (1944), in which the Court lent its imprimatur to incarcerating in concentration camps tens of thousands of Japanese-Americans, many of whom were native-born citizens of the United States. It is proof positive that the Supreme Court, during times of all-out emergency, becomes a part of the executive juggernaut. This is a large chink in the armor of judicial supremacy.

With the end of the Civil War, the third period of judicial review was ushered in. Three important amendments were added to the Constitution—the Thirteenth, Fourteenth, and Fifteenth —mainly to protect the newly freed slaves. But government, including the Supreme Court, was much more interested in promoting economic growth than in enforcing the Bill of Rights and the Civil War Amendments during the period that followed.

The war had given an immense forward thrust to capitalism. After the war, judicial review became a de facto arm of the propertied (business) class. To be sure, this was by no means a major realignment of judicial interest: judges and the law they promulgate have always been class-oriented and far from neutral, as Holmes acknowledged in 1873. Noting the criminal penalties imposed on laborers striking in England, Holmes maintained that the idea that the law is neutral, impartially imposed by judges, presupposed an identity of class interests that did not actually exist. The lack of social unity was eventually transmuted into a similar lack of unity in law. To Holmes, the decisions of courts represented the interests of the strongest in society: "Whatever body may possess the supreme power for the moment is certain to have interests inconsistent with others which have competed unsuccessfully. The more powerful interests must be more or less reflected in legislation [and judicial decisions]: which, like every other device of man or beast, must tend in the long run to aid the survival of the fittest" (quoted in Miller, 1982, 198). That early statement of social Darwinism epitomized a judicial system that neatly turned the Civil War Amendments into protections of corporate industry; the Fourteenth Amendment soon became a barrier behind which corporate officers could hide from the onslaught of regulatory measures.

Nationalism having become triumphant, business protectionism became the polestar of judi-

cial review. This was accomplished in two ways: the Court invented a new constitutional principle, substantive due process, and cavalierly rewrote such statutes as the Sherman Antitrust Act of 1890. The Court thereby helped the few against the many who would do to the few, via legislation, what the few had done to them. No abrupt shift was announced. If there is a major turning point, it came in 1886 when Chief Justice Morrison Waite casually announced for a unanimous Court, without hearing argument on the question, that the business corporation was a person within the meaning of the Fourteenth Amendment's due process clause. Soon thereafter, the justices became the final arbiters of what they considered to be sound national economic policy.

During that same three-quarters of a century, the Supreme Court interpreted the Civil War Amendments in ways that ensured that blacks would be consigned to a condition of virtual peonage. The Court invented the concept of "state action," which means that the Constitution runs against governments only. This meant that corporations had the protection of the Constitution (as of 1886) but had no concomitant duty to adhere to constitutional norms. The status of black Americans became starkly clear with the Court's invention of the "separate but equal" doctrine in *Plessy* v. *Ferguson* (1896), a case that tolled the end of the first Reconstruction.

As for business protectionism, two strands of judicial review may be discerned in the third historical period. First, the justices discovered, through an intuition belonging only to them, that the liberty protected by the due process clause included not only a guarantee of procedural safeguards when governments took action —the historical understanding—but also a requirement that the regulation itself not be arbitrary. Substantive due process was born, a lusty infant that established the Court as a little lunacy commission sitting to determine whether state legislation was "reasonable" in particular circumstances. The content (substance) of legislation was reviewed to determine if it was arbitrary. Reasonableness or arbitrariness were ascertained not by objective criteria but by the personal philosophies of the justices. Moreover, when Congress did enact statutes aimed at regulating railroads and other corporate entities "affected with a public interest," its efforts were sabotaged by the judiciary. Again, reasonableness became the magic formula to test the specifics of statutes.

This breathtaking intervention into the very center of government was accomplished by judges who, in contrast to John Marshall, struck out boldly and forcefully. Judicial hegemony in socioeconomic matters of course met opposition, but not from those who wielded effective control over the levels of power in the political order. Thus, for three-quarters of a century the justices ruled on the wisdom of economic legislation—all the while denying that they were doing so.

Constitutional judicial review in the 1865–1937 period was paralleled by like actions when the justices dealt with federal statutes. Realizing that invalidating too many statutes on the grounds of substantive due process could lead to public disapproval, the justices cannily played fast and loose with statutory programs, all to the same end of protecting corporate capitalism. But along with the Great Depression came the introduction of the American version of the welfare state. Not without difficulty, however, for the Court still stood like King Canute commanding the tides of social discontent to stop. And halt they did, at least at the legislative level, but only for a brief time. After a series of decisions early in the 1930s that eviscerated much of President Franklin Roosevelt's New Deal, the justices saw a new light in 1937. Without announcement or fanfare, they came to see that legislation that was unconstitutional prior to 1937 was now within constitutional boundaries. The fourth period of historical judicial review emerged.

Abdication of economic policymaking responsibility marks a major turning point in the history of judicial review. Since 1937, the Court has been quick to defer to Congress in economics. A Constitution that popular wisdom had called one of rights or limitations became a Constitution of powers. The "positive state" was born, one in which the Court constitutionalized the affirmative powers of government in social-welfare matters.

Abdication of economic sovereignty left the Supreme Court with an obvious task: to be a Court of statutory interpretation of the many laws passed in the 1930s and 1940s. The Court also began to search for a new constitutional role. This role was found, after some pulling and hauling, in judicial protection of civil rights and liberties. The "revolution" in civil rights and civil liberties that has occurred since 1937 is essentially one concerned with egalitarianism. Suddenly human rights and liberties became a preeminent concern as the Court dealt with cases involving racial discrimination, legislative reapportionment, and more protection for those caught in the toils of enforcement of the criminal law.

Attacks on judicial review have always characterized the American policy, from Thomas Jefferson down to the present day. Academics today argue over the legitimacy of an appointed body of judges making policy decisions; some maintain that this violates the principles of democracy. These attacks have a subtle but significant impact upon the manner in which the Court acts. As political actors, Supreme Court justices are fully aware of the ebb and flow of public opinion. Judicial review will doubtless continue, at least in form, although it is more than a little odd to think in terms of government by lawsuit in a complex technological society. A fast-changing society with planetary interests, such as the United States, simply cannot—indeed, will not—permit policy that really matters to be settled by an eighteenth-century institution using ancient methods of operation (the adversary system). The modern debate over the legitimacy of judicial review is curiously unsatisfactory: it argues yesterday's problems when today's and tomorrow's should be first on the agenda. Much of the debate is reminiscent of medieval Scholasticism, and like the Scholastics, the contestants in today's intellectual controversy over judicial review may be passed by. The Supreme Court and judicial review are—at least for the moment—important parts of American governance, but they are not sovereign. This is the age of the administrative or bureaucratic state as well as the national security state. All but a handful of the millions of governmental decisions never receive judicial scrutiny, a condition not at all likely to change.

CASES

Bonham's Case, 77 Eng. Rep. 646 (1610)
Brown v. Allen, 344 U.S. 443 (1953)

Brown v. Board of Education, 347 U.S. 483 (1954)
Chisholm v. Georgia, 2 Dallas 419 (1793)
Cohens v. Virginia, 6 Wheaton 264 (1821)
Dred Scott v. Sandford, 19 Howard 393 (1857)
Fletcher v. Peck, 6 Cranch 87 (1810)
Gibbons v. Ogden, 9 Wheaton 1 (1824)
Korematsu v. United States, 323 U.S. 214 (1944)
McCulloch v. Maryland, 4 Wheaton 316 (1819)
Marbury v. Madison, 1 Cranch 137 (1803)
Martin v. Hunter's Lessee, 1 Wheaton 304 (1816).
Plessy v. Ferguson, 163 U.S. 537 (1896)
Prize Cases, 2 Black 635 (1863)
Roe v. Wade, 410 U.S. 113 (1973)

BIBLIOGRAPHY

Paul M. Bator, Paul J. Mishkin, David L. Shapiro, and Herbert Wechsler, eds., *Hart and Wechsler's The Federal Courts and the Federal System*, 2nd ed. (1973), is a valuable collection of cases and materials dealing with judicial review, with emphasis on the procedural side. Raoul Berger, *Government by Judiciary* (1977), is a leading but tendentious attack on modern judicial review, focusing on the Fourteenth Amendment. Alexander Bickel, *The Least Dangerous Branch* (1962), is an important account of the development of judicial review; and *The Supreme Court and the Idea of Progress* (1970), is an attack on decisions of the Warren Court. Charles L. Black, *The People and the Court* (1960), is a defense of judicial review by a thoughtful scholar. Jesse Choper, *Judicial Review and the National Political Process* (1980), is a valuable study.

John Hart Ely, *Democracy and Distrust* (1980), presents the argument that judicial review should be limited to decisions "reinforcing voter representation" at the polls. Stephen C. Halpern and Charles M. Lamb, *Supreme Court Activism and Restraint* (1982), is a collection of articles by leading scholars on the pros and cons of judicial review. Learned Hand, *The Bill of Rights* (1958), is a prominent federal judge's discussion of the merits of judicial review. Robert H. Jackson, *The Struggle for Judicial Supremacy* (1941), is a well-written account of the development of judicial review; although somewhat out of date, it is still useful. Leonard W. Levy, ed., *Judicial Review and the Supreme Court* (1967), offers nine especially useful articles on judicial review.

Robert G. McCloskey, *The American Supreme Court* (1960), one of the best shorter accounts of the development of judicial review, is particularly useful when read with the Black volume. Arthur Selwyn Miller, *The Supreme Court: Myth and Reality* (1978), is a collection of the author's articles questioning the conventional wisdom about the Supreme Court and judicial review; *Democratic Dictatorship: The Emergent Constitution of Control* (1981), presents an argument that the United States is moving into an era of authoritarianism; and *Toward Increased Judicial Activism: The Political Role of the Supreme Court* (1982), is an astringent view of the history of judicial review, coupled with a suggestion for an even greater judicial role in the political order. Michael J. Perry, *The Constitution, the Courts, and Human Rights* (1982), a forceful argument for judicial protection of human rights, is an antidote to the John Hart Ely book above.

Martin M. Shapiro, *The Supreme Court at the Bar of Politics* (1964), is an interesting analysis of the political role of the Court; and *Courts: A Comparative and Political Analysis* (1981), is a ground-breaking study of the role of courts in several legal systems. Symposium, "Constitutional Adjudication and Democratic Theory," in *New York University Law Review*, 56 (1981); Symposium, "Judicial Review Versus Democracy," in *Ohio State Law Journal*, 42 (1981); and Symposium, "Judicial Review and the Constitution—The Text and Beyond," in *University of Dayton Law Review*, 8 (1983), cover the entire range of the modern debate about judicial review, with articles written by leading scholars. Laurence H. Tribe, *American Constitutional Law* (1978), is the leading text treatment of the ways in which the Supreme Court has interpreted the Constitution.

[*See also* APPEALS AND APPELLATE PRACTICE; CONSTITUTIONAL INTERPRETATION; COURTS AND CONSTITUTIONALISM; DUE PROCESS OF LAW; FEDERAL COURT SYSTEM; FEDERALISM; FRAMING THE CONSTITUTION; JURISDICTION; LEGAL REASONING; MARSHALL COURT AND ERA; RACIAL DISCRIMINATION AND EQUAL OPPORTUNITY; SUPREME COURT OF THE UNITED STATES; *and* TANEY COURT AND ERA.]

PRIVACY

David M. O'Brien

THE importance of privacy in American law and politics is unique from both a historical and a comparative perspective. The view of liberal legalism in the twentieth century has been that privacy merits special legal protection. Even as late as the seventeenth and eighteenth centuries, privacy received no recognition in Anglo-American common law. Although the United States Constitution and the Bill of Rights embody the principle of limited government—and hence the idea that individuals in some sense have a "right to be let alone"—neither specifically singles out privacy for special attention. Only after the development of new technologies, the growth of the administrative state, and the movement toward a more information-oriented society in the twentieth century did privacy appear crucial and related to fundamental and intimate decisions by which individuals discriminate and achieve some measure of self-definition. Privacy emerged and remains a concept rooted in liberal legalism's celebration of individual liberty and response to technological and socioeconomic changes.

PRIVACY AS A LEGAL-POLITICAL CONCEPT

What do we mean by "privacy"? Why is it important, and what and when do our privacy interests deserve legal protection? These questions prove especially vexatious and render the developing law of privacy problematic.

In his treatise *The Law of Torts* (1888), Judge Thomas Cooley planted the seed for the legal recognition of privacy by noting for the first time a "right to be let alone." Two years later, Samuel Warren and Louis D. Brandeis, in an article in the *Harvard Law Review,* cultivated the idea. Anticipating the emergence of new rights, they argued that the common law had evolved protections against invasions of privacy in the areas of contract and industrial property. They believed that the expansion of common-law property rights constituted a "recognition of man's spiritual nature." "The principle that protects personal writings and all other personal productions, not against theft and physical appropriation, but against publication in any form, is in reality not the principle of private property, but that of an inviolate personality."

The Warren and Brandeis article provides the watershed analysis of privacy as "the right to be let alone." Their assumptions about privacy largely structured subsequent discussions and indeed the development of the law of privacy. Specifically, it was assumed that privacy denotes the voluntary seclusion or withdrawal of an individual from public affairs and is an intrinsically important value and legally recognizable right. No less important, Warren and Brandeis gave social and legal status to privacy. In fact, what remains remarkable about the law of privacy is that their article prompted the development of that area of law. Between 1890 and 1941, courts in twelve states extended legal protection to privacy claims; the number increased to eighteen by 1956 and then to more than thirty-one states by 1960.

The expanding law of privacy, however, only perpetuated the problems of defining privacy. In 1960, William Prosser reexamined the concept only to conclude that there was actually no independent privacy interest and hence no right of privacy per se. "The law of privacy comprises four distinct kinds of invasion," Prosser argued, "which are tied together by the common name, but otherwise have almost nothing in common except that each represents an interference with the right . . . 'to be let alone.' " The four interests that Prosser found in the common law related to privacy are interests against intrusions on an individual's seclusion or solitude, not otherwise covered by the law of trespass, nuisance, or intentional infliction of mental distress; against public disclosures of embarrassing private facts; against publicity that places an individual in a false light and injures his or her reputation; and against appropriation for commercial purposes of an individual's name or likeness.

Prosser's classification of the protected privacy interests in tort law remains widely accepted. His reexamination of the concept, however, exposed a continuing controversy and presented a paradox for the law of privacy: either there is no single privacy interest and the concept of privacy is inherently ambiguous, or privacy can be adequately ensured by other legal doctrines, in which case a right of privacy is superfluous. In other words, there is nothing distinctive about privacy that deserves legal recognition in either common law or constitutional law.

A number of legal scholars tried to resolve this paradox by giving greater precision to the concept of privacy. When analyzing Prosser's classification, Edward J. Bloustein (1964), for one, sought to show that "inviolate personality" is the fundamental interest in privacy cases. "The injury is to our individuality, to our dignity as individuals, and the legal remedy represents a social vindication of the human spirit thus threatened rather than a recompense for the loss suffered." Like Warren and Brandeis, Bloustein's claim is that privacy has an intrinsic value and for this reason deserves specific recognition in law. Yet, Bloustein likewise offers not so much a definitional analysis of privacy as an explanation as to why we value privacy: privacy is in some way associated with human freedom and dignity.

Charles Fried similarly responded that privacy provides "the rational context for a number of most significant ends, such as love, trust and friendship, respect and self-respect" (1970, 138). Unlike Bloustein, however, Fried suggests that the normative value of privacy arises from its utility, its instrumental value. Privacy is "a necessary element of those ends [love, respect, and trust], it draws its significance from them"; but more than that, privacy is chosen, and therefore, violations of individuals' privacy expectations constitute deprivations of their basic liberty. Privacy, according to Fried, "is not simply an absence of information about us in the minds of others; rather it is the *control* we have over information about ourselves." Privacy, in short, "is control over knowledge about oneself" and that control enables individuals to enjoy intimate relationships as well as have a sense of human dignity (1968, 483).

From the broad, admittedly ambiguous definition of privacy as a "right to be let alone" offered by Warren and Brandeis, by the 1960s and 1970s most social scientists and legal scholars had come to view privacy as "control over access to information about oneself." Psychologists Oscar Ruebhausen and Orville Brim, for instance, define privacy as "no more, and certainly no less, than the freedom of the individual to pick and choose for himself the time and circumstances under which, and most importantly, the extent to which, his attitudes, beliefs, behavior and opinions are to be shared with or withheld from others." Pushing this line of analysis to the limit, Richard Parker concludes that "privacy is control over when and by whom the various parts of us can be sensed by others." More specifically, "control over who can see us, hear us, touch us, smell us, and taste us, in sum, control over who can sense us, is the core of the concept of privacy. It is control over the sort of information found in dossiers and data banks."

There are a number of appealing reasons for defining privacy as "control over personal information." The definition embraces a broad range of privacy interests that have come to be protected in tort and common law, appears appropriate and applicable to many of the problems associated with concerns about expanding governmental data banks and America's information-oriented society, and lends itself to normative and legal arguments for legislating privacy safeguards.

Defining privacy as "control over personal information" is nevertheless both too narrow and too broad. On the one hand, not every loss of control over information about ourselves is a loss or gain of privacy. Taken seriously, the definition leads to absurdities. By merely observing a person entering a room, the viewer gains some information about that person, but does that observation constitute an invasion of privacy? On the other hand, such definitions are too narrow.

Many privacy interests involve neither the dissemination nor the acquisition of personal information. The Supreme Court, for example, has confronted privacy claims ranging from challenges to music on public buses, loudspeakers in public streets, and door-to-door salesmen, to restrictions on the use of contraceptives and the permissibility of abortions. In all of these instances, the interests in privacy have nothing to do with disclosures of personal information but rather with an individual's freedom from intrusions on his or her activities.

Another problem with such definitions is the emphasis placed on individual control or voluntary deprivation. Defining privacy as "control over personal information" confuses privacy as a condition with legal claims to privacy protection. Privacy is not identical with a person's control over access to himself, because not all privacy is chosen; some privacy is accidental, compulsory, or even involuntary. As a logical and a practical matter, moreover, privacy differs significantly from a right to privacy. A person may have a large degree of privacy without having chosen it, let alone having a right to choose it. A right of privacy does not necessarily include the right to choose where, when, and how a person will have privacy.

Privacy is fundamentally a nonlegal concept that denotes an existential condition of limited access to an individual's life experiences and engagements. As such, privacy is a condition about which individuals may have a range of interests as well as make a range of claims to legal protection. When individuals' privacy expectations about their life experiences and engagements are compromised, they may seek the vindication of their privacy interests through litigation and the political process. Not every intrusion upon, or disclosure of, personal affairs gives rise to a privacy interest of sufficient weight to warrant legal protection. Privacy interests and claims must be balanced with other interests, administrative needs and costs, and broader societal objectives, such as crime control and efficient delivery of social services. Judicial and political institutions thus must determine whether a reasonable expectation and claim of privacy exists and whether society through its institutions should afford protection and compensation for invasions of personal privacy.

Contrary to the traditional view of privacy, then, there is not a single privacy interest underlying claims to a right of privacy or "the right to be let alone." Indeed, it is somewhat misleading to talk about a right of privacy, since individuals enjoy privacy rights in tort and common law, under state and federal statutes, and in constitutional law. Because privacy is a condition of life, individuals have, and may claim, a broad range of privacy interests—interests that run from control over personal information to control over personal engagements and activities as well as to control over fundamental decisions about personal life-style.

The nature and scope of legal rights of privacy depend on the practice of rights in society—that is, which claims to particular privacy expectations are legally recognized, under what circumstances, and with regard to what other legal, moral, and political considerations. Given the nature of privacy and the practice of claiming rights, "the right of privacy" is a broad, open-ended concept amenable to expansion and to the changes brought by new technological developments and unforeseen intrusions on private affairs. The legal contours of protected privacy thus may shift as individuals raise, and courts and legislatures legitimize, new claims to a right of privacy.

Privacy is more complex and multidimensional than "the right to be let alone." The Warren and Brandeis article in 1890, nonetheless, led to the development of privacy rights in tort and common law. The right of privacy was "an idea whose time had come," and developments in computer technology and telecommunications in the mid-twentieth century prompted not merely a new responsiveness of courts to privacy claims but also state and federal legislative enactments designed to regulate governmental and business information practices and thereby the creation of state and federal statutory rights of privacy. In addition to tort, common-law, and statutory rights of privacy, the Supreme Court responded to increasing claims that individuals have legitimate expectations of privacy against the government, by developing the constitutional law of privacy.

PRIVACY AND THE CONSTITUTION

The Supreme Court's creation of a constitutional law of privacy is controversial and paradoxical because neither the Constitution nor the

Bill of Rights specifically guarantees a right of privacy. Yet, the Court in *Griswold* v. *Connecticut* (1965) created out of whole constitutional cloth a right of privacy. Since only constitutionally permissible governmental activities may constrain the exercise of citizens' basic liberty, from the standpoint of the government citizens enjoy a right of privacy, or what Warren and Brandeis called "the right to be let alone." Once elevated to the Court, Justice Brandeis, in *Olmstead* v. *United States* (1928), explained his view and the basic rationalization for a constitutional right of privacy:

> The makers of our Constitution undertook to secure conditions favorable to the pursuit of happiness. They recognized the significance of man's spiritual nature, of his feelings and of his intellect. They knew that only a part of the pain, pleasure and satisfactions of life are to be found in material things. They sought to protect Americans in their beliefs, their thoughts, their emotions and their sensations. They conferred, as against the Government, the right to be let alone—the most comprehensive of rights and the right most valued by civilized men.

The rationalization for the creation of a right of privacy offered by Justice Brandeis and written into constitutional law by the Court in *Griswold* entails a degree of judicial creativity that many find an impermissible exercise of judicial power. As Justice Hugo Black, dissenting in *Griswold*, cautioned, "Use of any such broad, unbounded judicial authority would make of this Court's members a day-to-day constitutional convention." Moreover, Justice Black correctly observed, "The Court talks about a constitutional 'right of privacy' as thought there is some constitutional provision or provisions forbidding any law ever to be passed which might abridge the 'privacy' of individuals. But there is not. There are, of course, guarantees in certain specific constitutional provisions which are designed in part to protect privacy at certain times and places with respect to certain activities."

The Court in *Griswold* opened the doors for the development of a constitutional law of privacy. Subsequent decisions based on the right of privacy, furthermore, tend to confirm Justice Black's fears of an ever-expanding definition of the constitutional right. In post-*Griswold* cases

the Court extended its newfound right of privacy to protect a woman's decision to have an abortion but, in doing so, also narrowly construed the range of other permissible claims to constitutionally protected privacy. Ironically, as Justice Black perceived, the emerging contours of the constitutional right of privacy are considerably narrower than the scope of constitutionally protected privacy under the First, Fourth, and Fifth Amendments.

Privacy and the Rights of Conscience. The First Amendment secured what James Madison called "the full and equal rights of conscience." Because the amendment guarantees that individuals may define for themselves their own beliefs, activities, and associations, it also provides a basis for citizens' constitutionally protected privacy interests in these areas as well. Under the amendment, the Court accordingly has often had to reconcile competing claims of privacy with those of freedom of speech, press, and religious exercise. Privacy claims actually crosscut express First Amendment freedoms in three areas that both oppose and complement the amendment's enumerated guaranties: claims for protection against solicitors and offensive public displays, for associational privacy, and against the public disclosure of private affairs.

In two late nineteenth-century cases, the Supreme Court alluded to possible First Amendment protection for personal privacy, but not until 1920 did a member of the Court articulate the view that privacy interests underlie the amendment's guaranties. In *Gilbert* v. *Minnesota* (1920), the majority acknowledged that freedom of speech is not absolute when upholding a law forbidding the teaching or advocacy of pacifism. In dissent, Justice Brandeis insisted that "the statute invades the privacy and freedom of the home. Father and mother may not follow the promptings of religious belief, of conscience or of conviction, and teach son or daughter the doctrine of pacifism."

Further development of First Amendment privacy litigation did not arise until later with claims against solicitors, door-to-door salesmen, and offensive public displays. In these cases, the Court confronted the dilemma of reconciling two First Amendment claims, a privacy claim not to be intruded upon and claims to free speech and religious exercise. The Court balanced these competing claims and fashioned a policy toward protected privacy by contrasting intrusions made for noncommercial and commercial purposes—as with the interruptions of the privacy of homeowners by solicitors for religious and political organizations. In the "Handbills Cases," for instance, the Court held that municipalities may not constitutionally prohibit religious groups from religious canvassing. Such ordinances prohibited the free exercise of religion. Subsequently, the Court forbade owners of a company town and a privately owned shopping center from prohibiting the circulation of religious and political literature.

By contrast, *Breard* v. *Alexandria* (1951) indicated that the Court would give priority to privacy claims against intrusions made for solely commercial purposes. Breard was convicted under an ordinance prohibiting solicitors from going onto private property without the owner's permission. The Court, balancing householder's property and privacy interests against those of publishers who wished to distribute publications, rejected Breard's claim that the ordinance unconstitutionally restricted his freedom of speech and press. *Breard* signifies that free speech may be regulated when its expression is designed primarily for commercial purposes and disturbs the privacy of individuals' activities in their homes.

Judicial line drawing nevertheless remains difficult. The question of when free speech becomes so intrusive as to constitute an overbearing intrusion upon interests in personal privacy must be considered. Two cases illustrate the problems of formulating a principle of First Amendment–protected privacy upon an evaluation of the relative intrusiveness of speech on personal privacy. *Saia* v. *New York* (1948) struck down as a prior restraint on speech an ordinance prohibiting the operation of loudspeakers on public streets except where matters of public concern were broadcast and advance permission was obtained from the chief of police. Yet, the next year, in *Kovacs* v. *Cooper,* another ordinance forbidding sound trucks emitting "loud and raucous noises" was upheld. The majority distinguished *Saia* on the ground that the ordinance in *Kovacs* provided adequate standards for issuing permits and found that the phrase "loud and raucous noises" provided a sufficiently definite guideline. The Court, moreover, maintained that the intrusion upon privacy by means of

loudspeakers and sound trucks was distinguishable from that presented in the handbills cases. Individuals need not read the handbills, whereas the intrusiveness of sound trucks is such that an individual "is practically helpless to escape this interference with his privacy by loudspeakers." Although conflicting in result, *Saia* and *Kovacs* illustrate the Court's balancing of privacy and freedom-of-speech claims upon a consideration of the relative intrusiveness of different modes of communication.

Cohen v. *California* (1971) and *Erznoznik* v. *City of Jacksonville* (1975) further illustrate the problems of fashioning the contours of constitutionally protected privacy under the First Amendment. In *Cohen* the Court rejected arguments that privacy claims justify a conviction for disturbing the peace. The offensive conduct there was that of a political protest by an individual wearing a jacket emblazoned with the words *Fuck the Draft* in the corridor of a Los Angeles County courthouse. Justice John Harlan, speaking for the Court, reiterated that claims of privacy and freedom of speech must be balanced not on the basis of the content of the speech (whether individuals regard certain speech or forms of expression as obscene or indecent) but on the basis of the manner and extent of the intrusion. In *Erznoznik* the manager of a drive-in theater challenged the constitutionality of an ordinance making it a public nuisance to show any motion picture containing nudity where the screen was visible from a public street. Justice Lewis Powell, for the Court, found the ordinance to discriminate unconstitutionally between movies on the basis of their content, adding that "this discrimination cannot be justified as a means of preventing significant intrusions on privacy. The ordinance seeks only to keep these films from being seen from public streets and places where the offended viewer readily can avert his eyes. . . . Thus, we conclude that the limited privacy interest of persons on the public streets cannot justify this censorship of otherwise protected speech on the basis of its content."

Whereas in *Cohen* and *Erznoznik* the Court found no reasonable expectations of privacy against offensive public displays, the Court in *Stanley* v. *Georgia* (1969) reaffirmed that individuals have First Amendment–protected privacy interests in their homes. In *Stanley* the Court ruled unconstitutional a statute prohibiting the mere possession of obscene materials, even in a person's home. Justice Thurgood Marshall, when announcing the Court's decision, emphasized that there is "something special" about individuals' activities in their homes. The Court later reinforced its treatment of claims and interests in this area. On the one hand, the Court rejected privacy claims when raised outside individuals' homes and where they engaged in selling obscene materials, transporting obscene materials, and viewing pornographic films in so-called adult theaters. On the other hand, the Court affirmed the right of householders to request the post office to order any mailer to stop sending advertisements that appear erotically arousing or sexually provocative.

While the Court largely limited First Amendment–protected privacy in this area to an individual's activities within his home, it has not escaped the dilemma in its balancing approach based on a consideration of the relative intrusiveness of different modes of communication. The Burger Court's ruling in *Federal Communications Commission* v. *Pacifica Foundation* (1978) illustrates well the problems of determining the relative intrusiveness on the privacy of the home. Here, the majority accepted the commission's finding that George Carlin's monologue "Filthy Words," a satire about "words you couldn't say on the public airwaves," as patently offensive but not necessarily obscene and upheld the commission's power to ban such indecent broadcasts. Justice John Paul Stevens, for the majority, found that "patently offensive, indecent material presented over the airwaves confronts the citizen, not only in public, but also in the privacy of the home, where the individual's right to be left alone plainly outweighs the First Amendment rights of the intruder." He continued, "To say that one may avoid further offense by turning off the radio when he hears indecent language is like saying that the remedy for an assault is to run away after the first blow. One may hang up on an indecent phone call, but that option does not give the caller a constitutional immunity or avoid a harm that has already taken place." Dissenting Justices William Brennan and Thurgood Marshall argued however that the majority misconceived the nature of individuals' interests both in privacy and listening to broadcasts as well as the nature of the intrusiveness: "The radio can be turned off."

In contrast with the problems of balancing competing privacy and free-speech claims, the First Amendment's provision for "the right of the people peaceably to assemble" provides a textual basis for the Court's construction of a right of association and associational privacy. The Court formally recognized the right in *National Association for the Advancement of Colored People* v. *Alabama* (1958), but its basis had been laid in the preceding forty years with judicial enforcement of claims to association regarding religious exercises, political parties, and collective bargaining. In the NAACP case the state required the NAACP to produce certain documents and records, but the organization refused to produce its membership lists and was found in contempt of court. When reversing the contempt citation, the Court held that the rights of association and associational privacy are ancillary to express First Amendment freedoms. Subsequently, the Court held that the right of associational privacy may be circumscribed by governmental regulations where associations are forced (for example, as a condition of employment) and where the nature and conduct of an organization are illegal, as well as where associations perpetuate invidious discrimination. Individuals thus have a broad First Amendment right of associational privacy, but the government may also intervene when associations are for unlawful purposes.

Claims of privacy against the publication of individuals' private affairs, unlike claims to associational privacy, compete with claims to the First Amendment's guaranty of freedom of speech and press. The balancing problem is especially difficult and one that the Court has thus far avoided by refusing to recognize such invasions of privacy as constituting a legal injury different from that covered by the constitutional law of defamation.

Individuals' privacy interests are nevertheless distinguishable from their interests against the publication of libelous and slanderous statements. Privacy claims register individuals' interests in determining for themselves to whom and what they disclose of their personal experiences and engagements. Hence, the truth or accuracy of a publication should not afford a legal defense (as in libel cases), because the privacy interest lies not with any inaccurate portrayal of one's private affairs but with their very disclosure.

Even though there are different interests

represented by actions for invasion of privacy and for defamation, the Court draws the same boundaries for both. Rather, the Court is reluctant to develop an additional standard for reconciling conflicts between freedom of the press and privacy. The Burger Court avoided the conflict in *Cantrell* v. *Forest City Publishing Company* (1974). Margaret Cantrell and her children brought an invasion-of-privacy suit against the Forest City Publishing Company because a follow-up story on the Silver Bridge disaster that had claimed the life of her husband inaccurately portrayed the Cantrells as destitute after the bridge collapsed. Mrs. Cantrell claimed that the story invaded her family's privacy and, through misrepresentation, demeaned the family. While allowing Mrs. Cantrell to prevail, the Court took pains to avoid the conflict between free press and privacy, concluding that the case presented "no occasion to consider whether a State may constitutionally apply a more relaxed standard of liability for a publisher or broadcaster of false statements injurious to a private individual under a false-light theory of invasion of privacy."

A Man's Home Is His Castle. Personal privacy attains perhaps its principal constitutional protection and the closest approximation to explicit recognition in the guaranties of the Fourth Amendment. Because the amendment guarantees the right to be secure from unreasonable searches and seizures, individuals have legitimate expectations of privacy with regard to the security of their "persons, houses, papers, and effects."

While the Court noted the relationship between privacy and the Fourth Amendment in an 1877 case, the first discussion of that relationship did not occur until *Boyd* v. *United States* (1886). Holding unconstitutional a statute permitting the government to order an accused to produce shipping invoices of allegedly illegally imported goods, the Court set a liberal construction as its standard for interpreting both the Fourth and Fifth Amendments and applying them "to all invasions on the part of the government and its employes of the sanctity of a man's home and the privacies of life. It is not the breaking of his doors, and the rummaging of his drawers, that constitutes the essence of the offense, but it is the invasion of his indefeasible right of personal security, personal liberty and private property."

The *Boyd* construction of the amendment and its underlying common-law property principles ensured rather extensive protection for personal privacy. Privacy interests associated with common-law proprietary interests received constitutional legitimacy under the amendment's safeguards for "persons, houses, papers, and effects." Subsequent holdings established protection for houses, business offices, stores, hotel rooms, apartments, automobiles, and taxicabs. Individuals have legitimate claims to privacy in such constitutionally protected areas.

In the early twentieth century the development of new technological equipment such as the telephone and radio made it possible to eavesdrop on conversations at great distances. Consequently, the question arose whether the Fourth Amendment could be asserted against such nontrespassory government intrusions by means of wiretapping, eavesdropping, and electronic monitoring devices. In the landmark case of *Olmstead* v. *United States* (1928), a bare majority implied that no legitimate privacy claims existed with regard to messages passing over telephone lines outside a person's house or office. The Court held that since the interception of such messages is carried out without actual entry into an individual's premises, there is no "search" of a constitutionally protected area and, further, telephone messages are not things that can be "seized" under the amendment. In short, the Court assumed that prior to determining the reasonableness of search and seizure, there must be a search involving physical trespass and a seizure of tangible material. Ironically, the *Olmstead* decision resulted from the Court's rigid adherence to *Boyd's* jurisprudential basis and emphasis on the property principles underlying the Fourth Amendment.

The Supreme Court did not effectively overrule *Olmstead's* twin requirement of a physical trespass or penetration of a constitutionally protected area and seizure of a tangible material until *Katz* v. *United States* in 1967. In *Katz,* federal agents attached an electronic listening device to the outside of a glass public telephone booth in which the defendant was making incriminating calls relating to gambling. Counsel for both sides argued the issue of whether the telephone booth was a constitutionally protected area in which Katz had a reasonable expectation of privacy. In Justice Potter Stewart's opinion, analysis of protected privacy in terms of the *Boyd*-fostered doctrine of constitutionally protected areas was deceptive. The doctrine was deceptive because recognizable claims to privacy were contingent upon the place of an individual's activities. Simply because Katz was in a public telephone booth did not mean that he had forgone all expectations of privacy.

Instead of analyzing constitutionally protected areas, Justice Stewart emphasized that the Fourth Amendment protects people rather than places. Still, the crucial question left open was, Under what circumstances does the amendment protect people and their privacy? When are individuals' expectations of privacy reasonable? *Boyd* had provided a relatively objective standard for evaluating individuals' privacy claims: constitutionally protected claims of privacy are justifiable in terms of the place of an individual's activities and his proprietary interests. By comparison, Justice Stewart invited difficulties by substituting a more subjective standard: "What [a person] . . . seeks to preserve as private, even in an area accessible to the public, may be constitutionally protected."

In *Terry* v. *Ohio* (1968) the Court attempted to clarify *Katz*'s holding that "wherever an individual may harbor a reasonable 'expectation of privacy,' . . . he is entitled to be free from unreasonable governmental intrusion," by explaining that "the specific content and incidents of this right [of privacy] must be shaped by the *context in which it is asserted*" (emphasis added). Reasonable expectations of privacy, like the reasonableness of a search, are context-dependent. Determination of reasonableness requires a juxtaposition of the government's interest in searching and individuals' interests in privacy within the context and circumstances of a particular search and seizure. Courts, for example, found justifiable expectations of privacy against warrantless intrusions into homes, apartments, dormitory rooms, business offices, and, with regard to materials sent through the mail, stored in rented lockers, or placed in garbage cans; but they rejected privacy claims in jails, open fields, yards, abandoned property, goods under bailment, financial records of bankrupt companies, records of long-distance calls, vehicle identification numbers, and social security numbers.

United States v. *Santana* (1976) illustrates the Burger Court's approach to the amendment and the attendant difficulties of defining the scope of Fourth Amendment–protected privacy. Santana, standing in the doorway of her house holding a paper bag containing heroin, retreated upon the approach of police officers into the vestibule, where she was subsequently apprehended. Justice William Rehnquist, for the Court, observed that while "under the common law of property the threshold of one's dwelling is 'private,' as is the yard surrounding the house, it is nonetheless clear that under the cases interpreting the Fourth Amendment, Santana was in a 'public' place. She was not in an area where she had any expectation of privacy." Because the doorway of her house was not in an area in which the Court recognized any expectation of privacy, the police, who had probable cause, lawfully made a warrantless arrest. Santana's retreat into the vestibule of her house provided the grounds for "hot pursuit" by the police and thus justified the warrantless entry of her home. Dissenting Justices Brennan and Marshall objected that the decision did not rest on the exigency of the situation but on the fact that notwithstanding Santana's presence in the doorway of her house, she was "as exposed to public view, speech, hearing, and touch" as to be "in the unprotected outdoors," a constitutionally unprotected area in which individuals have no reasonable expectations of privacy.

Santana illustrates the Burger Court's strict application of the amendment to privacy claims. Although Katz had reasonable expectations of privacy in a public telephone booth, Santana did not in the doorway and vestibule of her house. Nor do citizens have reasonable expectations of privacy, though they have assertable proprietary interests, in their family automobiles. The Court has contrasted individuals' expectations of privacy in their houses and automobiles in several cases, generally finding no basis for an expectation of privacy in a car.

The property bias of the Court's construction of the Fourth Amendment thus continues, but with the opposite effect of limiting protection for personal privacy. Property considerations—ownership, possession, and occupancy—have become the standards for evaluating claims to constitutionally protected privacy. Still, the Court's assessment of privacy interests remains context-dependent and therefore yields few bright lines as to the scope of Fourth Amendment–protected privacy.

No Man Is Bound to Accuse Himself. By comparison with the relatively broad range of privacy interests that may receive protection under the First and Fourth Amendments, a considerably narrower range is embraced by the Fifth Amendment guaranty that no person "shall be compelled in any criminal case to be a witness against himself." The provision gave constitutional effect to the common-law maxim "No man is bound to betray [accuse] himself." Because the amendment proscribes the government from coercing and compelling individuals to divulge personal information about their thoughts and activities, the Fifth Amendment provides some basis for claims to informational privacy.

The text of the Fifth Amendment indicates that the guaranty applies only "when the accused is *himself compelled* to act, either by testifying in court or producing documents" (Comment). Inclusion of the phrase "in any criminal case" literally limits the scope of the guaranty. The Court however has never felt bound by such a strict construction of the amendment. The Court, for example, extended the contours of the amendment beyond criminal trials to grand jury proceedings, to legislative investigations, and, in some circumstances, to witnesses or parties in civil and criminal cases where truthful assertions might result in forfeiture, penalty, or criminal prosecution. The Warren Court's landmark decision in *Miranda* v. *Arizona* (1966) extended the right to police interrogations at the time of arrest or in the station house. Hence, as a product in judicial policies, the Fifth Amendment extends from the time the inquiry has begun to focus on a particular suspect, through custodial interrogation, to the trial itself as well as to other quasi-judicial and nonjudicial proceedings. The judicially fashioned contours of the Fifth Amendment and protected privacy are thus broader than entailed by the logic of a literal reading of the amendment. However, although constitutional interpretation broadened the scope of the amendment in terms of the contexts in which individuals may invoke their right to remain silent, loose construction of the amendment also fostered policies that compromise the amendment's potentially broad protection for personal privacy.

The Court's narrow construction of the fundamental purpose of the Fifth Amendment as the preservation of an adversary system permits an individual to invoke the amendment only when it has been demonstrated that a defendant has been compelled to testify. The consequences for the contours of Fifth Amendment–protected privacy are well illustrated by the Court's treatment of claims with regard to private papers, documents, and business records.

In *Couch* v. *United States* (1973), for instance, the petitioner was denied any reasonable expectation of privacy and claim under the Fifth Amendment to intervene with an IRS summons to her accountant for her business records. The Court held that "no Fourth or Fifth Amendment claims can prevail where, as in this case, there exists no legitimate expectation of privacy and no semblance of governmental compulsion against the person of the accused. The criterion for Fifth Amendment immunity remains not the ownership of property but the 'physical or moral compulsion exerted.'"

The Court's treatment of privacy claims with regard to private papers and documents arguably disregards the testimonial nature of private papers by drawing a distinction between speech and writing. The amendment, the Court has held, prohibits compelling a person to speak and incriminate himself but does not prohibit compelled revelation of written thoughts. The Court thereby circumvents claims to informational privacy by holding that the amendment prohibits only governmental compulsion of an individual's oral testimony or personal production of papers containing testimonial declarations, but not other documents in the possession of an individual's lawyer, accountant, bank, or employer.

Another exception to the potentially broad contours of Fifth Amendment–protected privacy is the Court's doctrine concerning "required records." *Shapiro* v. *United States* (1948) held that records required to be kept under the regulatory powers of Congress have "public aspects," and hence, personal (and even incriminating) information contained therein is not subject to Fifth Amendment protection. The required-records doctrine was later applied in *California* v. *Byers* (1971), where a plurality upheld California's hit-and-run statute requiring a driver of a motor vehicle involved in an accident to stop at the scene and give his or her name and address.

The limited utility of the Fifth Amendment for

claims to constitutionally protected privacy turns fundamentally on the Court's literal interpretation of the nature of personal compulsion. If individuals are not physically compelled to forego their privacy interests in an incriminating fashion, the Fifth Amendment offers little protection for their interests in informational privacy.

The Court's Constitutional Right of Privacy. Whereas prior to 1965 the Supreme Court had legitimated claims to constitutionally protected privacy under the First, Fourth, and Fifth Amendments, in *Griswold* v. *Connecticut* it denominated a constitutional right of privacy per se. *Griswold* struck down as a denial of individuals' interests in privacy a Connecticut birth-control statute, which prohibited the use of birth-control devices and made it a criminal offense for anyone to give information or instruction on their use. In announcing the Court's ruling, Justice William Douglas proposed a "penumbra" theory for the newly created constitutional right:

> [Previous] cases suggest that specific guarantees in the Bill of Rights have penumbras, formed by emanations from those guarantees that help give them life and substance. . . . Various guarantees create zones of privacy. The right of association contained in the penumbra of the First Amendment is one, as we have seen. The Third Amendment in its prohibition against the quartering of soldiers "in any house" in time of peace without the consent of the owner is another facet of that privacy. The Fourth Amendment explicitly affirms the "right of the people to be secure in their persons, houses, papers, and effects, against unreasonable searches and seizures." The Fifth Amendment in its Self-Incrimination Clause enables the citizen to create a zone of privacy which government may not force him to surrender to his detriment. The Ninth Amendment provides: "The enumeration in the Constitution, of certain rights, shall not be construed to deny or disparage others retained by the people."

A constitutional right of privacy thus emerged out of the background of the Constitution and the Bill of Rights. Justice Douglas' penumbra theory attempted to forge a general, not a specific, jurisprudential basis for the right of privacy and to circumvent criticism from within and without the Court.

Seven years after *Griswold* the Burger Court

invalidated a Massachusetts statute that made it illegal for single persons, but not married persons, to obtain contraceptives. In *Eisenstadt* v. *Baird* (1972), Justice Brennan found no rational basis for distinguishing between married and unmarried persons, observing that "if the right of privacy means anything, it is the right of the *individual,* married or single, to be free from unwarranted governmental intrusion into matters so fundamentally affecting a person as the decision whether to bear or beget a child."

The extension of the right of privacy in *Eisenstadt* presaged subsequent rulings in not only failing to distinguish between considerations of privacy and liberty but also in assuming a broad connection between individuals' privacy interests and their use of contraceptives. In instances in which individuals buy or sell contraceptives (let alone, as in *Eisenstadt,* in which individuals acquire contraceptives at a free public lecture), their expectations of privacy appear minimal and are, indeed, comparable to cases where the Court denied privacy claims to buy and sell obscenity and pornography. In *Eisenstadt* the Court could have reached the same result simply by finding no rational relation between the statute and the activities regulated. The Court would thereby have avoided the conceptual difficulties of justifying the enforcement of privacy claims with regard to the buying and selling of contraceptives, but not obscenity or pornography. Government regulation of marketing either contraceptives or obscene material affects individuals' liberty and may consequently influence their activities and expectations of privacy. In both instances, the issue nevertheless is basically one of infringing upon individuals' liberty. By substituting a privacy analysis for that of an evaluation of when and for what purposes the government may regulate individuals' activities, the Court blurred the concepts of privacy and liberty.

In 1973 the Court went further with its analysis of individual privacy interests when concluding that the right of personal privacy includes a woman's decision to have an abortion. *Roe* v. *Wade* (1973) dramatically extended the right of privacy yet failed again to clarify the nature of privacy and its legal protection. Dissenting Justice Rehnquist emphasized the "difficulty in concluding, as the Court does, that the right of 'privacy' is involved in this case. . . . If the Court means by the term 'privacy' no more than that the claim of a person to be free from unwanted state regulation, . . . there is no doubt that similar claims have been upheld in our earlier decisions on the basis of that liberty." *Roe*, like *Eisenstadt*, collapsed interests in privacy with more-general interests in individual liberty—interests in personal autonomy and self-determination.

The Court's extension of the constitutional right of privacy in *Eisenstadt, Roe,* and subsequent cases severed the right of privacy from *Griswold*'s analysis of the marital privacy between husband and wife, primarily to protect a woman's decision to use contraceptives or terminate a pregnancy. In so doing, the Court narrowly limited the scope of its constitutional right of privacy. It rejected the broader implication that the constitutional right of privacy establishes protection for individuals' sexual autonomy and freedom from governmental restrictions on choice of life-styles. The Court has likewise been unwilling to extend the right of privacy to claims of informational privacy.

PRIVACY AND LEGAL POLICY

Personal privacy emerged as an issue of legal policy in response to technological and socioeconomic changes in America's increasingly information-oriented society. State and federal courts accordingly extended common-law and tort-law protection to claims of privacy. The Supreme Court broadly construed guaranties of the First, Fourth, and Fifth Amendments to protect some interests in personal privacy and created out of whole cloth a constitutional right of privacy. The privacy interests that receive protection are diverse and wide-ranging. Still, neither the Court nor lower courts have adequately responded to privacy concerns. As the United States Privacy Protection Study Commission concluded, "Current law is neither strong enough nor specific enough to solve the problems that now exist" (p. 10). The problems of safeguarding interests in information privacy remain largely matters for Congress and state legislatures. The Fair Credit Reporting Act of 1970 (regulating consumer reports), the Crime Control Act of 1973 (regulating access to individuals' criminal records), and the Family Educational Rights and Privacy Act of 1974 (regulating access to student educational

records), for instance, safeguard specific kinds of interests in informational privacy. The Privacy Act of 1974 embodies the most comprehensive statutory scheme for safeguarding privacy interests by regulating the collection and utilization of personal information by federal agencies.

When passing the Privacy Act in 1974, Congress, like the Supreme Court, acknowledged that "the right to privacy is a personal and fundamental right protected by the Constitution of the United States." Given the nature of privacy and the practice of rights in the United States, privacy promises to remain an important and controversial area of litigation, legislation, and developing constitutional law.

CASES

Boyd v. United States, 116 U.S. 616 (1886)
Breard v. Alexandria, 341 U.S. 622 (1951)
California v. Byers, 402 U.S. 424 (1971)
Cantrell v. Forest City Publishing Company, 419 U.S. 245 (1974)
Cohen v. California, 403 U.S. 15 (1971)
Couch v. United States, 409 U.S. 322 (1973)
Eisenstadt v. Baird, 405 U.S. 438 (1972)
Erznoznik v. City of Jacksonville, 422 U.S. 205 (1975)
Federal Communications Commission v. Pacifica Foundation, 438 U.S. 726 (1978)
Fisher v. United States, 425 U.S. 391 (1976)
Gilbert v. Minnesota, 254 U.S. 325 (1920)
Griswold v. Connecticut, 381 U.S. 479 (1965)
Katz v. United States, 389 U.S. 347 (1967)
Kovacs v. Cooper, 336 U.S. 77 (1949)
Miranda v. Arizona, 384 U.S. 436 (1966)
National Association for the Advancement of Colored People v. Alabama, 357 U.S. 449 (1958)
Olmstead v. United States, 277 U.S. 438 (1928)
Roe v. Wade, 410 U.S. 113 (1973)
Saia v. New York, 334 U.S. 558 (1948)
Shapiro v. United States, 335 U.S. 1 (1948)
Stanley v. Georgia, 394 U.S. 557 (1969)
Terry v. Ohio, 392 U.S. 1 (1968)
United States v. Santana, 427 U.S. 38 (1976)

BIBLIOGRAPHY

Edward J. Bloustein, "Privacy as an Aspect of Human Dignity," in *New York University Law Review*, 39 (1964); and *Individual and Group Privacy* (1978), reprints four essays that examine the nature of privacy in individual and group action. Comment, "The Protection of Privacy by the Privilege Against Self-Incrimination: A Doctrine Laid to Rest?" in *Iowa Law Review*, 59 (1974), discusses the Court's interpretation of privacy claims with regard to private papers and records. Charles Fried, "Privacy," in *Yale Law Journal*, 77 (1968); and *An Anatomy of Values* (1970), both explore the nature of privacy. Arthur S. Miller, *The Assault on Privacy* (1971), discusses the problems of safeguarding privacy posed by computer data banks.

David M. O'Brien, *Privacy, Law and Public Policy* (1979), analyzes the concept of privacy and the developing constitutional law of privacy; and *The Right of Privacy: Its Constitutional and Social Dimensions* (1980), is a comprehensive bibliography of books, articles, government documents, and Supreme Court rulings. Richard B. Parker, "A Definition of Privacy," in *Rutgers Law Review*, 27 (1974), presents an analysis of privacy as control over who can sense oneself. Don R. Pember, *Privacy and the Press* (1972), offers an excellent treatment of the tensions between privacy and freedom of the press. Roland J. Pennock and John W. Chapman, eds., *Privacy, Nomos XIII* (1971), presents a collection of essays exploring the nature of privacy and its relation to liberty, personal autonomy and democracy. William Prosser, "Privacy," in *California Law Review*, 48 (1960), provides the classic treatment of privacy and tort law.

Oscar M. Ruebhausen and Orville Brim, Jr., "Privacy and Behavioral Research," in *Columbia Law Review*, 65 (1965), examines privacy and social research. United States Privacy Protection Study Commission, *Personal Privacy in an Information Society* (1977), reports the major study of state and federal laws governing privacy and public- and private-sector information practices. Samuel D. Warren and Louis D. Brandeis, "The Right of Privacy," in *Harvard Law Review*, 4 (1890), gives the initial and classic treatment of privacy and the common law. Alan F. Westin, *Privacy and Freedom* (1970), examines privacy from anthropological, sociological, and political perspectives.

[*See also* FREE SPEECH AND EXPRESSION; RELIGIOUS LIBERTY; *and* SEXUALITY AND THE LAW.]

PRIVILEGES AND IMMUNITIES

Gordon A. Christenson and Wendy E. Holschuh

T HE United States Constitution mentions "privileges" and "immunities" of citizens in two places. One is located in Article IV, Section 2 of the original Constitution and provides, "The Citizens of each State shall be entitled to all Privileges and Immunities of Citizens in the several States." The second clause is found in the Fourteenth Amendment, adopted after the Civil War, and reads, "No State shall make or enforce any law which shall abridge the privileges or immunities of citizens of the United States." The first provision, the "comity clause," tied the states together by linking the treatment of citizens of all the states to that of the citizens of any state. The second provision, the clause in the amendment, is a negation, a limit on the power of states to abridge those privileges and immunities attributed to national citizenship, aimed mainly, but not exclusively, at "black codes," which perpetuated racial discrimination against former slaves and blacks. Both clauses harbor themes that are central to the constitutional scheme. These themes, taken collectively, reflect overlapping and sometimes contradictory political claims; they reveal an uneasy equilibrium of the historical tensions that produced the two clauses. The relationship between the clauses has been doubted and asserted, but both clauses embody these tensions and themes.

One theme is national unity—the effort to forge "a more perfect union" from a collection of sovereign states that were loosely organized in the Confederation but often behaved more like separate nations than one unified country—a unity to be achieved through a system of primary and secondary allegiances and protection between individuals, states, and the national government. A second, related theme is the creation of a single economic entity; the framers sought to create an economic, as well as political, union by reducing barriers to trade, travel, and other intercourse of citizens, thereby increasing internal economic efficiency and strengthening the United States in dealing with other countries in the external marketplace.

Third, the framers guaranteed a republican form of government to the states based on concepts of civil allegiance and civic virtue. Elected representatives in the states and in the federal government make laws through deliberation and debate, seeking to advance the public good, not just private interests. The framers recognized that a government based on liberty is threatened by factions—the capture of governmental power or the exclusion of others from power or privilege by a group of citizens united by a common private purpose adverse to the interests of other citizens or to the interests of the community. To guard against the danger of factions and purely private interests capturing power, the framers separated the powers of the national government into different branches and distinguished between limited national powers and reserved state powers, thereby creating checks on natural human vices. The privileges-and-immunities clauses furthered this skeptical view of centralized power by forging practical links of power between classes of citizens. Under the comity clause, citizens of one state who lacked political power in other states would not be at a disadvantage when confronted with powerful factions in the other states, because their private interests were to be protected as if they were state citizens. Similarly, the Fourteenth Amendment invoked the protection of the national government to prevent the states from denying the privileges and immunities of national citizenship to their own citizens as well, thereby ensuring their participation in a republican form of government.

A fourth theme is the concern for the fundamental rights and liberties of all persons and the relationship between protection of those freedoms and the federal system, which entails a structural division between national and state governments in the protection of rights.

BACKGROUND TO THE COMITY CLAUSE

Article IV, Section 2 of the Constitution (the comity clause) was drawn from Article IV of the Articles of Confederation, which was one of the key sources of unity among the sovereign states and covered the commerce powers as well as a clearer statement that slavery as an institution of status and property was not to be touched. The relevant section of the Articles of Confederation reads,

> The better to secure and perpetuate mutual friendship and intercourse among the people of the different states in this union, the free inhabitants of each of these states—paupers, vagabonds, and fugitives from justice excepted—shall be entitled to all privileges and immunities of free citizens in the several states; and the people of each state shall have free ingress and regress to and from any other state, and shall enjoy therein all the privileges of trade and commerce, subject to the same duties, impositions, and restrictions as the inhabitants thereof respectively, provided that such restrictions shall not extend so far as to prevent the removal of property imported into any state, to any other state of which the owner is an inhabitant.

While bound together for certain purposes, such as common defense, the states of the Confederation remained separate sovereign entities. The role of the federal government was limited to ensuring that these states worked as a unity externally and to minimize conflicts and disputes between the states internally. The states of the Confederation saw themselves as distinct sovereignties, as separate nations with a common heritage. When the respective interests of several states collided, each would protect and favor its own citizens, often to the detriment of

aliens or citizens of other states who did business within its borders. Conflicts over the economic institution of slavery also needed accommodation before any national unity was possible. Article IV of the Articles of Confederation attempted to achieve unity but deferred to state sovereignty as its basis and avoided conflict over the substantive question.

Current commentators, looking back at this early period of American history, have remarked that the states at that time exhibited interstate jealousies and parochial tendencies that threatened to tear apart the newly created nation. A citizen of one state traveling in another was treated as an alien, just as though traveling in a foreign country. If the United States was to become a union and not a mere league of states, some provision was needed to remove the disabilities of alienage from citizens of one state present in, or passing through, another. The diplomatic processes and official forms of reciprocal sanction and retaliation used by nations to address conflicts in the international sphere were too uncertain and destructive to be of much use to states bound together as one nation seeking a common defense against European powers. Some system of decentralized order was needed for citizens venturing beyond their own state's borders.

The disparity between the treatment accorded a state's own citizens and that accorded visiting citizens of other states was especially pronounced in the economic area. Instead of the free flow of trade and business between the states that would be necessary for the nation to become a single economic entity, trade barriers between the states and protectionist attitudes favoring private interests close to home had developed, as had a belief in the necessity of slavery as the economic basis for southern trade with Europe. In business matters as well as others, the states favored their own citizens and protected their own economic institutions against strangers and free trade. Provisions were needed to bring down trade barriers and promote free trade and travel so that the newly emerging economics of comparative advantage could be used to maximize the wealth of everyone in the new nation.

The privileges-and-immunities clause of Article IV of the Constitution addressed those concerns. Some call it the clause that was the basis for union. It was briefer in form than its parent provision in the Articles of Confederation and changed nothing of substance or intent except to hide under greater generality the acceptance of slavery. The Federalists and the Antifederalists alike accepted the clause as a basis for achieving unity.

The clause establishes a "norm of comity" or reciprocity among the states in regard to the treatment of each others' residents. The concept of comity had developed in international law among European nations. As travel and trade among these nations had increased, conflicts resulting from activities of the nationals of one country in another were adjusted by reciprocal dealing, custom, and treaties to maximize the interests of all and to reduce friction that could lead to war. Gradually, the European nations developed more-sophisticated methods of dealing with conflicts to promote commerce and to reduce the possibility of war, although a state of war was considered a legitimate instrument of national power. The "law of nations" was well established by the time of the American Revolution. One aspect of this system was the notion of comity, by which one nation respected the legislative, executive, or judicial acts of another country, on the basis of certain reciprocal customs and practices. A second aspect was the development of the law of state responsibility, which dealt with the treatment of aliens within a country's borders in accordance with certain minimum standards of international law. The influence of these concepts of mutual respect and treatment of aliens is apparent in the commands of Article IV. Since each state is required to accord the citizens of other states the same privileges and immunities given to its own citizens, the clause places the citizens of all states on "the same footing," according to the Supreme Court in *Paul* v. *Virginia* (1869), assuring all citizens within any state equality of treatment as regards privileges and immunities.

Laurence Tribe has called the comity clause the "bridge between federalism and personal rights" (p. 404). By foreclosing the imposition of special burdens based on noncitizenship, the clause purports to vindicate the individual's right to nondiscriminatory treatment and yet maintain the structural balance necessary for a federal republic. Conflict is inevitable, however. State political processes may fail to check state parochialism when it manifests itself in laws that discriminate against those who are unrepresented in the state legislature and have no right to vote in state elections, which would of course include citizens of other states. The clause remedies this potential problem by requiring both residents and nonresidents within a state to bear the same general burdens, thus tying the fate of nonresidents to those inside the state possessing political power.

In the economic sphere, the clause demands that the citizens of each state be treated on an equal basis with the citizens of every other state, making unconstitutional any special burdens placed on the citizens of one state doing business in another. In conjunction with Article I, Section 8, known as the commerce clause, it provides that the states may not place an undue burden on commerce between the states.

Since the states were forbidden to treat out-of-staters differently from their own citizens in business matters and forbidden to burden commerce unduly, it became difficult to maintain protectionist policies. Nationally, these limitations led to a reduction of barriers to trade and commerce, which could not have occurred earlier except by an agreement between individual states based on reciprocity, as in the European system. The resulting increased economic competition encouraged each state to promote and concentrate on the businesses, industries, and products for which it was particularly well suited —an early example of Adam Smith's doctrine of comparative advantage—thereby increasing the wealth of all. The Article IV privileges-and-immunities clause and the commerce clause thereby contributed to the creation of a free market and the promotion of free trade among the states, as well as improving the economic efficiency of the new nation, which was responsible to other nations for a single tariff. This strengthening of the internal economy in turn strengthened the position of the United States in the international marketplace, allowing the nation to promote and encourage free trade on an international level and eventually a more rapid internalization within the Union of the burdens and benefits of that trade as an instrument of national policy.

The comity clause thus reflects the four underlying constitutional themes. It promoted national unity and the creation of a single economic entity by demanding equal treatment for the citizens of every state and by breaking down barriers that the states had erected between themselves. Republican ideals were advanced, because lawmakers could no longer bow to demands of preferential treatment by their constituents without running afoul of the Constitution unless they could justify such discrimination against outsiders as necessary for the public good as a whole. The clause also ensured that the interests of noncitizens lacking political power would enjoy protection from local factionalism. Finally, the clause protected a nonresident's right not to be treated differently on that account from state citizens but also maintained the balance of power necessary to a federal system. All states were placed on an equal basis, and while a noncitizen's rights might be enforced by the national government through the federal courts, the rights protected were still referred to as "Privileges and Immunities of Citizens *in the several states*" (emphasis added).

JUDICIAL INTERPRETATIONS OF THE COMITY CLAUSE

The contours of the privileges-and-immunities clause are still being shaped by judicial interpretation. In *Baldwin* v. *Fish and Game Commission of Montana* (1978) the Supreme Court found it unsurprising that the contours of the Article IV clause remain unclear. That clause has been historically overshadowed by the similarly worded clause in the Fourteenth Amendment and the litigation and controversy that has accompanied it. Prior to 1868, there were two differing opinions as to how the privileges and immunities protected by the Article IV clause were to be defined.

One view was based on the "natural rights" doctrine, which was the dominant political philosophy of the time, influenced by John Locke and other social-contract thinkers. According to this doctrine, all persons, while still in the state of nature, possessed certain inalienable rights (including "Life, Liberty and the pursuit of Happiness," as enumerated in the Declaration of Independence) that they did not entirely yield when they entered into society. Governments were created to protect these rights, not to abridge them. Some judges who subscribed to

this doctrine believed that an inherent limitation on state and federal legislation existed that compelled courts to strike down any law contrary to the principles of the social compact between the people and the government they created.

Another, different version of the natural-rights doctrine emanated from Thomas Hobbes and Jean-Jacques Rousseau. The latter thought that to avoid the war of each against all others, all freedom must be given to the state, which in turn must pass freedoms and recommendations back to citizens through the government on the basis of strict equality. Rights, however, were not reserved by law to the people; the people had to take them back by revolution rather than being protected through inherent limits on power through natural law.

The influence of natural-rights doctrine and the tensions between the two versions were evident in the earliest lower federal court interpretation of the privileges-and-immunities clause in the 1823 case of *Corfield* v. *Coryell*. Justice Bushrod Washington, author of the *Corfield* opinion, interpreted the clause as recognizing that natural rights belong to the citizens of every state and are guaranteed against infringement by any state because they had not been fully delegated. Thus, inherent natural rights of state citizens were given a national protection against abridgment by any state through which the citizen passed.

A second, much narrower interpretation of the clause was also widely held. Some courts, advocates, and scholars were of the opinion that the rights to which citizens were entitled under the clause were not inherent natural rights but positive rights granted under a state's constitution and laws, not the central government's. But under this construction, an interesting issue arose: Which state's laws defined the rights to which the citizen was entitled? Did citizens carry into other states the rights enjoyed in their home states? Or when citizens entered another state, were they merely entitled to those rights enjoyed by that state's citizens?

The debate over the meaning of the Article IV clause inevitably raised questions about the hidden meaning of the status of slaves, free blacks, slaveholders and their rights when they left their home states to travel in others. How the language was to apply was unclear. Because the Article IV clause was derived from the Articles of Confederation wording, the tacit exclusion from the protection of the clause of those blacks who were not "free citizens" probably carried forward, despite a change in language.

The parent clause in the Articles of Confederation stated that "the *free inhabitants* of each of these states . . . shall be entitled to all privileges and immunities of free citizens in the several states" (emphasis added). It is generally agreed that the word *free* was inserted to modify *inhabitants* by the Continental Congress to ensure the agreement of the slave states; the word *free* precluded any argument that slaves could claim any rights under the clause. However, because the Articles of Confederation were not in effect very long, these issues were not brought to light or settled.

The debates in the Convention of 1787 about including a similar clause in Article IV of the Constitution were very limited. Charles Cotesworth Pinckney of South Carolina, a cousin of the author of the clause, did express dissatisfaction with it, desiring that "some provision should be included in favor of property in slaves," a suggestion that was not pursued. The remark probably arose because the provision in the Articles clause protecting removal of property imported into a state was missing from the constitutional clause. Pinckney thought that questions about the rights of slaveholders who traveled to free states with their "property" would arise, but the issue was not pressed, for there was an unspoken gentleman's agreement to pursue union and defer the issue of slavery.

Questions concerning transit with slaves did arise as the views of slave states and free states grew farther apart during the mid-1800s. The privileges-and-immunities clause did not provide an answer, because the ambiguity had been conscious. When a slaveholder entered a free state with his slave, did the free state have to recognize the slave relationship sanctioned by the law of the traveler's home state? Or could the free state forbid entry—or even extinguish the slave relationship—because it was repugnant to its own laws and policy? It was a prominent enough concern but was avoided.

The hidden issues were not limited to the rights of slaveholders. The rights of free blacks from the North traveling in the South were also uncertain. Did a southern state have to recognize the privileges and immunities that a free black person enjoyed in his home state, or did a southern state need only to recognize those very limited rights it granted to its own free black residents? And what was the status and property interest in indentured servants, whether black or white?

These problems raised issues of comity under international law and how they were to apply in relations between the states. The rights of slaveholders, escaped slaves, and free blacks depended upon which state's law was applied. When was one state required to respect the law or policy of another? Under international law, comity is not an absolute obligation; in deciding whether to respect the law of another country in a particular situation, a country will consider international relations, the protection of its own citizens or persons within its jurisdiction, the extent to which the other country shows reciprocal respect for its laws and acts in similar situations, and whether the laws of the other country are similar or repugnant to its own. Whether these same considerations applied among the states of the Union was an open question.

Both proslavery and antislavery forces soon discovered that the principles of comity, and the clause itself, could be construed to support either cause. Either side could point out that comity was a matter of grace, not obligation, so neither could be forced to respect the laws of the other. But had the Article IV clause—aptly called the "comity clause" from the international usage—changed this rule in such a way that comity was now an overriding obligation of federalism in the relations of one state with another? Slaveholders argued that the clause expressed priority for interstate harmony and a cohesive union; therefore, the northern states were bound by the clause to respect, and not interfere with, the institution of slavery to avoid interstate conflict. Northern states argued that comity required respect for their policies of freedom for blacks, which were based on common law and natural law. Just as a nation would consider the effect that recognition of a certain law or act would have on international relations, it was even more imperative for union that every state consider the effect that recognition or nonrecognition of another state's laws would have on interstate harmony.

Both sides could deny recognition of the other's laws, based on their reciprocal concern for protection of persons within their jurisdiction. Some northern states argued that they did not want their citizens corrupted by the immorality of slavery and therefore would not permit a master to travel with slaves through their states. The slave states argued that if they granted to visiting free blacks rights that their own black residents did not enjoy, the slave uprisings that might ensue would endanger persons and public order within the state. For similar reasons, many slave states had laws requiring the jailing of free black seamen while their ships were in port in the state. They could not take the risk that their own black populations might be incited by the presence or agitation of free blacks.

Early nineteenth-century cases involving the slave trade ruled that the trade was not outlawed as piracy, because although it violated the law of nature, it did not offend the law of nations. As noted in *The Antelope* (1825), the slave trade at that time was practiced by many nations and had not been banned either by general treaty or by custom. Article I, Section 9 of the United States Constitution protected the slave trade until that provision expired in 1808. Congress did enact a statute on 2 March 1807, effective beginning in 1808, making the slave trade to American ports piracy. Then, in 1862, the United States entered into the Treaty of Washington with Great Britain, each country conferring upon the other a reciprocal right of visit, search, and detention of ships suspected of engaging in the slave trade on the high seas.

This was the general backdrop against which the privileges-and-immunities clause was interpreted before the Civil War. Antislavery advocates urged that slavery was against natural law and that the comity clause protected the fundamental, natural rights of citizens wherever they traveled in the United States. Therefore, slave states had to respect the natural rights of blacks, as well as whites, under the clause. But the southern states also used this interpretation to claim that the right of property was a natural right that must be respected in the North. Both sides might hold that citizens carried with them the rights they enjoyed under their home state's laws or at least some minimally protected fundamental rights. Therefore, free blacks from the North should be entitled to enjoy whatever rights they had in their home states, even while traveling in the South, and slaveholders should be entitled to enjoy their property rights in slaves granted

under southern law, even while traveling in the North. That natural-law basis for interpreting the clause solved nothing and revealed the contradictions and divisiveness masked by the privileges-and-immunities clause in the name of unity. Still another position that minimized the conflict was that the visitor only enjoyed whatever rights were granted to the citizens of the visited state. This view is now the accepted jurisdictional basis for conflicts of law, and it would have been more effective had blacks been citizens. But the natural-rights perspective was still strongly held in the nineteenth century, and slaveholders could not take slaves into free states with impunity if the citizens of those states had no such property right. Visiting northern blacks in the South were entitled to enjoy only those rights the slave state gave to its own free blacks. The comity clause lacked a definitive interpretation by the United States Supreme Court, although lower federal courts had begun to favor a natural-rights interpretation.

The debate over "natural rights" versus "rights under state law" was settled by the Supreme Court after the Civil War, in the 1869 case of *Paul* v. *Virginia*. The Court rejected the view that a citizen of one state carried with him into any other state certain fundamental privileges and immunities because of his citizenship in his home state, although the Thirteenth Amendment had abolished servitude. The now-settled interpretation of the comity clause is that in any given state every citizen of any other state is entitled to the same fundamental privileges and immunities enjoyed by the citizens of the state being visited. The clause limits a state's power to grant its own citizens greater preferences under the state's constitution and laws than accorded citizens from other states in privileges and immunities fundamental to interstate harmony, such as travel and business.

The Supreme Court has, however, retained one aspect of the natural-rights thinking of *Corfield*. The equality between the citizens and noncitizens in any particular state does not extend to all rights enjoyed by the citizens of that state but, rather, only to the exercise of fundamental privileges and immunities. A state may give to its own citizens certain nonfundamental preferences without providing equal treatment for outsiders. The limitation to those privileges and immunities thought fundamental stems from the reason the framers included the clause in the first place —to form a cohesive union from a collection of independent, sovereign states—and from the nature of federalism. Discrimination against noncitizens may be tolerated if it is based on certain distinctions that support the fact of the existence of individual states. For example, the right to vote or to hold elective state office may be restricted to citizens of the state, as these matters relate to the existence of the state as a separate entity in the federal system of government. But when the discrimination against citizens of other states hinders the formation, purpose, or development of a single union of states, it is prohibited.

Although the privileges-and-immunities clause is phrased in terms of state "citizenship," the Supreme Court has held that the terms *citizen* and *resident* are essentially interchangeable for purposes of analysis under the clause. Therefore, discrimination against nonresidents on fundamental matters triggers close analysis under the privileges-and-immunities clause (*Austin* v. *New Hampshire,* 1975).

The determination of exactly what privileges and immunities are fundamental and therefore protected by the clause has been done on a case-by-case basis. In *Corfield,* Justice Washington listed various circumstances in which the states must treat each other's citizens equally; the courts have relied heavily upon *Corfield's* illustrations. Privileges and immunities often recognized by the Court that were initially noted in *Corfield* include the right of free ingress and egress, or of passage through other states; the right to acquire, hold, enjoy, and dispose of real or personal property; the right to maintain actions in state courts; and the right to be exempt from higher taxes or excises than those imposed on citizens of the state.

The cases have dealt most often with discrimination against nonresidents seeking to "ply their trade [or] practice their occupation" where the state has attempted to bias employment opportunities in favor of its own residents, as was the situation in *Hicklin* v. *Orbeck* (1978). The Supreme Court has labeled the pursuit of an occupation a fundamental privilege protected by the clause. Thus, as the Court declared in *Toomer* v. *Witsell* (1948), one of the privileges guaranteed by the clause to a nonresident is that of doing business on terms of substantial equality with citizens of the state. This protection has been extended to the opportunity to work for private employers engaged in public-works projects, and "professional pursuits" (for example, practicing law, in *Supreme Court of New Hampshire* v. *Piper,* 1985). The privilege of engaging in an occupation or profession on equal terms has been said to stem from the intent of the privileges-and-immunities clause "to create a national economic union."

Although many cases involve commercial matters, the clause protects more than just economic interests. It protects the right to enter another state to seek medical services, the right of interstate travel (as in *Paul*), and the right of access to state courts (*Canadian Northern Railway* v. *Eggen,* 1920).

Just as the Court narrowed the scope of the privileges-and-immunities clause to protect only those thought fundamental, it began in the late nineteenth and early twentieth centuries to create exceptions for discriminations against nonresidents that seemed to have a reasonable basis other than mere hostility to the citizens of other states. Nonresidents might create special problems that require reasonable discrimination in state policies. For example, while nonresidents have access to state courts, a requirement that nonresidents appoint an agent for service of process is a valid burden, since it seeks to put nonresidents on the same footing as residents concerning amenability to process. The criteria for determining the reasonableness of laws that discriminate against nonresidents, however, remained vague and unpredictable.

The Supreme Court began to develop a more structured standard of review in the 1948 decision of *Toomer,* enunciating the "substantial reason" test. While the privileges-and-immunities clause, like so many other constitutional provisions, is not an absolute, the Court interpreted it to forbid discrimination by a state against nonresidents where there is no substantial reason for the discrimination other than the fact that they are citizens of other states. But such discrimination is not prohibited where "perfectly valid independent reasons" exist to support it. What criteria or policies undergird those independent reasons are being developed case by case.

Whether the state has substantial reasons for discrimination depends on whether "there is something to indicate that non-citizens constitute a peculiar source of the evil at which the statute is aimed" *(Toomer)*. The degree of discrimination against the nonresidents must bear a close relation to the reasons for the disparity of treatment. Any apparent and less restrictive alternatives available to the state to achieve its objectives will be considered. Thus, the substantial-reason test permits reasonable discrimination, but only where the fact of nonresidency demonstratively creates problems for legitimate state objectives that cannot be resolved in less discriminatory ways. The burden of persuasion rests with the state to justify the discrimination. In judicial review, the federal courts insist on a close connection between the end sought by the state and the means used to accomplish it.

In cases involving discriminatory state taxes, the Supreme Court has not specifically applied the substantial-reason test, although the reasonableness of the discrimination is an implicit part of the analysis. As Justice Washington noted in *Corfield*, one of the fundamental immunities to which nonresidents are entitled is exemption from higher taxes than are paid by the state's citizens. In reviewing the validity of a discriminatory tax, the Court will consider a reasonably fair distribution of tax burdens with no intentional discrimination against nonresidents. This standard was set out by the Court in *Austin*, which in turn referred to earlier cases. *Austin* states that the "practical effect and operation" of a taxation scheme are reviewed by the Court. If the nonresident is actually being asked to make his ratable contribution, considering other taxes imposed solely on residents, a tax that appears discriminatory on its face may stand. In this way, the cases have established a rule of substantial equality of treatment for citizens and noncitizens in matters of taxation.

A statute does not fall outside the scope of the clause merely because it is couched in terms of "residence" rather than "citizenship." The clause is used, for example, to invalidate distinctions based on municipal residence: a person who does not reside in a particular state does not reside in a city within that state, and therefore, it makes little difference whether the discrimination is based on state or municipal residency, as the Court held in *United Building and Construction Trades Council* v. *Mayor of Camden* (1984). The clause applies to municipal ordinances as well as state statutes, a municipality merely being a political subdivision of a state, from which it derives

authority. By looking beyond the literal wording of the clause to its underlying purposes, the Supreme Court has preserved the clause's power to demand substantial equality of treatment for citizens passing through, visiting, doing business in, or temporarily residing in a state other than their own.

THE COMITY CLAUSE AND OTHER PROVISIONS

The privileges-and-immunities clause has ties and similarities to several other constitutional provisions. In addition to its close relationship with the Fourteenth Amendment privileges-or-immunities clause, to be explored in the following section, the Article IV clause is related to the commerce clause and the equal protection clause.

The clause shares its origin—in Article IV of the Articles of Confederation—with the commerce clause. The two clauses share many of the same goals and purposes. They enjoy a mutually reinforcing relationship arising from their common origin and from their shared view of federalism. The similarity of the concerns of the two clauses is apparent in the following statement, made in 1935 by the Supreme Court in *Baldwin* v. *Seelig*, which used the commerce clause to strike down New York regulations setting minimum prices for milk in order to protect New York dairy farmers: "[The regulations could result in] rivalries and reprisals that were meant to be averted by subjecting commerce between the states to the power of the nation. . . . [The Constitution] was framed upon the theory that the peoples of the several states must sink or swim together, and that in the long run prosperity and salvation are in union and not division." The themes of union and prevention of retaliation between states thus appear in cases under both the commerce clause and the privileges-and-immunities clause.

As explained by Tribe, the modern understanding of the privileges-and-immunities clause, with its emphasis on the right of noncitizens to enjoy equality in employment and business opportunities in any state, has brought the courses of the two clauses even closer. Some members of the Supreme Court shared this opinion. Justice Robert Jackson's concurrence in *Edwards* v. *California* (1941) supported striking a state law prohibiting the transportation of nonresident indigent persons into the state. The majority relied on the commerce power, the concept of "commerce" including the movement of persons. Justice Jackson expressed concern that basing the right of an indigent person to travel from state to state on the commerce clause would eventually result in either "distorting the commercial law or in denaturing human rights." He believed the statute should be invalidated because it contravened the privileges-or-immunities clause of the Fourteenth Amendment by abridging a privilege of national citizenship, a view shared by three other justices.

While the commerce clause and the Article IV clause may have had similar origins and purposes, there have been differences in their applications. Corporations, for example, can invoke the protection of the commerce clause, but not the privileges-and-immunities clause. Different factors trigger the operation of the clauses. The commerce clause contains an implied restraint on state regulatory powers, and its application is therefore triggered by state regulation unduly burdening commerce between the states. The privileges-and-immunities clause is a direct restraint on state conduct, which serves to facilitate interstate comity; it is triggered by state discrimination against nonresidents on fundamental matters. For the commerce clause to be violated, the state must be acting in a regulatory capacity; if it is acting as a market participant by, for example, setting conditions on its expenditures for goods and services in the marketplace, no concern is raised under the commerce clause. A problem may arise under the privileges-and-immunities clause, however, because the state can discriminate against nonresidents on matters of fundamental importance when it is acting as a market participant by restricting jobs on public-works projects to residents. Therefore, while there are instances in which the clauses overlap, there are also circumstances in which state conduct may be perfectly valid under one clause but unconstitutional under the other.

Similarities also exist between the privileges-and-immunities clause and the equal protection clause of the Fourteenth Amendment, which states, "No State shall . . . deny to any person within its jurisdiction the equal protection of the laws." The concerns underlying the clauses are similar. The equal protection clause traditionally has been used to protect minorities against injury that may be inflicted by the majority through suspect classification schemes. Minorities need such protection because of their lack of political power and representation. The privileges-and-immunities clause is also concerned with injury that could be inflicted upon persons who lack representation—nonresidents, who are disfranchised in states other than their own.

The privileges-and-immunities clause has been called a "specialized type of equal protection provision" (Nowak, 414). The equal protection clause is triggered by classification under a state law imposing some burden or disadvantage by reason of membership in a class, such as blacks, women, and certain businesses. The privileges-and-immunities clause is concerned specifically with classifications in state laws that burden persons because they are not citizens or residents of the state.

Courts use various standards for reviewing statutes that contain classifications. As noted above, if the Court is reviewing under the privileges-and-immunities clause a statute that discriminates against nonresidents in matters of fundamental concern for national unity, it will try to determine if the classification reasonably and substantially relates to legitimate state purposes. This substantial-reason test influenced the Court's development of standards of review under the equal protection clause, and similarities may be seen between standards of review under the two clauses.

The most lenient standard of review in equal-protection cases, the "rational basis" test, is employed when reviewing statutes that classify people for purposes of economic and social regulation. The classification will be upheld so long as it arguably relates to some legitimate function of government; much deference is given the state legislature in determining the solutions for the state's problems in matters of economic and social concern. Compared with the privileges-and-immunities standard, the rational-basis test is easier to pass because it is not difficult to construct some arguable relationship between the classification and the state's objective, even after the fact. Under the privileges-and-immunities standard, a close relationship is required between the class of nonresidents and a legitimate objective for the different treatment.

In equal-protection analysis, when a statute classifies persons in a way that burdens a fundamental right or when the classification distinguishes between persons on a suspect basis (such as race or national origin), regardless of whether a fundamental right is at stake, the standard of judicial review is strict, in effect shifting the presumption of validity. The statute will be upheld only if it is necessary to promote an extremely important or compelling state interest. If the state's objective could be achieved by other means not involving a suspect class or impinging upon a fundamental right, a review of the means least restrictive is required. Comparing the privileges-and-immunities standard with the "strict scrutiny" standard, the former is not as demanding as the latter. Under a strict scrutiny, there must be a "necessary" connection between the classification and the state objective; privileges-and-immunities review requires only a "substantial" connection, permitting greater deference to a state's interests. Furthermore, under strict scrutiny, a "compelling," rather than simply a "legitimate," state interest is required.

A third standard of review sometimes used by the Supreme Court in equal-protection analysis is an intermediate standard; the Court independently reviews the state law, not giving the utmost deference to the legislature, but the standard is not as rigorous as strict scrutiny. The main use for this standard is in review of gender-based classifications, although variations have been used in classifications based on alienage, illegitimacy, and sometimes age or handicapped status. The statute will be upheld when the government can demonstrate that the classification is "substantially related" to an "important governmental objective." This intermediate standard of review is probably closest to that employed in the privileges-and-immunities context, requiring, as it does, a "substantial relationship" between the classification and objective. In contrast, privileges-and-immunities analysis requires a "legitimate" state purpose in discriminating against nonresidents.

Several differences also exist between equal-protection and privileges-and-immunities analyses. The equal protection clause protects alien residents and corporations; the privileges-and-immunities clause protects only citizens of American states and natural persons (that is, individuals). Nonresidence and out-of-state citizenship have never been deemed suspect classifications under equal-protection analysis, but they are the very core of privileges-and-

immunities analysis. The equal protection clause concerns a much broader range of discrimination. Still, the two clauses do have the basic goal of ensuring equal treatment among persons included in classifications, although the specific concerns of each may differ.

THE FOURTEENTH AMENDMENT

The United States Supreme Court decided in the notorious *Dred Scott* v. *Sandford* (1857) that black persons were not protected under the privileges-and-immunities clause or under any other constitutional provisions, because they were not, nor could they ever be, citizens of the United States. Only citizens of states were protected as United States citizens. One of the contributing causes of the Civil War was the polarizing effect of the *Dred Scott* doctrine; the amendments sought in part to cure this defect to ensure national protection for all persons and to authorize constitutionally valid enforcement by the national government. The Fourteenth Amendment provides the following:

> *Section 1.* All persons born or naturalized in the United States, and subject to the jurisdiction thereof, are citizens of the United States and of the State wherein they reside. No State shall make or enforce any law which shall abridge the privileges or immunities of citizens of the United States; nor shall any State deprive any person of life, liberty, or property, without due process of law; nor deny to any person within its jurisdiction the equal protection of the laws.
> . . .
> *Section 5.* The Congress shall have power to enforce, by appropriate legislation, the provisions of this article.

The Civil War established the supremacy of the national government over the states, a concept reflected in the Fourteenth Amendment. For the first time, the amendment defined national citizenship as primary and not derivative of state citizenship. No longer dependent on state citizenship, national citizenship was dominant. It transformed the reciprocal duties of allegiance and protection into those between the citizens of the United States and their national government. The federal government was given specific power to protect certain fundamental rights of all United States citizens, whether black or white. States no longer were able to limit national protection only to those persons having state citizenship. Aimed mainly at protecting blacks who were not citizens of some slave states, the amendment was broader in its concept. The second clause seemed clearer than it turned out to be: "No State shall make or enforce any law which shall abridge the privileges or immunities of citizens of the United States." The terms *privileges* and *immunities* are the same as in the Article IV clause. The relationship between the two clauses, however, has never been entirely clear, nor was it clear whether the clause was meant to unify minimum substantive standards of protection as well as national status for protection.

William Crosskey has argued that there is no connection between the clauses other than a similarity in language. There is some evidence in congressional debates, however, that the Fourteenth Amendment privileges-or-immunities clause was intended to cure certain deficiencies in the Article IV clause, which protected rights for citizens only under state law. It became obvious after the Civil War that the southern states, at least, were not going to be generous in the rights granted to the freedmen. Indeed, discriminatory "black codes" were being enacted. The Article IV clause provided no protection to citizens against discrimination practiced by their own states; clearly, this was now a major problem. Also, some congressmen had doubts that the Congress had power under the Constitution or the Thirteenth Amendment to ensure that black persons would not be denied civil liberties openly by their states or tacitly by private groups under color of state law. The Fourteenth Amendment at least would provide that authority and enforcement power.

The congressional debates surrounding the civil rights bill of 1866, the Freedmen's Bureau bill, and the proposed Fourteenth Amendment show that the members of Congress saw a connection between the Article IV clause and the privileges-or-immunities clause of the Fourteenth Amendment. Many congressional Republicans believed that the southern states for years had violated the Article IV clause by abridging the privileges and immunities of blacks and of white northern citizens traveling in the South. Congressman John Broomall of Pennsylvania told the House of Representatives that "for

thirty years prior to 1860 everybody knows that the rights and immunities of citizens were habitually denied in certain states to the citizens of other states." Among the rights denied were the rights of speech, transit, and domicile; the right to sue; the writ of habeas corpus; and the right of petition. This disregard of these privileges and immunities, the Republicans felt, made the civil rights bill, the Freedmen's Bureau bill, and the Fourteenth Amendment necessary.

The speeches of the principal draftsman of the amendment, Congressman John Bingham of Ohio, and many of its other supporters indicate that the dominant opinion among them was that the Article IV clause guaranteed to United States citizens their fundamental rights in every state and that the Fourteenth Amendment was needed because the states had ignored the demand of Article IV. Some congressmen believed that the federal government had no power under the original Constitution to prevent these transgressions by the states. Section 5 of the amendment closed this gap in protection by declaring Congress's power to enforce the amendment's provisions by appropriate legislation.

The Fourteenth Amendment privileges-or-immunities clause, then, was to complement and fulfill the promise of its sister clause in Article IV. Article IV had been read only to afford protection to citizens of one state from incapacitating legislation by other states; the Fourteenth Amendment expanded this protection for all citizens so that citizens (and residents) could demand recognition of certain minimum rights by their home states as well. The Article IV clause demanded equality of privileges and immunities for citizens of all states in each state. The Fourteenth Amendment clause not only guaranteed equal protection of the laws for all United States citizens but provided a minimum substantive standard, whether by incorporating the Bill of Rights or by narrower privileges or immunities. The Fourteenth Amendment also resolved the comity problems that had arisen under the Article IV clause; for example, the former slaves were now citizens of the United States and so could demand respect for their privileges and immunities no matter where they traveled throughout the country. Blacks were also made citizens of the respective states in which they resided, so the states were obliged to recognize their rights of citizenship and to grant comity to black citizens of other states temporarily within their borders. Their own states also would have to treat them with the minimum privileges and immunities due, subject to federal enforcement. And, if blacks were protected against their own states, the same principle would apply to protect whites as well if these same privileges and immunities were denied them. That question, rather than the protection of blacks, presented the first test of the amendment in the *Slaughterhouse Cases* (1873).

While there was some agreement that the rights protected by the Article IV clause—and, by extension, by the privileges-or-immunities clause of the Fourteenth Amendment—were natural, fundamental rights, there was less agreement on what these specific rights were. Among those privileges and immunities widely accepted were life, liberty, property, the pursuit of happiness, and the rights enumerated in the Civil Rights Act. Senator Jacob M. Howard of Michigan believed all the personal rights in the first eight amendments to be included. Other legislators selected certain of these rights for inclusion but not others. The comprehensiveness of the language of the amendment and the views of its supporters convinced its opponents that the power of the federal government would now obliterate that of the states. They feared that the federal system was at an end and that in reality all that remained was to consolidate the national government. Even the opponents of the amendment recognized its great breadth of meaning, although their overstatement was a strategic attempt, no doubt, to narrow the outcome.

Within five years of ratification of the Fourteenth Amendment, the Supreme Court effectively nullified it, succumbing to the strategy. In the *Slaughterhouse Cases,* either the meaning of the amendment's privileges-or-immunities clause was lost or the Court intentionally refused to recognize it for fear of what it would mean to the federal system. This first case was an odd one to address issues under the Civil War Amendments. The Louisiana carpetbag legislature had passed a statute through corruption by a crass private pact among monopolists, creating a corporation and granting a monopoly to the corporation for the purpose of maintaining slaughterhouses within New Orleans parishes. This monopoly, created in part for public health reasons but mainly for practical reasons of market

efficiency in centralizing distribution and rebuilding industry, effectively excluded many butchers of long standing from their lawful calling. An association of these butchers challenged the statute as a violation of the Thirteenth and Fourteenth Amendments. The history of the *Slaughterhouse Cases* is complex but is important today in the search for a workable theory for limits on legislation and in the consideration of economic liberties once again.

This first test of the amendment was brought not by blacks, clearly its beneficiaries, but by southern whites, a curious turn of fate. The butchers' specific argument was that by granting a monopoly in slaughtering to the state-created corporation, the legislature had deprived them of the opportunity to pursue their own slaughtering businesses—that is, their "property"—and thereby had abridged a privilege or immunity belonging to them as United States citizens.

The Supreme Court ultimately found that the butchers' property interest or economic liberty was not a privilege or immunity of citizens of the United States protected from state action. The majority opinion by Justice Samuel Miller observed that the first sentence of the Fourteenth Amendment made a definite distinction between national and state citizenship. The privileges-or-immunities clause speaks only of privileges and immunities of citizens of the United States, not those of citizens of the several states. Rights such as those mentioned by Justice Washington in *Corfield* belonged to the individual as a citizen of the state; they were "the class of rights which the state governments were created to establish and secure." The Court refused to believe that the purpose of the privileges-or-immunities clause of the Fourteenth Amendment had been to transfer the protection of these rights from the states to the federal government. The consequences of such a contention, said the *Slaughterhouse* Court,

are so serious, so far-reaching and pervading, so great a departure from the structure and spirit of our institutions; when the effect is to fetter and degrade the State governments by subjecting them to the control of Congress, in the exercise of powers heretofore universally conceded to them of the most ordinary and fundamental character; when in fact it radically changes the whole theory of the relations of the State and

Federal governments to each other and of both these governments to the people; the argument has a force that is irresistible, in the absence of language which expresses such a purpose too clearly to admit of doubt.

The Court was "convinced that no such results were intended by the Congress which proposed these amendments, nor by the legislatures of the States which ratified them." The evident concern of the Court was the revolutionary change that a different interpretation of the Fourteenth Amendment would have worked in the federal system, transferring protection of basic rights to the federal government and giving Congress the affirmative power to protect those rights, not just a negative check on the states whenever they abridged the amendment. Yet, it is arguable, in light of the problem that prompted the amendment—continual and blatant violation of rights by the state governments—as well as the statements of the drafters of the amendment, that such a radical change is exactly what was intended.

If the privileges-and-immunities clause did not protect fundamental rights of United States citizens, what exactly did it protect? While declining to define the protected privileges and immunities in detail, the Court "venture[d] to suggest" some of them, "which owe their existence to the Federal government, its National character, its Constitution, or its laws." The Court quoted language from *Crandall* v. *Nevada* (1868) that the citizen has a right to approach the seat of government to assert any claims he may have upon the government, to transact business with it, to seek its protection, to share its offices, and to engage in administering its functions. The citizen also has the right of free access to the seaports, subtreasuries, land offices, and courts in the several states. Aside from those rights mentioned in *Crandall,* the citizen also has the privilege to demand the care and protection of the federal government over life, liberty, and property while on the high seas or within the jurisdiction of a foreign country. Furthermore, the Constitution guarantees the right to peaceably assemble and petition for redress of grievances and the writ of habeas corpus. Other rights enumerated by the *Slaughterhouse* Court included the right to use the navigable waters of the United States, rights secured by treaties with other nations, and the right to become a resident and citizen of any state.

While this list may at first glance seem impressive, the dissent of Justice Stephen Field in the *Slaughterhouse Cases* pointed out that if the clause refers only to those privileges and immunities "specially designated in the Constitution or necessarily implied as belonging to citizens of the United States, it was a vain and idle enactment, which accomplished nothing, and most unnecessarily excited Congress and the people on its passage." The states could never have interfered with such privileges and immunities, because of the supremacy of the Constitution and laws of the United States over those of the states. The privileges-or-immunities clause of the Fourteenth Amendment, under the Court's interpretation, added nothing to the protection of rights of American citizens.

An opportunity still existed for the Court to give the clause a more expansive interpretation. Certain of the rights mentioned in the *Slaughterhouse Cases* as being "privileges and immunities of citizens of the United States" were found in the first eight amendments—namely, the rights of free assembly and petition, and the privilege of the writ of habeas corpus. Before the *Slaughterhouse Cases,* in *Barron* v. *Baltimore* (1833), the Bill of Rights had been held not to apply to the states, and here was an opportunity to do what some later thought the Fourteenth Amendment clause was intended to do—reverse that wrongly decided case—but the Court did not even consider the meaning of the Fourteenth Amendment in light of *Barron.* Such an interpretation of the privileges-or-immunities clause would have avoided the later development of substantive due process and its criticism for improperly incorporating the Bill of Rights in a procedural clause.

The Court, however, has rejected all attempts to interpret the clause more expansively. The *Slaughterhouse Cases* majority did not believe the clause protected fundamental substantive rights against state intrusions. Later decisions continued to construe the "privileges and immunities of citizens of the United States" very narrowly. According to the Supreme Court in *United States* v. *Cruikshank* (1876), the rights of free assembly and petition were not protected under the clause unless the assembling related to matters of national concern or the petitioning was of the national government. The Court has determined at various times that the Seventh Amendment right of trial by jury in civil cases was not a privilege or immunity of national citizenship. Neither were the Fifth Amendment requirement of indictment or presentment in capital and otherwise infamous crimes, or the Sixth Amendment requirement of trial by jury in criminal prosecutions. The right to be confronted by witnesses and the exemption from compulsory self-incrimination have been held not to be privileges or immunities of United States citizenship. Nor was the right to vote in state elections protected.

The Court has articulated some privileges and immunities of national citizenship. Among these are the right to pass freely from state to state, the right to petition Congress for the redress of grievances, and the right to vote for national officers. Other rights that the Court has attributed to national citizenship include the right to enter public lands, the right to be protected against violence while in the custody of a United States marshal, and the right to inform the United States authorities of violation of its laws. While the Court recognized these rights as privileges and immunities of citizens of the United States, it did not rest its decisions specifically on the privileges-or-immunities clause. In only one case, *Colgate* v. *Harvey* (1935), did the Court hold a state statute invalid as a violation of the Fourteenth Amendment clause. The Court there held that the privilege to transact business, lend money, or make contracts anywhere in the country was a privilege of national citizenship protected by the clause. Five years later, the Court overruled *Colgate* in *Madden* v. *Kentucky,* finding the right to "carry on" incident to a trade, business, or calling not to be a privilege of national citizenship. As Justice Harlan Stone concluded in *Hague* v. *Committee for Industrial Organization* (1939), the privileges and immunities of United States citizens have been restricted to "those which arise or grow out of the relationship of United States citizens to the national government" a definition severely limiting their content.

Perhaps the most forthright discussion by the Court of its interpretation of the clause occurred in *Twining* v. *New Jersey* (1908). Counsel had tried to argue that the privileges and immunities of United States citizens protected against state action by the clause included the fundamental personal rights protected by the first eight amendments. The Court observed,

> There can be no doubt, so far as the decision in the *Slaughterhouse Cases* has determined the question, that the civil rights sometimes described as fundamental and inalienable, which before the war Amendments were enjoyed by state citizenship and protected by state government, were left untouched by this clause of the Fourteenth Amendment. Criticism of this case has never entirely ceased, nor has it ever received universal assent by members of this court. Undoubtedly, it gave much less effect to the Fourteenth Amendment than some of the public men active in framing it intended, and disappointed many others. On the other hand, if the views of the minority had prevailed it is easy to see how far the authority and independence of the States would have been diminished, by subjecting all their legislative and judicial acts to correction by the legislative and review by the judicial branch of the National Government.

This statement is about as close as the Court has come to admitting that the standard interpretation of the clause may be wrong. Nevertheless, the Court refused to take a fresh look at the clause, choosing instead to adhere strictly to precedent. Past decisions were the law and would stand, whether right or wrong.

SOME QUESTIONS FOR THE FUTURE

While the rights expressed in the first eight amendments, along with other personal rights such as the right of privacy, have not been found to be protected by the privileges-or-immunities clause, many of them have received protection against state action under other constitutional clauses, such as the due process and equal protection clauses. Those clauses have come to serve the function that some commentators thought were better served by the privileges-or-immunities clause of the Fourteenth Amendment. The courts found a way by judicial activism to protect personal rights against state action. With the privileges-or-immunities clause seemingly foreclosed as a vehicle, they turned to the other clauses of the Fourteenth Amendment, in spite of some difficulty in finding a substantive meaning in their language and anomalies that some critics thought were activist abuses of principled decision-making (Bobbitt, 151–153). It also took more than a century to evolve a structure for these substantive limitations. With the reaction against subjective activism, the question of whether the Fourteenth Amendment properly incorporated selected rights has reappeared, and a new interest in economic liberty and property is accompanying the reaction against Court-made constitutional law. How much simpler constitutional doctrine protecting personal rights might have been if the Supreme Court had held in *Barron* that the original Bill of Rights excluding Article I applied to the states or if the words of the privileges-or-immunities clause had been adopted as the principled basis for the national protection of basic rights of all United States citizens, whether by judicially construed limits or under congressional authority.

Some have begun to call for reconsideration of this clause as a basis for minimum rights of work, education, subsistence, and health care, to parallel a rapid development of international human rights policy on these matters. As we turn to a future where cooperative activity will require positive expectations of all states for minimum standards of living for all human beings, the moral stance of United States constitutional doctrine, especially reexamining privileges and immunities of national citizens in relating to national governments in an international community, will make the history and future opportunities of the Civil War Amendments worthy of rigorous scrutiny. Rather than debate whether to reverse the troublesome cases using the due process and equal protection clauses to incorporate Bill of Rights protections against state action, we should be debating whether the Supreme Court decided the *Slaughterhouse Cases* properly.

CASES

The Antelope, 10 Wheaton 66 (1825)
Austin v. New Hampshire, 420 U.S. 656 (1975)
Baldwin v. Fish and Game Commission of Montana, 436 U.S. 371 (1978)
Baldwin v. Seelig, 294 U.S. 511 (1935)
Barron v. Baltimore, 7 Peters 243 (1833)
Canadian Northern Railway v. Eggen, 252 U.S. 553 (1920)
Colgate v. Harvey, 296 U.S. 404 (1935)
Corfield v. Coryell, 6 F. Cas. 546 (C.C.E.D. Pa. 1823) (No. 3,230)
Crandall v. Nevada, 6 Wallace 35 (1868)
Dred Scott v. Sandford, 19 Howard 393 (1857)
Edwards v. California, 314 U.S. 160 (1941)
Hague v. Committee for Industrial Organization, 307 U.S. 496 (1939)
Hicklin v. Orbeck, 437 U.S. 518 (1978)
Madden v. Kentucky, 309 U.S. 83 (1940)
Paul v. Virginia, 8 Wallace 168 (1869)
Slaughterhouse Cases, 16 Wallace 36 (1873)
Supreme Court of New Hampshire v. Piper, 105 S. Ct. 1272 (1985)
Toomer v. Witsell, 334 U.S. 385 (1948)
Twining v. New Jersey, 211 U.S. 78 (1908)
United Building and Construction Trades Council v. Mayor of Camden, 104 S. Ct. 1020 (1984)
United States v. Cruikshank, 92 U.S. 542 (1876)

BIBLIOGRAPHY

Chester James Antieau, "Paul's Perverted Privileges or the True Meaning of the Privileges and Immunities Clause of Article Four," in *William and Mary Law Review*, 9 (1967), discusses the legislative history of the Fourteenth Amendment as it relates to the Article IV privileges-and-immunities clause. Philip Bobbitt, *Constitutional Fate* (1982), interprets the privileges-and-immunities clause of the Fourteenth Amendment as a limit on government rather than a source of substantive rights. William W. Crosskey, "Charles Fairman, 'Legislative History,' and the Constitutional Limitations on State Authority," in *University of Chicago Law Review*, 22 (1954), argues that the purpose of the Fourteenth Amendment clause was to make the Bill of Rights applicable to the states and was therefore unrelated to the purpose of the Article IV clause. William W. Crosskey and William Jeffrey, Jr., *Politics and the Constitution in the History of the United States*, 3 vols. (1953; 1980), argues historically that the privileges-and-immunities clause of the Fourteenth Amendment overturned *Barron* v. *Baltimore,* which held that the original Bill of Rights did not apply to the states. Franciscus de Victoria, *Reflections in Modern Theology,* in Classics of International Law series (1917), was the first exploration of the doctrine of state responsibility in relation to the treatment of North American Indians by the Spanish. John Hart Ely, *Democracy and Distrust: A Theory of Judicial Review* (1980), explains the functioning of the Article IV clause and suggests that the privileges and immunities protected by the Fourteenth Amendment clause are not limited to those enumerated in the Bill of Rights.

Charles Fairman, "Does the Fourteenth Amendment Incorporate the Bill of Rights?—The Original Understanding," in *Stanford Law Review*, 2 (1949), rejects the incorporation theory of the Bill of Rights under the privileges-and-immunities clause of the Fourteenth Amendment; and *Reconstruction and Reunion, 1864–1888, Part One,* vol. 6 of the Oliver Wendell Holmes Devise History of the Supreme Court of the United States (1971), reviews the historical facts and procedural background of the *Slaughterhouse Cases* in depth.

Daniel A. Farber and John E. Muench, "The Ideological Origins of the Fourteenth Amendment," in *Constitutional Commentary*, 1 (1934), describes some of the natural-law background of the Fourteenth Amendment debates. Max Farrand, *The Records of the Federal Convention of 1787*, 4 vols. (1911), discusses the Article IV clause and its relationship to its parent provision in the Articles of Confederation. Paul Finkelman, *An Imperfect Union: Slavery, Federalism, and Comity* (1981), extensively covers the breakdown of comity between the states over the slavery issue, with a thorough treatment of the slave transit issue and related cases. Mitchell Franklin, "The Foundations and Meaning of the *Slaughterhouse Cases*," in *Tulane Law Review*, 18 (1943), is an exhaustive economic and political history of the *Slaughterhouse Cases* and the political interpretation flowing from the conflict between the president and the radical wing of Congress.

Robert J. Kaczorowski, *The Politics of Judicial Interpretation: The Federal Courts, Department of Justice, and Civil Rights, 1866–1876* (1985), discusses the use of natural-rights theories in case law before and after the Fourteenth Amendment. Philip B. Kurland, "The Privileges or Immunities Clause: 'Its Hour Come Round At Last?'" in *Washington University Law Quarterly* (1972), discusses the inconclusive nature of the Fourteenth Amendment clause. John E. Nowak, Ronald D. Ro-tunda, and J. Nelson Young, *Constitutional Law*, 2nd ed. (1983), discusses the similarities and differences of the equal protection clause and the privileges-and-immunities clause. Donald Robinson, *Slavery in the Structure of American Politics, 1765–1820* (1971), discusses the drafting of the Article IV clause.

Cass R. Sunstein, "Naked Preferences and the Constitution," in *Columbia Law Review*, 84 (1984), argues that the privileges-and-immunities clauses restrain the allocation of naked preferences by legislatures. Jacobus ten Broek, *The Antislavery Origins of the Fourteenth Amendment* (1951), discusses the congressional debates regarding the Fourteenth Amendment. Laurence Tribe, *American Constitutional Law* (1978), discusses the Article IV clause, its judicial interpretation, and its relationship to both the commerce clause and the equal protection clause. Gordon S. Wood, *The Creation of the American Republic* (1969), develops a general history of the events leading to the creation of the Constitution and the framing of its provisions.

[*See also* ARTICLES OF CONFEDERATION; CHASE AND WAITE COURTS AND ERAS; COMMERCE CLAUSE; CONSTITUTIONAL INTERPRETATION; DUE PROCESS OF LAW; EQUAL PROTECTION CLAUSE; FRAMING THE CONSTITUTION; MARSHALL COURT AND ERA; *and* SEX EQUALITY UNDER THE CONSTITUTION.]

RACIAL DISCRIMINATION AND EQUAL OPPORTUNITY

Charles M. Lamb

STUDENTS of the judicial system agree that racial minorities in America have historically experienced various kinds of discrimination. Before the 1950s, racial inequality prevailed in much of the nation, despite occasional antidiscrimination decisions by the United States Supreme Court. Since the 1950s, however, the Supreme Court has often played a crucial civil rights role, affecting both law and social policy. Indeed, in few other areas of law has Supreme Court policymaking been more manifest and pronounced since the 1950s. The Warren Court demonstrated an unprecedented judicial commitment to combat racial discrimination. The Burger Court had a more mixed record, but on balance it, too, supported the legal rights of racial minorities. This has meant dramatic changes since the watershed case of *Brown* v. *Board of Education* (1954), in which the Warren Court embraced the position that segregation in public schools is unconstitutional. For example, a striking break with the past is reflected in the removal by the Court of key impediments to minority voting rights and equal access to public accommodations. Yet, discrimination based on race still persists, especially in education, employment, and housing.

Linked with attempts to combat racial discrimination is the idea that minorities should receive equal opportunity. Equality of opportunity has emerged as a principal component of the law of discrimination as courts have attempted to resolve controversies over its meaning and scope. Considerable legal and political debate swirls around difficult issues such as school desegregation and busing, affirmative action in employment and higher education, and provision of more housing opportunities for minorities in predominantly white communities. The Warren and Burger Courts found a denial of equal opportunity in a number of cases as a result of constitutional or statutory violations. Most of these decisions have involved blacks, for they were the litigants in the vast majority of these cases. Other racial groups have of course encountered unjust discrimination in the United States, but far fewer Supreme Court decisions have arisen from their mistreatment.

Just as efforts to overcome discrimination and to promote equal opportunity largely explain how minorities have fared in the past, so, too, will they profoundly affect their future plight. The areas of education, employment, and housing are particularly important, and failure to recognize and enforce legal rights in one has a marked impact on the other two. Their interlocking nature is not difficult to understand. Because many minority-group members receive weak schooling, they cannot find good jobs; without such jobs they often cannot afford to live in better neighborhoods; and because they often live in less desirable communities, they are less likely than whites to have access to good schools. Thus, there exists a self-perpetuating circle of discrimination, rooted in public policies and private practices, that decreases the prospect for a better life for minorities. Additionally, this circle of discrimination is linked to other problems such as poverty, poor health, feelings of inferiority, and inadequate government benefits and services. Because illegal practices in one of these areas often have consequences for the other two, the courts—particularly the Supreme Court—must deter discrimination in education, employment, and housing. That responsibility is also shared by the legislative and executive branches because of their constitutional duties and policymaking roles.

RACIAL DISCRIMINATION AND EQUAL OPPORTUNITY

HISTORICAL BACKGROUND

Since the largest number of race-related discrimination and equal-opportunity decisions by the Supreme Court has involved blacks, one must understand their legal status prior to the Court's pathbreaking decision in *Brown.* Racial inequality in its most extreme form in the United States may be traced to the institution of slavery, under which blacks had no legal rights. Many black Americans' ancestors were taken by force from Africa in the seventeenth and eighteenth centuries, brought to North America in captivity, and sold into slavery mainly in the southern colonies. At first, some blacks were legally free or were indentured servants, but as slavery spread in the South, even blacks who had possessed some legal rights found themselves in a position of virtual subjugation. Relatively little strong opposition to slavery existed prior to the American Revolution, except that posed by several small abolitionist groups. As the leaders of the Revolution began to fight for their independence in the name of the "inalienable rights of all men," inevitably they were confronted by the blatant hypocrisy of refusing to extend even the most fundamental rights to slaves.

While some states outlawed slavery after the Revolution, the Constitution of 1787 did not give slaves anything like the legal rights enjoyed by whites. Indeed, the Constitution bestowed legitimacy on the institution of slavery, though not mentioning it by name. Slaves ("all other persons") were to be counted as only three-fifths of "free" persons for purposes of representation and taxation under Article I, Section 2. Article I, Section 9 permitted the slave trade to continue for at least two decades without congressional restrictions, while Article IV, Section 2 required that fugitive slaves be returned to their owners. The influence of the southern delegations to the Constitutional Convention is clearly evident in these provisions. Yet, most of those who wrote the Constitution were not neutral on the issue of slavery, and the seeds were sown for a fierce political battle over abolition that would be resolved only by the Civil War. During the period before the war, the Supreme Court consistently upheld the rights of slaveholders. In its most infamous decision, *Dred Scott* v. *Sandford* (1857), the Court declared that slaves were not citizens under the Constitution and therefore possessed none of the rights of citizens.

Three amendments of critical civil rights importance were added to the Constitution after the Civil War. The Thirteenth Amendment abolished slavery, and the Fifteenth Amendment guaranteed the right to vote irrespective of race, color, or previous servitude. It is the Fourteenth Amendment, however, that has proven to be the most important of the three in promoting basic legal equality for minorities. Its most momentous provision states,

> All persons born or naturalized in the United States, and subject to the jurisdiction thereof, are citizens of the United States and of the State wherein they reside. No State shall make or enforce any law which shall abridge the privileges or immunities of citizens of the United States; nor shall any State deprive any person of life, liberty, or property, without due process of law; nor deny to any person within its jurisdiction the equal protection of the laws.

The realized and potential significance of these two sentences, and particularly of the equal protection clause, for safeguarding fundamental racial equality as a matter of legal right in the United States cannot be overstated.

Supreme Court decisions examined in the following pages make it apparent that two legal systems operated in the United States from the post–Civil War period to the 1950s. Outside the South, the rights of blacks were recognized by government, although discrimination did occur. Such discrimination was usually covert in nature and is referred to as de facto discrimination—that is, discrimination that existed in fact but was not required by law. In the South, de jure discrimination—that is, discrimination stipulated by law—was common. But even where not required by law, separation of the races and differences in their treatment were deeply entrenched in state and local practices throughout the nation. These legal and political realities ultimately led to Supreme Court intervention.

EDUCATION

Progress toward overcoming racial discrimination in education is reflected in a line of Supreme Court decisions, most of which addressed different facets of school desegregation. As in employment and housing discrimination, these cases largely involved black litigants, but the legal standards derived from them generally apply to other racial minorities as well. Before these decisions, state-supported segregation in elementary and secondary schools was widespread. Nor did the 1954 *Brown* decision lead to the immediate abandonment of segregation. To illustrate, in the early 1960s less than 5 percent of black pupils throughout the South attended school with whites, although border states such as Delaware and Missouri had partly desegregated school systems. After implementation of these Court decisions in the 1960s, however, desegregation proceeded rapidly. By 1970, between 75 percent and 93 percent of black students in southern states were attending school with whites.

These dramatic changes in school desegregation during the 1960s cannot be attributed solely to Supreme Court policy. Congress passed some critical statutes that had a significant impact, such as the Civil Rights Act of 1964. President Lyndon Johnson and his administration also pushed to implement desegregation. But the Supreme Court played a key role because it acted long before the other branches, setting standards for both government and society. Had the Court's breakthrough policies not emerged when they did, progress toward desegregation would undoubtedly have been delayed many years.

To understand this progress, one must begin with the case of *Plessy* v. *Ferguson* (1896). Although *Plessy* did not directly involve the question of school desegregation, it did establish the legal concept of "separate but equal," which stood as a barrier to educational desegregation for nearly six decades. According to this doctrine, racial minorities could be legally segregated from whites if their treatment was equal to that afforded whites—which was very seldom the case. The Supreme Court specifically held in *Plessy* that a Louisiana statute requiring separate but equal railroad accommodations for blacks and whites was not a violation of either the Thirteenth or the Fourteenth Amendment. The Court majority stressed that the Thirteenth Amendment applied strictly to slavery and that the Louisiana law imposed a burden, not servi-

tude. "Separate but equal" accommodations did not "constitute badges of slavery or servitude," according to the majority, or if they did, "it is not by reason of anything found in the act, but solely because the colored race chooses to put that construction on it."

The Court opinion also asserted that the Fourteenth Amendment's equal protection clause required only political, not social, equality. States therefore had the right under their police power—the power to promote the public good—to separate blacks and whites if the traditions and customs of the states indicated that such a law was not unreasonable. In a passing reference to states that maintained separate schools for blacks and whites, the Court majority suggested that educational segregation was a reasonable exercise of the police power. Justice John Marshall Harlan took the dissenting position that "in view of the Constitution, in the eye of the law, there is in this country no superior, dominant, ruling class of citizens. . . . Our Constitution is color-blind."

Once the Court had adopted the separate-but-equal doctrine for public railroad accommodations, a majority of the justices increasingly accepted an extension of the *Plessy* principle to permit segregated public schools where the constitutionality of the separate-but-equal doctrine was not directly challenged in litigation. By the late 1930s and early 1940s, however, President Franklin Roosevelt's new appointments substantially altered the Court's conservative orientation, and so changes in constitutional policymaking were beginning to emerge.

A fundamental problem with the separate-but-equal doctrine, as indicated above, was that the treatment afforded blacks was virtually never equal to that afforded whites. Given this glaring reality, in *Missouri ex rel. Gaines* v. *Canada* (1938) a more liberal Supreme Court departed somewhat from prior decisional trends. Here the Court invalidated a Missouri statute that prohibited blacks from attending the University of Missouri Law School, even though the statute provided tuition payments for blacks to study law in neighboring states where segregation was not enforced. Missouri thus could not abdicate its responsibility to provide public legal education to qualified black students by making agreements with other states. Similarly, in *Sipuel* v. *Board of Regents of the University of Oklahoma*

RACIAL DISCRIMINATION AND EQUAL OPPORTUNITY

(1948), the Court held that a qualified black woman was denied equal protection when refused admission to the Law School of the University of Oklahoma solely on the ground of race.

These decisions, which struck down racial segregation in state law schools without reconsidering the constitutionality of the separate-but-equal rule, were extended in two 1950 decisions also pertaining to higher education, *McLaurin* v. *Oklahoma State Regents* and *Sweatt* v. *Painter.* In *Sweatt,* the more notable of the two, the Court ruled that it was difficult, if not impossible, for a state to meet the separate-but-equal requirement where there were disparities in vital tangible and intangible aspects of education. Thus, a new state law school exclusively for blacks but not substantially equal in terms of tangible qualities (faculty, library, and courses offered) and intangible qualities (the school's reputation and prestige) did not meet the minimum expectations of separate-but-equal under *Plessy.* Clearly, then, by 1950 the Court was underscoring the "equal" component of *Plessy* and casting doubt on the continued existence of racial separation in public elementary and secondary schools.

Equal educational opportunity for racial minorities then took its most profound step forward in the Warren Court's landmark 1954 decision in *Brown* v. *Board of Education (Brown I).* Here the justices first directly reconsidered the separate-but-equal concept as it pertained to elementary and secondary education, sounding its death knell as part of American constitutional law. *Brown* grew out of cases involving de jure school segregation in four states but ultimately applied to public elementary and secondary education nationwide. Like many black students, Linda Brown had been denied by law the right to attend white schools in her hometown. The Court, permitting extensive oral arguments, addressed in *Brown* one of the most explosive and emotion-laden legal questions of the 1950s, formulated by the Court in these words: "Does segregation of children in public schools solely on the basis of race, even though the physical facilities and other 'tangible' factors may be equal, deprive the children of the minority group of equal educational opportunity?"

The justices unanimously answered in the affirmative, sparking what is often referred to as the civil rights "revolution" of the 1950s and 1960s. Chief Justice Earl Warren's short opinion took the position that on the basis of findings of various social science studies, school segregation creates feelings of inferiority in black children and retards their intellectual motivation and development. Reversing *Plessy* in no uncertain terms, Warren concluded that under the equal protection clause, segregation in state-supported elementary and secondary schools could no longer be tolerated, "that in the field of public education the doctrine of 'separate but equal' has no place. Separate educational facilities are inherently unequal."

Therefore, educational segregation was unconstitutional even though the facilities and other tangible characteristics of black and white schools might in fact be equal. The most apparent reasons for this striking change in Supreme Court policy were the directions taken by the higher-education cases leading up to *Brown,* the fact that many members of the Warren Court were generally more liberal and inclined to activism than justices of earlier decades, and the brilliant leadership of Earl Warren, who ably forged the unanimity in *Brown* that was obviously necessary to secure public acceptance of school desegregation.

Chief Justice Warren and his colleagues realized that their decision in *Brown* would be immensely difficult to carry out, particularly in the South. Sensitive to the complexities inherent in desegregation and aware that considerable time would be required for implementation, the Court did not immediately order school desegregation but, instead, directed the plaintiffs and other interested parties to come before it again during the following term to argue how the new standard should be effectuated. In the 1955 follow-up case of *Brown* v. *Board of Education (Brown II),* Warren again authored the Court's unanimous opinion, which accepted a slow, ad hoc approach to desegregating public schools. The Court gave local school authorities the responsibility to "make a prompt and reasonable start toward full compliance" and directed the federal district courts to determine whether school officials were making a "good-faith implementation." But, fatefully, and more important, the district courts were also to recognize the practical problems that schools would encounter in desegregation, which was required only to take place "with all deliberate speed," not within a specified period. This "all deliberate speed" standard permitted hundreds of schools to delay desegregation for well over a decade, though it seemed essential at the time in light of the political, social, and legal upheaval caused by *Brown I.* Given the flexibility inherent in the *Brown II* implementation directive, lower federal court judges in the South witnessed myriad efforts to delay or circumvent desegregation.

The Warren Court subsequently avoided accepting cases that would require its direct involvement in dismantling segregated schools. The major exception was *Cooper* v. *Aaron* (1958), where authorities in Arkansas refused to comply with district court desegregation decisions and violence threatened the educational process. *Cooper* unanimously reaffirmed *Brown I,* stressing that state governors, legislatures, and courts could not nullify the 1954 decision either directly or indirectly. Nonetheless, only token desegregation had occurred in much of the South a decade after *Brown I,* and additional Supreme Court directives became necessary.

Gradually the Court was forced to reenter the arena. In 1964 it noted that "the time for mere deliberate speed had run out" *(Griffin* v. *School Board of Prince Edward County).* In 1969 the justices unanimously stated that " 'all deliberate speed' for desegregation is no longer constitutionally permissible. . . . The obligation of every school district is to terminate dual school systems at once and to operate now and hereafter only unitary school systems" *(Alexander* v. *Holmes County Board of Education).* These decisions clearly indicated that the Court had lost its patience with the countless delaying tactics used throughout most of the South after *Brown.*

School desegregation continued to experience a number of obstacles, however, and with the advent of the Burger Court in 1969 a volatile new issue had emerged: court-ordered busing of students to eliminate segregated schools. The Burger Court, which proved to be more reluctant than the Warren Court to initiate major social change, became involved in the question as federal district courts ordered bus transportation in certain cases to alleviate intentional segregation.

The first case to draw the Burger Court directly into the busing controversy was *Swann* v. *Charlotte-Mecklenburg Board of Education* (1971).

Charlotte, North Carolina, had once legally required separate schools for blacks, and the school board had failed over the years to develop a plan that would have allowed roughly half of Charlotte's black students to attend school with whites. Facing an unquestionable intent to discriminate, the federal district court in the end stipulated a specific racial balance for individual schools—71 percent white students to 29 percent black, which reflected the racial composition of the entire school system—and ordered busing to effectuate this balance.

The Burger Court unanimously upheld the limited use of both a mathematical ratio and busing, by recognizing broad equitable powers for federal district courts to remedy purposeful discrimination. A specific balance reflecting the racial makeup of the entire school district was not necessitated by the Constitution, said the majority opinion, but such a requirement could be imposed by a district court under the circumstances in Charlotte. The Court also decided that constitutionally, busing was "one tool of school desegregation. Desegregation plans cannot be limited to the walk-in school." In other words, although it was desirable for children to attend the school nearest their homes, because of an obvious history of uncorrected racial separation, remedies that placed children in more-distant schools could be required by lower federal courts. The Burger Court added, however, that busing should not be mandated if the time and distance involved presented a risk to a child's health or to the educational process.

The *Swann* decision applied only to school segregation required or permitted by law, as was that found in the South, but the busing remedy was extended to northern segregation in *Keyes* v. *School District No. 1, Denver* (1973). Blacks and Hispanics in Denver's central city had long been segregated from whites, and a black neighborhood had expanded to an adjacent white area known as Park Hill. By techniques such as gerrymandering attendance zones, the school board had prevented desegregation of the Park Hill schools. The Court ruled that the use of such techniques constituted intentional segregation by a governmental body and that it could be remedied by a federal district court through busing. Thus, the Burger Court majority seemed to expand the traditional meaning of de jure segregation by indicating that it may exist wherever there is intent to segregate, even if statutes requiring or permitting separation by race had never been enacted, as was the case in Colorado. This position triggered separate opinions by two justices who contended that the distinction between de jure and de facto segregation was no longer viable. The Court's opinion also held that desegregation might be required throughout the school district even though segregation was evident only in substantial portions of it, because discriminatory actions have an impact beyond the schools specifically segregated. When a school board sanctions an intentional policy of segregation in a sizable portion of a school district, the Court majority asserted, the board has the burden of proving that its policies in the rest of the district are not motivated by an intent to segregate and do not contribute to existing segregation.

Less complicated than *Keyes* was the 1974 case of *Milliken* v. *Bradley (Milliken I),* the next prominent Burger Court decision concerning educational desegregation and busing. In *Milliken* the Court addressed the question of whether the equal protection clause could require busing between different school districts (unlike *Swann* and *Keyes,* which had involved only single districts). The claim in *Milliken* was that illegal segregation in Detroit's school system was caused by actions by local and state officials and that desegregation required busing children between the predominantly black city schools and the overwhelmingly white suburban schools outside Detroit.

The federal district court had ordered cross-district busing between the city and the suburbs, but the Burger Court reversed for two reasons. First, it had not been demonstrated that district lines were drawn on the basis of racial considerations; and second, unconstitutional segregation in any school district had not been shown to have a significant effect on segregation in an adjacent district. The majority opinion therefore emphasized that "before the boundaries of separate and autonomous school districts may be set aside by consolidating the separate units for remedial purposes or by imposing a cross-district remedy, it must first be shown that there has been a constitutional violation within one district that produces a significant segregative effect in another district." These requirements have been met in some cases since *Milliken,* and the Supreme Court has upheld some cross-district busing ordered by lower federal courts.

Other education cases deserve brief attention. *Lau* v. *Nichols* (1974), a major decision involving bilingual education, required school districts to provide instruction in the native language for non-English-speaking pupils. *Pasadena City Board of Education* v. *Spangler* (1976) held that a specific ratio for the racial mix in a desegregating school system need not be adjusted each year because of population shifts so long as the school board had not assigned students on the basis of race. In the 1977 *Milliken* v. *Bradley (Milliken II)* decision, the Court upheld a lower court order for remedial education programs, such as remedial reading and student counseling, to make amends for past segregation. *Dayton Board of Education* v. *Brinkman* (1979) ruled that there may be a causal relationship between current segregation and past attempts by school boards to segregate and that compliance by school boards could be determined in the future by the effectiveness of their actions to eliminate segregation. In *Washington* v. *Seattle School District No. 1* (1982) the Court ruled against a state initiative that prohibited school boards from assigning pupils to schools for racial purposes, holding that the initiative overly burdened those advocating desegregation; but in *Crawford* v. *Board of Education of Los Angeles* (1982) the justices upheld a state referendum forbidding state courts from ordering busing to desegregate schools unless it was required to remedy a violation of the equal protection clause.

Affirmative action as a means for achieving equal opportunity in higher education goes beyond the issues examined thus far. Affirmative action involves the use of race-conscious actions to provide some degree of preferential treatment to minorities to compensate for past discrimination. *De Funis* v. *Odegaard* (1974) was the first case in which affirmative action in higher education might have been substantively addressed by the Supreme Court. De Funis, a white, had twice been denied admission to the University of Washington Law School, which had developed an affirmative-action program to recruit minority students. Since minority applicants were accepted to the law school who had weaker academic credentials than his, De Funis claimed he had been denied equal protection. The Court, however, dodged the issue by ruling that the case was moot, since a state court had earlier ordered the admission of De Funis, and by 1974 he was about to graduate from the University of Washington Law School. Presumably in 1974 the Court was still very reluctant to make a firm decision involving racial quotas in higher education.

While not establishing precedent, *De Funis* set the stage for the key affirmative-action case in education decided by the Supreme Court by the mid-1980s, *Regents of the University of California* v. *Bakke* (1978). It arose when Bakke, a white applicant, was twice denied admission to the Medical School of the University of California at Davis. The school's admissions procedure included a set-aside quota that reserved sixteen of one hundred entering places for minorities. Bakke alleged that the denial of his opportunity to compete for these seats violated his rights under the equal protection clause and the 1964 Civil Rights Act. Although the justices were thoroughly divided, a majority agreed that Bakke must be admitted to the school but also that institutions of higher education may rely on admissions procedures designed to promote affirmative action as long as quotas are not used.

Justice Lewis F. Powell's opinion was pivotal in *Bakke*. He reasoned that although the Fourteenth Amendment requires equality of opportunity, it does not require equality of results. Equal opportunity must be provided to all, without regard to race or color. Thus, although affirmative action is permissible, an admissions quota for minorities is legally unacceptable. Ultimately, according to Powell, the quota in *Bakke* could not be justified on the grounds that a small percentage of minority applicants were accepted to medical schools, that the quota helped to counteract the effects of past societal discrimination, that the quota would tend to increase the number of physicians practicing medicine in underserved minority communities, or that the quota promoted a more racially diverse student body. Therefore, for Powell, as for a majority of the justices, race could be one factor considered in admissions policy, but not the decisive factor.

EMPLOYMENT

Racial discrimination has long existed in the American job market. Minorities have been poorly represented in prestigious professions such as medicine and law, in part because of discrimination in higher education. Various forms of discrimination have also hindered access to the more numerous but less prestigious jobs that require little or no higher education. In the 1970s, whites were almost twice as likely as blacks to be employed as white-collar workers, with blacks more often found in blue-collar or service positions. Furthermore, blacks who find jobs often encounter discrimination in promotions and seniority. Frequently, as suggested by Supreme Court decisions, minority-group members were simply passed over for advancement or transfers to higher-paying jobs for which they were qualified, and seniority plans have also tended to favor whites. The combined impact of discrimination in hiring, promotions, and seniority, as well as high rates of unemployment, have kept many minorities on the lower rungs of the American economic ladder. The median income for all black families in 1964 was only half that of white families, and that figure had increased by only 8 percent to 10 percent in the early 1980s. These income disparities have in turn significantly limited the access of many minorities to better education and housing.

In contrast to education, where Warren Court decisions initially led the federal government into the fight against discrimination, executive and congressional leadership was evident in the early stages of combating unfair employment practices. For example, President Franklin Roosevelt, by an executive order of 1941, created the Fair Employment Practices Committee to help fight job discrimination by defense contractors; President Harry Truman, by an executive order of 1948, established the Fair Employment Board within the United States Civil Service Commission to affirm that equal opportunity would be required in federal employment; and President Lyndon Johnson, by an executive order of 1965, set up the Office of Federal Contract Compliance in the Department of Labor to prevent discrimination at the work sites of contractors and subcontractors responsible for federally supported projects. These and other presidents have exercised leadership to promote fairness in both federal employment and those parts of the private sector engaged in work funded by the federal government, as well as establishing boards, offices, and committees for equal-employment enforcement, research, and advice.

That these presidential initiatives served a purpose is undeniable, although they were often symbolic gestures with ephemeral and limited consequences. Just as undeniable is the real and lasting importance of Title VII of the Civil Rights Act of 1964, the leading weapon in the federal legal arsenal to deter job discrimination. Title VII forbids employment discrimination on the grounds of race, color, religion, sex, or national origin by private employers, labor unions, and employment agencies. Title VII also created the Equal Employment Opportunity Commission (EEOC) to carry out many requirements of the law, giving it the power to investigate job-discrimination complaints, to seek to conciliate such disputes, and to refer cases of discrimination to the Department of Justice for lawsuits on behalf of the federal government. In 1972, Congress passed amendments to Title VII that gave the EEOC the power to take cases directly to federal court without having to rely on the Justice Department and broadened the scope of the original legislation to include employees of state and local governments, private employers and unions with at least fifteen employees or members, and persons working for private or public educational institutions.

Although presidents and Congress took the lead, the Supreme Court has handled certain types of employment-discrimination cases since at least the 1940s. Early on, the Court prohibited unfair employment practices by labor unions based on its interpretation of federal labor-relations statutes. In *Steele* v. *Louisville & Nashville Railroad* (1944), a union and an employer had agreed on a contract under which blacks' opportunities for employment as firemen had been restricted. The Court declared that labor legislation forbade unions from participating in such forms of discrimination. A union must represent all of its members equally and has "the duty to exercise fairly the power conferred upon it in behalf of all those for whom it acts, without hostile discrimination against them." The concept of fair representation by unions became noteworthy and was subsequently extended in other cases. Beyond labor-relations statutes, the Court has upheld the basic employment rights of minorities under other legislation, such as the Civil Rights Act of 1866. As one aspect of *Jones*

v. *Alfred H. Mayer Co.* (1968), for example, the Court explained that the 1866 act ensures the same basic rights for blacks and whites to contract for work.

But in contrast to the Court's approach to discrimination in education and housing, it was not until the early 1970s that the Court began to announce its leading equal-employment decisions. The main reason for this delay was that many of these cases involved rights created under statutory law, not the Constitution, and before Title VII, there was no comprehensive federal statute explicitly designed to ban job discrimination throughout most of the economy. Fair-employment provisions existed in various federal laws but received relatively little emphasis in litigation accepted by the Court for decision. For several years after the passage of Title VII, the Warren Court also relied heavily on the lower federal courts to interpret the new law. Consequently, it was the Burger Court that forged judicial policy in equal employment.

The Burger Court's first celebrated decision in this area was *Griggs* v. *Duke Power Co.* (1971). In *Griggs,* black employees of the Duke Power Company of North Carolina presented a Title VII challenge to the company's ostensibly neutral requirements for a high school diploma or an acceptable grade on an intelligence test for both new employees and job transfers. As in many cases, job transfers in this instance were equivalent to promotions because they involved higher-paying positions and better working conditions. Diploma and testing requirements are used by many employers to predict the general abilities of job applicants. However, Title VII specifically prohibits practices that limit or classify persons in such a way as to affect adversely their employment opportunities on grounds of race, color, religion, sex, or national origin. Clearly the diploma and intelligence-test requirements had a disproportionately negative impact on black employment opportunities because of past segregation in North Carolina's public schools, the fact that nearly three times as many of the state's white males completed high school than did black males, and the fact that whites were ten times more likely than blacks to make acceptable scores on the standardized intelligence tests administered by the company. Most important, the diploma and test requirements were not demonstrably and reasonably related to the abilities or skills necessary for successful performance on the jobs in question, and the Duke Power Company had a long record of discrimination in hiring blacks and refusing to transfer them to certain jobs after they had been hired.

The Court held that Title VII prohibited practices that may be neutral on their face but have a discriminatory effect. In other words, discriminatory intent did not have to be proven for Title VII to be violated. The majority opinion stated, "Good intent or absence of discriminatory intent does not redeem employment procedures or testing mechanisms that operate as 'built-in headwinds' for minority groups," and "Congress directed the thrust of [Title VII] to the *consequences* of employment practices, not simply motivation." Hence, the Court unanimously accepted the so-called effect test regarding Title VII, but no constitutional question was addressed.

The outcome of the case probably would have been different if the Duke Power Company had been able to demonstrate that the diploma and intelligence-test requirements were directly job-related. The Court's opinion consequently noted that "the touchstone is business necessity. If an employment practice which operates to exclude Negroes cannot be shown to be related to job performance, the practice is prohibited." The legal standards suggested in *Griggs* have been refined in numerous cases since 1971 as litigants in fair-employment controversies have sought to clarify their rights relative to valid tests in light of "business necessity" and how statistics may be used to show disparate impact or treatment.

Title VII was the legal anchor for *Griggs*, but the Constitution was the focal point in the watershed case of *Washington* v. *Davis* (1976). This challenge under the due process clause of the Fifth Amendment concerned a written qualifying examination that was originally developed by the United States Civil Service Commission and was required for police recruitment training in the District of Columbia. Four times as many blacks as whites failed the test. The court of appeals, relying on *Griggs*, held that the examination's disproportionate impact was sufficient to establish a constitutional violation and thus it was not necessary for the black litigants to prove intent to discriminate.

The Burger Court reversed, ruling that the legal standard that the lower court used was appropriate for Title VII claims, as in *Griggs*, but not for those brought under the Fifth and Fourteenth Amendments. In other words, the Court majority held that to make an acceptable employment-discrimination claim under the Constitution, it was not enough to show that a law or practice had a disparate discriminatory effect. Although disproportionate impact and other relevant facts in a case may suggest intent, to reach the conclusion that a law or practice is unconstitutional requires proof that there was a specific intent to discriminate in the official conduct of those who framed the law or were responsible for administering it. The majority opinion explained, "Our cases have not embraced the proposition that a law or other official act, without regard to whether it reflects a racially discriminatory purpose, is unconstitutional *solely* because it has a racially disproportionate impact."

Furthermore, in the eyes of the Court majority in *Davis*, the police recruit examination was sufficiently related to the job to be performed that no denial of equal employment was evident, and the District of Columbia Police Department had in fact made efforts to recruit black officers. Nor did the Court stop here. Its opinion pointed out that in at least seventeen cases the lower federal courts had relied on the effect test in finding a constitutional violation, and the Court noted its clear disagreement. The Court also indicated that the process of validating tests for measuring the likelihood of successful job performance is not a simple one, a point that has predictably led to additional cases raising this difficult issue. But the lasting importance of *Davis* lies in the Court's insistence on the need to show intent, and as will be seen, this strict constitutional standard was later applied to fair-housing litigation.

Several other fair-employment decisions that suggest the diversity of issues brought before the Burger Court during the 1970s and 1980s need to be mentioned briefly. In *McDonnell Douglas Corp.* v. *Green* (1973) the Court ruled that under Title VII a complainant may establish a prima facie case of racial discrimination by demonstrating that he or she is a member of a racial minority, that the complainant had applied for a job opening and was denied it despite adequate qualifications, and that the position remained unfilled while the employer continued to seek applicants with the same qualifications as the complainant. In *Albemarle Paper Co.* v. *Moody* (1975) the Court decided that where Title VII had been violated, back pay cannot be denied if the employer's discriminatory actions conflicted with the statute's basic goals of deterring racial discrimination and remedying injuries resulting from past discrimination. *McDonald* v. *Santa Fe Trail Transportation Co.* (1976) announced that whites are protected by Title VII, and employers must apply the same standards in firing white and minority employees. In *International Brotherhood of Teamsters* v. *United States* (1977) the Court said that a seniority system, otherwise neutral on its face, did not violate Title VII even though it perpetuated discrimination practiced against minority truck drivers prior to the passage of Title VII.

In *Hazelwood School District* v. *United States* (1977), the Court decided that a prima facie case of discrimination may be based on statistical evidence demonstrating an obvious imbalance in the racial composition of the faculty of a school when compared to the racial makeup of the general community population. *California Brewers Assn.* v. *Bryant* (1980) upheld a seniority plan as legal under Title VII even though it favored permanent employee categories from which blacks had often been excluded. And in *American Tobacco Co.* v. *Patterson* (1982), the Court said that the intent test applied to discrimination claims involving seniority systems adopted before and after the passage of Title VII. On balance, these cases indicate the variety of equal-employment controversies appealed to the Burger Court and its mixed record on decisions for and against claims made by racial minorities.

After the mid-1970s, an increasing number of Burger Court cases involved the widely debated issue of affirmative action in employment. Four of these cases, decided between 1976 and 1984, will be discussed here because of their importance. In *Franks* v. *Bowman Transportation Co.* (1976) the Court confronted a Title VII controversy in which the employer had discriminated against black applicants for jobs as truck drivers and against black employees wishing to transfer within the company to more desirable positions. The lower federal courts found in favor of the black litigants, ordering that they be given preference in future job openings. The Burger Court went beyond this form of preferential treatment and ruled that retroactive seniority could be awarded to racial minorities who had been discriminated against in violation of Title VII. A major objective of Title VII, the Court majority noted, is to provide appropriate compensation for those injured because of discrimination in the workplace. One way to compensate justly is to provide retroactive seniority, and "federal courts are empowered to fashion such relief as the particular circumstances of a case may require to effect restitution." Although the Court said that the awarding of retroactive seniority may not be called for in some cases, neither is it an impermissibly extreme form of preference to compensate for past discrimination, as decisions of the National Labor Relations Board suggest.

One of the most historic affirmative-action decisions in employment in the 1970s was *United Steelworkers of America* v. *Weber* (1979). In this case an on-the-job affirmative-action agreement was collectively bargained by the Kaiser Aluminum and Chemical Corporation and the United Steelworkers of America at a plant in Gramercy, Louisiana. There were no skilled black craftsmen at the plant, and a voluntary affirmative-action plan was developed to avoid the possibility of litigation by black employees, even though no past discrimination by the Kaiser Company had ever been proved. Under the agreement, half the slots for in-plant craft training programs were reserved for black employees until the proportion of black craft workers approximated that of blacks in the local labor force. Weber, a white denied admission to the training program, claimed that because this preferential treatment involved a specific quota, it constituted racial discrimination in violation of Title VII. The relevant portion of Title VII provides that an employer cannot be "required" to give preferential treatment to any racial group because of a racial imbalance in the work force.

The lower federal courts ruled in favor of Weber, but the Burger Court upheld the lawfulness of the affirmative-action program at the Gramercy plant. There was no violation of Title VII, the Court's majority concluded, because obviously the affirmative-action plan was not required. Put differently, Title VII does not forbid private employers and unions from agreeing voluntarily on a bona fide affirmative-action plan involving racial quotas intended to eliminate a conspicuous racial imbalance in segregated job categories. One chief goal of Congress in enacting Title VII was to improve the economic plight of racial minorities by opening new job opportunities, and the legislative history of the law suggested that this could be accomplished by voluntary local means. Thus, according to the Court majority, the general purpose of Title VII and the voluntary affirmative-action program at the Gramercy plant were consonant—namely, to dismantle traditional patterns of racial discrimination and segregation in employment. "It would be ironic indeed," the Court majority concluded, "if a law triggered by a Nation's concern over centuries of racial injustice . . . constituted the first legislative prohibition on all voluntary, private, race-conscious efforts to abolish traditional patterns of racial segregation and hierarchy."

Furthermore, the Court did not think that the rights of whites such as Weber had been severely infringed. The preferential program at the Gramercy plant did not "unnecessarily trammel the interests of white employees" for at least three reasons: it did not require that white workers be discharged or replaced by newly hired blacks; it did not "create an absolute bar" on the promotion of whites, because half of the program's trainees were white; and it was a "temporary measure" that was "not intended to maintain racial balance, but simply to eliminate a manifest racial imbalance." In the final analysis, however, Weber was decided narrowly because the Court refused to reach constitutional conclusions and avoided speculating about what types of affirmative-action plans would be legally permissible or impermissible in the future.

Following Weber was Fullilove v. Klutznick (1980), involving congressionally mandated affirmative action for minority-owned businesses where federal contract funds were at stake. Fullilove emerged out of a constitutional challenge to the minority business enterprise (MBE) provision of the Public Works Employment Act of 1977. The MBE provision required that in the absence of an administrative waiver, a minimum of 10 percent of federal grant funds provided for local public-works projects be spent by the grant recipient to purchase services or supplies from minority-owned businesses. The legislation had been enacted in light of past discrimination under which minority businesses had not been allowed to compete on equal footing with nonminority businesses, and statistics clearly demonstrated that a small percentage of federal public-works funds had been received by minority firms.

The Burger Court determined that the objectives of the MBE provision were within the powers of Congress and that the quota was a valid means of accomplishing those objectives. Dismissing the assertion that the 10 percent set-aside was an impermissible burden on nonminority businesses, the Court explicitly approved of the constitutionality of Congress legislating racial quotas under these conditions. The MBE provision was upheld as being within Congress's powers, including the power to enforce the Fourteenth Amendment, to remedy the effects of past discrimination, and to curtail it in the future. Paying great deference to Congress, the Court majority emphasized that "in no organ of government, state or federal, does there repose a more comprehensive remedial power than in the Congress, expressly charged by the Constitution with competence and authority to enforce equal protection guarantees. . . . Where Congress has authority to declare certain conduct unlawful, it may, as here, authorize and induce state action to avoid such conduct."

Another prominent affirmative-action decision was announced by the Burger Court in Firefighters Local Union No. 1784 v. Stotts (1984). The Memphis Fire Department had been found in violation of Title VII and was under court order to hire and promote more blacks to make amends for past discrimination. Later, anticipating a budget deficit, the city planned to lay off public employees with the least seniority, an action that would have most directly affected recently hired black firemen. Stotts, a black fireman challenging the proposed personnel actions, received a favorable decision from the federal district court, which granted an injunction enjoining the Fire Department from strictly adhering to seniority in layoffs. As a result, the union appealed to protect its seniority plan and white union members. The Burger Court reversed the lower court by ruling that because no intentional discrimination had been proved, "Title VII protects bona fide seniority systems, and it is inappropriate to deny an innocent employee the benefits of his seniority in order to provide a remedy in a pattern or practice [discrimination] suit such as this." The district court injunction was unjustified because white employees would have been improperly denied their seniority. The Court thus held against the continuation of affirmative action under these circumstances, despite a past discriminatory effect and the fact that the firemen most injured by the layoffs would be the blacks most recently hired. "Even when an individual shows that the discriminatory practice has had an impact on him," the Court majority noted, "he is not automatically entitled to have a non-minority employee laid off to make room for him."

HOUSING

Segregated housing patterns are found in most large and medium-sized metropolitan areas in the United States. Such segregation often emerges from deliberate discriminatory efforts on the part of some white homeowners, real estate interests, local governments, banks, and home builders to exclude minorities from white communities. Therefore, less progress has been made in the area of fair housing than in employment and education, and the possibility for genuine change appears remote.

The principal reasons for continued discrimination and segregation in housing are generally understood. Fair housing evokes controversy because desegregation is thought by many whites to lower the value of their homes. Whether myth or reality, this may become a self-fulfilling prophecy: panic selling by whites leads to an increased supply of housing in white neighborhoods, which naturally results in a decline in the prices of homes. Housing desegregation is also thought to lead to more interracial social contact or marriage, which many whites dislike or fear. Some whites additionally receive psychological benefits from housing segregation: because of it, they may feel "above" minorities both socially and economically. They have access to housing in neighborhoods that are by and large off limits to minorities. Psychological insecurity and prejudice may thus be linked, breeding opposition to desegregation and attempts to eradicate discrimination. Others worry that crime, juvenile delinquency, and vandalism will escalate if their neighborhoods become desegregated. These and other factors have led to various practices to keep minorities out. When desegregation does occur, powerfully negative reactions by whites, including violence, still occasionally result.

Because there is virtually no affirmative action to promote housing desegregation, the Supreme Court has announced no housing decisions equivalent to *Bakke*, *Weber*, or *Fullilove*. Nevertheless, its decisions have mapped a course of constitutional development curbing the most flagrant discrimination.

Buchanan v. *Warley* (1917), the first leading fair-housing case handed down by the Supreme Court, involved a Louisville, Kentucky, city ordinance that prevented blacks and whites from residing on the same city blocks where mixed living patterns had not already developed. The stated purpose of the ordinance was to promote the public peace and general welfare by preventing conflict and ill feelings between blacks and whites, but the Supreme Court declared it to be in violation of the due process clause of the Fourteenth Amendment. Because the ordinance obviously promoted exclusive residential blocks for blacks and whites, this was a violation of the right to dispose of property freely, and the ordinance was therefore unconstitutional.

Few housing-discrimination cases were accepted for decision by the Court during the following three decades. The next important case was *Shelley* v. *Kraemer* (1948). At issue in *Shelley* was whether state courts could enforce "restrictive covenants," private voluntary agreements that prohibited blacks from purchasing housing in white neighborhoods. The critical distinction between *Buchanan* and *Shelley* was that the former involved a public law and the latter involved agreements between private citizens. The Supreme Court ruled that although private citizens could legally agree not to sell their homes to a particular racial group, state courts could not enforce such agreements without violating the equal protection clause, because enforcement by courts is a form of state action. In the companion case of *Hurd* v. *Hodge* (1948), the Court extended *Shelley* by holding that restrictive covenants could not be enforced by federal courts.

After *Shelley* and *Hurd* the Court was once more quiet on the question of fair housing; the matter rested for nearly two decades before the next notable case. Then the Warren Court handed down significant decisions in three consecutive years. *Reitman* v. *Mulkey* (1967), the first of the three rulings, involved an amendment to the California constitution that repealed the state's fair-housing statute. The amendment provided that the state could not limit a person's discretion to sell or rent his or her property to whomever he or she wished. Mulkey, a black, challenged the state amendment after Reitman refused to rent him an apartment, asserting that the refusal was based solely on his race, in violation of the equal protection clause. The Warren Court upheld both Mulkey's claim and the California Supreme Court's judgment that the amendment would tend to increase discrimination in housing. By essentially declaring it a constitutional right to discriminate in housing, the California amendment constituted state action that encouraged private discrimination on the grounds of race. Because of the amendment, minorities would also be unable to rely on regular political channels, such as the state legislature, to remedy unfair housing practices.

The case of *Jones* v. *Alfred H. Mayer Co.* (1968) appeared during the following term of the Warren Court. It arose after the Mayer Company's refusal to sell homes to blacks, including Jones, solely because of their race. Because the company operated a private development and realty business that received no government aid, no state action was involved in the litigation. The Warren Court broadly decided, however, that a provision of the Civil Rights Act of 1866 prohibits all public and private discrimination in the acquisition and rental of property. Additionally, Congress possessed the power to pass such legislation under the Thirteenth Amendment because housing discrimination constitutes a badge of servitude. The Court majority noted, "When racial discrimination herds men into ghettos and makes their ability to buy property turn on the color of their skin, then it is a relic of slavery."

Before Earl Warren stepped down as chief justice, the Court decided one other relevant case, *Hunter* v. *Erickson* (1969). Voters in Akron, Ohio, amended the city charter to prohibit implementation of a fair-housing ordinance passed by the city council, unless implementation was first approved by a majority of citizens voting in a local election. Akron's standard procedure had been that ordinances automatically went into effect after passage and could be repealed later through a referendum. The Warren Court ruled that the provision violated the equal protection

clause because it made "an explicitly racial classification treating racial housing matters differently from other racial and housing matters." Put otherwise, the amendment clearly had a negative effect on racial minorities, who would benefit from the fair-housing ordinance, without having a similar impact on persons seeking other changes in Akron's housing laws.

The Burger Court dealt more conservatively than the Warren Court with housing-discrimination claims. These claims became more frequent during the early 1970s and often involved various exclusionary devices not specifically challenged during the Warren Court era. This conservatism is reflected in the related decisions of *James* v. *Valtierra* (1971) and *City of Eastlake* v. *Forest City Enterprises, Inc.* (1976), both of which allowed local techniques that tend to exclude minorities from predominantly white neighborhoods. In *Valtierra* low-income residents of San Jose and San Mateo County, California, challenged a provision of the state constitution that required a majority of citizens to approve through a local referendum any low-rent housing project before it could be constructed or acquired. When the plaintiffs were denied housing, they alleged a violation of the equal protection clause on the grounds that the referendum requirement constituted wealth discrimination and imposed a heavier burden on minorities than on other groups seeking housing, since a higher percentage of nonwhites than whites is poor. But the Burger Court detected no constitutional violation in the California provision, which was said merely to uphold the state's history of allowing citizens to participate in public policymaking through the election process. Indeed, the Court opinion concluded that the referendum requirement exemplified a "devotion to democracy, not to bias, discrimination, or prejudice." Therefore, if a law discriminates solely on the basis of wealth, no matter how much in reality it burdens racial minorities, it would be declared constitutional.

The general principle enunciated in *Valtierra* was carried over in *Eastlake,* wherein the Court approved a restrictive referendum process to prevent the building of low-cost housing in affluent areas. Upheld was a city-charter provision in Eastlake, Ohio, requiring that all proposed zoning changes be submitted for final endorsement by a citywide referendum in which a 55 percent favorable vote was necessary. As in *Valtierra*, the Court approved the referendum provision, noting that it reflected the essence of democracy because all citizens of a locality were provided with a mechanism to express their views. In neither *Valtierra* nor *Eastlake* did the Court thoroughly address the argument that such laws perpetuate residential segregation because voters in white communities are unlikely to approve of low-income housing that will be occupied mostly by nonwhites.

After the appointment of Chief Justice Warren E. Burger in 1969, the Court also announced decisions affecting standing in fair-housing litigation—that is, whether the Court will recognize litigants and the issues presented to the Court. In *Trafficante* v. *Metropolitan Life Insurance Co.* (1972) black and white tenants in an apartment complex claimed that their landlord discriminated against minorities. The tenants contended that this deprived them of the social benefits of a desegregated living environment and of business advantages that would have materialized if it had not been for discrimination. The legal claims in *Trafficante* were predicated on the Fair Housing Act of 1968, which prohibits discrimination in the sale or rental of housing on the grounds of race, and the Court held in favor of the tenants. The tenants had standing as aggrieved persons under the 1968 act because they had experienced the claimed injuries resulting from discrimination.

However, contrast *Warth* v. *Seldin* (1975), an important case in which four different categories of plaintiffs challenged a zoning ordinance in Penfield, New York, an affluent white suburb of Rochester. The ordinance was typical of those enacted in other communities faced with the possibility of an influx of low- and moderate-income residents from the urban core. Specifically, the petitioners alleged that the town's zoning ordinance, by its terms and as enforced, had the effect of excluding low- and moderate-income persons from living in Penfield, in violation of both constitutional and statutory law. In other words, the ordinance made it virtually impossible to build the kind of housing needed to accommodate some groups wishing to move from Rochester to Penfield. Yet the Court refused to rely on *Trafficante* and other relevant precedents, denying standing to the plaintiffs.

In articulating a new legal standard, the Court

majority held that there was no "substantial probability" that minorities would have been able to find acceptable housing in Penfield had the zoning ordinance not been in effect. Because the petitioners did not contend that they had a "present interest in any Penfield property," were "subject to the ordinance's strictures," or had been "denied a variance or permit by respondent officials," they failed to show a direct causal connection between their asserted harm and the actions of Penfield officials. Noting that the desire of minorities to live in Penfield had always depended on the efforts of developers to construct low- and moderate-income housing suitable to their needs, the Court viewed the case as in fact raising the third-party rights of developers, and only two efforts had been made by developers to build low- and moderate-cost housing in Penfield. Employing a substantial-probability test, the Court found that the proposed projects were inadequate to meet the financial and dimensional needs of the plaintiffs in *Warth*. The Court majority thus concluded that each petitioner's inability to reside in Penfield was "the consequence of the economy of the area housing market, rather than of respondents' asserted illegal acts." The impact of the decision against the plaintiffs' standing in *Warth* was to limit the opportunities for minorities to challenge the exclusionary nature of local zoning laws in various parts of the country.

If the Burger Court was hesitant to vindicate fair-housing claims in *Valtierra*, *Eastlake*, and *Warth*, it was even more reluctant in *Village of Arlington Heights* v. *Metropolitan Housing Development Corp.* (1977), in which a majority of the justices placed their constitutional imprimatur on the intent test in fair-housing litigation. This was the first instance in which the Court addressed directly the substantive equal-protection issue in exclusionary zoning litigation, and its decision suggested that the Fourteenth Amendment was of little value to persons opposing exclusionary zoning practices through federal courts.

Arlington Heights involved the refusal of an affluent Chicago suburb to rezone certain property from a single-family to a multifamily classification so that a low- and moderate-income housing project could be erected. The Metropolitan Housing Development Corporation planned to build federally subsidized townhouse units in predominantly white Arlington Heights so that low- and moderate-income tenants might live there, but the zoning request was rejected by the town's planning commission. The corporation and blacks who wanted to work and live in Arlington Heights then filed suit under the Fourteenth Amendment and the Fair Housing Act of 1968.

The Burger Court held that no clear intent to discriminate had been demonstrated and thus no legal violation was evident. Although the majority opinion admitted that the refusal to rezone did "arguably bear more heavily on racial minorities," it concluded that "little about the sequence of the events leading up to the decision would spark suspicion." In determining intent in *Arlington Heights,* the Court relied heavily on *Washington* v. *Davis,* reaffirming its strict standard of proof of discriminatory purpose. Reliance on *Davis,* of course, makes a finding of racial discrimination extremely difficult by precluding courts from inferring intent from disproportionate impact except in the most egregious cases and particularly by requiring a specific showing of intent to discriminate.

These Burger Court rulings, generally decided against the position of fair-housing proponents, were offset in part by two prominent cases. The first was *Hills* v. *Gautreaux* (1976). The Chicago Housing Authority and the United States Department of Housing and Urban Development (HUD) had selected sites for the location of federally supported public housing in Chicago in a discriminatory manner and had also discriminated in assigning tenants to that housing. As a result, nonwhites in public housing were found almost exclusively in minority neighborhoods of the city. Such policies obviously perpetuated segregation in Chicago by making suburban public-housing opportunities for minorities virtually nonexistent.

The Burger Court held that these actions and practices constituted illegal discrimination. Because HUD exercised authority in both Chicago and the surrounding suburbs, it had a legal responsibility to make housing options available to minorities throughout the larger metropolitan housing market. This meant, of course, that HUD would have to locate some public housing for nonwhites in the overwhelmingly white suburban areas of Chicago. In *Milliken I* the Court had refused to order a cross-district remedy for school segregation in Detroit and its suburbs,

but in *Gautreaux* the Court said that the appropriate remedy for discriminatory site selection and tenant assignments should involve both the city and suburbs. The main distinction between *Milliken I* and *Gautreaux* was that in the former case the school districts had not been found to violate the Constitution but in the latter HUD had acted unconstitutionally. An interdistrict remedy in *Gautreaux* would not interfere impermissibly with the proper exercise of local governmental power, but it would have done so in *Milliken I.*

The second Burger Court decision reflecting more sympathy toward advocates of fair housing was *Havens Realty Corp.* v. *Coleman* (1982). The case involved the practice of some real estate agents to show to minorities only property that is already predominantly minority-occupied or racially changing—a practice known as steering. The plaintiff was a tester—a person who seeks to gain evidence of illegal steering by pretending to want to rent or purchase property. Coleman, a black tester hired by a fair-housing organization known as Housing Opportunities Made Equal (HOME), had been falsely told that there were no vacancies in a Havens Realty apartment complex in Richmond, Virginia, but a white tester had been informed that apartment units were available in the same facility. The testers, along with HOME and others, alleged specific injuries resulting from steering as prohibited by the Fair Housing Act of 1968, but the federal district court ruled that the testers lacked standing.

The Burger Court unanimously overturned the lower court by holding that Coleman had been denied accurate information regarding the availability of the property, in direct violation of the Fair Housing Act, and that standing existed under statutory law. The Court further concluded that HOME had standing to challenge the steering in this case because these practices interfered with the organization's counseling and referral services to persons of low and moderate income, causing a drain on its limited resources. *Havens* therefore provided encouragement for fair-housing groups in their endeavors to gain standing in federal courts to fight racial steering.

CONCLUSION

The Warren and Burger Courts made definite imprints on the development of American law pertaining to racial discrimination and equal opportunity. The Warren Court announced several notable decisions that ushered in an era of greater racial equality. Yet, it must be emphasized that much of the change in the legal status of minorities during the 1960s is attributable to presidential and congressional actions that were perhaps influenced and supported, but not shaped, by Warren Court policies. For example, it was President Lyndon Johnson who vigorously implemented school desegregation, and it was Congress that passed two critical laws—the Civil Rights Act of 1964 and the Fair Housing Act of 1968.

Broadly speaking, the Burger Court followed Warren Court policy in school desegregation and handed down important decisions involving busing and, secondarily, affirmative action in higher education. In addition, the Burger Court molded the major contours of equal-employment law and interpreted the meaning of Title VII of the 1964 Civil Rights Act. In fair housing, following a few liberal decisions during the late Warren period, the Burger Court was often reluctant to sympathize with those advocating significant legal change in housing discrimination and segregation. Moreover, since the advent of the Burger Court, Congress and presidents generally have not gone substantially beyond the efforts of the 1960s. No new legislation has affected racial equality in education, employment, and housing to the degree that the 1964 and 1968 statutes did, and no president's zeal to implement Supreme Court decisions and congressional statutes has matched that of Johnson. Developments of the 1970s and 1980s therefore indicate that in some ways the drive for racial equality in the United States has slowed since the 1960s, despite overall incremental progress against discrimination.

Some observers have suggested that the solution to racial inequality in the United States lies largely in a three-pronged attack on discrimination in education, employment, and housing. If such a solution is possible, certainly the Supreme Court will play a role. But, in a system of separation of powers, it is axiomatic that only so much can be accomplished by even the most activist Court. No one Court, no one president, no one Congress can alone shape the legal destiny of America's racial minorities. Deterring racial discrimination and promoting equal opportunity must be the joint responsibility of the Supreme Court and the remainder of the political system.

CASES

Albemarle Paper Co. v. Moody, 422 U.S. 405 (1975)

Alexander v. Holmes County Board of Education, 396 U.S. 19 (1969)

American Tobacco Co. v. Patterson, 456 U.S. 63 (1982)

Brown v. Board of Education, 347 U.S. 483 (1954) [Brown I]; 349 U.S. 294 (1955) [Brown II]

Buchanan v. Warley, 245 U.S. 60 (1917)

California Brewers Assn. v. Bryant, 444 U.S. 598 (1980)

City of Eastlake v. Forest City Enterprises, Inc., 426 U.S. 668 (1976)

Cooper v. Aaron, 358 U.S. 1 (1958)

Crawford v. Board of Education of Los Angeles, 458 U.S. 527 (1982)

Dayton Board of Education v. Brinkman, 443 U.S. 526 (1979)

De Funis v. Odegaard, 416 U.S. 312 (1974)

Dred Scott v. Sandford, 19 Howard 393 (1857)

Firefighters Local Union No. 1784 v. Stotts, 81 L. Ed. 2d 483 (1984)

Franks v. Bowman Transportation Co., 424 U.S. 747 (1976)

Fullilove v. Klutznick, 448 U.S. 448 (1980)

Griffin v. School Board of Prince Edward County, 377 U.S. 218 (1964)

Griggs v. Duke Power Co., 401 U.S. 424 (1971)

Havens Realty Corp. v. Coleman, 455 U.S. 363 (1982)

Hazelwood School District v. United States, 433 U.S. 299 (1977)

Hills v. Gautreaux, 425 U.S. 284 (1976)

Hunter v. Erickson, 393 U.S. 385 (1969)

Hurd v. Hodge, 334 U.S. 24 (1948)

International Brotherhood of Teamsters v. United States, 431 U.S. 324 (1977)

James v. Valtierra, 402 U.S. 137 (1971)

Jones v. Alfred H. Mayer Co., 392 U.S. 409 (1968)

Keyes v. School District No. 1, Denver, 413 U.S. 189 (1973)

Lau v. Nichols, 414 U.S. 563 (1974)

McDonald v. Santa Fe Trail Transportation Co., 427 U.S. 273 (1976)

McDonnell Douglas Corp. v. Green, 411 U.S. 792 (1973)

McLaurin v. Oklahoma State Regents, 339 U.S. 637 (1950)

Milliken v. Bradley, 418 U.S. 717 (1974) [Milliken I]; 433 U.S. 267 (1977) [Milliken II]

Missouri ex rel. Gaines v. Canada, 305 U.S. 337 (1938)

Pasadena City Board of Education v. Spangler, 427 U.S. 424 (1976)

Plessy v. Ferguson, 163 U.S. 537 (1896)

Regents of the University of California v. Bakke, 438 U.S. 265 (1978)

Reitman v. Mulkey, 387 U.S. 369 (1967)

Shelley v. Kraemer, 334 U.S. 1 (1948)

Sipuel v. Board of Regents of the University of Oklahoma, 332 U.S. 631 (1948)

Steele v. Louisville & Nashville Railroad, 323 U.S. 192 (1944)

Swann v. Charlotte-Mecklenburg Board of Education, 402 U.S. 1 (1971)

RACIAL DISCRIMINATION AND EQUAL OPPORTUNITY

Sweatt v. Painter, 339 U.S. 629 (1950)

Trafficante v. Metropolitan Life Insurance Co., 409 U.S. 205 (1972)

United Steelworkers of America v. Weber, 443 U.S. 193 (1979)

Village of Arlington Heights v. Metropolitan Housing Development Corp., 429 U.S. 252 (1977)

Warth v. Seldin, 422 U.S. 490 (1975)

Washington v. Davis, 426 U.S. 229 (1976)

Washington v. Seattle School District No. 1, 458 U.S. 457 (1982)

BIBLIOGRAPHY

Henry J. Abraham, *Freedom and the Court: Civil Rights and Liberties in the United States* (1984), contains a chapter describing the legal rights of racial minorities as declared in leading Supreme Court decisions, written in an entertaining but scholarly way. *Boston College Law Review* offers a detailed annual survey of judicial decisions in employment discrimination, including those made by the Supreme Court. Charles S. Bullock III and Charles M. Lamb, eds., *Implementation of Civil Rights Policy* (1984), assembles up-to-date research on how federal civil rights law and policy in education, employment, and housing have been carried out by federal administrative agencies and courts. Paul Burstein, *Discrimination, Jobs, and Politics: The Struggle for Equal Employment Opportunity in the United States Since the New Deal* (1985), provides an overview of interactions between Congress, public opinion, and political movements to promote equal employment opportunity from the New Deal through the 1970s.

Michael N. Danielson, *The Politics of Exclusion* (1976), is an insightful examination of the law, politics, and economics of exclusionary practices to keep minorities and the poor out of predominantly white suburbs. Anthony Downs, *Opening Up the Suburbs: An Urban Strategy for America* (1973), is an excellent advanced study probing the problems associated with making suburban housing available to the poor and minorities, presenting alternative approaches for possibly achieving that goal. David Falk and Herbert M. Franklin, *Equal Housing Opportunity: The Unfinished Federal Agenda* (1976), briefly covers many basic legal aspects of housing segregation and discrimination in the United States. Richard Y. Funston, *Constitutional Counter-Revolution? The Warren Court and the Burger Court: Judicial Policy Making in Modern America* (1977), provides an overview of the civil rights policy trends of the Warren Court and the early Burger Court.

Alan H. Goldman, *Justice and Reverse Discrimination* (1979), is among the more prominent advanced studies on affirmative action in employment and related issues. Lino A. Graglia, *Disaster by Decree: The Supreme Court Decisions on Race and Schools* (1976), criticizes Supreme Court policy in school desegregation in this interesting but controversial book. Jennifer L. Hochschild, *The New American Dilemma: Liberal Democracy and School Desegregation* (1984), assesses problems and disadvantages associated with desegregating the schools, as well as possible solutions.

David L. Kirp, *Just Schools: The Idea of Racial Equality in American Education* (1982), provides detailed case studies of school desegregation in five United States cities. Samuel Krislov, *The Negro and Federal Employment: The Quest for Opportunity* (1967), probes the early movement toward equal employment opportunity in the federal government. Richard Kruger, *Simple Justice: The History of Brown v. Board of Education and Black America's Struggle for Equality* (1975), is an easily read and thorough treatment of the *Brown* decision that also provides insights into that historic case and Supreme Court decision-making generally. Lee Modjeska, *Handling Employment Discrimination Cases* (1980), is a comprehensive book addressing the entire scope of equal employment law and includes regular supplements with recent case descriptions. Paul H. Norgren and Samuel E. Hill, *Toward Fair Employment* (1964), offers a solid analysis of equal employment opportunity through the early 1960s.

Gary Orfield, *Must We Bus? Segregated Schools and National Policy* (1978), provides one of the most thorough treatments of the political and legal dimensions of the busing controversy. J. W. Peltason, *Fifty-Eight Lonely Men: Southern Federal Judges and School Desegregation* (1961), presents a classic analysis of the lower federal courts' problems in implementing the *Brown* decision, while simultaneously illuminating aspects of the judicial process. C. Herman Pritchett, *Constitutional Civil Liberties* (1984), offers an authoritative chapter on the legal rights of racial minorities in the context of Supreme Court decisions and at times suggests their relevance to broader political developments. Harrell R. Rodgers, Jr., and Charles S. Bullock III, *Law and Social Change: Civil Rights Laws and Their Consequences* (1972), contains short but valuable descriptive chapters on the politics and law involved in educational, employment, and housing discrimination as of the early 1970s.

Allan P. Sindler, *Bakke, De Funis, and Minority Admissions: The Quest for Equal Opportunity* (1978), addresses questions inherent in affirmative action in American higher education while focusing on the Supreme Court's most famous cases on that topic. Michael I. Sovern, *Legal Restraints on Racial Discrimination in Employment* (1966), is a widely recognized early study of law as it relates to equal employment opportunity. Karl E. Taeuber and Alma F. Taeuber, *Negroes in Cities: Residential Segregation and Neighborhood Change* (1965), presents an exceptional sociological analysis of housing segregation against blacks, emphasizing the Chicago metropolitan area. Clement E. Vose, *Caucasians Only: The Supreme Court, the NAACP, and the Restrictive Covenant Cases* (1959), is a path-breaking study of the functioning of the judicial process in the context of the Supreme Court's restrictive-covenant decisions. J. Harvie Wilkinson, *From Brown to Bakke: The Supreme Court and School Integration, 1954–1978* (1979), is among the best-known book-length treatments of Supreme Court decisions on school desegregation.

[*See also* BURGER COURT AND ERA; DUE PROCESS OF LAW; EQUAL PROTECTION CLAUSE; LAW AND SOCIAL SCIENCE; *and* WARREN COURT AND ERA.]

RELIGIOUS LIBERTY

H. Frank Way

THERE has always been a degree of tension in the American formula for religious liberty. It stems, in part, from two seemingly contrary notions: on the one hand, the civil equality of all religions and, on the other hand, the belief that the state has a vested interest in a religiously based society. The seeds of this ambiguity were evident throughout the greater part of the colonial era. Consider for a moment the following: Colonial America, as a group of Protestant communities, challenged the religious orthodoxy of the Old World and, in the process, spurred the individualism and dissenting patterns central to the acceptance of the idea of the civil equality of all religions. Religious individualism, the "priesthood of all believers" in Protestantism, gradually raised the civil equality of all Protestant churches to the level of an ideological commitment. The idea of religious equality worked its way through late colonial America and finally contributed to the disestablishment of state-supported churches. Religious individualism also had another consequence, religious pluralism— that is, the multiplication of Protestant sects. American religious pluralism made it increasingly untenable for a state to support a single religious dogma. Not only was state support of a single church contrary to the idea of the civil equality of all Protestant religions, but it became a source of social strife. The Baptists, Methodists, Lutherans, Quakers, and Presbyterians of eighteenth-century America objected mightily to the privileged position of the Congregational church in New England and the Episcopal church in the South. These churches were not content with religious toleration; they demanded not only freedom of conscience and worship but civil equality. By the end of the Revolution, all state-supported churches had been disestab-lished except in Massachusetts, where final disestablishment did not occur until 1833, and Connecticut, where disestablishment took place in 1818.

While disestablishmentarianism carried with it a certain anticlericalism, it did not signify a rejection of the importance of religion to society. Whatever the numbers of the unchurched and religiously indifferent in late colonial America, there was a strong Protestant culture in most colonial towns. Religious freedom had of course been an important factor in bringing many settlers to America. The idea of America as God's perfect kingdom on earth may have died in the Massachusetts Bay Colony, but a religiously influenced culture remained an enduring feature of America. For generations, large numbers of Americans, while accepting the principle of no establishment, nonetheless expected the state to do nothing injurious to the churches and to religious life; indeed, the state was expected to provide a comfortable, if not cozy, relationship. An examination of early state constitutions gives some support to this conclusion.

At the outset of the Republic, there was a clearer legal and political consensus on matters of freedom of worship and conscience than on church-state relations. The disparity among state constitutional provisions on freedom of religion and no establishment illustrates this point. With the exception of Louisiana, every state constitution adopted between 1776 and 1895 had a provision guaranteeing freedom of worship and conscience. Furthermore, this guarantee was often augmented by additional provisions prohibiting compulsory religious attendance and compulsory support of churches and ministers; proscriptions against religious tests for public office; and proscriptions against enlarging or diminishing an individual's civil rights because of religious beliefs. In short, state constitutions contained rather extensive provisions guaranteeing religious belief and worship.

It is noteworthy, however, that these same constitutions did not contain similarly extensive provisions on church and state. Twenty-eight out of the forty-five eighteenth- and nineteenth-century state constitutions contained only a single provision that prohibited the state from giving preference to any religious establishment or mode of worship. Seven constitutions provided that no religious society or mode of worship could receive preference over any other sect. Six constitutions had no provision on church and state. The remaining four states either had a provision against the use of public money for religious societies or a no-establishment provision parallel to the federal provision.

What is reasonably clear from the language of these eighteenth- and nineteenth-century constitutions is that the states did not foresee as a constitutional policy Thomas Jefferson's idea of a wall of separation between church and state. Beyond the policy of disestablishment of state-supported churches, revolutionary America and the early Republic did not support a policy of separatism, and indeed, the states continued to support the ancillary activities of churches, such as schools, orphanages, and hospitals. Herein, then, lies the ambiguity of the American solution to religious liberty. At least after the removal of suffrage and public-office disabilities against Roman Catholics and Jews, state constitutional provisions clearly indicated a legal fabric strongly committed to the freedom of conscience and worship.

But if religious liberty is an equation composed of both personal rights of conscience and worship and a state obligation to separate itself from the corporate life of religious societies, then the equation was not fully formulated until well after the end of the nineteenth century. Disestablishment of state-supported churches did not carry with it any commitment to divorce the state from the religious life of the people. The "no preference" provisions of most state constitutions presumed that all religious groups would be treated equally. The provisions did not presume that the legislature would be unable to encourage and support equally all religions; on the contrary, it was not uncommon for eigh-

teenth- and nineteenth-century state constitutions to contain provisions stating that the security of the state depended on the legislature encouraging religion and morality, such as the Ohio Constitution of 1802, Article VIII, Section 3.

The provisions on religious liberty in early constitutions reflected a consensus that was not greatly disturbed until well after the Civil War. Although religious pluralism was a fact of colonial life—indeed, the constitutional provisions were pragmatic reflections of that pluralism—the religious population of pre–Civil War America did not contain large numbers of groups with unusual religious needs not accounted for in the late eighteenth-century constitutional settlements. The mainline Protestant churches—Methodists, Baptists, Presbyterians, Anglicans, Lutherans, and Congregationalists—could easily practice their religions without further judicial elaboration and refinement of the rights of religious conscience and worship. Only the historic peace churches, the Quaker and the Mennonite, pressed for greater legal accommodation. Some early state constitutions made the necessary accommodation by exempting from militia duty those who had conscientious scruples against bearing arms (for example, the Indiana Constitution of 1816, Article VII, Section 2) and, more commonly, by allowing an oath to be affirmed rather than sworn (for example, the Alabama Constitution of 1819, Article VI, Section 1).

For well over one hundred years after the signing of the Declaration of Independence, the American judiciary, both state and federal, was generally silent on issues of religious liberty. Although there were occasional challenges by Jews to Sunday-closing laws and by Roman Catholics to Protestant-inspired prayer and Bible reading in the public schools, the nineteenth century was not marked by frequent legal contests over issues of religious liberty. The state solutions of disestablishment and freedom of conscience and worship that had evolved during the colonial and revolutionary eras worked well for mainline Protestant America. However, after the early years of the Republic, the solutions did not always work well for the noncolonial religions, such as Mormonism, and for the increasing numbers of Roman Catholic and Jewish immigrants. By and large, members of these groups were not parties to the original agreements hammered out in early state constitutional conventions, and consequently their needs were either ignored or could not have been anticipated.

In 1790 there were only 1,243 Jews and approximately 50,000 Roman Catholics out of the total United States population of 2.8 million. By 1900 there were 12 million Roman Catholics and 1 million Jews in the United States. The rapid growth of these non-Protestant groups and the rise of what might be called indigenous American religions, such as Mormonism, Christian Science, and Jehovah's Witnesses, strained the original constitutional formula and eventually produced litigation and the gradual development of a body of appellate decisions on both no-establishment and free-exercise issues. It is not without significance that the precedents that provide the major underpinning for current case law generally do not antedate the 1940s.

FEDERALISM AND RELIGIOUS LIBERTY

By the 1980s the United States Supreme Court had become an active interpreter of the constitutional provisions on free exercise and no establishment; it was not always thus. The Court had few occasions in the nineteenth and early twentieth centuries to render opinions in these areas. The text of the First Amendment, which includes the religion clauses, limits only the federal government, not the states. Since the jurisdiction of the federal judiciary does not normally extend to claims made under state constitutional provisions, the long silence of the federal courts on issues of religious liberty is understandable.

It was not until the United States Supreme Court "incorporated" free-exercise and no-establishment principles as substantive parts of the Fourteenth Amendment's due process clause (an amendment that does apply to the states) that the federal judiciary gained jurisdiction over claims of state violations of religious liberty. This incorporation did not occur until the free-exercise decision of *Cantwell* v. *Connecticut* (1940) and the no-establishment decision of *Everson* v. *Board of Education* (1947).

Thus, for almost 150 years, judicial interpretation of the rights of religious liberty was largely a matter for the separate state judiciaries under their own constitutional provisions. The result of incorporation has been not only to open the federal courts to state claimants but also to bind state courts to the authoritative decisions of the United States Supreme Court on issues of religious liberty. These decisions establish the minimum or base standard of no establishment; state courts are free under their own constitutional provisions to expand or enlarge on the federally defined base. In requiring a higher standard than is demanded under the federal constitution, however, a state may not transgress other federally protected constitutional rights (*Widmar* v. *Vincent,* 1981).

PRAYER AND BIBLE READINGS

Given the largely Protestant composition of the American population in the early nineteenth century and given the fact that public education only gradually replaced the church-supported schools, it is not surprising that Protestant-based religious exercises were common to the public schools. Protestant religious hymns, Protestant-inspired readings, the King James Version of the Bible, and the Protestant version of the Lord's Prayer were commonly used in the public schools in the nineteenth century. It was not until a substantial Roman Catholic population arrived in America that these practices were legally challenged in the state courts. Nor is it surprising, given Protestant suspicion of the Roman Catholic church, that these challenges met with little success. From 1854, the date of the first recorded court challenge in *Donahoe* v. *Richards,* to the eve of the 1962 United States Supreme Court decision in *Engel* v. *Vitale,* seventeen states upheld the constitutionality of prayer and/or Bible readings in the public schools. In only one state, Illinois, were both prayers and Bible readings declared to be in violation of a state constitution.

The intensity of this dispute can be best captured from the trial record of a mid-nineteenth-century Boston case, *Commonwealth* v. *Cooke* (1859). Thomas Wall, an eleven-year-old Roman Catholic student at a public school, refused to recite the Ten Commandments. The boy offered as an excuse that his priest had recently addressed the nine hundred children of the boy's parish and had told them that they should not be cowards to their religion and should refuse to read or repeat the Commandments in the public school. The priest further told the students that if they did, he would read their names from the altar. Some sixty boys thereafter refused to do the required recitation. However, when Wall refused, his teacher caned his hands with a rattan stick for thirty minutes until the boy submitted. In upholding the punishment, the judge reasoned that to grant Wall an excuse from the exercises would lead others to request the same excuse, with the consequence of a war on the Bible. Furthermore, the judge argued, an excuse system would bridge the gulf separating church and state.

The insensitivity of the Boston court—indeed, of most courts prior to the *Engel* decision—to the non-Protestant community was evident. The new immigrants were told to adjust to American culture rather than seek legal exemptions from historic Protestant practices. As the Maine Supreme Court said in *Donahoe*, "Large masses of foreign population are among us, weak in the midst of our strength. Mere citizenship is of no avail, unless they become citizens in fact as well as in name."

This backward glance to the Boston case serves more than an antiquarian purpose. Whether it was the Irish Catholics of the mid-nineteenth century, the Mormons of the late nineteenth century, or the Jehovah's Witnesses and Hare Krishnas of more recent years, the judicial task of interpreting the constitutional rights of religious liberty has been complicated by occasional outbursts of popular intolerance. The judiciary risks its own fragile support if it ignores popular sentiment. On the other hand, for the judiciary merely to reflect popular sentiment would be to entrust written constitutional guaranties to vagaries of mass opinion. In the early 1960s the prayer and Bible-reading decisions of the United States Supreme Court attempted to lead, rather than follow, public opinion and to reshape historic practices rather than legitimate them.

In 1962, in *Engel* v. *Vitale*, a case of first impression, the Supreme Court, by a 6–1 majority, struck down as a violation of the federal no-establishment clause the following public school prayer: "Almighty God, we acknowledge our dependence upon Thee, and we beg Thy blessings upon us, our parents, our teachers and our Country." The prayer had been officially composed by the New York State Board of Regents, the body that governs the state's public schools, and had been transmitted to the various school districts as a recommended part of the curriculum. In the majority opinion written by Justice Hugo Black, the Court concluded that

> the constitutional prohibition against laws respecting an establishment of religion must at least mean that in this country it is no part of the business of government to compose official prayers for any group of the American people to recite as a part of a religious program carried on by government. . . . Neither the fact that the prayer may be denominationally neutral nor the fact that its observance on the part of the students is voluntary can serve to free it from the limitations of the Establishment Clause.

One year after the *Engel* decision, the Court addressed the related issue of Bible readings in the public schools. In companion cases arising in Pennsylvania and Maryland (*Abington School District* v. *Schempp,* 1963), the Court confronted the issue of voluntary Bible reading and recitation of the Lord's Prayer in the public schools. For the first time, the Court proposed a test for resolving issues presented by the no-establishment clause. In an opinion written by Justice Tom Clark, the Court noted,

> The test may be stated as follows: what are the purpose and the primary effect of the enactment? If either is the advancement or inhibition of religion then the enactment exceeds the scope of legislative power as circumscribed by the Constitution. That is to say that to withstand the strictures of the Establishment Clause there must be a secular legislative purpose and a primary effect that neither advances nor inhibits religion.

Applying the test to the two situations, the majority opinion concluded that the exercises were religious in nature rather than secular and therefore transgressed the no-establishment principle of state neutrality.

Neither the *Engel* nor the *Schempp* decision left much room for subsequent maneuvering in appellate litigation. The *Engel* decision did contain a footnote that distinguished public school religious exercises from public ceremonial occasions containing religious references. The

Schempp decision also made a distinction between religious exercises and an objective, secular study of the Bible or of religion. Throughout the 1960s, however, the Court gave no indication that a retreat from the ban on prayers and devotional Bible readings would be accepted.

Some softening in the positions of individual justices of the Supreme Court could be seen by the early 1980s. In 1980 the Court reversed the state courts of Kentucky, which had upheld a state statute requiring the posting in all public school classrooms of a copy of the Ten Commandments. The majority rejected the state's contention that the posting of the Ten Commandments primarily served a secular purpose; it concluded that the purpose of the posting was plainly religious *(Stone* v. *Graham)*. This time, however, four justices dissented from the Court's per curiam order, with two of the dissenters, Justices Potter Stewart and William Rehnquist, indicating that they were prepared to support the posting on the basis of its secular purpose.

One year later, in 1981, the Court struck down a University of Missouri ban on equal access to university facilities by a registered student religious group *(Widmar* v. *Vincent)*. The Court reasoned that to exclude the student group from equal access solely on the basis of the religious content of the organization violated the constitutional principle that state regulation of speech be content-neutral.

In 1983 there was further evidence of a break in the Court's position. In *Marsh* v. *Chambers* the Court upheld, by a vote of 6–3, the Nebraska legislature's practice of opening each legislative day with a prayer led by a chaplain whose salary was paid out of state funds. The Court noted that this was common practice, long accepted in many states and the federal Congress. Indeed, the Court noted that the same Congress that proposed the Bill of Rights also authorized the appointment of paid chaplains. The majority concluded that since the drafters of the no-establishment clause saw no threat to it from prayers and chaplains in the First Congress, therefore the Court ought not to impose on the states a more stringent standard than the draftsmen imposed on themselves. The majority entered a caveat, however, that the state legislator claiming injury in the *Marsh* case was an adult and thus presumably not readily susceptible to peer pressure or religious indoctrination. Although the intent of this caveat was not entirely clear, it does serve to distinguish legislative prayers from religious exercises in the public schools.

The school-prayer issue is not likely to disappear. Although there was some evidence after the *Engel* and *Schempp* decisions that a majority of elementary school teachers did stop the practice of morning prayers and Bible readings, the issue has become sufficiently political that short of a new United States Supreme Court ruling reasserting *Engel* and *Schempp,* litigation will continue. Groups seeking school board authorization for classroom silent meditation, preschool-hour prayers and Bible readings, or preschool-hour religious study clubs will likely continue to press their cause.

RELIGIOUS INSTRUCTION IN PUBLIC SCHOOLS

While prayers and Bible readings had been common in American schools from the outset of public education, sectarian religious instruction has become uncommon. Indeed, in the rare nineteenth-century cases in which the judiciary did have occasion to confront denominational instruction in the public schools, the practice was banned, generally as a violation of state constitutional provisions prohibiting the use of public funds for sectarian instruction. In the early part of the twentieth century, however, the weekday Sunday-school movement pressed school districts to allow the various denominations to provide religious instruction on a voluntary basis either outside the school or on the school premises.

One such program in Champaign, Illinois, became the center of a court challenge that led to a Supreme Court decision in *McCollum* v. *Board of Education* (1948). Under the Champaign program, pupils whose parents signed a "request card" were released during school hours to attend religious instruction in the school building offered by outside teachers furnished by a local interdenominational religious council. Attendance records were kept, and the outside teachers were subject to approval by the school superintendent. Students who did not enroll were sent from their classrooms to other rooms where they continued their secular education. In striking down the program as a violation of the no-establishment clause, Justice Black's opinion for the majority concluded that the facts

> show the use of tax-supported property for religious instruction and the close cooperation between the school authorities and the religious council in promoting religious education. The operation of the State's compulsory education system thus assists and is integrated with the program of religious instruction carried on by separate religious sects. Pupils compelled by law to go to school for secular education are released in part from their legal duty upon the condition that they attend the religious classes. This is beyond all question a utilization of the tax-established and tax-supported public school system to aid religious groups to spread their faith. And it falls squarely under the ban of the First Amendment.

Just four years later, the Court retreated from its *McCollum* decision. In *Zorach* v. *Clauson* (1952) a so-called dismissed-time program came before the Court for review. The challenged New York City program did not provide for instruction on the school premises but, rather, dismissed students during school hours to go to religious centers for religious instruction or devotional exercises. The Court, seizing on this as the critical difference, refused to extend the *McCollum* decision to off-campus programs conducted during school hours. Justice William O. Douglas' majority opinion warned that to have held otherwise would have indicated a judicial hostility to religion. He wrote,

> We are a religious people whose institutions presuppose a Supreme Being. We guarantee the freedom to worship as one chooses. We make room for as wide a variety of beliefs and creeds as the spiritual needs of man deem necessary. We sponsor an attitude on the part of government that shows no partiality to any one group and that lets each flourish according to the zeal of its adherents and the appeal of its dogma.

AID TO SECTARIAN EDUCATION

As the Roman Catholic population in the United States increased dramatically in the mid-nineteenth century, Catholics encountered a public school system with a strong Protestant bias. When they were unsuccessful in obtaining accommodation from school boards to their religious views, they began an ambitious program of parochial school education. Over the years, however, financially strapped sectarian schools have pressed for a variety of forms of public support. Roman Catholics and Lutherans have maintained that the double costs of public school taxes and private tuition are unjust. If they relieve the public from the financial burden of educating several million students, then, they argue, simple justice should dictate some public support. Opponents, on the other hand, point out that enrolling students in a private school is a choice freely made by parents and whatever costs that decision entails were necessarily known when the decision was made. Furthermore, they argue, any system of substantial state support for private schools would undermine the quality of the public school system, not only in financial terms but also by leaving in the public schools a greater proportion of pupils who have the greatest educational needs—that is, children from disadvantaged homes.

Transportation and Textbooks. It was not until 1947 that the Supreme Court decided a case involving the use of tax monies to support sectarian education. In *Everson* v. *Board of Education* a narrowly divided Court sustained a New Jersey board of education's payment to parents of the costs of transporting children in the public transit system to schools, both public and parochial. Justice Black's majority opinion, often characterized as a "high wall of separation" opinion, asserted that the no-establishment clause means that

> neither a state nor the Federal Government can set up a church. Neither can pass laws which aid one religion, aid all religions, or prefer one religion over another. Neither can force nor influence a person to go to or to remain away from church against his will or force him to profess a belief or disbelief in any religion. No person can be punished for entertaining or professing religious beliefs or disbeliefs, for church attendance or non-attendance. No tax in any amount, large or small, can be levied to support any religious activities or institutions, whatever they may be called, or whatever form they may adopt to teach or practice religion. Neither a state nor the Federal Government can, openly or secretly,

participate in the affairs of any religious organizations or groups and *vice versa*. In the words of Jefferson, the clause against establishment of religion by law was intended to erect "a wall of separation between Church and State."

There probably would be little disagreement with Black's assertion that neither a state nor the federal government may establish a church and none with a rule prohibiting preferential treatment of one religion or rules prohibiting compulsory church attendance or compulsory acceptance of religious beliefs. To the extent, however, that the *Everson* opinion suggested that the government may not equally aid all religions, the opinion was challenged (Howe). Indeed, the actual result in the *Everson* case bore little resemblance to this "high wall" assertion. Characterizing the New Jersey program as a religiously neutral act of general welfare for the safe and expeditious transportation of schoolchildren, the majority upheld the program. In other words, the majority argued that a state may not in some instances (such as fire protection), and need not in other instances (such as public bus transportation), exclude individuals and even organizations from receiving the benefits of religiously neutral general state law simply because the benefit received may have an incidental positive effect on the religious life of an organization or individual. It could be argued further that to deny the benefits of religiously neutral general-welfare legislation solely on the basis of religious orientation would bring the no-establishment clause of the First Amendment into conflict with its free-exercise clause.

On the other hand, determining that legislation is religiously neutral on its face does not preclude a legislative intent to target benefits so as to aid individuals in the exercise of their religious beliefs. In other words, merely because a statute does not employ religion as a standard for action or inaction under the statute does not mean that the statute was not written with any intent to aid religion. The parochial-school textbook cases are illustrative of the point.

In 1965 the New York legislature passed legislation requiring all local school boards to lend secular textbooks without charge to all children in grades 7–12 enrolled in a public or private school in the district. In 1968 a divided United States Supreme Court upheld the law in *Board of Education* v. *Allen*. Writing for the majority, Justice Byron White reasoned that since parents have a constitutional right to send their children to private schools, since religious schools do perform a secular educational function, since the statute had a secular purpose, and since its principal beneficiary was not the religious school but rather the parents and children, the statute was constitutional. Of course, as in many no-establishment cases, locating the primary effect or principal beneficiary is a matter of degree. Drawing a line between the primary secular effect for parents and children and the incidental or indirect benefits that may accrue to a religious school is at best problematic. In any event, loans of secular textbooks to parochial-school students have been approved by the Court twice since the *Allen* decision.

Shortly after World War II, when the costs of education began to increase sharply, proposals were made in Congress to enact a federal program to aid the states' public schools. Roman Catholics objected, however, to any aid program that did not include the parochial system. The effect of Roman Catholic objections was to foreclose a federal aid bill until a compromise formula could be reached. The formula, adopted in the Elementary and Secondary Education Act of 1965, was to channel federal funds to state public education agencies in order to meet the special needs of low-income families. The Title I formula of the 1965 act avoided the issue of public versus private schools and instead assumed that educationally deprived children could be found in either system.

With the passage of the act, some state legislatures assumed that the door was opened to state subventions to parochial schools. In the late 1960s the legislatures of Rhode Island and Pennsylvania passed legislation offering substantial financial benefits to the private schools. The Rhode Island act provided for a 15 percent salary supplement to teachers of secular subjects in schools in which the expenditure per pupil for secular education was below the state average. No teacher receiving a supplement could teach any religion course and the teacher could use only teaching materials used in the public schools. The Pennsylvania act authorized the state to reimburse nonpublic schools for specified secular educational services, including teacher salaries, textbooks, and instructional materials, and the aid was limited to courses in mathematics, the physical sciences, physical education, and modern foreign languages.

The Rhode Island and Pennsylvania acts were successfully challenged in companion cases decided by the Supreme Court in 1971. Writing for the majority in *Lemon* v. *Kurtzman,* Chief Justice Warren Burger adopted a three-part test for considering the constitutionality of the state acts. Under the test the state action must have a secular purpose, the principal effect of the action must neither advance nor inhibit religion, and the action must not foster excessive government entanglement with religion. The Court agreed that both statutes had a secular purpose. The opinion, however, did not make any determination about the principal effect of the statutes but, rather, concluded that both statutes failed to meet the requirement of no excessive entanglement. Because each statute had specific restrictions aimed at guaranteeing separation between religious and secular education and because these restrictions were subject to ongoing state monitoring and auditing, the Court concluded that the cumulative effect was excessive entanglement between the state and church-related schools.

One year after the *Lemon* decision, the New York legislature adopted a program to aid low-income nonpublic schools with grants of $30–$40 per pupil for the maintenance and repair of buildings. The legislation contained no provision restricting the grants to the secular areas of the schools. While agreeing that the legislation had a secular purpose, the Court nonetheless held the grants in violation of the no-establishment clause, asserting that the inevitable effect of the grants would be to subsidize and advance the religious mission of the church schools (*Committee for Public Education* v. *Nyquist,* 1973).

Similarly, in 1975 a narrowly divided Court struck down Pennsylvania's program for the loan of instructional materials and equipment to nonpublic schools *(Meek* v. *Pittenger).* Employing the three-part *Lemon* test, the majority concluded that loans of maps, charts, and laboratory equipment to schools whose religious mission was pervasive had the impermissible primary effect of advancing religion. Two years later the Court, again narrowly divided, struck down Ohio's program for lending nonpublic school students and parents secular instructional equipment and

materials of an unspecified nature *(Wolman* v. *Walter).* Again the majority concluded that given the dual responsibility of separating the sectarian and secular functions, the program inevitably would advance the religious role of the schools.

By the late 1970s it was apparent that a majority of the Court thought that in religion-pervasive elementary and secondary schools any substantial aid necessarily resulted in aid to the sectarian enterprise as a whole. On the other hand, there was some reason to conclude that a majority of the Court might support secular auxiliary services to nonpublic schools. In 1973 the Court struck down a New York program for reimbursing nonpublic schools by an annual allotment ranging from $27 to $45 per pupil for certain record-keeping and testing functions. Part of the services covered state-mandated tests and state-mandated records and reports. However, part of the funds were to cover teacher-prepared tests without regard to whether these normal classroom tests covered religious as well as secular topics (*Levitt* v. *Committee for Public Education).* The Court again found that the primary effect of the program was to advance religious education. Furthermore, the Court rejected any argument that state-mandated secular requirements could be reimbursed. There was, however, a hint in the *Levitt* case that some reimbursement might be possible for certain secular services.

The *Levitt* hint in 1973 became almost a full suggestion in the 1975 opinion in *Meek.* The Pennsylvania statute under consideration in *Meek,* had, among other provisions, one for so-called auxiliary services. The act authorized the state to provide public personnel and supportive materials and equipment for remedial and accelerated instruction, as well as for guidance counseling and testing and for speech and hearing services for nonpublic schools on the premises of the nonpublic school. The majority concluded not only that the proposed auxiliary services had the potential to advance the religious mission of the schools but also that the service would excessively entangle the state with church-related schools because "to be certain that auxiliary teachers remain religiously neutral, as the Constitution demands, the State would have to impose limitations on the activities of auxiliary personnel and then engage in some form of continuing surveillance to ensure that those restrictions were being followed." Nonetheless, the *Meek* opinion pointedly suggested in footnote 21 that general-welfare services to children could be provided regardless of any incidental benefit to a church-related school.

The footnote hint in *Meek* became the conclusion two years later in *Wolman* v. *Walter*. The Court had before it an Ohio program that, among other things, provided for standardized tests and scoring services as used in the public schools for pupils attending nonpublic schools; pupil diagnostic services parallel to those available to public school pupils in the areas of speech, hearing, and psychological services conducted by public personnel on the premises of nonpublic schools; and therapeutic psychological, speech, hearing, guidance, counseling, and remedial services and programs for the deaf, blind, emotionally disturbed, and physically handicapped, with programs and services to be conducted off nonpublic school premises or in mobile units by public personnel.

All three programs were upheld by the Court. While the Court was divided, a majority of the justices agreed there was little threat that either the testing program or the diagnostic services could be used to promote religion or foster ideological views. Similarly, the majority agreed that the therapeutic and remedial services offered at a neutral site would not serve to promote religion or excessively entangle church schools with the state. The neutral-site requirement will undoubtedly play a role in future litigation before the Supreme Court.

Tuition and Tax Credit. In addition to direct state support for the core educational program or state support for auxiliary services, proponents of parochial schools have proposed a variety of state-supported tuition grants and tax credit programs. In the 1973 *Nyquist* decision the Court struck down New York's program that gave a partial tuition reimbursement to low-income parents of students attending nonpublic schools. For parents who did not qualify for tuition reimbursement, the legislation allowed parents to receive a limited tax credit for each dependent attending a nonpublic school. Over the objection of three justices, the majority concluded that both programs failed the "effect test" propounded in the *Lemon* decision. The majority observed that in the absence of any

means of guaranteeing that a tuition grant would be used exclusively for neutral, nonideological, and secular purposes, the primary effect would be to provide financial support for sectarian education. Similarly, the tax benefit scheme was ruled to be a financial charge upon the state for the purpose of supporting religious education.

On the same day on which the Court handed down its *Nyquist* decision, the Court also struck down Pennsylvania's Parent Reimbursement Act. In *Sloan* v. *Lemon* the Court reviewed a tuition grant program that would have allowed qualifying parents of nonpublic school students to receive tuition reimbursement grants ranging from $75 to $150 for each enrolled dependent. Again the Court concluded that the primary effect of the grants was to advance religious education. Writing for the majority Justice Lewis Powell observed,

> We look to the substance of the program, and no matter how it is characterized its effect remains the same. The State has singled out a class of its citizens for a special economic benefit. Whether that benefit be viewed as a simple tuition subsidy, as an incentive to parents to send their children to sectarian schools, or as a reward for having done so, at bottom its intended consequence is to preserve and support religion-oriented institutions.

Ten years after striking down New York's tax credit scheme, a new Supreme Court majority upheld Minnesota's income-tax credit plan. By a narrow majority of 5–4, the Court upheld a plan that allowed all parents to deduct from their state income taxes the expenses incurred for a dependent's school tuition, textbooks, and transportation. Maximum deductions ranged from $500 to $700 per dependent. The majority concluded that the significant difference between the New York law and the Minnesota law was that the latter did not single out nonpublic schools for a special benefit but, rather, allowed all parents to claim the deductions without regard to whether their dependents attended private or public schools (*Mueller* v. *Allen*). While public schools rarely charge tuition, sectarian schools do, and even though tuition would be the largest deductible item, the majority dismissed the argument that sectarian schools would be the principal beneficiary of the legislation. On the contrary, the majority concluded that the legislation was facially neutral and intended to benefit a broad class of citizens. An even more interesting part of Justice Rehnquist's majority rationale was the observation that the deductions were a "rough return" to the parents who supported private schools. The rough return was for the benefit given to the state and all taxpayers that, he argued, flows from providing healthy competition to the public schools and the reduced tax burden.

Sectarian Higher Education. Throughout the 1970s the Court was skeptical of state financial aid to parochial schools; nonetheless, a slim majority (sometimes only a plurality) of the Court sustained state and federal aid to sectarian institutions of higher learning. In 1971, in a case challenging the validity of federal construction grant loans to certain Roman Catholic colleges, a plurality of the justices distinguished such loans from aid to parochial schools *(Tilton* v. *Richardson).* The loans were offered under the federal Higher Education Facilities Act of 1963, which expressly excluded loans for facilities primarily intended for divinity programs. Other than imposing these restrictions, the legislation did not preclude religious institutions from obtaining loans.

The plurality opinion in *Tilton* suggested that the important point to be determined in cases of state aid to sectarian institutions of higher learning was whether in such an institution the religious mission so permeated secular education as to make it impossible to separate the secular and religious missions of the colleges. The justices concluded that in the case before them there was no such pervasive religious mission. Furthermore, they observed,

> There are generally significant differences between the religious aspects of church-related institutions of higher learning and parochial elementary and secondary schools. The "affirmative if not dominant policy" of the instruction in pre-college church schools is "to assure future adherents to a particular faith by having control of their total education at an early age." . . . There is substance to the contention that college students are less impressionable and less susceptible to religious indoctrination. Common observation would seem to support that view, and Congress may well have entertained it.

Finally, the justices agreed that since the particular proposed facilities under review were secular and not likely to support or advance religious activities, the likelihood of excessive entanglement between church and state was minimal. The Court did, however, strike a provision in the act limiting the religious use of the facilities only to twenty years. The plurality opinion indicated that the restriction could not expire while a funded building had a substantial value. The *Tilton* decision was followed in several cases in the 1970s.

PROPERTY TAX EXEMPTION

For a number of reasons, many rooted in colonial American history, churches and religious organizations have often enjoyed what amounts to special consideration in the area of taxes. Legislatures have long given special tax classifications to groups and organizations whose influences or services are thought to be beneficial to the life of the community. Thus, houses of religious worship, nonprofit schools and colleges, public museums, libraries, and nonprofit hospitals are generally exempt from property taxes in all states. Similarly, the federal government exempts organizations operated exclusively for religious purposes from payment of income and gift taxes. Churches and their associations are subject to the unrelated federal business tax— that is, to taxes on income-producing property unrelated to the church, such as a commercial rental property or business enterprise.

Although there is little doubt that the tax structure often benefits religious organizations and in effect offers them a tax subsidy, the issue has not been widely litigated. The United States Supreme Court has considered the constitutional issue of no-establishment and church-property tax exemption on only one occasion: in *Walz* v. *Tax Commission* (1970) the Court upheld a New York tax exemption for properties of religious organizations where the properties were used exclusively for religious purposes. In answer to the contention that such an exemption indirectly required taxpayers to support religion, the Court noted,

> The general principle deducible from the First Amendment and all that has been said by the

Court is this: that we will not tolerate either governmentally established religion or governmental interference with religion. Short of those expressly proscribed governmental acts there is room for play in the joints productive of a benevolent neutrality which will permit religious exercise to exist without sponsorship and without interference.

Furthermore, the Court pointed out that such tax exemptions assist in guarding against the latent dangers to the free exercise of religion inherent in the imposition of taxes. The exemption transfers no public revenue to a church, and there is no real connection between the exemption and the establishment of religion. Indeed, the opinion argued that exempting religious property may promote separation by restricting fiscal contact between church and state.

RELIGIOUS SYMBOLS AND LANGUAGE

Given America's religious heritage, it would be unusual not to anticipate the occasional use of religious symbols and language in the public arena. Thus, calling for God's protection and deliverance has been a part of American public life from the Declaration of Independence to the present. Indeed, since 1864 all coins of the United States have had imprinted on them the phrase "In God We Trust," and since 1955 all currency has carried this national motto. On the rare occasions when federal courts have confronted the use of religious language and images on currency and stamps they have consistently upheld their use. In the currency cases, the courts concluded that there was no religious impact and that the language was purely ceremonial and not a religious exercise.

A somewhat more difficult problem arises when religious monuments and symbols are displayed or used on public property. A common problem has been the placing of Christian crosses on public property or the use of a nativity scene as a part of a Christmas display thereon. In those situations where a court has upheld placing a Christian cross on public property, the court has concluded either that the commercial setting of the cross negated any religious message (*Meyer* v. *Oklahoma City*, 1972) or that the

cross was used in conjunction with an otherwise valid secular purpose, such as a war memorial (*Eugene Sand and Gravel* v. *City of Eugene*, 1976). Where the courts concluded that the crosses were intended as a religious message, they have disallowed their use (*Fox* v. *City of Los Angeles*, 1978; *American Civil Liberties Union* v. *Raban County Chamber of Commerce*, 1981).

The cross cases suggest that religious symbols can be transformed by their setting into secular symbols—that is, that a given setting can neutralize the religious origin of a symbol and, in the process, give such symbols an independent status. This was the approach used in several nativity-scene cases decided by the lower courts in the 1960s and 1970s and adopted by the United States Supreme Court in 1984 in *Lynch* v. *Donnelly*.

In short, the judiciary has concluded that putting the nativity scene to the service of the Christmas trade secularized the religious symbol. In a 5–4 decision in *Lynch*, the Supreme Court upheld the right of a city to include a nativity scene as a part of an annual Christmas display. The display was part of a merchants' effort, and the crèche was placed among traditional secular holiday objects such as reindeer, a Christmas tree, and a Santa Claus house. The Court noted that the purpose of the crèche was to depict the origins of the holiday and that any benefit to religion was remote and incidental to this secular purpose. The opinion concluded by pointing out that there are many forms of official recognition of the Christmas season and that to strike down a passive symbol would be a stilted overreaction.

This review of some of the major areas of church-state law suggests something of the nature of the judiciary's struggle to give contextual meaning to the constitutional principle that the government must not sponsor religion. The dilemma for the judiciary has always been that it must not place the wall separating church and state so high that the no-establishment principle would run counter to the free-exercise clause. The no-establishment and free-exercise clauses are points on a continuum; the consequence of pushing one set of rules too far would be to run over the complementary principle. While the results of particular cases may provoke criticism, making clear distinctions and drawing precise lines in this area will always be hazardous.

FREE EXERCISE

Just as the body of no-establishment case law is of recent vintage, so is the body of free-exercise case law. As noted previously, the early state constitutions made extensive provisions for the protection of freedom of worship and conscience. One must presume that these provisions adequately served the needs of the major Protestant religious groups of pre–Civil War America. The removal in the early nineteenth century of some implicit political disabilities against Roman Catholics and Jews ensured that all the major religious denominations were not only free to worship but free to enjoy equal civil rights. While anti-Semitism and anti–Roman Catholicism were problems throughout the nineteenth century, religious bigotry did not prevent Jews and Roman Catholics from exercising their religion. They built their churches and temples, flourished, and became a part of the dominant religious culture. In short, throughout the greater part of the nineteenth century the free exercise of religion was simply not a problem for those religious groups within the Judeo-Christian mainstream. Even nonconformity of religious beliefs posed no problem; what became a problem was nonconformity to the law motivated by religious belief. The major example of this kind of behavior was the Mormon practice of polygamy.

It was the accident of the federal territorial status of Utah that led to the first and for decades the most important single free-exercise case. George Reynolds, a Utah Mormon, faithful to what was then a tenet of his church, had taken more than one wife. In doing so, he violated an act of Congress prohibiting bigamy in the territories. Reynolds offered the defense of religious belief and duty, a defense rejected by the trial court and subsequently rejected by the Supreme Court in *Reynolds* v. *United States* (1878). It is hardly surprising that in 1878 the judiciary rejected a defense of religious freedom to a charge of bigamy. Indeed, it would be surprising in the late twentieth century for the judiciary to accept such a defense. What is noteworthy about the *Reynolds* opinion is its lack of any recognition that there could be circumstances in which an otherwise valid secular law would yield to freedom of religious exercise. Instead, the Court reasoned that "laws are made for the government of actions, and while they cannot interfere with mere religious belief and opinions, they may with practices."

The *Reynolds* opinion came very close to reducing the free exercise of religion to mere freedom of religious belief without any constitutional right to act on, or exercise, individual beliefs, at least in the face of contrary law. The problem in free exercise is not laws that are direct and conscious violations of the right of free exercise, for these are rare. Indeed, the only recent example is compulsory chapel attendance administratively required for cadets at the national military and naval academies, which was successfully challenged as a violation of free exercise in *Anderson* v. *Laird* (1972). The problem, rather, is whether the free-exercise clause offers any protection to religiously motivated conduct that conflicts with a neutral secular law or regulation. The *Reynolds* opinion implicitly suggests that it does not. In a society in which few religious groups have unusual religious needs, the *Reynolds* opinion will work reasonably well. Where there is a sharp differentiation between the religious and the secular—that is, where religion does not inform its communicants how they must act in their secular lives—there will be little conflict with social or legal norms. The *Reynolds* opinion fell short of addressing the needs of marginal religious groups. For many sectlike religions the consequential dimension of religious beliefs extends deeply into the daily secular lives of communicants.

Uniform Behavior. The *Reynolds* decision failed to recognize those situations in which it would be possible to exempt religiously motivated conduct without jeopardizing the effectiveness of a given law or administrative regulation. While the effectiveness of a bigamy statute might well be seriously undermined by any exemptions, it does not follow that all secular law has the same need for uniform enforcement as a bigamy statute. The absence of an absolute need for uniform behavior can be seen in the flag-salute cases.

Beginning in the late nineteenth century it became increasingly common in public schools to begin the school day with a flag salute and pledge of allegiance. In some jurisdictions the ceremony became compulsory. This created a problem for the Jehovah's Witnesses, who concluded that participation would violate their religious duty to abstain from worshipping graven images. When the issue was litigated in *Miners-*

ville District v. *Gobitis* (1939), the Supreme Court rejected the plea of abstention based on religious freedom. In 1943, however, the Court overturned its earlier decision and concluded in *West Virginia State Board of Education* v. *Barnette* that a state does not have the power to coerce patriotism by a compulsory flag-salute exercise. The opinion, however, rested broadly on the First Amendment rather than merely on the free-exercise clause. Justice Robert Jackson, writing for the majority, concluded,

> If there is any fixed star in our constitutional constellation, it is that no official, high or petty, can prescribe what shall be orthodox in politics, nationalism, religion, or other matters of opinion or force citizens to confess by word or act their faith therein. If there are any circumstances which permit an exception, they do not now occur to us.

The *Barnette* case, however, had virtually no impact outside of the immediate issue of the compulsory flag salute. Indeed, it was not until 1963 that the United States Supreme Court directly confronted the issue of whether a free-exercise claim may supersede an otherwise valid administrative regulation or state law. In *Sherbert* v. *Verner* the claimant had been discharged from her employment because, as a member of the Seventh-Day Adventist church, she refused to work on Saturdays. She was subsequently offered other suitable employment and refused when the offers also involved Saturday work. She then filed a claim for state unemployment compensation. Her claim was rejected under a state regulation that denied benefits to those who reject available suitable employment without good cause.

In reversing the denial, the Court pointed out that refusal to work on Saturday on religious grounds was not analogous to those situations in which the government had validly regulated overt acts prompted by religious beliefs, such as polygamy. If the claimant's conduct was not a substantial threat to peace, order, or public safety, then, the Court reasoned, the denial of a benefit had to withstand a twofold test. First, did the denial constitute an infringement or burden on the rights of free exercise? Second, if there is a burden, is it nonetheless justified by a compelling state interest? Since the state ruling forced the claimant to choose between the precepts of her religion and the possible forfeiture of benefits, the burden was real, even if indirect. Equally, the Court argued, no compelling interest had been established by the state to justify the denial. The state had merely raised the abstract possibility that by granting Sherbert unemployment compensation, the state unemployment compensation fund could be diluted in the future by fraudulent claims filed by those feigning religious objection to Saturday work.

The Supreme Court underscored the *Sherbert* formula in *Wisconsin* v. *Yoder* (1972), wherein the Court considered whether Amish parents could be found guilty of violating the state's compulsory-education law by refusing on religious grounds to send their children to school beyond the eighth grade. Employing the *Sherbert* balancing test, the Court accepted the contention that it was a matter of deep religious conviction in the Amish faith that secular education beyond the eighth grade would expose Amish children to worldly influences alien to their religion. Thus, a compulsory-education law beyond the eighth grade was in fact a burden on a sincerely held religious belief. Furthermore, the Court concluded that the state had failed to establish that its law was so compelling that an established religious practice had to give way to the state interest. Since Amish parents continue to provide their children with practical, vocational education for a life in a closed community, there was no evidence that Amish children either grew up in ignorance or became burdens on society.

Both the *Sherbert* and *Yoder* cases stress that once a claimant has established that a government regulation burdens the claimant's religion, the government must demonstrate by more than an abstract argument its compelling interest in not exempting the claimant from its regulations. Thus, in *Thomas* v. *Review Board* (1981), the Court rejected the argument of the Indiana Employment Security Review Board that denying Thomas' claim to unemployment compensation was based on a compelling state interest. Thomas, a member of Jehovah's Witnesses, quit his job when he was transferred by his employer to a company unit engaged in fabricating parts for military tanks. The review board argued that its denial was based on the compelling need to avoid widespread unemployment and the consequent burden of the unemployment fund that would result if individuals were allowed to quit jobs for personal reasons. The board also argued that by refusing to accept Thomas' reason for leaving his job, the board would thereby discourage employers from probing into the religious beliefs of employees. As in both the *Sherbert* and *Yoder* cases, the majority in the *Thomas* case simply observed that there was no evidence in the record to support either argument.

It should not be inferred from the above opinions that any state burden on the free exercise of religion will be overturned by the judiciary. In *Heffron* v. *International Society for Krishna Consciousness* (1981) the Supreme Court upheld a Minnesota state-fair regulation restricting distribution, sales, and solicitation activities to a fixed booth location. The Hare Krishna sect challenged the fixed-booth rule because of its religious belief in *sankirtán,* a peripatetic ritual requiring members to proselytize and beg for alms.

While the Court accepted that the regulation burdened the Krishna religion, it concluded that the regulation was a valid restriction on the place and manner of exercising a First Amendment right. Given the need to control the flow of crowds within a congested area, the regulation served to prevent disorder, a goal that could not be achieved if all groups at a fair who were entitled to First Amendment protection were granted exemption.

A similar result was reached in a 1982 case involving the payment of social security taxes by a member of the Amish faith. In *United States* v. *Lee* a member of the Old Order Amish operated a farm and a carpentry shop, employing several members of the Amish faith. Lee argued that he should not be required either to withhold social security taxes from his employees or pay the employer's share of the tax; the Amish faith requires its members to provide collectively the kind of social assistance contemplated by the tax, and therefore it would violate the Amish faith to either pay or receive social security taxes or benefits.

The Court, while agreeing that payment of the tax would burden members of the Amish faith, concluded that there was a compelling government interest in maintaining mandatory and continuous participation in the social security system. Recognizing that to grant Lee's request for an exemption would open the door to requests for religious exemptions from the taxes, the Court observed,

> The obligation to pay the social security tax initially is not fundamentally different from the obligation to pay income taxes; the difference—in theory at least—is that the social security tax revenues are segregated for use only in furtherance of the statutory program. There is no principled way, however, for purposes of this case, to distinguish between general taxes and those imposed under the Social Security Act. If, for example, a religious adherent believes war is a sin, and if a certain percentage of the federal budget can be identified as devoted to war-related activities, such individuals would have a similarly valid claim to be exempt from paying that percentage of the income tax.

The *Sherbert-Yoder* line of cases does not suggest that mere proof of burden in the free exercise of religion was all that was necessary to gain exemption from a valid government regulation. The tax cases make it clear that it is possible for the government to establish a compelling-interest argument. Further illustrations of this can be seen in drug-use cases. While the United States Supreme Court has never ruled on a case involving a claim of religiously motivated drug use, other courts have made rulings in this area. Without exception, the judiciary has rejected pleas of religious motivation in marijuana and LSD cases (*People* v. *Crawford,* 1972; *State* v. *Brashear,* 1979). However, there have been occasional cases where a state court has upheld the use of the drug peyote in religious ceremonies by adult members of the Native American church (*People* v. *Woody,* 1964).

In contrast to tax and drug cases, medical care cases are often more difficult to resolve. There is little difficulty in demonstrating a compelling state interest in cases where parents make a religious claim on behalf of a child. Since the turn of the century the judiciary has consistently refused to accept a religious excuse for parental medical neglect of a child, as in *People* v. *Pierson* (1903). Thus, while Jehovah's Witnesses object on religious grounds to blood transfusions, as parents they have been unsuccessful in their objections to transfusions for minor children, as in *In re Green* (1971). However, adult Jehovah's Witnesses have occasionally been successful in arguing that the state has no compelling interest in forcing an adult of sound mind to be transfused, as in *In re Melideo* (1976). Similarly, religious groups that object to the immunization requirement for students entering public schools have occasionally been successful in demonstrating that where a particular communicable disease no longer poses a danger to the public, religious exemptions should be granted, as in *Brown* v. *City School District of Corning* (1976).

Sincerity and Authenticity of Religious Claims. Opening the door to religious claimants under the free-exercise clause has undoubtedly given increased vitality to religious liberty; the new vitality, however, raises a potential problem for religious freedom. The increased protection of religious exercise may prompt frivolous claims—for instance, claims not based on sincerely held religious beliefs or on an authentic religion. Since the Constitution specifies that it is religion that may be freely exercised, the judiciary faces a dilemma. If religion is the predicate for a constitutional claim of free exercise, may the judiciary determine the constitutional meaning of the word *religion*? In the vast majority of free-exercise cases, there is no problem in determining the bona fides of a claim or whether the claim is in fact an authentic religious claim. There is little doubt, however, that in the 1970s a certain number of "churches" or "religions" emerged for the primary, if not the sole, purpose of taking advantage of the free-exercise clause. This has been particularly evident in certain tax and drug cases and in some cases involving the religious rights of prisoners.

Inquiry into the bona fides of a claim and especially inquiry into the authenticity of a religion poses serious problems for the judiciary. Good faith does not depend on the truth or falsity of a religious belief; indeed, inquiring into the truth or falsity of a religious belief has been long foreclosed by the Supreme Court (*United States* v. *Ballard,* 1944). But courts occasionally find it necessary to inquire into the sincerity of a claimant's assertions. For example, in a criminal prosecution for violation of the income tax law, a federal court allowed the government to demonstrate that the defendant lacked sincerity in claiming a religious-order exemption, because he set up a church solely for purpose of tax avoidance (*United States* v. *Peister,* 1980). If the judiciary were precluded from any inquiry into the bona fides of a claim, a claimant would be able, under the guise of free exercise, to draw a conjurer's circle around illegal conduct.

On the other hand, judicial inquiry into authenticity of a claim—that is, whether the belief, however sincerely held, is in fact an authentic religious belief—is fraught with problems. For example, must a claimant demonstrate that the religion, in order to qualify as a religious belief, has a written theology or that it is based on belief in a Supreme Being (*Missouri Church of Scientology* v. *State Tax Commission,* 1977)? It is one thing to hold that the free-exercise clause does not protect mere personal or philosophical beliefs and quite another thing to suggest that a belief must rest on a theological conviction. In recent years it has become apparent that many trial-court judges are puzzled by the religious claims of American Indians, in part because the claims rest on an oral tradition of beliefs rather than a written theology (*Badoni* v. *Higginson,* 1977). Is a belief to be dismissed legally because to the observer within the Judeo-Christian tradition it is irrational or superstitious? On the other hand, phenomenological definitions of religion would likely introduce a large measure of flimflam into free-exercise litigation.

CONCLUSION

From 1789 until the 1940s, religious liberty in the United States was defined more by custom than by case law. The original state and federal constitutional provisions broadly delineated the principles of religious liberty, and these provisions in turn reflected the broad consensus that shaped the course of religious liberty for well over one hundred years. The explicit understandings arrived at in the late eighteenth and early nineteenth centuries were no state support for sectarian dogma; no state financial support for a particular church or clergy; and no state interference with an individual's religious beliefs or with the right to worship, always assuming that religious liberty would not excuse acts of licentiousness or justify practices inconsistent with public peace and safety. The implicit understanding was that organized religion continued to be important to the community and that the government, while remaining denominationally neutral, was not foreclosed from encouraging a broadly based interdenominational Christianity.

RELIGIOUS LIBERTY

For its part, the judiciary largely confined its role to confirming existing arrangements—that is, to legitimating specifically Protestant or generally Christian customs and laws, such as Sabbath closing, prayer, Bible reading, and laws against blasphemy. Indeed, with the exception of the issue of Mormonism, the nineteenth century was not marked by great legal struggles over religious liberty. In consequence, as the United States moved into the twentieth century there had been little judicial activity in anticipation of the problems facing an increasingly pluralistic society and a positive state prone to greater regulation. It was not until the *Cantwell* decision in 1940 and the *Everson* decision in 1947 that the religion clauses of the First Amendment were made applicable to the states. After this incorporation, however, the United States Supreme Court began the process of adjusting the clauses to a post-Protestant society.

Whatever course the Supreme Court charted after the *Everson* decision was likely to meet with opposition, an opposition that necessarily stemmed from the tension inherent in the religion clauses. In point of fact, the religion clauses are not conceptually coherent, merely complementary. The clauses offer no single residual principle but a congeries of reflections and perspectives on how religious liberty can best be maintained. From the point of view of results, the course charted by the Court through the early 1980s was a midcourse. It upheld bus transportation for parochial-school students, tax exemptions of churches, Sabbath laws, private-school tuition tax credits, some auxiliary services for parochial schools and students, legislative prayers, and a "secular encased" public nativity scene. Yet, the Court also struck down prayers and Bible readings in the public schools, sometimes gave preferential treatment to the exercise of religious beliefs, and generally disapproved of direct government subventions to church schools, at least where the religious mission dominated the enterprise. Such seemingly inconsistent results were not likely to produce a coherent jurisprudence. And as always, judicial incoherence was an open invitation to criticism, and the Court did not want for critics.

The critics faulted the Court for its lack of doctrinal coherence, its failure to be historically accurate in its opinions, and its lack of faithfulness to the intention of the framers of the First Amendment. Yet, each of the criticisms fails, although for different reasons. The search for a neutral principle that would substitute for doctrinal incoherence presumes not only a single residual principle in religious liberty but a cohesive society. The first presumption tortures the multiple and sometimes conflicting goals of the religion clauses, and the second presumption defies the reality of contemporary America. The argument that the Court failed to understand the evangelical rather than the political basis in colonial history for the religion clauses is unpersuasive. Nowhere is it required that history be elevated into constitutional law. The contemporary meaning of the religion clauses cannot be tied exclusively to Roger Williams', James Madison's, or Thomas Jefferson's understanding of religious liberty. Surely we underestimate these men of politics and vision if we do not concede to their ideas the vital capacity for growth. To bind the idea of religious freedom to the warp of time would destroy it. There have been numerous additions to the configuration of religious freedom since the late eighteenth century that the judiciary must necessarily factor into its decisions. The state, the churches, and the individual do not stand in the same relationship to one another today as they did two hundred years ago.

The decisions of the Supreme Court are natural and appropriate targets of criticism, and in no area has this been truer than in the often emotion-filled area of religious liberty. Indeed, many of the decisions reviewed above do raise valid questions that deserve further study and reflection. However, some critics of the Court fear that decisions such as those banning prayers and Bible readings in the public schools or those denying direct state subventions to parochial schools are a part of the broader process of secularization that is eroding the spiritual and religious basis for society (Neuhaus). Such fears are a legitimate basis for examining the social impact of judicial decisions.

What is puzzling about some criticism is its selective nature. Critics of the Court who argue for a benevolent neutrality in separating cases, a neutrality that would extend the mammon of the state to well-organized religious groups, are often indifferent or even hostile to extending constitutional protection to unconventional religious groups or to protecting nonbelievers from majoritarian religious impulses.

A strong argument can be made that benevolent neutrality and a restricted view of free exercise were operative facts throughout the greater part of American history. What cannot be successfully argued is that these positions were constitutionally enshrined. Customary practices are not necessarily constitutional. The Supreme Court is free to weigh any number of factors in arriving at its decisions, including custom, precedent, constitutional language, abstract principles, and social utility. A fair assessment of the Court's overall record in religious liberty since the 1940s suggests that it followed a moderate course in separatism and free exercise. While the Court has not been unmindful that religiously motivated conduct can have negative social consequences, still it has at long last restored the word *exercise* to religion clauses. Similarly, the Court has steered a middle course between those religious groups that wish to receive ever-increasing amounts of the state's benevolence and the village atheist who seeks judicial assistance in purging society of its religious impulse.

CASES

Abington School District v. Schempp, 374 U.S. 203 (1963)
Allen v. Morton, 495 F.2d 65 (D.C. Cir. 1973)
American Civil Liberties Union v. Raban County Chamber of Commerce, 510 F. Supp. 886 (1981)
Anderson v. Laird, 466 F.2d 283 (D.C. Cir. 1972)
Badoni v. Higginson, 455 F. Supp. 641 (1977)
Baird v. White, 476 F. Supp. 442 (1979)
Barron v. Baltimore, 7 Peters 243 (1833)
In re Bartha, 134 Cal. Rep. 39 (1977)
Battle v. Anderson, 376 F. Supp. 402 (1974)
Bender v. Williamsport Area School District, 741 F.2d 538 (3rd Cir. 1984)
Board of Education v. Allen, 392 U.S. 236 (1968)
Brown v. City School District of Corning, 429 N.Y.S.2d 620 (1976)
Cantwell v. Connecticut, 310 U.S. 296 (1940)
Committee for Public Education v. Nyquist, 413 U.S. 756 (1973)
Commonwealth v. Cooke, 7 Am. L. Reg. 417 (1859)
Cruz v. Beto, 405 U.S. 319 (1972)
Dearle v. Frazier, 173 P. 35 (Wash., 1918)
Donahoe v. Richards, 38 Maine 379 (1854)
Engel v. Vitale, 370 U.S. 421 (1962)
Eugene Sand and Gravel v. City of Eugene, 552 P.2d 596 (Or., 1976)
Everson v. Board of Education, 330 U.S. 1 (1947)
Florey v. Sioux Falls School District, 619 F.2d 1311 (8th Cir. 1980)

Fox v. City of Los Angeles, 587 P.2d 663 (Cal., 1978)
Freeman v. Scheve, 91 N.W. 846 (Neb., 1902)
Gilfillan v. Philadelphia, 637 F.2d 924 (3rd Cir. 1980)
In re Green, 286 A.2d 681 (Pa., 1971)
Heffron v. International Society for Krishna Consciousness, 452 U.S. 640 (1981)
Lemon v. Kurtzman, 403 U.S. 602 (1971)
Levitt v. Committee for Public Education, 413 U.S. 472 (1973)
Lynch v. Donnelly, 465 U.S. 668 (1984)
McCollum v. Board of Education, 333 U.S. 203 (1948)
Marsh v. Chambers, 463 U.S. 783 (1983)
Meek v. Pittenger, 421 U.S. 349 (1975)
In re Melideo, 390 N.Y.S.2d 523 (1976)
Meyer v. Oklahoma City, 496 P.2d 789 (Okla., 1972)
Minersville District v. Gobitis, 310 U.S. 586 (1939)
Missouri Church of Scientology v. State Tax Commission, 560 S.W.2d 837 (Mo., 1977)
Mueller v. Allen, 103 S.Ct. 3062 (1983)
People v. Crawford, 328 N.Y.S.2d 747 (1972)
People v. Pierson, 176 N.Y. 201 (1903)
People v. Woody, 40 Cal. Rptr. 69 (1964)
Perry v. School District No. 81, 344 P.2d 1036 (Wash., 1959)
Reynolds v. United States, 98 U.S. 145 (1878)
Schnapp v. Lefkowitz, 422 N.Y.S.2d 798 (1979)
Sherbert v. Verner, 374 U.S. 398 (1963)
Sloan v. Lemon, 413 U.S. 825 (1973)
Smith v. Smith, 523 F.2d 121 (4th Cir. 1975)
State v. Brashear, 593 P.2d 63 (N.M., 1979)
Stone v. Graham, 449 U.S. 39 (1980)
Thomas v. Review Board, 450 U.S. 707 (1981)
Tilton v. Richardson, 403 U.S. 672 (1971)
United States v. Ballard, 322 U.S. 78 (1944)
United States v. Kahane, 396 F. Supp. 687 (1975)
United States v. Lee, 455 U.S. 252 (1982)
United States v. Peister, 631 F.2d 658 (10th Cir. 1980)
Walz v. Tax Commission, 397 U.S. 664 (1970)
Weiss v. District Board, 44 N.W. 967 (Wis., 1890)
West Virginia State Board of Education v. Barnette, 319 U.S. 624 (1943)
Widmar v. Vincent, 454 U.S. 263 (1981)
Wisconsin v. Yoder, 406 U.S. 205 (1972)
Wolman v. Walter, 433 U.S. 229 (1977)
Zorach v. Clauson, 343 U.S. 306 (1952)

BIBLIOGRAPHY

Sidney E. Ahlstrom, *A Religious History of the American People* (1972), presents an exhaustive and thorough one-volume history of American religion from colonial times through the 1960s. Robert L. Cord, *Separation of Church and State* (1982), is a critical attack on the Warren and Burger Court decisions. Robert O. Drinan, *Religion, the Courts and Public Policy* (1963), examines questions about church-school and public-aid issues and religious education. Edwin Gaustad, *Historical Atlas of Religion in America* (1976), is the seminal study of the development and geographic location of religious groups in America. Donald Giannella, ed., *Religion and the Public Order*, reviews religion and the law, published annually under the auspices of the Institute of Church and State, Villanova University School of Law.

Evarts B. Greene, *Religion and the State* (1941), includes useful chapters on seventeenth- and eighteenth-century developments. Mark De Wolfe Howe, *The Garden and the Wildness* (1965), argues that the Warren Court's use of a Jeffersonian theory of separation ignores the theological bases of the religion clauses. Paul G. Kauper, *Religion and the Constitution* (1964), offers a thoughtful and scholarly examination of the constitutional problems surrounding the religion clauses. Dean M. Kelley, ed., *Government Intervention in Religious Affairs* (1982), collects essays on such issues as tax exemption for churches and government restraints on political activities of religious groups. Milton R. Konvitz, *Religious Liberty and Conscience* (1968), includes especially thoughtful chapters on the legal meaning of religion. Philip B. Kurland, *Religion and the Law of Church and State and the Supreme Court* (1962), offers an organizing principle for judicial interpretation of the religion clauses.

Michael I. Malbin, *Religion and Politics* (1978), examines the contributions of Jefferson and Madison to the religion clauses. Richard E. Morgan, *The Supreme Court and Religion* (1972), makes a sometimes persuasive argument in favor of an accommodationist approach to church-state issues. Gustavus Myers, *History of Bigotry in the United States* (1943), details the history of religious bigotry from the Middle Ages in Europe through the 1930s in the United States. Richard J.

Neuhaus, *The Naked Public Square* (1984), gives a Christian American view of issues of religion and democracy. Leo Pfeffer, *Church, State, and Freedom* (1967), is a clear and lucid argument about religious liberty written by a major church-state attorney.

Frank J. Sorauf, *The Wall of Separation* (1976), investigates the group politics of separation litigation. Murray S. Stedman, Jr., *Religion and Politics in America* (1964), inquires into the role of organized religion in politics. Anson P. Stokes, *Church and State in the United States,* 3 vols. (1950), provides an indispensable sourcebook on church and state from the colonial period through the 1940s. H. Frank Way, "Survey Research on Judicial Decisions: The Prayer and Bible Reading Cases," in *Western Political Quarterly,* 21 (1968), examines elementary-school teacher compliance with the prayer and Bible-reading decisions. H. Frank Way and Barbara Burt, "Religious Marginality and the Free Exercise Clause," in *American Political Science Review,* 77 (1983), studies the impact of two Supreme Court decisions in redefining free exercise for marginal religious groups. Paul Weber and Dennis Gilbert, *Private Churches and Public Money* (1979), argues for fiscal neutrality as a middle ground in the controversies surrounding the public aid and taxation questions.

[*See also* BURGER COURT AND ERA; CIVIL LIBERTIES AFTER 1937; FREE SPEECH AND EXPRESSION; STATE CONSTITUTIONAL LAW; STONE AND VINSON COURTS AND ERAS; *and* WARREN COURT AND ERA.]

SEX EQUALITY

UNDER THE CONSTITUTION

Beverly B. Cook

UNDER law in the United States, women and men do not have the same status. The inequalities exist in American constitutions, statutes, judge-made doctrines, and rules written by popularly elected representatives and their appointed bureaucrats. The relation of sex identity to legal rights and duties varies from national to state governments and between states and between localities. The minimum standards of equality of treatment by government, however, are set by the United States Supreme Court in the interpretation of the equal protection clause of the Fourteenth Amendment. Some states have equal rights amendments in their constitutions, and some state high courts use a strict standard for sex equality under state law. Congress and state legislative bodies have passed some statutes to ensure equity in practice that go beyond the Supreme Court's standards. But the Supreme Court provides a baseline for these other policies that is more visible and more compelling to the American public. Justices are expected to articulate the contemporary norms of the society on sex roles in deciding cases. This essay will provide an overview of the status of women under the United States Constitution as interpreted by the Supreme Court.

HISTORICAL PERSPECTIVES

The framers of the Constitution created and assigned powers to the national government and paid little attention to individuals except to protect them from mistreatment and intrusion by that government. For those rights of expression and due process guaranteed against national denial in the Bill of Rights there were no sex classifications. The Constitution did not take sex into account at all until the passage, in 1868, of the Fourteenth Amendment, which provides for the reduction of a state's representation in Congress as punishment for denying the right to vote to adult male citizens. The response of the all-male Congress to the efforts of women to expand their political rights after the Civil War was to denigrate their political role in the basic political document.

The first United States feminist movement, usually dated from the Seneca Falls convention of 1848, focused its efforts upon the state and local governments, which denied women the right to participate in government, legalized superior statuses for men in family relationships, and refused to recognize or protect women's rights to education, to recreation, and to jobs. The gradual transfer of the slave issue from the state to the national agenda and its legal resolution after the war through amendments to the federal Constitution showed women how their state-level problem could also be transformed into a national issue to be settled by national legal norms. The attempts of feminists to add "sex" to the categories of race, color, or previous condition of servitude of citizens whose votes were protected against federal and state denial in the Fifteenth Amendment failed in 1870. It was not until 1920, after making their contribution in World War I and bringing political pressure to bear upon President Woodrow Wilson, that American women won the guarantee of their voting right with the Nineteenth Amendment.

The equal rights amendment (ERA) passed by Congress in 1972 fell short of ratification in 1982 by three states. That amendment—which simply says, "Equality of rights under the law shall not be denied or abridged by the United States or by any state on account of sex"—would have given sex the same constitutional status as "suspect classes" (such as race, ethnicity, and national origin), which cannot be employed for differential treatment under law except for overriding public purposes or for remedial, temporary aid. The Constitution now explicitly protects sex class interests only in the area of voting. Nevertheless, women have been able since 1971 to expand their constitutional rights through precedents established in court cases based upon the equal protection clause of the same Fourteenth Amendment that was once interpreted to deny them federal protection for basic civic rights.

The story of the expansion of women's rights under the Constitution has moved through five phases: before the Fourteenth Amendment, from the Fourteenth Amendment to the Nineteenth, from the Nineteenth Amendment to the 1971 *Reed* decision, from 1971 to the 1976 *Craig* decision, and the contemporary period, which will last until either the ERA passes or the Court announces that sex is a suspect class. Neither the ERA in the Constitution nor the suspect label on sex would necessarily strike justices sex-blind and guarantee the same legal status for women as men.

Before the Civil War, women turned to the federal courts for relief unavailable under state law and, unlike blacks, found that their identity was not a constitutional bar to their use of the federal courts. The post–Civil War period of constitutional interpretation of women's rights is characterized by federal approval of the differentiation and segregation of women and men by governments, first by denying political feminists' claims to participate and later by approving social feminists' protective policy demands. The period of the two world wars is characterized by the failures of women with a variety of complaints of unequal social, economic, and political treatment to bring themselves under the umbrella of the equal protection clause; and the contemporary period involves the unfolding of the meaning of that clause in relation to women's various claims in the landmark decisions of *Reed* v. *Reed* in 1971 and *Craig* v. *Boren* in 1976.

The equal-protection doctrine has proved to be the most useful legal tool for Supreme Court justices who wish to extend sex equality into new policy areas, but they have also used their own powers to supervise lower federal courts and to remake common law. The Court has recognized three types of classifications used by legislatures —suspect, semisuspect, and nonsuspect. Suspect classes are those defined by the Constitution as

unacceptable—race, color, and previous condition of servitude—and those added in the Court's discretion by analogy, such as ethnicity, national origin, and religious affiliation. The semisuspect classes have been considered suspect by some justices or for some purposes; they include alienage, illegitimacy, and sex. The characteristic that usually distinguishes suspect from nonsuspect is immutability; in other words, there is no personal control or responsibility for one's race, sex, place of birth, parents' citizenship, religion, or economic status. If government provides for different treatment of a suspect class, the Court places a heavy burden on government to show a vital public interest to be served, such as national security in wartime.

The constitutional rights of women will be traced here over time and under the broad topics of women's rights to participate in public life as citizens, workers, and consumers. These public roles could once have been categorized into the separate spheres of the political world, the work world, and the social world, but the boundaries of these arenas are no longer clear. Political, military, and civil service positions have become well-paid and semipermanent jobs rather than part-time and short-term assignments for amateurs, so that the denial of equal opportunity in government may also result in the loss of economic opportunities. The denial of access to education for certain skills and to places where workers congregate directly impedes equal opportunity in employment. The Supreme Court, which makes constitutional law out of its own reading of the document and its own precedents and understanding of the new moral and practical arguments of those affected, has in modern cases recognized the weblike context of the real world in which the principle of equality is to be applied. The following separate discussions of political, economic, and social rights allow for a sharper focus, but the implications of equality won or denied in one arena must be kept in mind when speaking of others.

POLITICAL RIGHTS

To raise women's issues before an authoritative tribunal in anticipation of a favorable response, individuals must gain recognition as proper participants by decision-makers. At minimum, personal participation includes the right to bring complaints into court and the right to vote on public issues and for public officeholders. Women made demands for such participation when they discovered that the "protectors" assigned by law to pursue their best interests provided inadequate representation for women as individuals and as a class. Women's pursuit of recognition under the Constitution as legitimate participants in public life was not inspired by theories of equality but by the distress and frustration caused by impotence to "right wrongs" for themselves and to improve the community environment. Republican ideals provided the theoretical grounding for women's claims to participate in those political institutions.

The claims of women before the Civil War to use the federal courts fared better than the claims of blacks. In *Barber* v. *Barber* (1859) the Supreme Court allowed a woman legally separated from her husband and living in another state to sue for alimony in the federal courts under the constitutional clause (Article III, Section 2) relating to diversity of citizenship, which involves controversies between citizens of different states. The Court solved the dilemma of women with a grievance who could not ask for relief in either a state or a federal forum, by revising the traditional definition of a married woman's citizen status and thereby providing her access to the federal judiciary. A majority of the justices accepted her independent choice of domicile and therefore of state citizenship in order to "do justice." The dissenters would have left her bound by her estranged husband's choice of domicile and therefore restricted her to whatever relief, if any, might be available or affordable in his state court system. The precedent in favor of allowing women more leeway in choosing their own state citizenship was followed in later cases.

A unanimous Court in 1875 pronounced that the national citizenship status of women, unlike that of blacks before the Thirteenth Amendment, was settled by historical experience. However, by the 1890s the State Department considered the citizenship of women married to aliens and living in their husbands' countries to be "suspended." In 1907, Congress clearly defined women's citizenship as second-class in fundamental ways. For example, an American woman would lose her United States citizenship involuntarily through marriage to a noncitizen

between 1907 and 1922 and through marriage to a man ineligible for citizenship even after 1922. The Court approved in 1915 the alienage of a woman born a United States citizen who had always resided in the United States but who had married a British subject (*MacKenzie* v. *Hare*, 1915). The loss of citizenship entailed the loss of that woman's California right to vote; her claim that expatriation must be voluntary except as punishment was rejected as subordinate to a higher principle—the oneness of husband and wife, an ancient principle of unity of interests and male dominance. The Court rationalized that in choosing her marital partner, she voluntarily chose expatriation. A man could marry a foreigner and retain his citizenship. In fact, from 1855 to 1922 a foreign-born wife automatically gained United States citizenship; after 1922, a female alien spouse went through a formal naturalization process that was less onerous than that required of males.

Women had the worst of both worlds. To keep her citizenship a woman could not marry the man of her choice. To gain citizenship, she had to promise to fulfill a man's military role. An alien woman was denied naturalization upon testifying that she was a pacifist who would not take up arms for the United States. A majority of the Supreme Court announced the fundamental principle that "it is the duty of citizens by force of arms to defend our government against all enemies" (*United States* v. *Schwimmer*, 1929). Justice Oliver Wendell Holmes noted in dissent the irony of denying citizenship to a woman more than fifty years old who, even if she wanted to, would not be allowed to bear arms because of her sex.

In 1978 the Supreme Court faced the issue of Indian tribal citizenship defined by sex and upheld the inequality by avoiding the dispute (*Santa Clara Pueblo* v. *Julia Martinez*). A 1939 tribal ordinance of the Santa Clara Pueblo denies citizenship in the tribe to the children of a tribal woman married to a noncitizen but provides citizenship to the children of a tribal man married to a noncitizen. Tribal citizenship carries the privilege of residence on the reservation, inheritance of the home, a share of communal lands, voting, and holding tribal office. A majority of the Court denied access to the federal court to a tribal woman who asked for an interpretation of the equal protection clause of the statutory Indian bill of rights in an effort to win for her children the same rights as a tribal man's children similarly situated. Only Justice Byron White was willing to examine her claims on the merits. The same federalist principle that stood in the way of female state citizens before 1971 still blocks national protection of the rights of female Indian tribal citizens.

Unless women put their national or state citizenship in jeopardy through marriage, free white women, like men, acquired citizenship by birth or naturalization. The citizenship status of women, despite their lack of suffrage and other political rights, was conceded in the case opinions in *Dred Scott* v. *Sandford* (1857), which denied persons of African descent, slave or free, any avenue to attain national citizenship and access to federal courts, short of constitutional revision. However, female citizenship did not carry the same rights and obligations as male citizenship. White women were second-class citizens, but even before the Civil War they could use the courts to adjudicate their claims. However, after the Civil War the Fourteenth and Fifteenth Amendments provided black males (on paper at least) with citizenship status superior to the constitutional status of females of any color.

Political rights are better described as responsibilities or duties, because their exercise directly provides only psychic goods, such as respect, belonging, and fulfillment, and often involves costs in time, money, or even life. But they are the instruments to gain, preserve, or redistribute all those statuses and goods under governmental control. Women do not have the same political responsibilities as men under the Constitution. Women's participation in voluntary political activities is now guaranteed, but women and men are not held to the same standard of duty. The United States, unlike some other nations that use elections to choose public officials, does not coerce its eligible citizens to vote by penalizing those who do not. Other forms of political activity, however, are mandatory, such as jury service, the payment of taxes, obedience to law, and military service. The Constitution is now interpreted to require women and men to contribute equally to the jury system, but not to government treasuries as taxpayers and not to law enforcement or to the armed forces. The view that women's tax burden could properly be less than men's is an idiosyncratic one (*Kahn* v. *Shevin,* 1974) and is

not expected to survive, but controversy over women's role in sex-related crimes and in the military is lively and continuing.

Electoral Duties. The inclusion of women in the political sphere has occurred gradually and against the strong resistance of men who thought women were ill equipped mentally and physically to engage in politics and of women who thought that politics was a crude and dangerous competition ill fitting their civilized standards. Organized women had to win the suffrage the hard way, through a long and exhausting campaign for a constitutional amendment, because they failed fifty years earlier to secure a Supreme Court decision that women's right to vote was protected by the Fourteenth Amendment. The National Woman Suffrage Association instigated court cases, including one involving the great leader of the women's movement, Susan B. Anthony. One case reached the Supreme Court, a civil action against a registrar of voters who refused to register Virginia Minor, a Missouri leader for women's rights (*Minor* v. *Happersett,* 1875). The Court denied her claim that the right to vote is a privilege of United States citizenship protected by the Fourteenth Amendment. Minor's lawyer-husband argued that only one kind of first-class citizenship should exist and that women citizens who could claim land, obtain passports, and pay taxes could not be denied the ballot by state governments. The Court, however, insisted unanimously that privileges and immunities of national citizenship did not include voting and that only the states, through their own legislatures or by ratifying a constitutional amendment, could revise women's political status.

The experience of the Civil War and the subsequent three amendments (Thirteenth, Fourteenth, and Fifteenth) had not persuaded the justices that the political power to protect individuals in their fundamental rights had shifted from the state to the federal courts. Minor's second argument—that, at minimum, voting for a federal officer, such as a member of Congress, must be a privilege of national and not state citizenship—did not stimulate the Court, absent a specific congressional act, to provide constitutional protection. Ten years later, in *Ex parte Yarbrough* (1884), the Court announced that voting for a federal officer was a privilege of national citizenship for black males. This decision should have overturned *Minor,* but the hidden rationale of women's biology and domestic role was more powerful in resisting change than the new view of federalism.

Leaving women's suffrage under state control meant that as late as 1914 women could vote in general elections in only eleven states; other classes excluded in one or more states were idiots, vagrants, paupers, felons, polygamists, soldiers, Chinese, and tribal Indians. The "Anthony" suffrage amendment, introduced in Congress in 1878 and finally passed in 1920, did not affect the Court-established principle in *Minor* that the meaning of citizenship could be different for women and men. As recently as the 1970s, state laws burdened a woman's suffrage with prerequisites not imposed upon a man, such as revealing her marital status, using her spouse's last name, and accepting his legal residence as hers for voting and running for office. Such sex discriminations rooted in common law have usually been struck down by lower courts and may disappear without reaching the Supreme Court. The states generally assumed that the right of women to hold elected and appointed public office was a corollary of the suffrage.

Jury Duty and Estate Administration. The duty of a woman to serve as juror is not her personal obligation but is the right of the criminal defendant to a cross-sectional jury. When in 1975 the Court finally did mandate the inclusion of women, it did so not on the basis of their equality of duty but on the basis of their differentness in perspective and experience *(Taylor* v. *Louisiana).* The constitutional rationale for women's presence in juries is not feminist.

As early as 1879 *(Strauder* v. *West Virginia),* the Court announced that states could exclude the class of women from jury duty without violating the Fourteenth Amendment's equal protection clause (but could not exclude the class of black males). Passage of the suffrage amendment did not guarantee women access to the state jury box. The Supreme Court refused to take the case of *Commonwealth* v. *Welosky* (1932), in which a state chief justice narrowly defined women's new political rights because their suffrage status was "radical" and did not imply any other civic duties. It was only in 1984 that the justices found "well-settled" constitutional law that purposeful discrimination at the state level was forbidden *(Hobby* v. *United States).*

Federal law directed federal trial judges to follow state rules on juror eligibility, so that until after World War II, state restrictions acceptable under the *Strauder* dictum affected federal juries. In *Ballard* v. *United States* (1946) the Court, by a narrow margin, exercised its supervisory power over lower federal courts and declared that the systematic and intentional exclusion of women deprived federal juries of their broad representative base. In 1968, Congress provided for a random procedure of calling persons to federal jury duty regardless of sex. Jury duty, although considered by Chief Justice Harlan Fiske Stone to be one of the highest duties of citizenship, was still not considered a right of women by state courts.

State laws could, and did, exclude or exempt women as a class without constitutional barrier until 1975. As long after the Nineteenth Amendment as 1961, a unanimous Supreme Court accepted Florida's system of requiring women, but not men, to volunteer for the jury list, over the complaints of a woman defendant that the procedure resulted in the all-male composition of her jury *(Hoyt* v. *Florida).* The Court approved the absolute exemption, combined with a procedure placing the initiative for rejecting the exemption upon each woman, as serving the state's policy recognizing woman "as the center of home and family life." The Court majority found the sex classification reasonable because no women who wanted to serve were arbitrarily denied participation and the state was saved the trouble of calling upon women who would then use their exemption. Placing the burden of volunteering upon women, of course, had the practical effect of eliminating them from participation.

In *Taylor* the arguments that the Court found unpersuasive in 1961 from a female defendant worked for a male defendant. Since the right of a defendant in a state courtroom to a jury trial had been established in 1968, the coordinate right to a cross-sectional jury could not be denied on the basis of old notions of women's family role or on the basis of administrative convenience. Only Justice William Rehnquist could not find what quality women brought to jury duty that would be lacking if women as a class were exempt. Rehnquist posed the logical dilemma that if men and women are equally qualified for service, then how does underrepresentation of one sex infringe upon impartiality. In 1979 the Court finally eliminated the privilege of women to take an exemption on the basis of sex after their involuntary random selection from the jury list *(Duren* v. *Missouri).* Again in dissent, Justice Rehnquist insisted that the Court majority had created a hybrid doctrine of the Fourteenth Amendment's equal protection and due process rights and was in fact recognizing the rights of women to participate in the judicial process as well as the rights of defendants to a representative jury. He thinks the doctrine of sex equality enters through the backdoor when fair convictions are overturned because of the exclusion of a group from jury service, and he won his point in 1984 when the Court refused to dismiss an indictment because of discriminatory selection of grand jury foremen *(Hobby).*

The equal entitlement of women to serve as estate executors or administrators was established in 1971 in the landmark case of *Reed* v. *Reed,* when the Supreme Court for the first time found the sex classification in a state law to be unconstitutional under the equal protection clause. Idaho law provided that a judge must give preference to the male relative whenever both sexes have the same entitlement to represent an estate in probate court. Upon the claim of a mother to the same consideration as her ex-husband in such an appointment, a unanimous Court declared that the law mandating preference for males did not meet the standard of rationality. Although Ruth Ginsburg provided arguments for the plaintiff to the effect that sex, like race, should be considered a suspect classification in law, the Court instead took only a modest step toward sex equality by using the weak test of equal protection. In refusing to apply the suspect-classification test, the Court invited future litigation over the appropriate parameters of sex distinctions in law. In finding dissimilar treatment of men and women "similarly situated" unconstitutional, the Court also revealed its new perspective and appreciation of the active participation of women in public roles. In the Court opinion, Chief Justice Warren E. Burger referred to the widows who handle estate matters. In addition, more than token numbers of women lawyers and judges worked in the probate specialty, which was considered especially appropriate for women. The *Reed* case is a watershed for equal-protection doctrine, but its practical effect was only to recognize women's competence in work often sex-assigned to them.

Women and Taxation. The obligation to pay taxes has been associated in American demo-cratic theory with the right to participate in political decision-making since the revolutionary period. Exemption from taxation, then, provides a rationale for denial of civic rights. In 1912, before women had any national guarantee of voting rights, the Court found no constitutional barrier to the Montana law that exempted women in small, hand-laundry businesses from the license tax *(Quong Wing* v. *Kirkendall).* A majority agreed that the state could place a lighter burden upon women doing work considered appropriate for their sex. The Court also noted that women were in a legal posture inferior to men in respect to other rights. The Court had earlier approved the use of the sex classification for differential treatment and now argued that the equal protection clause was not intended to create a "fictitious equality" between the sexes. The lone dissenter insisted that it was arbitrary to levy taxes on the basis of the characteristics of the owner instead of the business.

After women won the vote in 1920, some states established rules that discouraged their exercise of the suffrage. Women who did not register to vote were exempt in Georgia from paying the poll tax levied upon men—a tax that also created a barrier to black male suffrage. The unanimous Court found this inequality in taxation by sex permissible because the discrimination favored women—at the price of their vote *(Breedlove* v. *Suttles,* 1937). The same reasoning that excluded or exempted women from jury service was employed to explain their tax exemption—"the burdens necessarily borne by them for the preservation of the race." The Court also took note of the responsibility of a husband as head of the family to provide the income and therefore pay his wife's tax; in effect, the Court approved a husband's control of his wife's suffrage.

States that offer women special consideration in taxation still do so with constitutional authority. In 1974 the Court approved an exemption on the annual property tax for widows on grounds that "the financial difficulties confronting the lone woman . . . exceed those facing the man" *(Kahn* v. *Shevin).* The use of the sex class in public policy was sustained over the objections of three justices who evaluated the law as irrational in its over- and underinclusion of others in need of tax relief. Justices William Brennan and Thurgood Marshall insisted that sex is a suspect class subject to strict judicial scrutiny. The majority ruling was narrow in that it limited the sex classification to policies that could be categorized as affirmative action. The precedent has proved awkward and will likely be ignored or overruled.

On the other hand, the Court found women responsible for their share of the federal income tax (unless covered by an innocent-spouse law which excuses liability in some circumstances for ignorance of income) when their husbands failed to pay. Although equal-protection analysis was not explicitly used, the unanimous Court found that women had the same obligation as men to pay their federal taxes; according to Justice Harry Blackmun, "If the wives were to prevail here, they would have the best of two worlds" (*United States* v. *Mitchell*, 1971).

Where the amount involved is minor, such as a poll tax intended to control access to the ballot or an exemption worth as little as $5 a year, the Court is more likely to allow sex inequality than when the raising of revenues may be severely affected, as with the income tax. The special treatment of women is approved when the cost to government is low.

A good citizen is also obligated to pay civil debts. As recently as 1966, the Court was willing to allow a wife to avoid repayment of a debt because of a state law (since repealed) that made her signature on a contract nonbinding unless a court had made a special finding of her competence (*United States* v. *Yazell*). The majority refused "to do battle to vindicate the rights of women," while Justice Hugo Black for the dissenters pointed out that her privilege to act irresponsibly carried a heavy penalty for her freedom of action. He interpreted the oneness rule to mean "the one is the man" and noted that the Court was behind social change: "It seems at least unique to me that this Court should exalt this archaic remnant of a primitive caste system to an honorable place among the laws of the United States."

Good Citizenship. Obedience to the law and cooperation with law enforcement officers is an obligation of citizenship that, under common law, fell more heavily upon men than upon married women. English courts developed the common-law notion of the oneness of the two parties to marriage, and American courts generally followed this doctrine in resolving cases. The oneness doctrine also served to protect a man from his wife's testimony, thereby reinforcing his authority as head of the family. The loyalty of spouses was not only protected but also coerced, often to the detriment of the wife. As late as 1958, the Court continued the ancient privilege barring testimony unless both spouses consented (*Hawkins* v. *United States*).

In 1960 the Court began invoking its supervisory power over the federal judicial process to set rules contrary to common law. It reworked the oneness doctrine by requiring a woman to testify against her husband over her objection when she was identified as the victim of the crime (*Wyatt* v. *United States*, 1960) and by holding a woman responsible for answering an indictment for conspiring with her husband to defraud (*United States* v. *Dege*, 1960). The Court no longer allowed her (or him) to escape prosecution by claiming "oneness." In *Dege*, Justice Frankfurter refused "to be obfuscated by medieval views regarding the legal status of women" and rejected the presumption that a wife acted under the coercive influence of her husband. He went so far as to call "self-deluding romanticism" Blackstone's characterization of woman's legal disabilities as beneficial to her. The minority was less eager to hold women to account through the conspiracy statute for joint criminal activity with their husbands because women might be unfairly implicated because of their actual loyalty and subordination within the marriage.

In 1980 a unanimous Court decided to leave the issue of domestic integrity up to the spouse who could provide adverse testimony; the spouse could not be barred by the defendant spouse's objection or coerced by the state for her or his own good. The Court unanimously rejected the notion of a married woman as without any legal identity or responsibility apart from her husband (*Trammel* v. *United States*, 1980). Adult obligations to obey the law and to support law enforcement may be the same for both sexes; however, sex equality in this area will remain uncertain until the Court takes cases involving sex crimes, such as prostitution and rape, with equal protection issues.

What constitutes criminal behavior by minors does differ by sex. The Court has approved well-established state law and practice in criminal justice to apply different standards to the same behaviors of boys and girls. A 1981 case involved the California statutory rape law, which held minor males, but not minor females, criminally liable for illegal sexual intercourse (*Michael M.* v. *California Superior Court*). Five members of the Court refused to find the law contradictory to equal protection, because state government had a strong interest in preventing illegitimate pregnancies. Since the penalty of pregnancy fell only upon the female partner of the illicit activity, the Court thought the state could designate the male partner for legal responsibility and punishment.

Justice John Paul Stevens, one of the four dissenters, insisted that the argument was illogical, since the party who risked the most harm needed the most deterrence; he found both sexes equally responsible and argued that the social interest in evenhanded law enforcement outweighed a policy unlikely to achieve the reduction of illegitimate births. The other dissenters accused the majority of using the weak test of equal protection, which places on the complainant the burden of showing the irrationality of the law. The purpose, which the Court accepted at face value, was superimposed by the state's attorneys upon a statute of 1850 that had its roots in notions of female weakness and chastity and male assertiveness and promiscuity. The contemporary Court is most likely to deny sex equality when the weakness and vulnerability of the female to become pregnant is involved, even here where pregnancy was only a speculative consequence of the criminal act.

Military Service. The responsibility of men for national security remains greater than that of women. The Court has not yet faced a direct challenge to the statutory barrier to female combat duty, but the Court in 1981 approved the policy of registering young men, but not young women, for a draft (*Rostker* v. *Goldberg*). The reasoning of the majority was quite pragmatic, based upon deference to congressional expertise in national defense and military affairs. As long as congressional policy bars women from combat duty, women are not "similarly situated" to men and may be treated differently with respect to registration and draft for military service. Two dissenters in *Rostker* found the different registration obligation to be unconstitutional discrimination with no practical justification but in dicta expressed their view that exclusion of women from combat would not offend equal protection. Only Justice Marshall indicated in a separate opinion that he might include women in all the obligations of citizenship.

The Court majority has consistently stayed a step behind the other two branches on the matter of including women in the military. However, once legislative or service policy places women and men in the same status, the Court insists upon nondiscriminatory treatment. In the section on employment, we will see how equal status increases women's work benefits and how unequal status multiplies their disadvantages in economic and social contexts.

ECONOMIC RIGHTS

Governments deny women the same work opportunities as men, and the second-class employment status is still found constitutional by the Supreme Court. In deciding controversies in the economic field, the Court has described with great precision the "inferior qualities" of women that provided the rationalization for sex classification. The aspects of work that have involved different treatment by sex are job assignments, job conditions, and job benefits.

Women's Work. Women have been excluded from many occupations, in particular those with the most prestige and income. At the same time that the Court refused to guarantee women's political rights, it rejected women's claims to the occupation most closely associated with politics —attorney-at-law. The Supreme Court first let stand a state court decision denying women the right to practice law in 1873. The opinion of the Court in *Bradwell* v. *Illinois* rested upon a narrow interpretation of the scope of rights and privileges of United States citizenship; the justices left to the states regulation of occupations. Justice Joseph P. Bradley (with Justices Stephen J. Field and Noah Swayne in agreement) found in the fundamental attributes and the historic social roles of women another reason for approving the Illinois court decision against Myra Bradwell's admission to the bar. He argued that the "privileges and immunities" of men and women were different in the common law and in contemporary social practice. He saw in women timidity and delicacy and in men firmness and energy, qualities that fit their respective spheres in the home and in the larger world. He brushed aside the rights of single women to an occupation of their choice, calling them "exceptions" to the "paramount destiny and mission of women . . .

to fulfill the noble and benign offices of wife and mother." Bradley gave credit to nature and to divine law for the complementary personality traits and roles of the sexes and so found that the state, in restricting the legal profession to men, had simply recognized the suitability of male attributes to a demanding occupation and had not denied to women a natural right. Only Chief Justice Salmon Chase, who was considered a friend of women's suffrage and who relied upon his assertive daughter for advice on his presidential ambitions, voted for Bradwell's claim. But he did not prepare an opinion to explain why exclusion from an honorable profession on grounds of sex and marital status was not constitutional.

Bradley's views on women, which reflected his wife's perspective and the mainstream culture, undergirded many subsequent opinions approving different legal statuses for men and women. Often, the Court, which had avoided the substantive issue in *Bradwell* by relying on the federalism doctrine, adopted the weak argument of customary practice to prevent women from appearing in court.

Shortly after the women lawyers' losses in judicial forums, the Illinois legislature and the United States Congress passed legislation to open the legal profession to women. Exclusion from the state bar after *Bradwell* continued to be a prerogative of state government, and the last continental state to accept women as lawyers was Delaware, in 1923, exactly fifty years after Bradwell's failure to gain national protection for women's right to an occupation.

In the twentieth century, women looked to the equal protection clause, instead of the privileges-and-immunities clause, for constitutional protection of their employment rights. The Supreme Court accepted the same reasoning based on female inferiority to find no denial of equal protection and to allow the exclusion of women from another kind of bar. The female's inferiority was not her incapacity to perform the work for her clients, as in *Bradwell,* but her inability to protect herself from the customers. Her very presence in a tavern was predicted to incite morally and socially inappropriate behavior. As late as 1948, long after women had entered the political arena, the Court continued to approve state rules that effectively prevented most women from bartending *(Goesaert* v. *Cleary).*

The *Goesaert* case was actually a test of the strategy of the bartender's union to restore its prewar male exclusivity. The Michigan law, which the Court found constitutional, restricted bartending to men and to women who were the wives or daughters of male bar owners. A woman bar owner would necessarily employ men. The Court approved these restrictions on women's work without finding any evidence in the record of recurring incidents in bars. Even if the moral concern was a serious one, the state solution was to punish the female victim and not the male perpetrator. Whether the purpose of the state legislators was to protect weak women and the moral climate of bars or to improve the job opportunities of returning veterans in response to union lobbying, the result was the same for women who lost their employment.

The three liberal dissenters, Justices Wiley B. Rutledge, William O. Douglas, and Frank Murphy, found exclusion arbitrary and not "motivated by a legislative solicitude for the moral and physical well-being of women." Justice Frankfurter for the majority pointed out that Michigan could forbid all women from working behind a bar; the old court standard for equal protection of women as a class was so weak that any legitimate purpose would support discrimination. In following the protection doctrine established by his mentor, Justice Louis Brandeis, Frankfurter ignored the social changes between 1908 and 1948 and did not follow the sociological jurisprudence that undergirded the protective doctrine and would have supported the new egalitarian policy.

The principle established in the bartending decision—that the state can exclude women from an occupation on the basis of the incapacity of the sex class to maintain a safe work environment for themselves and others—remains viable, even though the Court after 1971 was willing to find that some sex distinctions in state law did deny equal protection. In *Dothard* v. *Rawlinson* (1977) the Court interpreted the Civil Rights Act of 1964 to allow the exclusion of women from contact guard jobs in maximum-security prisons for males under a narrow exception (bona fide occupational qualification). Although the decision was based upon statutory interpretation, the reasoning fits equal-protection analysis as well. State policy excluded all women regardless of size, strength, appearance, or experience from applying for the job while including men meeting minimal requirements. The justices who approved the state policy denied any romantic paternalism; the justices who found the policy inequitable insisted that the job applicant was disqualified simply by her "womanhood." The Court of the 1970s, like Courts early in the century, took into account the conditions of work as they affected women, but not men. Alabama's maximum-security prison was a jungle with inadequate facilities and no segregation of dangerous sex offenders. Two justices in the minority argued that as in the past, the state policy served to punish the potential victim by denying her the occupation for which she had trained rather than to hold lawbreakers to account and to improve the inhumane conditions of their environment.

Justice Rehnquist in his concurring opinion offered advice to attorneys who might take cases similar to *Dothard.* He suggested that height and weight restrictions that excluded most females from consideration could be defended as reasonable and necessary when the "appearance" of strength was a job qualification. Regardless of individuals' objective strength, some charisma associated by others with size would deprive them of jobs. Such a doctrine, based on the psychological reaction of prisoners to the size of guards, would transfer the power of defining women's economic role to wrongdoers, since most persons of small size are women. The Rehnquist doctrine would also require subtle judgments by the justices about the motivations and competency of legislators in imputing attitudes to male prisoners as a class toward shorter, lighter-weight (female) guards. The effect of Rehnquist's advice is to allow the state to adjust its policies and norms to the perspectives of prisoners who see smaller persons (women) as (sex) objects to defy and harm. Apparently Rehnquist assumed the mental set of prisoners to be in tune with the American culture of the 1870s when Justice Bradley characterized the female sex as weak, dependent, and vulnerable. Thus, the ancient rationale is restated in a contemporary psychological format to allow government to deny high-risk work roles to women.

The Court's balancing of interests is even more difficult when a First Amendment right conflicts with a legislative policy of affirmative action. In *Pittsburgh Free Press* v. *Human Relations Commission* (1973) a bare majority gave prefer-

ence to principles of federalism and sex equality over freedom of the press. The Court settled a similar conflict without dissent in 1984, upholding a state law applied to integrate a job-related association over a freedom-of-association claim (*Roberts* v. *United States Jaycees*).

The Court has also found constitutional the indirect exclusion of women from occupations through the legislative preference given to veterans. In 1979 the Court approved the most extreme form of veterans preference, in which Massachusetts offered an absolute, lifetime preference to veterans, defined as those who served at least one day during wartime (*Feeney* v. *Massachusetts*). The impact of the law was to prevent most women from consideration for supervisory civil service jobs, since almost half of the male state citizens, but less than 1 percent of the women, were war veterans. A majority of the Court, however, found no legislative intent to use the veteran classification as a pretext for sex discrimination. The Court did not recognize any responsibility to deal with the institutional sexism that resulted from the relationship between women's historical exclusion from military service and their sparse numbers among veterans. A minority (Justices Brennan and Marshall) recognized that the consequence of the state policy was a male-dominated civil service hierarchy and found the preference unconstitutional under the new middle-level equal-protection standard. The joint effect of the *Feeney* and *Rostker* decisions is to allow legislatures to box women into a second-class economic status in government, which historically has included a larger proportion of women workers than the private sector.

However, elected officeholders may not make sex a qualification for working in their offices. The Court in 1979 found in the Fifth Amendment (the federal due process guaranty which subsumes equal protection) the right of a woman to sue a congressman for damages for sex discrimination. Members of Congress had not covered their own behaviors as employers under Title VII of the Civil Rights Act, which restricts most private companies and state governments. Despite the concern of the Court minority over separation of powers, a bare majority approved a private cause of action by a young woman fired explicitly because the congressman decided to make male sex identity a qualification for her position as deputy administrative assistant (*Davis*

v. *Passman,* 1979). A similar decision was made under the Fourteenth Amendment's equal protection clause by the Fourth Circuit Court in favor of a female law student who was not allowed to apply for work as a state senate page (*Eslinger* v. *Thomas,* 1973). Although the Supreme Court has never accepted a case involving sex discrimination in the federal courts, the *Eslinger* opinion did describe the new attitude toward integration of the courts: "We have only to look at our own female secretaries and female law clerks to conclude that an intimate business relationship, including traveling on circuit, between persons of different sex presents no 'appearance of impropriety' in the current age, graduated as we are from Victorian attitudes."

Conditions of Women's Work. The distinctive nature and domestic roles of the female sex described by Justice Bradley in 1873 became the explanation in a unanimous opinion in 1908 for approving a paternalistic state policy toward working women (*Muller* v. *Oregon*). Women leaders of the National Consumer's League gathered data for the *Muller* brief about the impact of long hours of work upon women's health and persuaded the Court to allow Oregon to restrict the working hours of women to ten hours per day in laundries and factories. This opinion firmly established the doctrine that woman "is properly placed in a class by herself" as inherently different from men because of physical structure, maternal duties, and a natural dependence upon men. The Court's reasoning was not altruistic toward the weaker sex but rested upon the public interest in "healthy mothers" to produce "vigorous offspring" as state citizens. The Court thus relied on biological nature as the unchangeable foundation for sex classification in law.

Although the Court later allowed state governments to extend their protection to male workers, the *Muller* precedent for special protection for the inferior sex still stands. That case supported the overt exclusion of women from "dangerous" occupations, described above, and their covert exclusion from more remunerative jobs through control over the time and places of their work (*Radice* v. *New York,* 1924). For example, the Court approved in 1915 a California law restricting work hours of women pharmacists who could not then freely compete for professional positions against men, who could contract to work for ten hours (*Bosley* v. *McLaughlin*).

What social reformers intended as protective labor legislation soon became, in the hands of male lobbyists and legislators, a new burden upon women in the job market. Just as husbands controlled women's personal lives under common-law doctrine, and not necessarily to their advantage, state government took control of women's economic role and directly and indirectly kept women subordinate and poor.

The *Muller* opinion had particularly stressed the reproductive role of women, and many state agencies, as well as private businesses, protected the domestic role of women by refusing to hire or retain married women (potential mothers) and pregnant women. In 1974 the Court announced in a case from the Cleveland, Ohio, school district that the broad policy terminating pregnant teachers at the end of their fourth month and not considering reemployment until three months after childbirth burdened the due process rights of the individual to choose to bear a child (*Cleveland Board of Education* v. *La Fleur*). Only Justice Lewis Powell applied the equal protection clause; he found no rational justification for the specific timing of the mandatory leave but would allow a more sensible rule for the class of pregnant women in preference to individualized treatment. Justices Burger and Rehnquist could "find no judicial standard of measurement" to strike down the rule as sex discrimination or interference with a basic right. Such claims of women workers against overprotection were, of course, new and contrary to the spirit and doctrine of *Muller.* Justices in the majority were trying to avoid equal-protection analysis in fashioning a new judicial remedy for pregnant workers.

When inequitable rules expedite women's careers, however, a majority of the Court is willing to recognize an affirmative-action exception. Some women in the military were allowed a longer period of years to move up in rank than men; the justices who approved the different treatment pointed out that the sexes were not similarly situated in the armed forces (*Schlesinger* v. *Ballard,* 1975). The minority was more concerned that the unequal status of women in the military created discrimination against men.

The Value of Women's Work. Women's wages for doing the same work as men or work of similar social value have been consistently lower than men's wages. Soon after the Court approved the progressive policies of maximum hours and safe conditions, it faced the issue of minimum pay. The Court followed the *Muller* doctrine in approving state policies setting minimum pay for women (*Hawley* v. *Walker*, 1914; *Simpson* v. *O'-Hara*, 1917). However, when the District of Columbia statute fixing minimum wages for women reached the Court soon after women's suffrage passed, a bare majority accorded the same freedom to contract over wages to women as to men (*Adkins* v. *Children's Hospital*, 1923). The oral argument against the protective law presented sociological data. The Court majority noted these arguments of the National Woman's Party, although its real concern was to prevent any state interference in business.

Conservative justices insisted that there was no longer any reason to place women in a different class, a point of view that has not been adopted by the conservatives sitting on the Court in the 1980s. The dissenters understood the Nineteenth Amendment as empowering women to work for social reform to benefit their own class and not as creating sex equality under law. They insisted that legislators could not avoid using the sex classification that was based upon immutable natural differences.

The *Adkins* precedent for sex equality lasted for only fifteen years. In 1937 the Court, in another close vote, returned to the *Muller* doctrine and approved the fixing of women's wages. The majority accepted the view that women were not powerful enough to protect their own interests in the market and that the suffrage created only a "fictitious equality" between the sexes, which did not prevent the state from interfering with women's free choice to protect their health and morals and "preserve the race." There is some doubt about whether the majority believed its own rhetoric about the advantages of differential treatment for women. They also introduced a pragmatic argument to the effect that women who were paid less than the cost of living would become the taxpayers' burden. Finally, they allowed the sex discrimination even when favorable effects were uncertain, as long as the policy was not entirely capricious.

The paycheck is only a part of the remuneration of many workers; other benefits may include housing, medical insurance, access to goods at low prices, credit, child care, paid leave and vacation, and pension at retirement. Women have found socially approved work in segregated jobs with the poorest benefit packages. Even token women in male-dominated occupations did not necessarily receive the same job benefits as their fellow employees. The assumption behind unequal economic treatment was similar to that behind women's unequal political status: all women marry adequate breadwinners. After 1971, however, the *Reed* precedent called into question laws that disadvantaged women workers.

In 1973 the Court struck down a federal statute that required women, but not men, in the military service to show proof of spouse's dependence, in order to receive housing, medical, and dental fringe benefits (*Frontiero* v. *Richardson*). The majority disagreed on the appropriate constitutional basis for the result. Four justices essentially proposed the standard of equality in the *Adkins* opinion; they declared sex to be a suspect classification, like race and national origin, which required strict judicial scrutiny of the legislation. The test of strict scrutiny, except in rare circumstances, results in the voiding of the class-based policy. These four justices (Brennan, Marshall, White, and Douglas) described the long and unfortunate history of sex discrimination and saw the practical effect of protective legislation as putting women "not on a pedestal, but in a cage." They directly repudiated Justice Bradley's view proclaimed one hundred years earlier that woman's destiny as wife and mother excused state control of her nondomestic occupation. The opinion notes the absence of women from positions of responsibility, including justice of the Supreme Court, because of discrimination in the work world. Eight years later a woman joined the Court.

The Court majority did not allow the state to defend its sex-based rule on grounds of administrative efficiency. Although the four other justices in the majority refused to adopt the strict test of equal protection, the impact of the decision was to void policies that treated women as an inferior and dependent class. The practical impact was not to benefit servicewomen as individuals but to extend the same benefits to their spouses and families as to those of servicemen. Only Justice Rehnquist dissented.

The *Frontiero* precedent was applied in 1975 to the social security provisions that allowed survivor's benefits to a wife, but not to a husband, left with the care of a dependent child (*Weinberger*

v. *Wiesenfeld*). The Court refused to approve a sex distinction based upon the presumption that women were not family breadwinners. The surviving husband in that case chose to stay home and raise the child. Two justices in concurrence rejected the sex distinctions in the law not because the value of women's work was denigrated but because the discrimination interfered with the purpose of the law to protect the family. Justice Rehnquist agreed with the result, but his reasoning ignored the sex discrimination and focused upon the need of a child for full-time parental care. The Court was also unanimous in finding unconstitutional the special program of Aid to Families of Dependent Children, which covered husband-fathers who had lost their jobs but not breadwinning wife-mothers (*Califano* v. *Westcott*, 1979).

Work and Pregnancy. From *Bradwell* through *Muller* to the modern case opinions, the central fact in the Court's reasoning is the potential of the female to become pregnant. The nineteenth-century justices assumed that most women would marry, that married women would bear children, and that pregnancy and child care would demand their lifetime energies. To place men and women in the same legal status for political and economic duties would double women's burdens and jeopardize the fitness of the next generation to protect the political community.

Cases about women's rights that do not involve pregnancy at all have often been argued as if motherhood was at stake. In its brief prepared for the *Hoyt* case in 1961, the state of Florida responded to the woman defendant, who thought fairness required women on her jury, with a homily on reproduction and child care: "Ever since the dawn of time conception has been the same . . . the gestation period in the human female has likewise remained unchanged. . . . The rearing of children . . . remains a prime responsibility of the matriarch." Progress in medical technology has given women better control over procreation and has protected their health during pregnancy and childbirth, thus shattering the factual foundations for treating women as a class determined by nature to be mothers throughout their maturity. The issue then becomes how to treat women who have chosen both the public roles formerly monopolized by men and the role of motherhood. Can govern-

ment equalize the opportunities of women who perform the public service of producing new citizens, without using the sex classification that has historically hampered, rather than emancipated, women?

The challenge of creating a doctrine that would guarantee sex equality and not penalize pregnant women for their personal choice and social contribution has brought about a crisis for contemporary feminist legal thinkers. The division exists between those who are convinced that equal status requires sex-blind treatment and those who think that a policy of preferential unequal treatment for childbearers could be fashioned that would avoid overprotection. This disagreement is a modern version of the bitter split during and after the suffrage movement between women social reformers who developed sex-specific programs to alleviate the hard lives of women laborers and the feminists concerned with the status of elite women who wanted equal rights in the Constitution to guarantee and symbolize their acceptance in American public life. The modern reformers, however, are asking for more than health, safety, and morals protection; they want "equality of effect" or the equalizing of the situation of those handicapped by pregnancy or other conditions. Some have a very personal concern with combining pregnancy and their professional lives, and others are thinking more broadly of all those in society with poorer natural and situational resources. Equality of effect is not like affirmative action, which assumes that groups historically discriminated against may need some short-term favorable treatment to catch up; there are limits upon the scope and duration of the affirmative-action measures. In contrast, equality of effect assumes that some groups will always need extra assistance. Pregnancy recurs within the class of women, and so, laws offering some positive assistance not provided for nonpregnant persons would be needed indefinitely for most members of the sex class at some time during their lives. Only the invention of gestating machines and nursing machines would change the situation of the female class. Meanwhile, the justices have not found a logic to suit nature. The justices have given up their simple and rigid doctrine of a sex hierarchy, with males superior to, and dominant over, females, but they have not found a satisfactory doctrine to replace it.

1242

While the Court would not be expected to adopt a radical doctrine of equality of effect in the contemporary political environment, neither has the Court announced the simple equality-of-treatment doctrine. Justice Powell's explanation for their failure to do so in *Frontiero* was that the ERA was under consideration by representative bodies. After *Frontiero* the Court had to resolve a number of controversies involving pregnancy, and the obvious difficulty of developing a theory that was intellectually satisfying and practical in application prevented the justices from reaching a consensus on sex equality. Instead, various members of the Court have offered different solutions, which have provoked reactions from mild support to scathing criticism from other justices.

Social Costs. In *Cleveland Board of Education* v. *La Fleur,* discussed above, the pregnant woman only asked to make her own choice about the timing of her leave and return; she did not demand paid leave or health care or even the same job back. Female complaints of wrongs with costly remedies seem to be more difficult for the Court to handle, despite the fact that many controversies among men, government, and corporations involve the redistribution of much larger sums of money. However, once the Court has established a principle, it follows its logic. In 1975 a woman collecting unemployment compensation who became pregnant was removed from the rolls after her sixth month on grounds that she was no longer in the job market *(Turner* v. *Department of Employment).* The state law allowed no payments to otherwise eligible unemployed women from three months before childbirth until six weeks after childbirth, and the Utah courts decided no right had been denied to her. A bare majority of the United States Supreme Court remanded the case to be decided by the *La Fleur* precedent that freedom of choice in family matters cannot be burdened except through more individualized means. In *Nashville Gas Co.* v. *Satty* (1977) the Court decided that a woman's job seniority could not be lost because she took leave during pregnancy but that the company did not have to pay for her leave.

The issue of paying for the pregnancy is somewhat different from the issue of working or collecting unemployment compensation during pregnancy and involves higher costs. The due process and basic rights analysis used in *La Fleur*

and *Turner* would have pointed toward maternity-care coverage in broad health plans. The Court instead used equal-protection analysis to examine a California state plan that covered private employees not under workman's compensation in *Geduldig* v. *Aiello* (1974). The plan covered almost all medical needs of both sexes except normal pregnancies, including ailments unique to the male sex and to the black race, voluntary procedures such as cosmetic surgery and sterilization, and injuries from risky athletic activities. The Court found that the exclusion of maternity benefits was not associated with a sex classification but, rather, that the division was between pregnant persons and nonpregnant persons. The Court had precedents in *Reed* and *Frontiero* for sex classifications but no precedent for this newly recognized classification to require more than weak scrutiny of the policy. The fiscal viability of the program was a legitimate state purpose reasonably related to the chosen pregnancy classification.

Writing for the Court, Justice Potter Stewart admitted that only women become pregnant, but he refused to treat pregnancy as a semisuspect class, absent proof of a hidden purpose to disadvantage the female sex. He argued that the exclusion of pregnant women from medical-care benefits improved the situation of the nonpregnant women as well as the men contributing to the insurance plan. The Stewart formulation fits the theoretical needs of those feminist legal theorists who want special advantages for pregnant women, since the precedent leaves the way constitutionally clear to persuade a legislative body to make policies advantaging, rather than disadvantaging, pregnant workers in relation to others in the same occupation or company.

In the *Geduldig* case, three justices who defined sex as suspect were in the minority; Justice White, who had signed the *Frontiero* opinion for strict scrutiny of the sex class, agreed with the majority that the pregnancy class was different. The dissenters argued that defining a class by a physical characteristic linked to only one sex was necessarily a sex classification and therefore discriminatory. Justice Brennan insisted that the cost of equal treatment could not override the constitutional value of equality.

The Court faced the same issue in a similar factual situation in 1976 when the claim was against General Electric for violating a statutory right (*General Electric* v. *Gilbert*). The majority followed its prior reasoning that sex discrimination was not involved in the denial of pregnancy medical benefits. Newly appointed Justice Stevens, taking Douglas' place among the dissenters, argued that pregnant condition implied that one was female. Congress responded to the *General Electric* decision by passing the Pregnancy Discrimination Act of 1978, clarifying its intention to cover pregnant women and overturning the decision. The reasoning and the precedent of *Geduldig* on equal protection, however, still stand. Members of the two branches disagreed on an issue that involves logic, biological facts, and policy preferences.

The congressional solution fits the thrust of the ERA and the legal theory of equality of treatment. If adopted as constitutional theory, it might stand in the way of legislation such as the California, Connecticut, and Montana statutes that guarantee reasonable pregnancy and childbirth leaves without loss of jobs to women, even in the absence of similar benefits for nonpregnant persons. On the other hand, even under strict scrutiny, the Court might evaluate the fostering of maternity and child health as a compelling state purpose, like national security in its significance, and find a necessary relationship to the special treatment of pregnant working women. Such an interpretation would be somewhat different from the *Muller* reasoning, which emphasized the physical weakness of women; under the new exception, the contribution to society that only women can make would be subsidized. This approach is more likely in an economic system that employs a high proportion of pregnant women and mothers across the full range of occupations.

The Court tries to imagine the impact of its precedents upon the linked institutions of society. The doctrine of equality of effect would bring the Court into the very heart of policymaking, distributing and redistributing social goods. The doctrine of equality of treatment has deep roots in case law interpreting the equal protection clause. Sex equality, whether embedded in the equal protection clause of the Fourteenth Amendment or in a new ERA, would allow for exceptions that go to the survival of the political system; policies that favor pregnant persons might qualify under some national conditions and not under others.

The Court's approval of the favorable treatment of veterans does not provide an exact model for its approach to pregnant women. The job-preference policy operates in a zero-sum context in which jobs offered to less-qualified veterans are not available for better-qualified nonveterans. One wonders if the Court would find discriminatory laws cutting in the other direction, against the employment of veterans, rational under the weak standard. None of the existing or proposed policies for keeping pregnant women workers in the work force do so at the price of removing other workers. Yet, the contribution of veterans that provides the rationale for their special benefits—risking one's life over a short period for national security—is analogous to the contributions of women who risk their lives and devote their energies over a long period to childbearing and nurturing to restock the polity with citizens. This perspective is common in foreign legal-political systems and provides the foundation for generous government support of families. Such a policy is antithetical to the American tradition of reliance on the male head of family to provide a decent standard of living for the women excluded, or at least discouraged, from taking responsible and remunerative public positions. The common law once fit this ideal family, but as noted in the section on political roles, the Court is gradually discarding those notions.

In the contemporary economic world, where women may be the only or the necessary second breadwinner, the Court's view of the sex class needs to move more radically away from earlier views of women. The Court's problem with pregnancy cases rests upon the traditional ideal of family life in which wife-motherhood and employment are incompatible. A new jurisprudence of sex equality of treatment may not be accepted until new justices with life experiences in new socioeconomic environments replace the old.

SOCIAL RIGHTS

The Supreme Court has limited power to monitor sex equality in social and domestic affairs. However, to the extent that citizens accept government service and protection, the range of state activities that must meet equal-protection standards expands. The equality standard covers state decisions on who is allowed to drive a car or receive a welfare check or change their marital status or matriculate at public schools or establish a parental relationship. Government has also defined for itself a special responsibility for minors, establishing schools and regulating their behavior in areas where adults are free of state control; and the Court has voided most of the sex discrimination relating to minors. The contemporary standards for sex equality in this quasi-private sphere will be addressed under the topics of social activities, marital relationships, education, and parent-child relationships.

Social Activities. Driving and drinking are social behaviors of special concern to state government, and their regulation has not been sex-neutral. The Supreme Court has generally restrained itself from entering these police-power areas in deference to the states and local communities. For example, the Court simply affirmed, without any explanation, the federal trial court's rejection of a woman's complaint that Alabama law required her to apply for a driver's license under her husband's last name (*Forbush* v. *Wallace,* 1972). Neither did a majority of the Court wish to address the unfairness of the cancellation of a woman's license after her husband had an accident in their uninsured car (*Perez* v. *Campbell,* 1971). Although this kind of denigration and oppression sets the tone for the treatment of women in the political and economic spheres as inferior and dependent, the Court left these problems for women to work out in the fifty state political systems. The Court's use of the federalism principle here, as in the early political cases, denied women a national standard of their equal worth.

The Court did decide, with considerable internal conflict, to void an Oklahoma state law that forbade male, but not female, minors from buying 3.2 percent beer (*Craig* v. *Boren,* 1976). The state argued that the purpose of the law—to reduce accidents among drinking and driving teenagers—could be achieved by concentrating on enforcement against male purchasers. Counsel for Oklahoma was not able to persuade the Court that traffic safety would be promoted through control of sales to (but not consumption by) one sex only. One of the archaic assumptions behind the state policy was that the male was always the driver; the other was that only males

had drinking problems. By the time the Court dealt with this form of sex discrimination among minors, most state legislatures had rewritten their codes to set the same parietal rules for boys and girls.

A much more important social issue for adult women in politics or business is their right of access to public accommodations and especially to civic associations where persons in related occupations become acquainted. The Court delayed facing this issue, refusing to hear the appeal of women who lost their claim to be served at the "men's grill" of a metropolitan hotel (*Millenson* v. *New Hotel Monteleone,* 1973). Only Justice Douglas voted for certiorari—that is, for the Court to take up the case and evaluate what women in the 1970s considered demeaning treatment. The 1948 *Goesaert* decision evidently had some vitality as late as the 1970s; the barrier to women who want to be served as customers is closely related in theory, practice, and state law to the old barriers against their employment in such places. Denied the support of the Court, women used direct action and state civil rights laws to win equal access to public places open to men.

The status of clubs or associations with all-male membership was left in doubt until 1984. Then the Court ruled unanimously that a state human rights act that protected women's interest in eligibility for membership in civic groups did not abridge the freedom of association of male members (*Roberts* v. *United States Jaycees*). When several local chapters of the Junior Chamber of Commerce admitted women, contrary to the national bylaws, the national organization challenged the state law that protected the local chapters' policy. The Court found the Jaycees to be a large organization with no selective criteria for membership, with no pursuits incompatible with female membership, and with many programs open to nonmembers. The circumstances of this case contrast with other sex-equality cases in ways that suggest that community norms have changed considerably. Women did not go to court with a complaint of exclusion as in earlier public-accommodations cases. Rather, the male members of the local chapter chose integration and challenged the segregationist policy of the national organization. Another difference was that the Court was not imposing a national standard upon a resistant state but was legitimating a state public-policy preference. The conservative justices on the Court, for whom federalism is a preferred constitutional principle, accepted Minnesota's nonsexist policy.

Socialization to Sex Roles. The Court has few opportunities to evaluate the way that parents discriminate between their children by sex. One occasion that brings government into domestic decision-making is the dissolution of marriage. In *Stanton* v. *Stanton* (1975) the Court voided a Utah statute that defined adulthood as commencing for females at eighteen and for males at twenty-one and thereby resulted, in the absence of individualized provisions in a divorce settlement, in males receiving child support for three more years than females. The Utah court rationalized the sex-specific outcome by projecting the future of boys as breadwinners and assuming that boys would therefore need more education than girls, who would marry earlier. Writing for the Court, Justice Blackmun rejected the ideas that had been persuasive to prior Courts: "No longer is the female destined solely for the home and the raising of the family, and only the male for the marketplace and the world of ideas." Justice Rehnquist was the only dissenter; he preferred to avoid the constitutional issue, which would have meant that the sexist statute would stand. By the date of the *Stanton* decision, only Utah and Arkansas fixed the age of majority by sex, so that the Court was placing its imprimatur upon new egalitarian standards already widely adopted by state governments. The decision is nevertheless significant in two respects: the Court articulated a national norm for the guidance of parents in making their private choices in distributing their family resources to children, and the Court took note of the relationship between the female's educational preparation and the performance of her political and economic duties.

Although the Court in 1954 established a doctrine against racial segregation in public schools, it accepted segregation by sex in education until 1982. In that year, when the segregated-school issue reached the Supreme Court after several affirmations of sex-segregated facilities in the 1970s, the first woman on the Court was assigned to write the majority opinion. In *Mississippi University for Women* v. *Hogan,* Justice Sandra Day O'Connor applied the middle-level test of equal protection to the complaint of the male nurse who was not eligible under state law to take a degree from the all-female nursing school. She did not find any "benign compensatory" purpose in maintenance of the single-sex school, since women already dominated the occupation. Indeed, the exclusion of men actually perpetuated the stereotype of nursing as woman's work. In several footnotes she provides a brief history of the constitutional law of sex equality. Of significance in Justice O'Connor's constitutional sex-equality case is that she undid the common-law maxim that the female is the "special favorite of the law." O'Connor showed how discrimination, regardless of intent, disfavors both sexes in its impact. The dissenters responded with their theories about the benefits to women of segregated education and introduced again the standard of consumer choice in public services.

Family Finances. The interest of the government in sex equality within the family comes to bear at the point of its dissolution. Otherwise, the state sets only minimal standards for the distribution of family income among family members. States have been slower in providing equal benefits or demanding equal responsibility for women in domestic relations than in political life. In 1979 the Court established that the sex of the spouse is no longer germane to alimony orders under state divorce laws *(Orr* v. *Orr).* The Court would not accept stereotypes of women as housewives and men as breadwinners to rationalize a law placing a financial liability for the ex-spouse only on men. The Court majority knew that its equality standard for spousal support would not place any administrative burden upon state government because the alimony decisions were already made by courts on an individualized basis.

The Court was not at the cutting edge of the law in the sex-equality cases affecting the social sphere but was simply voiding the consequences of old statutes or was bringing the last state with a sexist rule into line with the reformed states. Thus, the Court was unanimous in finding unconstitutional in 1981 a Louisiana statute that gave the husband the unilateral right to dispose of property owned jointly with his wife *(Kirchberg* v. *Feenstra).* The equal-protection test used was the middle level; the Court could find no important government interest in assigning autonomous power over joint property to the common-law "head-and-master." Two justices —Stewart, who left the Court later in the year to be replaced by O'Connor, and Rehnquist— based their agreement with the result on the fact that the marital partners were "similarly situated" under other state laws on marital property. This test of similar situation means that one sexist law may be the reason for approving another sexist law, which was the basis for the Court's denial of equal rights for women in military, prison, and civil service jobs. The similar-situation requirement can be applied to case facts in a strict or a loose fashion. Since women and men are often not in the same situation because of historical discrimination (*Schlesinger* v. *Ballard),* this formulation could easily be employed to maintain the unequal status quo.

PARENTAL RELATIONS OUTSIDE MARRIAGE

Although the Court has settled that the sex of a child is not a constitutional consideration in governmental distribution of goods (except punishment), the sex of a parent still makes a difference in relation to the child. The Court's hesitation in establishing a sex-blind standard draws from the same tradition as its pregnancy and work rulings. From the fact of gestation and lactation the tie of mother and child is assumed to be closer than father and child outside of marriage. In this issue area, the Court deals with the sex class plus one or more other semisuspect classes. The major social problems are the social ties of the parents to the illegitimate child and the financial responsibilities attached to the relationship.

Family Ties. The Court has seldom decided in favor of the father of illegitimate children on equal-protection grounds. In 1972 a Court majority provided a hearing on fitness for a father who claimed custody of his illegitimate children after their mother died (*Stanley* v. *Illinois*). The Court provided a procedural due process right but did not place him in the same legal position as a mother, whose custody of illegitimate children is assumed from birth. In dissent, Chief Justice Burger was willing to stereotype unwed fathers for differential class treatment; he wrote of unwed fathers that "many of them either deny all responsibility or exhibit no interest in the child or its welfare." He also stereotyped all mothers, claiming that the physiological experience "in carrying and nursing an infant creates stronger bonds." The source of his knowledge was the same as Justice Bradley's a century earlier, for Burger, too, turned to nature and to custom for authority: "Centuries of human experience buttress this view of the realities of human conditions and suggest that unwed mothers of illegitimate children are generally more dependable protectors of their children than are unwed fathers."

The Court does not provide procedural rights to natural fathers without taking account of the behavior of the complaining father. In 1979 the Court struck down a New York law that gave the natural mother, but not the natural father, the power to withhold consent to the adoption of the child (*Caban* v. *Mohammed*). The majority relied upon the reasoning in other sex equality cases, although they also considered the special attention of the father in that case to his child. Justice Stevens in dissent developed an argument about the female parent's special capacity to become pregnant that he had also utilized in the employment-benefit and abortion cases. His argument is biological in a more focused way than Bradley's, Brandeis', Harlan's, or Burger's. He wrote,

> Both parents are equally responsible for the conception of the child out of wedlock. But from that point on through pregnancy and infancy, the differences between the male and the female have an important impact on the child's destiny. Only the mother carries the child; it is she who has the constitutional right to decide whether to bear it or not.

His reasoning is palatable to many feminists who place a high value on autonomy for women in relation to pregnancy and children.

The Court takes a case-by-case interest in the father-child relationship while continuing to assume the goodness of the mother-child relationship. The father's relationship to the child is treated as optional, but the mother's, as mandatory. Equal treatment could mean extending to unwed fathers the same assumptions about loving concern credited to unwed mothers or reducing unwed mothers to the contemporary legal status of unwed fathers. Only one semisuspect classification would then be involved in state statutes—the child's legal status. Since most justices are concerned about the burden placed upon innocent children, illegitimacy and sex may eventually be defined as suspect, but unwed parenthood will continue to be treated differently from marital parenthood. To date, the Court has not found a satisfactory basis for defining the natural father's rights and obligations; the effect is to leave the mother with both a stronger legal right and a larger responsibility.

There is a consensus on the Court, however, that state law must provide the illegitimate child with an adequate opportunity to use the judicial process to make its paternity claim (*Mills* v. *Habluetzel,* 1982). If state laws required the identification of a legal father like a legal mother at birth, then the Court would have been freed of its trepidation in these cases of assigning the paternal obligation to the wrong person. As Justice O'Connor pointed out in her *Mills* concurrence, courts now have scientific evidence available to them to reduce the likelihood of error in paternity cases. The confusion of the Court in this area simply reflects the fact that changes in family life, including the large percentage of births outside of wedlock, have outstripped the development of new cultural norms and the formulation of legislative policy. The Court will have less difficulty in guaranteeing sex equality in the benefits and burdens of parenthood after other social institutions recognize the legal problems associated with this behavior and define new statuses and relationships.

For alien fathers or children the problem is compounded by the existence of three crosscutting semisuspect classes—sex, illegitimacy, and alienage. A majority of the Court refused in 1977 to void federal immigration policy that gave preferential treatment to unwed mothers and their children over unwed fathers and their children. A citizen father was not allowed an immigration visa for his illegitimate son, whereas a citizen mother or stepmother enjoyed a special preference in bringing children into the country *(Fiallo* v. *Bell).* The minority protested that deference to Congress over foreign policy should not be sufficient excuse for overriding the integrity of the family, even a family composed of an unwed father and child.

Child Support. The different legal status of male and female unwed parents has put a greater burden upon the mother to support her children. The Court has established no consistent formula for setting the limits of a natural father's obligations. The Court, for example, equalized the entitlement of legitimate and illegitimate children to recover for the wrongful death of their mother (*Levy* v. *Louisiana,* 1968) but approved the same state's law providing an unequal inheritance right from the father (*Labine* v. *Vincent,* 1971). Dissenting in *Jimenez* v. *Weinberger,* which allowed social security payments to some illegitimate children, Justice Rehnquist in 1974 was concerned, as he was in the *La Fleur* case, that the Court was placing upon government the administrative burden of individualizing case resolution. The Court accepted his view in a later social security case approving a provision that required some illegitimate children to prove dependency to receive survivor's benefits (*Mathews* v. *Lucas,* 1976).

The establishment of the paternal relationship to an illegitimate child entails certain obligations for support. The Court found a state law that denied illegitimate children the same right to their father's support as legitimate children a denial of equal protection (*Gomez* v. *Perez,* 1973). But the Court is not willing to guarantee the mother the same avenues to collect child support for illegitimates. This unwillingness to back the unwed mother with governmental power to collect often places upon her the full burden for support. A mother lost her class-action suit against Texas for failing to enforce the support duties of unwed fathers while pursuing them in the interests of legitimate children (*Linda R. S.* v. *Richard D.,* 1973). The principle of equal treatment lost in this instance because Justice Marshall, usually a stalwart for equality, questioned the soundness of the coercive policy in achieving the desired result of child support. As the progressives in an earlier period accepted sex inequality as the price of establishing their preferred economic policy, so he accepted sex inequality at the expense of illegitimate children and their mothers in order to retain his preferred criminal justice policy. Until sex equality is established under the Constitution, there will be no guarantee that the interests of women and children will not be sacrificed to other policy ends considered more important by legislators and judges.

SEX EQUALITY UNDER THE CONSTITUTION

SUMMARY

The United States Supreme Court shares in the making of public policy with other branches of national government and the states, although the Court also has a special duty to articulate the national principles and rules discovered in the Constitution. When Congress has acted on sex-equality issues, the Court has either not been drawn into the controversy or has made interpretations of policy subject to legislative revision. Congress mandated sex equality in credit, and the Court did not enter that arena; Congress also set standards for equal treatment in education and employment. The Court did, however, make sure that women could use the lower courts to vindicate those new rights, and when women have shown a prima facie case of discriminatory treatment, the Court has made the employer meet the burden of proof. The Court has also insisted upon sex-blind job opportunities even when the resistance was from the legal profession.

However, the Court has also protected educational institutions from the full penalties provided by Congress for infringing upon women's equal rights and has not pushed employers into creative affirmative-action programs beyond the Title VII (Civil Rights Act of 1964) prohibitions. And neither the Court nor Congress has been willing to face up to the institutional sexism that restricts job opportunities for women because of contining discrimination in the military.

The Court's decisions have consequences for the integration of women and men into social organizations and for their rights as individuals. The Court has been much more supportive of equality in individual behavior than of equality of participation in mixed groups. The Court's trepidation about the mixing of the sexes in the public arena is revealed most clearly in the cases on bartending, prison, and military jobs, where the Court placed the Constitution behind male resistance to women's entrance. Where the Court has mandated integration, the decisions have been made since the mid-1970s and, in most instances, because men would benefit.

Allowing persons to act autonomously regardless of sex in ways that do not involve integration is a recent concern of the Court. Earlier Courts refused to apply the Constitution to guarantee to qualified women the right to vote or to practice law, activities that are at the heart of the political system. However, the Court is gradually insisting upon sex-blind rules over personal activities that have nothing to do with politics, such as buying beer, paying alimony, receiving child support, or controlling property. On other issues of personal life, such as the responsibility of minors for sexual behavior or of adults for their illegitimate children, the Court is not ready to set firm constitutional standards of equality.

The theme that runs throughout the justices' opinions over time is that women gestate and men do not. Even where there were no relevant facts in the case on the pregnant, maternal, or marital condition of specific women, the species mode of reproduction and the related cultural expectations for maternal care of family members provided the biological and sociological argument for the Court's approval of sex-specific legal rights and duties. The decisions on sex crimes, on prison jobs, and on illegitimate children all rest upon the biology of procreation. The focus has narrowed considerably from treating all women as mothers, regardless of age or condition, to treating some women as particularly vulnerable to rape and therefore in need of "protection," even at the cost of their jobs and their responsibility for their own choices. Sex equality under the Constitution across the political, economic, and social spectrum depends upon the resolution of the pregnancy and motherhood issues by the American people and their institutions; the Court has been the defender of inferior and dependent women but has shown only a modest inclination toward treating women and men as equal in their virtues and vices and in their claims to institutional membership and to personal autonomy.

CASES

Adkins v. Children's Hospital, 216 U.S. 525 (1923)
Ballard v. United States, 329 U.S. 187 (1946)
Barber v. Barber, 62 U.S. 582 (1859)
Bosley v. McLaughlin, 236 U.S. 385 (1915)
Bradwell v. Illinois, 16 Wallace 130 (1873)
Breedlove v. Suttles, 302 U.S. 277 (1937)
Caban v. Mohammed, 441 U.S. 380 (1979)
Califano v. Westcott, 443 U.S. 76 (1979)

Cleveland Board of Education v. La Fleur, 414 U.S. 632 (1974)

Commonwealth v. Welosky, 276 Mass. 398, 177 N.E. 656 (1931), *cert. denied* 284 U.S. 684 (1932)

Corning Glass v. Brennan, 417 U.S. 188 (1974)

Craig v. Boren, 429 U.S. 190 (1976)

Davis v. Passman, 442 U.S. 228 (1979)

Dothard v. Rawlinson, 433 U.S. 321 (1977)

Dred Scott v. Sandford, 19 Howard 393 (1857)

Duren v. Missouri, 439 U.S. 357 (1979)

Eslinger v. Thomas, 476 F.2d 225 (1973)

Feeney v. Massachusetts, 442 U.S. 256 (1979)

Fiallo v. Bell, 430 U.S. 787 (1977)

Forbush v. Wallace, 405 U.S. 970 (1972)

Frontiero v. Richardson, 411 U.S. 677 (1973)

Geduldig v. Aiello, 417 U.S. 484 (1974)

General Electric v. Gilbert, 429 U.S. 125 (1976)

Goesaert v. Cleary, 335 U.S. 464 (1948)

Gomez v. Perez, 409 U.S. 535 (1973)

Hawkins v. United States, 358 U.S. 74 (1958)

Hawley v. Walker, 232 U.S. 718 (1914)

Hobby v. United States, 104 S.Ct. 3093 (1984) No. 82-2140

Hoyt v. Florida, 368 U.S. 57 (1961)

Jimenez v. Weinberger, 417 U.S. 628 (1974)

Kahn v. Shevin, 416 U.S. 351 (1974)

Kirchberg v. Feenstra, 450 U.S. 455 (1981)

Labine v. Vincent, 401 U.S. 532 (1971)

Levy v. Louisiana, 391 U.S. 68 (1968)

Linda R. S. v. Richard D., 410 U.S. 614 (1973)

MacKenzie v. Hare, 239 U.S. 299 (1915)

Mathews v. Lucas, 427 U.S. 495 (1976)

Michael M. v. California Superior Court, 450 U.S. 464 (1981)

Millenson v. New Hotel Monteleone, 414 U.S. 1011 (1973)

Mills v. Habluetzel, 456 U.S. 91 (1982)

Minor v. Happersett, 21 Wallace 162 (1875)

Mississippi University for Women v. Hogan, 458 U.S. 718 (1982)

Muller v. Oregon, 208 U.S. 412 (1908)

Nashville Gas Co. v. Satty, 434 U.S. 136 (1977)

Orr v. Orr, 440 U.S. 268 (1979)

Perez v. Campbell, 402 U.S. 637 (1971)

Pittsburgh Free Press v. Human Relations Commission, 413 U.S. 376 (1973)

Quong Wing v. Kirkendall, 223 U.S. 59 (1912)

Radice v. New York, 264 U.S. 292 (1924)

Reed v. Reed, 404 U.S. 71 (1971)

Roberts v. United States Jaycees, 104 S.Ct. 3244 (1984)

Rostker v. Goldberg, 448 U.S. 1306 (1981)

Santa Clara Pueblo v. Julia Martinez, 436 U.S. 49 (1978)

Schlesinger v. Ballard, 419 U.S. 498 (1975)

Simpson v. O'Hara, 243 U.S. 629 (1917)

Stanley v. Illinois, 405 U.S. 645 (1972)

Stanton v. Stanton, 421 U.S. 7 (1975)

Strauder v. West Virginia, 100 U.S. 303 (1879)

Taylor v. Louisiana, 419 U.S. 522 (1975)

Trammel v. United States, 445 U.S. 40 (1980)

Turner v. Department of Employment, 423 U.S. 44 (1975)

United States v. Dege, 364 U.S. 854 (1960)

United States v. Mitchell, 403 U.S. 190 (1971)

United States v. Schwimmer, 279 U.S. 644 (1929)

United States v. Yazell, 382 U.S. 341 (1966)

Weinberger v. Wiesenfeld, 420 U.S. 636 (1975)

Wyatt v. United States, 362 U.S. 525 (1960)

Ex parte Yarbrough, 110 U.S. 651 (1884)

BIBLIOGRAPHY

Barbara A. Babcock, Anne E. Freedman, Eleanor Holmes Norton, and Susan C. Ross, *Sex Discrimination and the Law* (1975), is a law school textbook prepared by women who were law professors and feminist lawyers in government and private practice, with sections of public policy analysis and proposals for legal reform. Judith A. Baer, *The Chains of Protection: The Judicial Response to Women's Labor Legislation* (1978), is a historical analysis of Supreme Court opinions on protective legislation for working women that probes the normative bases for the legal arguments and addresses contemporary concerns about the roles of women in the family and workplace. Sophonisba P. Breckinridge, *Marriage and the Civic Rights of Women* (1931), reviews the federal law provisions affecting the citizenship of women. Barbara Brown, Thomas Emerson, Gail Falk, and Anne Freedman, "The Equal Rights Amendment: A Constitutional Basis for Equal Rights for Women," in *Yale Law Journal*, 80 (1971), evaluates three methods of assuring equal rights for women: statutory reform, strict scrutiny under equal protection, and passage of ERA.

Comment, " 'A Little Dearer than His Horse': Legal Stereotypes and the Feminine Personality," in *Harvard Civil Rights—Civil Liberties Law Review*, 6 (1971), shows the extent to which differential treatment of women by law is based upon a belief in the inferiority of women. Beverly B. Cook, "Lecturing on Woman's Place: 'Mrs. Jellyby' in Wisconsin, 1854–1874," in *Signs: Journal of Women in Culture and Society*, 9 (1983), discusses the theory of sex roles developed by Edward G. Ryan, chief justice of the Wisconsin Supreme Court. Ruth B. Cowan, "Women's Rights Through Litigation: An Examination of The American Civil Liberties Union Women's Rights Project, 1971–1976," in *Columbia University Human Rights Law Review*, 8 (1976). Blanche Crozier, "Constitutionality of Discrimination Based on Sex," in *Boston University Law Review*, 15 (1935), provides a benchmark for the changes that have and have not occurred in respect to sex equality over fifty years.

Mary Eastwood, "The Double Standard of Justice: Women's Rights under the Constitution," in *Valparaiso University Law Review*, 5 (1971), reviews the status of women in constitutional law prior to the *Reed* decision and argues for the ERA. Leslie F. Goldstein, *The Constitutional Rights of Women* (1979), the only available case book for women-and-law courses at the undergraduate level, provides historical material and doctrinal analyses that are excellent. Winifred L. Hepperle and Laura Crites, eds., *Women in the Courts* (1978), contains two essays, one by Ruth Ginsburg and the other by Beverly Cook, that examine women's rights cases from the perspectives of a law professor and litigator and a political science professor. John D. Johnston and Charles D. Knapp, "Sex Discrimination by Law: A Study in Judicial Perspective," in *New York University Law Review*, 46 (1971), examines the relationship between judge's attitudes toward female roles and their opinions.

SEX EQUALITY UNDER THE CONSTITUTION

Leo Kanowitz, *Sex Roles in Law and Society* (1973), the first case book on the subject available for law school students, includes historical materials not available in some more recent texts. Herma H. Kay, *Sex-Based Discrimination,* 2nd ed. (1981), the most up-to-date of the law school case books, presents an overview of constitutional issues in the opening chapter (supplements are available). Linda J. Krieger and Patricia N. Cooney, "The Miller-Wohl Controversy: Equal Treatment, Positive Action and the Meaning of Women's Equality," in *Golden Gate University Law Review,* 13 (1983), analyzes two competing legal theories of sex equality, equality of treatment and equality of effect, in relation to pregnant women workers. Burnita S. Mathews, "Women Should Have Equal Rights with Men: A Reply," in *American Bar Association Journal,* 12 (1926), is by a woman who worked for the Nineteenth Amendment and for the ERA when first proposed in 1923 by the National Woman's Party and who became the first woman to serve as a federal district judge.

Karen O'Connor, *Women's Organizational Use of the Courts* (1980), makes a major contribution to the scholarship of women and the law by tracing and analyzing the types of litigation strategies followed by women's organizations before the Supreme Court. Deborah L. Rhode, "Equal Rights in Retrospect," in *Journal of Law and Inequality,* 1 (1983), examines the process of amendment through which the pro-posed norm of sex equality is debated as an exercise in symbolic politics. Susan Ross and Ann Barcher, *The Rights of Women,* 2nd ed., (1983), is a handbook sponsored by the ACLU and especially useful to young women looking for answers to practical questions, with appendices that include lists of organizations that may be able to provide information or legal assistance.

Virginia Sapiro, "Women, Citizenship, and Nationality: Immigration and Naturalization Policies in the United States," in *Politics and Society,* 13 (1984), relates the changing legal status of women to their own political efforts. Ann Scales, "Towards a Feminist Jurisprudence," in *Indiana Law Journal,* 56 (1980–1981), proposes an "incorporationist" approach to the meaning of sex equality and law that would allow positive rights for women different from men for sex-specific conditions of pregnancy and breast-feeding. Faith A. Seidenberg, "The Submissive Majority: Modern Trends in the Law Concerning Women's Rights," in *Cornell Law Review,* 55 (1970). Wendy Williams, "The Equality Crisis: Some Reflections on Culture, Courts, and Feminism," in *Women's Rights Law Reporter,* 7 (1982), explains the equal treatment theory of the meaning of the equal protection clause of the Fourteenth Amendment.

[*See also* DUE PROCESS OF LAW *and* EQUAL PROTECTION CLAUSE.]

SEXUALITY AND THE LAW

Judith A. Baer

THE relationship between law and sexuality in contemporary America reflects an inescapable paradox: sex is at once both a public and a private concern. There are few aspects of human life that people regard as more intimate and personal than their sexual behavior. But sex is too important to the functioning of society to be left exclusively in the private sphere. The United States, like all societies of which we have any knowledge, has laws relating to sexual activity. Indeed, these laws existed long before there was a United States. All the original colonies had statutes that delineated, sometimes in minute detail, what sexual activities were illegal; even now, most of the fifty states have laws of this kind.

Some of these laws forbid sexual relations between certain people, such as homosexual acts, adultery, incest, or fornication. Other laws proscribe certain types of activity, such as "sodomy" (that is, oral or anal intercourse), whether heterosexual or homosexual. In the states where such laws do not exist or, as happens more often, where they go unenforced, law often imposes indirect sanctions—for example, loss of a job or child custody—on people who engage in these behaviors. The predictable consequences of sexual activity are of great concern to society, as laws about birth control and abortion reveal. Laws against rape and sexual abuse reflect society's awareness that sexual expression can take violent, exploitative forms.

Today, controversy surrounds most of these laws. The most vehement opposition attaches to direct or indirect sanctions on what are known as "victimless crimes." But laws regulating sexual behavior are much older than opposition to them. A colonial American would not have proclaimed, "You can't legislate morality," nor would that person's English cohort have derided efforts to "make the people virtuous by Act of Parliament." These phrases belong to the nineteenth and twentieth centuries.

The conflict over the legal enforcement of sexual morality can be understood in terms of conflicting notions of the relationship between public and private life and between the individual and society. Many explanations have been advanced for society's efforts to control sexual behavior. Sigmund Freud claimed that society must control sexual drives in order to maintain civilization (1961). Followers of Karl Marx believed that capitalism required the forced redirection of sexual energy into production and the establishment of the nuclear family. However, both Freudian theory and Marxist theory are just that—theory. Each makes highly dubious use of history and anthropology, and neither has earned total acceptance.

Whatever else society needs to do, it must preserve itself. Human reproduction is essential to the continued existence of any society. Therefore, all societies must at least permit, if not encourage, heterosexual intercourse. It is not surprising, therefore, that laws dealing with sexual conduct do not forbid genital intercourse between males and females, at least not between spouses. This societal need may also help explain why another term for sodomy is "the crime against nature" and why the law has traditionally been hostile to contraception and abortion. But the reproductive imperative alone cannot explain why some states have forbidden nearly every kind of sexual activity except that which can result in conception or have restricted even this activity to marriage. It might seem reasonable that society should have to discourage other forms of sex, in order to keep the population stable, but in fact no relationship has been shown between the incidence of nonreproductive sexual activity and the birth rate.

Societies confront other imperatives besides physical ones, however, and some thinkers have argued that sexual laws arise from these needs. In the 1950s, an English judge defended laws against prostitution and homosexuality in this way: "What makes a society of any sort is a community of ideas . . . about the way its members should behave and govern their lives. [These ideas] are its morals" (Devlin, 9). Without shared morals, whatever these morals are, no society could survive, any more than it could survive without reproduction.

A particular version of this general thesis insists that the preservation of the traditional nuclear family is essential to American society. In 1878, when the Supreme Court upheld a law banning polygamy, it wrote, "Marriage, while from its very nature a sacred obligation, is nevertheless, in most civilized nations . . . regulated by law. Upon it society may be said to be built" (*Reynolds* v. *United States*). Nearly a hundred years later, two law professors maintained that "the state ought to be concerned that if allegiance to traditional family arrangements declines, society as a whole may well suffer" (Wilkinson and White, 595).

If we evaluate the "community of ideas" thesis according to Oliver Wendell Holmes' famous dictum that the best test of an idea is its power to gain acceptance in the marketplace of ideas, then the thesis has a consistently good track record. It has persuaded large numbers of people as long as it has been in the marketplace. But its acceptance has never been universal, and, indeed, the idea appeared only in response to challenges to traditional morals legislation. In this realm reason must remain separate from rationalization, and the views of lawmakers from those of their post hoc defenders. The thesis is not without both conceptual and empirical difficulties. There is no good evidence, let alone proof, that society in any way suffers if people are allowed to deviate from traditional family life. We can agree that American society will certainly have changed if alternatives to heterosexual family life become acceptable, but it is hard to equate change with suffering or to argue that society should punish all behavior that might change it.

None of the various arguments that society ought to legislate sexual morality suffice to explain the laws that exist and have existed. But the idea that society should use law to promote moral values goes back at least as far as the ancient Greeks. Aristotle's *Nicomachean Ethics* asserts that law is an appropriate means of moral education, of inculcating virtue by requiring virtuous behavior. Conceptions of virtue have changed greatly since Aristotle's time, but whatever virtue is, society has viewed law as a useful means of promoting it. Laws that regulate private sexual conduct are often viewed as efforts to encourage virtue by forbidding vice. Antiobscenity laws have typically been motivated by the desire to protect morals from corruption (Clor, 1969). This view of law's proper function has encountered strong opposition since the 1850s, but the view that law can and should promote virtue is still widely held in American society. The contemporary "religious Right" is the latest in a long series of proponents of this view.

Among the most widely accepted of sex-related laws are those which forbid injury to others. Laws against rape and child molestation are of this type. Sodomy laws can indirectly serve a similar function. A person who forces another to perform "unnatural acts" may be charged with, or plead guilty to, the lesser charge of consensual sodomy. Similarly, a man who forcibly rapes a female who is below the "age of consent" may be charged with "statutory rape" or "unlawful sexual intercourse." The earliest laws against abortion arose not from a "Victorian social concern" with morality (*Roe* v. *Wade,* 1973) but from the recognition that abortion was far more dangerous for a woman than childbirth. Abortion was made legal in large part because medical advances virtually eliminated this risk.

In general, however, society's condemnation of harmful sexual conduct is far from being complete or unambiguous. The crime of rape has historically been defined in ways that exclude much actual violence. Until very recently, for instance, a husband could not be accused of raping his wife if he forced her to have intercourse, even though he is obviously as capable of doing so as any other man. Society has also been more willing to forbid sexual violence than to punish it or even to recognize it when it occurs. The inescapable truth is that society tolerates much sexual abuse even as it punishes voluntary choices.

Those who oppose laws regulating private

sexual conduct argue that there are limits to the state's legitimate authority. One of the foremost proponents of this position was the nineteenth-century English philosopher John Stuart Mill. In *An Essay on Liberty,* Mill asserts the individual's sovereignty "over his own mind and body." Almost a century after Mill, a committee appointed by the British government recommended the liberalization of the laws against homosexuality. The *Wolfenden Report* echoed Mill's essay. "Unless a deliberate attempt is to be made by society, acting through the agency of law, to equate the sphere of crime with that of sin, there must remain a realm of private morality and immorality which is, in brief and crude terms, not the law's business." In demarcating this realm, the report contributed to the debate a now familiar phrase; it referred to activities "in private between consenting adults." (The committee's recommendations did not become law until 1966, in part because of opposition led by the English judge quoted earlier.)

Both Mill and the *Wolfenden Report* have been popular among American advocates of liberalization. However, those who believe that society needs a shared morality do not agree that private acts are harmless to others, and those who believe that law can promote virtue are even less willing to accept the premise that law cannot legitimately coerce people for their own good. The debate over law and morality continues primarily in these terms. The liberals have won some impressive victories; indeed, the law has sometimes gone even beyond Mill and Wolfenden.

CONSTITUTIONAL BASES FOR SEXUAL FREEDOM

In the American context, laws about sex are part of the police power: the power of the government to protect the health, safety, welfare, and morals of the people. In the American federal system, police power traditionally belongs to the individual states rather than to the national government. Therefore, the United States has not one but fifty sets of sex-related laws. (Actually, it has fifty-one, since the national government deals with sex in allocating its own funds, as with Medicaid, and in regulating exclusively national concerns, such as immigration.)

Conduct that is legal in one state can be, and often is, forbidden in others. Even if the Supreme Court rules that a particular state law conforms to the United States Constitution, the top appellate court in another state can rule that an identical law violates that state's constitution. The state court can even reject the Supreme Court's interpretation of the federal Constitution, and if the losing party drops the case or the Supreme Court refuses to review it, that decision stands. Each of these possible situations has occurred more than once; therefore, variety and confusion abound.

Even greater confusion is caused by the fact that the states have been far more likely to proscribe than to enforce. People have often been free to engage in forbidden acts, because arrests and prosecutions for violation of these laws have been rare. (This was not true with respect to male homosexual relations in England.) The Supreme Court recognized this fact in 1961, when it dismissed a challenge to Connecticut's ban on the use of contraceptives because of the state's "undeviating policy of nullification" of the law *(Poe* v. *Ullman).* Only when these acts became public in some way did the police power make itself felt. Laws against polygamy and abortion are obvious examples. People may not have been prosecuted for using birth control in Connecticut, but the state had no public birth control clinics, which meant that a woman who could not afford a private physician was at a disadvantage. When the Planned Parenthood Federation opened a clinic in New Haven and its executive director was arrested, the Supreme Court found it necessary to consider the limits of state power over private morality.

The Constitution does not limit the scope of police power to what Mill called "other-regarding activities." The constitutional limits on this power come from the individual freedoms listed in the Bill of Rights and made applicable to the states through the Fourteenth Amendment. These limits are basically of two kinds. First, the due process guarantee has been interpreted to forbid any governmental action that is arbitrary, unreasonable, or extralegal. The states may not punish acts that the law does not forbid; for example, adulterers may not be punished if their conduct is not illegal. Legislation must be reasonable; that is, a law must bear a rational relationship to a legitimate state purpose. Government cannot arbitrarily interfere with individual freedom. Second, government may not invade protected rights; thus, no state may deny freedom of speech or conduct unreasonable searches and seizures.

Reynolds disposed of the rationality issue. Courts still assume that the preservation of marriage and the discouragement of extramarital sexual relations are legitimate state goals. Therefore, any prohibition reasonably related to these ends may still be sustained. Some of the provisions in the Bill of Rights, notably those in the First Amendment, have an indirect relationship to sexual behavior. The polygamists in *Reynolds* alleged, unsuccessfully, that the law violated the free exercise of religion clause. Many obscenity laws have run afoul of the free speech guarantee. But nothing in the Constitution directly protects sexual freedom.

The Connecticut law that reached the Supreme Court in *Griswold* v. *Connecticut* (1965) was far from typical of laws regulating sexual behavior. First, it was a true relic of a bygone age: specifically, the age of Anthony Comstock, the nineteenth-century crusader against "vice." Most states had passed "little Comstock laws" banning the use or distribution of birth control devices—these were essentially obscenity laws—but only two states, Connecticut and Massachusetts, still had them by the 1960s. (By contrast, all fifty states still forbade sodomy and adultery.) Second, there was a clear conflict between the law and the growing public concern with overpopulation. The Court made few enemies by overturning this law, but it did make constitutional law. *Griswold* found a right of personal privacy in the Constitution.

"Various guarantees contain zones of privacy," Justice William O. Douglas wrote in *Griswold.* The First Amendment had a "penumbra" that protected the privacy of association, including marriage. The Third Amendment ban on the quartering of soldiers in private homes in peacetime, the Fourth Amendment prohibition of unreasonable searches and seizures, and the self-incrimination clause of the Fifth Amendment all recognized personal privacy. The Ninth Amendment guarded rights not specified in the text. Taken as a whole, these provisions established a general right of privacy that included the right of a married couple to use contraceptives.

Griswold established the principle that the Bill of Rights contained constitutional bases for sexual freedom. That ruling departed from the usual mode of deciding constitutional questions, which was to interpret clauses one by one rather than to read them together for broad implications. *Griswold* also departed from the usual terms of the law-and-morality controversy. The Court did not invalidate the law because it thought that birth control was not the state's business. Instead, *Griswold* declared that contraceptive choice was a constitutional right. This ruling meant that government could not ordinarily interfere with this choice even if family planning did affect society (as it obviously does). Constitutional rights are not absolute, but it is an established rule that government may infringe these rights only when there is a pressing need for such limitation. Judged by this standard, the arguments in favor of legal enforcement of sexual morality fall short. Although the holding in *Griswold* was limited to the right of a married couple to use contraceptives, the language of the opinion left ample room for recognition of other rights within the zone of privacy.

Twenty years later, the zone of privacy was wider than it was in that case, but the privacy principle had not been expanded as far as it might have been. The Court applied *Griswold* in a truly controversial way, but it did so only once. Thus, the reach of the precedent in cases that have been less controversial has been limited. Subsequent cases have placed a high value on marriage and on reproductive choice, but these rights have not been given the status of other constitutional rights.

A few decisions absorbed *Griswold*'s commitment to marital autonomy. *Loving* v. *Virginia* (1967) used both the right to privacy and the equal protection guarantee of the Fourteenth Amendment to invalidate a law against interracial marriage. A 1978 decision overturned a law requiring court approval before a noncustodial divorced parent under court order to pay child support could remarry (*Zablocki* v. *Redhail*). A combination of privacy and race resulted in one of the Supreme Court's rare ventures into child-custody cases. In 1984, *Palmore* v. *Sidoti* reversed a Florida ruling depriving a white divorced mother of custody of her daughter when the mother married a black man.

The Court has extended the right of reproductive choice beyond the marital relationship.

Eisenstadt v. *Baird* (1972) ruled that single people, too, had the right to use contraceptives: "If the right of privacy means anything, it is the right of the *individual,* married or single, to be free from unwarranted governmental intrusion into matters so fundamentally affecting a person as the decision whether to bear or beget a child" (emphasis in the original). *Carey* v. *Population Services* (1977) ruled that states could not forbid the sale of contraceptives to minors, effectively granting freedom of choice to anyone who could get access to the devices. In 1983 the Department of Health and Human Services proposed the Public Health Service Act, which soon became known as the "squeal rule": the regulation would have required all clinics that received federal funds to notify parents or guardians if the clinic had provided devices for a minor. This rule died when a federal district court granted an injunction against it (*State* v. *Schweiker,* 1983). A landmark ruling preceded these two decisions when in 1973, *Roe* extended the *Griswold* principle to protect a woman's right to an abortion:

> The Court has recognized that a right of personal privacy, or a guarantee of certain areas or zones of privacy, does exist under the Constitution. . . . These decisions . . . make it clear that the right has some extension to activities relating to marriage, procreation, contraception, family relationships, and child rearing and education.
>
> This right of privacy . . . is broad enough to encompass a woman's decision whether or not to terminate her pregnancy. The detriment that the state would impose upon the pregnant woman by denying this choice is apparent.

The Court acknowledged that the right was not absolute. A compelling state interest could justify limitations on it. That acknowledgment could have undercut the whole argument. If, as many opponents of reproductive choice argue, life begins at conception, the state's compelling interest in preserving human life begins there, too. But the Court's review of medical, legal, and ethical authorities showed that the question of when human life begins has historically been viewed as unanswerable. Therefore, the compelling interest had to be something other than simply the protection of the fetus. The Court did find two such interests, each of which became pressing at a different stage of pregnancy. In determining these stages, the Court referred to three "trimesters" of three months' duration each. (The Court has been criticized for this conceptualization, but the justices did not create it; obstetricians did, long before *Roe.*)

First, the state had a compelling interest in protecting the lives of fetuses able to survive outside the uterus. This point of viability came at about the seventh month of pregnancy; therefore, the state could forbid abortions in the third trimester except when necessary to save the mother's life. The second compelling interest was the protection of maternal health. By 1973, abortion was less dangerous than pregnancy until about the fourth month. Therefore, beginning in the second trimester, the state could regulate abortion in ways that were reasonably related to maternal health. In the first three months of pregnancy, no compelling need to regulate abortions existed. The decision to continue or terminate a pregnancy "must be left to the medical judgement of the pregnant woman's attending physician."

The wording of that last sentence is troubling. It suggests, as does much of the opinion, that reproductive choice belongs not to women, but to doctors, who are assumed throughout *Roe* to be men. Even in the absence of laws, the medical profession has often severely limited women's choices. Until the 1970s, for example, obstetricians and gynecologists made voluntary sterilization difficult for a woman to obtain, while at the same time women welfare recipients were often sterilized without their knowledge or informed consent (Cisler, 255–257). Nothing in *Roe* could have prevented doctors from imposing similar constraints on abortion. However, this possibility has not materialized. Since *Roe,* legal abortion has been generally available to adult women who can pay for it. Even with those far-from-trivial limitations on the right of a woman to have an abortion, the decision has greatly increased women's freedom.

The effects of *Roe* may help to explain why public controversy over the decision continued with undiminished ferocity into a second decade. Although public opinion polls indicated that a majority of Americans support legalized abortion, a large, vocal, and well-funded minority continued to oppose it. This self-styled "Right to Life" movement spurred the enactment of numerous restrictions on reproductive choice. As of the mid-1980s, efforts to amend the Constitution or to secure a federal law declaring that human life begins at conception had failed, but the antichoice forces had succeeded in denying access to abortion to many poor women and may succeed in denying it to minors.

The Supreme Court has reviewed several direct or indirect limitations on abortion. *Planned Parenthood* v. *Danforth* (1976) invalidated a Missouri law requiring prior consent of a married woman's husband and a minor's parent or guardian: "The state does not have the constitutional authority to give a third party an absolute, and possibly arbitrary, veto over the decision." This holding was reaffirmed in 1983, when *Akron* v. *Akron Center for Reproductive Health* struck down a parental-consent requirement for girls under fifteen. But other decisions have jeopardized the autonomy of minors. The Court has tended to worry whether teenagers are sufficiently "mature" to exercise this right. (A similar concern pervades other decisions on the rights of minors.)

Akron rejected the "blanket determination that *all* minors under the age of 15 are too immature to make this decision or that an abortion never may be in the minor's best interests without parental approval." But *H. L.* v. *Matheson* (1981) upheld a law requiring parental notification—and unemancipated minors have a legal obligation to obey their parents. Two years earlier, *Bellotti* v. *Baird* invalidated a Massachusetts law requiring the consent of both parents or a judge, but a companion case to *Akron* sustained a similar requirement where the minor had a chance to show that she was capable of mature decision-making (*Planned Parenthood* v. *Ashcroft*, 1983). It is difficult to envision how a person could prove her own maturity when challenged. It also seems curious that decision-making capacity is emphasized rather than the consequences of the decision for the individual involved. Perhaps one can grasp the point better by imagining the opposite situation: a girl who believes abortion is immoral who is forced to get one. A minor's decision remains free from absolute veto, but these rulings clearly compromise her freedom of choice.

The end of the 1982–1983 term brought another set of rulings from the Court. Five cases from Ohio, Missouri, and Virginia weighed several state-imposed conditions on abortion (*Akron; Akron Center for Reproductive Health* v. *City of Akron; Ashcroft; Ashcroft* v. *Planned Parenthood; Simopoulos* v. *Virginia*). Essentially, the Court reaffirmed *Roe*. In addition to Akron's parental-consent rule, the Court invalidated a mandatory twenty-four-hour waiting period, a rule that all second-trimester abortions be performed in hospitals, a requirement that doctors must counsel patients about the possible adverse effects of abortions, and a requirement of "humane" disposal of the fetus. At the same time, the Court upheld requirements for a pathological examination of the fetus (at the patient's expense) and a second medical opinion for second-trimester abortions. The factor that distinguished the constitutional conditions from the unconstitutional ones was the presence of a reasonable health-related justification. An *Akron* dissent by Justice Sandra Day O'Connor attacked the Court's doctrine at one of its weakest points, the trimester approach. O'Connor labeled this tactic "completely unworkable," especially in the light of technological advances that have extended the time of viability. But her reasoning convinced only two other justices. Trimesters included, *Roe* remains law.

Thus, government cannot legitimately ban abortion, nor is the discouragement of elective abortions a legitimate enough end in itself to justify restrictive regulations. Government can, however, refuse to pay for abortions. A series of decisions since 1977 has established that principle. In that year, the Court sustained state and local regulations banning the use of public funds, such as Medicaid, for elective abortions (*Beal* v. *Doe; Maher* v. *Roe; Poelker* v. *Doe*). Even more destructive to poor women's freedom was the 1980 decision upholding the "Hyde amendments" to congressional appropriations acts. These provisions bar federal Medicaid funding for all abortions except those necessary to save the mother's life. *Harris* v. *McRae* reaffirmed the principles of the 1977 cases: "Although government may not place obstacles in the path of a woman's exercise of her freedom of choice, it need not remove those not of its own creation. Indigency falls in the latter category."

The Court's absolution of government from responsibility for poverty is a view far from universally held, as Rosalind Petchesky shows. None of the dissenters challenged this statement, however, despite its crucial importance to the majority's reasoning. The Court has consistently held that government may distribute public assistance in ways that discourage abortion and encourage childbirth, even though the latter alternative costs the government, and thus the taxpayers, more money.

Subsequent to the *Harris* decision, states remain free to fund abortions if they wish, and several continue to do so. In two states that have restricted this funding, courts have even intervened under the authority of state constitutional provisions. The California Supreme Court overturned that state's restrictions, while its New Jersey counterpart construed a "little Hyde amendment" to allow funding for abortions necessary for the mother's health as well as her life (*Committee to Defend Reproductive Rights* v. *Myers*, 1981; *Right to Choose* v. *Byrne*, 1982). Nothing prevents other state courts from following suit. Presently, however, the reproductive rights of indigent women are far more seriously compromised than even those of minors. Neither group enjoys the freedom so confidently proclaimed in 1973.

The *Griswold* privacy doctrine has been invoked in still another type of situation: cases involving prohibitions of certain kinds of extramarital sexual conduct. At first glance, these activities seem unambiguously private and victimless in a way that abortion is not. That court decisions protecting extramarital privacy could produce anything like the anger stimulated by *Roe* seems unlikely, but the Supreme Court has not extended the right of privacy to private consensual sexual acts.

Not long after *Roe*, the Court upheld two sodomy laws: a Florida statue applied to homosexuals and a Tennessee provision applied to heterosexuals (*Wainwright* v. *Stone*, 1973; *Rose* v. *Locke*, 1975). Neither decision addressed the privacy issue. The facts of the Tennessee case were such as to make even the staunchest libertarian uncomfortable, for that defendant allegedly forced a woman at knifepoint to engage in oral sex, but had been charged only with the "crime against nature." Presumably, however, anyone convinced that an act is proscribed unconstitutionally could argue that the prohibition should not be available as the basis for a lesser charge.

A 1976 holding reaffirmed these cases. The Supreme Court summarily affirmed a lower court decision that, whether one agreed or disagreed with it, constituted a clear abuse of judicial power. *Doe* v. *Commonwealth's Attorney* had rejected a male homosexual's claim that Virginia's sodomy law was unconstitutional as applied to the private acts of consenting adults. Two of the three federal judges deciding the case seemed unaware of related decisions since 1965. Distinguishing *Doe* from *Griswold*, they stressed *Griswold*'s emphasis on marriage—a relationship that law itself restricts to heterosexual couples. The judges ignored *Eisenstadt* and *Roe*, which had made clear that the right of privacy belonged not to couples but to individuals. Despite this glaring error, the Supreme Court sustained the ruling without opinion.

The Supreme Court's reluctance to decide this issue persists to the present, occasionally to the advantage of individuals. Courts in Pennsylvania (*Commonwealth* v. *Bonadio*, 1980) and New York (*People* v. *Onofre*, 1981) invalidated those states' sodomy laws. Both statutes forbade "deviate" sexual intercourse between people not married to each other; both courts overturned them on both privacy and equal protection grounds. Although these interpretations of the federal Constitution contradict those of the Supreme Court, review was denied in the Pennsylvania case and not even sought by New York.

The nation's highest court has not ruled on the constitutionality of laws banning adultery or fornication. However, it refused to review two cases where states indirectly punished such conduct. In *Hollenbaugh* v. *Free Public Library* (1978), two public employees who lived together and had a child while one was married to someone else were fired, and in *Jarrett* v. *Jarrett* (1979) a woman lost custody of her three daughters to her former husband when her lover moved in with her. Neither case has been uniformly followed by state courts as precedent. Even in *Jarrett*'s home state, Illinois, mothers have retained custody in similar cases (*In re Marriage of Olson*, 1981). *Cord* v. *Gibb* (1979) reversed at the state level a Virginia court's decision that an unmarried woman law-school graduate who lived with a man lacked the "good moral character" needed for admission to the bar. But, as we shall see, homosexuals are far more likely than heterosexuals, however independent-minded, to suffer indirect penalties for their conduct.

The constitutional right to privacy announced in *Griswold* has had a complicated history. Perhaps the only generalization that can safely be made about this right is that subsequent decisions have given constitutional priority to reproductive choice. Both within and outside marriage, individuals have the right to decide whether or not to have children and to use available means to control their fertility. In effect, *individual* means "women," because they are the childbearers and the users of most methods of fertility control. This right is more vulnerable to governmental inhibition than are other constitutional rights. The state must pay for a copy of a poor defendant's trial transcript to aid in an appeal and must pay unemployment compensation to support a Seventh-Day Adventist's First Amendment right not to work on Saturdays, for example, but it may refuse to pay for an abortion that a Medicaid recipient has the right to choose. Furthermore, the Supreme Court has, often on dubious grounds if grounds at all, refused to apply the principles of *Griswold, Eisenstadt,* and *Roe* to private, nonreproductive sexual choices. Sexual expression outside of family planning remains the state's legitimate concern.

If the law confined its involvement with homosexuality to sodomy laws, gay people might have little to worry about. These laws are as little enforced as was the Connecticut birth-control law. But state and federal governments do not stop with statutes proscribing homosexual activities. Instead, homosexuals are subjected to numerous and severe indirect penalties for exercising their choices. These restrictions are so many and so great that they effectively make homosexuals a sexual minority in American law.

HOMOSEXUALS AND THE LAW

"The concepts of 'majority' and 'minority' necessarily reflect temporary arrangements and political judgments" (*University of California* v. *Bakke,* 1978). Those words of Supreme Court Justice Lewis Powell refer to racial and ethnic groups, but they apply with equal validity to sexual preference. Most Americans—that is, more than 50 percent—are heterosexually active and marry at some time during their lives; but many are members of one or more "minorities." They may be temporarily single, divorced, or widowed; they may have homosexual relationships or become what the Census Bureau calls POSSLQs (persons of the opposite sex sharing

living quarters). To complicate matters further, some celibates and some homosexuals enter into heterosexual marriages.

Of course, the term *sexual minority* is not commonly used to refer to those who, permanently or temporarily, are celibate, unmarried, or homosexual, any more than the term *racial or ethnic minority* describes those whose ethnic heritage is shared by less than half the population. Just as law and custom single out certain racial groups as minorities, and stigmatize and oppress them, so American society has isolated one group, homosexuals, as a disadvantaged sexual minority. This is not to say that all others who deviate from the "majority" escape social sanctions. Celibates, especially outside the religious life, may be the targets of ridicule; calling a woman a spinster is rarely a compliment. The phrase *living in sin,* once commonly used to refer to those now labeled POSSLQs, indicates the displeasure once visited on this conduct, as do the *Jarrett* and *Cord* cases.

These terms are mild as compared with epithets commonly applied to homosexuals. Neither celibates nor unmarried heterosexuals have consistently been labeled "deviant" or subjected to legal discrimination the way homosexuals have been. The notion that homosexuality is a disease has been so widespread that government officials once seriously proposed that homosexuality be included among the "handicaps" covered by federal civil rights statutes (Baer, 225). The emergence of a homosexual civil rights movement has increased awareness that homosexuals, like blacks, women, and the disabled, are a disadvantaged group within American society.

The legal deprivations visited on homosexuals are too numerous to list, but among the most burdensome are these: sodomy laws invade the most intimate aspects of gay people's lives; homosexuality has often been a disqualification for, or grounds for dismissal from, some government jobs; gay activists have been denied their First Amendment rights; state courts have deprived homosexual parents of custody and visitation rights; and the national government has refused to allow homosexual aliens to become citizens or even to enter the country. One of the commonest and most pervasive forms of discrimination against homosexuals is the prohibition, in every state, of same-sex marriages. Society has defined marriage as a relationship of preeminent importance but has denied this relationship to homosexual partners. The ramifications of this policy are enormous. If one partner dies without making a will, for example, the survivor does not inherit any of his or her lover's estate, as a spouse would. While making a will might solve that particular problem, same-sex partners are also denied a host of other benefits, such as social security and medical insurance, which spouses receive as a matter of course and which a person cannot "will" to others.

Those who make these rules have the power, formally at least, to change them. Amendments to the Social Security Act have given some divorced spouses the right to certain benefits; Congress is free to make similar changes on behalf of same-sex partners. States have the power to allow same-sex marriages, a decision that would make partners eligible for various kinds of work-related benefits. But to put these possibilities into words is to realize how remote are the chances of such occurrences. Only one state, California, has even forbidden discrimination against homosexuals in state employment by executive order.

In the absence of such actions, federal, state, and local governments can still pass civil rights laws for homosexuals, as they have done in the past for racial minorities, women, and disabled people. So far, only a few municipalities across the country have taken this step; however, these include such major cities as Atlanta, Boston, and Los Angeles (Altman). The New York City Council has recently accepted such an ordinance. In San Francisco, home of the most politically active gay community in the country, the mayor vetoed a measure that would have allowed insurance coverage for unmarried partners. Considering the deep and pervasive homophobia that characterizes American society, it is not surprising that gay activists have suffered some political defeats while winning other important victories.

Homosexuals—like blacks, women, and the disabled—have also used litigation as a means of changing disfavored treatment. In the absence of obvious infringements of constitutional rights, courts judge this kind of policy by the "rational basis" test described earlier. Since the states can make homosexual acts criminal, discouraging these acts is considered as legitimate a purpose as is discouraging any other crime. Even in the absence of sodomy laws, the states are free to discourage extramarital sexual relations, including homosexual acts. However, the acceptance of traditional morality as a legitimate concern of government does not mean that any policy that discriminates against homosexuals will withstand judicial scrutiny. These laws cannot be arbitrary, must limit governmental power, and must not invade recognized constitutional rights. The law is changing so rapidly in this area that it is difficult to make accurate generalizations about it.

At times, constitutional rights have given less protection to homosexuals than to heterosexuals. This remains true of the right to privacy in all but a few states. First Amendment rights constitute one area in which homosexuals have won significant gains. The freedoms of speech, press, assembly, and petition are as crucial to gay activists as to any other interest group; these activities are necessary means of getting support and publicizing demands. But homosexuals have not always been treated like any other interest group. On college and university campuses in particular, where vestiges of the in loco parentis philosophy remain, gay activists have run into problems. These difficulties have been the exception rather than the rule, at least in public institutions, but some administrators have been reluctant to allow these groups to use campus facilities.

One of these cases, *Gay Lib* v. *University of Missouri* (1977), is worth examining, because this eight-year struggle reveals the opposing views involved. In 1971, the university refused to recognize the group as an official campus organization, an act that would have entitled it to use campus facilities and to publicize its activities on campus. Administrators gave two reasons for this decision. First, recognition would encourage violations of Missouri's sodomy law —which means that because a law is rarely enforced, it is not, therefore, harmless. Second, they argued, homosexuality is a mental illness, and the gay group would spread it. When the conflict began, this opinion was shared by no less an authority than the American Psychiatric Association, whose *Diagnostic and Statistical Manual of Mental Disorders* listed homosexuality. The group's decision in 1973 to declassify homosexuality met with strong opposition from some of its members.

The university won in the district court, but

the appeals court sided with the students on the grounds that the possibility of illegal activity was too remote and the psychiatric testimony too mixed to provide the compelling justification necessary for abridgment of First Amendment rights (1977). The university then asked the Supreme Court to review the case. The Court refused, but in unusual circumstances. Three justices, one short of the necessary four, wanted to hear the case; one of the three, William Rehnquist, wrote a dissent that revealed his sympathy with the administration's position (*Ratchford* v. *Gay Lib,* 1978). If a subsequent case gets the fourth vote needed for review, it is quite possible that the Court will overrule the lower courts and abridge homosexuals' freedom of expression.

If direct limitations on these rights have met with defeat, policies that indirectly inhibit the First Amendment rights of homosexuals are common. The gay activist employee who loses his job (*McConnell* v. *Anderson,* 1971; *Gish* v. *Board of Education,* 1976) or the lesbian mother forced to choose between keeping her children and living with her partner (*Schuster* v. *Schuster,* 1978) speak out only at great personal cost. A Missouri judge who ordered a noncustodial father not to take his son to services at the gay church that he attended appeared unaware of any conflict between this order and the father's freedom of religion (*J. L. P.* v. *D. J. P.,* 1982).

In other areas that concern homosexuals, the government has considerably more leeway to legislate than is the case with recognized rights. Courts recognize no fundamental rights to employment, child custody, immigration, or naturalization. Although these interests tend to be of utmost importance to the individuals concerned, government may infringe them as long as it does so in conformity with due process. Indeed, it is not clear that even the due process limitation really applies to custody and immigration. Federal courts have viewed child custody as almost exclusively a state matter; *Palmore* is a very rare exception. Federal courts are reluctant to grapple with immigration cases for just the opposite reason: Congress' power is viewed as nearly plenary, leaving little room for judicial intervention. Nevertheless, the law is slowly changing even in these areas. Some state judges are questioning traditional assumptions about what children require, and some reinterpretation of congressional intent is going on in the federal courts.

Employers have often fired or refused to hire known or suspected homosexuals. In the absence of vigorously enforced antidiscrimination laws, the private sector is largely beyond judicial control; but when government is the employer, its actions are subject to review by the courts. The federal civil service, the military, and the teaching profession have been fruitful sources of cases since the early 1960s. With two exceptions, courts have upheld the power of public employers to discriminate against homosexuals. However, this power has been subjected to procedural and substantive limitations. Until very recently, the Supreme Court has refused to hear any of these cases.

Many reasons have been advanced for refusal to hire homosexuals. It is possible that any reason is merely a rationalization, a smoke screen for bigotry. However, the reasons given sound plausible on their face, although they turn out on analysis to be inadequate. School officials have feared that homosexual teachers would seduce or even molest students. The armed forces have worried about the effects of homosexuals on discipline and security. The national government has feared that homosexual employees, especially those in security-sensitive positions, would be vulnerable to blackmail or extortion.

As homosexuals have "come out of the closet," this last rationale has lost force; the threat of disclosure becomes empty when everyone knows an employee is gay. But employers have claimed that gay activists attract "embarrassing" publicity. In 1970, for example, the University of Minnesota withdrew a job offer to a librarian when a newspaper story revealed that he and his lover had applied for a marriage license. A federal appeals court upheld the university on the grounds that this man was not entitled to "foist tacit approval of this socially repugnant conduct upon his employer" (*McConnell* v. *Anderson,* 1971). The gay worker may face a choice between withholding information about his or her sexual preference, which employers may interpret as dishonesty, or candor, which employers may find embarrassing. For Joseph Acanfora, a Maryland junior high school teacher, this became a classic double bind. After Acanfora appeared on network television as a gay activist, he was transferred to a nonteaching position. The courts vindicated his First Amendment rights, but upheld the school authorities because Acanfora had "practiced deception" by omitting his membership in a homophile organization from his list of extracurricular activities on his job application (*Acanfora* v. *Board of Education,* 1974). Thus, he was punished for both secrecy and notoriety. Any choice that a gay employee makes may be the wrong choice.

The first employment cases to reach the courts came from the civil service. Eventually, the District of Columbia Court of Appeals established a rule that people could not be rejected or dismissed solely on the basis of unsubstantiated charges (*Scott* v. *Macy,* 1968; *Norton* v. *Macy,* 1969). As for the military, the widely publicized case of *Matlovich* v. *Secretary of the Air Force* (1978) established that the armed services could not dismiss homosexuals unless the services adopted formal rules to guide their decisions.

Later rulings have subjected both civilian and military policy to critical scrutiny. In 1976 the Supreme Court summarily remanded a decision upholding the dismissal of an activist employee (*Singer* v. *Civil Service Commission*). A Wisconsin district court invalidated an army regulation providing for the discharge of any soldier who "evidences homosexual tendencies, desire, or interest, but is without overt homosexual acts," finding it in violation of due process, privacy, and freedom of expression. As a result, Miriam ben Shalom, a drill instructor with an outstanding record, was permitted to remain in the Army Reserves. Although she had acknowledged her sexual preference, there was no evidence that she had had homosexual relations, made advances to other women, or been active in homosexual organizations. The court indicated that the result might have been different had she violated a rule forbidding homosexual acts (*Ben Shalom* v. *Secretary of the Army,* 1980). Federal courts have upheld dismissals for violation of similar rules against overt acts.

State and local governments have more autonomy in this area than does the national government. School boards, for example, may fire gay teachers on grounds of "unfitness." Such dismissals reflect a widespread fear of the effects that such teachers will have on children. To worry that a teacher may influence a child to become homosexual implies, of course, that there is indeed something wrong with being homosexual; it also implies that sexual orientation is something one learns by example. Those

who consider homosexuality evil or sick, those who find it unexceptional, and those who find it laudable are equally entitled to their opinions, but it seems unreasonable to fire homosexual teachers if there is nothing more than speculation to indicate that sexual orientation is shaped in childhood or adolescence by role models. Expert opinion is widely divided on this point, as it is on most other aspects of human sexuality. The columnist Russell Baker deserves the last word. Reflecting on his own schooling, he wrote, "It was curious, perhaps perverse, that I have not turned out to be a spinster."

The fear that homosexuals might sexually molest students is more difficult to address. It seems that every year, if not every week, we learn of more instances of sexual abuse of children by adults. Society's growing awareness of this problem is welcome, for child abuse is intolerable—although it is all too obvious that this conduct has been tolerated. However, it makes no difference whether the abuser is of the same or opposite sex as the victim; and there is no evidence that homosexuals are more likely than heterosexuals to molest children. The fact that administrators' and parents' fears are often strong does not make them valid bases for public policy. These fears are groundless, and the dismissal of teachers simply for being gay appears arbitrary and capricious in the extreme. But the dismissals continue, and the teachers usually lose in the courts (Baer, 242–249). As with the rulings on privacy, the Supreme Court's inaction and the presence of state constitutions create some room for new developments in public employment. Perry Aumiller may have been reinstated in his job because he was a university theater manager rather than a schoolteacher, but the district judge's statement that "the decision not to renew Aumiller's contract because of his public statements contravenes these most basic teachings of the First Amendment and cannot be tolerated" has wide implications (*Aumiller* v. *University of Delaware,* 1977). In 1979 the California Supreme Court held that a public utility's refusal to hire homosexuals violated the equal-protection clause of the state constitution—because such discrimination was "arbitrary exclusion of qualified individuals" (*Gay Law Students Association* v. *Pacific Telephone and Telegraph*). At present, however, these decisions represent minority views. In 1985, the Supreme Court heard a case from the Tenth Circuit that had invalidated, on the grounds of unconstitutional vagueness, an Oklahoma law allowing local school districts to fire teachers who advocate homosexual activity in a manner that creates a risk of their students' learning about it. With Justice Lewis Powell not participating, the Court divided four to four on the case. This tie affirmed the decision but did not establish a stable precedent.

Another severe deprivation that many homosexuals risk is the loss of the company of their children. Divorced homosexual parents often have to fight for custody or visitation rights. Traditionally, judges have used two criteria for making custody awards where divorcing parents cannot agree: the fitness of the parents and the best interests of the children. American courts have progressed from a nineteenth-century presumption in the father's favor to a twentieth-century presumption in the mother's favor, to a slow movement toward a presumption of neutrality. Nevertheless, most minor children of divorced or separated parents continue to live with their mothers. The factor that has changed is that judges no longer automatically favor mothers in custody disputes.

Whatever presumptions prevail, parents with unorthodox life-styles have often suffered. Thirty years before the *Jarrett* case was decided, when mothers were virtually always favored, a New York woman lost custody of her children to her ex-husband under similar circumstances (*Bunim* v. *Bunim,* 1949). But now *Jarrett* is an idiosyncrasy. Heterosexual parents rarely lose custody because of their sexual conduct, but homosexual parents remain in great danger. Custodial parents are more likely to lose custody than to keep it when challenged by their former spouses; most of these parents are lesbian mothers. Noncustodial parents, both lesbians and gay men, are more successful in keeping their visitation rights.

The cases decided since the 1970s do not reveal a general judicial presumption that homosexual parents are unfit or that living with a gay parent is contrary to a child's best interests. But neither do the courts presume that homosexuality is irrelevant to these issues. Judges take parental sexual preference into account in making these judgments, sometimes relying on expert testimony—which means that gay parents are at a disadvantage in court.

These custody decisions have expressed three major concerns about the possible effects of homosexual parents on children. Two of these fears are familiar from the disputes over gay teachers: sexual abuse (more often from parents' gay friends than from the parents themselves) and influence on children's sexual preference as adults. The first worry influenced the Missouri judge who ordered a father not to take his son to his own church or to gay social gatherings (*J. L. P.*). Although some judges have acknowledged that there is "insufficient expert testimony" on gay parents' influence on the sexuality of their children (*Jacobson* v. *Jacobson,* 1981), this concern seems to get at least tacit recognition in rulings like *Dailey* v. *Dailey* (1981), where a Tennessee court deprived a mother of both custody and visitation rights because she "flagrantly flaunted" her relationship with her lover in front of her child. It is important to remember that society approves of the publicizing, if not the flaunting, of heterosexual relationships; what else is a wedding ring, after all, but a public announcement?

A third fear, however, has been more powerful than either of these: the concern that the parent's homosexuality will "stigmatize" the child, exposing him or her to public ridicule, ostracism, and shame. Because of this fear, the gay-activist mother or the mother who lives openly with her partner is more likely to lose custody than her less active counterpart. The assumption seems to be that the more widely the parent's homosexuality is known, the more likely the child is to suffer.

A major victory for a lesbian mother involved a woman who, though "an admitted practicing homosexual," neither lived with another woman nor belonged to any gay organizations (*M. P.* v. *S. P.,* 1979). Despite this apparent isolation, S. P. somehow found an able, sympathetic lawyer when her former husband sued for custody of their two daughters. A New Jersey court declared, "Neither the prejudices of the small community in which they live nor the curiosity of their peers about defendant's sexual nature will be abated by a change of custody. . . . These are matters which courts cannot control, and there is little to gain by creating an artificial world where the children may dream that life is different than it is." A case like this remains the exception. Even when the homosexual parents win, their access to their children is often contingent on the acceptance of inhibitions on their life-styles. They are forced to choose between their children and their freedom.

Although the record in employment and parental rights remains bleak for homosexuals, they have won significant victories in the area of immigration and naturalization. Two federal appellate courts have ruled that aliens can no longer be excluded from the United States or, once here, be denied citizenship solely because of homosexuality. These are bold decisions, for they depart from both Supreme Court precedent and the last expressed wishes of Congress. The lower courts have defied both of their masters.

The Constitution states that Congress has the power to "establish an uniform Rule of Naturalization" (Article I, Section 8). The last major law passed under this rubric was the Immigration and Naturalization Act of 1952, known as the McCarran-Walter Act. This law reaffirms the traditional requirement that a new citizen be a person of "good moral character." This language provides a possible basis for refusing to let homosexuals become citizens. The law also establishes conditions for temporary entry that, compared to those of most Western European countries, are quite restrictive. All foreign visitors, however brief their intended stay, must get a visa and must be questioned by officials of the Immigration and Naturalization Service (INS).

The law forbids entry to several classes of aliens for medical reasons; among these are all applicants "afflicted with a psychopathic personality." An INS examiner who suspected that an entrant had such a disorder was to refer him or her to the Public Health Service (PHS), which had the power to issue a "Class A certificate" excluding the person. The INS and PHS had license to ask highly personal questions about sexual behavior. The law's legislative history indicates that Congress' conception of psychopathology included homosexuality. This evidence of intent, like all legislative history, is inconclusive, but the INS routinely excluded known homosexuals until the 1980s.

Congress' power over immigration and naturalization is traditionally considered plenary—that is, all but absolute. It is not usually limited by other constitutional provisions like those in the Bill of Rights. This fact has inhibited constitutional challenges to the immigration laws.

However, the McCarran-Walter Act, like any other federal statute, is subject to judicial interpretation. The Supreme Court has dealt with the homosexual issue only once, in 1967. *Boutilier* v. *INS* sustained the exclusion of a Canadian man who "had continuously been afflicted with homosexuality for over six years." But in 1983 the Court of Appeals for the Ninth Circuit ordered the INS to admit a homosexual whom it had excluded. The legal reasoning was adroit and intricate, as were the interrelationships of court and agencies.

The PHS had stopped issuing Class A certificates on the grounds of suspected homosexuality in 1979, by order of the surgeon general. In 1980 the INS instructed its examiners to stop asking questions about applicants' sexual orientation, but allowed them to exclude any alien who made a voluntary statement. *Hill* v. *INS* (1983) held that the INS could not exclude homosexuals without a medical certificate from the PHS. Since the PHS no longer issued such certificates, the ruling effectively ended the practice of keeping homosexuals out of the country. Of course, a new surgeon general or INS director is free to reinstate old policies.

There is no reason to believe that homosexuality would ever have become a problem in society if the heterosexual majority had not made it one. There is no evidence that homosexuals pose a threat to population growth or family life, that they have any bad influence on others, or that they suffer from any moral or mental defect. By stigmatizing homosexuals, society has forced them into concealment, has denied itself the fruits of much individual talent by frustrating its expression, and has caused an immeasurable amount of human misery. The law, like medicine and other professions, has enforced and reinforced social prejudice through repressive policies. The gay rights movement is slowly winning partial, tentative victories, but, as the twentieth century draws to an end, homosexuals remain a disadvantaged minority.

THE LAW OF RAPE AND ABUSE

If any development in the relationship between law and sexuality can be described as a trend, it is American law's slow move away from its concern with the private, voluntary sexual choices of adults. Both direct and indirect sanctions are gradually being dropped. However, law has yet to come to terms with the fact that not all sexual activity is voluntary. People can be coerced, either by the superior physical strength of an attacker or attackers or by weapons. Children are at least as vulnerable as adults to sexual assaults and are easier to cajole and manipulate into less than voluntary participation.

The criminal law has traditionally classified certain types of sexual coercion as rape. The classic common-law definition of rape is "unlawful carnal knowledge of a woman without her consent" (Thomas, 328–329). (Penetration by the penis constitutes rape; ejaculation is not necessary.) The qualifier *unlawful* is necessary because at common law there could be no rape between husband and wife. Traditionally, a male cannot be raped, although in reality he can be forcibly sodomized; nor can a female rape, although in reality she can sexually abuse anyone whom she can subdue. (These acts are sometimes punishable, however, as sodomy or assault.)

If all we knew about rape were what the penal codes provided, we would believe that American society has always unequivocally condemned it. In every state, rape is a felony, punishable by long prison sentences. But in fact most rapes—estimates vary from 50 percent to 90 percent—are not even reported to the police, and approximately seven out of eight reported rapes go unpunished. One study estimates that between 20 percent and 30 percent of American females now in their teens will experience a sexual assault at some time during their lives.

Perhaps the best explanation for this disjunction between law and practice is the fact that rape has often been denied or trivialized. "Blaming the victim" has been a common approach to rape. A typical way of blaming the victim is by not believing her. In the seventeenth century, Lord Chief Justice Matthew Hale of England declared that "rape is an accusation easily made and hard to be proved" (Brownmiller, 413). This belief persists to the present day.

We would like to know, of course, whether Hale's conclusion is supported by the facts. Unfortunately, the biases of those who receive reports of rape bias the data. In the 1970s, police statistics indicated that the national average of unfounded rape accusations was 15 percent—

but, in the same years, police textbooks trained officers to distrust rape complaints (Brownmiller, 190, 408). When police are taught to disbelieve accusations, it is hardly surprising that they do so.

Rape and racism are closely connected in American society. Although most rapes involve perpetrators and victims of the same race, black men convicted of raping white women get the heaviest sentences of all sexual-assault defendants, while rapists whose victims are black get more lenient treatment than those who rape white women (Feild and Bienen; Wriggins, 121). As shameful as these facts are, they do not constitute evidence that women who make rape accusations usually lie. What appears to have happened is that the usual disbelief of women complainants and trivialization of their experience have been abandoned in favor of racist thinking.

The extent to which social myths about rape have changed and continue to change is well illustrated by the history of such old saws as "there's no such thing as rape" or "when rape is inevitable, relax and enjoy it." These remarks, once common, are now considered offensive. A transformation is occurring in social attitudes about rape, a transformation for which much credit belongs to the feminist movement. Thanks to such studies as Susan Brownmiller's landmark book *Against Our Will,* we now take rape seriously; we have a better understanding of it, and we know that it is not unusual and not limited to psychopaths, strangers in alleys, or black men seeking white women. Indeed, Brownmiller and other experts have shown that rape is not primarily a crime of sexual desire or mental illness and that most rape occurs between people already acquainted. These changes in public knowledge and opinion are reflected in the fact that since 1969 every state legislature has changed its rape and sexual-assault statutes in ways that shift the focus from victims to perpetrators and make convictions easier to obtain ("Rape Reform").

Common law and, until recently, statutes have put rape in a class by itself. In no other crime is so much attention paid to the victim's behavior and so many excuses established for the offender. The law has endorsed society's suspicion of rape victims in a variety of ways. Perhaps the most significant difference between the way the legal system treats rape and the way it deals with other crimes is the fact that the typical defense to a rape charge is consent—that the woman was not forced to have sex but participated willingly. The spousal exemption arose from the common law's presumption, articulated by Hale, that "by their mutual matrimonial consent and contract the wife hath given herself up in this kind to her husband, which she cannot retract" (Brownmiller, 427). Unless the prosecutor can find witnesses to the act or show that the woman was injured, the consent defense effectively amounts to the complainant's word against the defendant's—who, of course, is presumed innocent like any other defendant. The whole issue is complicated by the nuances and ambiguities inherent in much sexual communication and because the man is usually expected to be the initiator.

That men accused of rape would attempt to defend themselves by alleging consent is not surprising; what is remarkable is that the law has often stressed the absence of consent rather than the presence of force. New York and Washington laws enacted in the 1960s were regarded as "reforms": both statutes dropped references to consent and defined the "forcible compulsion" necessary for a rape conviction as "physical force which overcomes resistance" ("earnest resistance" in New York) or a "threat, express or implied," of "death or serious injury." Similarly, the Model Penal Code proposed by the American Law Institute in 1962 has two degrees of rape: first degree, where the victim was not the "voluntary social companion" of the accused or where she sustained physical injury; second degree, where the victim is compelled to submit by "force or threat of force." Ten states revised their laws to incorporate the code's definition of rape.

These laws focus on the behavior of victims, asking such questions as whether the victim offered earnest resistance and why she was with the man in the first place. Saying "No"—even screaming it—has never been held to constitute sufficient resistance. Resistance requirements may force women to endanger their lives, and demand an atypical response to force: victims often "freeze" (Schwartz).

Considerations like these and pressure from feminists persuaded the New York legislature to abandon the earnest-resistance requirement in 1982. Eight years earlier, Michigan had revised its law in a way that has provided a model for at least eight other states. Its Criminal Sexual Conduct Act of 1974 expressly eliminates the resistance standard and defines criminal sexual conduct as penetration where force or coercion is used to accomplish it ("Rape Reform," 1537–1539). Consent is still available as an affirmative defense against the charge of forcible compulsion, but the prosecution need no longer prove the absence of consent. These reforms represent a trend toward treating rape like other violent crimes, where physical force is presumed to occur without the victim's consent.

A related common-law notion is becoming obsolete much faster than is the resistance standard. Traditionally, evidence about the complainant's sexual history has been admissible in rape trials, because the law has considered her prior "chastity" or lack thereof relevant to the issue of consent. But by 1984, forty-eight states passed "rape shield" laws, which typically exclude all evidence about the victim's prior sexual conduct except relations with the defendant himself. The Federal Rules of Evidence contain a similar provision. So far, these laws have survived judicial scrutiny (Thomas, 334–336). However, Massachusetts' highest court ruled that the Sixth Amendment right to confront witnesses required the admission of such evidence where it might show bias or a motive to lie (*Commonwealth* v. *Joyce,* 1981). The effects of such an interpretation were revealed in 1984, when several men were tried for raping a woman in a New Bedford bar. This crime, which allegedly occurred in the presence of cheering witnesses, received nationwide media coverage. The trial was even shown on cable television. The defense, in cross-examining the complainant, somehow managed to introduce evidence about her past, including her sex life. The fact that this trial ended in a guilty verdict for all defendants may indicate that jurors are becoming skeptical about the relevance of the victim's sexual experience. However, any drawing of conclusions must be cautious. This was a single case, and a study found that in hypothetical rape cases, the less prior experience the victim had, the harsher the sentence was (Feild and Bienen).

Any prosecutor knows that it is easier to obtain a rape conviction when rapist and victim are strangers than when they are acquainted. The Model Penal Code's distinction between first- and second-degree rape embodies this social attitude. Yet "date rape" is a common occurrence. Rape occurs even in situations where the couple has previously had a sexual relationship. Indeed, in every sense but the old legal definition, husbands have raped their wives. The old rule is gradually being abandoned, however. Twenty-three states and the District of Columbia now allow prosecutions for marital rape. In September 1984 a Florida man was convicted of raping his wife; what made this decision unique was that they were actually living together at the time. However, some states still specifically exempt husband-wife rape from prosecution; Texas has even extended the exemption to cohabiting unmarried couples (Thomas, 335–337). Changes in the law may help to produce changes in behavior, for they represent a welcome departure from the notion that a husband has an absolute right to his wife's sexual services.

Rape emerged as a public issue in the 1970s. The 1980s have seen the emergence of a related issue, the sexual abuse of children. Many studies have shown the prevalence of this behavior (Armstrong; Butler; Rush). The National Center on Child Abuse and Neglect estimates that 200,000 children are sexually abused every year (Geiser, 6), and this estimate is likely to be revised upward, not downward. Like rape, child molestation usually involves an offender known to the victim; this is why warning children against strangers does not end the abuse. Incest has become a subject for popular drama (as rape and homosexuality were in the 1970s). Wherever they are, both boys and girls, and even infants, are in danger of being molested.

For a male to force a female not his wife to have sexual intercourse with him is always rape, whether the victim is a child or an adult, and regardless of any blood relationship they might have. However, the law has three other classes of sex crimes that supposedly make it easier to convict those who victimize children: child molestation, or lewd and lascivious conduct with a child; statutory rape, or intercourse with a female below a certain age (ranging from seven to eighteen); and incest, or intercourse between persons so closely related by blood that marriage between them would be illegal. Thirty-seven states now have gender-neutral statutory rape laws, changing the crime to unlawful sexual intercourse with a person below the age of consent.

Prohibitions against child molestation, statutory rape, and incest are assumed to protect the young and vulnerable. Children are presumed to lack full capacity to make independent decisions to consent to, or to refuse, sex. They are also especially subject to manipulation, to superior intellectual force as well as to physical force, and to all the kinds of influence that adults have over children. Penalties for acts that would not be criminal with an adult partner recognize these circumstances.

Unfortunately, these laws rarely do what they are designed to do—protect children. They do make it possible to punish adults who exploit vulnerable young people, but they also allow offenders to get lighter penalties for greater harm. Children are forcibly raped. Because their bodies are small and immature, rape inflicts greater physical damage on them than on adult victims. But child-rapists who are prosecuted at all are often charged not with the forcible rape that they committed but with incest or statutory rape, which carry lesser penalties.

Moreover, punishment for any sexual abuse is the exception, not the rule. Like adult rape, child rape and molestation often go unreported and unpunished. Denial and trivialization have operated here, too. Children are often even less likely than adults to be believed. The law is suspicious of children as witnesses or accusers. This distrust accords with the law's general presumption that children are less competent than adults. Indeed, in a sense the law turns on itself: the same considerations that lead to special severity toward sexual conduct with children lead authorities to discount accusations made by them.

Even when a young victim is believed, sexual abuse has been reinterpreted in ways similar to the treatment of adult rape. Some studies have suggested that molested children behave seductively or attract attention by their unusual charm or that being molested really is not so bad after all. Alfred Kinsey's pioneer study of female sexual behavior in the 1950s trivialized his own findings that four-fifths of his interviewees reported unwanted sexual attention as children by criticizing their parents for overreaction (Brownmiller, 305–307). Even now, when this problem is being taken more seriously, adult-child sex has its defenders—all of whom are adults and none of whom are children (Rush, chap. 15).

The attention now being given to the sexual abuse of children may produce change in the laws, as has happened with rape. But unless authorities begin believing children and stop blaming them, there is little reason to expect the incidence of these crimes to decline. At present, the law in effect condones much sexual abuse of children. The future of the law is inextricably connected with the general treatment of children in American society.

Law must, of course, draw a somewhat arbitrary line between childhood and adulthood. It has often been suggested that some statutory-rape laws put the age of consent unreasonably high. When the age is eighteen, perhaps such critics are right; however, seven, or even the Model Penal Code's recommendation of ten, seem unreasonably low (Thomas, 327). Another problem is essentially a question of gender discrimination. If it is illegal for a male to have sex with a female below a certain age, what about the opposite situation? Although only thirteen states continue to punish only males for sex only with young females, the Supreme Court upheld such a law in 1981. *Michael M.* v. *Superior Court of Sonoma County* is worth discussion, for it reveals much about the phenomenon of rape in American society.

The case shows beyond cavil that Michael, charged with unlawful sexual intercourse with sixteen-year-old Sharon, was a forcible rapist. Intercourse took place only after the seventeen-year-old youth had repeatedly struck her. But Michael's violent behavior had no relevance to the offense with which he was charged. Justice Harry Blackmun, who cited Sharon's pretrial testimony in his concurring opinion, saw fit to remark that Sharon "appears not to have been an unwilling participant, in at least the initial stages of the intimacies." The fact that a Supreme Court justice could make such a statement is a good indication of why rape convictions are difficult to obtain. The availability of a lesser charge that made consent immaterial made it possible for the state to punish Michael.

However, the conclusion of five justices that a male-only statutory-rape law was constitutional is disturbing because of the grounds on which it relied. The majority concluded that the law was sufficiently related to the important state purpose of discouraging illegitimate teenage pregnancy. Since women's childbearing capacity has so often been used as a justification for their subjection, a reemergence of "outmoded sexual stereotypes" is no more welcome than a ruling in favor of Michael would have been. For women, *Michael M.* was an unwinnable case.

The picture that emerges from such a case is that of a legal system frantically trying to correct itself. Forcible rape continues to occur. Because authorities often impute consent to victims, rape goes unreported, and, when reported, unpunished. Because authorities view this situation as unacceptable in certain contexts, lesser charges like statutory rape or unlawful sexual intercourse are created. But, because these offenses depend not on the defendant's behavior but on the victim's age, such statutes are both too broad and too narrow: they punish people for consensual sex, and they punish violence too lightly. To the extent that the criminal law reflects traditional attitudes about rape—which is to say, in large part, traditional attitudes about sex roles—the state will continue to condone violent expressions of sexuality. Conversely, although the New Bedford trial and the *Michael M.* case show that attitudes about rape can no more be "legislated" than can attitudes about sexual morality in general, legislative reforms have shown that society can make it harder for these attitudes to dictate results. Many states have taken giant steps toward making rape a de facto as well as a de jure crime.

CONCLUSION

To discuss sexuality and the law is to aim at several moving targets, all moving at different speeds. It is a truism to say that changes in the law result from broader social changes, but it is less obvious that the relationship is never simple. American laws once reflected the view that sex was something to be hidden, reluctantly tolerated for the sake of procreation. Twentieth-century society is more open about sex, viewing it as good in itself. Slowly, America's laws have changed to allow people to con-

SEXUALITY AND THE LAW

trol their fertility and enjoy sex without reproduction. The legalization of contraception and abortion and changes in the laws relating to private sexual conduct reflect and reinforce these changes.

But if American society is no longer Puritan or Victorian, it is still patriarchal. The nuclear family, dominated by the husband and father, is regarded as the basic social unit. Much law about sexuality stems from the institution of patriarchy. Acceptable sex is still heterosexual sex, preferably within marriage.

The Supreme Court gave constitutional sanction to this patriarchal, heterosexist bias in *Bowers* v. *Hardwick* (1986). The Court upheld Georgia's antisodomy law as applied to homosexuals. The law forbids all oral and anal sex, even between wife and husband, but a suit filed by a married couple was dismissed for lack of standing. Hardwick had been charged with committing sodomy with another adult male in his own bedroom. The Supreme Court's ruling, therefore, explicitly refused to include the principles of the *Wolfenden Report* within the constitutional right of privacy.

Justice Byron White, writing for the majority, distinguished this case from *Griswold, Roe,* and their successors: "No connection between family, marriage, or procreation on the one hand and homosexual activity on the other has been demonstrated." A divided Court has thus interpreted the Constitution in line with the "profamily" bias of the New Right—although hardly in line with its "prolife" bias.

That bias, too, has patriarchal roots. Some opposition to elective abortion may well reflect fear of the possibility that women can control their own fertility. The proposed squeal rule and the attempts to limit minors' access to abortion seem to incorporate a notion that sex is a privilege to be reserved for adults, rather like smoking and drinking (and these indirect prohibitions on sex are about as effective as direct prohibitions on those activities, too). It is not surprising that a society in which men have dominated women would refuse to recognize rape, which is male domination in an extreme form, as a grave problem. More condemnation has been visited on those who voluntarily depart from the patriarchal norm, such as homosexuals, than upon those who violently act out the norm.

The 1970s and 1980s brought revelations too unpleasant for even the staunchest patriarchs to accept. Rape, child abuse, and incest are far more common than society has believed. Moreover, these crimes do not fit popular conceptions about them: they are not victim-initiated, and they are not the products of a few diseased, sex-crazed minds. Like violence in general, sex crimes could be termed "as American as apple pie."

The feminist movement is trying, and sometimes succeeding, in eroding patriarchy. With this slow, complex change have come changes in laws relating to sex. Violence is condemned more strongly, while the law is abandoning its restrictions on private choices outside the family. But if notions about the relationship between men and women are changing, notions about adults and children still endorse adult domination and child subordination. Some such acceptance, undeniably, is necessary and even desirable. But the survival of this particular hierarchical relationship may make it more difficult to deal with sexual violence against children and with the sexuality of youth. The legal developments that have occurred are welcome; they increase women's control over their lives and permit a healthy sexual pluralism. Unfinished business remains, however, if freedom is to increase and violence to decline.

CASES

Acanfora v. Board of Education, 491 F.2d 498 (1974)
Akron v. Akron Center for Reproductive Health and Akron Center for Reproductive Health v. City of Akron, 103 S. Ct. 2481 (1983), 462 U.S. 416 (1983)
Aumiller v. University of Delaware, 434 F. Supp. 1273 (1977)
Beal v. Doe, 432 U.S. 438 (1977)
Bellotti v. Baird, 443 U.S. 622 (1979)
Ben Shalom v. Secretary of the Army, 489 F. Supp. 964 (1980)
Boutilier v. INS, 387 U.S. 118 (1967)
Bowers v. Hardwick, 106 S.Ct. 284 (1986)
Bunim v. Bunim, 298 N.Y. 391, 83 N.E.2d 848 (1949)
Carey v. Population Services, 431 U.S. 678 (1977)
Committee to Defend Reproductive Rights v. Myers, 172 Cal. Rptr. 866, 652 P.2d 779 (1981)
Commonwealth v. Bonadio, 490 Pa. 91, 415, A.2d 47 (1980)
Commonwealth v. Joyce, 81 Mass.Adv.Sh. 39, 415 N.E.2d 181 (1981)

SEXUALITY AND THE LAW

Cord v. Gibb, 254 S.E.2d 71 (Va. Sup. Ct. 1979)
Dailey v. Dailey, 635 S.W.2d 391 (Tenn. Ct. App. 1981)
Doe v. Commonwealth's Attorney, 403 F. Supp. 1199 (1975), 425 U.S. 903 (1976)
Eisenstadt v. Baird, 405 U.S. 438 (1972)
Gay Law Students Association v. Pacific Telephone and Telegraph, 156 Cal. Rptr. 14, 595 P.2d 592 (1979)
Gay Lib v. University of Missouri, 558 F.2d 848 (1977)
Gish v. Board of Education, 366 A.2d 1337 (N.J. Super. Ct. 1976) cert. den. 434 U.S. 879 (1977)
Griswold v. Connecticut, 381 U.S. 479 (1965)
Harris v. McRae, 448 U.S. 297 (1980)
Hill v. INS, 714 F.2d 1470 (1983)
H.L. v. Matheson, 450 U.S. 398 (1981)
Hollenbaugh v. Free Public Library, 578 F.2d 1374 (1978)
Jacobson v. Jacobson, 314 N.Y. 2d 78, N.D. Sup. Ct. (1981)
Jarrett v. Jarrett, 78 Ill.2d 337, 400 N.E.2d 421 (1979)
J.L.P. v. D.J.P., Mo. WD 33116, 643 S.W.2d 865 (1982)
Loving v. Virginia, 388 U.S. 1 (1967)
Maher v. Roe, 432 U.S. 464 (1977)
McConnell v. Anderson, 451 F.2d 193 (1971)
In re Marriage of Olson, 98 Ill. App. 316 (1981)
Matlovich v. Secretary of the Air Force, 591 F.2d 852 (1978)
Michael M. v. Superior Court of Sonoma County, 450 U.S. 464 (1981)
M.P. v. S.P., 169 N.J. Super. 425, 404 A.2d 1256 (1979)
Norton v. Macy, 417 F.2d 1161 (1969)
Palmore v. Sidoti, 104 S. Ct. 1879 (1984)
People v. Onofre, 51 NY.2d 476, 415 N.E.2d 931 (1981)
Planned Parenthood v. Ashcroft and Ashcroft v. Planned Parenthood, 103 S. Ct. 2517 (1983), 462 U.S. 476 (1983)
Planned Parenthood v. Danforth, 428 U.S. 52 (1976)
Poe v. Ullman, 367 U.S. 497 (1961)
Poelker v. Doe, 432 U.S. 519 (1977)
Ratchford v. Gay Lib, 434 U.S. 1080 (1978)
Reynolds v. United States, 98 U.S. 145 (1878)
Right to Choose v. Byrne, 91 N.J. 287, 450 A.2d 925 (1982)
Roe v. Wade, 410 U.S. 113 (1973)
Rose v. Locke, 423 U.S. 48 (1975)
Schuster v. Schuster and Isaacson v. Isaacson, 90 Wash.2d 626, 585 P.2d 130 (1978)
Scott v. Macy, 402 F.2d 644 (1968)
Simopoulos v. Virginia, 103 S. Ct. 2532 (1983), 462 U.S. 506 (1983)
Singer v. Civil Service Commission, 530 F.2d 247 (1976)
State v. Schweiker, 557 F.Supp. 354 (1983)
University of California v. Bakke, 438 U.S. 265 (1978)
Wainwright v. Stone, 414 U.S. 21 (1973)
Zablocki v. Redhail, 434 U.S. 374 (1978)

BIBLIOGRAPHY

Dennis Altman, *The Homosexualization of America* (1983), predicts the eventual integration of homosexuals into the American mainstream. Louise Armstrong, *Kiss Daddy Goodnight* (1978), is a victim's account of father-daughter incest. Judith A. Baer, *Equality Under the Constitution: Reclaiming the Fourteenth Amendment* (1983), presents a theory of constitutional equality.

Susan Brownmiller, *Against Our Will: Men, Women, and Rape* (1975), offers a theory of the functions of rape in a patriarchal society. Sandra Butler, *Conspiracy of Silence: The Trauma of Incest* (1978), is an early study of sexual abuse within the family. Lucinda Cisler, "Unfinished Business: Birth Control and Women's Liberation," in Robin Morgan, ed., *Sisterhood Is Powerful* (1970), is a feminist analysis of fertility control.

Harry M. Clor, *Obscenity and Public Morality* (1969), argues for censorship in a liberal society. Patrick Devlin, *The Enforcement of Morals* (1959), is a critique of the Wolfenden Report. Hubert S. Feild and Leigh B. Bienen, *Jurors and Rape: A Study in Psychology and Law* (1980), is a study of the attitudes of simulated juries. Robert L. Geiser, *Hidden Victims: The Sexual Abuse of Children* (1979), investigates the prevalence of child molestation.

H. L. A. Hart, *Law, Liberty, and Morality* (1963), makes the case against legal enforcement of sexual morality. Nan D. Hunter and Nancy Polikoff, "Custody Rights of Lesbian Mothers: Legal Theory and Litigation Strategy," in *Buffalo Law Review*, 25 (1976), is an early study of this area of law. Rosalind P. Petchesky, *Abortion and Woman's Choice* (1984), is a socialist feminist analysis of reproductive freedom.

"Rape Reform and a Statutory Consent Defense," in *Journal of Criminal Law and Criminology*, 74 (1983), discusses recent changes in criminal law. Florence Rush, *The Best Kept Secret: Sexual Abuse of Children* (1980), takes a theoretical approach to a "dirty little secret." Susan Schwartz, "An Argument for the Elimination of the Resistance Requirement from the Definition of Forcible Rape," in *Loyola of Los Angeles Law Review*, 16 (1983), makes the case for reform of rape statutes.

Claire Sherman Thomas, *Sex Discrimination in a Nutshell* (1982), is a useful sourcebook for students. J. Harvie Wilkinson, III, and G. Edward White, "Constitutional Protection for Personal Lifestyles," in *Cornell Law Review*, 62 (1977), argues in the tradition of Devlin and Clor. *Wolfenden Report*, more precisely *Report of the Committee on Homosexual Offences and Prostitution* (1957), is a recommendation to Parliament for liberal reform. Jennifer Wriggens, "Rape, Racism, and the Law," in *Harvard Women's Law Journal*, 6 (1983), explores the relationships of racism and sexism.

[*See also* DUE PROCESS OF LAW; FAMILY LAW; LAW AND MORALITY; PRIVACY; *and* SEX EQUALITY UNDER THE CONSTITUTION.]

STATE CONSTITUTIONAL LAW

Shirley S. Abrahamson

"I N writing about or discussing American constitutional history there is a tendency to magnify unduly the importance of the federal government in comparison with the governments of the states." With this sentence J. Q. Dealey began his book *Growth of American State Constitutions.* The indifference toward state constitutional law that Dealey described in 1915— before national power expanded considerably— changed little over the years. The political climate of the 1970s, however, gave rise to greater emphasis on the state in the American federal system. This "new federalism" has brought a greater interest in state constitutions, especially in the possibility of state constitutions' offering protection of individual rights beyond that offered by the federal Constitution. For the most part, however, the public, the bench, and the bar continue to associate constitutional law with the federal Constitution more than with state constitutions. Constitutional law texts reflect and reinforce this association.

Nevertheless, state constitutional law continues to grow. States amend their constitutions and adopt new ones. State courts interpret their state constitutions and develop constitutional standards that the courts of other states may adopt in interpreting their state constitutions and that the United States Supreme Court may adopt in interpreting the federal Constitution. Scholars of state constitutional law have emphasized three subjects. First, some have attempted to set forth the principles underlying constitution-drafting and have attempted to judge the conformance of the products of constitutional conventions and revisions with the principles. Others have studied political behavior present in the process of state constitutional lawmaking and revision. Finally, scholars have discussed se-

lected state constitutions or state constitutional law issues. As a result of these three approaches, there are compilations of state constitutions and excellent material on the principles of drafting state constitutions, on the politics of amending a constitution, and on selected constitutions and subjects of state constitutional law. There is not, however, any modern treatise on state constitutional law comparable to the numerous treatises on federal constitutional law.

This essay will explore the importance of state constitutional law in the American legal system, the historical development of state constitutions, and the constitutional provisions establishing the framework of state government and the process for constitutional change. It will conclude with a discussion of the state constitutional provisions protecting individual liberties. Note at the outset that while the basic similarities of state constitutions make discussion of state constitutional law possible, their diversity forecloses the possibility of universal definitive discussion of state constitutional law.

STATE CONSTITUTIONS AND FEDERALISM

State constitutions have historical, legal, and political importance in the American federal system. Their historical significance lies in the fact that several preceded the federal Constitution and became models for the constitutions of other states. Indeed, the federal Constitution embodies most of the essential features of governmental organization found in the charters and constitutions of the colonial and revolutionary periods.

From a legal standpoint, a state constitution

establishes the framework of state government and thus may determine to a large extent the state's efficacy in dealing with problems facing government. The state constitution is the supreme state law, and the highest court of the state is the final arbiter of that constitution's meaning. The state court's interpretation of state law is binding on state and federal courts. The United States Supreme Court is "powerless to interfere" with a state court's decision regarding the constitutionality of state action under the state constitution (*Powell* v. *Alabama,* 1932). Thus, where a state court bases its decision on independent and adequate state grounds, the decision is unreviewable by the United States Supreme Court so long as no federal question is at issue (*Michigan* v. *Long,* 1983). By relying on their state constitutions, state courts are therefore able to insulate their decisions from federal judicial review.

The state constitution is, however, subordinate to federal law. While the American federal system is based on the existence of independent and sovereign state governments, federal law is nevertheless supreme. Article VI of the federal Constitution, the supremacy clause, provides,

> This Constitution, and the Laws of the United States which shall be made in Pursuance thereof; and all Treaties made, or which shall be made, under the Authority of the United States, shall be the supreme Law of the Land; and the Judges in every State shall be bound thereby, any Thing in the Constitution or Laws of any State to the Contrary notwithstanding.

In addition to interpreting the state constitution and state law, state court judges must interpret the federal Constitution and are bound by federal law on a federal question. State constitutional provisions or interpretations thereof that contravene the federal Constitution or federal law are unenforceable. State constitutional law is thus vulnerable to developments in federal law. This essay shall not, for the most part, discuss the federal Constitution or laws. In thinking about state constitutional jurisprudence, one must, however, keep in mind the limitations that the supremacy clause imposes on the states.

Politically, state constitutions are important because they reflect the movements, the struggles, and the political climate of the state. The length, the complexity, and the details of state constitutions frequently manifest a disillusionment with representative institutions and a desire to build into the constitution provisions that will prevent evil and promote good. Many constitutional provisions show that certain groups—whether they be good-government reformers, business interests, labor unions, environmentalists, or others—want their interests protected by special constitutional provisions, which are beyond easy legislative tinkering.

HISTORICAL DEVELOPMENT OF STATE CONSTITUTIONS

During colonization the English fostered the concept of a basic written document for government by granting colonial charters to trading companies that were establishing settlements in the New World. During the period of independence, eleven of the original thirteen states adopted written constitutions based substantially on the colonial charters. Connecticut, whose automobile license proclaims it the "Constitution State," and Rhode Island used their royal charters as constitutions, substituting the authority of the people for the authority of the king under the Lockean concept that government is a social compact.

The federal Constitution does not expressly require a state to have a constitution. Article IV, Section 4 guarantees "to every State in this Union a Republican Form of Government," and Congress determines whether a state has a republican form of government when it admits the state into the Union and admits senators and representatives to Congress. But while the Constitution itself is silent on the requirement, congressional practice has conditioned entrance of a new state on the adoption of a satisfactory constitution.

A generally accepted wisdom is that state constitutions should, like the federal Constitution, be relatively brief documents that set forth the structure of government and fundamental principles rather than detailed legislation. This view of state constitutions is espoused by the good-government reform movement epitomized by the National Municipal League, which had led the fight for state constitutional reform for many years. Although granting that there can be no model constitution because there is no model state, the league published six model state constitutions over the years, the first edition in 1921 and the last in 1968.

Most of the original state constitutions drawn in the eighteenth and early nineteenth centuries satisfied these prerequisites. The earliest constitutions were short documents, ranging from fifteen hundred words (Virginia) to twelve thousand words (Massachusetts). The two most recently adopted state constitutions, those of Alaska and Hawaii, have approximately twelve thousand and fifteen thousand words, respectively. The constitutions adopted or revised in the mid-nineteenth century were longer and reflected the new problems the states were facing on such issues as banking, corporations, local government and education, and the legislature (which was widely regarded as incompetent and corrupt with respect to taxation and finance and the passage of special legislation).

During the period 1860–1880 the southern states revised their constitutions several times: for secession, for readmission into the Union, for undoing changes made during Reconstruction, and for meeting new needs. After the Civil War many state governments were concerned with the railroads. By the 1880s the major issues were interstate corporations and trusts. The major constitutional revisions were spaced at intervals of a generation, suggesting that the revisions emerged from generational changes in social, economic, or political thinking.

The turn of the century brought more changes in state constitutional law: the secret ballot; women's suffrage; the initiative, referendum, and recall; reforms in labor law; reforms in tort law. In the first quarter of the twentieth century, an era of political reform, states attempted to give their legislatures power to deal with economic and social issues. Although by 1920 many states operated with anachronistic constitutions that unduly impaired their ability to meet the crisis of the Great Depression, the period from 1921 to 1945 was a relatively dormant time for constitutional revision. Revision of state constitutions from 1945 through the 1950s did not introduce any major innovative concepts.

The 1960s saw a renewed interest in state constitutions, with more than two-thirds of the states involved in constitutional revision. Many factors converged to create this trend, including the United States Supreme Court's one-person, one-vote apportionment decisions and the mounting concern about the adequacy of state constitutions to meet new problems created by urbanization, population growth, and increasing demands of society. A 1955 report of the United States Advisory Commission on Intergovernmental Relations summarized the weaknesses of the state constitutions and issued a call for constitutional revision as follows:

> The constitutions' greatest shortcomings lie in the hobbles placed on state and local government. . . . These self-imposed constitutional limitations make it difficult for many states to perform all the services their citizens require, and consequently have frequently been the underlying cause of state and municipal pleas for federal assistance. . . . The Commission believes that most states would benefit from a fundamental review and revision of their constitutions to make sure that they provide for vigorous and responsible government, not forbid it.
>
> (pp. 37–38, 56)

In the 1970s and 1980s, state constitutional changes reflected such concerns as race and gender discrimination, invasion of privacy, water and air pollution, gambling, and redress against governments for injuries and damages.

Many constitutions are filled with outmoded provisions of historical interest only. For example, the Oklahoma Constitution establishes the flash point for kerosene oil designed for illuminating purposes and the specific-gravity test for such oil (Article XX, Section 2). The Kentucky Constitution proscribes dueling (Section 239), and the Oregon Constitution prohibits titles of nobility (Article I, Section 29). Some constitutions contain regulations that one would expect to find in the statutes rather than in a constitution. The South Carolina Constitution, for example, provides the grounds for divorce (Article XVII, Section 3). The Hawaii Constitution was amended in 1978—in the midst of a plain-meaning movement in legal writing—to provide that "insofar as practicable, all governmental writing meant for the public, in whatever language, should be plainly worded, avoiding the use of technical terms" (Article XVI, Section 13).

More significant than the outdated or curious clauses are the provisions creating an overelaborate system of checks and balances and a proliferation of prohibitions that impede the effective operation of government. These provisions are legacies from an earlier age when the people imposed restrictions and constraints on state governments because they found the government unworthy of trust.

THE STRUCTURE OF STATE GOVERNMENT

A state constitution determines to a large extent the structure of state government. It decides how the powers of government are distributed among the branches of government and between the state and local governments. Because the framework of each state government is much like that of the federal government (which was patterned after the states), many state constitutional law issues relating to the respective powers of, and relations between, the three branches are similar to those arising under the federal Constitution. Yet, the interpretation of a state constitution need not duplicate the interpretation of the federal constitution. The federal government is a government of delegated powers, as set forth in the federal Constitution, whereas the state government has plenary powers except as restricted by the federal Constitution, federal law, or the state constitution. State constitutions are thus frequently characterized as documents limiting governmental power, while the federal Constitution is characterized as a document that grants power. Furthermore, considerations of federalism may affect the United States Supreme Court's interpretation of the federal Constitution, but these considerations do not affect a state court in interpreting its constitution.

Separation of Powers. All state constitutions establish three branches of government—legislative, executive, and judicial—and grant legislative, executive, and judicial power to the respective branches. Several constitutions, moreover, explicitly provide that the three branches "shall be separate and distinct, so that none exercise the powers properly belonging to the others" (Virginia, Article III, Section 1; see also Article I, Section 5). Even though the United States Supreme Court has not interpreted the federal Constitution as mandating that states adopt the doctrine of separation of powers and

even though a state constitution may not expressly state the doctrine of separation of powers, a state court will typically infer the doctrine from the constitution's creation of three branches and distribution of powers to each.

Although the doctrine of separation of powers is stated in unqualified terms, state courts generally recognize that the three branches are not absolutely separate and distinct; the branches have overlapping powers and functions. State governmental action is challenged with some frequency as violating the constitutional doctrine of separation of powers. Several state courts have held that challenged legislative action interfered with judicial power or executive power. The New Hampshire Supreme Court, for example, declared a statute requiring judges to permit law enforcement officers to wear firearms in any courtroom in the state an unconstitutional invasion of judicial power; the court, not the legislature, controls the conduct of trials (*State* v. *La France,* 1983).

The Wisconsin Supreme Court invalidated a statute requiring the governor to include a particular matter in the budget. The court held the statute to be an unconstitutional encroachment on the governor's constitutional power to communicate to the legislature at every session and to recommend such matters as he may deem expedient (*State ex rel. Warren* v. *Nusbaum,* 1973).

The state legislatures, like Congress, have created administrative agencies and delegated quasi-legislative and quasi-judicial functions to them. The state courts have generally upheld these delegations of power. Some state courts, however, are more willing than the federal courts to declare that the statute sets forth inadequate standards for the exercise of administrative authority and is invalid. The New Jersey Supreme Court invalidated a statute allowing, with certain limited exceptions, the legislature to veto by a concurrent resolution of both houses rules proposed by a state agency. The court held that the statute interfered excessively with the constitutional mandate that the executive branch faithfully execute the law and with the constitutional power of the governor to participate in amending or repealing laws (*General Assembly* v. *Byrne,* 1982). In November 1985 the voters of New Jersey rejected a state constitutional amendment providing for a legislative veto of administrative rules.

By contrast, the Connecticut voters amended their constitution to provide that "the legislative department may delegate regulatory authority to the executive department; except that any administrative regulation of any agency of the executive department may be disapproved by the General Assembly or a committee thereof in such manner as shall by law be prescribed" (Amendment Article XVIII). Thus, the people of Connecticut and New Jersey reached different conclusions regarding the powers they wished to give the legislature over rules promulgated by administrative agencies.

The Legislative Branch. State constitutions vest the legislative power of the state in the legislature and also grant power to legislate in particular spheres. An accepted state constitutional doctrine is that a state legislature has all the legislative powers of the state necessary to govern the people of the state except to the extent that the legislature's powers are limited by federal law or the state constitution and that a state constitution is therefore a document of limitations on legislative power, not a document granting power. While state constitutional provisions purporting to grant the legislature power to legislate in a particular sphere appear redundant and harmless in light of this accepted doctrine, grants of power have proved troublesome. Courts often infer a negative intent from constitutional grants of power. For example, provisions authorizing the legislature to levy certain taxes may be construed to imply that the legislature does not have power to levy other taxes.

To avoid such negative implications, a few constitutions, like Alaska's, expressly provide that "the enumeration of specified powers in this constitution shall not be construed as limiting the powers of the State" (Article XII, Section 8).

The state constitution also typically provides for the houses of the legislature; the number, qualifications, and compensation of legislators; the districts from which they are elected; periodic reapportionment; and terms of office. The legislature is generally made the final judge of the election and qualifications of its members. Many state constitutions provide "privileges" for legislators, such as immunity from arrest or civil process while the legislature is in session and from liability for words spoken in debate.

A state constitution usually sets forth the procedure by which a bill becomes a law and the "style" of a law—for example, the bill must have an exacting clause, the title must describe the contents, and the bill must be limited to one subject. Constitutions frequently also set forth substantive limitations on the enactment of special or local laws or on the enactment of substantive laws through appropriation acts. Courts will strike down legislation that does not comply with one or more of these constitutional requirements. The Kansas Supreme Court, for example, invalidated a law whose enacting clause read, "Be it resolved by the Legislature . . ." instead of the constitutionally required clause "Be it enacted by the Legislature. . . ." The court was unwilling to say that there was substantial compliance with the constitutional mandate (*State* v. *Kearns,* 1981). The Wisconsin Supreme Court invalidated part of the budget bill as a private or local law (*Milwaukee Brewers Baseball Club* v. *Wisconsin Department of Health and Social Services,* 1986). Some commentators criticize courts for invalidating laws on technical "style" grounds. Others believe that these constitutional requirements should be enforced because they may reduce legislative abuses such as logrolling and special-interest legislation.

A major trend in the nineteenth century was the curbing of the powers of the state legislatures to prevent misuses of power. Thus, many state constitutions include detailed limitations and restrictions on legislative power in regard to such issues as state and local governmental debt; the adoption of special, private, or local legislation benefiting private interests or particular local governmental units; and the sessions of the legislature. Limiting legislative sessions reflects the belief that the less frequently the legislature meets, the less mischief it can do. Several state constitutions have provided for direct legislation by the people through the initiative and referendum. These provisions are another indication of public dissatisfaction with state legislatures. Since the 1960s, however, the trend has generally been toward strengthening, not limiting, the legislature.

The Executive Branch. State constitutions vest the executive power of the state in a governor, and many provide that the governor "shall see that the law is faithfully executed" (California, Article V, Section 1). The constitution may also assign a variety of functions to the governor.

The governor may exercise only those powers

granted by the constitution. The term *executive power* is not self-defining and has been given meaning by the functioning of the executive and the decisions of the courts. Executive power includes those powers necessarily or fairly implied in, or incident to, the powers expressly granted and those inherent in the office of chief executive.

Certain executive actions have been challenged as falling outside the powers of the governor. For example, the Massachusetts Supreme Judicial Court held that the governor's inherent executive powers did not include the power to issue an executive order suspending the operation of a statute in the absence of legislative authority (*Massachusetts Bay Transportation Authority Advisory Board* v. *Massachusetts Bay Transportation Authority,* 1981).

Despite the separation-of-powers doctrine, the state constitutions provide for the governor's involvement in the legislative process. In some states, the governor must deliver a state-of-the-state message to the legislature and may recommend measures to the legislature that the governor considers necessary or desirable. State constitutions generally require that bills passed by the legislature be presented to the governor. A bill generally becomes law if the governor either signs the bill or fails to veto it within a fixed time period. A bill vetoed by the governor may be reconsidered by the legislature. In many states the governor may veto or reduce items in appropriation bills. This technique, the "item veto," was originally designed to prevent legislative logrolling. The governor's exercise of the veto, especially the item veto, has given rise to litigation. Courts have had to rule on what is an appropriation bill, what is an item in an appropriation bill, and whether the governor may veto language in the bill without vetoing the appropriation itself.

While scholars studying executive organization recommend that administrative power and responsibility be concentrated in a single popularly elected chief executive who would appoint the heads of the state executive departments and take responsibility for their action, many state constitutions provide that the heads of departments, such as the treasurer, attorney general, superintendent of education, and commissioner of agriculture and industries, are chosen by the electors. In many states, the constitutions addi-

tionally create governmental agencies and offices, state their powers, and provide for the selection of the officers. The Georgia Constitution establishes the Public Service Commission, the State Board of Pardons and Paroles, the Board of Natural Resources, the Veterans Service Board, the State Personnel Board, and the State Transportation Board. In other states, the executive departments are established by statute rather than by the constitution.

The American tradition of hostility toward a strong executive branch that is evident in state constitutions has roots in the colonial and revolutionary periods. Nevertheless, during the last half of the nineteenth century and continuing into the twentieth century, the executive branch has been strengthened in relation to the legislature. Constitutions were amended to strengthen the executive branch, as the executive branch became the champion of the people against the legislature, which was perceived as controlled by special interests. This trend has continued to the present.

The Judicial Branch. The state constitutions vest judicial power in the highest court of the state (ordinarily but not invariably called the supreme court) and other courts established by the constitution or the legislature. Some constitutions use the term *unified judicial system* to connote the intention to create a uniform court system all over the state, with the highest state court being the single administrative head authorized to promulgate rules to govern the administration, practice, and procedure of the courts. In contrast, some constitutions create numerous courts and prescribe their jurisdictions.

The constitution ordinarily provides for the selection and retention of judges and their qualifications, tenure, retirement, and removal. In the 1970s and 1980s, with increased interest and concern about the ethics of public officers and public accountability, several states adopted constitutional provisions establishing a commission on judicial discipline.

The courts generally act in the context of adjudicating disputes; they develop the common law and interpret statutes and the state and federal constitutions. Although the state constitutions are generally silent on this issue, the state judiciary has the power to declare legislative or executive action unconstitutional under the state constitution, as well as under the federal Constitution. Indeed, state courts developed the concept of judicial review of the constitutionality of governmental action before Chief Justice John Marshall adopted the doctrine in *Marbury* v. *Madison* (1803).

Several state constitutions authorize or require the highest court of the state to render advisory opinions to various government officials. Thus, the legislature may seek advice as to the constitutionality of a proposed bill. Ordinarily, in rendering advisory opinions, the justices do not have the benefit of adversarial briefs or argument, and the precedential value of advisory opinions may not be clear.

Despite the separation-of-powers doctrine, an increasing number of constitutions vest administrative, "quasi-legislative," nonadjudicative functions in the highest state court as the head of the court system. Since the beginning of the twentieth century there has been a nationwide reform movement to vest control of the operation of the state's judicial system in the state's highest court. In the 1970s, several states amended their constitutions to grant the highest state court rule-making power governing practice and procedure and to place responsibility for judicial administration in that court. There is a continuing tension between a state legislature and a state's highest court concerning what matters are legitimately court administration and practice and procedure within the domain of the court and what matters are legislative concerns within the legislature's power to legislate for the public good. The courts, however, are the final arbiter of the scope of their own and the legislatures' powers.

Although the state's highest court has the final word in a conflict between it and the executive or the legislative branches because the court interprets the constitution and the powers of each branch, there are checks on the court. One check is the people. In many states, the people elect the judges. Furthermore, the people can amend the constitution to overturn judicial decisions.

Another check on the courts is the legislature's control of the purse strings and the executive's power over the budget. Because inadequate funding may endanger the operations of the judicial branch and may threaten the independence of the courts, some courts and commentators are paying increased attention to whether the highest state court has inherent

power to assure that the judicial branch is adequately funded. If the states continue to have financial difficulties in the future and the legislatures reduce court appropriations or fail to fund programs requested by courts, confrontations between the judicial and legislative branches on the issue of financing the state courts may surface.

STATE AND LOCAL GOVERNMENT

State-Local Relations. Local governments—cities, towns, villages, counties, boroughs, parishes, townships, towns, special-function districts—are almost universally regarded as creatures of the state, having no inherent power of self-government and being subject to the complete control of the states in which they are located. The state's power over local governments is limited only by the state's constitution.

Local governments have evolved from entities that were not recognized in the state constitutions to entities receiving constitutional recognition as having some degree of local governmental autonomy. This doctrine of local autonomy is referred to as "home rule," an oft-used term that has no readily agreed upon definition. Home rule rests on the idea that some governmental functions can be assigned to local government and others to the state. It is a method of distributing power between the state legislature and local governments. The distribution has two ramifications—a grant of power to the local government and a restriction of the power of the state legislature.

The home-rule movement began in 1875 in Missouri. It originally arose out of a grass-roots concept of government and the malapportionment and consequent rural domination of state legislatures. The ideal of local self-government continues to have a considerable following. The critics contend, however, that home rule emphasizes a multiplicity of small local units of fixed geographic boundaries whereas contemporary problems call for cooperation cutting across boundaries. Furthermore, they question the assumption that governmental powers are inherently either state or local.

Constitutional provisions on home rule differ from state to state and are undergoing continual revision. Some state constitutions have self-executing provisions that directly confer powers on certain types of local governments. The constitutions in these states may contain detailed lists of home-rule powers and detailed provisions on the manner and adoption of home-rule charters. The local government may then enact a charter, which serves as a constitution for that government. Other state constitutions authorize the legislature to adopt laws that confer powers on local governments.

Much of the litigation and controversy regarding home rule has centered on the powers of the state and local governments and the conflict between state and local legislation. A state statute is usually declared invalid under a self-executing constitutional home-rule provision when the state statute deals with local concerns and is in conflict with the laws of the local government; a state statute usually prevails when state and local legislation conflict on a matter of statewide concern or when the state has preempted a particular field of regulation of statewide concern. The judicial interpretation of state or local relations and home-rule powers has not been uniform or consistent within a state or from state to state.

Whether or not the constitution protects powers of local governments, many state constitutions have a list of restrictions on the state legislature's exercise of control over local governments. Many constitutions require that laws be of a general nature and operate uniformly throughout the state or prohibit special and local laws. These restraints on the legislature are designed to protect local government from legislative control. Nevertheless, local communities do have different needs, and when the state legislature acts, it may have to adopt different laws for different communities. The constitutional restraints generally do not prevent the legislature from treating municipalities differently according to classifications it establishes, such as cities with a population over five hundred thousand, so long as the classification is reasonable and germane. Other than home rule and express restraints on the legislature, the state constitution does not protect local government from legislative action. The state due process clause affords the local governments few if any rights against the state except perhaps to protect municipally owned property held in a proprietary capacity.

State and Local Fiscal Powers. Because of inequities and abuses perpetrated by state and local legislatures in the railroad-bond era of the nine-teenth century, state constitutions generally impose detailed restrictions on the otherwise plenary state legislative power to tax, borrow, and spend and on the fiscal powers of local governments. Apparently when these constitutional limitations have interfered with legislative efforts, they have given way to piecemeal constitutional exceptions and legislative circumventions. Thus, despite elaborate constitutional limitations upon the legislature designed to ensure fiscal prudence, state taxes, outstanding debt, and expenditures grew enormously in the last half of the twentieth century.

From the 1940s through the 1980s the subjects of tax and finance accounted for much of the substantive change in state constitutions. The end of the 1970s brought a taxpayer revolt and state constitutional amendments to limit state and local taxation.

State and local revenues are raised by various taxes—property, income, sales, use, gift, inheritance, and business. State constitutions may prohibit or authorize the use of certain taxes and may specify exemptions from taxation. Most state legislatures' taxing powers are restricted by a uniformity clause, by an equality clause, or by both, at least with respect to ad valorem taxes (that is, taxes imposed upon the value of the items subject to taxation). Such clauses typically require "a uniform and equal rate of property assessment and taxation" (Indiana, Article X, Section 1), to attain equitable apportionment of the burden of taxation. The phraseology and interpretation of the uniformity or equality clauses are diverse. An understanding of these clauses requires studying numerous court decisions as well as the constitutional text. While these constitutional provisions were intended to achieve an equitable apportionment of the tax burden, they have often produced confusion and litigation instead.

Uniformity and equality provisions have been interpreted as requiring all real property—whether residential, industrial, or commercial—to be assessed at the same percentage of value and then taxed at the same rate. These provisions have hampered the legislature in developing an effective and equitable property taxation system that differentiates between classes of property. To enable the legislature to tax classes of property differently, the electorate has adopted numerous constitutional amendments relating to the taxation of certain properties, such as agricultural land, open space or forest lands, and urban redevelopment areas. While freeing the legislature to respond to specific needs, the amendments also tend to create narrow layers of exceptions that make the taxing power more inflexible.

Personal income tax statutes have been the subject of challenges under the uniformity and equality provisions. Several courts have viewed personal income as property and held the tax unconstitutional if it is graduated. Other state courts, holding that income taxes on individuals are excises levied on the privilege of domicile or doing business, have construed the uniformity and equality provisions as inapplicable to income taxes and applicable only to property taxes. In a number of states, the electorate has amended the constitution to authorize the levy of graduated personal income taxes. In several states, repeated efforts to amend the constitution to authorize a graduated personal income tax have failed.

A state constitution may allocate the power to use certain tax sources between state and local governments. These allocations may limit the legislature's efforts to formulate social policy. In *Buse* v. *Smith* (1976) the Wisconsin Supreme Court invalidated efforts to change a public school financing system that was based on local property-tax revenues. The court held that the law violated the constitutional requirement that a tax must be spent at the same level at which it is raised.

State constitutions constrain state and local governments from borrowing and prescribe debt ceilings. These provisions, which date back to the nineteenth century, were enacted to attain "intergenerational equity" by limiting the capacity of state and local officials to incur long-term financial commitments, to protect the taxpayers of the future. The states borrowed anyway. The history of borrowing in the twentieth century is a history of evasion of these constitutional restrictions by the issuance of moral obligation bonds, industrial development bonds, and revenue bonds requiring the lender to look to pledged revenues from the completed projects rather than to the general taxing authority of the government for repayment of the bonds. State courts are called upon to pass judgment on the validity of these creative techniques.

Many state constitutions require the state's financial powers to be used to serve public rather than private purposes and prohibit public assistance to private enterprise. Even in the absence of such a requirement or limitation, a state court may view the public-purpose doctrine as an inherent limitation on the powers of state or local government. Furnishing utilities to the public, establishing a state grain elevator, and granting tax exemptions to attract business have been held in some cases to be proper governmental purposes. The public-purpose doctrine may, however, prove an obstacle to urban-renewal programs and programs for industrial or economic development.

State constitutions frequently require a balanced state budget: the executive branch estimates anticipated revenue, and the legislature provides taxes sufficient to defray the estimated expenses and may not appropriate in excess of that figure. The executive branch may not expend any funds except pursuant to legislative appropriation.

Commentators suggest that sound judicial interpretation of the fiscal provisions and the adoption of amendments by the electorate of constitutional limitations on state and local taxation, borrowing, and spending are needed to prevent the state constitutional provisions from putting state and local government in a fiscal straitjacket and from hampering economic development.

AMENDMENT AND REVISION OF THE CONSTITUTION

Thomas Jefferson said that the earth belongs to the living and urged that each generation be given an opportunity to adopt its own constitutional documents. Successive generations of Americans have revised state constitutions. Americans have considered and adopted about 150 state constitutions and thousands of constitutional amendments in two hundred years of state constitutional history. In 1984, for example, the voters in forty-two states and the members of the General Assembly of Delaware (where constitutional amendments are not submitted to the electorate) acted on a total of 200 proposed constitutional changes and adopted 127. Proposed alterations relating collectively to the three branches of government accounted for more than a third of the total proposed amendments.

Provisions for changing the state constitution are an integral part of every constitution, and at least three methods of initiating constitutional change exist. First, state constitutions generally provide that the legislature (sometimes by a special majority and sometimes by two consecutive sessions of the legislature) propose amendments, which are then submitted to the electorate for adoption by the majority of those voting on the amendment or of those voting in the election for a specified state office or by special majorities.

Second, about a third of the states allow the people to propose constitutional amendments directly. Direct constitutional amendment—"the initiative"—is a distinctly western phenomenon, virtually unknown in the eastern and southern states. In Oregon the constitution has been amended more than one hundred times by initiative measures. The California Constitution is frequently amended by initiative to include statutorylike programs and to overrule judicial interpretation of the constitution or statutes. A state constitution may restrict the subject matter that may be addressed by initiative measures. The Massachusetts Constitution, for example, prohibits the use of the initiative on such subjects as the right to trial by jury, protection from unreasonable search, and freedom of the press.

A third method of initiating constitutional changes for ratification by the people is through the convention process. Approximately three-fourths of the state constitutions provide for a constitutional convention. Most of these state constitutions authorize the legislature to adopt legislation proposing a referendum for calling a convention; the electorate then decides whether to authorize a convention. Several state constitutions mandate a periodic referendum on whether a convention should be held. A convention may have a limited or unlimited mandate. The work of the convention is generally submitted to the electorate for ratification either as a single package or as multiple questions.

The constitution generally prescribes requirements for proposed amendments (depending on how the proposal is initiated), such as that the title must express the contents of the amendment or that the amendment must relate to a single subject. Opponents frequently challenge a proposed amendment's compliance with these requirements. Much has been written about the form of amendments; relatively little has been said about whether proposed amendments are subject to substantive limitations.

Ideally, the constitutional provisions empowering change should strike a balance between making change too easy or too difficult. Change should be easy enough to allow the constitution to be adapted to emerging needs. At the same time, change should be difficult enough to attain constitutional stability and to prevent the constitution from becoming a statute book. Because state constitutions are amended more easily than the federal Constitution, state courts interpret the constitution and develop state constitutional jurisprudence under a popular supervision not present at the federal level.

PROTECTION OF INDIVIDUAL LIBERTIES

All state constitutions contain a bill or declaration specifying individual rights. Many of the rights are substantially similar to those in the first eight amendments of the federal Constitution. Although the federal and state constitutional provisions may be similar, state courts have the power to interpret their own constitution independently of the United States Supreme Court's interpretation of the federal Constitution. The California Constitution expressly provides, "Rights guaranteed by this Constitution are not dependent on those guaranteed by the United States Constitution" (Article I, Section 24). This declaration is a reaffirmation of existing law. The federal Constitution does not preclude the states from granting greater protections to individuals through state constitutions, statutes, or rules than those granted by the federal Constitution. The federal Constitution, however, sets forth guaranties of individual rights that the state cannot violate, even if the state constitution grants an individual less protection than the federal Constitution.

Independent interpretation of state constitutional provisions paralleling federal constitutional provisions is part of the double security of having both federal and state bills of rights. United States Supreme Court Justice William J. Brennan, Jr., and other federal and state judges and commentators have urged state courts to interpret their own constitutions and to become a new "font of individual liberties" (p. 491).

A state court's independent interpretation of

the state bill of rights may mean that a person has different rights under the federal and state constitutions and may have different rights under the constitutions of the various states. For example, a law enforcement officer's search of a car with a warrant obtained on an informant's tip might be evaluated on the basis of one test under the United States Supreme Court's interpretation of the Fourth Amendment to the federal Constitution (*Illinois* v. *Gates,* 1983); on the basis of another test under the Washington Supreme Court's interpretation of the search-and-seizure provision of the Washington Constitution (*State* v. *Jackson,* 1984); and on the basis of the federal test under the Illinois Supreme Court's interpretation of the Illinois Constitution (*People* v. *Tisler,* 1984).

Between 1970 and the mid-1980s, state courts issued more than two hundred published opinions declaring that the state constitutions offered individuals more protection than did analogous provisions of the federal Constitution. Justice William J. Brennan has described these state court cases as probably the most important development in constitutional jurisprudence in the mid-1980s. Many commentators criticize a court's use of a state constitution to expand protections beyond those afforded by an analogous federal constitutional provision.

Although every state probably has at least one case in which the highest state court has extended individual protections further than the federal Supreme Court would, such cases are probably still the exception rather than the rule. These two hundred state court cases and the debate surrounding them demonstrate the changing roles of the state and federal constitutions in protecting individual liberties. The following sections examine state constitutional jurisprudence in the field of civil liberties, first historically and then in relation to selected rights.

Historical Background. As originally drafted, the federal Constitution did not enumerate protections of individuals. Upon ratification of the Bill of Rights in 1791, it was assumed that the first eight amendments would limit only the federal government's exercise of power. There was no need to limit state powers, for the state constitutions did that. Nevertheless, since the beginning of the nineteenth century, litigants have repeatedly requested that the United States Supreme Court interpret the limitations in the first eight federal amendments as being limitations on state powers as well as on federal powers. Beginning with *Barron* v. *Mayor of Baltimore* (1833), the United States Supreme Court refused to adopt such an interpretation. Not until 1925 did the Court recognize in dictum that the free-speech and free-press guaranties of the First Amendment of the federal Constitution "are among the fundamental personal rights and 'liberties' protected by the due process clause of the Fourteenth Amendment from impairment by the States" (*Gitlow* v. *New York*).

Thus, for most of the history of the country—for 138 years—the federal Bill of Rights offered little or no protection to individuals in their relations with state and local governments. The state constitution provided the people with protection against infringement upon their individual rights. In interpreting their state constitutions, courts could develop their own body of state constitutional law, free from the federal Supreme Court's interpretations. Sometimes the state courts did adopt the federal rule as the state rule; other times they did not; sometimes they adopted a rule of another state.

The protection of individual rights in the years from 1787 to 1925 was not uniform within each state or from state to state. Commentators have noted that the states' failure to protect individual rights adequately in this period created a void that the United States Supreme Court began to fill.

After *Gitlow,* the United States Supreme Court adopted the doctrine of selective incorporation: certain aspects of the Bill of Rights were so necessary to a scheme of ordered liberty that it was reasonable to conclude that they were encompassed within the Fourteenth Amendment and applicable to the states. By the beginning of the 1970s the United States Supreme Court had held that many, but not all, provisions of the Bill of Rights were applicable to the states.

The nationalization of individual rights through the Fourteenth Amendment seems to have arrested the development of state constitutional law. As the federal constitutional guaranties grew during the 1950s and 1960s, most lawyers tended to assert federal constitutional rights in state courts, and neither they nor the state courts examined the state constitutions to determine what rights were afforded the litigants. Either the court and the litigant simply forgot the state constitution or they assumed that the state constitution offered the same protections as the federal Constitution.

The 1970s saw renewed interest in state constitutions and in state courts acting as guardians of civil liberties. Observers attributed this renewed interest to a growing concern that the Supreme Court was retreating from its aggressive position in protecting the rights of individuals against state encroachments and was adopting procedural devices to limit adjudication of federal constitutional claims against state action in the federal courts.

Critics of independent state constitutional interpretation contend that the state courts that rely on state constitutions to protect individual rights are merely engaging in a result-oriented jurisprudence designed to give individuals greater rights than the federal Constitution offers. The critics argue that the United States is a nation, not a conglomerate of states; that the rights protected by the federal Constitution pertain to national citizenship, not state citizenship; and that all individuals deserve uniform protection as interpreted by the federal Supreme Court.

Advocates of independent state constitutional interpretation counter that reliance on state constitutions in regard to individual rights is a process-oriented approach, not a result-oriented approach, and that examining state law before turning to federal law is the legally sound way of analyzing a constitutional question. The advocates argue that state constitutions preceded the federal Constitution in protecting individual rights and that the process of looking to the state constitution prior to looking to the federal Constitution is as old as the nation itself and conforms to generally accepted legal rules of hierarchical sources of law. They urge that uniformity of rights between the federal and state constitutions is not always necessary or even beneficial. Diversity, they contend, allows for state experimentation, a desirable thing in a federal system composed of diverse states. State courts using different approaches to protect individual rights might make a valuable contribution to the development of federal constitutional law.

The emerging prominence of state constitutional law in protecting individual rights is a return to the concept of states' rights and a re-emphasis of the states on American federalism.

States' rights in this context, in contrast to the historical connotation of the doctrine, is identified with safeguarding individual rights.

State Constitutional Analysis. While all state courts would acknowledge their power to interpret their state constitutions independently of the United States Supreme Court, state courts in fact vary in their approaches to the development of state constitutional law. Some state courts look only to the federal Constitution and ignore the state constitution; others examine closely the text and history of the state constitution and apply the state constitution. In addition to state-to-state variations, the approach of a state's highest court to state constitutional law may vary from case to case.

In the 1980s many, if not most, state court opinions in criminal cases, for example, referred only to the federal Constitution. They made only passing reference or none at all to the state constitution. On the other hand, a good number of courts are interpreting their respective state constitutions.

Even if a state court undertakes to interpret and apply state constitutional law, there still remains a question about the significance the state court will attach to the decisions of the United States Supreme Court. A repeated refrain in the cases is that similarity of language in parallel federal and state constitutional provisions does not mean that federal decisions necessarily control the meaning of the state constitution. While some courts adopt, apparently in perpetuity, federal decisional law as the governing interpretation of a parallel state constitutional provision, others adopt federal decisions in case-by-case consideration, and still others adopt an independent interpretation of the state constitution.

Courts examining and applying their own constitutions have taken three approaches toward an analysis of state and federal constitutional rights. Under the "primacy" or "self-reliant" approach, the court decides the state constitutional claim first and then decides the federal claim, if necessary. Federal law and analysis are not presumptively correct; they are no more persuasive than the decisions of other state courts. Under the primacy approach, the state court necessarily must interpret its own constitution, and this independent examination of the provision in question may lead the court to a result that diverges from, or coincides with, existing federal interpretation. If a defendant's rights are protected under state law, the court need not examine the federal Constitution. If a defendant's rights are not protected under state law, the court must then review the matter in light of the federal Constitution. In this way, the parties are assured that federal requirements are met. Some courts and commentators view the primacy approach as faithful to the historical sequence of state and federal constitutions and as consistent with the historical role of state and federal courts. They prefer this approach because it avoids unnecessary construction of the federal Constitution and appeals to the United States Supreme Court. Oregon, New Hampshire, Maine, and Vermont have indicated a preference for this approach.

A second approach is the "interstitial" or "supplemental" approach. Under this approach, when deciding whether state action is valid, a state court looks first to the federal Constitution. If the government action cannot be upheld as a matter of federal constitutional law, it is struck down and the analysis ends; the court does not reach the state constitutional question. If, however, the status of the litigant's rights is questionable under the federal Constitution or if no violation of rights is found under the federal document, then the state court consults the state constitution. Some courts and commentators view the interstitial approach as consistent with the roles of federal and state constitutional law since 1925. New Jersey has preferred this supplemental approach.

The third approach is "dual sovereignty." When deciding whether state action is valid, a state court looks to both the federal and state provisions. This analysis reflects the policies underlying the American federal system by making available the maximum protection both levels of government offer to citizens. Rhode Island has used this dual-sovereignty approach. Even more than the other approaches, dual sovereignty generates "advisory" opinions. Of necessity, a court adopting the dual-sovereignty model will construe federal constitutional provisions even when the court explicitly bases its decision affirming an individual's rights on adequate and independent state grounds.

Criminal Procedural Rights. Many state court decisions expanding individual rights under state constitutions involve procedural rights of the criminally accused. The federal constitutional law of criminal procedure guides federal and state criminal proceedings. Almost every state constitution contains some form of most of the criminal procedural protections in the Fourth, Fifth, Sixth, and Eighth Amendments to the federal Constitution, including those relating to search and seizure, self-incrimination, speedy and public trial, confrontation, assistance of counsel, impartial jury, and double jeopardy.

State courts have differed with the federal Supreme Court on numerous criminal procedural issues. Suppose, for example, a state law enforcement officer seizes papers on the basis of a search warrant that a state court later holds had been issued without probable cause. The prosecutor wishes to use these papers as evidence in a state criminal trial; the defendant moves to suppress the evidence on the ground that the search and seizure violated her federal and state constitutional rights that no warrant shall be issued but upon probable cause. In *United States* v. *Leon* (1984) the Supreme Court created a good-faith exception to the exclusionary rule: if the evidence was seized in objectively reasonable reliance on a subsequently invalidated search warrant, the Fourth and Fourteenth Amendments do not prohibit the use of evidence in a criminal trial. The Mississippi Supreme Court refused to adopt the good-faith exception as part of the state's exclusionary rule. The Mississippi Supreme Court suppressed the evidence, concluding that the good-faith exception violated the fundamental logic of the exclusionary rule (*Stringer* v. *State,* 1985). Other state courts have adopted the *Leon* good-faith exception as part of their state constitutional criminal law. The battle being fought in the United States Supreme Court over excluding illegally seized evidence is also being fought in state courts. In addition to questions of search and seizure, state courts have differed with the federal Supreme Court on such questions as double jeopardy, self-incrimination, and right to counsel.

The state courts' expansion of individual rights in criminal procedure has probably been the most controversial area of state constitutional jurisprudence. United States Supreme Court Chief Justice Warren Burger in a concurring opinion criticized one state court for interpreting its own constitution to require more protection for individual criminal defendants than the federal Constitution provides (*Florida* v. *Casal*, 1983). The chief justice coupled his criticism with the suggestion that the people amend state law to override state court opinions that extend individual rights. Several states (for example, California, Florida, and Massachusetts) have adopted constitutional amendments overturning state court decisions that had expanded individual rights in criminal cases. Nevertheless, the current cases indicate that the state courts will continue to play a role in the development of state constitutional criminal procedural rights.

Rights of Expression. In the mid-1980s, all fifty state constitutions protected some aspect of freedom of expression. Many state constitutions affirmatively protect freedom of speech in comprehensive terms and do not, as does the First Amendment to the federal Constitution, merely place a restraint on governmental action. The California Constitution, for example, is fairly representative in declaring, "Every person may freely speak, write and publish his or her sentiments on all subjects, being responsible for the abuse of this right. A law may not restrain or abridge liberty of speech or press" (Article I, Section 2).

State courts have occasionally interpreted the state constitutions as precluding infringement of speech by private parties as well as by state action. The Supreme Court of California, for example, held that the California Constitution protects the collection of signatures for a petition in a privately owned shopping center (*Robins* v. *Pruneyard Shopping Center*, 1979). The highest courts of Connecticut and New York have not followed California's lead. Those courts have concluded that the full-expression provisions of the state constitutions protect expressive activity from actions of the state, not actions of private parties, such as owners of shopping malls (*Cologne* v. *Westfarms Associates*, 1984; *Shad Alliance* v. *Smith Haven Mall*, 1985).

State courts have interpreted their own state constitutions in numerous other free-expression areas, such as defamation and journalist privilege, and have led the Supreme Court in guaranteeing public access to judicial proceedings under either the state constitution free-speech provision or a state constitutional provision requiring all courts to be open.

Religion. The states have a variety of constitutional clauses respecting government and religion. About a fifth of the state constitutions echo the First Amendment prohibition against any law respecting an establishment of religion or prohibiting the free exercise of religion. A second type of clause provides that no person shall be compelled to attend or to support any ministry or place of worship without his or her consent. A third prohibits the state from practicing any preference or discrimination with respect to a religious denomination or mode of worship. A fourth prohibits state governments from giving public financial support to religious institutions. A fifth prohibits religious tests for witnesses, jurors, or public officers.

The Utah Constitution provides a broad statement of free exercise of religion and separation of church and state:

> The rights of conscience shall never be infringed. The State shall make no law respecting an establishment of religion or prohibiting the free exercise thereof; no religious test shall be required as a qualification for any office of public trust or for any vote at any election; nor shall any person be incompetent as a witness or juror on account of religious belief or the absence thereof. There shall be no union of Church and State, nor shall any church dominate the State or interfere with its functions. No public money or property shall be appropriated for or applied to any religious worship, exercise or instruction, or for the support of any ecclesiastical establishment.
>
> (Article I, Section 4)

One of the most frequently litigated church-state issues relates to religion and the public schools. State constitutions forbid religious instruction in schools and appropriations to aid parochial schools. State cases predating the 1962–1963 United States Supreme Court school-prayer decisions have prohibited Bible reading in school. States differ on the issue of furnishing publicly financed bus transportation to parochial school students.

Some state courts view their state constitution as requiring stricter church-state separation than the United States Supreme Court has required under the First Amendment. In interpreting state constitutional provisions, the state court must take care not to impose burdens that violate the free-exercise clause of the federal Constitution.

STATE CONSTITUTIONAL LAW

Equal-Protection Guaranties. While few state constitutions contain an equal-protection clause similar to that of the Fourteenth Amendment, state constitutions generally have several provisions relating to equality—that is, providing like treatment for like persons—which state courts generally interpret as equal-protection clauses. A state constitution typically has a provision that prohibits laws that grant certain citizens privileges or immunities not belonging equally to all citizens (Oregon, Article I, Section 20) or a provision that declares people to be "born equally free and independent" (Wisconsin, Article I, Section 1) and to have "certain inherent and indefeasible rights" (Pennsylvania, Article I, Section 1).

The original constitutions of Wyoming and Utah recognized the equal rights of women, and in the 1970s several states adopted some form of constitutional guaranty against sex-based discrimination, often referred to as the "state equal-rights amendment." The 1973 New Mexico amendment (Article II, Section 18) provides, "Equality of rights under law shall not be denied on account of the sex of any person."

Several states have broader equal-rights provisions. The Connecticut Constitution, for example, states, "No person shall be denied the equal protection of the law nor be subjected to segregation or discrimination in the exercise or enjoyment of his or her civil or political rights because of religion, race, color, ancestry, national origin, sex or physical or mental disability" (Amendment Article XXI). By the mid-1980s, state courts had decided relatively few cases on the basis of these constitutional provisions.

State courts seem to be using federal equal-rights analysis under the federal equal-protection clause in interpreting their state constitutional equality provisions. The state courts have not, for the most part, strayed from the federal decisions to develop an independent state jurisprudence under their equality provisions.

In reviewing state economic legislative regulation, some state courts, however, have used the state equal-protection clauses with more vigor than the federal courts have used the Fourteenth Amendment. After the late 1930s, federal judicial review of state economic regulations appears to have become a dead letter. Nevertheless, state courts have been willing to use a state's equal-protection guaranties rigorously to review regulatory economic legislation and to determine whether the legislative objective is proper and whether the means chosen by the legislature bear a reasonable relation to the end. Cases invalidating economic regulatory statutes, including cases striking down state fair-trade laws, frequently rest on the judicial determination that under the state constitution the legislation in question has the impermissible purpose of unreasonably impeding competition in the marketplace.

Thus, state courts are keeping the doctrine of substantive due process alive by occasionally—albeit not consistently—using their equal-protection and due process provisions as a substantive curb on legislative action in the economic area. Commentators are divided in their appraisal of this state constitutional law development. Those who look favorably on this development view the state courts as the last bastions of equal protection in economic matters and as having a special responsibility not to allow arbitrary and unreasonable discrimination to go unremedied. Critics fear that the state courts will substitute their judgment for that of the state legislature on debatable questions of public policy.

Access to Courts. About two-thirds of the state constitutions contain provisions guaranteeing the right of all persons suffering injury to seek redress through the civil courts conformable to the laws "without sale, denial, or delay" (Montana, Article I, Section 16). The Missouri Constitution provides, "The courts of justice shall be open to every person, and certain remedy afforded for every injury to person, property or character, and that right and justice shall be administered without sale, denial or delay" (Article I, Section 14). These provisions, referred to as "access to the courts" provisions or as "remedy guaranties," are derived from the Magna Charta. The federal Constitution does not have an equivalent provision.

The case law interpreting and applying this constitutional right has not been consistent within the states and from state to state. At times, courts rely on the remedy guaranty in a procedural manner to fashion a remedy to resolve disputes where no adequate procedure exists. At other times, courts use the remedy guaranty in a substantive manner (for example, as a new basis of tort theory). State courts have relied on the provision to grant a remedy for prenatal injuries. The Wisconsin Supreme Court used its constitutional provision to allow an injured person to continue her suit against manufacturers of diethylstilbestrol (DES), even though she was not able to meet the usual requisite burden of proving which entity manufactured the substance allegedly causing the harm (*Collins* v. *Eli Lilly Co.*, 1984).

The remedy guaranty, sometimes in combination with the state equal-protection and due process clauses, has been used to challenge legislation and court rules requiring the payment of fees to gain access to the courts. The same combination of state constitutional guaranties has been used to challenge tort-reform legislation—such as medical malpractice reform statutes, statutes of repose, and automobile no-fault insurance statutes—on the basis that such statutes deny or limit access to judicial remedies for certain claimants or claims.

The remedy guaranty, either separately or with the equal-protection and due process clauses, may take on growing importance as state legislatures adopt proposals to modify the common-law tort system and to establish alternative dispute-resolution systems. Only time will tell whether the remedy guaranty will be a stumbling block to what some see as a need to reshape the common law to be responsive to modern needs or will be a protection against what others see as a plot by special interests to limit the rights of innocent injury victims who need traditional judicial protection.

Other Liberties. While education is not mentioned in the federal Constitution, all state constitutions contain an education clause. Most require the legislature to establish and maintain public schools. The state constitution may also guarantee equal disbursement of educational benefits by requiring public schooling to be provided for all children or by ordering that school systems be established on a common or uniform basis. Some state courts have used the education provisions to prohibit fees for education and to invalidate local property taxes as the basis for financing education. Other states have not relied on the education provisions of the state constitution to enlarge rights over those guaranteed by

the due process or equal-protection clauses of the federal Constitution.

Approximately forty state constitutions guarantee the right to keep and bear arms, and only five track the Second Amendment to the federal Constitution. The United States Supreme Court has not yet held that the Second Amendment applies to the states. Some courts interpret the state constitutional provision as a collective right; others, as an individual right. The Oregon Supreme Court held that the state constitution's guaranty of the people's right to bear arms in defense of themselves and the state (Article I, Section 27) includes the right to possess a billy club in one's home. Accordingly, the court reversed a conviction for violating a statute making possession of a slugging weapon a crime (*State* v. *Kessler,* 1980).

About ten state constitutions expressly recognize a right of privacy—that is, a right to be free from government. The Florida Constitution provides that "every natural person has the right to be let alone and free from governmental intrusion into his private life except as otherwise provided herein" (Article I, Section 23). In other states, the courts have relied on the due process and equal-protection clauses as the basis for privacy rights.

State courts have sometimes been more expansive than the federal courts in protecting abortion rights, including invalidating legislative prohibitions on governmental payments for therapeutic abortions, and in protecting nontraditional living arrangements. In years to come, individuals may be relying on state constitutional privacy guaranties to challenge the state's control of such matters as drug use, dress, grooming, termination of medical care, and sexual activity between consenting adults.

CONCLUSION

Many state courts follow United States Supreme Court decisions in interpreting their state constitutions—even when the federal constitutional provision is not binding on the state and even when the texts or histories of the two constitutions are notably different. There is, however, a significant movement in the state courts away from exclusive reliance on the United

States Supreme Court's interpretations of the federal Constitution in interpreting state constitutions. The wisdom of the state court's self-reliance in interpreting its own constitution or of the state court's following the lead of the United States Supreme Court will continue to be debated as a jurisprudential issue. Whatever the resolution of this question, the result of the debate is a renewed interest in state constitutional law. State constitutional law is coming out of the legal archives into the legal literature, into court decisions, and into popular consciousness.

CASES

Barron v. Mayor of Baltimore, 7 Peters 243 (1833)
Buse v. Smith, 74 Wis. 2d 550, 247 N.W.2d 141 (1976)
Collins v. Eli Lilly Co., 116 Wis. 2d 166, 342 N.W.2d 37 (1984)
Cologne v. Westfarms Associates, 192 Conn. 48, 469 A.2d 1201 (1984)
Florida v. Casal, 462 U.S. 637 (1983)
General Assembly v. Byrne, 90 N.J. 376, 448 A.2d 438 (1982)
Gitlow v. New York, 268 U.S. 652 (1925)
Illinois v. Gates, 462 U.S. 213 (1983)
Marbury v. Madison, 1 Cranch 137 (1803)
Massachusetts Bay Transportation Authority Advisory Board v. Massachusetts Bay Transportation Authority, 382 Mass. 569, 417 N.E.2d 7 (1981)
Michigan v. Long, 463 U.S. 1032 (1983)
Milwaukee Brewers Baseball Club v. Wisconsin Department of Health and Social Services, 130 Wis. 2d 56, 387 N.W.2d 245 (1986)
People v. Tisler, 103 Ill. 2d 226, 469 N.E.2d 147 (1984)
Powell v. Alabama, 287 U.S. 45 (1932)
Robins v. Pruneyard Shopping Center, 23 Cal. 3d 899, 592 P.2d 341, 153 Cal. Rptr. 854 (1979), aff'd, 447 U.S. 74 (1980)
Shad Alliance v. Smith Haven Mall, 66 N.Y.2d 496, 488 N.E.2d 211 (1985)
State v. Jackson, 102 Wash. 2d 432, 688 P.2d 136 (1984)
State v. Kearns, 229 Kan. 207, 623 P.2d 507 (1981)
State v. Kessler, 289 Or. 359, 614 P.2d 94 (1980)
State v. La France, 124 N.H. 171, 471 A.2d 340 (1983)
State ex rel. Warren v. Nusbaum, 59 Wis. 2d 391, 208 N.W.2d 780 (1973)
Stringer v. State, 454 So. 2d 468 (Miss. 1985)
United States v. Leon, 104 S. Ct. 3405 (1984)

BIBLIOGRAPHY

William J. Brennan, Jr., "State Constitutions and the Protection of Individual Rights," in *Harvard Law Review,* 90 (1977), applauds state courts' extending individual protections through state constitutions. Ronald K. L. Collins, "Bills and Declarations of Rights Digest," in *American Bench* (1985), presents commentary and comparative charts and tables on state constitutional guaranties. Columbia University Legislative Drafting Research Fund, *Index Digest of State Constitutions,* 2nd ed. (1959), is a comparative analysis of state constitutional subjects; and *Constitutions of the United States: National and State,* 2nd ed. (1986), is a multivolume, looseleaf, up-to-date compilation of state constitutions. James Quayle Dealey, *Growth of American State Constitutions* (1915), discusses the history of, and trends in, state constitutions and analysis of state constitutions.

James M. Fischer, "Ballot Propositions: The Challenge of Direct Democracy to State Constitutional Jurisprudence," in *Hastings Constitutional Law Quarterly,* 11 (1983), discusses popular contribution to state constitutional law. Frank P. Grad, "The State Constitution: Its Function and Form for Our Time," in *Virginia Law Review,* 54 (1968), discusses the changing role of the state and the function of the state constitution. James Willard Hurst, *The Growth of American Law: The Law Makers* (1950), provides a history of American law, including state constitutional law. Bradley D. McGraw, ed., *Developments in State Constitutional Law* (1985), presents essays on state constitutional law prepared for a Williamsburg National Conference on Developments in State Constitutional Law. National Municipal League, *Model State Constitution,* rev. 6th ed. (1968), is a valuable resource on existing and proposed constitutional provisions with commentary. Wade J. Newhouse, *Constitutional Uniformity and Equality in State Taxation,* 2 vols., 2nd ed. (1984), provides state-by-state analysis of state constitutional provisions and judicial interpretations. Note, "Developments in the Law: The Interpretation of State Constitutional Rights," in *Harvard Law Review,* 95 (1982), is a student commentary analyzing the role of the state bills of rights. *Publius,* 10, no. 1 (1982), provides essays exploring the constitutional arrangements of the constituent polities in a federal system.

Barbara F. Sachs, ed., *Laws, Legislature, Legislative Procedure: A Fifty-State Index* (1982) and *Fundamental Liberties and Rights: A Fifty-State Index* (1980), are special subject indexes to the Columbia University *Constitutions of the United States: National and State,* referred to above. Special Section, "State Constitutional Law," in *National Law Journal,* 12 March 1984 and 29 September 1986, presents commentary on the resurrection of reliance on state bills of rights and on researching state constitutional law. Albert L. Sturm, "State Constitutional Developments During 1984," in *National Civic Review,* 74 (1985), is a state-by-state update, which regularly appears in a winter issue of this journal. Albert L. Sturm and Janice C. May, "Constitutions," in L. Edward Purcell, ed., *The Book of the States,* vol. 25 (1984), updates state constitutional change and data. Symposium, "The Emergence of State Constitutional Law," in *Texas Law Review,* 63 (1985), presents articles adapted from a national conference on state constitutional law. Symposium, "State Courts and Federalism in the 1980's," in *William and Mary Law Review,* 22 (1981), contributes articles exploring the relation between state and federal courts. Symposium, "The Washington Constitution," in *University of Puget Sound Law Review,* 8 (1985), includes articles on the new federalism and the Washington Constitution.

United States Advisory Commission on Intergovernmental Relations, *The Question of State Government Capability* (1985), provides in chapter 3 a brief history of state constitutions and critical analysis of modern state constitutions, with further resource materials in footnotes. United States Commission on Intergovernmental Relations, *A Report to the President for Transmittal to the Congress* (1955), includes a discussion of the federal system, the role of the states, and intergovernmental relationships in selected functional responsibilities. John P. Wheeler, Jr., ed., *Salient Issues of Constitutional Revision* (1961), is one of a series of lengthy essays published by the National Municipal League (now called the Citizens Forum on Self-Government), on state constitutions. Robert F. Williams, "State Constitutional Law Processes," in *William and Mary Law Review*, 24 (1983), analyzes state constitutional law development in selected subject areas.

[*See also* AMENDMENTS TO THE CONSTITUTION; BURGER COURT AND ERA; CONSTITUTIONAL INTERPRETATION; COURTS AND CONSTITUTIONALISM; CRIMINAL PROCEDURE; EQUAL PROTECTION CLAUSE; FEDERALISM; FREE SPEECH AND EXPRESSION; PRIVACY; *and* STATE COURT SYSTEMS.]

Part VI
METHODOLOGY

AMERICAN JURISPRUDENCE

Jerome Hall

From Plato to Hegel, jurisprudence was an important part of a wide-ranging philosophy. But beginning in the mid-nineteenth century, many specialized disciplines arose, among them the philosophy of law. Just as there are many philosophies, so, too, are there many schools of jurisprudential thought. One might classify legal philosophies in terms of the general philosophy they reflect, such as realism, idealism, utilitarianism, pragmatism, phenomenology, and existentialism. But with the development of jurisprudence as a specialized discipline, legal philosophies have been classified into one of three schools by reference to their typical emphasis and their view of the relevant subject matter. These schools have become known as natural-law philosophy, analytical jurisprudence, and the sociology of law. It is very important to distinguish a legal philosophy from positive law. Positive law, let us say for the present, consists of constitutions, statutes, regulations, and judicial decisions. Jurisprudence is theorizing about positive law and relevant actions and events.

As a preliminary to the discussion of these three schools of jurisprudence in the United States, it is important to note that jurisprudence is an international discipline. English and German legal philosophers have influenced American scholars, just as American contributions have had wide international influence. Finally, the immortals among philosophers—Plato, Aristotle, Thomas Aquinas, and Kant—have influenced the jurisprudence of all countries. The domestic participants in this international exchange of ideas have not supinely followed in the paths laid down by foreign writers. They have accepted some theories, modified others, and rejected still others. The consequence is that any adequate discussion of American jurisprudence must take account not only of the work of the international classics in the field but also of the lesser lights who were influential in determining the course and character of legal philosophy in the United States.

NATURAL-LAW THEORIES

The common bond of natural-law theories is their restriction of positive law to codes, statutes, and judicial decisions that are morally valid. Since moral philosophies differ in important respects, so, too, will the corresponding theories of natural law differ. Accordingly, in reading treatises on natural law, one should bear in mind that such common dismissals of it as laws "written in the sky" are exaggerations of a particular type of natural-law philosophy. A second caveat is that the term *nature* as it is employed in natural-law philosophies does not mean physical or biological nature; instead, it means moral values—a value cosmos.

Plato. Alfred North Whitehead said that all Western thought consists of footnotes to Plato. That may have been an exaggeration, but anyone who reads Plato's dialogues will appreciate the beauty of his style and the subtlety of his far-ranging thought. The enduring product of Plato's genius is the philosophy that laid the foundations of political theory and jurisprudence.

To understand Plato's legal philosophy, one must consider the questions that engaged his most imaginative efforts. Everyone agrees that science is important and this implies the existence of a certain kind of knowledge. But what is knowledge, and can there be any knowledge without ideas? Almost everyone agrees that communication is a fact, and this implies that many persons know "the same things." But how is communication possible? What is there in the world or in the brains or minds of men that permits common understanding to exist? How explain the complex structures of modern science and the uniform responses of scientists to them?

Since the senses cannot apprehend what things "have in common," Plato insisted that that and other "immaterial things . . . are shown only in thought and idea, and in no other way" (*Statesman*, 286a). Plato tried to discover "what that nature is which is common to both the corporeal and incorporeal, and which they [people] have in their mind's eye" (*Sophist*, 247d). In more prosaic language, what is involved in relationships, for example, of cause and effect, equal or unequal, opposites, correlatives, or parent-child? For example, one sees a woman and a child and sees her carrying the child; but one does not see their relation as parent and child. What of order, structure, system, and regularity? Surely, these terms do not represent mere sounds or physical things? They obviously are not tangible. Plato held that they are incorporeal entities, "forms" that exist objectively in reality and are apprehended in mental processes.

Plato's *Statesman* represents the great discovery of a basic limitation of positive law—the limitation inherent in the generality of law. There is no escaping the fact that "the law does not perfectly comprehend what is noblest and most just for all and therefore cannot enforce what is best. The differences of men and actions, and the endless irregular movements of human things, do not admit of any universal and simple rule. And no art whatsoever can lay down a rule which will last for all time" (294a–b). Although Plato holds that positive law cannot be perfect, he never says that law is an evil.

Plato's theory of law is also developed in his longest dialogue, *Laws*. When we turn to the "greater bulk" of the *Laws*, it is evident that the discussion differs markedly from that of other dialogues. Much of the discourse is concerned with specific legislation. It is this part of the *Laws* that has suggested the observation that the dialogue is a code of law. But it is certainly not a "code" in the modern sense. The theory of legislation expounded in the *Republic* is restated in practical terms. The gist of it is that the legislator's function is to educate citizens by persuading or coercing them to live a good life. This requires the legislator, first, to understand the relevant empirical and moral knowledge. Second, the legislator must look from the model to the clay; he must use his knowledge in drafting laws to direct the conduct of the citizens toward right ends. Finally, the legislator himself is a member of the political community; unlike the "philosopher-king," he is only an erring mortal, subject to law like other citizens.

Legislation is, for Plato, the best kind of law. He identifies the purpose of legislation with that of gymnastics, and he contrasts these with the judicial process and medicine. Medicine is, for him, a practical science used to restore the balance of health, whereas gymnastics habituate the body to the development and maintenance of health. Only when that is disturbed is the physician summoned. So, too, legislation disciplines human nature and habituates it to a rational integration of the components of the soul—the condition of justice. Only when the dominance of reason is upset by ignorance or passion is recourse to the law courts necessary. Coercive sanctions are used, just as doctors administer bitter drugs. In short, legislation is a constructive, educational process, implementing the ideal pattern, whereas adjudication is only remedial.

Did Plato hold that positive law is morally valid, that there is no such thing as "an unjust law"? Certain passages seem to support this thesis—for example, "virtue and justice and institutions and laws being the best things among men" (*Crito*, 53c). However, when Plato is discussing certain positive laws, he evaluates them as most modern critics would. They are good or bad; hence, we "praise and blame the laws" (*Laws*, 770e). He criticizes Cretan laws, for example, because they were designed only for war.

These attitudes derive in turn from Plato's view of the relationship between Nature and law. For Plato, Nature is a moral, purposeful, rational, divine order, to which rational beings should conform. Thus, "the true ruler is not meant by nature to regard his own interest, but that of his subjects" (*Republic*, 347d). In the *Republic*, Plato argued that justice is "real and natural and not merely conventional" (367c). Coming closer to later usage, he said in the *Laws* that "the individual, attaining to right reason . . . should live according to its rule; while the city, receiving the same from some god or from one who has knowledge of these things, should embody it in a law'' (645b). After he had challenged the still current naturalistic meaning of *physis,* he uttered words that later philosophers adopted almost verbatim: "Our general view of law will be more in accordance with nature" (858c), and "A legislator who has anything in him . . . ought to support the law and also art, and acknowledge that both alike exist by nature, and no less than nature, if they are the creations of mind in accordance with right reason" (890d). His final categorical imperative is to copy the "divine pattern," a perfect "unchangeable pattern" (*Timaeus,* 28b), an "eternal nature" (39d), for "happiness can only come to a state when its lineaments are traced by an artist working after the divine pattern" (*Republic,* 500e).

Was Plato inconsistent in his use of the word *law*? Was he only saying that positive law ought to conform to Nature? Or was he speaking in different levels of discourse—one in terms of ordinary language, the other, as a philosopher and scientist who in that context gives *law* a congruent, restricted meaning?

Aristotle. Aristotle made further contributions to the realistic theory of natural law. While Plato's orientation was in mathematics, Aristotle's was in biology. Nature, accordingly, was the development from potentiality toward the actualization of the ideal. Aristotle emphasized the difference between "natural laws," which were everywhere the same, and "conventional laws," which differed from city to city.

For Aristotle, justice is manifested in two ways. Corrective justice, exemplified by criminal law or breach of contract, calls for compensation, restitution, or punishment that is proportionate in that the gravity of the sanction is proportioned to that of the harm committed. Distributive justice deals with the allocation of goods, not only economic but also other values. It is proportioned to merit, a standard different from that of Marxism, which is that of need.

Aristotle agreed with Plato regarding the imperfection of law because of its generality, which was not suited to the uniqueness of the individuals involved or to the particularity of the relevant situations. He was the founder of equity, which comprised a set of principles whereby the judge could modify or supplement the generality of laws by ethical adaptations to particular persons and situations.

Aquinas. Saint Thomas Aquinas in his *Summa Theologica* presented a synthesis of his view of

Christianity and Greek philosophy, mostly that of Aristotle. Law "is a rule and measure of action, hence reason directs action toward ends," and "in order that the volition of what is commanded may have the nature of law, it needs to be in accord with some rule of reason." Then he states his theological doctrine: "Granted that the world is ruled by Divine Providence . . . the whole community of the universe is governed by Divine Reason." Thus, for believers who may have had problems regarding "law in the sky," faith steps in to give Plato's separated forms a more persuasive meaning. God's government of the universe has the nature of law, and it is perfect and eternal. Man is a rational animal and his "participation" in the eternal law—that is, man's understanding and internalization of the eternal law—is "natural law." For believers, revelation is the other principal way in which the divine law becomes known to man. Human law (that is, positive law) is not coterminous with natural law. Passion, ignorance, and selfish interest influence legislation. In addition, law cannot deal with many minor matters. What is important for Aquinas is that positive laws should not contradict natural law by commanding what natural law forbids.

Consistent with the foregoing premises is Aquinas' definition of positive law: "It is nothing else than an ordinance of reason for the common good, made by him who has care of the community, and promulgated." The "common good" implies the restriction of positive law to morally valid commands of the ruler. Aquinas makes this explicit in his quotation from Augustine: "That which is not just seems to be no law at all." Then he makes the statement that seems to contradict this use of *law.* "Laws," says Aquinas, "framed by man are either just or unjust." Here we encounter the same problem met in Plato's dialogues. Is Aquinas inconsistent in his use of *positive law*? Or is he in one context defining positive laws and in another saying what they ought to be? Or, finally, is he, like Plato, using ordinary language when he speaks of "unjust laws" and on another level, the philosophical, using the term in a scientific sense when he restricts "positive law" to morally valid commands?

In sum, the classical natural-law realism of Plato, Aristotle, and Aquinas holds the following: (1) Forms (that is, relations and values), which are universals, subsist in reality. (2) In ordinary language, positive laws may be said to be good or bad, just or unjust, but on a philosophical or scientific level of discourse, positive laws must conform to natural law—that is, to relevant moral principles. (3) Man is rational and social, and he alone is able to discover and understand, though imperfectly, the moral principles necessary for sound legislation and personal conduct in extralegal realms.

Kant. Taking a very different direction from that of classical natural-law realism, Immanuel Kant centered his philosophy on human beings. It is not externally subsisting values but man's practical reason that legislates. Kant's rigorous pietistic religious training made duty paramount in this context. He spoke of duty as "sublime and mighty." Both of these aspects of his scholarship were expressed in a memorable statement: "Two things fill the mind with ever new and increasing admiration and awe . . . the starry heavens above me and the moral law within me" (1956, 166). Accordingly, for Kant, there were two worlds—that of physical, biological nature in which cause-effect is the dominant feature, and the world of morality, characterized by human freedom, which must be presupposed if praise and blame are to have meaning. In the human world, one must assume not only a sufficient degree of autonomy but also authorship, not causation, as the reason or ground of action.

Kant classified ethics into two divisions: virtue and justice. Virtue is internal (conscience), and the sole imperative is to act in conformity with one's duty as directed by practical reason. Since this is internal and free, it cannot be coerced. One can be forced to do an evil act, but reason cannot be forced to think an evil act is in accord with moral duty. Justice, on the other hand, deals with duties that are expressed externally, as in obedience to laws; hence, external action can be coerced. In other words, one can be forced to behave in a morally correct way, and that is the purpose of law, but the motive to act morally cannot be coerced.

Kant's ethical theory was deontological as opposed to utilitarian. It is the intrinsic value of good actions that is important, not their consequences. In his retributive theory of punishment, for example, Kant insisted that the only justification for punishing anyone was that he deserved to be punished, and he deserved to be punished because he had deprived another person of his freedom. That, and not the deterrence of others or even the reformation of the offender, was the

only justification Kant recognized. He drove this home in his supposed case of inhabitants in a colony who are about to leave it when one of them commits a murder. The murderer must be executed, said Kant, before the inhabitants leave the colony, regardless of the fact that there will be no possible benefit to anyone.

Kant did not provide or defend a substantive natural law, as did Plato, Aristotle, and Aquinas. The test of the validity of a law was not its conformity with moral values. Instead, the test was conformity with the "categorical imperative," the dictate of practical reason to "act only according to that maxim by which you can at the same time will that it should become a universal law" (1959, 53). Accordingly, if Kant is to be included among the natural-law thinkers, he must be distinguished from the other members in that his theory is a formal or procedural natural-law theory. Unlike the realists who interpret Nature in objective terms of goodness (for example, life, liberty, and property), Kant holds that the validity of positive laws is determined by whether they conform to the categorical imperative.

The German historical school rose as part of the romantic movement, based on the earliest myths, poems, linguistic forms, and other expressions of the *Volksgeist,* the spirit or ethos of the people. Its legal representatives, notably Frederich Karl von Savigny, thought of law as they did of language and other cultural artifacts —namely, as arising from the consciousness of the people, first expressed in custom, then in judicial decisions, that is, "by internal silently-operating powers, not by the arbitrary will of a lawgiver." It followed that law cannot be made. The legislator, if he wants to enact laws that will not be merely paper laws, must discover and enact in conformity with the *Volksgeist.* So, too, the historical school scornfully dismissed the natural-law theories, which assumed that sound laws could be manufactured from the airy filaments of armchair speculation. Instead, the historical school advocated resort to the historical method based on the premise that there is an organic connection between past legal institutions and present ones. Legal scholars should by detailed investigation trace these various bonds to the *Volksgeist,* and thence to the manifested customs and on to current law.

As will more fully appear, the great natural-law philosophies have become part of American jurisprudence—often modified, sometimes criticized or simplified in terms of "due process" and "civilization." American neo-Scholastics have adopted Aquinas' theory and applied it to American law. Kant has distinguished supporters. And the realism of Plato and Aristotle permeates much of American jurisprudence, although some of its exponents are unaware of their adherence to the thought of the founders of their discipline. Further elucidation of natural-law theories depends on the differences between them and legal positivism. First, we shall present the structural features of analytical jurisprudence and then the criteria that distinguish it from natural-law theories.

ANALYTICAL JURISPRUDENCE

Analytical jurisprudence, also called legal positivism, has been defined as a "formal" science of the structure of basic concepts common to all advanced legal systems; it has also been likened to grammar. While there is an element of truth in these characterizations, they are somewhat misleading, and they oversimplify the functions of analytical jurisprudence. Relatively formal sciences such as mathematics and logic are said to be "formal" because they do not deal with facts, as do physics and biology. They deal with numbers and letters, which can represent anything or nothing, and they deal with the formal interrelations of propositions containing numbers or letters. But since analytical jurisprudence consists of statements about positive laws, which do refer to persons, facts, and actions, it has factual referents.

Analytical legal philosophers have been concerned with the structure and meaning of certain concepts (for example, "law," "right," and "duty"), on methods of legal reasoning, on classification, and on the characteristics of a legal system. It is because of the logical overtones of these interests that some writers have called jurisprudence a "formal science."

Austin. John Austin, a seminal figure of this school, produced a two-volume treatise, *Lectures on Jurisprudence, or The Philosophy of Positive Law,* that has been the focus of later jurisprudence. The principal thrust of Austin's jurisprudence is his statement that a positive law is a command by the political sovereign of an independent political society to his subjects, the violation of which entails an "evil," or sanction. The subjects are in the "habit of obeying" the commands, but the sovereign does not, and need not, obey any other political sovereign; indeed, he cannot be limited by any law. The sanction is an essential element of Austin's concept of law: unless there is an evil annexed, there is really no command. There might be advice, suggestion, or exhortation, but *command* implies an evil that will be imposed for disobedience. Austin also distinguished positive laws from other types of commands, such as those of God and those of public morality, by reference to the distinctive character of the "determinate source" of the commands— that is, the political sovereign.

Legal duty or obligation is simply being liable to have the sanction imposed for violation. Duty and right are correlatives; that is, there is one legal relation whether it is looked at from the pole of the holder of a right or from the viewpoint of the person having a duty. Duty is essential, but not every duty has a correlative right; for example, in criminal law, the victim does not have a legal right against the offender.

Although Austin wrote respectfully of "God's laws," which he thought were in accord with the principle of utility, he followed his utilitarian predecessor Jeremy Bentham in excluding the moral validity of a statute from his definition of "positive law." "With the goodness or badness of laws . . . it [jurisprudence] has no immediate concern" (1873, 1107).

Austin's effort to free the sovereign from any limitation by positive law aroused criticism. The political heirs of men who had risked their lives to wrest the Magna Charta and other bills of right from the hands of reluctant monarchs vigorously rejected Austin's thesis regarding the independence of the sovereign from control by positive law. One of Austin's most severe critics was Frederic Harrison, who argued that "command," the central notion in Austin's theory, was far from being an apt description of a legal system. Far more characteristic are the rules of law that do not command but, instead, grant powers to people that enable them to achieve many objectives, such as to marry or to make contracts. Indeed, these rules, he said, outnumber the commands "ten to one." They comprise rules that "the courts of justice recognize."

Gray. John Chipman Gray, an early American representative of this school and the author of a classic essay on property law, was also a legal positivist but with important differences that distinguish his work from that of Austin and Hans Kelsen (discussed below). He was a legal positivist because, for him, law is "something which actually exists. It is not that which is in accordance with religion, or nature, or morality" (p. 94). The law of nature is an "exploded superstition," and to bring it into the concept of law "is to take a step backward in Jurisprudence" (p. 309). Even if a tyrant like Caligula issued the most outrageous commands and his judges enforced them, they would be law.

Gray was influenced by Austin, but as is typical of American legal philosophers, he was also very critical of some aspects of Austin's jurisprudence. He criticized the thesis, originating with Bentham, that "the law is only the aggregate" of all the laws. He rejected "habit of obedience" because judges have often decided cases in which the habit was disobedience. Austin's concept of a sovereign was not germane to the United States.

Gray also disagreed with Austin's allocation of the morality of law to legislation. He agreed that jurisprudence should not deal with the question of what the law ought to be, but he insisted that jurisprudence must consider both rules actually adopted and questions concerning cases that have previously not been brought within the rules, to determine whether the adopted rule should be extended to other facts. He thought Austin was inconsistent in excluding questions of moral principle from jurisprudence but at the same time devoting a large part of his treatise to the discussion of ethics.

Gray's major criticism was that law is not, as Austin argued, the command of the sovereign; "law," for Gray, consists of the rules laid down by judges in their decisions "for the determination of legal rights and duties." He consequently rejected the then prevalent view that courts only interpret legislation by reference to the intention of the legislators. Often, said Gray, questions arise that are never considered in the legislature. He discussed many cases in which, to a clear and precise property lawyer, like Gray, there was not even a remotely relevant statute or precedent; these were obvious cases of judicial legislation.

This much, however, was only preliminary. What stirred wide interest and criticism was Gray's thesis that "the true view . . . is that the Law is what the judges declare; that statutes, precedents, the opinions of learned experts, customs, and morality are the sources of the Law" (p. 283). Gray did not deny that statutes and precedents influenced judges and were in that sense "binding," but his theory focuses on what is most important for the litigants in any case—the judge's decision in the case. From this perspective, precedents and statutes are only past laws (which Gray called "sources"). A lawyer's interpretation of relevant statutes and precedents leads him to predict what a judge will do—that is, how a judge will decide a particular case. This is a prediction of probable law, and that is what citizens and especially prospective litigants rely on.

The discussion thus far has focused on the concept of law. There are other basic concepts such as right-duty, which received relatively little attention. Moreover, "right" was rather loosely construed by the above analysts to include any legal advantage. Wesley Newcomb Hohfeld concentrated on these concepts. He presented and analyzed four legal relations: right-duty, privilege–no right, power-liability, and immunity-disability, which he called "correlatives." He also constructed a table of "opposites," namely, right–no right, privilege–duty, power–disability, and immunity–liability. Since *liability* has a negative connotation, as when it is commonly said that it means to be liable to subjection to a negative sanction, later analysts prefer "susceptibility."

The major criticism of Hohfeld's system has been that there are really only two legal relations, namely right-duty and power-susceptibility, and that the other alleged jural relations merely negate these actual legal relations. For example, to say that one is privileged to defend himself against an assailant is tantamount to saying that he has no duty not to lay hands on him. "No right" is obviously the negative of right, and likewise regarding the negation of power by disability. Although this criticism is logically valid and also apt as regards litigants, a sociological view of the negations leads to a different conclusion. In this perspective, it does not suffice to say that one who has a privilege has no duty. One who exercises a privilege may act in certain ways, such as defend himself, walk on land regarding which the owner has given him an easement, and so on.

Everyone agrees that right-duty is a necessary

relation. That is what everyone who is a prospective or an actual litigant is interested in; that is the crucial issue in any litigation. But what about power-susceptibility? That relation is the essential determinant of the existence of a right-duty relation. This relation does not drop down from the sky; it is created by the use of the prior relation of power-susceptibility. For example, if P sues D for breach of contract, he must prove that there is a contract between him and D. The only way he can do that is to go back in time and show (or have it assumed) that he and D were normal adults, he made D an offer that D accepted (that is, that they were in a power-susceptibility relation), D's acceptance created a right-duty relation, and D violated the duty the contract imposed on him.

Kelsen. Hans Kelsen is the greatest of the analytical jurisprudential thinkers of the twentieth century. Born in Vienna, he became a leading scholar in Europe, was the author of the Austrian Constitution, and enjoyed an international reputation. In 1939 he left Germany, a refugee from Nazi persecution, and went to the United States in 1940. He spent the second half of his life there, most of it as a professor in the political science department of the University of California at Berkeley.

Kelsen's *Pure Theory of Law* would more aptly be called *Theory of Pure Law* because the central focus and subject of his theory are legal norms. For Kelsen, legal norms are concepts or ideas; Kelsen excluded from norms all facts except those referred to by them. Kelsen also insisted on the exclusion of moral values, especially justice, from his definition of positive law. Legal norms, said Kelsen, give meaning to facts. For example, if A shoots and kills B, a physicist might be interested in the mass and velocity of the bullet. But seen through the norms of the criminal law, A's act is "murder."

The *Pure Theory* also distinguishes the causal character of the natural sciences from what Kelsen calls "imputation," which is a basic feature of legal rules. For example, when a gas is heated, a physicist will say that the volume of the gas expands in direct proportion to the increase in temperatures; that is, a scientific law is cast in terms of "is." But a rule of law has a different structure and meaning. It states, for example, that if a person violates his duty to keep a certain promise specified in a contract, he must pay cer-

tain damages. He may be insolvent or he may hide his assets, but that does not affect the meaning of the relevant law. In sum, a scientific law is descriptive; a legal rule is prescriptive or normative. The structure of a legal rule is such that if certain circumstances occur (including a violation of a legal duty), a certain sanction must be imposed. The sanction is coercive, and this characterizes a legal system as an external compulsive order, "an apparatus of compulsion."

In what has become one of his most famous contributions, Kelsen delineated the logical features of a legal system. A system must express the unity of its components. Kelsen achieved this by postulating a "basic norm," which prescribes how laws must be made. Below the basic norm is the constitution; below that are codes and statutes; and finally, at the bottom of the hierarchy are judicial decisions. Law, then, must conform with the procedure prescribed in a higher norm. For example, the validity of a judicial decision depends on its conformity with the procedure prescribed in a relevant statute; that of the statute depends on its conformity with the procedure prescribed in the constitution; and the constitution is valid by reference to the basic norm.

Hart. The felicity of style of *The Concept of Law* by H. L. A. Hart has made it one of the most widely discussed jurisprudential books of the twentieth century. Hart criticized Austin's thesis that law consists only of commands of the sovereign. Hart argued that law also consists of rules that are not commands. He distinguished "primary" rules from "secondary" rules. Primary rules are rules like those of criminal law, which prescribe duties and to which sanctions are attached. Secondary rules, far from commanding, confer powers, "facilities," to do many things, such as make contracts, wills, get married, make or change laws. No sanction is attached to the unsuccessful use of these powers. Plainly, a legal system is poorly—indeed, misleadingly—described if it is characterized as comprising only commands. Hart emphasized the thesis that the "key" to understanding "law" is the union or combination of primary and secondary rules.

One of the most difficult problems in jurisprudence is that of identifying positive laws. It will be recalled that Austin's answer was to point to the political sovereign of an independent society as the source of laws. For Kelsen, it was the hypothetical basic norm and the coercive sanction. For Hart, it was "the rule of recognition" that identifies positive laws. The rule of recognition cannot be a primary rule because it lacks a sanction. Secondary rules confer powers. But the rule of recognition does not confer powers; it identifies. This suggests that the rule of recognition is a third kind of rule. Is it only a reformulated Kelsenian "basic norm"?

While acknowledging his indebtedness to Kelsen, Hart disagreed with the *Pure Theory of Law* in two important respects. He thought that Kelsen's concept of law in terms of a hypothetical judgment (if certain circumstances, then a sanction must be imposed) is oversimple and misleading. What needs equal emphasis in an adequate description of a modern legal system is the importance of the secondary rules.

Hart's rule of recognition, like Kelsen's basic norm, is the ultimate criterion for identifying positive laws. It differs from Kelsen's basic norm, states Hart, in that the rule of recognition is "an empirical, though complex, question of fact." The most important fact is the practice of the courts, but it may also be, or include, an authoritative text, the acknowledgment that a text is "authoritative," as well as long customary practice or enactment by a specific body.

Much of the criticism of Hart's theory has been directed toward the rule of recognition. The claim of factuality is said to be vague and unsupported. The reliance on courts and legislatures assumes that they are competent to make or change laws; and if that competence is derived from statutes or constitutions, then the competence of those documents is assumed, or it is derived from an assumed still higher authority. In sum, the question is, What "authorizes" the rule of recognition to identify laws? If it only identifies certain rules as laws, what is it that makes those rules laws? This criticism of the rule of recognition suggests that it, too, serves as an ultimate postulate.

Hart held that only the primary rules are sanctioned, but that the secondary rules are not. Lon L. Fuller went farther. He held that sanction is not a necessary element in the (his) concept of law, but he conceded that sanctions must exist somewhere in a legal system. Hart's position is the necessary result of his assumption that secondary rules are rules of law. From the perspective of ordinary language and also of that of lawyers, Hart's view of secondary rules is obviously correct. On the other hand, the sanction has been held essential in the concept of law not only by such legal positivists as Austin and Kelsen but also by such natural lawyers as Aquinas and Kant. This involves the wider question noted above in the discussion of Plato's and Aquinas' philosophy: Should not ordinary usage be distinguished from scientific or philosophic usage?

Kelsen insisted that the coercive sanction of positive law is the only factual way to distinguish it from other norms. Fuller directed most of his criticism against the thesis that the sanction is a measure of physical force. That criticism is supported by reference to many legal sanctions that are plainly not measures of physical force, such as reprimand and posting the name of a corporation that violated rules of the Securities and Exchange Commission. But it is equally clear that coercion is a distinctive mark of government, and it is therefore at least one of the ways of distinguishing positive laws from other rules, especially from the rules of voluntary associations. But as will be discussed later, coercion must be given a wider meaning than "physical force."

There is another, equally important reason to include the sanction in the concept of law, namely, the scientific reason that necessitates generalization over a uniform field of data. To say that some legal rules are sanctioned but that others are not sanctioned includes disparate, not uniform, data. To hold that it is essential that there be sanctions somewhere in the legal system but that that does not necessitate its inclusion in the concept of law is equally unsatisfactory because, apart from the scientific reason noted above, it contradicts the widely, perhaps universally, accepted thesis that a rule of law cannot be understood except as part of a legal system. If the sanction is essential in a legal system, the rules of law that comprise it are sanctioned, and the concept of law must represent that characteristic.

Are we, then, driven to acceptance of Kelsen's basic norm as the unifying concept and necessary base of a legal system? What seems persuasive is that if an infinite regress is to be avoided, there must be a basic postulate or an agreement to which all can subscribe. Is it possible to adhere to the logic of the basic norm and to an initial agreement regarding the identification of positive laws that can open the door to their description? The suggested initial agreement is that if there is positive law in any society, it must be found in its constitution, legislative enactments, and judicial decisions.

Given the above conditional agreement, the following are submitted as the criteria for identifying positive law: (1) The enactments and judicial decisions must be ethically valid. (2) This quality must be reflected in public attitudes and in the function of those statutes and decisions. (3) The regularity of the administration must be given greater weight than the systematic character of the legal order. (4) Laws must be concerned with public interests. (5) The system must by and large be effective. (6) When challenged by other norms, law must prevail; this implies the supremacy of law. (7) The law must be inexorable, unlike the law of voluntary associations from which one can resign and avoid the imposition of sanctions. There is no resignation from the political society known as "the state." Law is inexorable vis-à-vis the will of any subject.

Since natural-law theories limit "law" to the coalescence of certain commands and rules with moral principles, they necessarily espouse a philosophy that relies on moral principles and values. Kelsen and others of the analytical jurisprudence school made a sustained frontal attack on this central thesis of natural-law theories. For Kelsen, ethical principles cannot, like legal norms, be known. Value judgments are mere expressions of feelings, emotions, and tastes. Thus, he held that justice is an "irrational ideal."

Bentham. Certain aspects of Jeremy Bentham's utilitarianism are important with respect to this debate. First is Bentham's advocacy of the principle of utility as the only test of the moral validity of any law, be it legislative or judicial, or, indeed, of any other act. His affirmation of that principle —the greatest pleasure or happiness of the greatest number—was accompanied by a fierce attack on ethical systems that stressed duty, conscience, and the intrinsic value or disvalue of certain actions.

Bentham had nothing but contempt for the contemporary moral philosophers who stressed duty, conscience, and intuition. His rejection of their moral philosophy was relentless when that philosophy was presented as natural law. Such terms as *right* and *fitting* are vague and only express emotions. Regarding moral obligation, he said, "The talisman of arrogance, indolence, and ignorance is to be found in a single word. . . . It is the word 'ought.'" "Natural Law, natural rights, are two kinds of fictions or metaphors." Proponents of that superstition write "as if there had been a real code of natural laws." "What is natural," he said, are "sentiments of pleasure or pain." These "inclinations," far from being laws, are subjected to laws.

For Bentham, pleasure is "good" and pain is "evil." Not content with such generalizations, he tried persistently to place his utilitarianism on a scientific foundation. He constructed a detailed table of pleasures and pains, together with directions for measuring them. Bentham applied the principle of utility and his calculus of pains and pleasures to legislation. Its purpose was to maximize the happiness of the greatest number.

Still, it is not fanciful to suppose that the happiness of the greatest number can be increased by persecuting an unpopular minority. This has impressed contemporary critics of utilitarianism who have espoused modified Kantian positions. They defend individual rights, especially those safeguarded by the Constitution, even though this protection does not advance, indeed, even if it opposes, the general welfare. To this, the utilitarian ploy is the "piggyback" strategy: the values Kant's descendants prefer are included in the general good.

Bentham's support of the utility principle and his rejection of any challenge to law on the ground that the statute in question was not really law because it was immoral have formed the core of utilitarian legal positivism that has persisted to this day: the moral validity (that is, the utility) of a statute or decision is not essential to its being law.

The Hart-Fuller Debate. The recent scene in Anglo-American jurisprudence is exemplified by the debate between H. L. A. Hart and Lon Fuller, the former an avowed utilitarian, the latter an avowed nonscholastic natural lawyer. Fuller defended the coalescence of law and morality, while Hart proposed their separation.

In *The Morality of Law,* Fuller distinguished the

"morality of duty" from the "morality of aspiration." The morality of duty is categorical and involves "shalls" and "shall nots." The morality of aspiration deals with the "good life," with excellence and the fullest development of one's potentialities. It is the latter that, in Fuller's view, constitutes the "inner morality" of a legal system. It is expressed in eight requirements: (1) There must be rules so that ad hoc decisions are avoided. (2) The rules must be published. (3) Legislation may not be retroactive. (4) The rules must be understandable. (5) The rules must not be contradictory. (6) The subjects must be able to obey the rules. (7) There must not be frequent changes in the rules. (8) The government must conform to the rules. A total failure in any one of these requirements, stated Fuller, results not simply in a bad legal system but in a system that cannot "properly" be called a legal system.

The principal response of Hart was that Fuller mistook efficiency for morality. The most ruthless dictator could comply with every one of Fuller's requirements but the result would not be a morally valid legal system. Hart charged that Fuller confused two realms—law and morality—that must be distinguished; clarity demands that. Moreover, Fuller's insistence on "purpose" likewise fails to distinguish morality from efficiency: a would-be assassin can plan his actions and proceed to attain his homicidal purpose.

Fuller replied that his critics used "efficacy" in a shortsighted way. He cited the Russian retroactive law imposing capital punishment for previously committed large-scale theft. In the short term, that was certainly very effective, but the concomitant loss of confidence in the system made the long-range results ineffective. He emphasized two differences between a legal system and a manager's instruction to his employees. First, a legal system is expressed in general rules; a manager gives specific instructions. Second, Fuller posited the reciprocity between government and citizens as opposed to the one-way direction of positivism—that is, commands or rules issued by government to its subjects.

Dworkin. The American scholar Ronald Dworkin also developed a critique of legal positivism. But, instead of directing his attention to the principal issue that characterized the perennial polemics between natural lawyers and legal positivists—whether law should be restricted to morally valid enactments—Dworkin criticized the legal positivists' restriction of "law" to legal rules. Dworkin insisted that law must also include principles. He also criticized legal positivists for their claim that judges make law. Even in "hard cases," states Dworkin, where there is no relevant legal precedent, judges rely on legal principles.

Dworkin distinguished between policies and principles. The term *policies* refers to goals such as social welfare. *Principle* refers to a "requirement of justice" or fairness or some other value; it prevails regardless of whether it advances or secures the public welfare or any economic or political goal. For example, to decrease accidents is a policy; that no one may profit from his wrongdoing is a principle. Dworkin acknowledged that this distinction can be "collapsed"; that is, a principle can be stated in terms of a social goal, and likewise, a policy can be stated in terms of a principle. Still, Dworkin insisted, the distinction between policies and principles is not a merely verbal one; it is important in some contexts. Since *policy* connotes utility, while *principle* means justice, the distinction has had basic importance in moral philosophy.

Dworkin also distinguished *principles* from *rules.* This is a necessary strategy, since his main thesis is that law does not consist only of rules, as the positivists maintain; it also consists of principles. Rules are specific; for example, they prescribe specific speed limits, that a will must have three witnesses, and so on. In addition, said Dworkin, rules operate in an absolute fashion; that is, either the facts in issue fall within a recognized rule or they do not. Principles, on the other hand, are much more general than rules (for example, manufacturers of automobiles have a special obligation to purchasers of their vehicles regarding safety); hence, they do not operate in the mechanical all-or-nothing way that rules operate but, rather, influence the process of judicial decision-making.

The above distinctions between rules and principles have a necessary corollary: Principles may conflict, such as freedom of contract versus the auto manufacturer's obligation to buyers, and they therefore must be given different weights in different contexts. But rules do not have this quality of weight, or general influence. If two rules seem to conflict, one of them must be rejected as invalid. Not so as regards principles. Dworkin admitted that "it is not always clear from the form of a standard whether it is a rule or a principle."

Dworkin's criticism of one positivist thesis—that when a rule does not cover a case, the judge legislates—raises the question of whether principles are law or whether they are extralegal. Dworkin held that principles are a type of law; the legality of principles, he said, is determined by practice, by other principles, by implications of legislation and judicial decisions, and by "community practices and understandings." He seeks the obviously needed precision by citing the doctrines of precedent and legislative "supremacy" and rests finally on "a sense of appropriateness" to support a judge's reliance on a principle.

A writer may, of course, define his terms, and *principle* offers many possibilities. *Principle* has been used in a precise way in the writer's theory of a science of criminal law. That law is comprised of rules, doctrines, and principles. Rules state the specific elements of numerous crimes. Doctrines, such as those regarding insanity, mistake, and coercion, qualify the partial definitions given by the specific rules; that is, they are thought of as excuses that exclude or limit liability. The criminal law of any country is stated when all the doctrines are applied to all the rules. In advanced legal systems there are also legal principles. These are derived from the union of rules and doctrines; that is, in examining that union of norms, one finds that certain broad principles are embodied or expressed in it, such as mens rea, act, harm, and causation. In a very complex system such as the American legal system, it is not easy to think of a principle accepted by a judge that cannot be derived from the union of rules and doctrines.

Dworkin insisted on a strict division of functions between legislators and judges. The former are concerned only with policy, such as the social welfare, while the judge applies only principles, especially those granting the rights of individuals even when they conflict with social interests. The distinction he drew has been employed by moral philosophers who contrast the utilitarian perspective of the legislator with the attention to justice that is allegedly the sole concern of the judge. But even if one grants that justice should

have priority in judicial decisions, it is difficult to avoid the impression that judges (notably those in criminal cases) also have in mind the utilitarian ends of deterrence and rehabilitation. Nor does the restriction of the legislature's function to policy (utility) take account of the fact that the legislature fixes the scale of penalties according to the gravity of the offenses and provides for probation and parole.

Dworkin joined other American critics of utilitarianism, such as Robert Nozick and John Rawls, in making "policy" or utility (the advance of social goals) subordinate to principles that safeguard individual rights. These writers argue that if a man has a legal right, based perhaps on the Bill of Rights, the courts should support that right, regardless of the social consequences of doing that. This position has long been maintained by scholars of criminal law who, like Kant, insisted that the justice of (retributive) punishment should take priority over the utilitarian goals of deterrence and rehabilitation.

Nonetheless, the reasons for the persuasiveness of the utilitarian formulation of legal positivism are obvious. In constitutional democracies it is commonplace to speak of "good laws" and "bad laws." It comes as a shock to users of ordinary language in such societies to be told that only "good laws" are law. Moreover, utilitarianism is a constructive moral philosophy. If a law is bad, the utilitarian will urge its repeal. If much of the system is grossly immoral, he will even endorse revolution. The insistence on clarity, which requires that law and morals be distinguished, also seems persuasive. Thus, the moderate positivism of utilitarianism has had much popular appeal.

The principal support of the natural-law theory that restricts "law" to morally valid enactments and decisions is that this is necessitated by scientific requirements, especially that the relevant generalizations, such as those comprising jurisprudence, must, if valid, be limited to uniform data. Moral principles and values are of maximum importance in the determination of uniformity of the data—that is, positive laws. To include among the data enactments that are morally valid and enactments that are iniquitous is a plain violation of that elementary scientific canon. This was indicated above in the discussion of the theories of Plato and Aquinas, where the use of *law* in ordinary language was distinguished from its philosophic, scientific use, where *law* was limited to conformity with natural law. That makes possible the advance of knowledge of positive law.

SOCIOLOGY OF LAW

An early American representative of the third major school of jurisprudence was Justice Oliver Wendell Holmes, who combined philosophical insight with a felicitous style. Said Holmes,

> Law should draw its postulates and its legislative justification from science.
>
> The prophecies of what the courts will do in fact, and nothing more pretentious, are what I mean by the law.
>
> For the rational study of the law the black-letter man may be the man of the present, but the man of the future is the man of statistics and the master of economics.
>
> It is perfectly proper to regard and study the law simply as a great anthropological document.
>
> We must think things not words, or at least we must constantly translate our words into the facts for which they stand, if we are to keep to the real and the true.
>
> The life of the law has not been logic: it has been experience. The felt necessities of the time, the prevalent moral and political theories, intuitions of public policy, avowed or unconscious, even the prejudices which judges share with their fellow-men, have had a good deal more to do than the syllogism in determining the rules by which men should be governed.

These pithy comments, written between 1895 and 1899, appealed at once to the practical sense of American lawyers and to the philosophical aptitude of the scholars and generated the sociological perspective of jurisprudence, which is the most uniquely American of the three schools.

Pound. Roscoe Pound, a botanist and lawyer, introduced the full stream of European legal philosophy into the United States, and he applied them to the American scene in original ways. In *An Introduction to the Philosophy of Law,* he introduced "sociological jurisprudence." The purpose of law, he proposed, is to protect and maximize social interests with the least possible "friction." His view of the lawyer as a "social

engineer," his pragmatic ethics, his contrast between law in books and law in action, and his theory that law is comprised not only of a prescriptive element but also of ideals, methods, and techniques of adjudication and administration opened many doors to sociological research. Pound's sociological jurisprudence was a composite of philosophical and sociological generalizations applied to legal problems.

In 1930 the publication of Karl Llewellyn's essay "A Realistic Jurisprudence—The Next Step" and of Jerome Frank's book *Law and the Modern Mind* emphasized the importance of facts, a perspective to which many Americans had contributed; and the existence of "American legal realism" was formally announced. In fact, legal realism was not a distinct school of thought; there were only some points of emphasis that distinguished it from the more general work of Pound and Holmes. First, the realists drew sharp distinctions between a court's written opinion and the actual decision. This perspective caused thinkers to consider the extralegal influences on judicial decision-making, especially the judge's philosophy and relevant social and economic problems. This approach to judicial decision-making contrasted sharply with the somewhat naïve view—held at that time in many countries—that the law is fully expressed in the codes and that judges merely find it there and apply it to cases.

A second major contribution, one as significant as that noted above, resulted from the realists' distrust of broad generalizations, their preference for intensive study of narrow problems and for what in American social science has come to be known as middle-range hypotheses. While Pound's work generated trend-generalizations (for example, Pound's five stages in the evolution of the law), the realists delineated and studied narrow sociolegal phenomena. Additional contributions to the sociology-of-law school have been made since the 1930s. Only a few will be noted here to illustrate such work.

Hall. Jerome Hall's *Theft, Law and Society* presents in its first part a cultural history of the law of theft in eighteenth-century England. Such a study necessitates an examination of social, political, economic, and ideological influences, as well as the extant law. The work underscores the need to study not only statutes and decisions but also the way in which law is administered and the relevant practices of lay persons and associations.

The second part of *Theft, Law and Society*, builds on the history in the first part and consists of a study of three current sociolegal problems—receiving stolen property, automobile theft, and embezzlement—from a sociological perspective. Concepts were examined in a functional way. Often, the same terms (for example, *larceny*) continued to be employed but in a very different sense from their previous meaning; and technical, frequently very peculiar, interpretations of statutes were couched in terms of the purposes sought. Several propositions were rigorously formulated, such as that the rate of automobile theft varies directly in proportion to size of population of cities, while that of the thefts "cleared by arrest" is in inverse proportion to the size of population of the cities, and that the percent of prosecutions of known embezzlers varies directly in proportion to the amount of the defalcation and the amount of publicity, and inversely in relation to restitution and the identification of employer with embezzler.

Llewellyn and Hoebel. The collaboration of the legal scholar Karl Llewellyn and the anthropologist Adamson Hoebel produced *The Cheyenne Way*, a work that raises important questions regarding the comparison of advanced legal systems with primitive ones. The book investigates "trouble cases"; the method employed was the interview. Through interpreters, elderly Cheyennes recalled important cases. The underlying notion of *The Cheyenne Way* is that the purpose of law is to prevent and settle serious conflicts that otherwise would threaten the continuity and, eventually, the survival of the group. Llewellyn and Hoebel contended that primitive law can be understood in terms of the functions of law common to it and to advanced systems. The book is replete with descriptive material produced by sensitive inquiry that reflects the authors' " 'feel' of the culture" and bares to intuitive understanding a knowledge of Cheyenne law.

One of the principal contributions of this book is its elucidation of "positive law" from the perspective of their sociology of law. The authors reject "the road of felt or known 'norms.' " The Indians do not think in such conceptual terms; there are wide divergencies between ideal and practical morals; and, in any case, the best way to discover actually operative norms is to study trouble cases, departures from norms, where one can see the violative conduct, what was done about that, how, and by whom—"these are sufficiently significant in what a developed society conceives of as 'law.' " Thus, the authors hold that "the techniques of use of any legal form or rule are, if anything, more important than the form and rule themselves." The only difference between advanced legal systems and primitive law is that the former "has a technical field of discourse." But if that discourse is viewed "as a batch of tools to get jobs done" and if that same instrumental view is applied to rules and methods of procedure, and all of this is set against objectives and problems—that is, seen as part of the machinery of functioning legal institutions—criteria can be discovered that are common to primitive and advanced law. For every legal concept is "an effort at diagnosis of a recurrent social trouble of some particular kind."

Any sociology of law, behavioral, psychological, or humanist, must by definition include factual data within its subject matter. Accordingly, positive law has been viewed as a kind of attitude, as official and other behavior, as decision-making, as a cultural fact, and as a type of action.

In the twentieth century, the expansion of the social sciences and their prominence in the work of scholars in this school have highlighted the need to include empirical, factual observations in any jurisprudence. Jeremy Bentley said that "law is specified activity"; Joseph Bingham, that it includes "principally human actions"; and Llewellyn, that law is "official behavior." But these definitions of law have met with wide criticism because they seem to omit the normativity of law. If the "ought" is taken out of law, what remains is no longer law, critics maintain.

CONCLUSION

A complete legal jurisprudence will include both the empirical-descriptive ("is") and the normative ("ought") dimensions of human behavior. Only a legal philosopher sensitive to these dimensions of experience will be able to construct a full-blown integrated jurisprudence.

Since 1945 many philosophers and social scientists have attempted to make human action the center of their work. This, in the writer's view, has made it possible to create an integrated jurisprudence. The coalescence of law as rules with the factual expression of law as action and with the moral value of action directed toward sound goals must be the postulate of an adequate jurisprudence.

Law as action provides opportunities for scholars to collaborate with moral philosophers and social scientists within the contours of the given datum. Given law as action as its subject matter, jurisprudence can become a genuinely dynamic discipline.

BIBLIOGRAPHY

John Austin, *Lectures on Jurisprudence, or The Philosophy of Positive Law*, edited by Robert Campbell, 4th ed. (1873), is a basic work on analytical jurisprudence. Jeremy Bentham, *An Introduction to the Principles of Morals and Legislation*, edited by J. H. Burns and H. L. A. Hart (1970), is the leading work on utilitarian legal positivism. Benjamin N. Cardozo, *The Nature of the Judicial Process* (1921), contains a great judge's wide-ranging theory of judicial decision. Ronald Dworkin, "Hard Cases," in *Harvard Law Review*, 88 (1975), deals with judicial legislation in difficult cases. Jerome N. Frank, *Law and the Modern Mind* (1963), is a Freudian interpretation of the law. Lon L. Fuller, *The Morality of Law* (1964), is the leading current work supporting a nonscholastic theory of natural law.

John Chipman Gray, *The Nature and Sources of the Law*, 2nd ed. (1921), is the work of an early American positivist, clear and challenging in his theory that law consists only of current judicial decisions. Jerome Hall, *Foundations of Jurisprudence* (1973), contains an analysis of the principal problems leading to a detailed discussion of integrative jurisprudence; and *Theft, Law and Society*, 2nd ed. (1952), emphasizes the context in which law is administered. Herbert L. A. Hart, *The Concept of Law* (1961), defends utilitarian legal positivism, in this most widely discussed book. Wesley N. Hohfeld, *Fundamental Legal Conceptions* (1919), is an acute analysis of jural relations; Arthur L. Corbin, "Legal Analysis and Terminology," in *Yale Law Journal*, 29 (1919), provides a simple summary of Hohfeld's system. Oliver Wendell Holmes, Jr., *The Common Law* (1881); and *Collected Legal Papers* (1920), is a forerunner of sociological jurisprudence, written in a superb style; includes "The Path of the Law" and "Law in Science and Science in Law."

Immanuel Kant, *Critique of Practical Reason*, Lewis W. Beck, trans. (1956); *Foundations of the Metaphysics of Morals*, Lewis W. Beck, trans. (1959); and *The Metaphysical Elements of Justice: Part I of "The Metaphysics of Morals,"* John Ladd, trans. (1965), presents a great philosopher's idealist theory of law. Hans Kelsen, *General Theory of Law and State* (1945) and *Pure Theory of Law* (1934), are major works by the century's leading analytical jurist. Karl Llewellyn, *Jurisprudence: Realism in Theory and Practice* (1962), is an influential work by the most eminent American realist; includes the article "A Realistic Jurisprudence—The Next Step." Karl Llewellyn and Adamson Hoebel, *The Cheyenne Way* (1941), compares advanced legal systems with primitive ones. Robert Nozick, *Anarchy, State, and Utopia* (1974), criticizes utilitarian subordination of the individual's rights to the social good. Plato, *Dialogues*, is here quoted variously in the translations of Benjamin Jowett (1892), A. E. Taylor (1934), J. B. Skemp (1952), and F. M. Cornford (1941). Roscoe Pound, *An Introduction to the Philosophy of Law* (1922), is an introduction by the dean of American legal philosophers. John Rawls, *A Theory of Justice* (1971), an important treatise in political theory, criticizes utilitarianism. Friedrich Karl von Savigny, *On the Vocation of Our Age for Legislation and Jurisprudence* (1831), contains criticism of natural law and advocacy of the historical method based on the spirit of the people.

St. Thomas Aquinas, *Treatise on Law from Questions 90–97 of the Summa Theologica* (1948), is a Christian philosopher's theory of natural law. Max Weber, *On Law in Economy and Society*, translated and edited by M. Rheinstein and E. Shils (1954), discusses the sociology of law by one of the greatest twentieth-century scholars. The Twentieth Century Legal Philosophy series, 8 vols. (1945–1970), offers translations of the leading European and Latin American legal philosophies of the first half of the twentieth century. The best textbooks on American jurisprudence are Edgar Bodenheimer, *Jurisprudence: The Philosophy and Method of Law*, rev. ed. (1974); Wolfgang Gaston Friedmann, *Legal Theory*, 5th ed. (1967); Edwin W. Patterson, *Jurisprudence: Men and Ideas of the Law* (1953); and Harold G. Reuschlein, *Jurisprudence: Its American Prophets* (1951).

[*See also* ADVERSARY SYSTEM; AMERICAN LEGAL CULTURE; BEHAVIORAL STUDIES OF THE AMERICAN LEGAL SYSTEM; CONSTITUTIONAL INTERPRETATION; COURTS AND CONSTITUTIONALISM; HISTORIOGRAPHY OF THE AMERICAN LEGAL SYSTEM; *and* LAW AND MORALITY.]

BEHAVIORAL STUDIES OF
THE AMERICAN LEGAL SYSTEM

Glendon Schubert

THE American "legal system" is much broader in scope than the American "judicial system." The system of courts and judges constitutes a major part of the legal system, the other major components of which include analogous constituent, legislative, executive, and administrative legal subsystems. The focus of discussion here will be on behavioral studies of judges and those with whom they interact.

The American legal system necessarily embraces, given both the developmental history and contemporary political realities of the American Constitution, several distinguishable levels of governance, which for present purposes can be described as national, state, and local. This means that the American "judicial system" subsumes one subsystem of national ("federal") courts; fifty differing (sub)systems of state courts; and, from a functional point of view, thousands of differing sub-subsystems of local courts. Similar remarks can be made about vertical differentiation between constituent assemblies or aggregations of voters; legislatures; chief executives; and administrative bureaucracies. All of these many and diverse subsystems of the American federal governmental system make law and thereby contribute to both the substantive and procedural content of the American legal system. Nor is that all; there are important horizontal interrelationships between various of these lawmaking centers, so that it is necessary to take into consideration the significance of inter-local, as well as interstate, interactions in lawmaking.

This essay is restricted to an understanding of the American legal system on the basis of the many "behavioral" studies that have been made of it, especially by political scientists but also, though to a lesser extent, by sociologists, psy-

chologists, anthropologists, and law professors. It will survey research that has been published since 1960. It is equally concerned with why research gets done (its theory), how it gets done (its techniques of inquiry), and what it purports to have discovered (its empirical findings).

Political behavioralism, the dominant methodology of the period surveyed, reflects the reincarnation, within political science, of theories and research methods developed initially in sociology, psychology, anthropology, and economics and an acceptance of scientific epistemology and the legitimacy of quantification as approaches to the understanding of empirical data. Thus, in the first major political behavioral study of the United States Supreme Court, C. Herman Pritchett began his preface with the remark that his office at the University of Chicago was "one floor above and some thirty feet west of the inscription on the Social Science Research Building which quotes Lord Kelvin's statement that 'When you cannot measure, your knowledge is meager and unsatisfactory' " (1948, xi).

Political behavioral research has been organized around a variety of concepts, including attitudes, culture, groups, personality, rationality, role, and systems. The latter, systems theory, has been extremely important and is the organizing concept for this essay. Systems theory came to political science from biological models of the physiology of complex organisms (such as the human body); but it came indirectly and primarily through the writings of sociologists such as George Homans and Talcott Parsons, as interpreted by such early and leading political systems analysts as David Easton (1953), Gabriel Almond, and William Mitchell (1962).

Easton's (1965) model of a generic political system depicts inputs in the form of both demands placed upon, and support for, decision-makers, which these persons (whom Easton calls the "authorities") convert into output decisions and policies that feed back through the total environment to become transformed (by means of processes that he does not analyze in detail) into new demands and support. Easton's model denotes certain "systems" (ecological, biological, personality, and social) as "intrasocietal"; other systems are described as "international" (political, ecological, and social) or as "extrasocietal." Easton's is one of several systems models of political behavior; alternative examples are Max Weber's bureaucratic model and the mixture of Eastonian and Weberian concepts proposed as a structural-functional approach to political systems by Almond and Coleman.

The systems approach must be understood as a reaction to the model of legal systems anchored in formal institutions, history, and philosophy that is taught in law schools. Sheldon Goldman and Thomas Jahnige remarked,

> A major contribution of legal realism, the sociology of law, and judicial behavior has been to show how great the deviation is between the real behavior of courtroom actors and that posited by the traditional model. Moreover, as an explanation, the traditional model simply cannot explain such crucial events as the "switch" in judicial policy during the Supreme Court's 1936 term or the Nixon Court's marked change of direction, particularly in the criminal procedures area. The killing blow . . . has been the quantitative work that shows better *prediction* of judicial behavior than does the traditional model.
>
> (1976, 290)

The use of Eastonian systems analysis to guide research in the American judicial process was discussed by Goldman and Jahnige (1976) and by Charles Sheldon (1974). One of the earliest explications of Easton's model per se, as applied to judicial systems, was by Walter Murphy in relation to Supreme Court decision-making. In a figure depicting his model, Murphy distinguished between "demands," "threats and sanctions," and "supports" as types of inputs and between "decisions," "opinions," and "informal personal influence" as types of outputs (p. 32). He also included judges in his figure, but other-

wise his drawing repeats Easton's general model, with an encircling environment and feedback (from the impact of outputs on the environment) to inputs.

The first book to be organized on the basis of the Eastonian model was a reader edited by Jahnige and Goldman (1968), which includes some four dozen selections grouped under the main concepts of Easton's theory. The introduction to the work summarizes the theory and presents a figure of the federal judicial system that differs from Murphy's model primarily in substituting three levels of courts (district, appeals, and Supreme) for the nine justices and in defining their outputs as "decisions" and "policies."

Sheldon's 1974 work provides a relatively extensive discussion of Eastonian models of the judicial system, including a figure that makes a different attribution of conversion roles (dividing them among judges; juries; and lawyers as officers of the court) and a much more detailed specification of input categories. It differentiates between "demands" in the categories of legal disputes; lawyers as litigant managers; facts; public opinion; and statutes, constitutions, and rules. It categorizes "supports" as being either "diffuse" (including image of law, respect, deference, consensus, and apathy) or "specific" (that is, winners and losers in dispute, elites, and media). Sheldon pointed out that an Eastonian system has been analogized to an organism that must cope with environmental stresses and strains. But that is of course a metaphor: it is a mistake to place literal interpretations upon analogies between the conditions of biological life and the circumstances under which social groups and institutions change through time. Sheldon also pointed out that "the judicial process involves a variety of delays, appeals, pleadings, counterpleadings, continuances, dismissals, reversals, and remands which are forms of feedback within the system itself. [Easton's] simple systems model concentrates on that feedback which occurs following decision, thus ignoring the many internal feedbacks" (p. 170). Every biological organism must stay within the limits of the respective ranges for a host of interacting organic systems if it is to continue to exist.

Schubert (1974a) proposed a systems model of judicial policymaking that differs from the others described above by putting much greater emphasis upon the psychological processes in terms of which individual decision-makers join together to convert into outputs their own cognitions and perceptions.

A MODEL OF THE JUDICIAL SUBSYSTEM

The major concepts of Eastonian systems theory include environment, inputs, conversion, outputs, and feedback. These concepts provide a convenient vehicle for organizing behavioral studies of the past generation. Of course, those studies themselves are by no means necessarily based on systems theory in either theory or method. Before beginning the survey, however, several caveats must be stressed. In systems theory, there is a postulated flow of behavioral communications and consequences as issues move from one of these conceptual states to another; the design of that flow is linear and unidirectional. But in the real world, judicial behavior and its communications and consequences are transactional, convoluted, and multidimensional —vastly more complex than any theory can encompass. Therefore, for both analytic and heuristic reasons a certain amount of oversimplification must occur in order to be able to reduce the complexity of the subject to what is feasible for exposition. Furthermore, the American judicial system, upon which we shall focus, is by no means the only American legal system. Law is made by a variety of nonjudicial actors, including voters, legislatures, chief executives, administrative agencies, and, from time to time, elected constituent assemblies that meet to propose or approve changes in the explicit language of constitutional documents. Lawmaking, then, in the political environment of the judicial system is a broader phenomenon than that which takes place through the agency of courts and judges.

Finally, the judicial system is a kind of megasystem, which itself includes diverse subsystems, such as the United States Supreme Court, the federal courts of appeals and district courts, specialized courts, offices of judicial management, military tribunals, and state and local court systems.

ENVIRONMENTAL CONSTRAINTS OF THE LEGAL SYSTEM

The environment for American courts and judges is a complex mixture of natural, cultural, social, economic, and political components, any of which may constrain judges at a particular point in space and time. As William Daniels has shown, geography always has influenced such policy decisions as who gets selected for appointment to the United States Supreme Court and where and how circuit boundaries are defined from time to time for organizing the lower federal courts. Daniels confirms what even a rudimentary understanding of American history would lead one to expect: the initial political division was between the northern and southern states, with the latter dominant in their influence upon the federal judiciary, but throughout the nineteenth century, change was primarily in the direction of movement to the west (and, secondarily, from south to north). But that observation in turn reveals that geography followed the lead of demographic change; and probably until the mid-twentieth century, much of the relevant environment for American courts could be explained in terms of such traditional socioeconomic variables as industrialization, urbanization, and national territorial expansion.

By the 1980s, however, such classical environmental phenomena no longer sufficed as explanations of the major external influences upon the judicial systems of the United States. The new environment for American courts is one conditioned by extraterrestrial national expansion not merely in the quest for communications and other technological superiority but also in the explicit context of a national political anxiety. Other widely accepted reinforcing components of American political anxiety include the domestic and international economy (with the exponentially escalating national debt), widespread recession and chronic underemployment, exacerbating foreign-exchange problems, and, of course, nuclear weapons. The period has also witnessed an unprecedented mobilization and voting participation of blacks, Hispanics, and women. Among the probable consequences for the judiciary is that the inequitable representation of blacks, Hispanics, and women in the Supreme Court and elsewhere in the court system will shift to less-biased membership in succeeding decades.

The kinds of attitudinal, political, and demographic changes noted above redefine the environment that constrains the kinds of policy issues that can get to all kinds of courts for decision and the kinds of social dispositions that are made of those policy issues. Such judicial dispositions in turn stimulate the feedback that determines what effect present decisions by courts will have upon subsequent inputs to courts.

Federal Courts. The specific political environment of the United States Supreme Court is discussed by Schubert (1970), and the federal courts generally, by James Eisenstein. For the federal district courts, there is an excellent book by Robert Carp and C. K. Rowland, in which both new and secondary information is presented about environmental influences. They focus on such "old environmental" components as court geography and urbanization and find that circuit and district boundaries tend to be based on historically important markers of subcultural sociopolitical differences and to segregate federal judges into groups that are differentiated in terms of their values and behavior. Though the sources of legal information currently make possible universal dissemination of at least formal law, district judges rely almost entirely on intracircuit (rather than intercircuit) information channels; these are adequate to inform, control, and provide support for judges within a circuit. This same process also operates (although almost entirely through informal channels) within districts where more than one judge is assigned.

Carp and Rowland made a systematic investigation of differences in the ideology of federal district judges in terms of major geographic regions and over a period of forty-four years, based on their analysis of these judges' decisions. The most liberal group consisted of those from the ten states classified as "eastern," and the most conservative, of those from the seventeen states designated as "southern." The eastern judges upheld claims of civil liberties at an overall average rate of 55 percent, and they decided in favor of economic liberalism at the even higher rate of 63 percent; the corresponding average percentages for judges from the South were about 10 percentage points lower for each category, at 44 percent for civil liberties and 53

percent for economic liberalism. But controlling for the political party affiliation of the federal judges, combining both civil liberties and economic cases, and focusing their attention only upon differences between judges from the South and all others (whom they designated as from "the North"), Carp and Rowland found that nonsouthern Democrats were the most liberal group of judges (49 percent pro) and southern Republicans were the least liberal, with only 33 percent support for general liberalism in their decisions. They concluded that there are regional differences within each of the two major political parties and that there are likewise political party differences in the South and elsewhere in the country.

Carp and Rowland expected to find a positive correlation between urbanism and judicial liberalism, because they hypothesized metropolitan centers to be "more pluralist" and heterogeneous than rural areas and (as they inferred from small-group theory) that urban federal district judges (because of their denser congregation) provide psychological support for each other while enjoying "a greater degree of anonymity" in their relationship to their district public. Their data show that the correlation that they hypothesized did not show up for most of the issues examined but did for racial discrimination and local economic regulation.

Carp and Rowland also ranked two dozen of the largest cities in the country in terms of their support for liberalism (that is, regarding civil liberties, criminal justice, and/or economic issues) of the federal judges in the districts that included these cities. Minneapolis and Milwaukee were tied as most liberal toward civil liberties and economic issues (and overall), although both were only moderate in their criminal-justice liberalism. At the other extreme, Saint Louis (followed closely by Oklahoma City) was in the least liberal rank (or the next one to it) across all three issues. Kansas City—closer to both Saint Louis and Oklahoma City than they are to each other, although all three are heartland cities—had a low-moderate score across all three issues. Chicago and Newark, both sites of political trials in the late 1960s, scored quite differently. Chicago ranked as liberal on criminal justice and high moderate on civil liberties, but Newark was in the least liberal group on both issues.

This research demonstrates that all American

court trials are "political"—that is, influenced by their political environments. All of them also are, from another perspective, "legal." Some cases will be minimally legal and minimally political; some few others will be maximally legal and maximally political; and alternatively there will be cases that are maximally legal but minimally political, and others that are minimally legal but maximally political. The vast majority of cases will fall in the more moderate ranges of both the legal and the political dimensions. But the (quantitatively very rare) cases involving revolutionary activists, such as the trial of the "Chicago Eight" in 1969–1970, will typically be minimally legal and maximally political.

Herbert Kritzer studied the impact of local environmental political factors on what he hypothesized to be a particularly sensitive aspect of federal district court decision-making: the sentencing of criminal defendants who had resisted selective-service induction during the Vietnam War. As an example of the effects of national cultural political factors, Kritzer observed that "as troop levels rose, prison sentences increased in length [but] that prison sentences began to drop *before* de-escalation actually started" (emphasis added). Kritzer found that the most important predictor of sentencing appears to be the local political culture, while the backgrounds of judges are the least important. Judges in more-progressive states tended to sentence more leniently.

Beverly Cook (1983) also discussed the effect of geographic differences upon the sentencing of conscientious objectors during the Vietnam War. She found that the most severe sentences were given in the fourteen states that she identified as "South," "Border," and "Frontier" and characterized as "traditional" in culture.

State Courts. The most elaborate study of environmental variables on state-level judicial policymaking was done by Burton Atkins and Henry Glick. They explicitly assumed that "courts share policymaking with legislatures and administrative agencies." Consequently, they took as their measures of the socioeconomic and political environment half a dozen factors that had been derived from extensive research in policy studies of all major branches of the state governments generally. Two of these factors, or independent variables, focused on political characteristics: "professionalism" measured the salary levels of

public officials and their staffs, and "competition" measured the extent of competition between (or within) political parties, in relation to the degree of electoral participation by voters. One socioeconomic dimension was "industrialization" (the proportion of a state's population involved in manufacturing and the contribution of manufacturing to per capita wealth); another, "affluence," was indexed by average degree of attained education, with the northern part of the country substantially higher than the southern—at the time of the original studies in the mid-1960s. Of the remaining two dimensions, "welfare" dealt with the relative amounts states spent on public assistance, and "highway/natural resources" compared the extent of state highway mileage and funding to expenditures for conservation and natural recreational purposes. These six independent variables were employed to examine state-level decision-making in the areas of civil liberties, criminal justice, and economic regulation. Atkins and Glick also studied the impact of these variables on cases that involved private economic and private noneconomic issues.

Their results showed that for judicial decision-making in favor of civil liberties, the most important positive environmental influences were affluence and professionalism; strong negative effects were attributed to highways and industrialization. Competition and welfare had little or no effect. Stated otherwise, the judges most supportive of civil liberties belonged to the highest state courts of wealthy but nonindustrialized states with well-paid governmental officials and with an emphasis on natural recreation rather than on highway development. But the pattern for economic liberalism in state judicial policymaking was quite different: the environment conducive to that result was one in which states were highly industrialized, with strong highway systems, and had substantial wealth but poorly paid public officials and civil servants; and for such states neither political competition nor welfare expenditures had much effect upon judicial economic liberalism in their highest state courts. The impact of these factors on criminal justice cases was inconclusive.

Relatively sparsely populated and rural states decided high proportions of cases concerned with private-issue policy problems, whereas in the densely populated, industrialized, politically competitive states, state supreme courts were preoccupied with the same types of policy issues that prevail in the federal courts: civil liberties, criminal justice, and economic regulation.

Atkins and Glick comment that

> as political and economic diversification generates alterations in the universe of litigation, supreme courts restructure their decisional priorities to meet changing demand patterns. . . . [Thus] the appearance of larger proportions of civil liberties, criminal law, and particularly economic regulation cases may be indicative of judicial systems which have remained attuned to changing patterns of demands entering the political system from the differentiated political and socioeconomic environment.

A comparative study of the social, political, and legal environments of three city courts also concluded that there were systematic differences in their degree of politicization, conformity to legal norms, and the professional aloofness of judges from the lawyers who practiced before them. John Paul Ryan and his associates conducted field survey research in 1976 in Philadelphia, Chicago, and Los Angeles. The Chicago courts were characterized as highly sensitive to local partisan politics and circuit-court litigation. Philadelphia also was politicized, but neither in the same way nor to the same degree as Chicago; the Republican party remained much stronger in many of the city wards as well as elsewhere in the state, and no mayor in modern times had been able to unite control of the Democratic party and control over the city as Richard Daley had in Chicago. Los Angeles was characterized as a metropolitan environment that was much more decentralized politically and, at the same time, much more professionalized legally, resulting in bipartisan selection of judges, more-formal relations between judges and lawyers, much more reliance upon jury (as compared to nonjury) trials, and an ethic of administrative efficiency (as contrasted to the Chicago ethic of political efficacy).

INPUTS TO COURTS

When the judicial process is considered in terms of systems theory, two major factors can be conceived in terms of inputs to the system—the judges, who are primary actors in the system, and the cases that are brought to the judges for disposition. Studies, then, that can be grouped under the rubric "input" consider who the judges are, what they believe, and how they are selected, since all of these factors clearly have an impact on the positions judges take in the system. Similarly, in considering cases as inputs, one must examine the structures and processes that allow cases into the system for processing as well as those which exclude some types of cases from judicial purview—the concept of "jurisdiction," for example. Also related to the notion of input is the part lawyers play in framing and arguing cases before judges, since the words, legal strategies, and attitudes of the lawyers can in turn affect the willingness of the judges to accept a case and decide it in a certain fashion.

Characteristics and Selection of Federal and State Judges. The background characteristics (attributes) of federal judges are discussed in books by the two leading authorities on the subject, John Schmidhauser and Sheldon Goldman (in Goldman and Jahnige). Of the more than one hundred Supreme Court justices to date, it could be said until very recently that virtually all were white males of northern European ancestry who had received the best training in law available at the time of their formal legal education; who tended to have been raised in civic-minded, politically active, economically well-off families; and most of whom had been raised in higher-status Protestant denominations and had had considerable-to-extensive personal political experience prior to appointment to the Supreme Court.

But that situation had begun to change by the time of the Warren Court, and most dramatically perhaps when the first black was appointed to the Supreme Court in 1967. For the next two terms (1968–1969), that Court reached its transitory peak in the representation of justices of "humble birth," with (for the first time in its history) a majority of five justices whose families were poor and working-class in socioeconomic terms, including one who was the great-grandson of a slave and the son of a Pullman conductor (Thurgood Marshall) and others whose parents included another railroad worker, poor Irish immigrants, an ill-paid minister who died when his son was five years old, and an impoverished storekeeper. But seventeen years later, at the opening of the 1984–1985 term, that majority had been reduced to only three persons—Marshall, liberal Democrat William J. Brennan, and conservative Republican Chief Justice Warren Burger. The data for the 1967–1969 terms are important because that period was also the first and only time in the history of the Supreme Court when an absolute majority of the incumbent justices were liberals. This implies a high positive correlation between a justice's having been raised in a working-class household and his own empathy in political and economic ideology as an adult. Other attributes that have been used to predict the attitudes and behavior of the contemporary justices of the Supreme Court are partisanship, education, legal training and experience, age, sex, ethnicity, religion, and residence.

Jerome Corsi reported systematic information concerning the attributes of all federal district and appeals court judges, grouped according to the appointing president (Dwight D. Eisenhower through Jimmy Carter). His data for Carter's appointments show that for from 45 percent to 47 percent of the district and appeals appointees their previous major occupation had been judicial, and for from 27 percent to 35 percent it had been work in a large law firm. From 54 percent to 55 percent had had judicial experience, and from 32 percent to 39 percent had been prosecutors. From 90 percent to 94 percent of them were Democrats—but for the earlier Richard Nixon appointments, from 92 percent to 93 percent were Republicans. From 60 percent to 73 percent had been political activists, and it was the appeals judges who constituted the more activist of the two groups. The Carter-appointee religious affiliations were predominately Protestant (58 percent to 61 percent,) with 23 percent to 28 percent Roman Catholic, and 13 percent to 16 percent Jewish. Their ethnicity is not given, but "race" was reported as white (79 percent), black (14 percent to 16 percent), Hispanic (4 percent to 7 percent), and Asian (0.5 percent to 2 percent). Sex was 80 percent to 86 percent male, and 14 percent to 20 percent female.

Female federal judges were discussed in two notable articles. Cook (1982) surveyed the complete universe of female Supreme Court candidates over the relevant period of half a century, beginning in the early New Deal era. The first serious female aspirant to the Supreme Court was Florence Allen, whose background and career Cook (1981, 1982) has described in some detail. Allen was preeminently well suited and qualified, at least in terms of social, educational, and legal-professional criteria, for appointment to the Court; her father was a lawyer-politician; her mother, a member of the first class at Smith College, was an early and active feminist; and Allen's personal and family friendships included the two justices who between them occupied the seventh position on the Court for more than twenty years—ultraliberal peace activist Democrat John Clarke of Ohio and ultraconservative Republican George Sutherland of Utah. Such credentials would seem more than sufficient today, but "Allen's active self-candidacy faltered against the resistance of public opinion and the disinterest of the president [Franklin Roosevelt]" (1982). Florence Allen had to settle for appointment, in 1934, as a judge of the Court of Appeals for the Sixth Circuit. Cook's article provides equivalent information about Sandra Day O'Connor, the first woman to be appointed to the Supreme Court. Among the virtues of Cook's article is the insight that she provides into the relevant changes in both the national legal and political cultures that made the appointment of O'Connor or another woman not merely possible but almost inevitable.

The next female federal judge (after Florence Allen) received her position fifteen years later when Harry Truman appointed Burnita Matthews to the District Court for the District of Columbia. Then it was thirteen years before Lyndon Johnson persuaded John Kennedy to appoint sixty-six-year-old Sarah T. Hughes—a longtime personal friend and political associate of Johnson—to the District Court for the Northern District of Texas. Johnson subsequently appointed Shirley Hufstedler, a California state supreme court judge, to the United States Court of Appeals for the Ninth Circuit and two women as federal district judges; Nixon and Gerald Ford each appointed one female district judge but no women as appeals judges. The modern era of fairer employment in the federal judiciary begins with Jimmy Carter, who appointed forty-one women to the federal courts: twenty-nine to district courts and eleven to courts of appeals, plus one to the Tax Court. This was four times the number of women appointed by all of his predecessors combined.

An analysis by Elaine Martin of Carter's appointments shows that women were much more likely than men to have had previous judicial experience, although men were much more likely than women to have been political activists, and that men were much more likely to have had experience working for large law firms, while women had worked in law firms of small to moderate size. Martin explained all of these differences in terms of the opportunities for legal practice open to women, as compared to men, during the 1950s and 1960s: the big law firms would not hire women, so it was difficult enough for them to get into any kind of private practice. Neither were women welcomed in other than a menial capacity by either the Democratic or the Republican party, so that few could become political activists, whatever their abilities or inclination. Consequently, female lawyers went into government practice, and since most of them had had to have superior academic abilities in order to have gotten into law school in the first place, they found it easier to pass bar screening and become judges than to go into politics.

Corsi also reported data on legal education and law-school admissions; and since all federal judges are lawyers and law-school graduates, who gets into law school is virtually determinative of who has any chance of becoming any kind of federal judge. Corsi's data show that in 1965, women constituted only 4 percent of total law-school enrollment; but by 1980, more than a third of all law students were women; and although Corsi's data end with 1980, it appears that that proportion has continued to increase since then. Clearly, then, environmental influences constrain the inputs—including what kinds of persons the judges themselves will be—of the American judicial system.

The attributes of state supreme court judges who held office during the 1960s were analyzed by Bradley Canon (1972). The average age of those judges was sixty-two, and their average tenure was thirteen years; just about all were white males, and they were predominantly of Anglo-Saxon ethnicity and Protestant in religious affiliation. Almost all of them were law-school graduates, a majority from state universities but about a sixth from the most prestigious law schools. They tended to be local in both birth and education (less than 9 percent had been socialized out of state) and to have originated in rural areas of their home state. Almost all of them had prior state governmental experience, as a prosecutor, legislator, trial or appellate judge, or attorney general (or assistant attorney general).

A subsequent study of state trial judges (Ryan et al.) surveyed the entire country in 1976. This study confirmed that, as in the case of state supreme court judges, the occupational route to the bench was through governmental service, with a majority having had private legal practice, 24 percent experience as a lower-court judge, about 10 percent as prosecutors, and slightly more than 10 percent as other types of public officials. But less than 3 percent had practiced criminal law as defense attorneys. A majority were Democrats, and more than a third were Republicans (as a nationwide average); but the proportion of Democrats was much higher in the South (82 percent) even in the mid-1970s—and obviously it would be substantially less than that a decade later, so the balance between Republicans and Democrats was closer elsewhere in the country except on a per state basis where many one-party states (such as Democratic Hawaii) obtained. Their average age at the time they became trial judges was forty-six; but their average age at the time of the survey was fifty-three. Almost all (96 percent) were white; only 3 percent of these trial judges were black, and they were concentrated in a few metropolitan centers outside the South; and less than 1 percent were Asian-American or Native American. In the late 1970s, 98 percent of American state trial-court judges were males; the women judges were concentrated, like the black males, in metropolitan regions of the West and the Northeast.

The study reports that both women and blacks —but especially the latter—allocate part of their own (unofficial) time to community relations work; but no statistical control for urbanization was mentioned, so the finding may reflect the concentration of women and blacks in highly urbanized environments as much as it does sociopsychological characteristics of blacks or women. In seeming confirmatory generalization of Schmidhauser's (1959) pioneering study of the attributes of United States Supreme Court justices, the Ryan study indicates that many state trial judges come from legal or political families, which is the "occupational heredity" of which Schmidhauser wrote. The study also noted complex interrelationships between subcultural regions of the country, political activism, and the career development of state judges, in that "in the Northeast, where judges are generally older at the time of their selection, a trial judgeship is likely to be a reward for past political service or lower court apprenticeship, whereas in the South the office of trial judge has proven to be a potential stepping stone to higher political office" (p. 141).

A study by Susan Carbon, Pauline Houlden, and Larry Berkson surveyed the entire population of 549 female state judges in 1980. These judges were found to be five years younger (forty-eight) than males, on the average, but not all that different ethnically: more than 92 percent were white, 7 percent black, and less than 1 percent Native American, Hispanic, or Asian-American. Neither did they differ substantially in partisanship, with almost two-thirds Democrats and about a fourth Republicans; but only 10 percent had been active in party politics. And they did differ from their male counterparts in ideology: these women judges were liberal in their attitudes by more than 2:1, with 31 percent either liberal or very liberal, and only 14 percent conservative or very conservative. One in seven had attended one of the best law schools, and about one in six had been a law professor; but two-thirds of the majority that had law firm experience had been associated with small law firms. Forty percent had experience working as government lawyers, but 31 percent had held office in state bar associations, and one in ten had clerked with a state judge. Most of them held office in large cities and in appellate courts rather than as trial judges or in less populous areas.

The selection of judges is a complex process that also has an impact on the makeup of the federal and state benches and, thus, on the inputs to the American legal system. The process centers around the political response to the stimulus provided by the likelihood or the certainty of vacancies arising in existing or, in the case of lower courts, potential judicial positions. Typically this involves the presidency; both major political parties; various interest groups (depending on the time and place); frequently, incumbent justices and/or judges; the Department of Justice; the American Bar Association; the news media (and in a major way in this age of investigative journalism); public opinion; indi-

vidual United States senators; and especially the Senate Judiciary Committee and its chairperson (although ultimately, the Senate generally). For lower-court federal judges (as compared to Supreme Court justices), the process usually is both less intense and less an issue of national public policy, but there have been many exceptions, involving either low-key Supreme Court appointments or high-key appointments to district judgeships.

William Hulbary and Thomas Walker undertook a systematic examination of the relevant data, most of which had been published since 1969. They were able to include the complete universe of eighty-four justices who were on the United States Supreme Court for at least five years from 1789 through 1967. Concerning the choice of particular nominees, they classified presidential motives into three categories of criteria: traditional, political, and professional. Their objective was to determine through statistical analysis the extent to which any or all of the criteria had an important effect upon the official performance of the justices. That performance was based on subjective interrater consensus among a group of sixty-five experts who had been asked (independently, by two other scholars, in studies published before the design of the 1980 article discussed here) to rank all of the justices on a scale using the categories "great," "near great," "average," "below average," and "failure."

For the independent variables, the "traditional" criteria included the candidate's ideology, geography, age, and religion, all in relation to the president's own preferences. The "political" criteria included membership in the same political party as the president, whether the president believed that making a particular appointment would benefit himself, whether the president wanted to make a particular appointment to pay off obligations incurred earlier, and whether the candidate was a crony of the president. "Professional" criteria included legal distinction, including (during the 1950s and 1960s) a favorable ABA report; the candidate's record of public service; and the candidate's judicial experience.

The evidence showed that presidents most frequently selected "outstanding" justices when they purposely ignored both geography and ideology (which these authors call "political philosophy") and when they disregarded any difference between the candidate's religion and their own preference. Indeed, a composite test for rejecting at least one of the traditional criteria also (necessarily) showed a similar result. Disregarding geography produced even more impressive judges, though sample sizes were very small (that is, three instances where presidents disregarded ideological differences, two where they disregarded religious differences, and fourteen where they disregarded geography). Overwhelmingly, presidents did seek ideological agreement in their appointees and were concerned with their nominees' religion; but they disregarded geography almost a third of the time, and they disregarded "optimal" age more than 85 percent of the time.

Presidents almost always considered ideological congruence more important than political selfishness or payoff considerations, but they did indulge in cronyism about a third of the time. All to little avail, however, because these political criteria were all poorly and insignificantly correlated with performance, as measured by Hulbary and Walker.

Most relevant of all turned out to be the professional criteria of legal distinction (which presidents favored in almost two-thirds of their choices) and judicial experience (which they paid no attention to half of the time). The best predictor of good performance came from the combination of preferring legal distinction but disregarding prior judicial service, which explained even more of the variance than did disregarding geography (and was equally significant). Their conclusion was that "Presidents who consciously make appointments consistent with the traditional norms tend to nominate persons approximating the average quality of the justices as a group. However, when a President specifically rejects the traditional criteria, when he consciously appoints individuals who would be disqualified under the traditional norms, the result tends to be a justice of superior quality." The authors found no instances of a president deliberately rejecting the professional criteria by looking for someone who would be poorly qualified in those terms—but they surely would have discovered some relevant examples if they had been looking also at the universe of appointments to the lower federal courts. Moreover, all of the authors' conclusions necessarily hinge

upon the validity of their dependent variable. More-objective measures of judicial "greatness" —such as would take into account the impact of the judges' decisions in other policy arenas than that of the elite audience of "Court-watchers" at a particular time—might result in very different conclusions about the relative importance of traditional, political, and professional criteria.

A 1980 behavioral study by Wayne Sulfridge on Senate action on presidential nominations to the federal judiciary concludes that "once a nomination becomes controversial, [then] the ideological position of a senator is a major factor in . . . how he will vote." Sulfridge discusses the principal reasons associated with rejections, which have been few during the twentieth century, observing that even nominees generally believed to be staunch conservatives proposed by conservative Republican presidents have been confirmed with little or no opposition by heavily Democratic and generally liberal Senates. His study then focuses on four controversial cases: those of Abe Fortas, William Rehnquist, G. Harrold Carswell, and Clement Haynsworth. The author studied the voting behavior of individual senators in relation to the above four nominees, using the scale (conservative–liberal) developed by the interest group Americans for Constitutional Action (ACA) based on legislators' votes on various issues. The nominees themselves are readily scaled from most liberal to most conservative in the sequence Fortas, Haynsworth, Carswell, and Rehnquist. They were grouped together for purposes of the analysis, so that a vote for Fortas was classified "liberal," as were votes against the other three nominees, and vice versa for "conservative" Senate votes.

The resulting information shows a clear and consistent relationship between the ACA ratings of individual senators and the extent to which those senators voted conservatively on the confirmation of these controversial nominations to the Supreme Court. The data presented indicate that charges of ideological extremism against a nominee are sufficient to generate a controversy over his nomination but, at least for these four cases, for rejection to occur, additional charges of unethical behavior had to be raised and supported with evidence.

Appointment by the governor (usually in combination with ABA preselection) is the state judicial-selection analogue of the presidential system for selecting federal judges. It is used in less than half of the states; a majority of the states use either partisan or nonpartisan elections.

Carbon and her associates presented data on the number of women selected for state judgeships, which, when matched with information about the numbers of states using various different methods, make possible the following observations: 115 women judges in Carbon's sample were elected (either partisan or nonpartisan) to office in the twenty-four states using that method, whereas 176 women became judges in the slightly lesser number (twenty-two) of states that use gubernatorial appointment (with or without the Missouri Plan). Evidently women are one and a half times more likely to become judges in states that rely on appointment than in those with popular election as the method of selection, no doubt because of the structural bias against the financing and institutional support of female candidates that has characterized state (and federal) elections generally in the past.

Sheldon (1977) surveyed the state bar associations to ascertain both the extent and manner of their organizations' participation in the selection of judges in their respective states and their opinions concerning the effectiveness of their activities. His data show that most states use one or more of three methods: rating polls by the bar membership that are publicized before elections take place; the Missouri Plan, whereby a bar committee makes nominations to the governor; and /or nomination by the governor in relation to the investigation and evaluation of nominees (or proposed nominees) by a bar committee. A few of the states that use one or more of these methods join with five other states in the use of one or more of the following much less commonly employed methods: solicited endorsements (by members of the bar) of candidates; rating polls (by bar membership) of candidates; and/or solicitation of candidacy (by leaders of the bar) of bar membership. In the remaining six states no formal bar activity is undertaken in relation to the selection of state judges.

Sheldon's data support the following generalizations: (1) the Missouri Plan succeeded in giving the largest degree of influence to state bar associations; (2) the other two most popular methods (publicized rating polls by bar membership, and investigation and selection by bar association committee of gubernatorial nominations)

and endorsement by bar leaders are the next most effective methods for state bars to use; and (3) relatively least effective were the solicitation of candidacies or of the endorsement of candidates. Sheldon also compared the degree of politicization of the five principal means of selection to the degree of influence that the bar had in each (which involved reordering of the data as organized for purposes of the eight categories of bar participation discussed above). The scale of "politicization" that he postulated was (ranging from most to least) (1) partisan election, (2) legislative selection, (3) gubernatorial appointment, (4) nonpartisan election, and (5) the "merit" (Missouri) plan. Sheldon concluded that "the inverse relationship between bar and political party appears not to be exact." In fact, the conclusion is clear that there is no relationship whatsoever between degree of politicization and the effectiveness of the bar in influencing judicial selection.

The selection of state judges by popular election (partisan; nonpartisan; and "merit retention," where an incumbent runs against his or her record) was studied by Philip Dubois, whose data confirm that voter participation in judicial elections is highest in partisan elections, markedly less in nonpartisan, and least in merit retention. He also found that in those states that changed from partisan to merit-retention elections, voter participation declined by about a third, on the average. If Dubois is correct, his findings imply that nonpartisan and merit-retention elections are much less democratic than partisan elections because they entail much lower voter participation, with the result that effective choice is turned over to a single interest group —and at that, the one that has the biggest stake in judicial elections: the professional organizations of lawyers.

Cases as Inputs. Questions of access to the Supreme Court and its jurisdictional decision-making are complex and the subject of considerable research. Gregory Caldeira (1981) studied the period between 1935 and 1976, using all of the criminal justice cases decided with opinion and on the merits, to test a dozen or so hypotheses about why the Court decided the volume of cases that it did, when it did so. He found that the Court does not appear to respond to the general level of crime or changes in that level in determining how many criminal cases it will decide from term to term. Nor does it respond to increases in the number of criminal cases appealed to it, at least from term to term. The Court does, however, respond to publicity about crime, but only after a four-year lag and then in an inverse manner, deciding fewer relevant cases as the level of relevant publicity increases. But it does not respond to changes in media publicity about crime, nor does it respond to the general level of public concern about crime. The Court ignores public opinion in determining how many criminal cases it will decide from term to term. Furthermore, changes in the rest of the Court's case load have no effect on the number of criminal cases decided, and the Court does not respond to policy-relevant criteria, in determining, for example. Democratic courts do not pay more attention to criminal cases than do Republican courts. However, ideology, rather than party affiliation, does make a difference: a Court dominated by liberals is significantly more likely to decide more criminal cases than one controlled by conservatives. The volume of criminal cases decided also varies with change in the chief-justiceship. Caldeira also observed that his data on four decades of cases support a "life-cycle" hypothesis: Supreme Court attention to any particular subject of public policy wanes over time.

It is notable that the only positive predictor of judicial response to a criminal case load revealed by Caldeira's analysis was that both the volume and direction of the Court's criminal justice decisions are determined by ideological differences in regard to that issue among incumbent justices. This confirms a considerable body of earlier behavioral research on the Supreme Court (such as Schubert, 1959, 1965a, 1974b).

Another kind of input comes from the participation of lawyers in their presentation of cases to courts. Neil McFeeley and Richard Ault undertook a pioneering exploratory study of oral argument before the Supreme Court, which had been virtually ignored in previous behavioral studies of the Court. Oral argument is important because it probably provides the most important source of inputs for directly influencing uncommitted justices as to how they should vote and may persuade a previously decided justice to change his or her mind. Oral argument also places the justices in an interactive mode in which they initiate questions (or comments) that

counsel must answer (or avoid or suffer) and thus reveals in a highly social context much behavioral (including cognitive) information about justices that cannot be observed through studies of opinion and/or voting behavior per se.

McFeeley and Ault analyzed the stenographic transcripts of the oral argument in ten of the eleven major obscenity decisions of the Supreme Court during the period 1957–1968. The authors coded the remarks of judges into the following categories: substantive questions; repetition; leading questions; procedural questions; tangential questions; hypothetical questions; and statements that were substantive/factual, rephrasal, challenging, distortive, or "asides"; and interruptions. They found that there were striking individual differences in the extent to which, and the manner in which, justices participated in oral argument in regard to the particular policy issue that was sampled. One of the fourteen justices, Felix Frankfurter, overwhelmingly preempted discussion on the Court's side of the bench in the four cases out of the ten in which he participated before his retirement; in those four cases his remarks constituted between 43 percent to 63 percent of all verbal behavior emanating from the bench. The authors also remarked that "there was a qualitative as well as a quantitative element to Justice Frankfurter's domination of the proceedings." Brennan, who had managed a participational rate of only 7 percent while speaking in Frankfurter's presence, managed to escalate his performance more than threefold with Frankfurter permanently in absentia. The other justices who tended to participate more than others included Fortas, Arthur J. Goldberg, Earl Warren, and Potter Stewart; evidently most of them (Frankfurter, Brennan, and Fortas) were moderates on the issue of obscenity, although not necessarily in their more general ideological posture, while two (Goldberg and Stewart) were liberals; Warren was the only conservative in regard to the issue of obscenity.

Three of the justices, two conservatives (Thomas C. Clark and Harold H. Burton) and one moderate (Charles Whittaker) were underparticipators. The remaining five justices (Hugo Black, William O. Douglas, John M. Harlan, Byron White, and Marshall) all participated closer to the average level for the group as a whole; but two of them were, in addition, highly selective in the cases in which they chose to participate at all.

Other students of the judicial process have also noted the effects of courts of appeal, which act as filters to control case input to the Supreme Court of the United States. J. Woodford Howard gave a detailed report on three federal courts of appeals based on interviews with thirty-five of the judges during 1969–1971 and extensive analyses of their decisions and related data. For one three-year sample of almost five thousand cases, the three courts affirmed two-thirds and reversed the decision below in about a fifth of the total. About 20 percent of these five thousand cases were appealed to the Supreme Court, which accepted 9 percent, of which it then reversed in whole or in part two-thirds (1.2 percent of the total sample). The three tribunals then became courts of last resort in 98 percent of the cases and made decisions that formally prevailed in 98.6 percent. Thus, "the Courts of Appeals normally went about their business without close surveillance by their superiors or effective challenge by their constituents" (p. 76). Inputs to the federal courts of appeals generally were discussed by Goldman and Jahnige, who summarized the findings of most of the behavioral studies on that subject through 1975.

Lawrence Baum, Sheldon Goldman, and Austin Sarat traced both the qualitative and quantitative changes in the case-load input of what are now three of the most important federal courts of appeals—the Second in New York, the Fifth in New Orleans, and the Ninth in San Francisco. The authors took fifty-case random samples at five-year intervals over a period of eighty years (1895–1975). The average annual case load for all of the federal courts of appeals increased from fewer than one thousand in 1895 to about eleven thousand in 1970. The qualitative changes in case loads were equally dramatic: during the initial two-decade period, the Fifth and the Ninth (but not the Second) courts decided relatively few criminal cases, and all three dealt primarily with real property, business, and tort cases. But by the most recent period all three dealt primarily with criminal and other public-law (that is, business regulation; labor regulation; taxation; aliens; abuse of governmental authority; racial discrimination; and patent trademark, and copyright) cases, with very few

private law (real property, business dispute, tort) cases. The authors asserted that there was a general shift through time for all three courts, from considerable diversity in case-load mix at the beginning to substantial homogeneity (in the transformed mix described above) at the end of the period.

Another factor that affects case-load input to the judicial system involves decisions by litigants and organized groups. One of the early and important findings of judicial behavioralism dealt with the success of what today is called public-interest-group litigation management in planning national campaigns and selecting favorable cases so as to induce favorable public policy decisions from the United States Supreme Court. The classic example was provided by the National Association for the Advancement of Colored People (NAACP) and by Thurgood Marshall as its chief counsel in presenting civil rights issues to the Warren Court during the 1950s. Steven Wasby questioned "the extent to which race relations litigation from the late 1960s through the early 1980s has been 'planned' by organizations and lawyers associated with them." Wasby's findings, based on interviews and other data sources, imply that either the cultural and social environment in which federal litigation management takes place have become considerably more complex during the past generation or the role of chance influences explain increased litigation in certain areas rather than the impact of organized group decisions. Perhaps all have played a role.

Victor Flango, Robert Roper, and Mary Elsner published an imaginative and comprehensive analysis of the inputs to, and decisions of, state courts. The monograph examines several popular notions about state court case loads and finds most to be incorrect. For example, it is often thought that criminal cases predominate at the state level. However, for 1978 and when parking violations are excluded, almost 64 percent of the cases dealt with traffic offenses, 21 percent with civil cases, 14 percent with criminal cases, and 2 percent with juveniles. Felonies constituted only 7 percent of total criminal filings, and for the four states that provided criminal trial data for all case types across all courts, only one in four criminal trials involved a felony charge. Three times (or more) as many civil cases, than criminal ones, were tried. The authors commented,

> This higher trial rate in civil cases may result from the fact that there is less management incentive for civil attorneys to settle during the pretrial phase than there is for prosecutors. There is probably a much higher caseload per prosecutor than per civil attorney. In short, the civil attorneys have much less to lose and perhaps more to gain financially by at minimum letting a case begin the trial process.
>
> (pp. 43–44)

CONVERSION: JUDICIAL DECISION-MAKING

The cases that are accepted by judges into the judicial system must then be transformed into decisions. This stage, the "conversion" stage, has been conceptualized by scholars who have studied the judicial system empirically in three different ways: they have examined the attitudes of judges toward specific types of cases and the impact of those attitudes on the postures of judges toward a case; they have commented on the interrelationship of a specific set of attitudes about the proper role of the judge in the judicial system and the effect that they can have in the conversion of case into decision; and they have examined the ways in which judges interact and group together over time (coalition behavior) to understand the complexities of the conversion of cases into decisions. Examples of each type of conversion study will be noted below.

Studies of the United States Supreme Court. Neal Tate (1983) provided an excellent survey and appraisal of the methodology of judicial-behavior research, in which he commented that *"The Judicial Mind* [Schubert, 1965b] marked the end of the pioneering and the beginning of the modern era because it represented the first full-scale, completely behavioral, methodologically sophisticated effort to develop a theory of judicial decision making in the world's most celebrated court. It . . . served as a reference point for later inquiries." *The Judicial Mind* developed the attitudinal approach to judicial decision-making, in which the attitudes of the justices toward issues of public policy are assumed to be implemented in their votes in cases. For the period

from 1946 through 1963, Schubert examined 1,657 cases that involved disagreement among members of the United States Supreme Court. Those cases were almost evenly divided between economic and civil liberties issues. Schubert then constructed "C" (political liberalism) and "E" (economic liberalism) scales. The C scale had five elements: political equality, political freedom, religious freedom, fair procedure, and individual privacy. The E scale encompassed fiscal claims, governmental regulation of business, union-management disputes, freedom of competition, and the constitutionality of state taxing. Justices Frank Murphy, Wiley B. Rutledge, Douglas, Black, Warren, and Brennan placed most prominently on the C scale (that is, they voted most often in favor of the extension of civil liberties). Justices Stanley F. Reed, Sherman Minton, Fred M. Vinson, Clark, Burton, and Whittaker ranked lowest on it. Liberal attitudes toward the E scale measured by votes on economic issues were most strongly held by Justices Murphy, Black, Douglas, Rutledge, Warren, and Brennan (that is, they voted most often for the economically underprivileged), and Justices Whittaker, Robert H. Jackson, Harlan, Frankfurter, Burton, and Stewart gave least support. The remaining justices fell between these two extremes. Tate (1981) reported an extension of the use of these scales to include an additional six years and two justices of the Warren Court and an additional nine years and five justices of the Burger Court. The two Warren Court justices (Marshall and Fortas) were C-scale liberals but E-scale moderates. Of the five Burger Court justices, four (Burger, Harry A. Blackmun, Lewis Powell, and Rehnquist) were conservative on both scales; the fifth (John Paul Stevens) was moderate on both scales.

Schubert (1983) also examined the effects of aging upon judicial attitudes, in terms of both cultural and biocultural models of attitudinal change. The research examined decisional voting behavior in relation to age at the time of the decision-making, for each of fifty-nine Supreme Court justices who participated in the Court's decisions over a period of ninety years beginning in 1890. The decisions were used to classify the justices' votes as conservative or nonconservative, for each of the ten decisional eras into which the overall period was divided in which each justice participated. The age of the justices was used to determine two different variables, a biological variable of aging and a biosociocultural variable, in relation to historical data about changes in the national culture through time. The latter variable divided the period 1765–1979 into fourteen "socialization eras" of variable length but defined in terms of the alternation between periods of relatively nonconservative ethos. The duration of the socialization eras had to be much longer than that of the decisional eras because several of the justices in the first of the latter were socialized during the nonconservative era of "frontier democracy" of 1801–1848.

With these data, it became possible to test two alternative hypotheses: that to the extent that justices became more conservative as their tenure on the Court increased, this was caused either by changes due to aging or by the prevailing cultural ethos into which they were socialized at their youthful "critical period" for learning. Analysis of the data shows no support whatsoever for the cultural hypothesis, but the biological hypothesis received modest support at a statistically significant level for the relationship between aging and decisional conservatism for all eras combined: that is, older justices vote more conservatively and younger ones vote less conservatively. But the latter tendency is strongest when both older and younger justices, for any decisional eras, were socialized in nonconservative rather than conservative eras, and that finding suggests, of course, that both hypotheses are true but at different probability levels. Socialization appears to interact with biological aging in contributing to decisional conservatism, although the biological effects are stronger than the cultural ones for most justices most of the time.

A second, complementary behavioral approach to judicial decision-making is offered by role theory, an offshoot of the structural-functionalism discussed earlier in this essay. With regard to the Supreme Court, it is assumed that all justices are not only politically socialized into national, regional, and local subcultures of whatever may have been the learning experience of their youth but that they are also lawyers who in all likelihood went to a very good law school and often clerked to a Supreme Court justice.

Much survey research involving interviews with both appellate and trial-court judges, including at least one (James) with a Supreme Court justice, indicates that judges profess to believe in such norms as the maintenance of an orderly judicial process, judicial independence, and judicial self-restraint. The thrust of role theory, at least as applied to Supreme Court justices, is to emphasize that whatever their personal ideological preferences in regard to public policy, all justices, as a result of their respective socialization processes, are to some extent motivated to uphold in their behavior the professional norms that the legal culture associates with their positions or at least to appear to do so. Consequently, all judges can be expected to qualify ideology with institutional role constraints that they also accept to some degree. Sidney Ulmer used this approach in his research.

A third approach is represented in the work of David Rohde, who studied coalition behavior (the tendency of judges to form voting blocs on specific issues over time) among Supreme Court justices. He studied civil liberties decisions of the Warren Court over a period of sixteen years. He classified more than three-fourths of these cases according to twenty-five policy-issue dimensions that were identified through cumulative scaling. Rohde's basic hypothesis was that majority-opinion coalitions would include only five justices, the minimum number needed to decide a case in a particular direction.

Rohde's second hypothesis was that the twenty-five policy dimensions would vary according to their contemporary political sensitivity, because some issues would be perceived as posing a threat to the Court as an institution. The degree of the threat associated with a particular dimension would be important because it would temper the extent to which justices would join, or refuse to join, coalitions.

Rohde's data indicate that in "nonthreat" situations, minimum-sized coalitions of five justices are the most frequent (40 percent), with a consistent linear decrease as coalition size increased until only 8 percent consisted of unanimous (nine-justice) decisions. In "threat" situations, by contrast, there was an almost perfect parabolic curve, with 23 percent five-justice and 26 percent nine-justice coalitions; 20 percent for both six-justice and eight-justice coalitions; and only 9 percent in the modal seven-justice coalitions. This curve indicates that the effect of role-related (defending the Court) attitudes was as strong on the justices as was that of ideology, with the consequence that about half of the justices were primarily influenced either by role or by ideology. The remaining half were cross-pressured in varying degrees both by attitudes toward role and by attitudes toward the substantive issues represented by the policy scales.

Saul Brenner studied another aspect of judicial decision-making, the extent to which changes occur in the votes of justices between the secret initial conference vote in a case and the final vote announced with the decision. He was able to obtain the conference votes in 153 civil liberties cases from the Burton docket books archived in the Library of Congress. Analysis of the data by Brenner revealed that only 35 of the conference decisions were by minimal winning voting coalitions, of which 20 became final decisions. In 22 cases, what were losing voting coalitions in the conference became converted into winning ones—12 minimally so and the other 10 with varying numbers of surplus votes. But in almost as many (18), what began as winning majorities in the conference vote were coalitions that lost sufficient votes to become converted into residual dissenting minorities; most of these were originally six- or seven-vote majorities, but 3 had been unanimous. The other 113 (75 percent of the decisions) began as majorities that either remained unchanged (15) or else increased in size (98). Thus, almost two-thirds (64 percent) of the changes in conference majorities resulted in increasing the size of these majority voting coalitions.

Roger Handberg studied interagreement in opinion behavior, which provides an alternative to the analysis of interagreement in voting. He measured the extent to which Supreme Court justices agreed in majority, concurring, or dissenting opinions for the 1965–1976 terms of the Court. He divided his data into subperiods defined by "natural" Courts (those in which no personnel changes occur). This resulted in two periods for the Warren Court and four for the Burger Court. Handberg's data show a liberal-to-center majority coalition linking Warren, Fortas, Brennan, Clark, and White in a cluster centering around the chief justice for the first Warren period (1965–1967); not included in the coalitional structure are the most extreme justices at that time, Douglas in the liberal direction and Stewart and Harlan in the conservative, and

Black, who by this time was extreme in a different sense—extremely idiosyncratic in his ideology. Handberg reported two dissenting coalitions for this first period, which fit very well the majority structure just described: Harlan and Stewart, who dissented together from liberal decisions, and Douglas, Warren, Fortas, and Brennan, the most liberal four, who dissented together against conservative decisions when Harlan, Stewart, White, and Clark succeeded in coopting Black, as they frequently did by this time. The second period of the Warren Court (1967–1969) was initiated by Justice Marshall's replacement of Clark, and the resulting majority coalitional structure is precisely the same as the one for the first period except that Marshall is substituted for Clark as a member of it. But the two dissenting coalitions differ from the ones for the first period. The conservative dissenting coalition, for example, now includes White as well as Harlan and Stewart, and the liberal one is reduced to two justices, Warren and the new justice Marshall, with the generally more liberal Douglas and Fortas no longer affiliated.

During the third period (1969–1970), Burger replaced Warren as chief justice and defined a new right wing for the Court, so that the liberal-to-center group that emerged during this first period of the Burger Court combined Marshall, Brennan, White, and Harlan. This group did not include an absolute majority of the justices; rather, it constituted a plurality of four justices who most frequently agreed on the moderate rationalization of center-to-liberal decisions during a period when one seat on the Court was unfilled. The strongest dissenting coalition against this four-man group involved Burger and Stewart. Black and the left-wing liberal Douglas did not participate in a routine way with either group. By contrast, for the 1976–1977 period, Handberg suggested three groupings: a conservative plurality coalition (Burger, Blackmun, Rehnquist, and Powell), a three-justice center bloc (White, Stewart, and Stevens), and a liberal minority coalition (Brennan and Marshall). Throughout the four periods of the Burger Court, Brennan and Marshall remained united in a highly cohesive nonmajority liberal coalition.

Studies of Federal Courts of Appeals and District Courts. Howard analyzed the processes of panel and opinion assignment for the federal appeals judges in three circuits for the triennium 1965–

1967. His data show that for all three circuits there was statistically significant variation in the differences between actual and randomly probable panel assignments for many of the judges. There was also variation for opinion assignment, but it was statistically significant for only two of the circuits. As a result of these observations, Howard concluded that the administrative discretion of the senior judge in an appellate court affected adjudication in certain ways: there was a bias toward seniority and experience in all three circuits in selecting panel members and spokesmen, and panels were created to reflect the policy preferences of chief judges.

Carp and Rowland, using a very large sample of almost 28,000 federal district court decisions, examined the relationship between judicial ideology and decision-making. They found that there was a modest but significant tendency for the judges who were Democrats to be more liberal than those who were Republicans. Stated differently, the odds are that any Democratic judge chosen at random will be liberal whereas a conservative will be Republican. Their data disclose that liberalism differences between judicial Democrats and Republicans were relatively higher during the mid-1950s and from 1967 to the end of the data in 1976. Democrat judges tended to be more liberal than Republican judges in eighteen of the nineteen policy issues examined, including local economic regulation and race discrimination.

Studies of State Appellate Courts. Craig Ducat and Victor Flango examined the relationship between leadership roles and dissenting behavior on selected state supreme courts. Their sample included fourteen such courts for the two decades 1951–1971, of which most were chosen because they use the rotational system for selecting the chief justice, thereby making possible analyses of differences in the dissenting behavior of judges while in the role of chief justice and after their incumbency. One of their basic hypotheses was that the concern of the chief justice for institutional stability will lead to his promotion of unanimity wherever possible and, to this end, he may suppress his own tendencies to dissent, even if the decisions go contrary to his own value preferences. Both permanent and temporary chiefs dissented less often than their associates, and the permanent chiefs did so relatively less frequently than the temporary chiefs; but

these differences are without statistical significance. Their data also show at a statistically significant level that seven of the eight associates who were promoted to life-tenure chiefships decreased their dissent rate after promotion. In the seven states providing rotating but long tenures for chiefs, 59 percent of the chiefs decreased their dissent rates after assuming that office.

The premise underlying Ducat and Flango's expectations regarding the suppression of dissent by chiefs stems from the experimental research of Robert Bales (1950, 1970) with small laboratory decision-making groups, which has been discussed frequently in both earlier (Danelski) and subsequent (Schubert, 1985, vol. 2) behavioral research in leadership theory applied to courts. Bales distinguished between the roles of effective ("task") and affective ("social") leaders, and both Danelski and Schubert demonstrated that such roles might, but did not necessarily, coincide with formal leadership status. Ducat and Flango developed a typology, which they present in a table (p. 21) that distinguishes between types of leaders as a function of whether the dissent rate of the Court (which they identified with effective leadership) is increasing (Ct +) or decreasing (Ct−) and whether the dissent rate of the chief justice likewise is increasing (CJ +) or decreasing (C−, which they identified with effective leadership). Thus, they defined "social leaders" as CJ− and Ct+—obviously the situation described above for both life-tenured and long-term chiefs. Conversely, CJ+ but Ct− defines chief justices who play the role of "task leaders." But a fourfold table produces two other types, and Ducat and Flango defined decrease in dissent for both the chief and the court as the consequence of a role of an "extraordinary leader," whereas mutual increase in dissenting identifies a chief as a "nonleader."

The authors related their own systematic empirical data to compare leadership roles to the methods of judicial recruitment for their judges and chiefs. They reported that the method of partisan selection was associated primarily (70 percent) with either social or task leadership; the Missouri Plan, predominantly (40 percent) with extraordinary leadership; and nonpartisan election with all four types, although it produced proportionately more nonleaders than either of the other two methods.

Studies of State Trial Courts. Two ideal-type

models of criminal trials were described by Pamela Utz. The first model is that of the "adversary trial," which evolved in English common law and still predominated in nineteenth-century America. The other, the "administrative model," is derived from organizational theory and analysis of a trial court as an organization whose component units interact but each in pursuit of its own goals. Roles are strictly defined by rules, and the common goal is the processing of arrests made by the police. To achieve efficiency in coping with large case loads, the traditional legal components of the adversary process (for example, the presumption of innocence, the right of trial by jury, the procedural safeguards subsumed under due process of law) become subverted to a cooperative enterprise. Even the defense attorney joins in with the prosecutor and other accoutrements of the court—including the judge who necessarily becomes an acquiescent party to such dispositions—in persuading the defendant to plead guilty to a lesser offense (or the same offense with an agreed-upon lesser sentence) than the formal charge. Thus, a compromise settlement is institutionalized for virtually all defendants, as a substitute for many being found innocent and others guilty as originally charged; and the adversary system is retained as a legal fiction that legitimizes the bargains struck through administrative processes. Utz asserted that "the abuses associated with plea bargaining are the result not of cooperation per se, but rather of a highly vulnerable species of cooperation under conditions of continued organizational conflict" (p. 6). She saw the adversary process as having been displaced out of the courtroom, into adversary group relationships throughout the courthouse as the working place for the organization at large. The bulk of her book is devoted to detailed discussions of two empirical approximations of her ideal types: San Diego as the more traditional adversary system, which discourages plea bargaining; and Alameda County (Oakland) as a well-developed demonstration of the administrative model, which builds upon plea bargaining.

A similar analogy was presented by Martin Levin, who contrasted what he calls a judicial decision-making model (Minneapolis) with an administrative one (Pittsburgh). But Levin's "administrative" model describes an empirically oriented, pragmatic decision-making process in the context of judges who tend to reflect the values imprinted by a working-class socialization and background, whereas his "judicial" model reflects upper-middle-class values of a law-and-order orientation, with judicial sympathies toward the victim of crime rather than toward the social and economic circumstances out of which criminals are spawned. In commenting upon Levin's case studies, Henry Glick remarked that the relatively lenient Pittsburgh judges were the products of a partisan ballot and close connections with the local Democratic party machine, whereas the civic and bar association goal in Minneapolis was to depoliticize judicial selection via a tradition of bipartisanship.

The question of the racial differences of trial judges as a possible biasing consideration in criminal sentencing was investigated by Thomas Uhlman. His universe of black judges was substantially smaller than the available sample of white judges in the same metropolitan judiciary, but it was large enough to permit some statistical comparisons. His major finding was that there were small and statistically insignificant differences overall in the sentencing behavior of black judges as compared to white judges; there was much greater variation between individual judges—either black or white—than between the means of the two groups. Indeed, the black judges were a more highly selected elite than were the white, in the sense that the blacks came from the more traditional sector of the black legal establishment, while whites were drawn from more heterogeneous backgrounds. Controlling for crime severity, Uhlman found that black judges agreed with white ones in sentencing black defendants more severely than white defendants, which raises, but does not resolve, the question of the possibility of discrimination against black defendants.

In a subsequent article, Cassia Spohn, John Gruhl, and Susan Welch undertook to reanalyze this question for the same large northeastern metropolis that had been studied by Uhlman, but with extensive methodological refinements, including the use of a large sample of cases over a period of time almost twice as long as Uhlman had studied, a larger number of different types of offenses, and a methodology that contained controls for both legal and extralegal variables. These authors found that black defendants are more likely than white ones to have a prior criminal record and more likely to be the subject of a serious charge, which is related to the likelihood of their receiving a more severe sentence; and they concluded that there was no statistical evidence of direct racial discrimination in determining sentence severity. On the other hand, black defendants were less likely than white ones to afford a private defense attorney or to avoid being jailed pending trial; thus, to the extent that socioeconomic discrimination was the cause of this disadvantage to blacks, it was reflected also in socioeconomic-status-based racial discrimination in determining sentence severity. And black males went to prison at a 20 percent higher rate than did whites, notwithstanding control for both legal and extralegal variables. Black males were discriminated against racially by being sentenced to prison more frequently than whites in the same range of the charge-severity scale; and conversely, white males were put on long probation more frequently than corresponding black males. So the authors concluded that there was racial bias in sentencing to the extent that blacks were imprisoned more frequently than whites.

Kritzer and Uhlman analyzed the possibility of sex discrimination, in terms of both judges and defendants, for the same northeastern metropolitan criminal court. They discussed various hypotheses gleaned from the research literature of sociology and social psychology, on the basis of which they stated a dozen hypotheses about expected differences in sentencing behavior on the part of female judges or in relation to female defendants. Their overall finding was that sex differences were not statistically significant for five of their seven offense categories but were for robbery and drugs, although at weak levels of correlation. The authors hypothesized that sentencing in rape cases would be of special importance in detecting possible sex bias in judges. The defendants at the time of the study were all males. The data show that female judges did indeed deal more harshly with rape defendants in terms of both conviction and also imprisonment, but not at a statistically significant level. What is significant, however, is the bias in assigning rape cases to female judges, who get twice the volume they could have been expected to get on a random basis. The authors' general conclusion was that there was no strong evidence indicating that female judges are more severe in their sentencing than male judges as a general pattern, de-

spite some significant differences for certain types of crime.

Candace Kruttschnitt focused on the effect of social-status differences upon the severity of sentencing of female defendants. Her study included more than a thousand women who were tried during the early 1970s in a northern California county criminal court and convicted of such offenses as disturbing the peace, assault, forgery, drugs, or petty theft. The theory with which she worked suggested that both a prior criminal record and youth are treated by judges as negative indices of respectability and punished accordingly. Her data confirm this for criminal records and for being poor, which likewise merits harsh sentencing, especially for forgery. Black women are sentenced more severely than white women for drug offenses or disturbing the peace. But being on welfare "is generally given the greatest weight and appears to have a more consistent impact than either race or income alone on the sentences accorded these women." Yet, race appears to have an effect directly and quite independently of the fact that relatively more black than white women are welfare recipients. On the other hand, poor women are given more severe sentences primarily because of their welfare status. Employed women, women students, and older women are sentenced relatively leniently.

JUDICIAL OUTPUTS

The modern judicial decision-making theory of outputs was developed during the quarter-century extending from 1941 to 1965, primarily through cumulative scaling studies of the voting behavior of Supreme Court justices (Pritchett, 1941, 1948; Schubert, 1962, 1965a, 1965b; Thurstone and Degan). These pioneering studies and techniques have been used to examine trends in judicial decision-making as it related to certain types of issues and litigants before courts. Examples of studies of this nature will be noted below to illustrate the kind of work done. This essay will note output trends as related to two groups of litigants—government administrative agencies and the economically disadvantaged.

Support of Administrative Litigants. Bradley Canon and Micheal Giles analyzed Supreme

Court decisions in regard to the six most frequent federal administrative agency litigants for the period 1957–1968. Their first question was whether the Court was more supportive of some agencies than others, and their finding was that the Court gave maximal support (91 percent) to the Federal Power Commission (FPC) and the Federal Trade Commission (FTC); modal support (73 percent–74 percent) to the National Labor Relations Board (NLRB) and the Internal Revenue Service (IRS); and relatively minimal support (56 percent–68 percent) to the Immigration and Naturalization Service (INS) and the Interstate Commerce Commission (ICC). Their second question was whether the Court's decisions reflected differences in the attitudes of justices toward the individual agencies. The data reported by the authors demonstrate that of their sample of twelve justices, six showed the most marked and consistent discrimination among the half dozen agencies, in terms of the percentages of support received. This is evident in the number of high or low levels of agency support, in relation to each justice's average, and the range of his support (that is, his highest level of support minus his lowest level). Thus, Fortas was maximally supportive of three agencies and high on a fourth, with a range of only 50; Douglas was high on one but very low on two other agencies, with a range of 84; Black also was high on one and low on two, with a range of 75; Warren and Brennan both were high on one and low on one, with a range of 70; Goldberg was low on two with a range of 68. These six justices had all been identified as liberals in considerably earlier behavioral research on the ideology of Supreme Court justices during the period analyzed by Canon and Giles, and correspondingly, the other six justices in the sample are recognized conservatives.

Of the six agencies, five could be differentiated in terms of individual-justice support levels on the basis of the number and direction of high-low support levels and/or significant differences in the average support level of the six liberal, as compared to the six conservative, justices. The agency least approved by liberal justices was the INS, which showed low levels of support by all six, as well as by Frankfurter. Next came the ICC, which received low support from three liberals and the conservative Clark. Third was the IRS, which got low support from two

liberals (Douglas and Fortas). On the other hand, four liberals gave very high support, while two conservatives gave very low support, to the FTC; and although the FPC attracted only moderate liberal support levels, the average support for it among the liberals was 87, while the average for conservatives was only 66. There was no important difference between liberals and conservatives in their support for the NLRB.

To sum up, there were important differences between the two groups of justices; the liberals favored the FTC and FPC, but not the IRS, the ICC, and the INS. Canon and Giles provided a rather different interpretation and findings than those suggested above, but they did agree that "in the case of the INS, obvious blocs of highly supportive and highly nonsupportive justices appear"; and although they did find "that in general differential levels of Court support result from justices' concurrent shifts in attitudes toward any given agency," they still did "not know what factors associated with the agencies evoke these attitudes." The obvious explanation is that they were studying the Warren Court at a time when majorities of liberal justices tended to predominate in regard to many issues; indeed, their scale of support by the Court for these six agencies, which puts the agencies in the same sequence as the analysis above premised on the ideological differences between the justices, suggests that as perceived by the Warren Court, the six major litigious administrative agencies were arrayed along a continuum (ranging from most liberal to most conservative) as follows: FPC, FTC, NLRB, IRS, ICC, and INS.

Support of the Poor. Gayle Binion focused on "the disadvantaged" in Burger Court cases. Her analysis included almost a hundred "poverty" cases decided during the first eleven years of the Burger Court (1969–1980); and her most important finding was that while the Burger Court had tended to continue the Warren Court's policies in regard to the access of indigents to fair criminal procedure and voting participation, the Court during the 1970s pioneered in developing new and increasingly negative policies affecting the material interests of indigents. Her data show that although about half of the decisions were proindigent overall, there were sharp differences in the Court's rates for unanimous, as distinguished from split, decisions: almost three-fourths (74 percent of 34) unanimous decisions, were pro, but only two-fifths (39 percent of 62) split decisions were pro. Hence, for reasons that her data and analysis did not enable her to explain, the Burger Court was almost twice as favorable to indigents in cases disposed of with only a single opinion for the Court as it was in cases where explicit proindigent views were confronted by those opposed to such an outcome. One can speculate that the reason must be found in the internal dynamics of the Court's decisional processes, but further research is needed to resolve this question. She did point out that there has been a distinct dropoff in support for the claims of the poor during the period since 1976 and since the appointment of Justice Stevens. Binion concluded that

> the distinction between the nonmaterial cases and those with a close and substantial connection to the life conditions of the poor is associated with the decline in success of the poor before the third Burger Court. . . . The Supreme Court of today is as likely as were its two predecessors (in statistical terms) to support the right of an indigent to fair criminal procedures, to the right to vote or run for office, and to the right to marry and divorce (despite inability to pay a fee or support one's children). But the Court of today is distinctly less likely to support the interests of welfare recipients, whether the issue is one of getting into court, challenging eligibility decisions, or attacking funding policies. . . . The result has not been equal protection, but the newest unequal protection.

Judicial discrimination against the poor was well known to American courts before it emerged in the 1960s as an issue of policy for the United States Supreme Court; and as James Eisenstein demonstrated so well, judicial discrimination against the poor in lower courts differs primarily in reflecting the overwhelming preponderance of what preoccupies lower-court policy outputs—not the tiny fraction of 5 percent of formal workload that it is now for the Supreme Court.

Eisenstein distinguished between symbolic and material outputs and then made the point that what is important about United States Supreme Court outputs are their symbolic significance for the vast audience not involved directly in the fragment of litigation that is disposed of by the Court and, to a decidedly lesser extent, by all state supreme courts, although more by some than by others. Symbolic overtones are unusual for appellate intermediate court decisions, which affect almost exclusively the "material" interests of the immediate parties to cases. Eisenstein explained that

> the relationship between the level of the legal process and the characteristics of citizens involved in it is . . . striking. The lower levels are for the less well-off strata of society. . . . Corporations, newspapers, universities, labor unions, governmental units, and other institutions and organizations of higher-status people rarely honor the lowest levels of the legal process with their presence . . . [and] those aspects of the legal process that higher-status individuals are likely to encounter are more likely to conform to popular beliefs about how it functions. The gap between myth and reality is smallest precisely where the most influential segments of society are likely to participate.
>
> (pp. 314–315)

Furthermore, Eisenstein pointed out,

> the poor, the young, the very old (especially if poor), and disadvantaged minority group members receive a disproportionately large share of the sanctions and a correspondingly small share of the benefits allocated by the legal process in comparison to other individuals in society.
>
> (p. 323)

He exemplified judicial discrimination against the poor at lower levels of the judicial system with discussion of research dealing with both criminal and civil case dispositions by trial courts. Concerning criminal trials, he states that

> the prevalence of the Poor in pretrial detention is shocking to anyone who believes in equal justice for all. In New York City, more people are in jail because they . . . [can] not make bail prior to trial than are sentenced to prison after conviction.
>
> (p. 327)

In regard to civil trials, Eisenstein remarked that

> by enforcing property rights, ensuring the smooth functioning of the political status quo, and delaying change, the civil process tends to perpetuate existing social and political condi-

tions. Since the Disadvantaged are by definition doing poorly, they certainly do not benefit and probably suffer as a result of its effectiveness in maintaining these conditions.

(p. 337)

FEEDBACK TO JUDGES

In terms of the judicial systems model, decision-making and policymaking are followed by a range of possible consequences for parties to the case, other courts, the legal profession, other branches of government, interest groups and segments of the general public, and the media. These consequences in turn generate or operate as feedback to the courts that originally rendered decisions. The behavioral studies of feedback from judicial decisions can be organized in terms of four major categories. First, feedback can be examined in terms of the impact of judicial decisions upon persons who are directly and indirectly affected by the implementation of the decision. Second, it can involve the issue of compliance, the actions subsequent to the decision taken by lower-court personnel, and/or administrative agencies, counsel to the parties to the case, the parties themselves, and any other persons who are legally responsible for putting into effect the decree of the deciding court. Third, public opinion, consisting of the attitudes of the general public (or select subpopulations of it) toward a decision or policy (or the prestige generally) of a court, can be generated. Finally, political responses are important because they focus upon actions taken by legislatures, executives, constitutional amendments, initiatives, referenda, and/or judicial recall elections. Any or all of these types of responses to court decisions may, and frequently do, result in newly felt input demands or supports to the court designed to provoke either reinforcement of an earlier decision or change—hence their collective designation as feedback "loops."

Impact. Richard Johnson analyzed the impact of the Supreme Court's decisions on public school religious activities, by studying a district in Illinois, to discover to what extent religion was practiced in the public schools of this district subsequent to the Supreme Court's decisions in *Engel* v. *Vitale* (1962) and *Abington Township School District* v. *Schempp* (1963). The first invalidated a prayer composed by state officials for use in the public schools of New York as violative of the separation of church and state; the second disapproved a state statute and a municipal school board administrative order that authorized Bible reading and/or the recitation of the Lord's Prayer in public schools, as contrary to the establishment clause of the First Amendment.

The community that Johnson studied in 1964 was overwhelmingly Protestant and most respondents claimed to attend church at least weekly. It had been the practice in the elementary schools of the district to have students recite prayers before lunch and as a morning devotional exercise. The superintendent at the time of both Court decisions discouraged any changes, but a new superintendent who took office soon after the *Schempp* decision agreed with the Court and ordered that organized group prayers be abolished. Johnson's subsequent survey research showed that 40 percent of the leading citizens of the community, 29 percent of the teachers, and 29 percent of the school board members disavowed a duty of compliance with the Court's policy. And a majority of leading citizens and educators disagreed with the new superintendent's policy by a margin of almost 5–1. Johnson found that "while the . . . district did comply with the Court's prayer rulings, the substance of the compliant behavior was in a form generally acceptable to the community," such as silent individual prayer (p. 150). Micheal Giles and Douglas Gatlin analyzed the extent to which, in the early 1970s more than a decade and a half after the Court's decision on public school desegregation (*Brown* v. *Board of Education*, 1954) that policy was being observed in the public schools of the state of Florida; by that time, desegregation plans had been implemented in all of the state's school districts. They surveyed three groups of parents: "avoiders" of public school desegregation, who withdrew their children and sent them instead to racially segregated private schools; "potential avoiders," those who replied to one of the survey questions in a manner indicating that they were thinking about becoming avoiders; and "compliers." The objective of the research was to evaluate differences between these three groups, on the basis of both attitudinal and socioeconomic-status variables.

The authors compared each group with the others. The most important variable was the parents' income; thus, the capacity to afford placing one's child in a private school distinguishes best between avoiders and potential avoiders and between avoiders and compliers. Three of four desegregation-policy component variables are next most important: (1) the distance students were bused distinguished avoiders and compliers; (2) the ratio of black to white students in a school distinguished avoiders and potential avoiders, and avoiders and compliers; (3) the previous status of the school (as black rather than white) distinguishes both avoiders and potential avoiders from compliers; but (4) busing (irrespective of distance) showed no statistical significance for distinguishing any of the groups.

Giles and Gatlin's study also demonstrated that the attitudes of parents concerning their social class and racial bias distinguished fairly well between potential avoiders and compliers. The authors concluded that "racist and non-racist respondents react in like manner to increasing distance, higher black enrollments and the onset of busing" and that "non-southerners appeared just as likely as southerners to think about and actually to avoid desegregation."

Kathleen Kemp, Robert Carp, and David Brady analyzed the impact of the Supreme Court's abortion decisions by testing their effect upon hospital policy, as measured in terms of the decisions of hospital administrators. The authors conducted interviews with almost seventy administrators in thirty-six general hospitals in Houston. These interviews indicated that before the Court's decisions, 60 percent of the administrators had authorized abortions only when necessary to save the mother's life, when her physical or mental health might be affected, or when her pregnancy was the result of rape or incest. However, after the decisions less than 14 percent relied on such reasons; instead, almost two-thirds then authorized elective abortions during the first trimester or even during the second, while only 5 percent would have done that before the Court's decisions. The opinion of these respondents concerning the Court's decisions was twice as important to the change in their collective behavior as their opinion of the Court itself. Almost as important to the decision to comply were two resource variables: a hospital's staff-to-bed ratio and occupancy rate. Some hospitals had available capacity to handle a substantial increase in abortions and patients; these additional operations provided new business for the hospitals.

Susan Hansen also analyzed the impact of Court abortion policy, but with a focus on how it affected the behavior of fecund women. One clear result of the Court's decisions, which drastically changed the law on abortion in half the states and further liberalized it in most of the others, was virtually to eliminate the previously substantial number of abortion-related maternal deaths, as abortion became at least legally available throughout the country as a medical procedure. Another clear result of the Court's decisions was substantially to equalize the availability of abortion as a surgical procedure.

Charles Johnson and Bradley Canon report public opinion concerning abortion over the decade 1972–1982, based upon survey responses to the question whether it should be possible for a married pregnant woman to obtain a legal abortion if she does not want any more children. The Court's decision in *Roe* v. *Wade* had come in 1973, and for that year there was a temporary increase in affirmative replies (of + 9.3 percent, from 37.6 percent in 1972) and decrease in negative replies; but the eleven-year-response means were as follows: yes, 43 percent; no, 52 percent; and other, 4 percent. These data suggest that the impact (if any) of the Court's decision was slight and transitory, with (a full decade after the Court's decision) a maximal average shift of no more than 5 percent in public opinion toward abortion.

Federal and State Court Compliance. Charles Johnson analyzed the extent of lower federal court compliance, during 1963–1967, with Supreme Court formal decisions of the 1961 and 1962 terms. He hypothesized that there would be a direct and positive correlation between the extent of compliance on the part of lower federal court judges and the degree of consensuality manifest in the Court's decisions. He measured consensuality in terms of five indicators: number of majority votes; number of judges joining in the opinion of the Court; number of dissenters; number of dissenting opinions; and whether the opinion of the Court was authored by the chief justice or by an associate justice. He reported separately the compliance behaviors of federal appeals judges and district judges—although there was not a large difference in their responses. The appeals-court data show overall that compliance, evasion, and discordance tended to be highly and positively intercorrelated. But it is by no means a simple matter of evasion and discordance being lowest and compliance highest when Supreme Court consensuality is maximal on any of the five indicators. Indeed, it is the 5–4 decisions that are associated with maximal compliance, but also with maximal evasion and maximal discordance. Conversely, unanimous decisions and majority opinions both result in minimal evasion and discordance, to be sure, but also minimal compliance. Similarly, maximizing the number of dissenting opinions results in maximizing compliance, evasion, and discordance; and opinions of the Court authored by the chief justice are associated with less compliance, as well as evasion and discordance, than those written by other justices.

The most remarkable aspect of the district-court data is that those judges evince very low discordance in comparison to the appeals judges and also less evasion, whereas their level of compliance is virtually identical with that of the federal appeals judges. There are other differences in detail in the district-judge data, but the data generally agree with the finding for the appeals judges that unanimous decisions and majority opinions evoke minimal compliance, evasion, and discordance, whereas dissensuality in Supreme Court voting tends to maximize all three types of responses, as does the number of dissenting opinions. The district judges agree with the appeals judges that opinions of the Court authored by associate justices result in higher compliance, evasion, and discordance than do opinions of the Court written by the chief justice. Johnson's stated conclusion was that "the degree of Supreme Court support or nonsupport for a particular case has little or no bearing on the eventual treatment of that case by the lower courts."

Johnson's data and explicit findings clearly suggest that lower federal court judges are more vigorously stimulated by maximal dissensus—not consensus—in Supreme Court decision-making and, further, that the resulting behavior of lower federal judges is intensified across the board: some lower-court judges are more manifestly compliant, others are more evasive, and still others (but especially among appeals court judges) are more discordant. This indicates that the lower-court federal judges become more aware of Supreme Court decisions that are more controversial, and therefore better publicized, than the (typically) more bland unanimous decisions, so lower-court judges behave in response to what they perceive as making a change that matters.

Donald Songer, C. K. Rowland, and Robert Carp studied the compliance of lower federal court judges with decisions of the United States Supreme Court for the period 1950–1975 in regard to three major policy components: political and religious freedom (PF+/RF+), fair procedure for criminal defendants (FP+), and labor relations (W+). The authors proposed first to determine any bench marks of statistically significant changes in the level of Supreme Court support for each of these policies and then to discover to what extent parallel changes of statistical significance could be observed for the federal courts of appeals and for the federal district courts. They also examined their data in relation to the political-party affiliation of the lower-court judges to see if differences could be attributed to partisanship. Finally, they proposed to ascertain whether there was statistically significant variation between the circuits, in terms of either their courts of appeals or district courts. The decisional samples consisted of approximately 1,300 formal decisions of the Supreme Court; almost 13,000 district-court decisions; and almost 8,200 decisions of the courts of appeals.

Two significant turning points were found for the Supreme Court; they coincided with changes in the chief-justiceship. According to these authors, "In each policy area the Supreme Court became significantly more liberal in the first decade after the appointment of Earl Warren . . . and then returned to a more conservative trend during the Burger Court." Actually, Warren had been chief justice for seven to eight years and so was in the middle of his tenure as chief before the first turning point, whereas the second turning point came (for two of the three issues) a year or two after Burger replaced Warren.

The authors' data show that the liberal change at the appellate level in regard to labor issues came in the 1959 term, while for the First Amendment and criminal justice issues it began with the 1961 term. The conservative change came first for First Amendment issues, beginning with the 1969 term, and not until the 1970 term for the other two issues. The federal district judges changed both times in the right direction for labor policy, but for the other two issues, the initial changes were extremely small and not statistically significant. The Burger Court changes —though significant—were in the wrong direction: increases in liberalism toward both First Amendment and criminal justice issues. Overall, the courts of appeals and district court judges alike behaved in a manner consistent with the hypothesis of compliance in only two of six instances.

Only between the first and second periods, and then only for labor issues, was there a statistically significant difference between Democratic and Republican appeals court judges—and that was in the wrong direction, with Republicans increasing their liberal voting at more than three times the difference rate for the Democrats. For district court judges, the changes between both the first and second periods and between the second and third were statistically significant in regard to labor issues for both Democrats and Republicans. But Democrats and Republicans changed by almost identical amounts, which seems to indicate that although both party groups changed significantly, there was no significant difference between them. For the Democratic district judges, there were statistically significant increases in liberalism for both criminal justice and First Amendment issues (while their Republican colleagues stood pat); and the authors remarked upon "the tendency of Democratic district . . . judges to oppose the increasing conservatism of the Burger Court in regard to criminal cases and also the rights of religion and expression while the decisional tendencies of Republican judges remained unchanged." The authors concluded that "policy changes in the courts of appeals have little immediate discernible impact on the decisional trends in the district courts." More generally, they stated that the Supreme Court "had virtually no discernible impact on the outcomes in criminal cases. Impact on freedom of religion and expression appeared to be confined to the courts of appeals."

Compliance by state supreme courts with United States Supreme Court policymaking was discussed by G. Alan Tarr. He undertook a quasi-empirical discussion of state supreme court compliance in relation to First Amendment (establishment clause) policy during the years 1950–1972. Tarr's sample consisted of fifteen cases in which he found what he considered to be deviations from full compliance. Judicial noncompliance occurred in only 15.5 percent of the cases decided during this period. Nine of the fifteen cases involved the "substitution of alternative standards for those of the Supreme Court," another nine (often the same cases) involved "misapplication of Supreme Court standards," only three constituted "failure to follow a determinative Supreme Court precedent," and only one showed "failure to address the establishment question in a related case." However, in most cases, state supreme court judges did not admit their noncompliance but rather attempted to portray their decisions as consistent with previous Supreme Court decisions and the standards enunciated in them. Noncompliance thus tended to take the form of evasion rather than outright defiance of Supreme Court mandates.

Corsi discussed an article by Canon (1974) dealing with state supreme court compliance with four of the United States Supreme Court's landmark fair-procedure decisions of the early to middle 1960s. Corsi pointed out that in the analysis of a relatively small sample of ninety-one opinions of state supreme courts, Canon found instances of resistance in two-thirds of the fifty state supreme courts during this period. In four states, the resistance went beyond the occasional unguarded comment; instead, the judges in the supreme courts of New Jersey, Utah, Nebraska, and Washington openly stated their denunciation of four Warren Court decisions in the criminal justice area. Canon concluded that in these four states "the counterpressures of public opinion and judicial identification with outside groups or claims have blunted organizational loyalty to the point of producing sustained organizational contumacy." At the very least, the sharp contradiction between Tarr's findings and those of Canon indicate that the state supreme courts follow diametrically opposed compliance practices in First Amendment establishment-clause cases than they do in fair criminal procedure cases. Awareness of such an unexplained difference in the behaviors of state supreme court justices certainly indicates a pressing need for further careful research to explore the reasons for the difference.

Public Opinion. Walter Murphy and Joseph Tanenhaus distinguished between two categories of "the public." The "attentive" public included almost a majority of the respondents to questions that the authors had placed in a 1966 Ann Arbor Survey Research Center national opinion survey; attentive replies showed specific likes and dislikes about the Supreme Court, as well as generalized attitudes toward it. To the same questions, slightly more than a fourth of the respondents provided only generalized ("diffuse") support and had no specific opinions about the Court; they were designated as the "marginal" public. The remaining quarter of the respondents were the possibly uninformed, perhaps forgetful, but indisputably nonresponsive residual public. In terms of a five-point scale ranging from strongly positive support to strongly negative, the two extremes of the scale showed reciprocal patterns of response: the least well informed "marginal diffuse" was most strongly positive, and the best informed "attentive specific" was most strongly negative, with medially informed "attentive diffuse" also in the middle in terms of support. The public who know the least about the Court like it the best.

Even in its prime, the Warren Court got little specific support from any part of the public, and its strongest institutional support came from persons who knew nothing specific about the Court's policies. Goldman and Jahnige reanalyzed the probable size of the different categories of the public, using a broader data base than had the initial Murphy and Tanenhaus survey; this led them to conclude that only about 40 percent of the public is "attentive," an equal proportion is "marginal," and the remaining 20 percent is "politically irrelevant"—actually, 20 ± 10 percent, depending upon which data set one observes. They also reported a series of Gallup polls that indicate increasing public sentiment throughout the late 1960s, ranging from not quite a bare majority in 1965 to 75 percent in 1969 who said that they thought that the courts did not treat criminals harshly enough; the authors asserted "that the Court in the late 1960s was approaching a crisis in its input of support" (p. 147).

Roger Handberg and William Maddox undertook to extend into the 1970s the linkages between public opinion and the United States Supreme Court that Murphy and Tanenhaus had begun during the 1960s. Unfortunately, the data upon which Handberg and Maddox relied—na-

tional surveys conducted by the Center for Political Studies in 1972, 1974, and 1976—overweeningly focus upon the political party system and hence include very little that is useful about the Supreme Court. Their analysis focuses upon diffuse support in the form of "trust in the Court," in relation to sets of selected social, partisan, psychological, and issues variables. Blacks had been the only social group that gave consistent positive support to the Court during the 1960s, but black support steadily decreased as the Nixon Court became structured. Education provided the highest and most stable basis of support for the Court. These findings indicate that the Warren Court image as the protector of minority rights faded in the face of Burger Court realities—and it is notable that when race was statistically controlled by education, in relation to trust, college-educated blacks made a better than fifty-point reversal, from most supportive of all blacks to least supportive.

A state public-opinion sample of support for the Supreme Court was reported by David Adamany and Joel Grossman. The survey was conducted in 1976 by the Wisconsin Survey Research Laboratory. The sample included almost six hundred respondents who were divided between those who had participated in at least two activities out of several dozen different possible ones involving support of an American political party (activists) and those who had not (inactives). A fourth of the sample were activists; the majority of the sample had never participated in any activity supportive of a political party. In regard to specific-decision support, the activists were twice as positive (that is, they liked specific decisions) as, and considerably less negative (disliked specific decisions) than, the inactives. Similarly, but to a lesser degree, activists favored the Court (as compared to either Congress or the president) when asked which should have the final authority to decide, whereas more inactives than activists favored both Congress and the president. When both activists and inactives were subdivided according to ideology into liberal, moderate, and conservative, the activists gave more positive specific-decision support and less negative across all three ideological groupings; but the relatively strongest positive support (and relatively weakest negative support) came from the moderate activists, with relatively less extreme support, both positive and negative, for liberal activists and least positive for conservative activists. But in regard to their overall performance rating, there was no difference between liberal activists or inactives or between conservative activists and inactives, although a majority of both categories of liberals were positive (while a majority of both categories of conservatives were negative) in their overall performance rating of the Supreme Court. There was a difference among the moderates, however: moderate activists were distinctly more positive, and moderate inactives correspondingly more negative, in their overall performance ratings.

Liberal activists were sharply and significantly more "confident in the Court" than inactives; but the only other difference was that conservative activists have less confidence than inactive conservatives. In the questions on final authority, liberal activists were pro-Court over either Congress or the president, moderate activists favored the Court over the president but not over Congress, while both liberal and moderate inactives favored Congress but not the president over the Court.

Caldeira (1977) surveyed both federal and state trial judges in regard to their attitudes toward the policy decisions of the United States Supreme Court. His sample consisted of 115 federal district judges whom he interviewed and 32 others, plus 84 state trial judges (from Colorado, New York, and South Carolina), who responded to a mail questionnaire. Both the interviews and the mail surveys took place in 1975–1976, so it was the Burger Court that made the decisions to which these lower-court judges responded. All of them "liked" the Burger Court's relatively more conservative criminal justice policies best. Criminal justice was also the most "disliked" policy of the Burger Court—presumably by different judges than the ones who liked it. About 17 percent of the state judges also disliked the Burger Court's First Amendment policies and its "style" of decision-making; federal judges disliked the Court's equal protection of the laws and other-than-First-Amendment Bill of Rights policies, as well as its style, equally at the rate of 10 percent. Federal judges tended generally, however, to give more extreme specific support—both strong and weak—to the Supreme Court, no doubt because the nature of their work required them to be better informed than state court judges, and likewise, the federal judges gave almost twice as much strong diffuse support to the Court as state judges did. Caldeira commented,

> Of the federal judges, more than half (55.5 per cent) rated the Court as "good" or "excellent"; of the state judges, a mere [sic] 39.8 per cent rated the Court in this manner. A majority (52.6 per cent) of the state judges and nearly one-third of the federal judges (32.7 per cent) found the performance of the Court "fair." . . . Almost two-thirds of the federal judges (63.9 per cent) and more than half of the state judges (53.9 per cent) felt that the Court is impartial in its decision making.
>
> (pp. 215–216)

Richard Lehne and John Reynolds studied the public-opinion response to a series of decisions made by the New Jersey Supreme Court in *Robinson* v. *Cahill,* a landmark case involving a major political dispute, in which the court invalidated on constitutional grounds the funding for the public schools in the state and then devoted much of the next couple of years to trying to force the legislature to enact a substitute source of revenue. Eventually the court ordered the closing of all public schools in the state; about a week later New Jersey adopted a state income tax, and the schools reopened. The first of the court's six formal decisions with opinions came in 1973, and the tax law was not enacted until July 1976; but little public attention was directed by the press to the court's role in the controversy until early 1975. The authors reported a table showing the percentages of responses to an opinion-poll question that asked respondents to evaluate the job the New Jersey Supreme Court was doing on four separate occasions over the period from September 1975 to October 1976. There was no change in the proportion (43 ± 4 percent) who approved of the court's performance, but as between the other two response categories, disapproval or no opinion, there was a consistent, if modest, shift of about 10 percent from "no opinion" to disapproval: no opinion began as 27 percent and ended as 17 percent, and disapproval began as 32 percent and ended as 40 percent. So, to the extent that change occurred, public opinion became less approving through time.

Political Feedback. The principal direct political check upon the United States Supreme Court is the Congress, which (at least, in constitutional theory) can revise, abolish (except for Court original jurisdiction), and manipulate the Court's legal right to decide cases; withhold funding, in whole or in part; remove justices by impeachment by the House and conviction after trial by the Senate; and refuse to confirm the appointment of any or all new justices. Very little of that has ever been done, but the little that has been, or might be, undertaken by Congress still represents the strongest available political constraint upon the Court.

There has been much discussion in the literature of public law and American politics concerning the extent to which the Supreme Court is an independent or dependent actor in the American political system. The dependent theory is exemplified by the thesis that the Supreme Court follows the election returns. The independent branch theory is well exemplified by Chief Justice John Marshall's decision in *Marbury* v. *Madison* (1803), where the Court placed itself in direct political and legal opposition to President Thomas Jefferson. This was the first of what by now are more than a hundred decisions in which the Supreme Court has ruled that acts of Congress were unconstitutional.

Jonathan Casper reported a table, in which he organized those cases by the length of time between enactment and invalidation, creating two groups of decisions, those from 1803 to 1957 and those from 1958 to 1974. The table demonstrates that in most of the Court's judicial review after the 1950s, there were significant time lags between legislation and Court action, whereas before 1957 the Court's rulings of unconstitutionality were much closer to the cutting edge of then contemporary congressional policy and personalities. However, the Court's decision of twenty-eight such cases in 17 years, as compared to seventy-eight over a period of 169 years, also constitutes a statistically significant relative acceleration in the Court's tendency to hold acts of Congress unconstitutional.

Richard Funston discussed an approach that relates Court decisions of unconstitutionality to their occurrence during either "critical" or "un-critical" periods of American political history. Critical periods involve major realignments of the American political party system. Funston identifies five major eras of party-system stability, in each of which a dominant coalition was established that retained control over the national government for a substantial period of time. These eras include the Jeffersonian Republican (twenty years); the Jacksonian Democrat (twenty-four years); the Radical Republican (twenty-eight years); the McKinley Republican (thirty-two years); and the New Deal Democrat (thirty-two years). These eras of stability alternated with shorter "phases" of realignment, which by Funston's reckoning were all eight years in length: 1820–1827; 1852–1859; 1888–1895; and 1928–1935.

Funston hypothesized that the Court is more likely to strike down new federal legislation during realignment phases because the Court's dominant majority represents the old political coalition that already has been, or is in the process of becoming, superseded in the presidency and the Congress; and conversely, Congress then retaliates against the Court. He reported Supreme Court cases declaring congressional legislation unconstitutional within four years of enactment for both critical and noncritical periods. He indicated sixteen cases decided in 32 years of critical periods and twenty-two cases decided in 136 years of noncritical periods, thus confirming his hypothesis.

This essay has selectively reviewed what amounts to a full generation of highly productive work by a large number of scholars of judicial behavior. Most of these persons are of the "second generation" of individuals who have worked in the empirical mode. Their work represents broad-ranging research that has asked and answered important new questions about the operation of the American judicial system. But this new generation of scholars has also raised many new questions about the complexities of the American judicial system for scholars of the next generation to address.

CASES

Abington Township School District v. Schempp, 374 U.S. 203 (1963)

BEHAVIORAL STUDIES OF THE AMERICAN LEGAL SYSTEM

Brown v. Board of Education, 347 U.S. 483 (1954)
Engel v. Vitale, 370 U.S. 421 (1962)
Marbury v. Madison, 1 Cranch 137 (1803)
Robinson v. Cahill, 62 N.J. 473 (1973)
Roe v. Wade, 410 U.S. 113 (1973)

BIBLIOGRAPHY

David Adamany and Joel Grossman, "Support for the Supreme Court as a National Policymaker," in *Law and Policy Quarterly*, 5 (1983). Gabriel Almond, "Comparative Political Systems," in *Journal of Politics*, 18 (1956). Gabriel Almond and James Coleman, *The Politics of the Developing Areas* (1960). Burton Atkins and Henry Glick, "Environmental and Structural Variables as Determinants of Issues in State Courts of Last Resort," in *American Journal of Political Science*, 20 (1976). Robert Freed Bales, *Interaction Process Analysis* (1950) and *Personality and Interpersonal Behavior* (1970). Lawrence Baum, Sheldon Goldman, and Austin Sarat, "The Evolution of Litigation in the Federal Courts of Appeals, 1895–1975," in *Law and Society Review*, 16 (1982). Theodore Becker, ed., *Political Trials* (1971). Gayle Binion, "The Disadvantaged Before the Burger Court: The Newest Unequal Protection," in *Law and Policy Quarterly*, 4 (1982). Saul Brenner, "Fluidity on the United States Supreme Court: A Reexamination," in *American Journal of Political Science*, 24 (1980).

Gregory A. Caldeira, "Judges Judge the Supreme Court," in *Judicature*, 61 (1977); and "The United States Supreme Court and Criminal Cases, 1935–1976: Alternative Models of Agenda Building," in *British Journal of Political Science*, 11 (1981). Bradley Canon, "Characteristics and Career Patterns of State Supreme Court Justices," in *State Government*, 45 (1972); and "Organizational Contumacy in the Transmission of Judicial Policies: The *Mapp, Escobedo, Miranda,* and *Gault* Cases," in *Villanova Law Review*, 20 (1974). Bradley Canon and Micheal Giles, "Recurring Litigants: Federal Agencies Before the Supreme Court," in *Western Political Quarterly*, 25 (1972). Susan Carbon, Pauline Houlden, and Larry Berkson, "Women on the State Bench: Their Characteristics and Attitudes About Judicial Selection," in *Judicature*, 65 (1982). Robert Carp and C. K. Rowland, *Policymaking and Politics in the Federal District Courts* (1983). Jonathan Casper, "The Supreme Court and National Policy Making," in *American Political Science Review*, 70 (1976). Beverly Cook, "Should We Change Our Method of Selecting Judges?" in *Judges' Journal*, 20, no. 4 (1981); "Women as Supreme Court Candidates: From Florence Allen to Sandra O'Connor," in *Judicature*, 65 (1982); and *Sentencing the Unpatriotic: Federal Trial Judges in Wisconsin During Four Wars* (1983). Jerome Corsi, *Judicial Politics: An Introduction* (1984).

David Danelski, "The Influence of the Chief Justice in the Decisional Process," in Walter Murphy and C. Herman Pritchett, eds., *Courts, Judges, and Politics* (1961). William J. Daniels, "The Geographic Factor in Appointments to the United States Supreme Court, 1789–1976," in *Western Political Quarterly*, 31 (1978). Philip Dubois, "Voter Turnout in State Judicial Elections," in *Journal of Politics*, 41 (1979). Craig R. Ducat and Victor E. Flango, *Leadership in State Supreme Courts: Roles of the Chief Justice* (1976). David Easton, *A Systems Analysis of Political Life* (1965). James Eisenstein, *Politics and the Legal Process* (1973).

Victor Flango, Robert Roper, and Mary Elsner, *The Business of State Trial Courts* (1983). Richard Funston, "The Supreme Court and Critical Elections," in *American Political Science Review*, 69 (1975). Micheal Giles and Douglas Gatlin, "Mass-Level Compliance with Public Policy: The Case of School Desegregation," in *Journal of Politics*, 42 (1980). Henry Glick, *Courts, Politics, and Justice* (1983). Sheldon Goldman and Thomas Jahnige, *The Federal Courts as a Political System*, 2nd ed. (1976). Roger Handberg, Jr., "Opinion Behavior on the United States Supreme Court, 1965–1977," in *Jurimetrics Journal*, 18 (1978). Roger Handberg and William Maddox, "Public Support for the Supreme Court in the 1970s," in *American Politics Quarterly*, 10 (1982). Susan Hansen, "State Implementation of Supreme Court Decisions: Abortion Rates Since *Roe* v. *Wade,*" in *Journal of Politics*, 42 (1980). George Homans, *The Human Group* (1950). J. Woodford Howard, Jr., *Courts of Appeals in the Federal Judicial System: A Study of the Second, Fifth, and District of Columbia Circuits* (1981). William Hulbary and Thomas Walker, "The Supreme Court Selection Process: Presidential Motivations and Judicial Performance," in *Western Political Quarterly*, 33 (1980).

Thomas Jahnige and Sheldon Goldman, eds., *The Federal Judicial System: Readings in Process and Behavior* (1968). Dorothy James, "Role Theory and the Supreme Court," in *Journal of Politics* 30 (1968). Charles A. Johnson, "Lower Court Reactions to Supreme Court Decisions: A Quantitative Examination," in *American Journal of Political Science*, 23 (1979). Charles Johnson and Bradley Canon, *Judicial Policies: Implementation and Impact* (1984). Richard M. Johnson, *The Dynamics of Compliance* (1967). Kathleen Kemp, Robert Carp, and David Brady, "The Supreme Court and Social Change: The Case of Abortion," in *Western Political Quarterly*, 31 (1978). Herbert Kritzer, "Political Correlates of the Behavior of Federal District Judges: A 'Best Case' Analysis," in *Journal of Politics*, 40 (1978). Herbert Kritzer and Thomas Uhlman, "Sisterhood in the Courtroom: Sex of Judge and Defendant in Criminal Case Disposition," in *Social Science Review*, 14 (1977). Candace Kruttschnitt, "Social Status and Sentences of Female Offenders," in *Law and Society Review*, 15 (1980). Richard Lehne and John Reynolds, "The Impact of Judicial Activism on Public Opinion," in *American Journal of Political Science*, 22 (1978). Martin A. Levin, *Urban Politics and the Criminal Courts* (1977).

Neil McFeeley and Richard Ault, "Supreme Court Oral Argument," in *Jurimetrics Journal*, 20 (1979). Elaine Martin, "Women on the Federal Bench: A Comparative Profile," in *Judicature*, 65 (1982). William Mitchell, *The American Polity: A Social and Cultural Interpretation* (1962). Walter Murphy, *The Elements of Judicial Strategy* (1964). Walter Murphy and Joseph Tanenhaus, "Public Opinion and the U.S. Supreme Court," in Joel Grossman and Joseph Tanenhaus, eds., *Frontiers of Judicial Research* (1969). Talcott Parsons, *The Social System* (1951). C. Herman Pritchett, "Divisions of Opinion Among Justices of the U.S. Supreme Court, 1939–1941," in *American Political Science Review*, 35 (1941); and *The Roosevelt Court: A Study in Judicial Politics and Values, 1937–1947* (1948). David Rohde, "Policy Goals and Opinion Coalitions in the Supreme Court," in *Midwest Journal of Political Science*, 16 (1972). John Paul Ryan, Allan Ashman, Bruce Sales, and Sandra

Shane-DuBow, *American Trial Judges: Their Work Styles and Performance* (1980).

John R. Schmidhauser, "The Justices of the Supreme Court: A Collective Portrait," in *Midwest Journal of Political Science*, 3 (1959); and *Judges and Justices: The Federal Appellate Judiciary* (1979). Glendon Schubert, *Quantitative Analysis of Judicial Behavior* (1959); "The 1960 Term of the Supreme Court: A Psychological Analysis," in *American Political Science Review*, 56 (1962); *Judicial Policy-Making: The Political Role of the Courts* (1965a); *The Judicial Mind: The Attitudes and Ideologies of Supreme Court Justices, 1946–1963* (1965b); *The Constitutional Polity* (1970); *Judicial Policy-Making: The Political Role of the Courts*, rev. ed. (1974a); *The Judicial Mind Revisited* (1974b); "Aging, Conservatism, and Judicial Behavior," in *Micropolitics*, 3 (1983); and *Political Culture and Judicial Behavior* (1985). Charles H. Sheldon, *The American Judicial Process: Models and Approaches* (1974); and "Influencing the Selection of Judges: The Variety and Effectiveness of State Bar Activities," in *Western Political Quarterly*, 30 (1977). Donald Songer, C. K. Rowland, and Robert Carp, "The Impact of the Supreme Court on Outcomes in the U.S. District Courts and the U.S. Courts of Appeals: A Longitudinal Exploration," paper presented at the annual meeting of the American Political Science Association, Washington, D.C. (1984). Cassia Spohn, John Gruhl, and Susan Welch, "The Effect of Race on Sentencing: A Re-Examination of an Unsettled Question," in *Law and Society Review*, 16 (1982). Wayne Sulfridge, "Ideology as a Factor in Senate Consideration of Supreme Court Nominations," in *Journal of Politics*, 42 (1980).

G. Alan Tarr, *Judicial Impact and State Supreme Courts* (1977). Neal Tate, "Personal Attribute Models of the Voting Behavior of U.S. Supreme Court Justices: Liberalism in Civil Liberties and Economics Decisions, 1946–1978," in *American Political Science Review*, 75 (1981); and "The Methodology of Judicial Behavior Research: A Review and Critique," in *Political Behavior*, 5 (1983). Louis Thurstone and J. W. Degan, "A Factorial Study of the Supreme Court," in *Proceedings of the National Academy of Sciences*, 37 (1951). Thomas Uhlman, "Black Elite Decision Making: The Case of Trial Judges," in *American Journal of Political Science*, 22 (1978). Sidney Ulmer, "Selecting Cases for Supreme Court Review: An Underdog Model," in *American Political Science Review*, 72 (1978). Pamela Utz, *Settling the Facts: Discretion and Negotiation in Criminal Court* (1978). Steven Wasby, "How Planned Is 'Planned Litigation'?" in *American Bar Foundation Research Journal*, 1 (1984).

[*See also* COMPLIANCE AND IMPACT; COURTS OF LIMITED AND SPECIALIZED JURISDICTION; FEDERAL COURT SYSTEM; JUDICIARY; JURISDICTION; LEGAL EDUCATION: LEGAL PROFESSION AND LEGAL ETHICS; STATE COURT SYSTEMS; *and* SUPREME COURT OF THE UNITED STATES.]

HISTORIOGRAPHY OF THE
AMERICAN LEGAL SYSTEM

Stephen B. Presser

For many years the writing of the history of American law was the ugly stepchild of legal scholarship. Lawyers had no use for the effete scribblings of academic historians, and historians mistrusted the hagiographic panegyrics produced by law professors or amateur chroniclers of local bench and bar. In a profession that prided itself on the glories of its past and ostensibly subscribed to an ideology involving precedent, this was something of a national disgrace.

There were some few exceptions to the general barrenness of production in the field, although like Oliver Wendell Holmes, Jr.'s *The Common Law* (1881), they were really more about Roman and English law than American. There was also a longstanding tradition of writing about the history of the federal Constitution, reaching back perhaps to Joseph Story's *Commentaries on the Constitution* (1833) or to Thomas Cooley's *Constitutional Limitations* (1868). Out of the philosophy of this writing of constitutional and doctrinal history there finally emerged an effort to produce an indigenous American legal history.

Story and Cooley were more or less openly writing history to advance an interpretation of particular constitutional doctrines and with clear political aims. Story was trying to mute sectional discord over the tariff and slavery issues. He sought to advance an interpretation of the United States Constitution designed to combat Southern advocates of the "compact theory." Those Southerners, principally John C. Calhoun and John Randolph of Roanoke, argued that the federal Constitution is a revocable agreement between equal and sovereign states, in the nature of a legal partnership. As such, according to the relevant legal doctrines, they argued, when any state or states feels that the others are breaching the agreement, the injured state is free to withdraw from the agreement and, if it chooses, to join in partnership with other withdrawing states or enjoy the benefits of nationhood alone.

Story argued that the federal Constitution is not an agreement between sovereign states but a political pact among the sovereign people of all the states themselves, a pact that limits the sovereignty of the individual states and that can be dissolved only by the acts of the entire nation, not by those of any state. Story's argument initially failed, of course, but following the victory of the North in the Civil War, it became part of the received national wisdom and helped lay the foundation for national commercial and social development in the next century. Similarly, if less dramatically, Cooley sought in his 1868 treatise to demonstrate that the federal Constitution imposes limits on the regulatory powers of the state governments, limits that are not to be exceeded if national commerce was to flourish. Story's and Cooley's works thus demonstrate how writing about the law's past could chart a course for the future.

Holmes's *Common Law* (1881), though it is both more and less than a work in the history of American law, was probably designed in part to offset some of what he believed to be the stultifying implications of the work of Story and Cooley. Holmes examined the development of the doctrines of Anglo-American private law and sought to illustrate how they evolved to serve different social purposes. In the famous opening words of the first chapter of his book, Holmes explained that the primary source of American law is not logic but "experience," that the content of legal systems reflects neither divine order nor abstract theorems but rather "the felt necessities of the times."

Holmes tried to show how judges, usually unconsciously or at least surreptitiously, take old legal maxims, rules, or doctrines and subtly alter them to serve new social purposes. Holmes felt that by such alteration of legal and constitutional precedents and rules, judges perform an entirely laudable task, transforming the law to meet the needs of the times. This means, to Holmes at least, that it is fruitless to try, as Story and Cooley had, to restrict the work of courts or legislatures by attempting to tie judges down to particularly abstract visions supposedly inherent in the original constitutional scheme. Rather, Holmes maintained, judges should be allowed to remain the great unsung legislators of American law.

Courts, Holmes pointed out, do not simply find but rather make American law in accordance with what they perceive to be the economic or social goals of their eras. Holmes's work as the great modern American judge, for twenty years on the Supreme Judicial Court of Massachusetts and then for thirty years on the United States Supreme Court, demonstrated that he meant to make the kind of history he wrote. His judicial philosophy, later to be interpreted by a group of acolytes as "legal realism," was, from the third decade of the twentieth century on, to mold both constitutional and private law in such a way as to expand the regulatory and planning powers of the state and national governments, in all their branches.

PRODDING THE SUPREME COURT

From that day to this, the writing of the history of American law has seized upon the legal-realist insights of Holmes and has concentrated on the role of American judges in forging new legal rules. More often than not, the most distinguished work of American constitutional and legal historians has been advanced with the aim of prodding contemporary courts or of scoring the kind of political points attempted by Story, Cooley, and Holmes. The early twentieth-century classics in this vein are Charles Warren's *The Supreme Court in United States History* (3 vols., 1922) and Roscoe Pound's *The Formative Era of American Law* (1938).

Warren's volumes show how the United States Supreme Court, particularly under the leadership of John Marshall, Joseph Story, and Roger B. Taney, had interpreted the Constitution in a manner that permitted the orderly expansion of the national economy but still protected the essential elements of private property. In keeping with the progressive politics of Woodrow Wilson and Theodore Roosevelt, Warren's work seems to demonstrate how the judiciary, at least in a golden age before the Civil War, had met the needs of a vital and robust nation. In Warren's time, the implication, of course, was that the American Supreme Court of the 1920s and 1930s, still mired in the laissez-faire philosophy limned in Cooley's treatise, ought to expand its horizons in order to support legislative efforts to invigorate state economies and thus provide protection to the social welfare of the laboring classes, which efforts progressive historians like Warren felt were necessary to achieve lasting national prosperity.

Pound's book, written in the depths of the Great Depression, is another effort to save the judiciary from itself and to recapture a glorious professional past. Pound concentrated on private rather than public law, but he transmitted a similar message regarding the need for legal creativity. In his slim volume Pound created a mythology of American legal development that still prevails in the majority of American legal minds. Pound wrote of what he called the "taught legal tradition," an adherence to basic principles of American private law—principles such as freedom of contract and freedom from tort liability without fault—that Pound claimed prevailed in the first half of the nineteenth century. These principles entered the mainstream of American law, replacing more restrictive English doctrines based on status and hereditary privilege, through the work of the great nineteenth-century judges, such as Marshall, Story, James Kent, and Lemuel Shaw. Pound tried to show how these judges evenhandedly applied these principles—in the case of Shaw, for example, to protect the rights of laborers as well as the rights of employers.

Pound expressly denied the validity of "Marxian" interpretations of American law, which had recently sought to demonstrate that the great nineteenth-century judges were no more than servants of a capitalist and domineering ideology. The "taught legal tradition," thundered Pound, constant over 150 years of American law, has much more to do with American legal rules than with the economic circumstances of time or place. Nevertheless, Pound's work belies some of his claims, and his particular political agenda also suggests difficulties with his notion that the legal system is capable, without fundamental restructuring, of meeting the needs of American society.

In the first place, Pound's analysis, insofar as it suggests that the greatness of American law is to be found only in a formative era running roughly from the American Revolution to the Civil War, by implication disparages the century and a half of colonial legal development before the Revolution and that of the three generations since the Civil War. Pound claimed that before 1776, American law was a shallow imitation or a rough frontier attempt at justice that could hardly be dignified as the work of a learned profession. Pound asserted that after about 1860 the creative spurt of legal doctrines ceased and a lesser race of judges took to the bench, a tribe committed to formalism and a rather unthinking adherence to mechanical legal logic and use of precedent. Why this occurred Pound never explained, but he appears to have admitted that something needed to be done to reverse the trend of judicial somnabulism and mechanistic jurisprudence.

By implication, Pound, like Warren, seemed to be calling for a rejection by the United States Supreme Court of its jurisprudence of substantive due process, of its practice of frustrating state efforts at reform through its adherence to the constitutional doctrine that individuals' contracts are immune from state regulation and of its cashiering of Roosevelt's New Deal. As befitted the dean of the Harvard Law School, Pound was relatively careful to refrain from overtly criticizing the Court. Pound's solution for what he perceived as a need for legal reform is the creation of a national ministry of justice, staffed by the country's best legal minds, who could engage in the same kind of rethinking of American law as that undertaken by Pound's early nineteenth-century heroic common-law judges.

Pound's effort to legitimate legal reform and his characterization of a formative era is echoed in two other notable works of legal history, which, beginning an important revision in his-

toriographical methodology, treat the jurisprudence of particular states. Oscar and Mary Handlin, in their *Commonwealth: A Study of the Role of Government in the American Economy: Massachusetts 1744–1861* (1947; rev. ed., 1969), and Louis Hartz, in his *Economic Policy and Democratic Thought: Pennsylvania, 1776–1860* (1948), sought to provide an historical pedigree for the interventionist philosophy of the New Deal. Reaching into the colonial era, these two works try to show that central planning and the conscious formation of legislative regulatory policy could occasionally be found in the colonial era and characterized most of the nineteenth century.

If state regulation of the economy is an American tradition, they reasoned, then the Supreme Court's ideology of social Darwinism and rugged individualism ought to be abandoned in the interests of progressive reform. In this manner, the Handlins and Hartz can also be read as legitimating the blatant reversal of the Supreme Court in 1937, when, following Roosevelt's Court-packing threat, the Court suddenly appeared more willing to tolerate federal and state regulatory schemes.

Pound's periodization, his characterization of a "formative era" or "golden age" of American law, continued to dominate legal historiography, such as it was, for the next generation. The work of legitimating the New Deal went on in such specialized legal-historical works as Felix Frankfurter's *The Commerce Clause Under Marshall, Taney and Waite* (1937), an effort to elaborate an American judicial tradition of inspired nationalist vision. To a great extent, the idea of the judges as the font of American law, made popular by Holmes and by the focus on the works of the Supreme Court justices and the great early nineteenth-century state judges, led to a narrowness in the field and a restrictive focus on legal doctrines applied by both lawyers and judges.

There were occasionally brilliant exceptions, such as the quixotic attempt at a new constitutional theory presented in two volumes by William Winslow Crosskey in 1953, *Politics and the Constitution in the History of the United States.* In an extraordinary effort at linguistic analysis resulting from decades of painstaking research, Crosskey sought to show that the meaning of the constitutional text and the debates of the framers ought to be interpreted very differently from the manner in which they had been in orthodox constitutional theory since John Marshall. Crosskey's effort was either savaged or ignored by orthodox scholars, and while some of his ultimate doctrinal conclusions may have been dubious, it took another twenty years before a new generation of historical scholars was able to profit from many of his astonishing insights.

WIDENING THE HISTORICAL RANGE

The orthodoxy and sterility of the field began to change dramatically with the appearance of the work of James Willard Hurst. Hurst accepted the periodization of Pound and still wrote about the first half of the nineteenth century as the great formative period of American law. Unlike Pound, however, Hurst found the wellsprings of American law not in the efforts of judges but in the work of executives, legislatures, administrative agencies, and private parties.

Hurst wrote with the same passion Holmes, Story, and Cooley had employed, but with a different purpose. The most important of a series of major works he produced is a legal history of the lumber industry in Wisconsin, *Law and Economic Growth: The Legal History of the Lumber Industry in Wisconsin, 1836–1915* (1964; 2nd ed., 1984). Hurst sought to show how, through manipulation of all the instrumentalities of legal change—courts, legislatures, executives, and administrative agencies—lumber in Wisconsin had been ravaged without much thought to the environmental or economic implications for Wisconsin's future. Hurst's theory is that the ostensible legal rules employed by courts tell only a very small part of the story of the development of American law. To a shockingly great degree, Hurst showed, the legal and constitutional rules have not been employed to serve stirring philosophical purposes, such as liberty or justice, but rather have served as tools of "bastard pragmatism," a sort of seat-of-the-pants philosophy of economic development at all costs. Even more darkly, Hurst hinted that much law had resulted from a lack of conscious planning altogether, which Hurst labeled simply "drift."

Hurst established the theoretical background for his magnum opus on the lumber industry with two broader works, encompassing the entire American legal system. In the first of these, *The Growth of American Law: The Law Makers* (1950), Hurst sought to revise the work of Holmes and Pound by illustrating how agencies of the law in addition to the courts had influenced legal history. Hurst followed this work on the methods of legal growth by a book on the substance and the themes of American law, *Law and the Conditions of Freedom in the Nineteenth-Century United States* (1956). In that book, Hurst, adopting the precise periodization used by Pound in his *Formative Era,* tried to illustrate how the demands of American economic growth had dictated the character of American legal development. He suggested that Pound's "taught legal tradition" is much less important than national desires for individualistic expression and economic change.

Hurst moved beyond Pound's simple characterization of the post–Civil War era as one of arid formalism. He showed that the end of the nineteenth century was a period of frenetic large-scale organizational activity, that there was still much legal development but at a very different level from that at the beginning of the century. In the antebellum era the growth of legal doctrines involved the property interests of individuals, Hurst suggested, but by the end of the century, unless the individual could align his legal interests with those of a larger organization, he was likely to be overwhelmed, since American law was principally promoting larger-scale enterprise and association.

By demonstrating the richness of the legal materials from a stunning variety of institutional sources, the extent to which economic theories and history could be used in the analysis of changes in the law, the power with which Holmes's legal-realist insight could be employed, and his willingness to share his theories and methodology with a succession of graduate students, colleagues, and correspondents, Hurst became the most influential figure in American legal history of the twentieth century. As others adopted his methods and came to study with him, there arose the first recognizable association of practitioners of American legal history, the "Wisconsin school."

Hurst and the other members of the Wisconsin school proceeded to perform empirical research on a variety of topics and, in the burgeoning academic environment of the 1960s, to assume positions teaching courses in American legal history at various law schools and colleges. At about this time the American Society for Legal History was founded; it provided an annual forum for discussion of research and eventually two professional journals that publish articles and review a rapidly appearing series of monographs.

By 1960, however, in other sectors of the academy, voices were beginning to be heard that challenged other aspects of Pound's treatment of American law, many of which were still accepted by Hurst and his school. Most prominent among these challenges was the questioning of Pound's implicit suggestions that nothing of value to the future course of American legal development occurred before the American Revolution and that the overwhelming source of American law is the materialistic desires of the American people. In 1960, George Haskins published his seminal *Law and Authority in Early Massachusetts: A Study in Tradition and Design.* Haskins suggested that what happened in the first twenty years of the colony of Massachusetts, culminating in the colony's "Laws and Liberties of 1648," helped set patterns that were to endure for the rest of American legal history. Haskins showed how even as early as the 1620s the Massachusetts colonists, several of whom had been trained at England's Inns of Court, were using wide legal knowledge to fashion new American means of furthering political and religious, as well as economic, goals.

Haskins and several others like him demonstrated that the American law used in the colonial period was not simply dictates from Deuteronomy or rough "frontier justice," as earlier American legal historians, following the lead of Pound, had claimed. Rather, the law of colonial Massachusetts, according to Haskins, was a sophisticated attempt to pick and choose from several different traditional varieties of English local and common law and to use the new combination to promote the colonists' designs for their lives in New England, their projects of spiritual salvation as well as their projects for material progress.

At about the same time that Haskins was writing, Joseph Smith, who for many years presided over the Society for American Legal History, began important projects in editing colonial and early American primary sources. He also produced an important monograph on the interaction of the courts in the American colonies and the English authorities, the magisterial *Appeals to the Privy Council from the American Plantations* (1950). Smith's book is an important demonstration, in the same manner as Haskins' work, that the most fundamental American constitutional doctrines (in Smith's case, the doctrine of judicial review) have colonial antecedents.

Some time later, in 1971, one of Smith's colleagues at Columbia University, Julius Goebel, published a massive book linking virtually all of early American constitutional law with its English antecedents. This, the first volume of the Oliver Wendell Holmes Devise History of the United States Supreme Court, *Antecedents and Beginnings to 1801,* capped a lifetime of work in the colonial and early national period for Goebel. Goebel's thesis, differing markedly from that of Hurst, seems to be that one cannot understand even postrevolutionary American development without an appreciation of the nature of English local and national legal institutions. The focus on English and American institutional development, principally courts and the English forms of action, was further elaborated by both Goebel and Smith in teaching materials, one volume of which was published by Smith as *Development of Legal Institutions* (1965) and became one of the first commercially available legal-history casebooks.

Smith's and Goebel's focus on legal institutions, on the formal aspects of the law, can be perceived as slighting the influence of particular personalities and of the social forces that the Wisconsin school had begun to study. Some notable works exploring these neglected aspects began to appear in the late 1950s. A new kind of judicial biography came to be written, one that sought to present judges as caught up in, and troubled by, the political and social forces of their times, rather than as Pound's noble expositors of scientific legal doctrines. Among the best of these were Leonard Levy's *The Law of the Commonwealth and Chief Justice Shaw* (1957), on the greatest of the Massachusetts early nineteenth-century state court judges; John P. Reid's *Chief Justice: The Judicial World of Charles Doe* (1967), the life of a New Hampshire judge in the late nineteenth century; and R. Kent Newmyer's *Supreme Court Justice Joseph Story: Statesman of the Old Republic* (1985).

Similar work detailing individual cases in American law and putting them in their ideological, political, social, and economic contexts was undertaken, often by students of Hurst or of others like him who had begun to teach American history in law schools. Excellent examples in this genre are Stanley N. Katz's *A Brief Narrative of the Case and Trial of John Peter Zenger, Printer of the New York Weekly Journal. By James Alexander* (1963), on the colonial law of freedom of the press; Stanley Kutler's *Privilege and Creative Destruction: The Charles River Bridge Case* (1978), on the law of competition and vested property interests; C. Peter Magrath, *Yazoo: Law and Politics in the New Republic* (1966), on the power of state legislatures in the early federal period; and Tony Freyer's *Harmony and Dissonance: The Swift and Erie Cases in American Federalism* (1981), on the allocation of substantive jurisdiction to state and federal courts.

Finally, the evolution of legal institutions in their social context, the staffing of institutional bureaucracies of the law, and the clash between formal bureaucratic structures of state and federal governments became a rich lode to be mined by practitioners of a "new legal history." Foremost in this area is the work of Harry N. Scheiber, a product of the Wisconsin school who began a prolific career with *Ohio Canal Era: A Case Study of Government and the Economy, 1820–1861* (1969) and continued to produce a stream of influential articles on federalism, the allocation of responsibilities between the state and federal governments, and legal historiography. The most prominent practitioner of the art of judicial prosopography, shedding light on the interaction between political parties and the evolution of law, is Kermit L. Hall, the author of *The Politics of Justice: Lower Federal Judicial Selection and the Second Party System, 1829–61* (1979) and a comprehensive multivolume bibliography of American legal history.

CONSOLIDATING THE GAINS

By the late 1960s a time for taking stock seemed to have arrived, and a host of works appeared that summed up the legal-history field or presented anthologies of articles. These surveys and anthologies still contain much of the best legal-historical writing available. The most important was a volume in Harvard University's Perspectives in American History series, edited by two members of Harvard's history department, Bernard Bailyn and Donald Fleming, and republished, to reach a wider audience, as *Law in American History* (1971). There is an eclectic quality to this book, as befits an effort to introduce a variety of young historians with wide-ranging interests. The book's orthodox introduction, written by a Supreme Court justice, acknowledges the rise of what was perceived to be a maturing new discipline; but the book contains some fundamental reevaluations of colonial and American law. The most notable of these is Stanley Katz's essay on colonial Chancery courts, which he showed to be proving grounds for American radicalism, and Morton Horwitz' piece on the emergence of "an instrumental conception of American law," in which he presented an elaborate statement of the manner in which early American jurisprudence came to differ from English and colonial models. Other essays treat topics ranging from two hundred years of American legal education to the workings of the mid-twentieth-century Department of Justice.

Two collections of topical essays, reprinting some classics of the field and introducing a "third generation" of American legal historians (the students of the students of "founders" such as Pound, Hurst, Smith, and Goebel) were soon published. The first of these, edited by David H. Flaherty and titled *Essays in the History of Early American Law* (1969), appeared just before the Bailyn and Fleming volume and is devoted to the colonial era, which was finally coming into its own after the pioneering work of Goebel, Haskins, and Katz. This collection was followed by *Essays in Nineteenth-Century American Legal History* (1976), edited by Wythe Holt. Both editors wrote long bibliographical essays introducing their volumes, and both essays are still indispensable guides for anyone seeking overviews of American legal historiography.

By the early 1970s, the accumulated weight of the classic works by Story, Holmes, and Pound; the monographs of the Wisconsin school; and the raft of articles produced by an increasing number of professional legal historians teaching in both colleges and law schools had reached a critical mass. This allowed the production of several surveys that could be used as texts, lending some unity of conception to the field; these texts could also be used, in the phrase of one of their authors, as "whipping boys" to propose a "tradition" for American legal history, which could then be attacked and revised. That is precisely what happened.

The contributor of the "whipping boy" phrase was the author of the self-proclaimed "first attempt to do anything remotely like a general history, a survey of the development of American law, including some treatment of substance, procedure, and legal institutions." Lawrence M. Friedman, a student of Willard Hurst, in his splendid and simply named *A History of American Law* (1973; rev. ed., 1986), did present the whole range of American legal development, concentrating on the nineteenth century but adequately sketching the colonial period and the twentieth century.

Friedman, as a product of the Wisconsin school, explained that his work had become possible because of "the important work of scholars of first rank, men like Willard Hurst," and "the development of modern social science." Friedman proceeded to present the story of American law as a mirror in which were reflected the political, economic, and sociological changes in society at large. The forms and the content of American law were revealed as shaped by the manifold struggles taking place in all sectors of American life.

Friedman's book became the subject of long review essays in virtually all of the major law reviews, most of which perceived it as inaugurating the period of maturity of the discipline. The appearance of these reviews also signaled an increased willingness on the part of the law reviews, and thus indirectly American law schools, to take seriously the writing and teaching of the history of American law. Friedman's general survey was followed by a less widely noticed but still quite good illustrated volume by Bernard Schwartz, *The American Heritage History of the Law in America* (1974), which brought the actual faces of the greats and near greats in American legal history to a much greater audience than ever before.

Three more general surveys, two in the form of long biographical profiles and one a general treatment of the institutions of the profession, soon appeared. G. Edward White, in *The American Judicial Tradition: Profiles of Leading American Judges* (1976), attempted to do for American judges what Richard Hofstadter had done for politicians, and continued the effort begun by Fried-

man to give shape to a general historiographical tradition. White argued that from John Marshall to Earl Warren there were common judicial determinants, supradoctrinal principles that restricted what judges could do and thus maximized their effectiveness in American society.

Both state and federal judges, according to White, were allowed broad freedom as individual shapers of private- and public-law doctrines, but federal and state constitutions came to be interpreted as forbidding the judicial institution from infringing on the most fundamental responsibilities of the executive or legislative branches. This allowed American judges to claim that they were not politically partisan and thus ought to be entitled to deference as oracles of supposedly neutral, objective legal rules. Like Friedman, White presented a sort of neo-Poundian form of consensus history in which there were, admittedly, political disagreements about the application of fundamental values in American life but broad fundamental agreement on those values.

Maxwell H. Bloomfield, in *American Lawyers in A Changing Society, 1776–1876* (1976), followed the same strategy as White, presenting short biographies of several American lawyers and explaining how each had dealt, with varying degrees of success, with the ideological and social struggles of his times. Differing somewhat with White's and Friedman's approach, however, Bloomfield suggested that there had been alternative political visions of the practice of American law, including deferential aristocratic attempts in the early national period and French-inspired reformist efforts shortly thereafter, both of which had been decisively rejected. Bloomfield also showed that even if lawyers had failed in implementing their grand political visions, they were successful in altering inequities present in the nineteenth century in the law of slavery and the law of families.

THE FAILURE OF LEGAL IDEALS

Bloomfield hinted at the existence of a darker side of American law, one of conformist pressures and materialistic insensitivity. Such themes had occasionally appeared in a very muted form in the work of Hurst and his students, but they now began to be sounded much more loudly. In Gerald Auerbach's *Unequal Justice: Lawyers and So-*

cial Change in Modern America (1976), the entire American legal profession was presented as an entity stubbornly and selfishly reluctant to change and committed to equal justice only for some—those able to pay for it.

The thesis of the failure of the American legal system to live up to its high ideals was given great visibility as national attention focused on the struggle of blacks for civil rights. It was pursued in several specialist studies, most often concerning the treatment of minorities in America. Among the best of these was Richard Kluger's Simple Justice: The History of Brown v. Board of Education and Black America's Struggle for Equality (1975), the story of the pursuit of school integration in the courts. Probably the most popular topic was a return to the root causes of racial discrimination, the history of the American law of slavery and constitutional problems at the time of the Civil War and Reconstruction. Some of the most sensitive and distinguished works on this theme were William M. Wiecek's The Sources of Antislavery Constitutionalism in America, 1760–1848 (1977), Mark Tushnet's The American Law of Slavery 1810–1860: Considerations of Humanity and Interest, and Harold M. Hyman's A More Perfect Union: The Impact of the Civil War and Reconstruction on the Constitution (1973).

The idea of a critical national self-examination, which seemed to dominate much of American politics from the assassination of John F. Kennedy through the presidency of Jimmy Carter and which was inherent in many of these works on constitutional issues, led also to inquiries into the nature of private law, to dissatisfaction with the kind of consensus history practiced by the Wisconsin school, and to research beyond the characteristics of the profession into the most basic questions about the nature of American law. Three such broad inquiries, among the most important works ever written on American law, appeared in the midst of this time of self-study; they uncovered much of the source of American legal difficulties in the immediate post-revolutionary period.

The first of these, Gordon Wood's The Creation of the American Republic, 1776–1787 (1969), was written by a student of Bernard Bailyn's who developed the insights of Bailyn's critically acclaimed Ideological Origins of the American Revolution (1967). Wood found that in the years between the Declaration of Independence and the federal Constitution, a distinctive national constitutional politics took form. The practice of this politics gave way to popular demands for the establishment of the ultimate sovereignty of the people and the abolition of aristocracy but tried simultaneously to control the worst excesses of democracy and to safeguard from popular legislative excesses individual rights to make contracts and own property. Accompanying this creation of the American Republic, Wood demonstrated, was a theoretical shift in the philosophical support for American systems of constitution and law, from divine inspiration and "natural law" to the "will of the people." Whereas, as Haskins and Smith had demonstrated, colonial legal systems were grounded in the ancient rights of Englishmen, the Christian religion, and the hegemony of the British monarch and aristocracy, the only basis left for America was the desires of the American people themselves.

The second two works, written by two former Harvard graduate students with both law degrees and doctorates in history—increasingly dual prerequisites for the writing and teaching of legal history—are William Nelson's The Americanization of the Common Law: The Impact of Legal Change on Massachusetts Society, 1760–1830 (1975) and Morton Horwitz' The Transformation of American Law, 1780–1860 (1977). Both of these built on the work of Bailyn, Wood, and others like them who had seen a "great transformation" in the nature of the American social order in the last part of the eighteenth century and the beginning of the nineteenth.

Nelson's work is confined to a single state but is a model of historiography, the result of a reading of virtually every manuscript and printed account of all the court decisions in Massachusetts for the period studied. It is an exhaustive treatment not only of substantive law but of civil and criminal procedures as well. Nelson's book dramatically shows the movement of the law in Massachusetts from a system based on colony-wide deferential equitable rules, grounded in the same religious order Haskins found in the late sixteenth century, to an individualistic, pluralistic, market-oriented and secular society in the nineteenth. Nelson, one of the most prolific and brilliant of American legal historians, followed up his trailblazing Americanization of the Common Law with a multivolume collection of Plymouth

County Court records and a monograph on dispute and conflict resolution in Plymouth.

Horwitz, concentrating on private-law doctrines in property, contracts, torts, and commercial law, expanded Nelson's themes to cover the law generally, or at least that of the Eastern Seaboard, from the Revolution to the Civil War. The first chapter of Horwitz' book is his essay from the Bailyn and Fleming collection; it shows how revolutionary theory had destroyed the natural-law basis of American doctrines and made possible an era in which judges could alter private law in the service of social change. The rest of the book demonstrates how Story, Shaw, Kent, and others had performed this transformation in the content of American law.

Horwitz, who repeatedly excoriated the type of "lawyer's legal history" practiced by Pound, had, curiously, returned to the very periodization and description used by Pound. He shared Pound's beliefs in the early nineteenth century as the formative era of American law and the late nineteenth century as a period of arid formalism. Unlike Pound, Horwitz found the source of both of these developments in the economic desires of merchants and entrepreneurs and of lawyers and judges who saw their future economic and social interests allied with them.

Horwitz' treatment of this "merchant-lawyer alliance" was not a conspiracy theory, although many reviewers of his book mistakenly believed it to be. Rather, Horwitz' point is that consciously or unconsciously, nineteenth-century American lawyers had altered the law in two great legal shifts. First, they secured in the early nineteenth century a set of private-law doctrines that could come to grips with the scarcity of capital in America, reward active entrepreneurs, and reduce their costs of investments by jettisoning doctrines that imposed harsh liability in contracts, torts, and corporations. Second, once this move had been accomplished, by about the time of the Civil War, the merchant-lawyer alliance needed to freeze in place its proentrepreneurial doctrines, and this need encouraged judges sympathetic to their goals to implement a system of stare decisis. Pound's interpretation had been turned on its head, or perhaps set on its feet: the only determinants of American law, it seemed, were the economic circumstances of time and place.

Horwitz' book received even more notice in the law schools and in history departments than had Friedman's. Most reviewers found something to criticize, particularly Horwitz' explicitly polemical argument that the result of the nineteenth-century transformations in general and the merchant-lawyer alliance in particular was to transfer resources from the weak to the strong and to reinforce and maintain the disparities in wealth and power that the market system produced. Essentially, Horwitz argued that merchants and lawyers had (extremely undemocratically) weakened the influence of the forces of morality and democracy in private law and, by calling the law a "legal science" fit only for professionals, had stolen it from the people.

Nevertheless, the subtlety and analytical brilliance of Horwitz' doctrinal analysis of a variety of substantive law areas; his creative use of such neglected primary sources as nineteenth-century legal treatises, periodicals, and pamphlets; and his incorporation of perspectives from political science, orthodox legal analysis, and the best in the recent writing of American and European history appeared to lift the practice of American legal history to a new peak. In 1978, Horwitz was awarded the Bancroft Prize for American history by Columbia University, the highest honor that the history discipline in the United States has to bestow. From then on, the practice of American legal history, even in the law schools, became something not only lawyers but historians had to regard seriously. Furthermore, the demographic decline in the college-age population and the temporary surge in law school applications led even more professional historians into teaching in the schools of law.

A MASS MARKET FOR LEGAL HISTORY

The influx to the law schools of students who in earlier years would have gone to graduate schools in the social sciences and humanities and the forced examination of the philosophical and ethical bases of law brought on by the involvement of so many lawyers in the Watergate affair created a market for "law and" courses—"law and philosophy," "law and economics," "law and literature," and "law and history." Three new readers, the first devoted exclusively to the history of American law, had appeared by 1980.

One of these, *Readings in the History of the American Legal Profession* (1980), was assembled by a law professor, Dennis Nolan, and presented the primary sources for students to build an evaluation of the practice of law such as that presented by Bloomfield. The other two were put together by historian-lawyer combinations. The first of these, a Wisconsin-school product edited by Lawrence Friedman and Harry Scheiber, *American Law and the Constitutional Order* (1978), consists of edited versions of legal-history articles on a wide range of constitutional and private-law topics. The second was put together by a law student of Horwitz' and a graduate student of Katz's, and chose the standard law-school "cases and materials" format. Stephen Presser and Jamil Zainaldin's *Law and American History* (1980), is a coursebook that tries to combine the insights of Katz with the economic realism of Horwitz and to push the analysis into the end of the twentieth century. The book is based on edited primary sources but is accompanied by a hundred-page teachers' manual that compares and contrasts the work of other legal historians in order to contribute to the building of a coherent historiographical field theory. The authors' argument, extracted from the materials presented, is that American public and private law rest on the same mutually inconsistent political and philosophical principles. According to Presser and Zainaldin, the basic principle of American law, taken from the struggles of the English against the Stuarts, is the restraint of all arbitrary power. Fundamental political rights were secured against arbitrary power by the principle of popular sovereignty established in the American Revolution, as suggested by Gordon Wood; and popular sovereignty was itself secured by social mobility and economic progress, as demonstrated by Willard Hurst. Finally, economic progress and social mobility were secured by maintaining an individualistic free market and the principle of a protected private sphere, as shown by Horwitz, Nelson, Bloomfield, and many other historians.

As Kermit Hall noted, Presser and Zainaldin's implicit premise is that American law ought to be studied as a matter of anthropology, as evidence of a variety of ideological assumptions that combined to form a distinctive American culture. The nature of those ideological assumptions, the extent to which the law is a tool of political or economic forces, and the countervailing extent to which the law is characterized by a sort of legal-cultural "relative autonomy" became the central question addressed in legal historiography in the late 1970s and 1980s.

LAW AS IDEOLOGY

Horwitz' 1977 work had effectively opened the next phase of historiography by arguing that nineteenth-century law had been manipulated in the service of economic ends and that this manipulation had been concealed behind a structure of supposedly neutral "scientific rules." A group of younger scholars, many students of Horwitz' and many products of a similar approach taken by legal scholars at Yale who called themselves the Conference on Critical Legal Studies, soon built upon, and went beyond, Horwitz. They sought to explain that much of American legal history is the product of American culture's artificial separation of the public and private spheres and reflects the incapacity of Western bourgeois liberalism to move beyond the "possessive individualism" and the atomistic market society conceived by the great English liberal and market theorists.

One of the most articulate spokesmen for this group is Robert Gordon, a Horwitz student who became a colleague of Hurst and later of Lawrence Friedman. In his three major historiographical essays, Gordon, one of the leading critics of legal history, showed a dramatic development of his thought from that of a fairly mainstream exponent of the Wisconsin school to that of a passionate advocate of critical legal studies and fundamental social change. The essays are "J. Willard Hurst and the Common Law Tradition in American Legal Historiography," in *Law and Society Review*, 10 (1975); "Historicism in Legal Scholarship," in *Yale Law Journal*, 90 (1981); and "Critical Legal Histories," in *Stanford Law Review*, 36 (1984). A similar progression of belief can be traced in the work of another of Gordon's former Wisconsin colleagues, Mark Tushnet, also a prolific critic and critical legal studies scholar, who combined work in legal history with contemporary constitutional analysis. For a review of Tushnet's work and that of other radical scholars, see A. Nash, "In re Radical Interpretations of American Law: The Relation of

Law and History," in *Michigan Law Review*, 82 (1983).

Inspired in part by the work of such critical legal scholars as Gordon, Tushnet, Jay Feinman, Wythe Holt, and Karl Klare, American legal historians in the 1980s seemed to be turning their attention increasingly to the period during which the basic ideological assumptions of American public and private law took form, the end of the eighteenth century. One of the most influential works in this vein is not ostensibly about American law at all but rather is an exhaustive analysis of Blackstone by a leading critical legal scholar, Duncan Kennedy: "The Structure of Blackstone's Commentaries," in *Buffalo Law Review*, 28 (1979). Kennedy argued that Blackstone's *Commentaries* reveal many of the antinomies and irrationalities that continue to plague American public and private law. Gordon suggested that this one work of Kennedy's has actually spawned a whole school of legal historians.

Other notable works exploring the formation of the ideological assumptions of the American legal culture in the late eighteenth and nineteenth centuries include three richly detailed monographs by John Reid on the American Revolution and English and American theories of constitutionalism. These are *In a Defiant Stance: The Conditions of Law in Massachusetts Bay, the Irish Comparison, and the Coming of the American Revolution* (1977); *In a Rebellious Spirit: The Argument of Facts, the Liberty Riot, and the Coming of the American Revolution* (1979); and *In Defiance of the Law: The Standing-Army Controversy, the Two Constitutions, and the Coming of the American Revolution* (1981). Also noteworthy are William Nelson's *The Roots of American Bureaucracy, 1830–1900* (1982); Henrik Hartog's book on the development of municipal corporation law in New York, *Public Property and Private Power: The Corporation of the City of New York in American Law, 1730–1870* (1983); Mary K. Bonsteel Tachau's work on the lower federal courts, *Federal Courts in the Early Republic: Kentucky, 1789–1816* (1978); two essays by Stephen Presser on the jurisprudence of the pre-Marshall Federalist judges, "A Tale of Two Judges: Richard Peters, Samuel Chase, and the Broken Promise of Federalist Jurisprudence," in *Northwestern University Law Review*, 73 (1978), and, with Becky Bair Hurley, "Saving God's Republic: The Jurisprudence of Samuel Chase," in *University of Illinois Law Review* (1984); and two articles by H.

Jefferson Powell revising our understanding of the intentions of the framers of the Constitution, "The Original Understanding of Original Intent," in *Harvard Law Review*, 95 (1985), and "Joseph Story's Commentaries on the Constitution: A Belated Review," in *Yale Law Journal*, 94 (1985).

THE FUTURE OF THE DISCIPLINE

In the mid-1980s it was unclear precisely what form or direction American legal historical scholarship would take. At the end of the 1970s, in Grant Gilmore's idiosyncratic and passionate *Ages of American Law* (1977), originally a series of lectures that supposedly left even jaded Yale law students gasping, Gilmore made dire predictions. In the nineteenth and early twentieth centuries, he suggested, there was room for titans of the law and legal history, such as Holmes, Cardozo, and Corbin, who could articulate brilliant theories of individualism and legal liberty. At the close of the twentieth century, he cautioned, we have entered an era of overpopulation, scarce resources, and irremediable shortages, and the unhappy task of the law will be somehow to soften the blows inflicted by economic despair.

Gilmore's note of pessimism can still be found in much legal history, particularly that of the critical legal studies writers, but that pessimism, which prevailed in much of the American academy, seemed curiously out of touch with mainstream American culture and a nation that in 1984 reelected the most optimistic American president in its history by one of the greatest landslides. The greatest need, then, seemed to be for an American legal history that could better explain, interpret, advise, and caution the American people and one that better reflected their political expressions.

Perhaps the most characteristic projects as the end of the twentieth century neared were mammoth stock-taking volumes. Several of these were the thousand-page gold-leafed volumes of the official Oliver Wendell Holmes Devise History of the Supreme Court, which in 1971 began to appear at several-year intervals. Goebel's book, mentioned above, was the first to appear; it was followed by the first of a projected two volumes by Charles Fairman, *Reconstruction and Reunion, 1864–88* (1971); by Carl Brent

Swisher's *The Taney Period, 1836–64* (1974); by George Haskins and Herbert Johnson's *Foundations of Power: John Marshall 1801–1815* (1981); and by the late Alexander Bickel and Benno Schmidt's *The Judiciary and Responsible Government, 1910–21* (1984). These volumes are exhaustive treatments aiming for definitive coverage, but their extraordinary bulk and narrow focus on constitutional doctrines makes them of limited interest. Worse, these books took so long to complete that the scholars who had spent decades on them often found that the interests of the community of legal historians and then prevailing historiographical assumptions had veered off in directions very different from those familiar to the authors when they began their projects. More immediately useful is Kermit Hall's five-volume *Comprehensive Bibliography of American Constitutional and Legal History, 1896–1979* (1984), which lists and classifies every book and article written in the field through the 1970s.

Finally, there seemed to be a movement to take advantage of the surge of monographic work. A series of short volumes published in 1983 was sponsored by the National Endowment for the Humanities (NEH) and the American Bar Association (ABA). Written principally by younger scholars teaching in history departments, the series includes Stephen Botein's *Early American Law and Society*, George Dargo's *Law in the New Republic*, Jamil Zainaldin's *Law in Antebellum Society*, Jonathan Lurie's *Law and the Nation 1865–1912*, and Gerald Fetner's *Ordered Liberty: Legal Reform in the Twentieth Century*. Each of these includes an interpretive essay and several readings from primary sources. Each treats a few generations in American history. They are all offered as supplements to undergraduate courses in American history, perhaps as a means of partially reclaiming legal history from the law schools.

These NEH-ABA volumes primarily examine private law, but in that same year, Herman Belz produced a new edition, a thorough and comprehensive revision of both the narrative and the interpretation, of a classic, Alfred H. Kelly and Winfred A. Harbison's *The American Constitution: Its Origins and Development* (originally published in 1948). As Belz indicated in his preface, what he had done was essentially to write "a substantially new book based on the extensive body of scholarship that in the past generation has altered our understanding of virtually every aspect of the American constitutional experience." Belz sought to grapple with the mood of the new legal historians and announced that he was rejecting the old Kelly and Harbison perspective, which confidently predicted that "centralized bureaucratic institutions [such as those of the New Deal] can fulfill the ideals of liberty, equality, and democratic self-government."

Instead, said Belz, his book was rewritten with an understanding of recent movements on the left and right that had made clear that there were deep skepticism about New Deal methods and philosophies and a heightened interest, which he proposed to trace, in "decentralist, democratic-participatory, and antigovernmental values in the American constitutional order." Finally, Belz suggested that he would treat constitutional law not as an expedient method of promoting class and economic interests (as Warren, Beard, and, to a certain extent, Hurst and Horwitz had done) but rather "as a basic ideology and approach to political life." Not the least part of Belz's comprehensive, lively, and lucid book was his seventy-page annotated selected bibliography, amounting to one of the best and most current essays on American legal historiography to be found.

As Belz's book appeared, there were increasing signs that the ideology of constitutionalism to which he referred was undergoing profound change. In 1974, in the aftermath of Watergate, following the conviction for corruption of the vice-president, widely televised Senate and House hearings, and the resignation of the president, there was a sense that democracy and the people's constitutional ideology had triumphed. But in the wake of the electoral "reforms" that flowed from Watergate and the Supreme Court's rejection of several of them, it slowly became clear that American society had become something very different from the "democracy" continuously invoked. The effect of the electoral reforms, as interpreted by the Supreme Court, was to shift the balance of power in national and local politics from the two major political parties to a series of "political action committees," or PACs, organized arms of business, fraternal, and labor organizations. Rightly or wrongly, many analysts saw in the triumph of the Republicans and Ronald Reagan in the late 1970s and the 1980s a triumph of wealthy "special interests." Such analysts, many of whom were in the academy, also decried the adventurism of the Reagan administration's foreign policy, which they saw as repeating what they believed to be the mistakes of the Vietnam War era.

In the middle of the 1980s, then, there were signs that the legal history about to be written would try to aid in the solution of national political dilemmas by casting light on remaining national iniquities. In particular, there was an increasing scholarly interest in women's issues and those of the family; some authors sought to elaborate a humanistic approach to the law that might serve as an antidote to the more rabid market-oriented approaches. Some earlier works in social legal history had suggested the richness inherent in such an approach, most notably Michael S. Hindus' *Prison and Plantation: Crime, Justice, and Authority in Massachusetts and South Carolina, 1767–1878* (1980). (Two pathbreaking works of this type were published as part of the American Society for Legal History's Studies in Legal History series, Michael Grossberg's *Governing the Hearth: Law and the Family in Nineteenth-Century America* (1985) and Marylynn Salmon's *Women and the Law of Property in Early America* (1986).

There were also signs in some of the law schools, most notably Harvard, Yale, Stanford, Berkeley, Columbia, Pennsylvania, Virginia, New York University, and Northwestern, where American legal historians had become involved in administration and curriculum reform, that legal educators saw the practice and learning of legal history as holding some promise for a needed fundamental restructuring of legal education. The work of almost three decades of legal history, from that of Hurst to that of critical legal studies, in uncovering the common economic, political, social, and ideological bases of a welter of constitutional- and private-law doctrines, had finally succeeded in throwing into question the artificial separation of doctrines as formerly taught in the law schools. One legal historian, Jay Feinman of Rutgers, even taught a course labeled "Contorts," combining and exploring the underpinnings of the two fundamental first-year subjects.

In the late 1980s a national shift in demographics and a national decline in the number of applications to law schools in the light of an apparent glut of the market for lawyers suggested the difficulties to be faced by those practicing legal history. It seemed that in the near future there would be an increase in the college-age population, and if Belz' observation about a national constitutional ideology is correct, a need to educate a new generation in the meaning of, and need for reform of, that ideology. There are signs that the educational and ideological crises in the law schools and the political and social struggles in the broader American society are being perceived as creating a need to articulate a new ideology. It has become increasingly common for legal historians in particular not only to remark on the artificiality of legal doctrines but to argue the artificiality of the separation of realms of public and private law. In both realms they see a need to create a new legal ideology to replace soulless and amoral "possessive individualism," the liberalism dominant in American public and private law since the New Deal years.

Legal historians' increasing interest in the formation of an American nationalist and liberal ideology in the late eighteenth and early nineteenth centuries seems to offer an understanding of possible alternative ideological approaches, and that understanding is being increasingly incorporated in their teaching and writing at both colleges and law schools. The fourth generation of American legal historians finds itself in possession of a field now accepted in all but the most reactionary enclaves as a vital part of the teaching and practice leading to the further evolution of American law.

BIBLIOGRAPHIC AFTERWORD

This essay, as a work on the history of the writing of histories of the American legal system, has itself had to be something of an extended bibliography. There is little need for extensive listings here, then, and the reader contemplating further research is best advised to read the relevant works already discussed. Yet, the approach to historiography taken here is hardly the only one possible, and there are several valuable historiographical essays that can profitably be consulted, both for their discussion of works in addition to those treated here and for the different perspectives they present. Probably the most influential such piece is Morton Horwitz' "The Conservative Tradition in the Writing of American Legal History," in *American Journal of Legal History,* 17 (1973), a discussion of biographies of Joseph Story by Gerald Dunne and James McClellan, which contains Horwitz' excoriation of Roscoe Pound and his now famous condemnation of "lawyers' legal history."

Two valuable surveys of the literature by Harry Scheiber, which stress the importance of the Wisconsin school's works and which illuminate both constitutional and private law, are "American Constitutional History and the New Legal History: Complimentary Themes in Two Modes," in *Journal of American History,* 68 (1981), and "Doctrinal Legacies and Institutional Innovation: Law and the Economy in American History," in *Law in Context,* 2 (1984). His Wisconsin-school colleague and one of the other leading figures in American legal history, Lawrence Friedman, also wrote a very readable short survey of the field, "American Legal History: Past and Present," in *Journal of Legal Education,* 34 (1984).

From time to time since the mid-1960s, New York University's *Annual Survey on American Law* has included an essay on developments in American legal history, several written by New York University School of Law faculty members John Reid or William Nelson. These essays, among the most comprehensive and insightful available, have been released in a single volume from the New York University Press as *The Literature of American Legal History* (1985). In 1981, that press also brought out a valuable compendium of review essays on leading works in American legal history edited by Hendrik Hartog, *Law in the American Revolution and the Revolution in the Law.*

Legal-history volumes are regularly reviewed in *Reviews in American History,* published by the Johns Hopkins University Press, the best collections of review essays on historical works as they are published. Shorter reviews can be found in the two legal history journals, *American Journal of Legal History,* now published at Temple University, and the American Society for Legal History's official journal, *Law and History Review,* published at Cornell University. Finally, for earlier attempts by the author of this piece at setting forth a historiographical field theory, see Stephen Presser's " 'Legal History' or 'The History of Law': A Primer on Bringing the Law's Past into the Present", in *Vanderbilt Law Review,* 35 (1982), and "Revising the Conservative Tradition: Towards a New American Legal History," in *New York University Law Review,* 52 (1977), a long review essay on Horwitz' *The Transformation of American Law,* discussed above.

The academic works referred to in the last part of this essay as indicating a new direction for historiography and for the law are Roberto Unger's *Knowledge and Politics* (1975) and Alasdair MacIntyre's *After Virtue,* 2nd ed. (1984), in philosophy; and Michael Perry's *The Constitution, the Court, and Human Rights* (1982), in constitutional analysis.

[*See also* AMERICAN JURISPRUDENCE.]

ALPHABETICAL LISTING OF ARTICLES

ALPHABETICAL LISTING OF ARTICLES

ALPHABETICAL LISTING OF ARTICLES

ALPHABETICAL LISTING OF ARTICLES

LIST OF CONTRIBUTORS

LIST OF CONTRIBUTORS

Shirley S. Abrahamson
Wisconsin State Supreme Court
STATE CONSTITUTIONAL LAW

James J. Alfini
Florida State University
TRIAL COURTS AND PRACTICE

Judith A. Baer
California State Polytechnic University,
    Pomona
SEXUALITY AND THE LAW

Howard Ball
University of Utah
THE FEDERAL COURT SYSTEM

Paul R. Benson, Jr.
The Citadel
THE COMMERCE CLAUSE

Loren P. Beth
University of Georgia
THE FULLER COURT AND ERA

Roger Billings
Northern Kentucky University
LEGAL SERVICES

Gayle Binion
University of California, Santa Barbara
THE FRANCHISE

David S. Bogen
University of Maryland
FREE SPEECH AND EXPRESSION

James Bolner, Sr.
Louisiana State University
THE STONE AND VINSON COURTS AND
    ERAS

Stephen Botein
College of William and Mary
COLONIAL LAW AND JUSTICE

Henry J. Bourguignon
University of Toledo
THE ARTICLES OF CONFEDERATION

Wayne D. Brazil and Gregory S. Weber
Magistrate, U.S. District Court, Northern
    District of California
Attorney, California Bar
DISCOVERY

John Brigham
University of Massachusetts, Amherst
CIVIL LIBERTIES AFTER 1937

W. Hamilton Bryson
University of Richmond
EQUITY AND EQUITABLE REMEDIES

Bradley C. Canon
University of Kentucky
COMPLIANCE AND IMPACT

Milton Cantor
University of Massachusetts, Amherst
THE TANEY COURT AND ERA

LIST OF CONTRIBUTORS

Lief H. Carter
University of Georgia
LEGAL REASONING

David F. Chavkin
Maryland Disability Law Center
PUBLIC-INTEREST ADVOCACY

Gordon A. Christenson and Wendy E. Holschuh
University of Cincinnati
PRIVILEGES AND IMMUNITIES

Roger S. Clark
Rutgers University
INTERNATIONAL HUMAN RIGHTS LAW

Beverly B. Cook
University of Wisconsin, Madison
SEX EQUALITY UNDER THE CONSTITUTION

William G. Coskran
Loyola Law School
PROPERTY LAW

David J. Danelski
Occidental College
THE HUGHES COURT AND ERA

William J. Daniels
Union College
IMMIGRATION, NATURALIZATION, AND CITIZENSHIP

Craig R. Ducat
Northern Illinois University
CONSTITUTIONAL INTERPRETATION

Henry W. Ehrmann
University of California, San Diego
CIVIL LAW SYSTEMS

Robert K. Faulkner
Boston College
THE MARSHALL COURT AND ERA

Malcolm Feeley
University of California, Berkeley
THE ADVERSARY SYSTEM

Jay M. Feinman
Rutgers University
LEGAL EDUCATION

David Fellman
University of Wisconsin, Madison
DUE PROCESS OF LAW

Peter G. Fish
Duke University
JUDICIAL ADMINISTRATION

Louis Fisher
Library of Congress, Congressional Research Service
CONGRESS

Tony Freyer
University of Alabama
FEDERALISM

Richard Funston
San Diego State University
THE BURGER COURT AND ERA

Michael J. Glennon
University of Cincinnati
ADMINISTRATIVE LAW

Henry R. Glick
Florida State University
STATE COURT SYSTEMS

Sheldon Goldman
University of Massachusetts, Amherst
JUDICIAL SELECTION

Thomas C. Grey
Stanford University
LAW AND MORALITY

Joel B. Grossman
University of Wisconsin, Madison
AMERICAN LEGAL CULTURE

Jerome Hall
University of California, San Francisco
AMERICAN JURISPRUDENCE

Stephen C. Halpern
State University of New York, Buffalo
TAX LAW

LIST OF CONTRIBUTORS

Dan Fenno Henderson
University of Washington
INTERNATIONAL ECONOMIC LAW

Louis Henkin
Columbia University
THE EXECUTIVE AND FOREIGN AFFAIRS

Milton Heumann
Rutgers University
PLEA BARGAINING

Herbert Jacob
Northwestern University
THE CRIMINAL JUSTICE SYSTEM

M. Ethan Katsh
University of Massachusetts, Amherst
LAW AND THE MEDIA

Nicholas N. Kittrie
American University
CRIMINAL PROCEDURE

Charles M. Lamb
State University of New York, Buffalo
RACIAL DISCRIMINATION AND EQUAL
    OPPORTUNITY

James Lare
Occidental College
THE EXECUTIVE AND DOMESTIC
    AFFAIRS

Abe F. Levy and Lewis N. Levy
Levy, Ansell & Goldman
LABOR LAW

Wallace D. Loh
University of Washington
LAW AND SOCIAL SCIENCE

James Magee
University of Delaware
THE COURTS AND CONSTITUTIONALISM

Robert J. Martineau
University of Cincinnati
APPEALS AND APPELLATE PRACTICE

Lynn Mather
Dartmouth College
PROSECUTORS

Gary L. McDowell
United States Department of Justice
CIVIL LIBERTIES TO 1937

Jerome E. McElroy
Vera Institute of Justice
THE POLICE

Albert P. Melone
Southern Illinois University, Carbondale
BAR ASSOCIATIONS

Arthur S. Miller
George Washington University
JUDICIAL REVIEW

Jeffrey Brandon Morris
University of Pennsylvania
THE CHASE AND WAITE COURTS AND
    ERAS

Paul L. Murphy
University of Minnesota
THE WHITE AND TAFT COURTS AND
    ERAS

Walter F. Murphy
Princeton University
THE SUPREME COURT OF THE UNITED
    STATES

David M. O'Brien
University of Virginia
PRIVACY

Jarret C. Oeltjen
Florida State University
COMMERCIAL LAW

Frances Olsen
University of California, Los Angeles
FAMILY LAW

Donald J. Polden
Drake University
CORPORATIONS AND THE LAW

Stephen B. Presser
Northwestern University
HISTORIOGRAPHY OF THE AMERICAN
    LEGAL SYSTEM

LIST OF CONTRIBUTORS

Doris Marie Provine
Syracuse University
CERTIORARI

David Robinson, Jr.
George Washington University
CRIMINAL LAW

Austin Sarat
Amherst College
ALTERNATIVES TO FORMAL
    ADJUDICATION

John R. Schmidhauser
University of Southern California
THE JUDICIARY

Glendon Schubert
Southern Illinois University, Carbondale
BEHAVIORAL STUDIES OF THE
    AMERICAN LEGAL SYSTEM

Bernard Schwartz
New York University
THE WARREN COURT AND ERA

Jeffrey M. Shaman
American Judicature Society
THE EQUAL PROTECTION CLAUSE

Edward F. Sherman
University of Texas at Austin
MILITARY LAW

Herbert L. Sherman, Jr.
University of Pittsburgh
TORTS

Harold J. Spaeth
Michigan State University
JURISDICTION

Victor L. Streib
Cleveland State University
JUVENILE LAW

Joseph P. Tomain
University of Cincinnati
CONTRACTS

S. Sidney Ulmer
University of Kentucky
FRAMING THE CONSTITUTION

Jon M. Van Dyke
University of Hawaii, Manoa
TRIAL JURIES AND GRAND JURIES

Clement E. Vose
Wesleyan University
AMENDMENTS TO THE CONSTITUTION

H. Frank Way
University of California, Riverside
RELIGIOUS LIBERTY

Russell R. Wheeler
Federal Judicial Center
COURTS OF LIMITED AND SPECIALIZED
    JURISDICTION

Peter Woll
Brandeis University
ADMINISTRATIVE AGENCIES

Calvin Woodard
University of Virginia
COMMON LAW AND COMMON-LAW
    LEGAL SYSTEMS

Frances Kahn Zemans
American Judicature Society
THE LEGAL PROFESSION AND LEGAL
    ETHICS

Elyce Zenoff
George Washington University
SENTENCING ALTERNATIVES

INDEX

INDEX

Abbate v. *United States* (1959), 1021b

Abbott Laboratories v. *Gardner* (1967), 239b

Abel, Richard, 460a

Abingdon School District v. *Schempp* (1963), 796a, 800b, 804a, 933a, 1215b, 1216a

A. B. Kirschbaum Co. v. *Walling* (1942), 946a–b

Ableman v. *Booth* (1859), 76b, 80b–81a, 85a, 1095a

Abney v. *United States* (1977), 1021a

abolitionism, 76b, 82b

abortion, 187b–188a, 421b, 425a, 484a,b, 592a,b, 1253b, 1256a–1258a; constitutional amendment, 935b–936a; federalism, 1102a; law and morality, 844b; legal aid, 647a; privacy right, 212b, 1176b–1177a; *Roe* v. *Wade* impact, 795b, 801b, 803b, 805b, 806b, 807a; social equality, 227a–b

Abraham, Henry, 212a, 558a

Abrams v. *United States* (1919), 127b, 206a–b, 1125a,b

absence without leave (AWOL), 388a–b

absentee ballot, 1108b

absolutism, 213b, 972b–976a, 1131a–b

abstention doctrine, 833b–834b

abused children, 356a–357a, 1267b–1268b

Acanfora v. *Board of Education* (1974), 1261b–1262a

accountability of police, 662a–663a

accreditation of law schools, 616b–617a

acquittal, 1021a

Act for Establishing Courts of Judicature (1691), 9b

Act for Supressing Immorality (1708), 4a

Action Programme (1974), 324a

Active capture, 22a, 24b

activism, judicial: Warren Court, 163a–164a, 172a

actus reus (wrongful act), 249b

Adair v *United States* (1908), 115b, 205b, 1034a, 1098b

Adamany, David, 779a

Adams, John, 39b, 46a; judiciary, 556b, 601b–602a, *Marbury* v. *Madison*, 42b, 1161a; Sedition Act, 200a; Supreme Court, 1160a

Adams, John Quincy, 39b, 41a,b, 60b, 78a, 1056a

Adamson Act (1916), 123b, 126a

Adamson v. *California* (1947), 154b, 974a

Adams-Onis Treaty (1819), 56b

Adams v. *Tanner* (1917), 126b–127a

adaptionist adjudication, 447b, 450b–451a, 720b, 776a

adjudication: administrative agencies, 233a,b, 237b, 238a, 437a, 438a–441a,b, 442a; adversary system, 753a–766b; juvenile law, 354a–b; social sciences, 869b, 870a, 872a; trial courts, 720b; *see also* Alternatives to Formal Adjudication

Adkins v. *Children's Hospital* (1923), 996b, 1034a, 1241a

Adler v. *Board of Education* (1952), 152b

administrative agencies, **435a–445b,** 510a, 776b, 969b; administrative law, 233a–244b; appeals, 564b; corporation regulation, 286b; delegation of powers, 960b, 961a–b, 962a, 963a, 964a, 965a–b; free speech, 1133a; judicial compliance, 799b–802b; public law advocacy, 913a; reorganization, 1061b–1962b

Administrative Conference of the United States, 442a,b

administrative law, **233a–244b,** 508a, 518b, 832a–b; constitutionality, 125b–126a; judges, 438b, 440b, 441

Administrative Office Act (1939), 571b–572a,b

Administrative Office of the United States Courts, 559a, 572a, 576a, 578b; circuit councils, 577a; Judicial Conference 574b, 575b; pages' lobby, 579a,b; budgets, 581b

Administrative Procedure Act (1946), 236b, 237a,b, 961a

admiralty courts, 504a, 520a; Fuller Court, 114b; inland waterways; 59b–74a, prize law, 20a,b–21a, 23a; wrecked or stranded ships, 71a

admission request (discovery), 816b–817a

adoption, 309a, 310b, 311a–312a

adultery, 314a, 315a, 430a, 856b, 1255a, 1258b; colonies, 5b; criminal law, 303b–304a

INDEX

American Declaration of the Rights and Duties of Man, 342a–b
American Farm Bureau Federation, 479b, 934a
American Federation of Labor, 137a
American Judicature Society, 476b, 521a, 525a, 580b, 591b
American jurisprudence, **1291a–1304b**
American Law Institute, 246a,b, 252b, 295a, 476b, 1011b
American legal culture, 761a, 763a, **767a–782b**; plea bargaining, 898a
American Medical Association, 479b
American Nazi Party, 214a–b, 797b
American Railway Union, 360b
American Revolution, 11b–12a, 13a–14b, 600b–601a, 737b, 738a; Articles of Confederation, 14b–25a; federalism, 1089a–1090a
American rule, 635b, 908a–b
American Sugar Refining Company, 941b
American Telephone and Telegraph Company, 727a
American Textile Manufacturers Institute v. *Donovan* (1981), 878a
American Tobacco Company v. *Patterson* (1982), 1204a
American Trading and Products Corp. v. *Shell International Marine* (Suez Canal Case, 1972), 270
Ames, James Barr, 615b, 619a
amicus curiae, 705b–706a, 710b, 788a, 806a, 1159a
Amish, 185b, 1224b, 1225a
Amistad: see United States v. *The Schooner Amistad*
Amnesty International, 338a
Amsterdam, Anthony, 1001b
analytical jurisprudence, 1295a–1302a
anarchy, 503b–504a,b
ancillary jurisdiction, 827a–b
Anderson v. *Dunn* (1821), 966a–b
Anglo-American law: adversary system, 753a, 755a–756a,b, 758a, 762a, 763b
Anglo-Saxons, 504a, 754b
animal regulation, 110b
Annapolis Convention (1786), 27b–28a, 30a
annulment, 301a,b, 308a, 314b–315a
Anslinger, Harry J. 529b
Antelope, The (1825), 54a,b, 1184a
antenuptial agreement, 316a
Anthony, Susan B. 1233b
Anti-Defamation League of B'nai B'rith v. *Federal Communications Commission* (1968), 357b–376a
Antifederalists, 37b, 196a–b, 198b, 554b–555a,b, 602a, 604a, 1181a
Anti-Slavery Society, 334a
antitrust laws, 116a–b, 124b–125a, 291a, 361a–b, 477a–481b, 727a, 1071b–1072a
Apartheid, 98a
Apodaca v. *Oregon* (1972), 746b

appeals and appellate practice, **462a–474b,** 517a, 518b–519a, 520b, 601b, 603a; administration, 571b, 576b; ambiguity, 877a; California, 685b, 686 (diagram); case load, 565b, 566 (chart); certiorari, 783a–794b; colonies, 9b–10a; criminal proceedings, 540b–541a, 1021a, 1022b–1023a; decision compliance, 795a; equal protection, 1046a; federal courts, 557a–558a, 560b–561a, 564b–567a; Fuller Court, 114a–b; habeas corpus, 94b; Indiana, 687 (diagram); judges, 589b, 596b, 605a–611a; jurisdiction, 478a–b, 480a, 827b, 828a; law of concepts, 107b; legal reasoning, 882a–b, 884a, 886b–887a; Louisiana civil code, 493b, 496a; military law, 387a–388a,b; national court of appeals, 559b–560b, 582b; plea bargaining, 893a–b; prize law, 20b–21a, 22a–24a; prosecutors, 679a; sentences, 918a, 920a; state courts, 682b–683a,b, 684a–b, 689b–690a, 692a, 693 (chart), 695a; Supreme Court, 704a–705a, 1159b; trial transcripts, 168b
appointments: ambassadors, 1078b–1079a; president, 1059a–1060b
apportionment, 124a, 167b, 175a, 178a–179b, 189a, 190b–191a, 831a; constitutional amendment, 932b, 933b–934a; equal protection, 1043a–b; federalism, 1101a
apprehension of criminals, 656b
apprenticeship, 311a; legal profession, 614a, 615a, 633a–b
appropriations: Congress, 968b–971a; president, 1066a–1068b, 1086b–1087a
arbitration, 331b–332a, 362a, 455b–456a,b, 458b, 520b
Argersinger v. *Hamlin* (1972), 181b, 523a, 636b, 644b, 645b, 730a, 758b
Aristotle, 1293a–1294a
Arizona, 953b, 1106b; *see also Southern Pacific Co.* v. *Arizona*
Arizona Train Case (1945), 951a,b
Arkansas, 551b, 597b, 729a
armed forces: blacks, 146b; homosexuals, 1262a; sex discrimination, 186a–b, 189a, 1049b; voting rights, 1109a–b
armistice treaties, 1080b, 1082b
arms, right to bear, 1286b
Armstrong v. *Athens County* (1842), 67b
Arnold, Thurman, 607a, 769a
arraignment, 536b, 564a, 1016a, 1019b
arrest, 301a–b, 1004b, 1010a–1012a; crime control, 656b–657a; juvenile law, 352a; police, 667a; prosecution, 534b–535a
Arrow v. *Dow* (1982), 487b–488a
arson, 303a–b
Articles for the Government of the Navy, 384b

blacks (continued)
Court, 133a; Warren Court, 164a–b; White Court, 128a–b, 129b
Blackstone, Sir William, 51b, 614a–b; common law, 502b, 503b, 508a, 510b, 512a, 514a; due process, 1027a; free press, 1122b; property, 850a,b
Blair v. *Commissioner* (1937), 414b–415b, 416a
blanket injunction, 360b
blasphemy, 5b–6a, 216a
Blatchford, Samuel, 113b
blockade, 55b, 85b–86a, 90b
Blockburger v. *United States* (1932), 1021a
blood tests, 307b, 310a
Bloustein, Edward J., 1168a
Blow, Peter, 83a
Blow, Taylor, 83a
blue collar class, 147a
blue laws, 108b
Blum v. *Stenson* (1984), 909a
Board of Curators of the University of Missouri v. *Horowitz* (1978), 224b, 243b
board of directors (corporations), 279b, 280a, 284a–285b, 289b–290a
Board of Education v. *Allen* (1968), 1218a–b
Board of Education, Island Trees Union School District No. 26 v. *Pico* (1982), 215b
Board of Regents of State Colleges v. *Roth* (1972), 220a, 397b
Boddie v. *Connecticut* (1971), 226b
body, human: law and morality, 845b, 848b–849a, 857b–858a
Body of Liberties, Massachusetts, 5b
Bolling v. *Sharpe* (1954), 188b
Bollman and Swartwout, Ex parte (1807), 46a
bonds, government, 91b, 98b, 116a, 138a–b
bond elections, 1107a–b
Bonham's Case (1610), 1155a
books: law and media, 373a–b
Booth v. *United States* (1934), 138a
Borah, William E., 143a
Borden Co. v. *Borella* (1945), 149b
Bordenkircher v. *Hayes* (1978), 679b
borrowing powers, federal, 76b
Bosley v. *McLaughlin* (1915), 1240a
Boston, 9a, 62a, 79b, 80a, 81a, 485b, 656a, 863b, 864a, 1214b–1215a; *see also Norris* v. *City of Boston*
boundaries, 15a,b, 16a, 17a–19b; interstate commerce, 73b; voting discrimination, 1114a–b, 1116a
Bowers v. *Hardwick* (1986), 1269a
Bowlin v. *Lyon* (1885), 112a
Bowsher v. *Synar* (1986), 971a
boycott, 129a, 360a, 361a,b, 364a, 367b, 482b
Boyd v. *United States* (1886), 1173a, 1174a
Bracero Program, 1145a,b
Bradfield v. *Roberts* (1899), 120b

Brady v. *Maryland* (1963), 823a, 1030b
Bradley, Joseph P., 92b, 103b, 113b, 114a; civil rights, 97a; due process, 101a; on females, 1048b; women's rights, 1237b–1238a, 1239a, 1240a, 1241b, 1247b
Bradley, Omar N., 386a
Brandeis, Louis B., 163a, 606b, 859b; clear and present danger test, 989b; employment agencies, 126b–127a; free speech, 132b, 144a, 206b, 207b, 1125a–1126a, 1130b; judiciary costs, 583a; liberalism, 130a; New Deal, 138a–139b, 142a–b, 143b, 144a, 558b; privacy, 1167a–b, 1169b, 1170a,b; separation of powers, 959a; Taft Court, 136a; wiretapping, 133b, 221b; women's rights, 1238b
Brandeis brief, 118a, 861a,b, 867a
Brandenberg v. *Ohio* (1969), 389b, 1126b, 1127a
Branzburg v. *Hayes* (1972), 184a, 739a, 804b
breach of contract, 265b–266a, 268b, 269a, 271b; remedies, 272a–273b
breach of peace, 153a, 301a
Breard v. *Alexandria* (1951), 151a, 1171a
Breedlove v. *Suttles* (1937), 1111b, 1235b
Breed v. *Jones* (1975), 349b
Brennan, William, Jr., 610a, 707b; certiorari, 788a; commerce clause, 947a,b, 953a, 954b; constitutional interpretation, 983a–b; executive power, 1087b–1988a; national court of appeals, 560a; obscenity, 215b, 216a, 1130a; privacy, 1172a, 1174b, 1176b; property rights, 219a, 220a; state constitutions, 1280b; Warren Court, 161a,b, 162a–b; women's rights, 1235b, 1239b, 1241b, 1243b
Bretton Woods Conference and era (1945-mid 1960s), 321a, 323a,b–325b, 327b, 328b
Brewer, David J., 114a, 116a, 992a
Brewer v. *Williams* (1977), 1015b
bribery, 857a
Bricker Amendment, 930b–931a
Bridge Proprietors v. *Hoboken Co.* (1864), 65a
Bridges, Harry, 483a
briefs, 463b, 471b–472b, 566a, 567b, 621b, 705b–706a, 787a, 859b
Brim, Orville, 1168b
British Empire: common law, 500b, 509b
Brinegar v. *United States* (1949), 155a
Briscoe v. *Bank of the Commonwealth of Kentucky* (1837), 69b–70a
broadcasting, 372b, 373b–381a, 429b
broad construction, 87a
Bronson v. *Kinzie* (1843), 66b–67a, 1094b
Brooks v. *United States* (1925), 131b
Broomall, John, 1189a–b
Brosman, Paul W., 387b
Brotherhood of Railway Trainmen v. *Virginia* (1964), 640a–b, 650a–b
Brougham, Lora, 755a

INDEX

Brownell, Herbert, 483b, 1063a
Brown Transport v. *Atcom* (1978), 560b
Brown v. *Allen* (1953), 1156a
Brown v. *Board of Education of Topeka* (1954), 128a, 153a, 164a–166a, 175a, 177b, 226a, 478a, 711b, 776a, 797b, 798a, 799a–b, 860a–b, 861a,b, 866b–867a, 868a–869b, 872a, 873a,b, 879a, 888a, 906a–b, 999b, 1040a,b–1041a, 1047a, 1101a, 1149b, 1159a, 1198a–1199a
Brown v. *City School District of Corning* (1976), 1226a
Brown v. *Maryland* (1827), 50a, 70b, 71b
Brown v. *Mississippi* (1936), 144b
Brown v. *New Jersey* (1899), 197a
Brown v. *Ohio* (1977), 1021a
Brown v. *United States* (1814), 52a, 56a, 55a
Bryan, William Jennings, 609a–b
Buchanan, James, 83a
Buchanan v. *Warley* (1917), 128a, 1040b, 1098a
Buchholz, Bernard, 779b
Buckley v. *Valeo* (1976), 189b–190a, 233b–234a, 707b, 779b, 1086a, 1134b
Buckner v. *Buckner* (1980), 227a
Buck v. *Bell* (1927), 132a
budget, congressional, 969a–971a
Budget and Accounting Act (1921), 968b–969a, 1064b, 1066b
Budget and Impoundment Control Act (1974), 968b, 969b–970a, 1066b, 1067a
bugging devices, 221b
buildings regulation, 110b–111a
bulk transfers, 253b–254a
Bullock v. *Carter* (1972), 226a
Bull v. *McCuskey* (1980), 430b
Bunim v. *Bunim* (1949), 1263a
Bunting v. *Oregon*, 126b
Burch v. *Louisiana*, 222b–223a, 746b, 1020a
burden of proof, 725b–726a
bureaucracy, 558b–559a, 800a; *see also* administrative agencies
Burford, Ex parte (1806), 52a
Burger, Warren Earl, 160a, 574a, 575a, 576a, 580b, 581b, 610a,b, 707a; "all deliberate speed," 166a; case load, 792a,b; delegation of powers, 961b; equal-time rule, 377a; free speech, 1128a; gerrymandering, 179a; judges and politics, 579a; judicial notice, 1158b; lay juries, 748a; Miranda decision, 181a; national court of appeals, 559b, 560a,b; obscenity, 216a; right to counsel, 730a; state criminal procedures, 1283b–1284a; women's rights, 1235a, 1247a–b
Burger Court and era, **174a–195b,** 557b, 808a; certiorari, 785b; civil liberties, 697a; conservatism, 773b; constitution interpretation, 983a; constitutionalism, 999a, 1000a–b; criminal rights, 605a; equal opportunity, 1195b, 1202b–1206a, 1209b–

1210a; federalism, 1101b–1102a; judicial employees, 582a; law and social sciences, 867b; legal reasoning, 886a; opinion writing, 612a; privacy, 1173a, 1174b, 1176a–b; racial discrimination, 1195a, 1199a–1200b, 1207b–1209a, 1209b–1210a; right to counsel, 223a
burglary, 303a, 350a
Burks v. *United States* (1978), 1021a
Burnet v. *Leininger* (1932), 415a
Burns Baking Co. v. *Bryan* (1924), 163a
Burns v. *Fortson* (1973), 1109a
Burns v. *Wilson* (1953), 387a–b
Burr, Aaron, 34b, 46a–b, 51b, 743b
Burton, Harold H.: certiorari, 786b, 788b, 789a,b, 790a, 791b–792a; desegregation, 164b; presidential powers, 150b; reapportionment, 156b
Burton v. *Wilmington Parking Authority* (1961), 1039b
Bushell's Case (1670), 735b–736a
Buse v. *Smith* (1976), 1279a
business: *see* corporations and the law; economy
business regulation, 1098b–1099a
busing, 175b, 176a, 225a, 805a, 806b, 862b, 863b, 864b, 866b, 867a,b, 1199a–1200b
Butchers' Benevolent Association, 96a–b, 101b
Butler, Pierce, 129b, 136a,b, 558a; New Deal, 138a–b; voting behavior, 140b
Buttfield v. *Stranahan* (1904), 1065b–1066a
Butz v. *Economou* (1978), 241
buy/sell agreements, 283b
Byrd, Harry F., 1056a
Byrd, Robert, 413b
Byrnes, James F., 142a, 151b, 156a

C

Caban v. *Mohammed* (1979), 1050a–b, 1247b
Cable Act (1922), 132b
cable television regulation, 377a–379a,b
Cadwallader, George, 86a–b
Cafeteria and Restaurant Workers Union v. *McElroy* (1961), 219b
Calhoun, John C., 60a, 1093a
Califano v. *Webster* (1977), 1051a
Califano v. *Westcott* (1979), 1242a
California, 112b, 177a, 211b, 215a, 223a, 309a, 310b, 312b, 316b, 351a, 355b, 369b, 529b, 585b, 597a, 617a, 648b, 735a–b, 747b, 784b, 815a, 816b, 822a–b, 909a–910a, 954b, 1207a,b; limited jurisdiction courts, 521 (table); see also *Adamson* v. *California*; *Almy* v. *California*; *Faretta* v. *California*; *Hurtado* v. *California*; *Oyama* v. *California*; *Robinson* v. *California*; *Rochin* v. *California*; *Stromberg* v. *California*; *Whitney* v. *California*

INDEX

Chicago, 101b, 115a, 485a–b, 531a, 1208b–1209a

Chicago Bar Association, 475b, 645a

Chicago Bureau of Justice, 645b

Chicago, Burlington & Quincy Railroad v. *Chicago* (1897), 1036a

Chicago Jury Project, 747b

Chicago, Milwaukee, and St. Paul Railway v. *Minnesota* (1890), 102a, 204b, 1033a–b

Chicago Reform School, 347b

chief justice of the Supreme Court, 574b–575a, 576b, 579b, 581b

child abuse, 356a–357a

child custody, 316a, 317b–318a, 699b, 719b, 764a–b; homosexuals, 1263a–b

Child Health Assurance Program, 913b

child labor, 108b, 127a, 129a, 130b, 928a,b, 929a, 930a, 932a–b, 935b

Child Labor Act (1916), 131b–132a, 943b

child marriage, 306b–307a

child molestation, 1253b, 1262b, 1267a–1268a, 1269b

child neglect, 356a,b, 357a

children, 422b, 425a, 530a,b; citizenship, 1151b; criminal law, 298a; equal protection, 1045b; income splitting, 414a,b, 415a,b–416a; juvenile law, 347a–358b; law and morality, 852a; parents and family law, 309a–312a, 313b, 314a,b, 318b–319a; as property, 132a–b; public interest advocacy, 913a–b; segregation effects, 860b–861a

children in need of supervision (ChINS), 349b

Children's Defense Fund, 912b–913b

child support, 226b–227a, 309b, 310b, 313b, 318b, 695b, 699b, 1248a–b

Chimel v. *California* (1969), 179b–180a, 1012b

Chinese, 112b, 133a

Chinese Exclusion Act (1882), 1141b–1142a

Chirelstein, Marvin, 413a

Chisholm v. *Georgia* (1793), 40b, 834b, 1903a, 1160b

Choate, Rufus, 71a

choice-of-court clause, 330b

Choy, Herbert Y.C., 606a

Christian Scientists, 1214a

church: *see* religion

Church, Thomas, 727a

church and state, 111b, 120b, 151b–152a, 191a, 217a,b, 1213a

Cipriano v. *City of Houma* (1969), 1107b

Circuit Court Act (1802), 41a, 43a, 556b

Circuit Court Executive Act (1981), 576b

circuit courts, 41a, 43a, 45b, 61a, 95b, 103b, 114b; administration, 579a,b, 580b, 581a; administrative agencies, 443b–444a; appeals, 465a, 565a; judges, 556a–b, 605b–606a, 607a; jurisdiction, 827b

circuit judicial councils, 572a–577a, 597b

citizens: criminal justice system, 532a, 541a–b

Citizens Against Rent Control v. *Berkeley* (1982), 190a

citizen's arrest, 301b

citizenship, 3a; blacks, 96a; corporations and, 76b; *Dred Scott* Case, 83b, 84a,b, 201a; exclusion, 207b–208a; expatriation, 1151b; Fourteenth Amendment, 96b, 203a; Indians, 132b; privileges and immunities, 1185a, 1188b–1189a, 1192a; racial bias, 133a; women, 132b, 1232a–1233a,b; *see also* immigration, naturalization, and citizenship

Citizenship Act (1824), 1150a–b

city government, 123a, 124a, 131a

City of Eastlake v. *Forest City Enterprises, Inc.* (1976), 1207b–1208a

City of New York v. *Miln* (1837), 70a–b, 72a

City of Oakland v. *Oakland Raiders* (1982), 398b

City of Philadelphia v. *New Jersey* (1978), 954a

Civil Aeronautics Board, 240a

Civil Code of 1870 of Louisiana, 491b–498a,b

Civilian Conservation Corps, 137b

civil law systems, **490a–499b**, 701a,b, 707b, 734b, 771a; certiorari, 784a; and common law, 500b; discovery, 810a–812a, 823a, 824a; district courts, 563b–564a (chart); insanity, 299a; juries, 120b, 745b, 747b, 748a, 760a; jurisdiction, 828a; limited and special jurisdiction courts, 517b, 519a, 521b 521 (table); right to counsel, 758b; state courts, 683b, 691 (chart), 692a–b, 694 (chart); torts, 418a; trial courts, 721b–724b, 726a, 728a; U.S. attorneys, 673 a–b

civil liberties and rights, 483a,b, 484a,b, 485b, 777b, 780a; commerce clause, 948b–949a; compliance with decisions, 805b, 806b; constitutionalism, 997a–1001a; due process, 224a–225a, 1036a–1037b; federal courts, 557b; federalism, 1096a–1097a, 1098a, 1100b, 1101a,b–1102a; Fuller Court, 118b–120b; homosexuals, 1260a–1261a, international law, 338a; judicial review, 1165a–b; police misbehavior, 663b–664a; public-interest advocacy, 901b, 902a, 906a–907a, 908a; state courts, 124a, 690a, 695b–697a; Taft Court, 132a–133a; Waite Court, 90a; Warren Court, 164a–166b, 170a, 171a, 175b; White Court, 127b; *see also* American Civil Liberties Union

civil liberties to 1937, **196a–210b**

civil liberties after 1937, **211a–229b**

Civil Rights Act of 1866, 93b, 96a, 1202a–b, 1207a

Civil Rights Act of 1875, 97b, 166a, 203b

Civil Rights Act of 1964, 166a, 932b, 1197a; affirmative action, 188b, 191b, 192a, commerce clause, 948b; equal pay, 227b; executive orders, 964a, job discrimination, 1202a, 1210a; voting, 1111a; women's rights, 1238b, 1239b

Civil Rights Act of 1968, 1150b

INDEX

INDEX

INDEX

INDEX

INDEX

Day, William R., 119a, 609b, 943b

Dayton Board of Education v. *Brinkman* (1977, 1979), 176b, 1200b

deadly force, 300b–301b, 665a0b, 1011b

Dealey, J. Q. 1271a

Dean Milk Co. v. *City of Madison* (1951), 953a

death, 109b; negligence, 425a–b, property interests, 403a

death penalty, 223b–224a, 1022a–b; deterrence, 530b; expert testimony, 867a; juveniles, 353b; sentencing, 917b–918a, 918b–919a; *see also* capital punishment

Debs, Eugene V., 116a

Debs, In re (1895), 116a–b, 360b

debt capital, 281b

debtor-relief, 66b–67a

debtors, 54a, 67a–b

debts, 92a,b, 93b

decedents: law and morality, 848b–849a

Decalogue Society of Lawyers, 476a

decision-making, judicial, 449a, 515a, 753a–766b, 859b, 860a, 867b, 870a; appeals, 473a–b, 566b; constitutionalism, 987a–1003b; juries, 734a, 748a–b; prosecutors, 673b–676b, 677a, 679a

Declaration of the Rights of the Child (1959), 336b

Declaration on Principles of International Law Concerning Friendly Relations and Cooperation Among States in Accordance with the Charter of the United Nations (1970), 337a

Declaration on Social Progress and Development (1969), 337a

Declaration on Territorial Asylum (1967), 337a

Declaration on the Elimination of All Forms of Intolerance and of Discrimination Based on Religion or Belief (1981), 337a

Declaration on the Elimination of Discrimination Against Women (1967), 337a

Declaration on the Establishment of a New International Economic Order (1974): *see* New International Economic Order (NIEO)

Declaration on the Granting of Independence to Colonial Countries and Peoples (1960), 336b

Declaration on the Participation of Women in Promoting International Peace and Co-operation (1982), 337a

Declaration on the Promotion of Peace, Mutual Respect and Understanding Between Peoples (1965), 336b

Declaration on the Protection of Women and Children in Emergency and Armed Conflict (1974), 337a

Declaration on the Rights of Disabled Persons (1975), 337a

Declaration on the Rights of Mentally Retarded Persons (1971), 337a

Declaration on the Use of Scientific and Tehnological Progress in the Interests of Peace and for the Benefit of Mankind (1975), 337a

decriminalization, 915b

defamation, 183a,b–184a, 429a, 1173a

defendant, 120a,b, 153b–155b, 756a; discovery, 821a,b–823b; court jurisdiction over, 836b–837a, 838a; plea bargaining, 80a, 891a–b, 892a, 893a,b, 894b–895a,b; pleadings, 812a; small claims court, 728b; trial courts, 723a–724a, 725a–726a, 730b, 731a–b; women's rights, 1234b

defendant in error, 463a

defense counsel, 527a, 528a, 529a–b, 533a, 534a, 536b, 538a–540a,b; plea bargaining, 537b–538a, 890a, 891a–b, 892a, 893a,b, 894a, 898a,b; *see also* public defender

defense of others, 300b–301a

defenses, 298a–301b; intentional torts, 421b–422a, 431a

defiance of Court decisions, 797b, 804b

De Funis v. *Odegaard* (1974), 188a, 828b–829a, 1200b

De Jonge v. *Oregon* (1937), 144b, 208b, 213b–214a

Delaney v. *United States* (1952), 967b

Delaware, 50b, 551b, 585a, 586b, 672b, 827a, 840a, 939a

Delaware v. *Prouse* (1979), 1011a

delegation of powers, 234a–b, 960b–961b, 963a

delinquency: *see* juvenile law

democracy, 715b–717a, 980a, 981a–b

democratic government, 36b

Democratic party, 58b, 60b, 143a, 147b, 479a, 529b, 590b, 609a–b, 1095b, 1112a,b

Democratic-Republicans, 1140a

demurrer, 723a–b

demography, 863a–b, 864a

denaturalization, 149a

denization, deeds of, 1138a–b

Dennis v. *United States* (1941), 153a, 214a, 389b, 1126a

Denver, 176a, 862a, 1199b–1200; *see also Keyes* v. *Denver School District*

dependent children, 356a

deportation, 133a, 208a, 1144a, 1151a–b

depositions, 724a, 811b, 814a,b–815b, 823a

depraved heart murder, 302a

desegregation, 175b–178a; compliance, 797b, 798a, 799a–b, 801a,b, 802a–b, 805a, 807a; education, 165b–166a; 1197a, 1198a–1200b, 1210a; federalism, 1101a, 1102a; housing, 1206a–b; social sciences, 860a–869b, 871b

detectaphone, 155a

desertion, 315a

deterrents, crime, 350b, 530a–b, 656b, 915a, 818b, 919a, 920b

INDEX

INDEX

Estes, Billy Sol, 217a

estoppel, 308b, 831b–832a, 835a,b

ethics: American Bar Association, 476b; public-interest advocacy, 902a; judicial discipline, 597b; *see also* legal profession and legal ethics

ethnicity: judge and jury selections, 606a, 703a, 746a

Eugene Sand and Gravel v. *City of Eugene* (1976), 1222b

Europe: adversary system, 762a–b, 863a,b; courts, 701a–702a; immigration, 1143a–b, 1144a; legal culture, 768a

European Commission of Human Rights, 342a,b

European Convention on Human Rights and Fundamental Freedoms, 342a

European Court of Human Rights, 342a,b

European Economic Community, 322a,b, 329a

Evans v. *Cornman* (1970), 1109b

evasion, 804b–805a, 818a

Everson v. *Board of Education* (1947), 151b–152a, 217b, 1214a, 1217b–1218a, 1227a

evidence: adversary system, 753a; against oneself, 144b; discovery, 758b–759a, 810a–824b; equity courts, 546b–547a; exclusionary rule, 169b, 757a–b; grand jury, 739a, 1017b; illegally seized, 128b, 133, 154a, 155a, 180a,b, 1017b–1019a; military law, 385b; negligence, 423a–b; prosecution, 535b, 536a–b, 537a, 540b, 677a; search, 1013b; small claims court, 524a; trial courts, 725a–b; wiretapping, 133b

evidence, rules of, 452a

Exchequer, Court of, 504b, 508a

exclusionary rule, 169b, 180a–181a, 222a, 532b, 533a, 757a–b, 798b, 801a, 860a, 1017b–1019a

executive and domestic affairs, **1055a–1073b**, 1275b–1276b; administrative agencies, 435–445b; agreements with Congress, 1083b; appointment of judges, 585a,b, 589a,b, 590a; judiciary, 43a, 46a,b, 47a, 720a; orders, 963b–964b; police, 653a; powers, 131a, 1081b–1082a, 1086b–1088a, 1163b–1164a; privilege, 967a–968b, 1062b–1063b; proclamations, 85b; prosecution, 671b

executive and foreign affairs, **1074a–1088b**

executory contracts, 270a

exhaustion of remedies doctrine, 240b–241b

exonerating evidence, 823a

expatriation, 1151b–1152a, 1232b

expectation interest, 261b, 262b, 264a, 268b–269a

expert witnesses, 181b, 815a, 822b–823a, 859b, 862b, 863a, 867a

exploitation, 853b

ex post facto laws, 918b

extended facilities (loans), 324b, 325b

extended families, 844b

extended impact cases, 720

extradition, 76b, 78a

extramarital sex, 1255a, 1258a

eyewitness identification, 1013b–1014b

F

Fair Credit Reporting Act (1970), 1177a

Fair Deal, 603a

Fair Employment Board, 1201b

Fair Employment Practices Act, 220b

Fair Employment Practices Committee, 1201b

Fairfax's Devisee v. *Hunter's Lessee* (1813), 44a–b

Fair Housing Act (1968), 1208a, 1209a,b

Fair Labor Standards Act (1938), 149a, 945a–948a

fair practice codes, 131b

fair representation concept, 367a–b

Fair Share Refugee Act (1966), 1146b

"fair trial" rule, 128b

Falk, Maurice and Laura, Foundation, 246a

false arrest and imprisonment, 418b, 419b

false-light cases, 430a

family-car doctrine, 314a

Family Educational Rights and Privacy Act (1974), 1177a–b

family law, 146b, 147a, **306a–320b**, 430a–b; colonies, 8a–b; courts, 517a, 520a, 719b; equal protection, 1045a–b; mediation, 764a–b; sex equality, 1246b–1247a; sexuality and, 1253a; state courts, 109b, 698a, 699a–b

Faretta v. *California* (1975), 772a

Fare v. *Michael C.* (1979), 352a

Farmer, Arthur E., 386b–387a

Farr, Bill, 217a

fascism, 483a

fathers, 309b–311a, 312a, 313b, 1050b

FCN treaties: *see* friendship, commerce, and navigation treaties

featherbedding, 363b

Federal-Aid Highway Act (1970), 186a

Federal Aviation Act (1958), 240b

Federal Aviation Administration, 238a

Federal Bar Association, 476a

Federal Bills of Lading Act, 254b

Federal Bureau of Investigation, 483a–b, 484a, 531a, 594b, 688b, 1060a, 1063a

Federal Circuit Court of Appeals, 565b

Federal Coasting Act (1793) 938a, 939a

Federal Communications Act, 439a

Federal Communications Commission, 347a–b,

Federal Communications Commission v. *Midwest Video Corp.* (1979), 378a

Federal Communications Commission v. *Pacifica Foundation* (1978), 872b, 876a, 1172a

finding of law, 242a–b

Finch, Heneage, Lord Nottingham, 550b

fines, 52a, 918b, 921a,b–922a

Firefighters Local Union No. 1784 v. *Stotts* (1984), 1205b

First Amendment, 487b–488a; administrative agencies, 240b; Burger Court, 182b–185b, 189b–190a,b, 191a; civil liberties; 200a, 206b, 208b, 209a, 213a, 218a; clear and present danger, 153a; common law, 510b; constitutional interpretation, 974a, 981a; free speech and press, 144a, 171a, 1120a–1136b; Fuller Court, 118b, 120a,b; homosexual rights, 1260b; 1261b; media, 371b–373a, 376a, 378b–379b, 381a; military, 389a–390b; prayer in schools, 932b–933a,b; privacy, 1170b–1171b, 1172b; religious liberty, 1214a, 1218a, 1224a, 1225a; Stone and Vinson Courts, 158a; Taft Court, 132b; Warren Court, 162a; women's rights, 1239a–b

First Continental Congress (1774), 14a–b

first-degree murder, 302a–b

First Employers' Liability Cases (1908), 115a

First National Bank of Boston v. *Bellotti* (1978), 190a

First National City Bank v. *Banco Nacional de Cuba* (1972), 1078b

Fiss, Owen, 448a, 449b

Flagg Brothers, Inc. v. *Brooks* (1978), 227b

flag salute, 151a,b, 1223b–1224a

Flast v. *Cohen* (1968), 830b, 886a

Fleming, Macklin, 759b

Flemming v. *Nestor* (1960), 219b

Fletcher v. *Peck* (1810), 52b, 53a, 218b, 711b, 1093b, 1161b–1162a

flogging, 384b

Flood v. *Kuhn* (1972), 880a,b

Florida, 55a,b, 56b, 187a, 315b, 821b, 912a–b, 953a

Florida Lime and Avocado Growers, Inc. v. *Paul* (1963), 954b

Florida Oil-Spill Prevention and Pollution Control Act, 186a

Florida v. *Casal* (1983), 1284a

Flynn, Elizabeth Gurley, 483b

Foley v. *Connelie* (1978), 1042a

food, 943a

Food and Agriculture Organization, 327a

Food and Drug Administration, 439a

Food, Drug, and Cosmetic Act (1938), 237b

football: franchise as property, 398b

foot patrols, community, 661a,b

Foran Act (1885), 1142a

Forbush v. *Wallace* (1972), 1245a

force, use of, 654b, 663b, 664b–666a

forced-share provision, 313a

Ford, Gerald R., 369a, 607a, 610b, 931b, 1057b, 1072a

Ford Foundation, 910b–911a

foreclosures, 48a, 66b

foreign affairs, 483a, 484b–485a; *see also* executive and foreign affairs

foreign corporations and interstate activities, 277b

foreign exchange, 329b

Foreign Intelligence Surveillance Act (1978), 1009b

Foreign Intelligence Surveillance Court, 1159a

foreign nationals, 126b

Foreign Sovereign Immunities Act (1926), 1083a–b

foreign trade, 50a, 55a, 56a, 73a–b; *see also* international economic law

formalism, legal, 109b

Fortas, Abe, 168a, 174b, 483b, 591a, 603a, 610a, 931b, 1030a

Fortescue, Sir John, 505b

Fortnightly Corp. v. *United Artists Television* (1968), 378a–b

forum state, 836b, 837a–838b

foster care, 311a, 348a, 355b

Fourteenth Amendment, 94a, 203a, 602b; adjudicated decision-making, 449b; administrative agencies, 236a–b; affirmative action, 189a; aliens, 1151a; arrest, 1010a–b, 1012a; Bill of Rights, 197a–198a, 207a, 208b–209a; blacks, 90a, 96a, 1110a–b, 1111a,b, 1112a,b, 1114b; citizenship, 1141a, 1149a–b; civil liberties, 205a–b, 207a, 208a,b; constitutional interpretation, 974a, 977a,b, 981a, 982b; constitutionalism, 992a–b, 993a, 997b, 998a; corporations as persons, 99a, 102a; criminal procedure, 128b, 221a,b; desegregation, 175b; due process, 212b, 1026a–1037b; electronic surveillance, 1009a; equality, 225a,b, 226b; equal protection, 1038a–1054b; exclusionary rule, 1017b; federalism, 1096a; franchise, 1106a,b, 1108b; free speech and expression, 144a, 1125b, 1127b; Fuller Court, 118b, 119b; Harlan on, 119b–120a; Holmes on, 118a; illegally seized evidence, 128b, 154a, 155a, 180a,b; incorporation theory, 144a, 175a, 211a; Indians, 1150b; juries, 746a; Marshall Court, 52a; naturalization, 1151b; police power, 137b; privacy, 1173a–b, 1174a,b–1175a; privileges and immunities, 1179a, 1188b–1193a; property law, 396b, 397a; racial discrimination, 1196b, 1197a–b, 1205b, 1206a; religious liberty, 208a, 1214a; right to counsel, 208a–b; school prayer, 933a; searches, 1012a; sex equality, 1230a,b; state guarantees of due process, 52a; Stone and Vinson Courts, 153b–154b, 158a; Taft Court, 128b; trial rights, 119b–120a; Warren Court, 164a–b, 170b; Waite Court, 101a; White Court, 126a, 127a, 128a; wiretapping, 133b

Fox v. *City of Los Angeles* (1978), 1222b

framing the Constitution, **26a–38b**

INDEX

INDEX

La Follette, Robert, 482b, 571a

Lamar, Joseph, 122a, 1066a

Lamar, Lucius Q. C. 113b

land: citizenship, 3a; colonies, 1b, 2a, 3b, 9b; dividing property, 400a–401b; income tax, 116a; negligence, 426a–b, 431a; trespass, 420a,b–421a

land claims, 39b, 95a; western lands, 16a–b, 17a

land grants, 52b–53a, 56b

Landis, James M., 143b

landlord-tenant courts, 517a, 518b, 646b

Landrum-Griffin Act (1959), 363b–364a

Lane v. *Newdigate* (1804), 551a

Langdell, Christopher Columbus, 107a–b, 615a–b, 633b

language, 132a, 1222a–b

Lanzetta v. *New Jersey* (1939), 1031b

La Raza Legal Alliance, 484a

larceny, 296a, 303b

Lassiter v. *Department of Social Services of Durham County* (1981), 357a, 1110b

Lasswell, Harold, 407a, 416b–417a

last-clear-chance doctrine, 426b

Lathrop v. *Donohue* (1961), 487b

Latimer, George W., 387b

Latin America, 1144b, 1145a

Lau v. *Nichols* (1974), 1200b

law and morality, **842a–858b**

law and order, 669b–670a

Law and Order Campaign Committee, 799a

law and social science, **859a–874b**, 892b, 898a

law and the media, **371a–382b**, 1135a

law clerks, 563a–b, 565a, 788a–b, 1158a

law enforcement, 482b, 653a–668a, 1068b–1070b, 1081a–b

Law Enforcement Assistance Administration, 656b

law firms, 625b, 630b–631b, 634b–635a, 777a, 778a, 791a, 904a–b, 907a–b, 909a, 911b

law merchant, 245a–b, 249b, 504a, 511b

law of nations: *see* international law

law review, 623b–624a

Law School Admission Test (LSAT), 617b–618a

law schools, 633a, 911b, 1197b–1198a; *see also* legal education

law students, 485b–486a, 505b, 617a–618b

law workers, 486a

lawyer–client relationship, 630a–b

lawyers: adversary system, 760a–b; advertising, 215b–216a; bar associations, 475a–489b; colonies, 11a–12a; common law, 501b–502a, 505b, 509a, 513a,b, 514a; contract process, 269a–b; corporations, 131b; defense counsel, 538a–540a; discovery, 817b–818b, 820a,b; discrimination, 112a; legal culture, 772a; public-interest advocacy, 900b, 901b, 902a, 904a–905a; small claims court, 728b; Supreme Court justices, 607a; tax attorneys, 411a–b;

work-product doctrine, 813a–b; *see also* legal profession and legal ethics

League of Nations, 334b

League of Women Voters Education Fund, 910b

Lebanon, 1086a

Lee, Richard Henry, 14b–15a

Legal Action Center of New York, 910b

legal aid: *see* legal services

legal culture: *see* American legal culture

legal education, 502a, **614a–626b**, 633a–b; access to profession, 634a–b; American Bar Association, 476a; civil law, 497a–b; common law, 512b–514a; judges' backgrounds, 607a; professional prestige, 632b

legal ethics: *see* legal profession and legal ethics

legal expense insurance, 651a–652a

legalism, 769b, 770b–771a

legalization, 773a

legal profession and legal ethics, **627a–643b;** adversary system, 760b; advertising, 189b; American legal culture, 776b–778b; bar associations, 475a–489b; colonies, 6b–7a, 10b–11b; common law, 510a, 513a; education, 625a, 644b–645a; law school curriculum, 624b; women, 1237b, 1238a

legal reasoning, **875a–889a;** education, 624a–b

legal services, 482b, **644a–652b;** availability, 636b–638a; costs, 635b–636a; legal aid societies, 644a–b, 645a–b, 646a–b, 648b–649b, 778a, 912a; legal clinics, 637b–638a; Office of Economic Opportunity, 647a

Legal Services Corporation, 637a, 646b–647b, 648a, 905a, 909a, 910a, 912a

Legal Services Program, 637a, 640b

Legal Tender Acts (1862, 1863), 92a–93a

Legal Tender Cases (1869, 1870, 1871, 1884), 91a–93a

Lehr v. *Robertson* (1983), 310b

legislative veto, 1068a–b, 1077b, 1086a,b

legislation, judicial, 870a–871b

legislation and legal reasoning, 880b–883a, 884b, 886b

legislatures, 39b, 42b, 109a, 156b, 720a, 915b–916a, 919b, 1275a–b

Leigh, Benjamin, 60a

Leisy v. *Hardin* (1890), 950a–b

Lemkin, Raphael, 339b–340a

Lemon v. *Kurtzman* (1971), 1219a, 1220a

Lenzner, Terry, 647a

Lerner, Max, 712a, 885b

letters of credit, 252b–253b, 256b

Lever Act (1917), 127a–b

Levi, Edward H., 482b, 883a, 884b

Levin, Martin, 726b, 773a

Levitt v. *Committee for Public Education* (1973), 1219b

Levy, Leonard, 1154b

Levy v. *Louisiana* (1968), 1051b, 1248b

Mentschikoff, Soia, 246b

mercantile courts, 504a

mergers, 125a, 291a

merit selection of judges (Missouri plan), 478b, 541a, 585a, 586a–587a,b, 588a,b, 589a, 595b–596a, 597a, 722b

Merryman, Ex parte (1861), 86a, 202a

Metropolitan Life Insurance Co. v. *Ward* (1985), 1101b

Mexican-American Legal Defense and Education Fund, 906a

Mexico, 490a, 1143b, 1145a

Mexico v. *Hoffman* (1945), 1078a

Meyer v. *Nebraska* (1923), 132a, 207a, 1034b

Meyer v. *Oklahoma City* (1972), 1222a

Miami Herald Publishing Co. v. *Tornillo* (1974), 184a, 377a

Michael M. v. *Sonoma County Superior Court* (1981), 187b, 1237a, 1268a–b

Michelle W. v. *Ronald W.* (1985), 310b

Michigan, 100a, 598a

Michigan v. *Long* (1933), 1272a

Michigan v. *Summers* (1981), 1011b

Michigan v. *Tucker* (1974), 181a

Middle Ages, 462b, 500a

"midnight" judges, 41a

Military Appeals, Court of, 561b

military commissions, 202a,b–203a

military discipline, 666b, 667a,b–668a

military exigency, 148b

Military Justice Act (1968), 388a–389a

Military Justice Act (1983), 388b

military law, **383a–393b;** and civil courts, 86b; Civil War, 90b–91a, 93a–b, 94a–b; martial law, 91a, 93a

Military Rules of Evidence (1980), 388b

military service, 127b, 217b, 1237a–b, 1240b, 1241b

Milk Wagon Drivers Union v. *Meadowmoor Dairies* (1941), 152b

Mill, John Stuart, 842a–858b; 1124a–b, 1125a, 1128a, 1130b, 1254a

Millenson v. *New Hotel Monteleone* (1973), 1245b

Miller, Arthur S., 409b–410a

Miller, Richard, 451b

Miller, Samuel, 85a, 93b, 96a–b, 103b, 113b, 114a, 992b–993a,b, 1028a, 1190b

Miller v. *California* (1973), 216a, 1129b

Miller v. *McQuerry* (1853), 80a–b

Milligan, Ex parte (1866), 86b, 90b–91a, 93a–b, 202b, 387a, 1069a

Milliken v. *Bradley* (1974, 1977), 175b–176a, 862b, 863a, 866a, 868b, 869a, 1200a–b, 1209a–b

Mills v. *County of St. Clair* (1850), 64b

Mills v. *Habluetzel* (1982), 1248a

Milwaukee Brewers Baseball Club v. *Wisconsin Department of Health and Social Services* (1986), 1275b

Mineral Leasing Act (1920), 908a

Minersville School District v. *Gobitis* (1940), 151a, 1223b–1224a

minimum contacts, 836b–837b, 841a

"Minimum Standards of Judicial Administration," 572b–573a

minimum wage laws, 124a, 139b, 140b–141a, 142b, 149a, 851a–b, 945a

mining, 109b, 110b, 149b, 363a, 495a, 947b

Minnesota, 126a, 217b, 729a, 1220b

Minnesota Gag Law, 208a

Minnesota Moratorium Act, 138a

Minnesota Rate Cases (1913), 126a, 993a–b

minorities, 482b; constitutional interpretation, 984a; judicial selection, 590b, 593a–594a, 595a; law schools, 618a; legal profession, 633a, 777a; preference programs, 188b;

minority business enterprise (MBE), 1205a–b

minors, 126b, 1257a

Minor v. *Happersett* (1875), 931b, 1096b, 1106a, 1110a, 1233b, 1234a

Minton, Sherman, 150b, 156a,b

Miranda v. *Arizona* (1966), 169a–b, 175a, 179b, 180a, 181a, 221b–222a, 533a, 690b, 757a, 795a,b, 796a, 800b–801b, 802a,b, 803b, 1007a–b, 1015a–b, 1175a

mirror-image rule, 267b–268a

miscegenation, 2b, 112a, 147a

misdemeanors, 293a, 297a,b, 301a, 303a, 522b–523b, 536b, 675a, 722a, 727b, 728b–731b, 760a

misrepresentation, 428b–429a

Mississippi: banking, 67a–b; black voting, 1114a–b, 1115b; equity, 551b; interstate commerce, 953a, 955a; jury service and blacks, 119b; manumission, 82a; railroad commission, 102a; Reconstruction, 94a; slave trade, 77a–b

Mississippi River, 64b

Mississippi University for Women v. *Hogan* (1982), 1050b, 1246a–b

Missouri, 81b, 82b, 83a–b, 86, 129a, 253a, 551b, 558a, 589a, 597a, 727b, 950a

Missouri Church of Scientology v. *State Tax Commission* (1977), 1226b

Missouri Compromise (1819), 44b, 83a–85a

Missouri ex rel. Gaines v. *Canada* (1938), 153a–b, 226a, 1032a, 1100b, 1197b

Missouri v. *Holland* (1920), 131a, 1079b

mistrial, 1020b–1021a

Mitchell, John, 936b

Mitchell, William D., 136a–b

Mitchell v. *Wells* (1859), 82a

M'Naghten's Case (1843), 298b–299a

Mobile v. *Bolden* (1980), 1113b, 1115b

Model Business Corporations Act, 279a–b, 281a

INDEX

National Association for the Advancement of Colored People, 124a, 137a, 225b–226a, 557b, 867a, 906b–907a, 911b

National Association for the Advancement of Colored People v. *Alabama* (1958), 1172b

National Association for the Advancement of Colored People v. *Button* (1963), 640a, 650a, 906b–907a

National Association for the Advancement of Colored People v. *Claiborne Hardware Co.* (1982), 1126b

National Association of Manufacturers, 477a, 479b, 481b

National Association of Women Lawyers, 476a

National Association of the Deaf, 910b

National Broadcasting Co. v. *United States* (1943), 374a

National Center for State Courts, 521 (table), 522a, 573a,b

National Child Labor Committee, 124a

National Commitments Resolution, 1083b

National Committee to Combat Women's Oppression, 487a

National Conference of Black Lawyers, 484a

National Conference of Commissioners on Uniform State Laws (1892), 246a–b, 255a

National Consumer's League, 124a, 1240a

National Council of U.S. Magistrates, 576a

national court of appeals, 792a–b

National Crime Survey, 531a–b

National Environmental Policy Act (1969), 806a, 908a

National Health Law Program, 905b

National Immigration Project, 485a

National Industrial Recovery Act (1933), 138a,b, 362a, 1099b

nationalism, 90a

nationality, 1143a

National Judicial College, 573b

National Labor Center, 484b

National Labor Relations Act (1935), 149b, 362b–364a, 944b–945a, 1060a

National Labor Relations Board, 362b, 363b, 364a,b–366a, 367a–b, 368a–b, 369b, 483a, 944b, 945a

National Labor Relations Board v. *Fainblatt* (1939), 945a

National Labor Relations Board v. *Friedman-Harry Marks Clothing Co.* (1937), 944b–945a

National Labor Relations Board v. *Highland Park Co.* (1951), 242b

National Labor Relations Board v. *Jones & Laughlin Steel Corp.* (1937), 142b–143a, 363a, 558b, 944b, 945a, 1100a

National Labor Relations Board v. *Babcock and Wilcox* (1956), 365a

National Lawyers Guild, 475a, 481b–487a, 624a

National Lawyers Guild Quarterly, 482b–483a

National Lawyers Guild v. *Attorney General*, 485a

National League of Cities v. *Usery* (1976), 947a–b, 948a, 1101b

National Legal Aid and Defender Association, 647a

National Motor Vehicle Theft Act, 877b, 943a

National Municipal League, 525a, 573a, 1272b

national-origins principle, 1143b, 1144a,b, 1148a

National Recovery Administration, 138b–139a, 1099b

nationals, U.S., 1148b

National Science Foundation, 901b

national security, 146a, 1068b–1070b, 1144a

National Welfare Rights Organization v. *Weinberger*, 913a

National Woman's Party, 132b–133a

National Woman Suffrage Association, 1233b

Native Americans Rights Foundation, 906a

Native Americans: see Indians, American

nativity scene, 1222a

naturalization: *see* immigration, naturalization, and citizenship

natural justice, 1027a–b

natural law theories, 1291b–1295a

natural resources, 106a, 113a

natural rights theory, 198b–199a, 1122a,b, 1123b, 1137a, 1182a–b, 1184a

navigation, 73a–74a, 938b, 939a,b

Navy, Department of the, 435a

Navy, U.S., 384b, 385a

Nazis, 149a, 213b, 214a–b

Near v. *Minnesota* (1931), 144a, 184b–185a, 208a, 216b

Nebbia v. *New York* (1934), 138a, 1034a

Nebraska, 102a–b, 112a, 117b, 132a, 178a, 185b, 1216a

Nebraska Press Association v. *Stuart* (1976), 183a

Nebraska v. *Scheve* (1903), 112a

necessary and proper clause, 47a, 48b, 92b, 93a, 200a

neglect, 356a,b–357a

negligence, 295a–b, 298b, 302a, 422a–427a, 428a–b, 431a

negotiable instruments, 249b–251a, 256a,b

negotiation, 265b, 266a–267b, 268b, 269b–270a, 454b–455a

neighborhoods, 661a–662a

Nelson, Samuel, 94a, 95b, 72a, 83b, 84a

Nereide, The (1815), 56a

Neubauer, David, 719b

neutrals, 55b, 56a–b

Nevada, 100b, 315b, 587a

Newark Foot Patrol Experiment (1981), 661b

New Deal: administrative agencies, 439b–440a, 443a–b; American Bar Association, 477a; constitutionalism, 996b; federalism, 1099b–1100a; law and morality, 844a,b; Hughes Court, 137b–141b, 142b–145a; Stone and Vinson Courts, 157b, 158a;

INDEX

Permanent Sovereignty Over Natural Resources (1962), 336b

Perry, Michael J., 989a

Perry v. *Sindermann* (1972), 243b–244a, 397b, 1032a

Perry v. *United States* (1935), 138a–b

personal autonomy, 1042b–1043a

personal injury cases, 644a, 830a–b

personal liberty laws, 78b, 80b

personal property, 256a, 395a, 396a; *see also* property law

Personnel Administration of Massachusetts v. *Feeney* (1979), 804a, 1051a

persons in need of supervision, 349b

petit larceny, 293a

petty theft, 729a

Philadelphia, 85b, 86a, 73a–b, 359b, 482b, 656a, 896a, 939b, 954a

Philadelphia Plan, 964a

Philippines, 116b, 1148a–b

physical disability, 422b

physical examination, 816a–b

Phoenix, 21b

Phoenix v. *Kolodziejski* (1970), 1107b

Pickering, John, 602b, 1161b

Pickering v. *Board of Education* (1968), 389a

picketing, 110a, 125a, 129a, 152b, 214b–215a, 360a, 364a, 365b, 367a,b–368a, 482b

Pickett v. *Brown* (1983), 1035b

Pierce v. *New Hampshire* (1847), 71b

Pierce v. *Society of Sisters* (1925), 132b, 207a

Pierce v. *United States* (1920), 206b–207a

Pike v. *Bruce Church, Inc.* (1970), 953b

pilotage, 73a–b, 939b, 940a

Pinckney, Charles Cotesworth, 29a, 31b, 33a, 35a, 51a, 1183a

Pinckney, William, 42a

Pinckney Plan, 29a, 31b, 32b

Piqua Branch of the State Bank of Ohio v. *Knoop* (1853), 68a

piracy, 27a, 56b

Pitney, Mahlon, 126b, 206b

Pittsburgh Free Press v. *Human Relations Committee* (1973), 1239a–b

plain-meaning rule, 881b

plaintiff, 723a–724a, 725a–726a, 728b, 812a,b, 816b, 817b, 828b, 836b–837a, 838a, 839b

plaintiff in error, 463a

plain-view doctrine, 1013a

planned economy, 322a, 328a–b

Planned Parenthood Federation, 1254b

Planned Parenthood v. *Ashcroft* and *Ashcroft* v. *Planned Parenthood* (1983), 1257a,b

Planned Parenthood v. *Danforth* (1976), 1257a

Planters' Bank v. *Sharp* (1848), 64a, 67a–b

Plato: and American jurisprudence, 1291a–1293a

plea bargaining, 455a–b, 457b, **890a–899b;** adversary system, 736b–764a; Burger Court, 181b–182a; criminal procedure, 536b, 537b–538a, 539b, 540a, 1019b–1020a; discovery, 820b, 821b; federal courts, 564a; juvenile law, 354a; legal culture, 771b; prosecutors, 671b–672a, 673b, 674b, 676a, 677a,b, 679a,b; sentencing, 916b

pleading, 811b–812a,b, 817b, 893b, 894b–895a,b, 1019b

pledge of allegiance, 151a,b

Plessy v. *Ferguson* (1896), 98a,b, 118b–119a, 128a, 164b, 165a, 203b, 225a–b, 860b, 873a, 999b, 1040a, 1096b, 1164b, 1197a–b, 1198b

Plumas County v. *Califano* (1979), 903b

Plumer, William, 53a,b

pluralism, 769b, 772b–773b

Plyler v. *Doe* (1982), 187a, 227a

Poe v. *Ullman* (1961), 171a, 1028a

Poelker v. *Doe* (1977), 1257b

Polar Ice Cream and Creamery Co. v. *Andrews* (1964), 953a

police, 517a, **653a–668b,** 671a–b; arraignment, 1016a; arrest, 1010a–1011b; behavior control, 663a–666b; compliance with Supreme Court decisions, 795a–b, 800b, 801a, 802a,b; courts, 517a; criminal justice system, 527a–b, 528a,b, 531b–534a, 535a–536a, 538b–539a, 543a, 1006a,b–1007a; criminal rights, 757a; deadly force, 301a–b; due process, 221a–222a; electronic surveillance, 1008b; evidence, 1018a–b; entrapment, 300a–b; interrogation, 1014b–1016a; job discrimination, 1203a–b; juvenile offenders, 351b, 352a–b; *Miranda* decision, 169a–b, 179b; misconduct, 300b, 484b, 485b; preliminary hearing, 1016a; search and seizure, 180a–b, 1012a–1013b, 1018b, 1019a; state regulation, 50b

police emergency number, 657a, 658b–659a

Police Foundation, 661b, 662a

police harassment, 537a

police powers: Chase Court, 100a–b, 101a; commerce clause, 70a, 939a,b, 942b–943a; contract clause, 64a; industrial legislation, 205a; interstate commerce, 71b; private property for public use, 405a–b; religious freedom, 151b–152a; segregation, 118b; sexuality and law, 1254a; state laws, 50b, 102a,b, 107b–108a,b, 109a, 110b, 111a, 116b, 124a, 126a–b, 130a, 131b–132a, 133b, 137b, 199b–200b, 201a,b; Taney Court, 87a; Waite Court, 90a–b, 98b, 101b

political contribution, 1134b

political debate, 376b

political participation, 1043a–1044b

political parties, 586a, 587b, 1044a–b

political protest, 666a–b

INDEX

Schmidt, Benno, 128a

Schander, William, 246a

Schneiderman v. *United States* (1943), 149a

Scholasticism, 505a

school districts: desegregation, 175b–176a,b; elections, 1107b

school prayer and Bible-reading, 217b–218a, 1214b–1215a

schools: commerce clause, 946b; due process rights, 224a–b; free speech, 215a

schools, parochial: aid to, 151b–152a, 217b, 1217a–1221b

schools, private, 119a, 132b

schools, public, 123b, 132b; desegregation, 175b–176a, 176b–177a, 860a–869b, 871b; loyalty and employment, 152b; and religion, 111b–112a, 152a, 185a–b, 1214b–1215a; segregation, 81a, 112a, 164b–166a; tax funding, 177a, 227a; *see also* education

Schooner Exchange v. *McFadden* (1812), 55b

Schuster v. *Schuster* and *Isaacson* v. *Isaacson* (1978), 1261a

Schwartz, Bernard, 108b

Schwenkfelders, 3a

Scott, John, Lord Eldon, 550b–551a

Scott, Winfield, 86a

Scottsboro Cases, 208a–b, 482b

Scott v. *Emerson* (1852), 83a,b

Scott v. *Illinois* (1979), 730a

Scott v. *Macy* (1968), 1262a

scrap metal, 954a

scrip, 109b, 110a

Scudder v. *Trenton Delaware Falls Co.* (1832), 66a

sea, law of the, 504a

search and seizure, 3b, 128b, 133a–b, 155a, 158a, 169b, 180a–b, 208a, 221a–b, 236a–b, 352a, 532b–533a, 1012a–1013b, 1173b

search warrant, 52a, 532b–533a

Searight v. *Stockton* (1845), 74a

seatbelts, 852a–b

secession, 91b, 1095a

Second Continental Congress, 14b

Second Employers Liability Cases (1912), 125b

Secor v. *Railway* (1877), 103a

secrecy, 440b, 740a, 793a

sectarian education aid, 1217a–1221b

securities regulation, 287a–289a

Securities Act (1933), 287a–b

Securities and Exchange Commision, 287a–289a

Securities Exchange Act (1934), 287a–288a

security, 769a

sedition, 478a

Sedition Act of 1918, 123b, 127b, 200b, 206a–b

segregation, 225a–b, 478a, 483a; affirmative action, 188b; Burger Court, 176a, 177b–178a; equal protection, 1040a–b, 1041a; federalism, 1100b, 1101a; Fourteenth Amendment, 203b; free blacks, 81a; Fuller Court, 112a–b, 118b–119a; housing, 1206a; public-interest advocacy, 906a–b; public schools, 1197a, 1198a–1200b; separate-but-equal doctrine, 203b–204a; by sex, 1246a–b; social sciences, 860b–682a,b, 863a–864a, 865a,b, 866b, 867b–868a,b; Stone and Vinson Courts, 150a, 153a–b; transportation, 98a; zoning, 128a

Sei Fujii v. *State* (1952), 344b

Selden, John, 550a

Selective Draft Law Cases (1918), 127b

selective incorporation theory, 144a, 154a, 170b, 998a,b

Selective Service Act (1917), 123b, 127b

Selective Service Board, 241b

self-dealing, 284b–285a

self-defense, 300b–301a

self-help remedy, 421a

self-incrimination, 533a, 1014b–1016a; administrative agencies, 236a; discovery, 820b, 821a, 823a–b; Fuller Court, 120a; privacy, 1175a–1176a; privileges and immunities, 1192a; Stone and Vinson Courts, 154b; Warren Court, 166b, 170b

Senate, United States, 30b–31a, 33a–b, 34a–b, 35a–36a, 37a, 38b, 40b, 45b, 136b–137a, 141b, 142a,b, 178a, 589b, 590a, 591a–b, 601a

Senate Judiciary Committee, 479a, 480a, 594b

Senate Subcommittee on Criminal Laws and Procedures, 481a

Senate Subcommittee on Investigations, 148b, 166b

senators, 929a, 935a; judicial selection, 589b, 590a, 592a, 593a

seniority, 1204a,b, 1205b

sentencing, 529a,b, 537a, 540b, 542a–543a, 695b, 719a–b, 726b–727a, 729a, 1021b–1022b, 1046a–b; plea bargaining, 671b–672a, 894b, 895b, 896b–897b, 898b; state courts, 112b, 698b–699a

sentencing alternatives, **915a–923a**

separate-but-equal doctrine, 119a, 164b, 203b–204a, 225b–226a, 1197a–b, 1198a–b; constitutionalism, 999b; equal protection, 1040a–b, 1041a; federalism, 1096b, 1100b, 1101a; social sciences, 860b, 861b, 868b; Vinson Court, 153b; White Court, 128a

separation agreements (divorce), 316a

separation of powers, 36a–37a; advisory opinions, 829a; appellate review, 462b; Congress, 958a–960b; delegation doctrine, 234a–b; judicial administration, 569a–b, 579a; judiciary, 601a,b; president and foreign affairs, 1086a; state constitutions, 1274a–1275a

Serrano v. *Priest* (1977), 909a,b

INDEX

INDEX

Social Security Court, 561a

society: *see* American legal cultures; compliance and impact; community; law and social sciences;

sociological jurisprudence, 123a–b

sociology of law, 130b, 1302a, 1303b

sodomy, 304a, 1253b, 1255a, 1258b, 1259b, 1260b, 1265a

Sohn, Louis B., 337b

"soujourner" statutes, 81b, 82a

Soldano v. *O'Daniels* (1983), 884a–b

Solem v. *Helm* (1983), 223b

solicitor, 11b

solicitor-general, 791a

Soliuson v. *Mississippi* (1975), 834a

Solomon, Maureen, 720b

Sosna v. *Iowa* (1975), 1045a,b

sources, news, 217a

South Africa, 339b

South America, 55a, 56a,b

South Carolina, 4b, 14b, 29a, 44a, 45b, 50a–b, 65b–66a, 520a, 551b, 585a, 597a, 1093a

South Carolina State Highway Department v. *Barmuch Brothers* (1938), 953b

South Carolina v. *Katzenbach* (1966), 166b, 1111a, 1113a

South Dakota, 727b

South Dakota Cement Commission, 954a

Southeast Asian immigrants, 1146b

Southern Pacific Co. v. *Arizona* (1945), 149b–150a

Southern Poverty Law Center, 911a

Southern Railway v. *United States* (1911), 115b

South-South trade, 327a

sovereign immunity doctrine, 241b–242a, 697b, 834b–835a, 1078a, 1083a–b

sovereignty, 63b, 1090b

Soviet Union and Soviet bloc, 148b, 321b, 322a, 323b, 328a, 500b, 1080b, 1151b–1152a

Spain, 24a, 55a,b, 56a,b, 77b–78a, 483a, 490a,b–491a,b, 494a, 498a,b–499a, 774a

Sparks v. *State of Texas* (1912), 112a

Spaziano v. *Florida* (1984), 182b

speaker of the House, 1058a

Specht v. *Patterson* (1967), 1022a

Special Committee on Administrative Law (ABA), 439b–440a

Special Committee on Public Interest Practice (ABA), 901a–b

Special Committee to Investigate the National Defense Program, 147a–b

specialized jurisdiction: *see* courts of limited and specialized jurisdictions

special court-martial, 385a, 386b, 388a

special drawing right (SDR), 324b

special master, 704a–b, 720a, 727a

specialties, legal, 628b, 631a–632b, 777a

speech or debate clause, 966b, 967a

speedy trial, 1019a–b

Speedy Trial Act (1974), 222b, 564b, 1019b

spouses, 430a,b, 431a

Springer v. *Philippine Islands* (1928), 960a

Stafford v. *Wallace* (1922), 131a,b

stagecoach, 59a

standardization of products, 131b

Standard Minimum Rules for the Treatment of Prisoners (1957, 1977), 336b

Standard Oil Co. v. *United States* (1911), 124b

Standards of Judicial Administration, 469a–b

standby letter of credit, 253a–b

Standing Committee on Federal Judiciary (ABA), 589b

Standing Committee on Jurisprudence and Law Reform (ABA) 478a, 480a

standing to sue, 239a–b, 710a, 828b, 830a, 831a, 832b

Stanford University, 911b

Stanley v. *Georgia* (1969), 184a, 1171b–1172a

Stanley v. *Illinois* (1972), 310b, 1247a

Stanton, Edwin M., 94a, 1058b

Stanton v. *Stanton* (1975), 186b, 1246a

staple courts, 245a–b

stare decisis, 87a, 193a, 512b, 879b–880b, 881a, 883a; *see also* precedent

Starnes v. *Albion Manufacturing Co.* (1908), 129a

State, Department of, 435a, 1140b

state, secretary of, 1058a

state constitutional law, **1271a–1288b;** due process, 1027b–1028a

state bar associations, 487b–488a

State, County and Municipal Employees v. *Woodward* (1969), 369b

state court systems, **682a–700b;** appeals, 465a–b, 567a, 1022b–1023a; case load, 561b; certiorari, 784a,b–785a,b; compliance and impact of Supreme Court decisions, 797b–798a, 799a, 807a–b; Constitutional Convention, 555a; constitutional law, 1280b–1283a; criminal procedures, 1008a–b discovery, 812b, 813a, 821a, 822a–b, 823b; evidence, 154a; federal courts, 555b–556a, 557a, 603b–605a; Fuller Court, 109a–113b; grand juries, 738b–739a; judicial administration, 572b–573b; judicial discipline, 578a; judicial review, 1159a–b; judicial selection, 587a–589a, 596b; judicial tenure, 596b; jurisdiction, 826a–827a, 828a, 830a, 832b–834b, 835b, 836b, 837b, 839a–841a; legal culture, 776b; legal pluralism, 773b; limited and special jurisdictions, 518a,b, 520a,b–522a; pleadings, 812a; prize law, 20b–21a, 23a,b–24a; Supreme Court, 42b, 571b, 702a–b, 705a; Taft Court, 133b–134a; trial courts, 721b, 722a, 723a–724a, 727a, 728b; trial juries,

INDEX

Thompson v. *Louisville* (1960), 1030b

Thompson v. *Utah* (1898), 746b

Thornhill v. *Alabama* (1940), 152b

Thurlow, Edward, Lord Thurlow, 550b

Thurlow v. *Massachusetts* (1847), 71a–b

Tiedeman, Christopher G., 108a

Till, Irene, 712a

Tilton v. *Richardson* (1971), 1221a–b

Time, Inc. v. *Firestone* (1976), 183b

Tinker v. *Des Moines Independent Community School District 393* (1969), 215a

Title VII (Civil Rights Act of 1964), 1202a–1206a, 1210a

tobacco, 4b, 115b, 948a

tobacco trust, 125a

Tocqueville, Alexis de, 39a, 488a, 633b–634a, 701a, 708a, 778b–779a, 1157a

Todd, Thomas, 41b, 45b, 608a

Tokyo Round (1973), 325a

tolls, 62a, 63a–b, 65a–b

tolerance, pure, 213b, 214b

Tollett v. *Henderson* (1973), 223a

Tonkin Gulf Resolution (1964), 1085a

Toomer v. *Witsell* (1948), 1185a–b, 1186a

torts, **418a–432b;** court jurisdiction, 838a–b; equity, 553a; exemptions from, 64b; legal culture, 776b; Louisiana courts, 496a; privacy, 1168b, 1169b; state courts, 697a–698a; victims, 762b

total incorporation, 154b

totality-of-the-circumstances test, 364b, 366b

Toth v. *Quarles* (1955), 391a,b

Townsend v. *Yeomans* (1937), 1034a

Toyota v. *United States* (1925), 208a

Trade Act of 1974, 235a

trade associations, 131b, 458b

trademark cases, 114b

trades, nonpecuniary, 263a–b

trade secrets, 398a, 440b

trading stamps, 111a

Trading With the Enemy Act, 953a

traditionalists, 720b, 775b

traffic cases and courts, 180a, 349b, 517a, 518b, 521 (table), 690b, 691 (chart), 692b, 722b, 728b, 729a

Trafficante v. *Metropolitan Life Insurance Co.* (1972), 1208a

Trammel v. *United States* (1980), 1236b

transcripts, trial, 168a–b, 181b, 471a–b, 739b

transportation, 58a, 59a–b, 64b, 74a–b, 1217b–1218a; federalism, 1092b; railroads, 110a; segregation, 98a, 118b, 165b; taxation, 955a

travel, right to, 212b, 1044b–1046a, 1109a, 1182b, 1187a

traveling salesmen, 955a

Traynor, Roger, 605a

treason, 46a–b, 148b–149a, 919a

Treasury, Department of, 435a

treaties, 39b–40a, 55a,b, 56b, 131a, 328b, 336a–b, 337a–b, 340b–341a, 343a,b–344a, 930b–931a, 1079a–1081a, 1983a, 1150a

Trenchard, John, 1123b

trespass, 64b, 420a,b–421a, 426a, 428a

triadic dispute processing, 455b–457b

trial by battle, 734b

trial by ordeal, 734b, 735a

trial courts and practice, **719a–733b;** appeals, 467a–468a; Articles of Confederation, 27a; Burger Court, 182a, 183b; certiorari, 784b, 787a; court-martial, 385a, 386b; district court, 563a; due process, 222a–b, 1031a; fair trial rule, 128b; Fourteenth Amendment, 119b–120a; free press, 217a; jurisdiction, 828a; law schools, 623a; limited and special jurisdiction courts, 517a–b; Louisiana courts, 495b–496a; Marshall Court, 52a; misdemeanors, 730b; plea bargaining, 897b–898a; prosecutors, 676a–b; speedy trial, 1019a–b; state courts, 683a–684a,b, 685–b, 686 (diagram), 687 (diagram), 690a–b, 691 (diagram), 692a–b, 694 (diagram), 698a–b; Stone and Vinson Courts, 154a; Supreme Court, 704a

trial de novo, 730b, 731a–b

trial juries and grand juries, 719a, 724b–725a, 726a, 727a–b, **734a–749b;** administrative agencies, 235b; adversary system 753a, 755a–756a, 762a; arrest, 1011a–b; Bill of Rights, 144b; blacks, 97b, 112a, 119b; colonies, 6b, 7a, 10b; common law, 510b, 547a–b; criminal procedure, 534a, 541b–542a, 1020a; death penalty, 1022; discovery, 822b; due process, 222b; evidence, 1018a; indictment, 1017a–b; instructions, 75a; juvenile law, 348b–349a, legal culture, 772a; privileges and immunities, 1192a; prize law, 20b, 22b; prosecutors, 671b, 675b; selection, 724b–725a; sentencing, 916a; Warren Court, 170b; women, 186b

Tribe, Lawrence, 218b, 227b, 1181a, 1186b

Trimble, Robert, 608a

truancy, 349b, 350a, 357b

Truax v. *Raich* (1915), 126b

Trubek, David, 768b

Truman, Harry S., 146a,b, 147a–b, 148a, 150a–b, 156a, 343a, 603a, 606a,b, 930b, 961b, 963b, 1060b, 1061a, 1062a, 1069b, 1082b, 1144b, 1146a, 1201b

trust funds, 651a

trusts, 108b, 115a, 116a–b, 124b–125a, 404a–b, 414b, 941b

TRW, Inc. (1979), 365a

Tumey v. *Ohio* (1927), 521a, 730b, 1030b

Turner, In re (1867), 96a

INDEX

United States v. *Hudson and Goodwin* (1812), 51a

United States v. *Jacoby* (1960), 387b

United States v. *Joint-Traffic Association* (1898), 1097a

United States v. *Judge Peters* (1809), 43b

United States v. *Klein* (1872), 95a

United States v. *L. Cohen Grocery Co.* (1921), 127b

United States v. *Lee* (1982), 1225a

United States v. *Leon* (1984), 180b, 860a, 1018b, 1283b

United States v. *Mara* (1973), 739b

United States v. *Midwest Video Corp.* (1972), 377b

United States v. *Mitchell* (1971), 1236a

United States v. *Nepstead* (1970), 1012b

United States v. *Nixon* (1974), 739a, 967b

United States v. *O'Brien* (1968), 1133a

United States v. *Peister* (1980), 1226a

United States v. *Perez* (1824), 1020b

United States v. *Priest* (1972), 390a

United States v. *Primrose* (1839), 68b

United States v. *Rabinowitz* (1950), 155a

United States v. *Randenbush* (1834), 52a

United States v. *Reese* (1876), 97a–b, 203b, 1096a

United States v. *Reynolds* (1914), 128a

United States v. *Robel* (1968), 167a

United States v. *Robinson* (1973), 1012b

United States v. *Rock Royal Co-operative, Inc.* (1939), 1034a

United States v. *Ross* (1982), 180b

United States v. *Santana* (1976), 1174a–b

United States v. *The Schooner Amistad* (1841), 77b–78a

United States v. *Schwimmer* (1929), 1232b

United States v. *Seeger* (1965), 217b

United States v. *The Ship Garonne* (1837), 76b

United States v. *Southeastern Underwriters Association* (1944), 149b

United States v. *Southwestern Cable Co.* (1968), 377b

United States v. *Spock* (1969), 214a

United States v. *Student Challenging Regulatory Agency Procedures* (1973), 444a

United States v. *Trans-Missouri Freight Association* (1897), 1097a

United States v. *Trottier* (1980), 391b–392a

United States v. *United States District Court* (1972), 1010a

United States v. *United States Steel Corp.* (1920), 125a, 1099a

United States v. *Voorhees* (1954), 389a

United States v. *Wade* (1967), 179b, 180a, 1013b, 1014a

United States v. *Watson* (1976), 1010a, 1012a

United States v. *Will* (1980), 569b

United States v. *Willow River Power Co.* (1945), 219a

United States v. *Wilson* (1833), 52a

United States v. *Winslow* (1913), 125a

United States v. *Yazell* (1966), 1236a

United States v. *Yoshida International Inc.* (1975), 963a

United States v. *Zenith Radio Corp.* (1926), 374a

United Steelworkers of America v. *Weber* (1979), 188b, 1102a, 1204b

United Transportation Union v. *State Bar of Michigan* (1971), 640b, 650b

Universal Declaration on the Eradication of Hunger and Malnutrition, 337a

Universal Declaration of Human Rights, 336b, 337b–338a, 342a

University of California at Davis, 188b

University of California at Davis Medical School, 1201a

University of California at Los Angeles, 911b

University of Chicago Law School, 619a

University of Maryland, 614b

University of Michigan, 911b

University of Missouri, 1216a

University of Missouri Law School, 1197b

University of Oklahoma Law School, 1198a

University of Pennsylvania, 911b

University of Washington Law School, 1200b–1201a

unjust enrichment theory, 273a

unwed fathers, 309b, 310b–311a

unwed parents, 1247a–1248a

Upshaw v. United States (1948), 155a–b

urban crime, 655b, 656b, 660b

use taxes, 955a

Utah, 586b

utilities, public, 108b, 110a, 123b, 129a, 220a–b, 227b, 290b, 905a,

Utz, Pamela J., 674b, 677a

V

Valentine v. Chrestensen (1942), 189b

Valentine v. United States ex rel. Neidecker (1936), 1082a

Vallandigham, Ex parte (1864), 86b, 202b, 1069a

Valley Forge Christian College v. Americans United for the Separation of Church and State (1982), 239ab

Van Buren, Martin, 61a

Vance v. Bradley (1979), 1048a

Vanderbilt, Arthur T., 572b–573a, 721a

Van Devanter, Willis, 122a, 125b, 136a,b, 137b–138a,b, 140b, 142b, 143a,b, 144a, 558a

Vanhorne's Lessee v. Dorrance (1795), 199a

Veazie v. Fenno (1869), 92a

Veazie v. Moore (1852), 73b–74a

Vera Institute of Justice, 677b

Verba, Sidney, 779a–b

Vermont, 17a, 63a–64a, 521 (table), 586b, 822b, 823a,b; free speech, 1123a

Vermont Yankee Nuclear Power Corp. v. Natural Resources Defense Council (1978), 444a

versial decisions, 808a; Court of Military Appeals, 387b; equal opportunity, 1195b, 1209b–1210a; equal protection, 1000a,b; federal courts, 567b; federalism, 1101a–b; judicial employees, 582a; law and social science, 867b; legal reasoning, 886a; racial discrimination, 932b, 1195a, 1198b, 1199a, 1206b–1207b, 1209b–1210a; reapportionment, 1116b–1118b; right to counsel, 223a

Warth v. *Seldin* (1975), 191a, 227b, 1208a

Washington, State of, 112a, 126b, 129b, 140b–141a, 142b, 223b, 521 (table), 822a, 955a

Washington, George, 14b, 20a, 29b, 40a, 384b, 601b, 1056a, 1066a–b, 1076b,

Washington, Harold, 485a–b

Washington v. *Davis* (1976), 176a–b, 179a, 1041a, 1203a, 1209a

Washington v. *Seattle School District* (1982), 176b–177a

Wasserstrom, Richard, 876b

watchmen, 655b

Watergate, 565b–566a, 639a, 777b, 1062b, 1063b, 1074a, 1077a

Watkins, Ex parte (1833), 52a

Watkins v. *United States* (1957), 166b–167a

Watts v. *Indiana* (1949), 155a

Watt v. *Community for Creative Non-Violence* (1983, 1984), 214b

Wayne, James M., 41b, 61a, 64a, 71a, 73b, 74b, 76b, 83b, 84a, 85a

wealth, 1052a–b

Webb-Kenyon Act (1913), 123b

Webb v. *Texas* (1972), 1031a

Weber, Max, 600a, 610b, 710b, 859a

Webster, Daniel, 42a. 49b–50a, 60a,b, 62a, 63b–64a, 67b, 69a, 71a–b, 72a,b–73a, 608a–b, 1029a

Wechsler, Herbert, 989b

Weeks v. *United States* (1914), 128b, 757a, 1017b, 1018a

Weicker, Lowell, 970b

Weinberger v. *Wiesenfeld* (1975), 186b, 802b–803a, 1241b–1242a

Weinstein, Jack, 561b

welfare, 163b, 219b–220a,b, 397a, 510a–b, 646a, 647a,b, 800b, 903b, 904b, 1047b

Weller, Steven, 728a–b

Welton v. *Missouri* (1876), 949b–950a

Wesberry v. *Sanders* (1964), 1117b

West Coast Hotel Co. v. *Parrish* (1937), 140b–141a, 142b–143a, 205b, 558b, 996b, 997b, 1034a

Westinghouse Electric Corp., In re (1981), 270b

Westmoreland v. *Columbia Broadcasting System* (1984), 907b

West River Bridge Co. v. *Dix* (1848), 63a–64b

West v. *Kansas Natural Gas Co.* (1911), 950a

West Virginia State Board of Education v. *Barnette* (1943), 151b, 217a, 977a,b, 979b, 988b, 1224a

Weyand, Ruth, 482b

wheat, 149b, 948a

Wheeler, Burton K., 142b, 143a

Wheeler, Russell R., 569a

Whig party, 58b, 60a,b, 72b, 73a, 608a–b

Whiskey Rebellion, 1070a

Whitcomb, Howard R., 569a

Whitcomb v. *Chavis* (1971), 178b

White, Byron, 174b, 224a, 376b, 378a, 560a,b, 591a, 610a, 737a, 953a, 1035b, 1129a, 1218b, 1233a, 1241b, 1243b, 1269a

White, Edward Douglas, 114a, 116a, 122a–129b, 1065b–1066a

White, James, 245a

White and Taft Courts and eras, **122a–135b**

white-collar class, 147a, 655a,b

white flight, 863b–864a, 870b

white primary, 153b, 1110a,b, 1112a–b

White Slave Traffic Act, 943a

White v. *Regester* (1973), 178b–179a

White v. *Weiser* (1973), 178a

Whitney v. *California* (1927), 207b, 1125b

Whittaker, Charles E., 786b

Wickard v. *Filburn* (1942), 149b, 948a, 1100a

Widmar v. *Vincent* (1981), 1214b, 1216a

widows and widowers, 9a, 1050a, 1235b

Wieman v. *Updegraff* (1952), 152b

Wiener v. *United States* (1958), 234a, 1060b

Wigmore, John 385b

Willard v. *People* (1843), 81b

Williams, Roger, 5a

Williamson, Hugh, 1122b–1123a

Williams v. *Florida* (1970), 222b, 745a,b, 746a

Williams v. *Mississippi* (1898), 119b, 1096a

Williams v. *New York* (1949), 1022a

Williams v. *Rhodes* (1968), 1044a

wills, 8b, 77a, 83a

Willson v. *Blackbird Creek Marsh Co.* (1829), 50b, 939b, 1093b, 1096b

Wilson, James, 24b, 30a,b, 33a, 35a

Wilson, James Q., 659b–660a,b, 661a

Wilson, O. W., 664b

Wilson, Woodrow, 49b, 123a, 125a, 606b, 609b, 703b, 1072a, 1079a

Wilson v. *New* (1917), 126a

Winship, In re (1970), 348b, 354a, 747a

Winthrop, William, 387a

Wireless Ship Act, 373b

wiretapping, 133b, 208a, 221b, 1008b, 1009a, 1078a, 1173b

Wirt, William, 42a

Wisconsin, 80b, 83a, 110b, 112a, 465b, 469a, 934b

Wisconsin v. *Weiss* (1890), 112a

Wisconsin v. *Yoder* (1972), 1224b